D0561122

GUARDIANS OF OUR HERITAGE

HERITAGE

(1724-1953)

EDITED BY

LEO JUNG

The Jewish Library

NEW YORK

BLOCH PUBLISHING COMPANY

5719-1958

Univ. of Tulsa Library
Tulsa, Oklahoma

COPYRIGHT, 1958, BY LEO JUNG

LIBRARY OF CONGRESS CATALOG CARD No. 28-25930

(PRINTED IN UNITED STATES OF AMERICA
BY THE AD PRESS, LTD.)

BM 45
.J8
v.7

sept - send Jewess C.C. - 2/11/60

DEDICATED TO THE SACRED MEMORY OF
SIEGFRIED STERN

PREFACE

The sixth and seventh volumes of The Jewish Library, "Jewish Leaders" and "Guardians of Our Heritage", are meant to preserve some very precious and too little known aspects of our recent history.

Yeshayahu Aviad-Wolfsberg, distinguished physician, thinker, scholar and diplomat, and Juda Ari Wohlgemuth, brilliant writer and devoted teacher of Torah, were called away from life and letters whilst this volume was being edited. Their last writings will enshrine them in the readers' highest regard.

I am humbly grateful for the zekhut *(privilege) of including the former's biography of David Hoffmann, of blessed memory, at whose hand I received my last and most cherished* Semikhah. *My first teacher was my sainted Father, from my youth to the last day of his life. At his yeshivah I sat also at the feet of Rabbi Isaac Landman of Smorgon. During World War I, in London, I was blessed by the wisdom of Rov A. I. Kook, the* Gaon, *mystic and Messianic dreamer. All these men have been called to the "Academy on High" for their timeless reward. But the teacher to whom I owe an insight into* Torah im Derekh Eretz *(the study of our sacred literature in accord with the assured results of modern research) was David Hoffmann—a selfless personality, matchless in assiduity, tremendous in knowledge. His luminous example—and occasional rebuke—challenged his disciples. We entertained for him profound respect and warm affection.*

My daughter, Rosalie Rosenfeld, my friends Nima H. Adlerblum (whose chapter in this book is of unique value and historical significance), Ethel Liebowitt, and Eugenie A. Propp, have been very helpful in preparing this book for the press, nor may I omit the efficient attention bestowed upon it by my secretary, Margaret Weiss.

This volume owes much to the generous cooperation of Arthur LeVine of blessed memory, patron of Yeshivah and Young Israel, president of synagogue and hospital, ever proud of his Anglo-Jewish traditions.

LEO JUNG

Iyyar 5718

CONTENTS

INTRODUCTION

THE RABBIS AND FREEDOM OF INTERPRETATION

BY LEO JUNG

THE RABBIS AND FREEDOM OF INTERPRETATION

INTRODUCTION

THE RABBIS AND FREEDOM OF INTERPRETATION

I. Two Realms

Judaism does not move in a vacuum, spiritual or intellectual. It is based on beliefs and attitudes which establish its theological locus. The one doctrine whence all arises is that of Revelation. That has its negative as well as its positive aspects. What had been conveyed by Torah is not the fruit of Moses' genius nor the summing-up or re-statement of the wisdom or insights of many, but the uncovering (that is what *reveal* means) of the nature of God and His role in the affairs of the cosmos and of men. The positive message of the revelation of Sinai is that God by His nature is just, merciful, all-powerful, perfect and utterly independent of time, space and circumstance. Indeed, He is unique therein, no other factor of existence being absolute, beyond any limitation or conditions as He is. The Creator is the Lawgiver. Man is to endeavor within his sphere to imitate Him, to try to approximate God's qualities of righteousness and mercy. The way to achieve, in however limited a manner, this God-likeness, is acceptance of the Torah, a set of principles and practice, faith, attitude, habituation, study as a method of worship, worship as a method of study, which cumulatively, through the cultivation of all its disciplines, would produce the ethical personality, group, and, finally, the perfect society.

The Torah contains terms and norms. The latter, grounded on the five books of Moses and complemented by the teaching of the other prophets, have been applied by the rabbis in the uninterrupted legal activity spanning Judaism's history and forming the skeleton of the national building. Together they shape the *Halakhah,* the Jewish way of life, literally the *walking* in the way of God. The *Halakhah,* based on its classic texts and progressing by the application of precedent and principle to new conditions, is objective, valid for any normal Jew, but it is never finished. Its processes will go on as long as Judaism stays alive as the *raison d'être* of the Jewish people. Whilst new chapters of *Halakhah* are being written—they are ever fresh fruit of judicial controversy and academic discussion—its results are binding upon Jews who accept the Torah as *Halakhah,* a guide for thinking and living.

But the Torah contains also non-preceptive material, philosophical, theological, clothing its ideas and metaphysical state-

5

ments in words, images, parables, which are capable of many interpretations. The Torah's single purpose is the teaching of moral and spiritual values, no matter what form that teaching takes. It is the core of these teachings and not their vesture which ultimately matters. No Jew can lawfully interpret laws, be they positive or negative, in the light of his special inclinations or insights.

But it is altogether different in the realm of creative thinking as it applies to the non-preceptive parts of the Torah texts. As long as one acknowledges the divine revelation, as long as one recognizes the timeless truth of its essential message, one has, within the traditions of Judaism, a very wide margin of freedom. Indeed, interpretation of such texts is not merely lawful, not merely tolerated as undeniable privilege, but throughout two millennia we have seen it encouraged and hailed as indications of religious loyalty. Otherwise, there would have resulted a deadening sameness and monotonous repetition of translations and comment. But because of that precious margin of freedom, Jewish literature as it dealt with Biblical texts, has been amazingly multicolored, refreshingly various and, as a consequence, of great value in keeping The Book as Books vital, influential, an unfailing source of intellectual and spiritual enrichment.

Throughout the two thousand years of Rabbinic Judaism that right has been taken for granted, just as the divine origin of the Revelation is presupposed throughout. In all the infinite range of the eight hundred years of discussion in the academies of Babylonia and Palestine, there is no hint at any doubt about this—so is freedom of interpretation of metaphysical passages taken for granted. Or else some of the statements or suggestions which I am presenting here would not have been either possible or, if offered, would not have been included in the texts of Talmudic literature. Elsewhere I have shown that e.g. the thought of rebellious angels was not found in any pre-Christian Jewish text, no matter how copious the sources were of such folklore.[1] Similarly, the most up-to-date research would fail to discover there any skeptical view of the origin of the Torah. But the wide divergencies of individual interpretations of non-preceptive texts are as instructive, inspiring as the right to offer them is considered self-evident. Or else there would be found in the minutes of the

---

[1]See my "Fallen Angels in Jewish, Christian and Mohammedan Literature," Dropsie College, 1926.

academies' meetings at least a definite type of criticism, some principles of remonstrance of such non-conformist opinion. The *argumentum de silentio* is persuasive.

More evidence of this self-evident attitude may be adduced from the classic commentaries on the Pentateuch. There is deposited not the give-and-take of many scholars which could account for divided views becoming perchance wider in the heat of discussion, but the deliberate, calm judgment of the scholar offering his comment to all his readers, and especially the youth and the common people. (Only Ibn Ezra, occasionally, and Ramban state an implicit *sod* [secret] rather than an explicit opinion). Scholars would be doubly careful not to disturb the faith of the unlearned, often the unthinking, did they harbor the slightest doubt that they might engage in activity not acceptable to the traditions of Israel. It was a type of sublime naiveté or *a priori* conviction that enabled them to offer often bold, utterly unique interpretation.

Rashi, the greatest, most learned, and most pious of all commentators on the Bible, in his animadversion on the first verse of the first chapter of Genesis, quotes R. Yitzhak, who declares the usual translation of that verse erroneous. It must not be rendered, he avers, *"In the beginning God created heaven and earth"*, as countless scholars before and after him have read it, as the whole house of Israel and Bible-studying non-Jewish savants have understood it. He reflects an early Tannaitic discussion in questioning, on philological grounds, both the translation AND THE NEED TO INCLUDE these metaphysical passages in the Torah: "As a book of law, it might fitly have commenced with Exodus XII." Then he offers his apposite contribution which sheds arresting light not only on the implications of the text, but on the prerogatives of the interpreter as well.

At least five hundred years earlier the Talmud (B. B. 15a, Men. 30a) states that the last eight verses of the Pentateuch—the Torah of Moses—could not have been written by Moses, since they report his death and the people's mourning for their great teacher. As a matter of course, a number of alternative interpretations are offered, among them, that Joshua wrote these verses (although there is no indication in the text to that effect), or that Moses wrote them, unaware of their meaning.

More than eight hundred years before Rashi, a sage in the Mekhilta ventured, without apology or consciousness of possible heresy, the statement that "the Lord (*Shekhinah*) never came down on Mount Sinai, nor did Moses ever go up to heaven." This, all supercommentaries notwithstanding, is an unliteral explanation, to say the least. About the same time another scholar did not hesitate to put a new meaning into the plain account of the Torah which described the flood as having overtaken the whole world. He stated that its waters never invaded the Holy Land. In spite of the privileged position of that portion of the earth, no such comment would have been permitted unchallenged, were not freedom of interpretation taken for granted.

In the schools of Babylonia from the sixth to the tenth centuries of the Common Era flourished great rabbis, whose character, no less than their learning, impressed the Jewish people everywhere. As long as communication was possible, there was a steady flow of questions on every aspect of life and lore addressed to them and of answers or decisions they sent. The latter were accepted as authoritative for the theory and practice of Judaism. The heads of the academies, called *Geonim* (Excellencies), enjoyed particular respect because of their learning and piety. One of them, Samuel ben Hofni, declared the account of the ass of Bileam to have been a vision in a dream; another great defender of the law, doughty champion of the Faith, interpreted in the same manner the vision of the three angels who came to see Abraham. This great thinker, Saadia Gaon, ventured the statement: "There are two sources of the knowledge of God: nature and Torah, the book of the created world and the book of revelation. Both, as coming from God, must be in agreement with each other. If they seem to disagree, it must be due to the fact that we misread the testimony of either of them."[1a] It was not occasional exhibition of "a heretic's courage." This freedom has been the happy asset of Jewish loyalists from Mishnah to our own days.

There are seventy meanings to Torah, said the rabbis, and they pointed to the well-nigh inexhaustible richness of its accounts: its philological, sociological, esoteric nuances, the emphases due to intellectual or emotional, religious or philosophical preoccupation.[2] Jews, in every generation, and in an amazing variety of climates, have put their own deepest thinking, searching, insight into the text of the Hebrew Bible, so that in addition to its plain meaning

---

[1a]Cp. for variations H. Malter, Saadia Gaon, p. 196, note 459 and M. Ventura, La Philosophie de Saadia Gaon a. 1.

[2]Otiot de R. A.; Men. ha-Maor 149; Resp. R. D. b. Zimra, III 1043; the last has significant observations on the inexhaustible wealth of meaning inherent in the Biblical text.

it has transmitted a riot of color and power in the incessant output of commentaries, supercommentaries, tangential observation and ever new effort at semantics. Just as the *Halakhah* is never finished but grows vertically and horizontally through the loving devotion of its authoritative scholars, so is the *Agadah,* or the non-preceptive part of the Torah, eternally subject to search, investigation, comparison, elucidation, an ongoing enterprise—a complementary progressive revelation of the message from Sinai—through Moses, Isaiah, Hillel, Saadia, Rambam, Ramban, Ralbag, Arama, Hirsch, Rab Kuk, to the dedicated students in all lands and cultures. Thus arose *Agadah,* bearing the stamp of many minds and milieus, but of one basic structure.

Only faith could have created that encyclopedia of the Jewish mind. Only freedom of interpretation made it possible.

II. About Agadah

"There are four reasons for the later scholars to interpret the books of earlier ones and to expound them:

(1) The superior quality of the earlier author who, because of his great perception, discusses profound and recondite mysteries in concise style, which to him is simple and not in need of any additional remark, but as he who comes after him endeavors to derive full understanding from that brief statement, he finds it difficult and, therefore, sees himself obliged to add certain explanation (of terms used in the article), so that a study thereof may make clear what the author had intended.

(2) The absence of premises which the author of the book knew, for the writer occasionally writes a book full of uncertainties or doubtful matter. He might think that the student of his book was aware of the premises, without which the subject in question could not be understood. Hence, the interpreter is obliged to mention briefly those premises and to smooth the path leading to them. In this process, the interpreter may expound an auxiliary science which the author had failed to mention.

(3) As to the manner of the essay involved: In any language, most essays call for interpretation, and it is possible that contradictory or changing subjects may be derived from the reading thereof. These changes may cause someone to infer a theory or a subject and to make the statement that the author referred only to

that, whereas another person may derive another theory or point
of view from it, so that the interpreter of that particular essay may
be obliged to decide between the various theories or views, to bring
evidence that one is correct and thereby to cancel all others.

(4) A thought may have occurred to the author before he had
given the matter careful consideration. He may be repeating himself, or the thought may be irrelevant. The interpreter would be
obliged to refer to that, to hint at it, to bring proof which will cancel
it, or to show that idea to be completely useless or a repetition, so
that it may be just considered not a true thought or notice."[2a]

"Our opinion is that everyone should investigate the principles
of his religious belief. As for the divine law, one who professes it
should also inquire whether it is temporal or eternal, and if it should
turn out not to be eternal, wherein the change is likely to occur.
This is also Maimonides' reason for saying in the fortieth chapter
of the second book of the "Guide of the Perplexed" that it behooves
everyone to investigate the religion which he professes. He must
examine the comments and prohibitions, and if he find that their
sole purpose is to remove wrongdoing and violence and to maintain order in the affairs of the state, he must know that it is a conventional and not a divine law. If, on the other hand, he find that,
in addition to removing wrongdoing and violence, it also takes
care to inculcate true ideas about God and angels and endeavors
to enlighten mankind and to awaken them to the nature of truth in
all things, that shows that it is divine."[2b]

"The Talmud contains:

(1) *Halakhah,* the discussions of Jewish laws and their results.
Any such result is binding for the traditional Jew. These *Halakhot*
extend and develop with the variety and increase of new conditions. In all such cases the principle which decided the more
primitive case is applied to the new situation.

(2) *Haggadah,* which has rightly been termed "religious
folklore." It contains stories, parables, maxims, interpretations,
grown neither out of a system, nor due to any definite method, but
originating from the occasion of the rabbi's sermon or from his
imagination which embellished the characters of Biblical stories,
or from his desire to comfort an afflicted congregation, or to arouse

---

[2a]Rambam—From his introduction to the chapter of Hippocrates.
[2b]"Ikkarim," by Joseph Albo—Book I, Chapter 24.

a new interest in their sacred lore. To give just a few telling
instances:[3] Rabbi Akiba, to cheer his downhearted congregation,
speaks of the virtues of Sarah, her kindness and purity, that she
lived 127 years, as innocent and youthful at the end of her life as
when she entered this world. The audience is not interested. Then
suddenly "127" suggests to him that Queen Esther reigned over
127 provinces and he excites their interest by asking: "What
caused Esther to reign over 127 provinces?"—"It is the fact that
she was a descendant of Sarah who lived 127 years." The meaning underlying this observation is obvious. The great qualities of
her ancestress which Esther inherited, eminently fitted her for
the post. Esther lived in the hearts of the people as a patriotic,
selfless woman, and the moral of the story was both clear and
impressive.

"What is the meaning of *Shaddai?*" asks a rabbi on another
occasion.[4] The etymology of this word was quite clear to him.
He knew the text (Isaiah XIII, 6) and also that *Shaddai* was
derived from *shaddad* ("to deal mightily"). But in telling his
audience about the meaning of *Shaddai* (Almighty) he looked for
a point which would immediately illustrate it. And thus he came
to explain: "The omnipotence of God is nowhere seen so clearly
as in the fact that He gave His universe a fixed law according to
which all change and action should take place. He said to His
world, 'Enough!', arresting its development, its laws and its forms
at a definite point. Now to remind yourself without delay of what
Shaddai means, think of *'she-amar dye'*, Who said 'Enough, no
further!' "—Most cases of *Al-tikre* serve as mnemotechnic devices. (Compare the very instructive essay on *Die Al-Tikre
Deutungen* by A. Rosenzweig, in *Festschrift zu J. Levy's 70sten
Geburtstag*, p. 240ff.) In a manner similar to the above, *Al-tikre*
inculcates a teaching, moral or ritual, by "misreading" a word in
a sentence, e.g.[5] "One should pronounce a hundred blessings
every day." That is a postulate or devout wish of some authority.
To impress this fact on your mind, remember the verse, Deb.
X, 12, *mah Hashem sha-el mi-mekha*, "*What doth the Lord thy
God require of thee*," but do not read *mah* "what" the Lord thy
God asks of thee, read instead *me-ah* "a hundred" the Lord
thy God asks of thee.

[3] *Esther Rabba* I.
[4] *Babli Hagigah* 12a.
[5] *Babli Menahot* 43b.

"A moral:[6] Isaiah LIV, 13 *ve-rav shalom banayikh,* *"And great will be the peace of thy children."* Do not read *banayikh,* "thy children," read *bonayikh* "those who build thee up."

"There are innumerable sentences and interpretations of this kind. In every case the 'change' is due to the idea underlying it. Hence such interpretations or translations must not be mistaken for philological truth. Yet that is exactly what happens. But none would have been more astonished than the rabbis on hearing that their mnemotechnical devices were taken as fullblown philology.

"Similar observations are necessary when we read the stories embedded in the rivers of *Haggadah.* Here again the purpose in telling them was to amuse, to cheer up, to let the people forget their present suffering by either leading them back to the glorious past or by painting in bright colors the fulness of time when there will be no enemy, no slander, no prejudice. There is no trace of a definite method, of any endeavor to weave these stories into a dogmatic texture, the *Haggadah* containing all that had occupied the popular mind, what they had heard in the *bet hammidrash,* or at a social gathering. Stories contradicting each other, theories incompatible with one another, are very frequent. They are recorded as the fruits of Israel's genius. Although stimulating, instructive, often inspiring, they have no authority, they form no part of Jewish religious belief. Nor may they be taken literally: it is always the idea, the lesson, and not the story, which is important. It is wrong to say that the *Haggadah* contains the doctrines of the rabbis, or that only orthodox views have been admitted to the exclusion of all the rest. There is nothing more unorthodox than some views on fundamental matters expressed in the *Haggadah.* Thus e.g. the idea of a personal Messiah is rejected,[7] the last verses of Deuteronomy are ascribed to Joshua.[8]"[9]

"Know ye that the words of *Agadah* are not like a *Halakhic* tradition (*shemuah*), rather does every (*Agadist*) say what occurs to him as a possible or acceptable thought, not a matter of a clear decision (*davar hatukh*). Hence we do not rely on (consider authoritative) *Agadic* statements.—About such Midrashic statements Rabbi Sherira says: 'They are guesswork; hence we do not, as a rule, rely on them, but accept what appeals to our

---

[6]*Babli Berakhot* 64a.
[7]*Babli Sanhedrin* 98a.
[8]*Babli Baba Batra* 15a.
[9]"Fallen Angels in Jewish, Christian and Mohammedan Literature", by Rabbi Leo Jung, Ph.D., Philadelphia, 1926.

mind or is supported by Biblical text.' R. Samuel ha-Nagid, in his celebrated introduction to the Talmud, supports Sherira's statement."[10]

With regard to *Agadah,* see Assaf, *Tekufat Hageonim,* Jerusalem, 1955, especially his quotations from Hai Gaon, Sherira Gaon, and Rabbi Samuel ben Hofni, as to the lesser significance of *Agadah.* Rabbi Sherira said, "We do not rely on the words of *Agadah.* They have no ultimate end or purpose." Rabbi Samuel said, "The *Halakhot* are fine flour. The *Agadot* are waste," a severe statement provoked, no doubt, by some homiletical extravagance. R. Saadia Gaon asserts: "One must not use *Agadah* as evidence."

"Rabbi Samuel ha-Nagid[11] in his introduction to the Talmud says: '*Haggadah* (that is any explanation in the Talmud on any subject outside the commandments)—you need not accept any of its teachings which do not appeal to your mind. You must know that of those laws which our Sages have decided as *Halakhah,* which are the traditions of Moses our teacher of blessed memory, nothing must be taken off, nor may anything be added to them. But when the Sages indulge in explanations of Biblical passages, each of them does according to what occurred to him and as it appeared good to his mind. Those explanations which appeal to us we accept, and the rest we do not consider authoritative.' "[11a]

"In his introduction to the *Haggadah,*[12] Rabbi Abraham, son of the great Maimonides, and himself a great scholar, says: "We are not obliged to defend the views of the Sages of the Talmud concerning natural science, medicine or astrology, or concerning any other subject, simply on the ground that our Sages were men of great knowledge in all matters and details touching the Torah.

"Whosoever propounds a certain theory or idea and expects it to be accepted on the mere ground of the author's eminence without substantiating its claims to truth and reasonableness, such a man acts against the Torah and contrary to human intelli-

---

[10]Rov Hai Gaon (quoted in *Otzar ha-Geonim, Hagigah* 59).

[11]Samuel Halevi Ibn-Nagrela ha-Nagid, scholar, poet, statesman, 993-1055.

[11a]Fallen Angels p. 5.

[12]*Maamar 'al odot Derashot Hazal,* translated from Arabic into Hebrew by an unknown scholar, published in *Kobetz Teshubot ha-Rambam,* ed. A. Lichtenstein, Leipzig, 1859.

gence. The Lord said: *'Thou shalt not respect the poor, nor honor the great person. In righteousness shalt thou judge.'*

"As far as the knowledge of the Torah is concerned, our Sages have arrived at the highest possible perfection, but that is not the case as to any other branch of knowledge. The rabbis themselves speak in that vein, when rejecting the medical theory propounded by a certain rabbi, declaring that it proved untrue (Talmud Babli Shabbat 66b)."

In the course of his valuable essay Rabbi Abraham speaks of *Derashot* (*Haggadic* explanations) which contain a figurative or hidden meaning, which are parabolical or hyperbolical expressions of some idea. Rabbi Abraham was mindful of the words of his illustrious father: "Beware that thou take not literally those sayings of our Sages, for thou wouldst thereby degrade religion and find thyself in contradiction with the holy teaching. Always look for the deeper meaning and if thou art unable to find the kernel, leave the shell alone."

Moshe Hayyim Luzzatto, in his famous essay on the *Agadot,* discussing progressive revelation in the paragraph on our teacher Moses and the influence of the Torah:

"Whatever a distinguished scholar will offer as a new light was already given to Moses on Sinai. At that time only that part of revelation was given to Israel which was suitable for them. In all generations there are such positions to be revealed through the Sages, all, however, coming from Moses. This is the inner meaning of the prophetic admonition, *'Remember the law of Moses, My servant'* (Mal. III, 22). Thus, the context (the matter or the content) of the Torah stays incomplete (unexhausted), and whenever a new individual arises, there is a revelation of the part due to him. That is the meaning of the Talmud statement, 'Let it rest until Elijah comes.' For it is he who will complete and prove the revelation for all."

Luzzatto refers to to Zohar, Raya Mehemna on Par. Tzav, 27.

In the introduction to the Talmud by Rabbi Tzevi Chayes, he describes many expressions and statements that must not be taken literally. In Gittin 58, 1, *Berakhot* 51b, *Avodah Zarah* 14b, reference is made to the use of round figures, like 400.—In *Erubin* 16b, the Talmud states the Sages "refer (not to abiding facts, but) to actual contemporary conditions," even as Scripture does. In

Shabbat VI, 6, the Mishnah states, "The scholars (in using the words 'Arabian woman') speak of the ordinary custom (not to the exclusion of other people)."—All so-called "popular etymology" has ethical or spiritual purposes. In such light must one view the naturalization of Greek words and their interpretation, as it were, on the basis of Semitic root meanings, as in Gittin 36a ("Prozbol") or, in *Berakhot* 62b ("Kapandria"—literally *compendiaria via,* a short path); similarly, the interpretation of proper names meant illustratively, rather than logically, such as Putiel in Sotah 43a, Petahya in Men. 65a, and Shobab in Sotah 11b. (The whole subject of free rabbinic interpretation of Bible passages in Talmudic and Midrashic literature was exhaustively treated by Dr. Israel Frankel in "Peshat," Toronto, 1956, especially in his introduction, pages 26-35.)

"The study of the holy Torah will produce two types of Jewish literary schools, united in the subject matter, separate in the source of knowledge they are seeking. The first will be charged with the understanding of the divine texts that are to govern our life and what they imply for the governance of our life. Its sources will be almost exclusively the tradition which hands down in written and oral form the divine texts and the ordinances of our Sages.

"The other will be charged with contemplation and study of these laws. The source of its knowledge will be, first of all, the spiritual light of each individual, burning more or less brightly.

"The first is found in *shemateta,* derived from *shema,* 'that which is heard or has been received.' The second we find in *agadeta,* derived from the spirit of each individual that which he expressed or relayed (*higid*). Everything belonging to the second circle implies no obligation because it is only the opinion of individuals and has authority only to the extent to which it corresponds with the content of *shemateta.* The first circle in its positions is completed in the *Gemara* as it completes the collection of the *shematetot.* The second, the circle of *Agadah,* is free and capable of enrichment at all times. In the sphere of the knowledge of the law, everything rests upon the principles transmitted in that field, and no private opinion about the meaning or the motive of any law can ever change its enactments, but in the search, the creation and formation of such opinions, the mind and spirit of every individual has unlimited margins of freedom. Indeed, from earliest times to our own day, the most varied opinions have been conveyed by men highly endowed. The scientific test of an *Agadah,* however, will be its conformity to *Halakhah* whenever it deals with a legal subject. Wherever an opinion or part thereof would violate any legal test, that opinion would have to yield."[13]

The late Dr. David Hoffmann, recognized as one of the greatest rabbinical authorities of our age, who combined a comprehensive knowledge of the whole range of Jewish literature with modern scholarship, may be cited for his view (see Hoffmann, *Leviticus,* vol. I, p. 6). "The sayings of our Sages called *Haggadot* contain a statement of moral import or an explanation of a scriptural passage not bearing upon Jewish law or something cognate. They are by no means to be considered divine traditions and we are not obliged to accept them."

The world-renowned *Gaon,* Rector Dr. J. J. Weinberg, in his volume, *"Das Volk der Religion,"* Geneva, 1949, describes it as a unique quality of Judaism that it combines obligation to tradition with creative freedom, explaining that conformity to the law allows infinite variety of interpretation (page 39 ff.). He indicates how the Mussar movement of Lithuania offers a fascinating example of that double orientation and how the history of Jewish thought presents many variants of interpretation, all not only not impeded, but protected, by the traditional forms of Jewish life.

The classification of the *mitzvot* to which Zunz, in his *"Gesammelte Schriften"* dedicates a whole chapter, presents another example of the freedom to use the inexhaustible treasure of the Torah for particular needs, from apologetics in face of attacks from foreign ideologies, theological or philosophical, to the endeavor to stimulate contemporary thinking by association with thoughts implied or expressed in the Biblical texts.

The Other Side of the Picture

"These two things have troubled us: 'Nature' and 'Peshat.' (The reference to Natural Philosophy—as against statements on this subject in the Jewish books; and simple text meaning as against symbolic and hyperbolic interpretation)."[14] We may dis-

---

[13]"Horeb," by S. R. Hirsch, Altona 1837 (Introduction, page vii).

[14]"Emunat Hakhamim," by Aviad Sar Salom, the son of Menahem Samson Bazilah, famous Gaon, published 1730, in Mantua. A book in defense of the teachings of the Sages of Israel, and opposed to any type of rationalization, and to the Freedom of Interpretation. Fond of quoting non-Jewish literature. Ch. II (p. 3).

agree with this opinion, but freedom of interpretation includes also its privilege.

"I am offering this as an example known to all our *poskim* (decisors of Jewish Law), who decide according to the Talmud by whose text we live. Whosoever is considered a Jew will never depart from a decision of the Talmud. One who does almost departs from life.

Nevertheless, there are other things (expressions, ideas) in which we ignore the word of the Talmud and guide ourselves according to other literature, the reason being that these things are not dependent on matters of *issur ve-heter* (prohibition or permissiveness) and, therefore, we have the right to accept the words of somebody who appears right to us, even though his opinion does not agree with that of the Talmud, *as long as the matter involved has nothing to do with Jewish precepts.* This is a principle to guide ourselves by."[15]

Rabbi Caro, in declaring his independence from the Talmud in the interpretation of non-preceptive matter, might have had in mind the statement in *Yerushalmi, Horayot* (at the end of Chapter III), on the text, *"Yet God giveth him not power to eat thereof"* (Ecclesiastes VI, 2): That refers to the teacher of *Agadah,* who neither prohibits nor permits, neither declares pure or impure.—

A modern Talmudist and classical scholar, the sainted Rabbi Heinrich Ehrentreu, in *"Sprachliches und Sachliches aus dem Talmud,"* CI, in discussion of the statement, *"Al ehad lo dak,"* emphasizes the Talmud's elastic attitude towards numbers. It literally means that in such instances the Talmud does not express itself with exactitude. In this fashion a number of difficult passages find satisfactory interpretation.

III. Contradictory Agadot

Since *Agadah* is individualistic and hence not objective, the following examples of its contradictory statements are not surprising. Most of them are culled from that indispensable Biblical Encyclopedia, Rov M. M. Kasher's *Torah Shelemah.*

The complete absence of an *Agadic* scheme or set of metaphysical doctrines will impress itself upon the reader.

---

[15]"Responsa Abkat Rokhel," 28, by Rabbi Joseph Caro.

I. About the Flood:

Talm. Zebahim 113a: One master holds that the flood descended in Eretz Israel, while the other holds that it did not descend there. The master whose opinion obviously ignores the Biblical account (*"Every living substance will I blot out from off the face of the earth"*, Ber. VII, 4), is quoted side by side with the colleague who records his own in conformity with the text. Complete freedom of interpretation is here taken for granted. A parallel passage in the Midr. Ral Gen. XXXII, reads: "Mount Gerizim (in Palestine) is blessed because it was not submerged by the flood".— Although the speaker is a Samaritan, his "fact" is not disputed. (Torah Shel. a.l. has colorful elaborations).

II. About Abraham:

Nahmanides, on Ber. XII, 10: "Father Abraham, by error, committed a great sin in that he brought his wife to the stumbling block of iniquity because of his fear that the Egyptians might kill him. He should have trusted in God that He would save him and his wife." His point of view, appealing to many, is, however, completely at variance with that held by the Tanhuma and of Pirke de R. Eliezer (quoted in Tor. Shel. a.l. CXLV).—Arresting is the heated argument of R. Berekiah against R. Levi for the latter's somewhat excessive use of *licentia homiletica!* Again: what matters is not the force of particular logic, but the freedom of interpretation.—In connection with the sin of Abraham, Samson R. Hirsch has a valiant and persuasive argument, just as Malbim and others have perceptively pleaded for a more lenient judgment. One may accept either or, in some cases, both as approximations to true evalution, yet not forget the fact that both are cited, welcomed, uncriticized on any dogmatic ground. No heresy-trial ever threatened the Sage, however freely he let his imagination roam in his homiletical efforts as they dealt with non-legal verses.

In Ber. 13a the Talmud Babli reads: "Anyone referring to Abraham as Abram transgresses—a prohibition." (Ber. XIII, 5), but in the Yerushalmi, Ber. I, it is recorded that the men of the Great Synod called him "Abram."

III. Re Isaac:

Ber. XXVII, reads: *"And it came to pass that when Isaac was old and his eyes were dim."* The Midrash R., XLV, 9-11, expounds the cause of his affliction in terms favorable to the patriarch, but the Tanhuma a.l. takes an opposite view: as resulting from his acquiescence in the wickedness of Esau, who bribed him with gifts of venison. In Kohelet Rabba, LXXXIV, the Lord is made to refer to his iniquity which He graciously overlooks, as Malakhi I, 2: *"I love Jacob,"* indicates.

IV. CONCERNING JACOB:

Commenting on Ber. XXXIII, 10, the Talm., Sobah 41b, quotes these opinions: (Jacob addressed Esau thus): *Receive my present at my hand forasmuch as I have seen thy face as one seeth the face of God and thou wast pleased with me.* R. Simeon ben Lakish would derive from this verse the right to flatter the wicked in this world (to escape the menace of their assault), whilst R. Levi explains the reference to God as an indirect warning of His inescapable retribution.

V. ABOUT REUBEN:

Ber. XXXV, 22 tells of his grave aberration. Yet the Talm. Shabb. 55a, avers that whosoever maintains that Reuben sinned merely errs. Torah Shel. a.l. quotes views which either interpret the Biblical passage as censuring him for injecting himself in his father's private affairs (such interference being tantamount to indecent abuse), or which emphasize his penitence that wiped the stain of the offense off his escutcheon.

VI. TOUCHING JOSEPH:

The text of Ber. XXXIX, 11 refers to his routine work, yet, according to Talmud Sotah 36b, Rab and Samuel differ in their interpretation: one said the text refers to his real work, while the other held that he went to satisfy his passion. Rov Kasher, op. cit., cites explanations which have much merit. Here again freedom of interpretation is extended equally to views which defend a Biblical figure and to those which attack him.

VII. MOSHEH RABBENU:

The Mekhilta has amazing interpretation of Shem. II, 21. As to IX, 24 ibidem: *The Lord met him and sought to kill him,* the Midrash cites His reproof: "I sent thee (Moses) to redeem my

children who are in trouble and you are relaxing at the inn!" Hence
He sought to slay him.—A passage in *Pesikta Zutarta* offers a
deviating account of the passage at the Red Sea. On the coming
up of the quails, *Bekhor Shor* suggests a dislocation of the text,
quite legitimate on the basis of *en mukdam umeuhar* (that in the
Biblical texts events or laws are recorded occasionally not chrono-
logically but logically or by associative considerations), yet illus-
trative of *Agadic* privilege.

Referring to: *"And the Lord came down upon Mount Sinaï"*,
the Talmud in Succah 5a states: "Neither did the *Shekhinah*
ever descend to earth, nor did Moses or Elijah ever ascend to
heaven." Though the further discussion in the tractate allows
for modification of this bold statement, it is but an instance of
free interpretation of metaphysical passages of the Torah. The
ebb and tide of classic versus romantic attitude, evident everywhere, is exemplified by the Targum's extreme precaution against
any anthropomorphic concept of the Deity, as against the Talmud's
extreme freedom in bringing Him nearer to the heart of the non-
philosophical average Jew by such liberties as recorded in Baba
M. 59b. Such action and reaction appear in the rigid rationalism
of Saadia and Rambam, by the peopling of the interstellar spaces
with the millions of ghosts, angels, *shedim* in the Zohar and its
literature, to be followed by two almost contemporary divergent
schools, the 19th century rationalism and the various nuances of
Hassidic imaginative doctrines, as reflected in the richness and
warmth of the stories from the Baal Shem Tov to the Kotzker.
The amazingly bold commentaries, exampla and maxims of the
Hassidic leaders defy with equal vigor grammatical or stylistical
categories, yet have not only added immeasurably to the treasury
of the Torah, but have also exhibited to marked degree the wide
margin the most pietistic thinker took for granted as a privilege
or duty of the student of the Torah. It is through such interpretation and re-interpretation—faithful to the fundamental doctrine
of the divine origin of the Torah and conforming to the duty
of investing one's deepest thoughts, bravest dreams and one's
blessed ingenuity in reading the text, between the lines, and beyond its obvious realm, whilst at large in the garden of the four
time-hallowed Jewish modes of interpretation of Holy Writ (the
PARDES)—that Jewish scholars, searchers, students have managed
to keep the Torah an effervescent source of inspiration, challenge,
and yet of profound peace.

The mystic Recanati (ad locum) and the rationalist Rambam (in Moreh I, 18) meet in amazing agreement in their interpretation of the last verses of Shem. XXIV.

VIII. CONCERNING THE MESSIAH:

In Sanhedrin 98b, R. Hillel is quoted as saying: "There shall be no Messiah for Israel because they have already enjoyed him in the days of Hezekiah" (derived the benefit of ease and prosperity). This statement belongs to the small group of astonishing disagreements with a basic Jewish teaching. Indeed, R. Joseph animadverts on the same page: "May God forgive him that utterance!" Other contradictary opinions are also cited. Again, the decisive point is the absence of any hesitation on the part of R. Hillel, although he may have anticipated his colleague's censure. Rashi explains him to mean that there shall be no human Messiah, but the Lord will redeem Israel and rule them. There is, beyond R. Joseph's exclamation, no comment from any member of the learned collegium. The privilege of *ad hoc* and individual interpretation is taken for granted. Again the commentators and the super-commentaries, from Rashi on, deal, rationally or mystically, traditionally or in new ways, with the words of R. Hillel. Together, they form the symphony of *Agadic* orchestration, each nuance justified and relevant in its locus and none compelling the loyal Jew to accept any particular version, reaction or interpretation. As Dr. I. Epstein (Soncino Edition of Sanhedrin, II, 669, note 5) suggests, R. Hillel may have been prompted to this declaration by Origen's professed discovery in the Hebrew Bible of Messianic passages referring to the founder of Christianity, but that only helps to support the margin of freedom of interpretation in non-preceptive verses of the *Tanakh*.

An outstanding example of this freedom, with courage to question God's greatness, is found in Yoma 69b:

R. Gidal said (with reference to Neh. VIII): *"'And Ezra blessed the Lord, the great God.'* He magnified Him by pronouncing the ineffable name." R. Mattena said: "He said: *'The great, the mighty and the revered God.'"* R. Mattena's view seems to agree with that of R. Joshua ben Levi who said: "Why were they called men of the Great Synod? Because they restored the crown of the divine attributes to its pristine completeness. For Moses had said: *'The great God, the mighty and the revered.'*

Then Jeremiah called out: 'Aliens are howling in His temple. Where, then, are His awful deeds?' Hence he omitted the attribute *'Awsome'* (revered). Daniel came and said: 'Aliens are enslaving His children. Where, then, are His mighty deeds?' Hence he (in his prayer, Dan. IX, 4) omitted the word 'mighty.' But they (the men of the Great Synod) came and said: 'On the contrary! His mighty deeds lie in the fact that He controls His anger, extending long suffering to the wicked. These are *'His mighty deeds'* for, were it not for the fear of Him, how could a single nation survive among the many (hostile) ones!" But how could those scholars (the prophets Jeremiah and Ezra) uproot something established by Moses? Said R. Eleazar: "Since they knew that the Holy One, blessed be He, insists on truth (and hates untruth), they would not pay lying homage to Him when (for reasons known to Him alone), he would not display His power (but His moral quality)."

No modern rabbi, nor any religious person of our day, would dare challenge, even by implication, His omnipotence or omniscience!

IV. Interpretation of Non-Preceptive Verses of Tanakh

"The Torah speaks in the language of man," Ket. 67b, Baba M. 31b. The expression *'lashan havay'* (exaggeration in rhetorical speech) in connection with Biblical passages is found in Hullin 90b, where also *'lashon guzma'* (figure of speech, hyperbole) is used in that connection. In Betzah 4a, the same phrase refers to hyperboles in Baraita or Mishnah. Most relevant in this connection is appendix 22, on *"Mikra ki-peshutto",* in the seventeenth volume of Torah Shelemah.

"Although in the *Gemara* the verse was interpreted otherwise, since, as far as Jewish Law is concerned there is no practical difference, it is legitimate to interpret it (differently, according to one's own view).

"For I see no difference between the interpretation of Mishnah and that of Scripture, where freedom has been granted to explain (Biblical) verses (freely), as we can see in the works of the interpreters from the time of the *Gemara;* provided there be no decision or interpretation to contradict the (legal) opinion of the scholars of the *Gemara.*"[16]

---

[16]Rabbi Yomtov Lipman Heller, (17th Century), in his commentary "Tosafot Yomtob" on the Mishnah (Nazir V5).

In his note on Ber. XLIX, Rabbi Yomtov Lipman says the Torah bears many interpretations, each of which are the words of the Living God, for it implies all proper explanations. In paragraph 45 on Genesis XLVIII, 14, he opposes the abuse for theological purposes of that freedom of interpretation. His comments on Shemot XXXIII, 13, offer similar suggestions.[17]

"And the Lord came down upon Mount Sinai. I might understand this to mean upon the entire mountain, but it says: 'To the top of the mount.' One might think that the Glory actually descended from heaven and was transferred to Mount Sinai, but Scripture says: *'That I have talked with you from heaven'* (Shem. XX, 19). Scripture thus teaches that the Holy One, blessed be He, bent down the lower heavens and the upper heavens of heaven, lowering them to the top of the mountain, and thus the Glory descended. He spread them upon Mount Sinai as a man who spreads the mattress upon the bed and speaks from the mattress. For it is said: *'as when fire kindleth the brushwood, and the fire causeth the waters to boil'* (Isa. LXIV, 1). Likewise it says: *'When Thou didst tremendous things'* (ibid., v. 2).—R. Jose says: "Behold, it says, *'The heavens are the heavens of the Lord, but the earth hath He given to the children of men'* (Ps. CXV, 16). Neither Moses nor Elijah ever went up to heaven, nor did the Glory ever come down to earth. Scripture merely teaches that God said to Moses: *Behold, I am going to call you through* (i.e., you will hear the call as if it came from the top of the mountain) the top of the mount and you will come up, as it is said: *'And the Lord called Moses to the top of the mount'* (v. 20)."[18]

" '*And it came to pass, when Moses held up his hand, that Israel prevailed; and when he let down his hand, Amalek prevailed.'* Now, did the hands of Moses wage war or crush the enemy? Not so. The text only signifies that so long as Israel turned their thoughts upwards and subjected their hearts to their Father in heaven, they prevailed, but otherwise they failed.

"The same observation applies to the passage Nu. XXI, 8: *'Make thee a fiery serpent and set it upon a pole; and it shall come to pass that everyone that is bitten, when he seeth it, shall live.'* Now, did the serpent kill, or keep alive? No. The verse teaches that when Israel turned their thoughts upwards and sub-

---

[17] The "Sefer Nitzahon" of Rabbi Yomtov Lipman of Muelhausen (early 15th Century).
[18] "Mekhilta de-Rabbi Ishmael," Volume II—Philadelphia, 1933, p. 224.

jected their hearts to their Father in heaven, they were healed, but otherwise they pined away."[19]

R. Abbahu said: "Were this verse not written, it would have been impossible to say (what it states): *'In the same day shall the Lord shave with a razor that is hired, namely, by the river side, by the King of Assyria, the head and the hair of the feet, and it shall consume the beard'*.[20] The RMA (Rabbi Moses Isserlis, co-author of the *Shulhan Arukh* and renowned philosopher) observes: "This statement is obviously farther from truth than the East is from the West, for the simple text contains many denials of His deity. Although R. Abbahu says: 'The Holy One, blessed be He, went and appeared before Sennaherib as an old man and spoke to him,'[21] * * *, I say, in spite of this being a Biblical text, it is impossible to quote or explain it according to its plain meaning, for *'God is in heaven and the earth He gave to the sons of man.'* He does not—God forbid—assume physical shape to come down to earth." RMA continues: "Since earlier scholars have failed to offer a satisfactory explanation of this strange statement, I said, 'I'll arise out of regard for my Creator's honor—blessed and holy forever—to remove such anthropomorphism. He is far above such terms, according to the basic principles of our faith.' " RMA then offers five interpretations, beseeching God to teach him the wonders of His Torah.[22]

Rabbi Jannai and Rabbi Ismael both say there is no *Gehinnom* in the world to come, but the sun comes forth, the righteous enjoy it, as it is said (Malakhi III): *"The sun of righteousness will arise, with healings in its wings,"* and the wicked shall be judged, as it is said: *"The day that cometh shall set them"* (Ib. 19).[23] These reports are interesting, but more significant is the fact that the whole statement could be offered without any protest or condemnation.[24]

" *'But then the anger of the Lord shall be kindled.'* Through anger, the body becomes heated and smoke, as it were, issues from the nostrils. Thus is it said in Psalms XXII, 9: *'Smoke arose up in His nostrils.'* Although this is not really applicable to

---

[19]Mishnah Rosh Hashanah 29a, referring to Exodus XVII, 11.
[20]Sanh. 95b.
[21]Ibid.
[22]Sanh. 95b.—In his preface to "Mehir Yayin."
[23]Midrash Koh. R. I, 5.
[24]See also Nedarim 8b, Aboda Zarah 3b and cp. the amazing interpretation of Rabbi Yehuda Liva (the Maharal of Prague) as reported in Rabbi Dessler's *"Mikhtav Eliyahu,"* p. 302.

the Omnipresent, Scripture makes the human ear hear the matter (tells it to humans) in the manner that it is accustomed and able to hear in accordance with the ordinary course of the world (i. e., when speaking of God, it uses language properly applicable only to human beings because it is the only language at our command)."[25]

"The sage keeps his eye in front. Let him not surrender his mind, no matter how imposing the personality or how attractive the suggestion. Each person should engage in his own search for the knowledge of God, his own way of finding God through the study of his creation and the search for the *ta'ame ha-mitzvot,* but—(Hilkh. Meilah VIII, 8)—let him never assume that failure to discover an adequate reason would in any manner justify violation of any law of the Torah."[26] For freedom of interpretation deals neither with the one a priori doctrine—the divine origin of the Torah—nor does it apply to the assured results of *Halakhah,* the precepts handed down from the past, finally edited in the Mishnah, illustrated in the decisions of the Talmud and applied by the ingenious loyalty and encyclopedic knowledge of the authorities of every age, the *Poskim,* whose legislative activity is never finished.

"On the one hand, there is freedom of interpretation, but consistently, on the other, there is no obligation to accept any individual's view—homiletical, philosophical, or theological—on any nonpreceptive matter."[27] This applies to all cognate literature, from Ibn Ezra's astrology through Rabbi Levi Ben Haviv's acceptance of *gilgul* (metempsychosis), which he considers obligatory upon Torah-true Jews.[27a]

"One who entertains a certain (alien) notion in relation to one of the miracles of the Torah because he thinks that he is not thereby denying any of the doctrines which it is obligatory upon us to believe by the authority of the Torah,—a person of this sort is not an unbeliever. He is classed with the sages and pious men of Israel, though he holds erroneous theories. His sin is due to error and requires atonement."[28]

In paragraph 9 of his introduction to his commentary on Job, R. Simeon bar Tzemah (14th Century), quoted in T. Sh.

---

[25]Rashi on Debarim XXIX, 19.
[26]Rambam—From "Maamar al Tehiyat ha-Metim".
[27]Rambam—From "Teshuvah to the Congregation of Marsilia."
[27a]Responsum on Gilgul.
[28]"Sefer Ha-Ikkarim" by Joseph Albo, Philadelphia, 1929; Book I, Chapter 2, Page 50.

XVI, 317, says: "Some of our scholars have reached foreign ideas which we must not accept. Nor may we, on that account, speak ill of them and say that they deny God, since they are loyal in their faith, observant and conforming. A man may interpret a midrash literally and arrive, e.g., at an anthropomorphic view of God. That, however, does not make him a heretic. (He is just in error about this matter)."

On the other hand, Rambam, in his *Moreh,* has a strange view about the ass of Bileam, contrary to the scriptural text. But one must not therefore say that because of this view he contradicts basic principles of the Torah, God forbid.

Gersonides had strange views about the origin of the world.

Abravanel in chapter XII of his *Rosh Amanah* observes: "If somebody, because of his literal reading of the text, comes to anthropomorphic views, he must not be called a *min* (heretic).

In similar vein does R. Mosheh Cordovero (in his *Pardes Rimonim*) express himself. Generous consideration is granted the conservative, as well as for the liberal view.[29]

V. ALLEGORY—A SPECIAL FORM OF FREE INTERPRETATION

For hundreds of years, from Philo through the Middle Ages, allegory was used as addition to the simple meaning (*peshat*). It could have been a mystical interpretation (justified by the famous passage in the book of Zohar, Par. Behal):

"So it is with the Torah itself. It is itself the supernal all-comprehensive Rule, yet in addition does each particular narrative, seemingly a mere story or fact, standing outside the all-comprehensive Rule of the Torah, teach us not only its own limited lesson, but supernal ideas and recondite doctrines applicable to the whole of the all-comprehensive Rule of the Torah. Thus when we read that *'the ark rested in the seventh month, on the seventeenth day of the month, upon the mountains of Ararat',* we assuredly find

---

[29]Prof. Goodenough in his edition of "The Politics of Philo Judaeus" and A. Wahrman in *Mis'tre ha-Agadah* (the latter following to some extent the trail blazed by J. D. Eisenstein in his book on Rabba b. b. Hana) account admirably for some seeming incongruities and baffling mysteries, in the writings of the Neo-Platonic philosopher and the tall stories of the Amora, respectively. The theme of both becomes clearer when viewed as satires of contemporary rulers. Rov Z'ev Katz (in *Tenuat ha-Mussar,* III, 219) quotes an interesting interpretation of difficult *Agadot* in Talmud B. Batra 73b, the emphasis being that only an intimate knowledge of contemporary local configuration would enable one to comprehend some apparently strange dicta.

here a particular statement, apparently a superfluous detail; for what matters it to us whether the ark rested in this or in the other place so long as it rested somewhere? Yet does it contain teaching applicable to the whole principle of the Torah. And happy are Israel to whom was given the sublime Torah, the Torah of truth. Perdition take anyone who maintains that any narrative in the Torah comes merely to tell us a piece of history and nothing more! If that were so, the Torah would not be what it assuredly is, to wit, the supernal Law, the Law of truth. Now if it is not dignified for a king of flesh and blood to engage in common talk, much less to write it down, is it conceivable that the most high King, the Holy One, blessed be He, was short of sacred subjects with which to fill the Torah, so that he had to collect such commonplace topics as the anecdotes of Esau, and Hagar, Laban's talks to Jacob, the words of Balaam and his ass, those of Balak, and of Zimri, and such-like, and make of them a Torah? If so, why is it called the 'Law of truth' Why do we read *'The law of the Lord is perfect . . . The testimony of the Lord is sure . . . The ordinances of the Lord are true . . . More to be desired are they than gold, yea, than much fine gold'* (Ps. XIX, 8-11)? But assuredly each word of the Torah signifies sublime things, so that this or that narrative, besides its meaning in and for itself, throws light on the all-comprehensive Rule of the Torah. See now what the resting of the ark comes to teach us. At the time when Rigor impends over the world and the Holy One, blessed be He, sits on His throne of Judgement to judge the world, within that Throne, in the King's chest, there are deposited ever so many records, notes and books, so that nothing is forgotten by the King. That Throne attains its full significance only in the seventh month, on the Day of Judgement, when all the people of the world pass before it for scrutiny. 'The Ark' thus 'rested in the seventh month', on the world's Day of Judgement, 'on the mountains of Ararat', that is, attended by the lords of Rigour, the lords of the hostile shout. Many are the executioners who bestir themselves on that day and place themselves underneath the Throne to take part in the world's judgement. Israel on that day offer up prayer and supplication before Him, they blow the trumpet, and the Holy One, blessed be He, takes compassion on them and changes Rigour into Mercy. Then all the upper and the lower beings proclaim: *'Happy is the people that know the joyful shout'* (Ps. LXXXIX, 16). Hence, on that day, whoever blows the trumpet should know the root of the matter, so as to concentrate his mind on the meaning of the blowing and to perform it with understanding. Thus, 'happy is the people that *know* the joyful shout', and not merely 'that *sound* the joyful shout'. "[30]

The allegorical or mystical interpretation was never meant to supersede the *peshat,* but to be additional to it. At times, it was obligatory, as in the Gan Eden story, and others, it was permissible wherever reason required it.

The use of allegory is referred to in Saadia Emunot VII, where he chastises and ridicules its abuse.

The Mishnah Yadayim III, 5 views the *Song of Songs* as a dialogue between God and the congregation of Israel. The Talmud, in Sanhedrin 92b, allegorizes Ezekiel's celebrated vision of the dead bones. Rashi, in Bamidbar VII, quotes from Rabbi Moshe Hadarshan's interpretation of every part of the consecration sacrifice as having symbolical reference to historical acts or personalities.

The *Maasseh Merkabah* of Ezekiel I and X has long ago been recognized as an effort to explain allegorically the infinite and inexpressible.

R. Salomo Adret, in Responsa 95 and 418, respectively, discusses the double aspects of allegorizing tendencies in rabbinic literature.

Redak. on Samuel I, 29, quoting the Gaon Rabbi Samuel ben Hofni: "For these things will not be accepted whenever there is contradictory evidence from the intellect." He also quotes Saadia Gaon, who says: "Intelligence will not accept that, and my interpretation is the proper one."[31]

Saadia justified allegory when literal translation would contradict sense perception or reason or other Biblical passages or traditional interpretation. Ibn Ezra, in his commentary on Exodus XVI, 28 holds that Biblical passages have also an inner mystical meaning, in addition to the simple natural one. Aramah appropriates this attitude and elaborates it. Joseph Albo, in "Ikkarim," does the same. Ralbag ad locum agrees, although in his commentary on Genesis III, he adventures in his own way. Nahmanides

---

[30]"The Zohar", translated by Maurice Simon and Harry Sperling, Vol. V, Soncino Press, 1949.

[31]Examples of freedom of interpretation found in the commentaries of Rabbi David Kimche on the Prophets:

Samuel I—XXV, 43; XXVIII, 24; Samuel II—XXI, 19; Melakhim I— VIII, 55;

Isaiah—V, 2; VIII, 1; XX, 2; XXII, 11; XXV, 8; XXIX, 13; XLII, 5; Jeremiah—V, 22; Ezekiel—XVIII, 6; XXXIX, 31.

(in *Zekhut Adam ha-Rishon,* Appendix III to Jellinek's edition of his famous *derashah,* Leipzig, 1853) would limit freedom of interpretation to historical parts of the Torah, like Jacob's ladder. The very fact of recognition of the four approaches of the Pardes (Peshat, Remez, Drash, Sod) emphasizes freedom of interpretation and the account of the three scholars who were hurt as they "entered the garden" (with only Rabbi Akiba escaping) indicates the perils involved. Rambam, in Moreh III, 29, had stressed the need of interpreting passages of metaphysical content. He was more liberal than Nahmanides. (Compare also his commentary on the Mishnah Sanhedrin I, s.v. *dibra Torah bilshon bne adam;* Yess. ha-Torah I, 9 and 12, and Moreh I, 26 and 59). Rabbi Moshe Isserlis, in his preface to his *"Mehir Yayin,"* follows the Rambam's attitude in Moreh III, 43, and advises that we concentrate on the kernel rather than on the form of the statement and stresses various meanings, obvious and esoteric. He emphasizes the religious obligation to offer an interpretation beyond the text and transcending its obvious form.

Yerushalmi K'tubot 28c: "This is one of the three passages to be explained allegorically or symbolically or in which the Torah uses metaphorical expressions (Shem, XXI, 19, XXII, 2, Deb. XXII, 17)." Babli Sanh. 92b.: "In truth, the fact of resurrection was a symbol for the redemption of Israel from captivity."

Bam. Rabah XIV: "God spoke to Balaam only through allegories or visions."

Cp. Leopold Dukes "Aelt. Jued. Exegeten," p. 92, note 3.

In Midrash Rabbah, Shem. LXXX, we read: "Do not interpret Jacob's request for bread and garment literally. It refers rather to his hope that the Lord will be with him and protect him."

Rabbi Isaac Aramah, of the 15th Century, the famous commentator on the Torah, states:

"The Torah deliberately hid the reason of certain *mitzvot,* in order that every person should recognize that every *mitzvah* in the Torah has a hidden motive beyond human reason. Thus, he will never permit himself levity with regard to the Torah nor modify his conformity in any manner. Every *mitzvah* has an obvious and a hidden motive. The hidden motive remains hidden forever." Cp. Ibn Ezra on Exodus XX, 1 and Rambam, Moreh II, 29.

As to the limits of interpretation, see Sanhedrin 99b, where the Baraita comments thus on the verse in Nu. XV, 31, *"because he hath despised the word of the Lord":* This refers to one who maintains that the Torah is not from heaven. Even if he asserts that the holy Torah is from heaven, excepting one verse, which (he avers) was not uttered by God, but by Moses himself—even excepting a single point or *kal vahomer* (argument ad majorem), he is included among those who despise the word of the Lord. Yet compare with this the statement that the last eight verses of the Torah (Deb. XXXIV) were written by Joshua and the text in Megillah 31b: "In the warnings of Debarim, Israel is addressed in the singular (*If thou shalt not hearken unto the voice of the Lord thy God*) and Moses uttered them *in his own name*. Tosaphot a.l. (sub voce: Mosheh) comments: "Moses uttered them in his own name and under prophetic inspiration" (or: in the holy spirit).

See long note of J. L. Krinsky's *"Mehokeke Yeduha"* on Ibn Ezra's commentary to Deut. XXVI, 5.

In Talpiot I, 384, Rabbi Kasher cites ten rabbinic passages referring to the Creation. All differ in important details and are quoted without limit of either primacy or any judgment as to authoritative opinion; without any emphasis on one or excuse for another. The basis of all scholars' view was the belief that God created the world. An infinite margin is left to individual ingenuity.

MEMOIRS OF CHILDHOOD—AN APPROACH TO JEWISH PHILOSOPHY

By Nima H. Adlerblum

CONTENTS

33

MEMOIRS OF CHILDHOOD—AN APPROACH TO JEWISH PHILOSOPHY

By Nima H. Adlerblum

If I seek to enter into the Jewish spirit through the gates of childhood, it is because one may better sense its force and palpable reality through the magnifying eyes of a child, who sees everything in its original freshness. It is like opening the faucets through which Jewishness flows in its freshness and spontaneity.

The panorama of great men unfolded in this and the preceding volume (*Jewish Leaders*) projects a view of those who helped keep Jewishness everlastingly vivid. With them it is not a system superimposed upon the centripetal forces of life. It is a continuum from one central force to another which for the Jew merge into one. Living Jewish life in its entirety was as natural to them as breathing the air or abiding by the laws of gravitation. If we seek for their underlying philosophy, we would find it to be one of implicit acceptance of Jewishness. The urge of fashioning the world into the image of God is the vital impetus of them all.

Their common foundation and outlook are not devoid, however, of colorful distinctions and richness of personality. Within the harmonious ensemble, the divergence of emphasis forms a colorful kaleidoscope reflecting a variety of temperaments, shades in the clarity of vision, moods and dangers of the times. The gamut runs from purely intellectual to deeply emotional notes, each carrying a tone and fidelity of the Jewish spirit. A suitable background for a Jewish canvas is the milieu in which I was reared in Jersualem, known as Sara Bayla's courtyard. It would add one more film to a cinematographic picture of the Jewish whole through those who expressed it in their own being. It is less my intention to draw individual sketches, than to paint the Jewishness that flows from the great and from the humble, from old and young.

My Jerusalem Milieu

The courtyard was built by Sara Bayla and her husband Reb Jacob Mordecai Hirschensohn in 1863, when they came there after a fifteen years' stay in Safed. The *Yeshivah,* the little cottages built for the scholars, the large dining room, the deep cistern for water supply, the terraces, the spaciousness, the large hill overlooking the town, with the Mosque of Omar facing it, the beauty of the natural landscape—all this gave it a unique place in the affection of the community. When the construction was under

35

way, the rabbis came there to make *She-heheyanu,*[1] that God
blessed them with such a locality for consecration to learning.
The terraces were the town's favorite place for the blessing of
the moon.[2] People of all walks of life would come to refresh
their minds with long or short visits to the *Yeshivah,* where learning went on uninterruptedly. This courtyard grew to be a meeting
place for weighing problems, for joint planning, for the reception
of prominent visitors, or for installing newcomers. There was
hardly a meal without some rabbis at the table, more absorbed
in discussions than in food.

The debates, especially in regard to upheavals in the Jewish
world, were sufficient in themselves to indicate the depths of their
Jewish concern—an essential trait of Jewishness. The turbulence
abroad caused by the blasting blows of Reform and assimilation,
were a source of great pain to the people of Jerusalem. In despair,
they sought comfort in isolation and in the hope that with the
multiplying of offspring and with the incoming of an increasing
number of refugees of the spirit, there would grow in the Holy
Land a perpetual remnant immune to the vicissitudes of the times.
But for Jacob Mordecai and Sarah Bayla to live on an isolated
island was not the proper solution. A prime factor in their leaving
Safed for Jerusalem was to help widen its Jewish horizon. They
pleaded with guests at the home to unite their efforts to revitalize
Jerusalem. It should become their religious center from which
sufficient strength would radiate to combat the dangers abroad.
Their own *Yeshivah* became, indeed, an intercommunicating
wire. Exchanges of commentaries, interpretations, *she'elot* and
teshuvot (rabbinical responsa) were established with scholars
from Germany, Austria, Russia and Poland. Among these were
Eliyahu Gutmacher, David Hoffmann, Ezriel Hildesheimer, Marcus
Horowitz and the Malbim.[3] This exchange of thought went on as
long as the *Yeshivah* lasted. Chief Rabbi Auerbach, Rabbi Samuel
Salant, *Hakham Bashi* Jacob ben Shaul Elyashar, and other
scholars would often come to participate in the discussion of
the comments that came from *hutz la-aretz* (abroad). The magazine *Ha-Misderonah,* edited by Avi,[4] had the same purpose.

----

[1] Blessing made on the attainment of a happy eposide in life.
[2] Blessing pronounced when the moon is in its waxing stage.
[3] Malbim: Initials for *Meir Leibush ben Jehiel Michael,* (1809-1879).
[4] In Hebrew: "My father"—referring to Rabbi Hayyim Hirschensohn
(cf. "Sara Bayla" in "Jewish Leaders").

Had this courtyard been only a rabbinic milieu, it could not have served as a diagram for a picture in proper perspective. There was hardly a person in town who was not familiar with it. No visitor from abroad ever skipped it. The local people who came there were from among Hassidim,[5] Mitnaggedim,[6] Sephardim,[7] Yemenites, outstanding scholars as well as humble people, constituting together a Jewish mosaic.

As I belong to the third generation in Jerusalem, my intimacy with the atmosphere and my own experiences of childhood may help project shades and colors of an integral Jewish life. With the camera focused on the life of a group of children who reflected that environment, Jewishness may be revealed to us with that spontaneity and poetry with which a child sees things for the first time. It would be viewing the depths of its richness as through a glass-bottomed boat.

Like some children of musical parents who strike harmonious notes on the piano as early as their first years, those of us born at the courtyard seem to have responded to the spiritual tone of the surroundings even before our articulation of words. I was told that my first vocal expressions were *koss* and *havdalah*.[8] The stretching for the *kiddush* goblet, or for the silver spice-box may have been not only for a pleasant sensation, but also a reflex of the sentiment of those holding us in their arms. Our early years were marked by cheer and play on a wide open hill. But the very manner of playing indicated an unusual precociousness in grasping Jewish life. There was no lack of competitive games such as running, rope-jumping, ball bouncing, but the leader of the group would be the one capable of imaginative and constructive ideas. We were building with Jewish material, just as children nowadays erect towers and pyramids with wooden blocks. Dolls, engines or balloons were not to be had. Our imaginative games with Jewish content drawn from the environment made up for lack of toys.

A favorite pastime was impersonating some great men whose names we would pick up from talks at the table. Our ideas were naturally vague, but we would clothe them with our own conceptions and enact them as such. Among the figures whom we tried

---

[5]Hassidim: Adherents of a mystical movement dating from the 18th century, with emphasis on piety, and joy of living.
[6]Mitnaggedim: Opponents of Hassidism.
[7]Sephardim: Jews of Spanish or Portuguese origin.
[8]*Koss:* The wine goblet used for *Kiddush* (sanctification of the Sabbath and festivals) and for *Havdalah*,—the benedictions recited at the termination of the Sabbath, separating the holy day from the week-days.

to reflect were the *Gaon* of Vilna, to whose memory a *Yahrzeit* lamp was lit in the dining room; Akiba Eger, whose letter,[9] in possession of Reb Jacob Mordecai, was shown at the table to *Hakham Bashi* Elyashar; Nahmanides,[10] for our association of him with the Blessing of the Moon; the Rambam,[11] whom we heard Avi call "the Guide"; and Rashi,[12] because my uncle Yitzhak was continually referring to him. Biblical figures were too sacred to be intermingled with play, except the Prophet Elijah who appeared at many occasions, and whom we loved so dearly. There was freedom in the choice of heroes we wanted to personify, but for Elijah lots had to be drawn. At our gatherings on a rock on top of the hill, he would be the one to introduce the Rambam to Rashi. Nahmanides to Akiba Eger, and so on.

My favorite hero was Jehudah Halevi, whose ode, *Tzion ha-lo tishali,* I knew by heart when I reached the age of four. At three, I impersonated him for days and days. Once, my grandmother Sarah Bayla called me by name across the terrace to offer me some honey cake. I did not reply. With her perspicacity she called out again, "Jehudah Halevi, I have some cake for you and your colleagues." I answered at once and fetched the cake.

Not being reared on Grimm's and Andersen's fairy tales, nor on the nursery rhymes of "Jack and the Beanstalk," we had to weave tales of our own, a mixture of what we heard and what we embroidered upon it. We re-fashioned the story of Hagar. It was a composite picture of Hagar crying for water, and of Sarah crying for having driven her into the desert. Sarah's cries were an atonement. God forgave Sarah and provided Hagar with water. Little Leah, our Moslem neighbor, agreed that Sarah was good and pious. Daniel was not a bit frightened by the lions in the den. The challenge was easy. All he had to do to scare them

---

[9]In a deep emotional tone his letter expressed reluctance to become a rabbi, for fear that the sins of his community might weigh upon him. (See "Jewish Leaders.")

[10]Nahmanides—commonly referred to as *RaMBaN* (Rabbenu Moshe ben Nahman)—came to Jerusalem in 1267 at the age of seventy, to gather ten Jews (a *minyan*) who would greet the moon at its reappearance each month, as required to give validity to the Jewish calendar. He found only two Jews in Jerusalem. From the various surrounding little villages he gradually succeeded in building a *minyan*. With supreme effort and at great sacrifice he eventually established a *yeshivah* at Acre, which attracted scholars from various countries.

[11]Maimonides, the greatest medieval Jewish philosopher, is called in Hebrew literature *RaMBaM*—initial letters of *Rabbenu Moshe ben Maimun.*

[12]Rashi (1040-1105) was the most eminent commentator on the Bible and the Talmud. His full name was *Rabbenu Shlomo Yitzhaki.*

away was to say *Shema Yisrael*. When the stars saw Jacob's ladder ascending, they dispersed so that he might pierce the sky and go up way above them as far as heaven itself. Even the stars knew that Jacob was destined to be the father of Israel. While these and many other stories were shaped and colored through our own prism, the spirit remained and they constituted the dynamic source of our behavior. These images were as visible to our minds as those reflected on the retina.

The colorful courtyard with its rich variety of people was a kind of interplay between the real world and the one we projected far into the past, a horizon blended of remoteness and nearness— a natural perspective at the age of three or four. As soon as we detected from the top of the hill some rabbis entering the yard, we rushed down telling each other, "Let us greet Hillel, Rabbi Akiba, Rashi." These and other names stuck to us through overheard conversations. The *ger* (proselyte) who drew water from the cistern for the families of the yard, was an enviable person. How could we possibly equal the number of *mitzvot* he earned, amounting to as many as the number of scholars for whom he was carrying the water. He declined to accept remuneration.

The *sopher* (scribe) whose little cottage was below the hill, stood out like a privileged character in a fairy tale. He, only he, could write the *Sefer Torah*. During his periods of silence, i.e., when he was writing, we would occasionally follow him on tiptoe, without even a whisper. As soon as he completed writing a scroll, he would climb up our hill, bring some candy, and beamingly exclaim: "Children, not a single mistake; no parchment sheet of mine is hidden in the synagogue, thank God."[13]

Israel Shimeon, the calligrapher, with a long quill pen in his hand, writing letters dictated to him, still found time to satisfy the children's requests. He would draw lines on our very thin sheets of yellow paper, and take dictation of the letters we addressed to "great men who continued their lives in heaven." One of my letters was for Elijah, saying that I would wait up all night at the *seder* in the hope of seeing him. This was shown to Rabbi Samuel Salant, who placed his hands on my head and blessed me. His words I still remember: *"Eliyahu ha-Navi* is always in our

---

[13]The scribe's profession is exacting as well as sacred. If he makes an error, the whole section of the parchment must be removed; but it must not be thrown away, for it is holy. There is a special place in the synagogue where such discarded sections are kept.

midst, but we have to wait for the Messiah until we can see him face to face." We started to wait for the Messiah from the age of three on.

The *melammed* who came daily to train the young girls in prayers and who would tell us that girls need not learn to write, had to yield to our insistence and write down for us the *alef bet,* which we copied assiduously. I wanted to compose a book on how the world could get along without money. At four, I acquired a little more wisdom, and my book was to be on the rebuilding of the Temple. I generously imparted my little knowledge of writing to others of my age.

One who in our eyes ranked next to the scribe, was the *parokhes-*man,[14] as we called him. He was a prosperous dry goods merchant, who traveled frequently to Beyrouth, and brought back on every trip some high-quality damask silk which he donated for mantles of the scrolls. Each time, he would invite us to his cottage and display the beautiful material he brought for *"parokheses,"* some for every synagogue. He exchanged with a Yeshivah scholar his spacious, relatively luxurious house in town for a small cottage in our yard, so that his six young boys and his little girl might absorb that atmosphere. I had to share my bedroom with his baby daughter, since the cottage could not accommodate them all.

Another mental photograph which has not yet faded is that of the repenting *meshummad* (apostate). His tears drew tears from our eyes, too. We jointly prayed that God might forgive him. I also recall our delight in the stories of the Messiah which were related to us by some fine old women who, through a lifetime's savings, were able to end their days in the Holy Land. The delectable stories of the Hassidim were another source of enchantment. We would interrupt our competitive games at the slightest sign of some story telling at the Hassidic *Bet ha-Midrash* across our terrace. We would patiently and silently sit on the stoop in the hope of some forthcoming ones. We loved to hear them even when we grew a little older, but we gradually became more impressed by the serenity of our *Yeshivah,* with the frowning foreheads and faces bent over thick volumes. We would follow the scholars on their way to and from the *Yeshivah,* and flood them with questions. "What does the Rambam say on this matter?" was steadily on our lips. Avi would retrace his steps, enter his library, and actually

---

[14]*Parokhes* is the curtain in front of the Ark of the Law.

open a Rambam volume and clarify the text. He would speak to us with the same care and earnestness as if he were addressing himself to the members of the *Yeshivah*. Some of us at the mature ages of eight to ten, experienced even fleeting moments of innocent perplexities. But Avi's "Guide" and my uncle's Rashi promptly pulled us out of our difficulties.

Children of such an environment and with poetical sensitiveness are bound to express the Jewish being with a strength of feeling and perception alike to that of the artist who brings out the heart of a landscape or the soul of people. Those who surrounded them were not as dramatic as Sholem Aleichem's coachman or Peretz's "silent Bontche." But they were nearest to the fountain of Jewishness through their study and understanding. The story of these children is a living document that the strength of Jewishness is in the blossoming of its own self. It is the divorce of the Jewish self from its source that brings about schizophrenia.

These memories are neither embellished nor co-ordinated, but reproduced as they pass before my mind, experiences from early childhood to the age of ten. At ten one was a full-fledged grown-up. Like plants that shoot up out of the soil that nourishes them, we grew Jewishly, as it were, out of our own inner selves. We imbibed the atmosphere in the same way as a child starts talking without formal lessons. At a little over two, we could already "reason out" Jewishly. At three we began to accumulate some knowledge from which our thinking proceeded. From four on, the Jewish seed met with a fertile soil; the tree grew as by the streams of water. In spite of their precociousness, these children should not be looked upon as prodigies, but as a natural sprouting on an island of learning. Early maturity, it is known, was a general characteristic of former ages, especially of Jewish youth.

THE LITTLE YELLOW FLOWER

In our courtyard, at the foot of the hill, grew a lonely tree with slender branches, embroidered leaves, covered with dainty, tiny flowers as with a soft yellow silken mantle. It had a charm and fragrance of its own. On Fridays, children would wake at dawn to vie with each other in picking these little flowers for the Sabbath table. When Immi[15] first took me outdoors in her arms,

---

[15]In Hebrew: "My mother."

still in my swaddling clothes at the age of eleven months,[16] this tree was the first object to attract my attention. When I started crawling, I crawled to it, and when I began walking, I walked to it. It is to this tree that I owe my first Jewish consciousness. Psychologists tell us that the human mind is like a flowing stream, and that consciousness arises only through a crisis, an interruption in the flow.

It was on a Sabbath day; I found myself alone in front of that tree, caressing a little flower, smelling it; finally I picked it. I softly passed it through my fingers with tender care, smelled it again, and enjoyed it far more than some candy melting in my mouth. In the midst of my delight, my sin dawned upon me: cutting was prohibited on that day of rest, and I had not heeded it. Only recently Immi had told us the story of Adam and Eve and the tree. My case loomed far worse than that of Eve, for there had been no serpent to entice me. I alone was responsible for desecrating the Sabbath. Where could I be driven to, since I was already out of the Garden of Eden on account of Adam and Eve? I threw away the little flower; at least no one had seen me. But I could not hide from God, as Adam and Eve tried to do, for He sees everything. What is more, through this strange act I also had separated myself from my world, the courtyard, and the people in it. I think now that this concept of separation born in a child's mind through a crisis, is a really fundamental basis of a philosophy of Jewishness, namely, that with each transgression, no matter how insignificant, we isolate ourselves from the Jewish whole, past and present.

When night-time drew near and we all gathered for the *Havdalah* ceremony, the little flower stood between me and the *Havdalah,* to which I had started to look forward when still in my cradle. While absorbed in confused thoughts, immediately after the *Havdalah* and the song *hatotenu hu yimhol* (He will forgive our sins), I found myself lifted in Avi's arms, with a severe look in his usually tender eyes. In the presence of all gathered, he put me on the table and punished me. To the amazement of everyone, not a tear came to my eyes, no resentment, my face relaxed, and I felt relieved. While I lay humiliated on that table, the thought

---

[16]With an abrupt change of climate from hot days to cold nights, and with the high infant mortality, there was fear of taking a child out until the eleventh month. Arabs would expose their newly-born infants for several hours outdoors, in order to toughen them.

crossed my mind that sin and punishment were correlated, and that when punishment is administered, the sin is obliterated. (The wording was simpler, but the thought identical). I was relieved through my punishment. Unaware that a neighbor had noticed me, I thought that it could have been only an angel who prompted Avi, so that I should not carry my sin too long with me. This correlation between punishment and forgiveness is another important seed of Jewishness that my plucking the flower from the tree had planted in me.

My Handkerchief

On a Sabbath, a little before *Minhah* (Afternoon Prayer) I asked Avi to take me for a short walk beyond the Gates of Zion. A walk carried with it some stories on the way, told on a child's level. By the time we reached the Gates of Zion, we were plunged in the exciting battle of Absalom against his father, King David. The "Shepherd King" was among our beloved figures. We sometimes played David and Goliath, with the panorama of the hills and wide-open spaces beyond the Gates as a background. The walk continued, and the story with it, for a long stretch of about ten blocks. I lifted my hands to clap and applaud David's victory over Absalom, when I noticed that my handkerchief was not tied around my wrist. Without losing an extra moment for even a single word, I ran back, with a pace beyond Avi's, to the exact spot, the divide between the inside and outside of the town. There I quickly took out the handkerchief from my pocket, tied it on my wrist, and started back towards Avi.

The two Turkish soldiers, one at each corner of the gate, immobile like statues, with a large sword on the right and left side, and sharp knives with colored handles strapped at their leather belts, cried out in Arabic (not in Turkish) "Hey, little girl, show us that handkerchief!" They saw no hidden marks on it to indicate some secret reference to the Sultan. A child, not fully three years old, could not be taken for a traitor, even with the irrational suspicion of the Turks at that time, fearing more the Arabs than the Jews. But some magic may have been injected into it. *"Tikhki Arabic?"* (Do you speak Arabic?) *"Ava"* (yes), I replied. "Tell us, then, why you left your father behind and ran like a deer to take your handkerchief out of a convenient place and tie it uncomfortably on your wrist." I explained, what they probably did not grasp, that in town there is an *eruv*[17] which makes carrying on the Sabbath permissible. As there can be no *eruv* in open spaces, we are allowed to carry only what we are wearing. As I was talking, it dawned upon me that by retracing my steps I carried the handkerchief a double distance. The excitement of the moment ran ahead of my thinking. "Is there really no magic to that handkerchief?" "Yes," I said teasingly, "there is." "It reminded me in the middle of the road that I was trespassing a commandment. I might have gone a still longer way, unaware that there was a sin in my pocket." By that time Avi reached the gates, and the two guards who usually looked like robots, said in Arabic: "Go by, you are all right. Salaam." "Salaam to you. Would you like me to play some magic tricks with my handkerchief?" The stony soldiers actually laughed aloud. I doubt whether anyone else had ever seen them laughing.

When we returned home, I asked Immi for another handkerchief. I did not want to be reminded with each blowing of the nose that I had carried it beyond the gates on a Sabbath.

The Taryag Mitzvot—(613 Commandments)

We learned to count at a rather early age. To reach 613, the number of precepts,[18] was a genuine concern with us. If all had to be performed during the waking hours of the day, it would mean at least one for every minute. How could this possibly be attained with time consumed in eating, playing, joint deliberations, or sitting on the stoop of the synagogue? Even for the boys, with the *mitzvah* of a whole day's study, it could not be easy, either. Yet, if some minutes are devoid of them, others could be filled with many simultaneously. We must redouble our chores, carry food to the destitute old people, and recite the *Shema* with great concentration. As the attainment of 613 is like a difficult climb, there must be fairness among the children in the opportunities for earning them. Each one had his turn, and we kept a scrupulous account.

---

[17]*Eruv:* A *halakhic* device of converting an open public domain into a closed one, usually by putting a symbolic wire to span the exit.

[18]Ramban showed that only sixty *mitzvot* are incumbent upon every Jew nowadays. The 613 Commandments were given to the whole nation, (including all circumstances, professions and businesses), and almost one half of them referred to services connected with the national sanctuary. To a non-merchant e.g. apply none of the laws governing fair prices or prohibiting monopoly; to a non-employer, no regulations settling wages and prohibitions of personal enslavement. (See the last paragraph in the first part of his "Sefer ha-Mitzvot"—Editor)

One day, sitting on the stoop of the synagogue while the others were playing, my grandmother Sarah Bayla asked me to carry some chicken soup to the feeble old woman who lived in the basement of the Hassidic headquarters. Delighted with the *mitzvah,* I carried that bowl with tenderness and utmost care. As I was way down the stairs I remembered that my cousin Anna fell a little short of *mitzvot* that week. I retraced my steps, went up the stairs, climbed up the hill, crossed the two terraces with the bowl tight in my hands, and passed it over to cousin Anna to deliver. Touched by my generosity, Anna assured me that I, too, earned a *mitvah* in procuring one for her, and that I lost none through my kindness. Our little Moslem friend Leah asked to join in our good performances. One of the boys remarked that allowing a share to Leah earned us an additional *mitzvah,* because the Torah commands us to be kind to "the stranger within thy gates."

With our growth, the number of *mitzvot* grew, and so did our understanding of them. We could not, however, reach a satisfactory solution as to the scale of values. Since all the *mitzvot* emanate from God, they have to be on equal footing. One of us hit upon a happy thought: If each morning we would arise with a readiness for *mitzvot,* it would be equal to the performance of them all. If we would not omit those within our reach, it would show that we were fully ready for the rest of them when the occasion arose.

Some of our other reflections are still fresh in my mind: They are to the Torah what the *Alef Bet* is to writing. (In more mature language this would mean that they are intertwined.) God gave them to us out of His goodness, so that we be as steady in our ways as the stars in heaven. (This indicates, I think, a sense for the unification of the spiritual laws with those of nature.) Following the commandments is like reaching the terrace through the stairs and its bannister, instead of taking a jump into the air. (The implication could have been no other than that they are guardians of the Jewish balance.)

Be-Yadkha Afqid Ruhi—("Into Thy Hands Do I Entrust My Spirit")

These Biblical words best express the inwardness of religion: the trust and kinship between the weak and the Universal Source of strength. It indicates an indissoluble link between the Creator and His creatures, and a longing on the part of the individual to be a worthy component of the large universe where all spirits are in the heart of God. If I could paint the warmth, sincerity, and innocence with which these words were uttered by the children of our courtyard, I would carry a refreshing breeze, blowing from Jewish inwardness.

After Immi recited the *Shema* with me, she would turn down the wick of the kerosene lamp, blow it out, close the door, and bid me good night. I did not feel lonely in the darkness, for I immediately entrusted my soul to God, and was deeply stirred by His willingness to have so many spirits entrusted to Him. When I awoke from sleep, gazing into the horizon with the multicolored sunrise and the chirping of the birds, I spontaneously thanked God that He had returned my soul to me. I would promise that at night, when I should entrust it again to Him, it would be far better than the one of the preceding day.

Our joy of living was overflowing with thankfulness to God. We thanked Him for our being happy, for having ordered such beautiful festivals, and for the fascinating excursions which often consisted of visits to tombs of great men with whose stories we were familiar, and who lived in us as if they were our playmates. The intellectual distinction between the ritual and the ethical did not enter our mind. To us, all commandments came from God, to teach us how to behave properly. We hoped that our ways, our thoughts, our dreams, and that even our games were pleasing to Him.

With all this intimate communion, our concept of God was not anthropomorphic, but neither was it abstract. One little girl remarked that God is much too great to be encompassed by the human mind, but we could learn of Him through His commandments. We also know Him through the song preceding the *Havdalah,* that He is the God of Abraham, Isaac and Jacob, and of course He is ours just as much. Years later, while I was studying the *Moreh Nebukhim,* these thoughts, which would have met, I think, with the approval of the Rambam, came back to me in full force.

The Covenant was for us an additional tie with God. Without knowing the Psalmist's exclamation *Mah enosh ki tizkerenu (What is man that Thou art mindful of him),* we were overwhelmed by God's goodness, that He, so great, should make a covenant with one who is less than even a little point when compared to Him. It was no doubt in order that man should lift himself up high. How could one fail Him when He shows such goodness? We resolved that every act of ours should be as if it were part of the Covenant, as if it had been contracted by ourselves, not solely by our ancestors. Whatever they promised and undertook to do, is also our obligation. Otherwise, we would be disloyal to God and to them as far back as Abraham, Isaac and Jacob.

Enjoying, as we did, the little birds which flew back and forth from our hill to the Mosque of Omar, the multicolored butterflies, the ants on their hills, we were naturally bound to ask ourselves whether or not they knew that God had created them. We pondered upon it a great deal, and the conclusion made us very sad: the most sorrowful distinction between animals and men is their not knowing that God created them and that they could lean on Him as we do. We ought to be doubly kind to them, to make up for their unfortunate ignorance. I had a little cat which I cherished and with which I shared my food. This single act is not sufficient; we must spread a larger quantity of grains for the little birds, and be attentive to the needs of some other animals in the yard. Would this *mitzvah* be among the 613, or did we increase the number by one?

The Passing of Jacob Mordecai

It was on a Wednesday morning. To my surprise there was no one around me when I awoke. I looked through one window, and no sound whatever came from the *Yeshivah*. I looked through the other, and no one was sitting at the tables of the *Hassidic Shul*. I opened the door, and the whole place was overflowing with people. I had never seen so many. I learned years later that all stores closed, studies in the *yeshivot* and *heders* were suspended. Even the Arabs in the *finstere kleiten* —stores in dark alleys—stopped their business. I ran out barefoot in my nightgown with hair disheveled, and leaned on the bannister of the upper floor. Subdued cries came from downstairs. Do grown-up people cry, too? Who could have hurt them? "Our master, our master, our crown is gone! Jacob Mordecai, we feel lost without you." Why does Jacob Mordecai not answer them? Why should he go away when all these people want him to stay? Did he cease to love Jerusalem, the heavy books on

the table, and the children who would follow him up the stairs?
I rushed down in my nightgown, pushed myself through the
crowd to ask Jacob Mordecai to stay. As I was approaching
the dining hall, I recognized Immi's voice: *"Mein Shwer, mein
Shwer,* (my father-in-law), you took my father's place, and now
you, too, are leaving me!" "He must not leave her, she is too
lonesome for him," I said to myself. At that very moment Immi
picked me up: "God called your grandfather away." If He
called him away, why do you cry? Like a flash, the concept of
death dawned upon me, but in terms of lonesomeness. *Gan Eden,
Gan Eden,* filled my ears,—a place with which I was already
familiar through the story of Adam and Eve. I construed that
Jacob Mordecai had left for there, and that the people were so
sadly lonesome for him.

At the second Yahrzeit of Jacob Mordecai, when several of
us had already reached the mature age of five, the thoughts
woven around him were about the soul, and about the impossibility of disappearing forever. So much learning, from morning
to night, could not get lost. It is no doubt preserved in some
form unknown to us. Perhaps this very preservation is the soul
itself. That could not be, for a soul is given to everyone, whether
learned or ignorant as the *ger,* and even to women who spend
most of their time cooking. Without their cooking, men could
not learn uninterruptedly; so women have a share in their study.
But what about children who have not studied yet, especially the
girls? Thereupon a six-year old boy offered to teach the girls
all he knew. In the midst of our perplexities, a little girl gave
a more satisfactory definition: "The soul is the spirit which
God breathes into the body at each one's birth; it is loaned
to the body for a time until it goes back to heaven." We had
already been told by the fine old women of the courtyard that
when the Messiah would come all bodies would be resurrected
and reunited with their souls. But does not this mean that
some bodies have to wait longer than others for the reunion?
Abraham, Isaac and Jacob have to be without a soul for a longer
time than ourselves, and we would have a longer wait than those
who come after us. Another perplexing question: which is responsible for our behavior, the soul or the body? If it is the soul,
then all people would be perfect and righteous. Tzipra, the landlady of the Hassidic terrace, was not so very kind, nor were
some of the Arab officials. How about the wicked Titus and

Nebuchadnezzar? If the body is responsible, how could something so physical and ephemeral be master over the soul, which is pure, indestructible and an inhabitant of heaven? As we could find no adequate answer, we thought it best to make a supreme effort to maintain harmony between body and soul through perfect behavior. To make it easier for us not to stray from the right path we should watch and help each other. For such weighty matters we would usually have recourse to Avi, whom we often notice absorbed in talks with *Hakham Bashi* Elyashar. We made Avi repeat many, many times what we heard him say once to the *Hakham Bashi*. We liked that explanation, and I think I could repeat it approximately in these words: "The mysteries of life are unfathomable. God revealed His Torah to us and in it are all the answers to our perplexities, but it requires much diligence to dig deep into it until the answers come to the surface. Meanwhile we must trust in God, and be thankful for the many revelations that we have already discovered."

Another perturbance about the soul came to us through stories from the Hassidim. Sitting on their stoop we heard a long discussion on how some souls would travel from one body to another, and assume even the shape of an animal. "If my soul has to travel, I prefer that it should enter into a cow, rather than into the body of an *apikores* (unbeliever)," I exclaimed tremblingly. But we reassured each other that if the soul has to enter into different bodies, it could go only into better ones. In this manner, little by little, the world would become a perfect one.

Gan Eden—(Paradise)

The stories about Paradise which our little friend Leah would tell us, made us fear that there might be two paradises—one for Jews and one for Arabs. Ours and her conceptions were so totally different, that we could not possibly imagine that the two kinds would ever meet, much as we would have loved to have Leah with us. Her father had told her that way beyond, on an endlessly flowing golden river, there is a paradise for the righteous ones, with most delicious food in golden plates, with beautiful dancing girls around the tables. One could eat uninterruptedly all day long, and choose what is most palatable to him. It felt awkward to us that Paradise should consist mostly in eating. We, too, are looking forward to the Leviathan banquet, but this is the only one, in order to welcome the Messiah and celebrate the resurrection of the bodies. After that, all of us would be studying day and night in an enchanted atmosphere of chirping birds, lots of these little yellow flowers, and all sorts of huge trees with large foliage—of course, not the apple tree. The bearded men will wear beautifully embroidered *talletim,* such as are worn by bridegrooms on the first Sabbath after the wedding-day. Difficult problems which we could not solve in this world would be revealed to us in a flash. Everyone would be a learned man, and maybe women, too, would be encouraged to study. We aired our views at the dining room table, and to our delight we were told that the great poet Jehudah Halevi said that the righteous of all nations have a share in Paradise, in one beautifully unified future world. We already knew of the variety of nations through the consuls who visited us frequently. There was the French consul who taught us to count in French up to one hundred; the German, the Austrian, the Russian. We also knew of the Russian pilgrims who came yearly to visit the holy sepulchre. They slept on the ground, ate dark rye bread and herring which they brought from Russia in their little sacks. That square was named the Russian Square, and we passed it frequently.

If all those people were not given the 613 precepts, by what can they be guided and how can they be tested for their righteousness? Anyhow, little Leah will not be parted from us, but she will have to admit that our conception of Paradise is the only possible one; otherwise it would be merely a replica of this earth. Avi sided with us and seemed to enjoy as much as we did the projected spiritual picture of the world to come. He paraphrased in a language of our own, the way the great masters have depicted it. The name of one of them stuck in my memory. He claims that the more we study in this world, the richer will be our life in Paradise, provided of course that our life on earth was a righteous one. The name of this great philosopher is Levi ben Gershon, and this led me a number of years later to make a study of his philosophy.

A Jewel from the Urim ve-Tummim[19]

At our times we were not aware of oil nor of archaeological findings. The children of our courtyard cherished the thought that ours was among the nearest places to the ancient Temple.

---

[19] Oracular jewels attached to the breast-plate of the High Priest.

Maybe some of the treasures were hidden from the wicked Titus under the ground; perhaps the layer underneath is holier than what we are treading on. The digging adventure started with nails, sharp pieces of wood, fingers (toy shovels were non-existent). A vow was solemnly taken that whoever finds something would bring it to the attention of the whole group. While digging, one of us detected, in a deep hole on the path to the stairs, a little object covered with earth, and yet shining through it. We all convened, and, with palpitating hearts, devised ways of pulling it up. A jewel so brilliant even under the dust, could not but belong to the *Urim ve-Tummim* of the High Priest. What a *zekhut* is ours! We washed it and wiped it. The shinier it became, the higher the pitch of excitement and the surer we felt that it must have belonged to the bejeweled breast-plate of the High Priest. Night was approaching; we should not keep such a holy object in our midst without confiding to Sarah Bayla. With what sympathy and tact she led us out of our illusion: "This is not from the Temple, but you have earned a *mitzvah* in finding the brooch which our neighbor cherished. It had been a wedding gift from her bridegroom's parents, *alehem ha-shalom*. She was under the impression that she had lost it on the street. So precious was it to her, that she wore it only on most festive occasions, usually at night: the last time at a *Huppah* of an orphan." At least we were comforted that we did not keep overnight an object that did not belong to us. The candy that was offered us as a reward was unanimously declined, with a slight hesitation, however, for they were candied almonds, a rare delicacy.

The Holy Earth

We learned that people abroad appreciated a little earth from the Holy Land, to have it placed in their coffins. We understood the reason, and we started to gather earth from as near the Temple site as possible. After sewing and neatly tying little bags, we would ask Israel Shimeon to open his address book, draw lots, and send them to the lucky numbers. The boys insisted that they should be the ones to fill the bags, since the sewing was done by the girls. It was a red-letter day when acknowledgments and blessings came from the recipients. But a difficult question arose, with serious debates pro and con. What if the possession of this little bit of earth should diminish their anxiety for the Holy Land?

The consensus of opinion was that no Jew would delay his coming when he could do so. The problem was solved by pinning a note, "You better come here yourself and give this bag to someone else for whom it is a physical impossibility to undertake the trip." Together with descriptions of excursions and visits to the tombs of saints, we added the inducement of free rent in our courtyard, and that we would even bring them some food if they had none. A fine old widow, Deborah from Dwinsk, assured us that she took our note seriously, sold her belongings, and came to our court-yard. She did get free rent.

Rebuilding the Temple

One day at the age of four, I saw Immi sitting on the floor, her shoes off, a book in her hands, and tears over her face. It was *Tish'ah be-Av*. She told me the dramatic story of the building of the first Temple, the joy in rebuilding it a second time, and how the wicked Titus destroyed it, and now we have none. God punished Titus with a fly continually buzzing in his ears. Long after midnight I awakened my parents, with a dreadful fear that Titus's fly had entered into my ear, because I felt a buzzing. They were forced to pour hot oil into it. The buzzing stopped, but the tumult in my thoughts went on. I lay awake in deep silence, except for the chirping of the crickets. "Why is such a sad event mourned on *Tish'ah be-Av* only? How could one bear the thought of the destruction of the Temple without attempts at rebuilding it a third time? There should be no further delay."

At the first sign of dawn I jumped out of bed, ran from cottage to cottage to awaken the children, so that we might convene on the hill before the boys left for *heder*. I announced it as an emergency meeting. They all agreed that we must purchase the Mosque of Omar, replace it by the Temple alike to that built by King Solomon at God's behest. Would the Mohammedans sell it? We could claim our right to it as the first occupant. What about the necessary funds for the purchase? We shall immediately begin to raise them. We could supplement our chores for *mitzvot* with those that need not be done gratis; we could also donate our Hanukah *geld*. No more candy with our pennies. We obtained a little metal box with a tight cover on which we had Israel Shimeon inscribe *"for the Bet ha-Mikdash."* Whatever coins we earned we inserted in the box. No one was asked the amount of his contribution; we were equal partners. It was an honor system with a pledge of dedicating the total sum of earnings. Any need for a personal withdrawal had to be approved by the whole group. Such a petition never came up, for what could be more urgent than the rebuilding of the Temple? Our Arab playmates might be of some assistance. One of them was taken into our confidence, and he promised to speak on our behalf to his father, his uncle, and even his grandfather, the Pasha (Governor). He assured us that it should not be hard to make them see our side. "After all, there is enough space on the Mount of Olives to build another Mosque, and free the site which belongs to King Solomon. Nor would it require much money, since by right the hill belongs to those who first owned it."

Encouraged by our playmate Abdallah, a little older than ourselves, we resolved to make an appeal to all the Jewish children in the world. For this we would have to write our own letters and not depend on Israel Shimeon, who might not impart the urgency with the same warmth as we would. We must learn how to write, and learn quickly; and indeed we did, to the amazement of the *melammed*. I bought notebooks for each child with the money my parents had given me to buy a bouncing ball which I very much desired. This was not diverting from the fund, as it was a necessary investment for enlisting the interest of children all over the world.

The grown-ups, too, would have to be awakened; we needed their assistance. They could perhaps give up eating cake after *kiddush;* maybe the *derasha-geshenk* (wedding gifts) could be turned over to us, and perhaps the brides would forego their jewelry. We once overheard that Reb Shemuel Salant received lots of money from abroad (*Halukah*). Why not ask him a large part of it? As we noticed from the top of the hill that he was entering our yard, we dashed for our inscribed box, and caught him on top of the stairs. "Reb Shemuel Salant, you have lots of money. Give us some for purchasing the Mosque of Omar." He looked at us in his usual calm way, nevertheless deeply affected by our earnestness. He rubbed his eyes so as to better reflect on how to handle a situation so delicate. One should not dampen such sacred enthusiasm, and at the same time he wanted to lead us to the reality of the situation. "Yes, children, our Temple must be rebuilt, and it will be when the Messiah comes." A child retorted: "Couldn't we meanwhile help a little? Maybe the Messiah will arrive sooner if he knew how eager and impatient we are. Maybe God will renew the miracle of the Maccabeans." Reb Shemuel Salant stretched his hands to bless us all, and deposited a madjideh ($1) in our inscribed box. *Hakham Bashi* Elyashar would deposit a little coin in it whenever he met us. Ussischkin probably never knew that he was preceded in his idea by children of a rabbinic milieu.

When we grew a little older—approximately six or more years of age—we had a clearer conception of money, and became fully aware of the complicated problems. Efforts should not be diminished, but the coins in our box are much too inadequate. Let us meanwhile allocate our joint funds for the writing of a *Sefer Torah* by Reb Meir the scribe. We would have liked to dedicate it to the memory of Jacob Mordecai, but the community had already done that, and it was marked by an elaborate ceremony. The scribe left some outlines of letters to be filled in by Reb Shemuel Salant, *Hakham Bashi,* Elyashar, other outstanding scholars, including *Yeshivah* students and a few Bar Mitzvah boys. We dedicated ours to "Our beloved Jehudah Halevi, who risked his life to come to the Holy Land." We could not imagine that a box filled with coins would not cover the cost of a *Sefer Torah*. We would not fail our *Sefer Torah* for the sake of some candy, and we would naturally prolong our period of economy. But Sarah Bayla offered to supplement the deficit, and assured us that it would be dedicated to Jehudah Halevi in our name, since we were the ones to initiate it. The silken mantle would be entirely our own work, and adorned with the finest embroidery.

When this *Sefer Torah* was presented to the synagogue, the children arranged a special celebration of their own, to which older boys were also invited. From Bar Mitzvah on, boys shunned the girls, fully conscious of the dignity of manhood. This was a special occasion with a *Berakhah,* of course. The *She-heheyanu* was the first to come to our mind, but a more selfless one would be *Barukh she-natan Torah* (Blessed be the One Who gave the Torah), which would comprehend thanks for the whole Jewish people, of the past, the present, and those to come. The refreshments were provided by ours folks—all the tempting things of which we had been depriving ourselves during the period of our financial economies. They consisted of roasted almonds coated with sugar, tiny roasted nuts, rock candy, halvah, a brownish marshmallow, and a few other delicacies which I do not recall.

Shimeon ha-Tzaddik's Grave and the Area Adjoining It

Shimeon ha-Tzaddik (the Righteous) ranked among our beloved heroes. The title *Tzaddik* evoked in us a quasi-mystical feeling. He was associated in our mind with the celebration of *Lag ba-Omer,* with the pleasantness of the day and the bonfires of the preceding night.[20] Children of the town, young and old people, Hassidim, Ashkenazim, Sephardim, Yemenites, would come up our hill and sit around a huge bonfire for which logs had been assembled days in advance. The air was filled with songs, cheerful Hassidic, monotonous Sephardic, touching Yiddish melodies, and colorful voices of Yemenites in Arabic rhymes. Next morning we would be out of bed before the cock's greetings to the sunrise, before the chirping of birds and their picking the grains on the window sills. We would wash our hands, dress quickly, say our morning prayers, and wait with feverish impatience for the grown-ups. The town's gathering center was at the foot of our stairs, as our courtyard was situated on the corner of the dark Arab alley leading to the gates of Shekhem. The children were usually cautioned not to pass that alley without an escort. At the gates, the donkeys with their Arab owners were ready to carry us to Shimeon ha-Tzaddik. (The word "grave" was omitted.) The softness of the early hours, the pure blueness of the sky, the rolling hills, the precipices, the vastness of space, the picnic on the field, the return at sunset with the sun like a red apple in the sky, the first shy little star coming out of its hidden abode alone in the firmament, the lanterns in each one's hands lighted for the passage through the dark alley, the goodbye greetings at the foot of our courtyard, and more than this, the colorful dreams at twilight welded with this intoxicating spiritual day— all this merged in the figure of Shimeon ha-Tzaddik.

I have a clear picture of my first pilgrimage at the age of two. I was seated on a burro, Immi walking on one side, the Arab on the other, both holding me tightly, while I looked at the hills, repeating to myself "Shimeon ha-Tzaddik, Shimeon ha-Tzaddik." A year later with my second pilgrimage, I had already learned from older children the romantic stories related to it. At the age of four, I wove many dreams of my own around him.

One night, when I was already in bed, I overheard my parents talking about the need of a land movement, and of their going the

---

[20]The grave of Shimeon ben Yohai was a chief attraction on Lag ba-Omer for those who could endure the hardship of travel between Jerusalem and Meron near Safed.

following day, together with *Hakham* Jacob Meir, to explore the possibility of land-buying on the road to Shekhem. As I was half asleep, their whispering merged with my dreams, and evaporated together with them when I awoke. I spent the morning playing with the children, had lunch at my cousin's home—a frequent treat on Tuesdays—and returned late in the afternoon, almost at dusk. When I entered the house with greetings and childish overbubblings, there was no reply. The conversation of the preceding night came back to my mind like a flash. Without hat and coat, nor communicating with anyone, I started to run in the direction of the Gate of Shekhem. I passed the Arab alley rapidly in order not to attract attention, continued running through the vast stretches of hilly land with but one single thought, to catch up with my parents and tell them what had brought me there. My feet began to tire but it mattered not, the silence was a little troubling, but it could not compare with the hardship of some *Tzaddikim* who lived all week long on dry figs and carobs. Now and then the silence would be relieved by the trotting of a well-trained horse with a luxurious saddle, a Turk with a red fez and sparkling belt riding it in the direction opposite to mine. I met also with a few bare-footed peasants with loads of vegetables on their heads for delivery to town the following day. The nights they would often spend sleeping on the street so as to be the earliest arrivals at the market. To their questioning as to where I was headed for, I replied "to join my parents on this road." I began to ask myself where are Avi, Immi and the rest of them? They may have stopped to pay a visit to the grave of Shimeon ha-Tzaddik. These thoughts gave speed to my feet, but when I reached the spot they were not there. No vestige of sun or moonlight, just the cheerful stars playing with each other in heaven. Maybe on a ground surrounding such a Tzaddik angels would pierce through the stars and pay an invisible visit to his grave. The lines "Twinkle, twinkle little star; How I wonder what you are" were not known to me. But with the brilliant firmament, the peacefulness of the hills, the long stretch of mountainous land, the multicolors left behind by the sunset and with no human being around, I had to share such profound emotion with the friendly stars. "Stars, you gay companions, shining like diamonds on a bride's neck—(I happened to have attended not long before a wedding of a wealthy Sephardic bride bedecked with jewelry)—hide yourselves for a moment that an angel may fly on the blueness of the sky."... "Angels, do you know what made me chase after my parents? It was not lonesomeness, for the children are still playing and my grandmother surely has a nice supper for me. I wanted to request that group, before it would be too late, that the first piece of land for a new Jewish settlement should be near the grave of Shimeon ha-Tzaddik, who deserves this testimony of appreciation."

As I was communing with the angels and stars above, the darkness below grew thicker and thicker. I could not remain with the stars and hidden angels, nor could I retrace my steps in the dark. The warning not to pass alone through that Arab alley came to my mind and added a little to the perplexity. The silence so pleasant and lulling to dream, suddenly became frightening. *"Ha-Shem, beyadkha afqid ruhi venishmati* (Lord, in Thy hand do I repose my spirit and my soul). You who watch over us when safely in bed, do surely guard those in peril." The prayer tranquilized me. I looked to the right, looked to the left, looked down the steep hill strewn with sharp rocks, and I saw little stars coming out of the earth, as if they were companions to those above. These were reflections of kerosene lamps of small sparse huts which appeared like points from the top of the hill. "These," I said to myself, "must be homes, either Jewish or Arab; not of Bedouins, for they travel from place to place by foot or donkey and sleep outdoors. Should they be Arab dwellings, I shall ask for their hospitality." I knew of the Arab custom that a host would never do harm to one who has been his guest. But what if there were a chasm at the foot of the hill and I remained alone in the valley? It required less courage to slide down at night than at daylight, with the looming danger. It was not easy to hold on to shifting rocks; I was even careful that my dress should not tear and that my shined brown shoes be not scratched. There was no chasm. A little hut which appeared like an Arab one was right at the foot of it. Instead of knocking at the door, I pushed it swiftly, breathlessly saying, "Salaam, may I have a cup of coffee?" This request would secure their hospitality, and I would be safe in their hands. As the owner closed the door behind me, I noticed a *mezuzah* on the lintel. "I want no coffee. Please take me home. I am Sarah Bayla's grandchild; she certainly will pay you a medjideh." He of course knew Sarah Bayla. He put away the necklace which he was twisting behind his back between the fingers of one hand and the other,[21] extinguished the nargile, locked the door carefully

---

[21]This is an occasional pastime with Sephardim.

and bade his wife not to open it to anyone whomsoever. There was danger of prowling Bedouins in such an isolated place.

Walking back safely with my hand in his, the anxiety about my family's worry increased, but the fear left me. The sense of beauty forced itself upon me. It felt like the taste of wine at *kiddush,* or some exquisite juicy fruit. There is a *Bore peri ha-etz* and *Bore peri ha-Gafen* (benedictions upon eating fruit or grapes). What *berakhah* (blessing) could I make at sensing beauty? I would have to ask Avi. Maybe there is none, because there is beauty everywhere, on our hill, on the Hassidic terrace, in Leah's orchard,—and one could not utter prayers all day long. I could almost hear now how I thanked God silently for letting the beauty hidden in heaven shine upon us here, just as the sun sends forth his rays. It dawned upon me that besides being all goodness, all wisdom, all power, as the older boys had told us, God is also all beauty. It was not the teleological argument of design that came to my mind. I did not question God's existence, and needed no proof. With such a deep experience of beauty, I searched its source and traced it to the bosom of God Himself. "The hills, with the heaps of rocks, could not have been beautiful in themselves, were it not for the rays of beauty coming from God which we perceive with something within us.

This inner experience is, I think, that of young and old, when climbing a mountain, walking through a forest, or witnessing the rising or setting of the sun. Beauty is no doubt at the basis of the mystical unity between man and his universe. If I were to seek for a definition of mysticism, I would go back to my experience of that evening. I would say it is a kind of intimacy flowing from us to the outer world and from it to us, with God as the source of this fellowship.

The Biblical hills, intimate companions of the psalmist, danced like rams to join him in the praises of God. Had I known the Psalms, I would have thought that the friendly hills were joining me in thanking God for the possible new settlement near them, with Shimeon ha-Tzaddik in their midst. The darker it grew as we were leaving the hills behind us, the closer heaven and earth seemed to touch each other. All the way long, the stars above intermixed with my dreams within.

My disappearance from home naturally caused consternation. A thorough search was made through town, particularly at places where I was apt to wander. The house of Reb Shemuel Salant was animated. I would sometimes crawl under the table and silently listen to the bearded men of the *Bet Din* (Law tribunal) sitting around it, patiently answering questions from people coming and going. The large house of the Brisker Rov Diskin also attracted me, as I enjoyed playing with the many kittens in the yard. The house of my uncle, the pharmacist, was another place where they looked for me. I enjoyed eating their delicious salads and playing with the toys. My cousins were the only children in Jerusalem who had a few toys, brought them from Germany by a relative of my uncle and of the renowned geographer, Joseph Schwartz. My uncle suggested that since his house was on the way to the *Kotel Ma'aravi,* I might have gone there in spite of the dark alley that leads to it. It was not easy to tear me away from the Wall whenever I was taken there. Our devoted Arab friend Leah suggested that I might have gone to the Mosque of Omar to figure out how to replace it with the Temple of Solomon. She insisted that her *Abba* (father) look for me there. Some went to the *Yad Avshalom* monument where Avi had taken me once. The story of a French general who blasted off the hand of the son who dared raise it against his father, had left a deep impression upon us. A little girl, not from our courtyard, with whom we were forbidden to associate on account of her preoccupation with *shedim* (demons), looked for me in every underground hole, pleading with the *shedim* to release me for her sake, and not take revenge for my disbelief in them. Our friend Abdallah urged his grandfather, the Pasha, to send out gendarmes on horses, which he did. The road to Shekhem was not thought of, as it was a total impossibility that a child would venture through the dark alley leading to it. People were running from one corner to another, and no supper was eaten anywhere.

When the search began to look futile, Reb Shemuel Salant ordered the beadle to knock at every door and gather the people to the *Hurvah* and other nearby synagogues. *Hakham Bashi* Elyashar and the Hassidic rabbis issued a similar call. The Hassidim of our courtyard joined our *porushic*[22] *Bet ha-Midrash* so that all prayers should reach Heaven jointly. The children went back and forth kissing the *mezuzah* and praying. The sheiks in their turbans and imposing costumes ascended the circular stairs to the minarets of their mosques. Their solemn chanting of

---

[22]The *Bet ha-Midrash* belonging to the *perushim* (consistent pietists, removed from every transgression of any minutiae of Jewish law).

"Allah, Allah," clearly indicated imminent danger. The Arabs, aware of what had happened, gathered in their mosques for prayers. Sweet Leah was divided between joining the prayers at our court-yard or going to the nearby mosque. The children suggested that she pray at her own place of worship.

Approaching the courtyard with the tall Sephardi holding my hand, I was bewildered to see from afar so many people coming and going. A Hassid who espied us pushed himself through the crowd, ran in front, snatched me and put me on his shoulders. Out of excitement he tossed me into Avi's arms. "Have you already bought the land?" "What land?" asked Avi, unaware that I had overheard their planning. I heaved a sigh of relief when he said that they had not yet come to a decision. "Since you want to organize a new settlement on the road to Shekhem, the first one ought to be adjoining Shimeon ha-Tzaddik's grave. It will be a kind of reward to him. Should the people feel lonesome far away from town, they will draw strength and courage from his being among them." The children, still in the dark of what it was all about, but confident that it was a worthy cause, echoed in unison "Yes, yes, buy the land there." Eventually a lot was bought in the vicinity of Shimeon ha-Tzaddik, but restrictions on immigration issued by the Sultan, diverted the building project.

The courage or foolhardiness of a young child is inconsequential, but the story carries with it some relevant points. Jews and Arabs could be brotherly, each with his own faith, tradition and customs. Leah went to pray in her own mosque, but she prayed for the safety of a Jewish child. Hassidim, Ashkenazim, Sephardim may have been at odds, but neither Hassidim, Ashkenazim nor Sephardim ate supper that evening. Of still deeper significance is the hold great men have on the heart and mind. Their impact is a dynamic force which molds into one, vicarious and personal experiences, memories and sense perceptions. The Jerusalem children could not have grasped Augustine's philosophy that the past is no more, the present a vanishing point, and the future not yet born. To us the past was not a static entity; it gave momentum and content to our thoughts and feelings. Like poets who bring forth a sense of beauty in others, Jewish leaders, with their keen sensitivity, awaken the sense of Jewishness within the Jewish self. There is grandeur in the double projection of oneself into the otherness of the past and that of the future.

An Expedition to the Lost Ten Tribes

Each time a Yemenite would come to our courtyard, we would run towards him to inquire whether he knew something about the lost ten tribes. We would even conjecture that unaware to himself, he might belong to one of them. The Yemenites were so different: they talked Arabic and spoke Hebrew with an Arabic accent. Owing to the scarcity of *siddurim* in Yemen, they were trained to read from the four sides of a page, so that one *siddur* could be used simultaneously by four people. At the *heder,* pupils would be seated on the floor, four in a group, with the teacher in the center. The Yemenites we met were dark, tall, slender, nimble and graceful. They resented our suspicion. "We belong to the faithful surviving tribes, not to those who wavered and erred." We knew that among those tribes there were some who worshipped Baal now and then, but being lost for such a long time is a sufficient punishment in itself. It was time that we should help them atone and lead them back to God. How could we retrace their steps? Were they lost in some special regions or among the crowds of Babylon and Assyria? Did they carry the Torah with them? Were they mindful not to lose it? Would the Messiah gather them from the jungles or wherever they might be? (We heard of jungles through the tales of the remote voyages of Jacob Saphir). What was the use of speculating? Let us start a search throughout the world.

One noontime the *heder* boys had to forego their lunch and be satisfied with the sandwiches we brought them. We had arranged to call on Reb Shemuel Salant while the *Bet Din* was in session. Accustomed to our fancies, he gently asked, "What is it this time?" "Very important and urgent. It cannot be postponed any longer. It is by now almost three thousand years, and no steps have been taken to trace our lost brethren. These tribes are like children lost in the woods, and we might prove to be God's messengers." "What are we to do?" asked Reb Shemuel Salant in an earnest tone of voice, with a smile under his beard. "Send your *meshulahim* (emissaries) everywhere, particularly to the jungles where no communication is possible. Let them also gather those who bear names of the tribes; they might be their descendants and have some information, no matter how scant. It could turn out to be like the story of Joseph." "Well," said he, "the *Bet Din* and I will give thought to your worthy expedition." We asked him not to delay, so that these unhappy people might return in time to have a share in the rebuilding of the Temple which we had just started to plan, and be retraced before the coming of the Messiah. "They are our brothers, and we should be our brothers' keepers."

The boys had to return to *heder,* the girls proceeded towards the residence of *Hakham Bashi* Elyashar with the same problem. He took us more seriously and pointed out some difficulties. With his philosophical bent he even gently hinted that the whole episode was wrapped in obscurity. We admitted that it was not an easy task; that they should have been looked for as soon as they disappeared. But blaming others is no valid excuse for shirking one's own duty. Moved by our earnestness, he said he would deem it a privilege (*zekhut*) to have a share in such a holy expedition, that he would come to our hill to deliberate, and that we should meanwhile search for some constructive plans. We took his advice, and our suggestions multiplied and fructified. He, indeed, came to meet us on the hill and listened patiently. The ten tribes are still lost! In every generation there are some who wither away with them, but those in whom Jewish concepts and beliefs are living realities, never die; their ideals perpetuate themselves.

My Excursion to the Yiddishe Gass—and the Jewelry Store

Shmerl, a friend of the family, obtained permission to take me with him on a tour of the Yiddishe Gass (Street). He was tall, handsome, sociable, and liked by the children. I was delighted with the anticipation of walking through the streets, looking at the shops, and meeting many people. Our first stop on the way was the Arab *Finstere Kleiten,* a row of stores on each side of a tunnel about ten blocks long, not too narrow, with kerosene lanterns hanging from the ceilings of the shops. The goods consisted of dry and fresh vegetables, fruit and spices, plus a fish market with very little fish. On Friday, the Moslem day of rest, and the cooking day for Jewish housekeepers, fresh fish was brought in from Jaffa. The long distance of twenty-four hours by coach, (a half hour now by plane), the wrapping of the fish in damp Turkish towels sprinkled with salt as a means of preservation, naturally raised the cost. When prices went up as high as a quarter of a medjida per pound, the people substituted baklava (of the cod family) soaked in water overnight and fried in olive or sesame oil. This was still fish *likhevod Shabbat* (in honor of the Sabbath). The only one among the Jewish women who would buy it even at such a price, was Tzevia, the step-mother of my uncle the pharmacist, daughter of the famous geographer Joseph Schwartz. It was known throughout Jerusalem that she served my uncle the unheard-of luxury of sardines for breakfast. Sarah Bayla, too, would buy fresh fish on Fridays, but she made gefillte fish, mixed with flour and onions, while Tzevia cooked it plain, with raisins and vinegar. Besides, the merchant set a specially reduced price for Sarah Bayla, as she bought large quantities. She treated everyone in the courtyard, including the Hassidim across the terrace, with a portion of gefillte fish on Friday evenings.

After I had scented the cinnamon, the branches of the sweet lemons, stretched myself on the owner's hammock or divan, way inside the store, and swallowed with my eyes the deep-red water-melon covered with flies (Jewish customers would buy them un-opened), Shmerl took me to the Yiddishe Gass. It was an open, narrow, up-grade street, shaded a little by the shops on each side. At the entrance, on the corner, was my uncle's pharmacy, with several benches filled to capacity and with many people standing. The one with a prescription had to wave it over the people's shoulders to reach the counter. The shop had become a center for discussion of events and a lively exchange of arguments. Opposite the pharmacy was a kosher butcher store with just a few chunks of lean beef, a slightly larger supply of mutton and lamb. However, meat for supper was customary; not broiled or baked, but stewed with vegetables or cooked in soup. Mrs. Moses Luncz, the wife of the blind editor of the geographic magazine *Yeru-shalayim*, was the only one who broiled the meat, on an outdoor charcoal oven of stones, improvised by herself. As she had to be her husband's guide, she could not spare the time to *kasher* the meat. Chickens for the Sabbath could be purchased alive, at not too high a price, from the peasants on the pavement of the Yiddishe Gass. We, and many others, raised our own chickens. The *shohet* would go from house to house for the slaughtering.

I was fascinated by the Arab women sitting on the ground, the baskets of vegetables in front of them, a baby in swaddling clothes strapped on the mother's back, the other four or five children with running noses, red eyes and muddy cheeks, sitting on their laps. The mother's large earrings, straw necklaces, inter-twined metal bracelets, and one hanging from the veil exactly on

Univ. of Tulsa Library
Tulsa, Oklahoma

top of the nose, or from a hole in the nostril, were like toys to me.
It was a sad spectacle to see the mother carefully watching that
her own children should not snatch some food from the basket.
The contents of these baskets, carried on their heads down the hill
from the farm to town, had to be sold to meet the rent and taxes
imposed by the Turks.   Their own lunch on the street was limited
to bread and green onions.

When I sat down to play with the children, Shmerl gently reminded me of the many dry goods stores where we could look at fine
material. These were well patronized, as ready-made clothes were
not thought of. The one with a reputation of over-charging and
with materials of inferior grade, had the largest number of customers. For the owner was the mother of a *bat yehidah* (an only
daughter) ; no son for *kaddish,* and no five or six children to cheer
the dining table. People felt that they ought to compensate her
with a little kindness. Whenever she would assure one that she
was selling below cost, her lips would be moving, silently praying
to be forgiven for her misstatements. The people knew it too well;
they forgave her because she was the mother of but a *bat yehidah.*

To the left of that store stood the *Hurvah,* the oldest synagogue
in Jerusalem. Shmerl took me inside. After I had admired the
ceiling, the walls, the *bimah,* he told me—and I was quite impressed—that it was Immi's father who had rebuilt the ceiling,
fixed the walls and redecorated the whole place.

We did not skip a single shop. Something still more exciting
awaited us on the flat little plateau, some yards further up: three
jewelry stores, and one for reparing watches, earrings and for
sharpening knives and scissors. Shmerl had to fix his watch. He
left me outside meanwhile to enjoy the jewelry display. He found
me glued to one counter, my eyes moving from one piece to another.
He looked around and saw a brilliant golden ring my size. He
probably spent more than he could afford. He purchased the ring
and put in on my finger. My eyes were gleaming with joy; my
fingers must have trembled with excitement. Everyone around
told me what a beautiful ring and how nice it looked on me. I
could hardly wait to show it to the children. I shall, of course, let
them take turns wearing it, but on Sabbath I should like to have
it to myself. I shall go to the women's section of the Hassidic Shul,
and display it before Tzipra, who wears on festive occasions a
golden tiara studded with large and small diamonds. I shall wave
my finger from far to the Hassidic boy who always keeps at a

distance from girls. All of a sudden a thought flashed through my mind. I let go of Shmerl's hand and ran back as fast as I could through the Yiddishe Gass and the *Finstere Kleiten*. Shmerl was not worried, as it was a simple way, with no bifurcations. He waited a little longer for his watch.

I came home in tears, and when I saw Immi, the tears grew into cries and sobs. "I do not want to get married without a *huppah, klezmer* (music), dances, especially those of the Hassidim who jump like into the sky, chant and clap hands. I want *derasha geshank* (wedding presents), a *badhen* (entertaining jester) who makes you cry and laugh in one breath. I want banquets for seven days, and have the helpless people of the *magrib* hall (immigrant Jews from Persia and Turkestan) come and eat all they want. I don't want my hair to be cut off yet, I want to play with the children on the hill. I do not want to get married so young. I do not want to be Shmerl's wife. He is nice, I like him, but he is so tall, I have to stand on tip-toes to look at him. I want to wait until I am eleven."

Immi answered it could be even at twelve, the age she was wedded. Without showing it, she became perturbed. "Stop crying and tell me exactly what happened." "He put the ring on my finger. I was so attracted by it that it escaped my mind that with a ring one becomes a bride." Immi, not less upset, but with a controlled, apparently calm tone, asked whether I heard him say *harei at mequdeshet li betaba'at zu* (Behold, thou art consecrated to me by this ring). "I do not know what he said. I was looking at the ring; he was talking to the people, and that was probably what he uttered." "Did the people see when he put the ring on your finger?" "Of course they did; they all admired it." Immi's uneasiness grew and I began to reflect it. "What am I to do now?" I was too excited to get her reply, except that the sound of the word *get* (divorce) reached my ears. I remained silent, her agony became apparent, when all of a sudden she exclaimed: "Let me see your ring." It was not on the finger specified for the wedding ring. As Immi regained her calm, she assured me that I was not wedded to him. She warned me, however, never to accept a ring from any man. My tears dried by the time Shmerl returned, and I thanked him affectionately. He swung me around his shoulders, "Oh you silly little girl, one does not get married without parents' permission. You think I would have deprived you of a *huppah?*"

It is only to people for whom the spiritual is as real as the physical, that the strength of words is equivalent to physical ties.

Through the simple formula of *harei at mequdeshet li . . . ke-dat Moshe ve-Yisrael*[23] husband and wife, the Torah of Moses and Israel, all become knitted into one sanctification.

PENITENTIAL DAYS

We would solemnly gather on our hill, boys and girls, taking a careful account of our deeds, lest we forgot some. We would try to recall what sins we may have committed towards each other or towards the grown-ups. My brother Benjamin, among the poets of our hill, had developed a dislike for a fine old woman, Haye Esther, whom in a moment of anger he called a *mekhashefah* (witch). We all insisted that he must apologize to her, in order to obtain God's forgiveness. He was adamant, but finally yielded to our plea that his sin may be borne by all of us, and even prevent the rebuilding of the Temple. Haye Esther not only forgave him, but also contributed to our Temple fund. Never again did he call her *mekhashefah*.

A more complicated problem was the one versus Tzipra, the owner of the Hassidic terrace, who was afraid that we would break her large square stones, and would chase after us with a broomstick. How could we ask her forgiveness, with the full knowledge that we would jump and run again, and even play some pranks? This particular terrace had a special fascination for us. There was the Hassidic *Shul,* and across the place was an Arab ground where several tall Arabs would kneel daily for their prayers. We would invariably stop our running as soon as they began with their ablutions. We even kept still at the sound of the muezzin announcing the prayer time. For the Hassidim we had a deep affection. But to Tzipra we were bad, teasing and spiting her, and crying out, "Tzipra, Tzipra, our running and jumping will break your stones." She would run after us, but in vain; we could run faster. On *Erev* Yom Kippur there was a load weighing on our chest. It was her property, and we took it over as if it were our own. Yet we neither scratched her stones, nor disturbed the Hassidim. Although it was her property, she also used ours as an exit to the street, and for an entrance to the men's and women's synagogues. We finally decided that it was Tzipra who was sinning, and not we. We gathered in front of her house and exclaimed in unison:

---

[23]"Behold, thou art consecrated to me . . . according to the Law of Moses and of Israel."

"Tzipra, Tzipra, we forgive you for chasing after us, for interrupting our games, and for your false accusations of breaking your stones." The air was filled with "We forgive you, we forgive you, Tzipra." Poor Tzipra was flabbergasted by such an onslaught, and in her bewilderment she accepted our forgiveness. On the spur of the moment one ventured to ask, "Will you let us play on your terrace after Yom Kippur?" Thereupon we ran as fast as we could, fearing her answer. In re-examining our conduct, there still remained a trace of remorse for irritating her. But she was unkind; never a smile on her lips nor a pleasant greeting, only the bitter refrain: "Get away from here."

It was not the knock of the beadle that would wake our parents for the *selihot* (penitential prayers for forgiveness). We were up long before. We wanted our prayers to illuminate the heavens before they were lit by the rays of the sun.

"Be-Ivrit! Be-Ivrit! (In Hebrew! In Hebrew!)"—This story, which made front page in the Jerusalem newspapers and was cited also in the Hebrew papers abroad, needs to be corrected in its interpretation. It was stated, and Ben Yehudah's influence was taken for granted, that a six-year old girl by the name of Nehama, decided to speak only Hebrew. Through her insistence, it became the language of the family, of the relatives, and of the residents of a most popular courtyard in Jerusalem. It was told that this caused a great alarm among the rabbis, who pleaded with the child to abandon it, and that an aunt of hers traced the cause of her malaria to that stubbornness. As I happen to be the one referred to, I should like to restate the facts in their proper contexts. Ben Yehudah's influence in the spread of the Hebrew language is not to be contested, but our respective modes of approach were from diagonally different angles. He was carried away by the wave of radicalism combined with nationalism which had swept over Europe. His ideal was to dissociate the language from its religious connotations and transform it into a completely secular one. Therein lay the antagonism of the rabbis, who felt that the sacredness of the content extended also to its instrument of expression. Hebrew was not just *ivrit,* but *lashon kodesh* (holy tongue).

With the children of our courtyard it was a religious impetus. Since the Torah was given us in Hebrew, it must be God's wish that the form, i.e., the language, should remain as intact as the content. We wanted to be one with the children who heard the voice of Moses at Mt. Sinai. The poem we intended to write in honor of King Solomon would have to be in the language spoken by him and his contemporaries who saw him build the Temple. The Shepherd King sang his praises in Hebrew, and so did Isaiah in his message *na'hamu, na'hamu ammi* (*Comfort ye, comfort ye, my people*). Should we ever be fortunate enough to meet Elijah during his invisible appearances, how could we address him in any other way? Not least, Jehudah Halevi's poem *Tzion halo tish'ali* (Zion, wilt thou not ask?) was one more inducement to banish jargon (a derogatory term for Yiddish) and replace it with *Ivrit*. We actually learned to speak it out of our own resources, without formal lessons for the girls. The boys got a great deal from their study of *hummash* (Pentateuch) at the *heder,* and would impart to the girls whatever knowledge they were capable of transmitting.

When the news spread that the children of our courtyard were like gendarmes, driving away jargon from anyone's lips, the rabbis thought that it was time to warn us not to be swayed by Ben Yehudah or some of the colonists who sought to make converts for radicalism. Reb Shemuel Salant came to our hill, and in one instant all the children flocked around him. No sooner had he started talking to us, than he saw from what deep Jewish sources our Hebrew speaking sprang. "With such sentiment," he said, "your Hebrew is *lashon ha-kodesh.*" He spoke in Yiddish, and we answered him in Hebrew. We lacked the courage to stamp with our feet and yell *lo be-jargon,* ("Not in Yiddish") as we did with everyone else. "You are an example of integral Jewishness." He warned us, however, not to forget that this is the language in which we address God in our prayers, and that we must keep ourselves as holy and pure as the language itself. "You should never fight in Hebrew." We replied that if we happen to fight, which is an extremely rare occurrence, we shall fight in pantomime and be careful not to utter a single word. If our hands are dirty from touching any polluted thing, we shall wash them, before speaking, just as we do before the *ha-motzi.* There shall be a jug of water on the hill to wash our hands before we start speaking to each other. He left us saying, *"Tov, tov, yevarekhekhem ha-Shem."* (Good, good, may God bless you.) Hakham Bashi

Elyashar was so delighted that he would climb our hill each time he visited our folks, so as to converse with us in Hebrew. He would patiently correct many of our grammatical mistakes.

The *Safah Berurah* Society for the spread of Hebrew throughout the world originated with Avi Hakham Jacob Meir (later *Hakham Bashi*), and a few others. Subsequently several members of rabbinic families joined it.

Free Lessons in English

One day, when we were already allowed to go out unescorted, we ventured outside the Gates of Zion, where a new suburb was rising. At the turning of a wide street we came across an ornate gate with rose-bushes and carnations on its sides, pointing to a luscious garden and a sumptuous house. On the door were sentences with the letters cut out of pressed flowers, spelled in Yiddish, Hebrew, Arabic, French, German and English, "Welcome! Do you wish to learn English? Knock at the gate; teaching free of charge." This was the first year of our crusade for Hebrew, but acquiring an additional language would not be in conflict with it. Should the children from America write to us, we would not be dependent on the British consul for the translation. Of course we would reply in Hebrew and bid them learn it. What fun also in surprising our folks. They might think another confusion of the tower of Babel. But, God forbid, we do not challenge Him. We dream of heaven, but do not seek to climb it like those who tried to build the Tower. With exciting anticipation we knocked at the gate and told the door-keeper in the little French we knew that we wanted to study English. *"Oui, oui, entrez mes enfants."* (Yes, yes, come in my children). It was dazzling. Never had we seen anything like it: marble floors, a brilliant ceiling, colored pictures of human beings with wings, and a heavy chandelier hanging from the center. The sky-blue walls were adorned with even brighter pictures than the ceiling. How can there be human beings with wings? They could not represent angels either, since no one in our days has beheld one. Even those who appeared to Abraham were disguised as travelers, and to Jacob they appeared only in a dream. The garden with its large variety of flowers and delightful fragrance intoxicated our senses. The gardener picked some blooms for each of us. Candied fruit—the kind we abstained from on account of our Temple fund raising—were passed around in profusion. We were told that in English this was called "candy"; this, a "flower"; and this a "picture." Our eyes fastened on a large one in a conspicuous corner. "Oh, this picture," the teacher remarked casually, "don't you know it? This is the portrait of our Lord Jesus." "Who is Jesus?" we asked. "He is God, our Savior." "How could God be painted," I exclaimed in amazement, "since no one has seen Him except Moses, and my grandmother told us that even Moses did not see Him in His fullness, God could not look like a man. We are created in the image of God, but He could not be the image of man. He could not be fenced into a picture on the wall. He is in Heaven, on earth and everywhere. The Bible says He soared over the firmament after He created the world. Then He must be a spirit, and you cannot paste a spirit on the wall."

The tall, slim teacher with golden hair—I clearly remember her large blue eyes—must have realized that she was going at too fast a pace. She merely said, "Come, let us pass into the other halls." We were ushered into a large, pleasant dining room with the windows opening on the garden. On the table was nicely-shaped almond pastry;—I knew its delicious taste, for Immi would buy it for me from a newly-opened German-Jewish bakery whenever malaria would make me dislike normal foods. There were also spread before us carobs, pieces of cane sugar, pomegranates sliced into quarters, peeled cactus fruit, deep-red apples with small silver knives, tiny jars with jelly, yellow cheese cut symmetrically (imported Swiss cheese), a kind we had never seen before. Our own homemade cheese looked like a thick piece of white chalk. The chairs around the table were upholstered with a fine ornate plush, like the kind I saw in Paris years later. The table was mahogany with carved pictures on the legs. We were asked to sit down and pick what we pleased. I felt like Alice in Wonderland, but it was not a dream. I could easily have stretched my hand and brought all it could hold in its grasp to my watering mouth and longing eyes. But a vague, almost unconscious suspicion took hold of me, without my knowing what I was suspecting. The children skipped the pastry and the cheese, but enjoyed the fruit, especially the dainty little silver knives with which to cut it. From the table we were led to the classroom, with pictures of small chairs, tables, vases, bottles, with English words underneath them. The classroom fascinated me, but the avidity to learn English become dampened by thoughts obscure even to my own self. These obscure sensations were suddenly illumined and translated into clearer thinking when the teacher said in French, "Before we start our lessons we must kneel, and you repeat after me our prayers to the Lord Jesus." "Kneel, little girl, kneel." She gently put me on my knees. Thereupon I gave out a shrill yell, began to run, and pointed to the bewildered children to run after me. We ran from hall to hall until we reached the gate locked with an inside chain. Pitying our panic, the teacher readily unlatched the chain and said in fluent Yiddish, "Go, you little fools; you are as stupid and stubborn as your ancestors."

This was our first and last lesson in English, with a secret feeling of guilt which we carried for a long while when we learned that this enchanted place was a missionary center, and that it was a sin to pass its threshold. It is hard to understand what prompted the hope of the missionaries of those times to center their activities among the Jews, when they knew at what risks those people came to Jerusalem in order to lead a fuller Jewish life.

We were too frightened and deeply stirred to bring this terrifying experience to our folks before regaining our equilibrium. But as soon as we returned home we looked for our *ger*. He happened to be in town, carrying jugs of water. We left word with each neighbor that he should meet us on the hill the moment he comes. The neighbors surmised that it was an emergency meeting, and the message was promptly relayed to him. "What news, children? I had a wonderful lesson in Rashi today." We loved Rashi and we would have wanted to know what his lesson was about, but there were more pressing questions. "Please tell us, did the rabbis hold out much inducement to you to become a Jew? Did they promise you a reward in heaven and a blessing in this life?" "No, children, the rabbis discouraged me and said that if I am motivated by the expectation of a greater share in the world to come, I could remain within my faith. Righteousness is the only badge for admission. They admitted me into your fold after putting me through one test after another." We related our experience to him, and relived it in its minutest details, with a fear which is usually magnified in retrospect. About Allah we heard from our little Arab friends, but no one had as yet told us about Jesus. We knew that the *ger* was not born a Jew and had chosen to become one. But somehow at the age of six our philosophizing had not yet gone beyond the Jewish frontier, and the antecedents of the *ger* had not yet entered our reflections. At this juncture we learned

from him about the birth of Christianity and its deviation from
Moses. Why didn't Jesus, we asked, remain with the Jews if he
wanted to make them better Jews? Did Moses leave us because
some worshipped the golden calf when he was on the mountain
with God? Did Isaiah forsake us when he scolded the bad women,
the bad kings, and those who were less than oxen for not knowing
their God? You don't make people better by deserting them. When
you stay, they may learn from you. Ezra did not despair of the
people's ignorance; he taught them patiently. We had learned only
recently about Ezra from the *ger* who imparted to us information
he acquired with a child-like pleasure. We said to each other that
the English teacher wanted us to part from the Jews because their
master Jesus had done so.

This confused experience came back to my mind, with clearer
notions that years bring with them, when, in 1927, I gave a series
of lectures on a philosophical (not theological) approach to the
genesis of Christianity. (There were twenty-three Catholic priests
among the audience.) I think the memory of the *ger* and that of
the missionary teacher helped me view in their proper perspective
the conflicting philosophies at the emergence of Christianity.

May I now express some views reached in my maturity, but
based on these experiences of my childhood. In a disintegrating
and menacing world, self-preservation becomes the concern of
all. But the challenge was met through roads wide apart which
could not possibly converge. One philosophy was that of self-
reflection, intensification, integralness, re-enforcement of the moral
strength within, and a tenacious holding to its structure—a structure which has engendered the Jewish mode of living and which
has become itself sanctified in the process of its fulfilment. The
other line of thought which eventuated into the philosophy of
Christianity was that of expansion, expanding its moral principles
even if they have to be torn from the organism that brought them
into being. Divorced from its own mechanism, the philosophy of
Christianity was faced with the problem of finding a substitute in
which to embody the moral principles abstracted from the Jewish
setting, from instructions (laws) so closely knit with it and
which grew from within. I have tried to show elsewhere[24] that
this transplantation into an alien soil resulted in some philosophical
dilemmas which the Christian scholastics found it hard to solve.
For, Jewish and Greek thought could at best be co-ordinated, but

---

[24]Journal of Philosophy, Vol. XXX, No. 17.

not fused into one. Philo's attempt at amalgamating them was artificial, and did violence both to the Jewish and the Greek essence. These dilemmas, however, (sensed by Thomas Aquinas, Duns Scotus; Augustine before them, and particularly by the Christian philosophers of the Renaissance) have remained solely within the domain of philosophy. Religion draws its nourishment and vitality not from philosophy, but from the faith embedded in human nature.

In the course of their historic developments, the language, too, reflected the respective philosophies of expansion and intensification. The one drew its strength from sculpture and painting, the other from interpretation and re-interpretation. The great painters and sculptors throughout the ages have been the masterbuilders in the Christian world, just as Rashi and other interpreters have enriched the Jewish world.

One should not mistake the Jewish leaning on words for verbalism. They have become translated into instruments of moral behavior. The unceasing search for the inward meaning of words in which to discover God's Revelation created an organic transition between the various stages of Jewish development. It has been like diving under its stream to bring forth to the surface the sustaining nutrients for continuous growth. Depth, length and breadth become unified into one dimension. A chief weakness of the Kabbalah is its tendency to transform words into independent entities instead of viewing them, as do our classic interpreters, as dynamic functions of a living system—a system in which the roots persist, even when branches and leaves wither.

She'erit Israel—the remnant of Israel, has been not just a a comforting concept, but a profound constituent of Jewish philosophy. The perpetuity of the Jewish flow is kept insured as long as there is a nucleus which remains intact. The Jewish sprouting in a courtyard such as ours, and in centers from which Jewish leaders have sprung, is for the philosophy of Jewishness a living testimony to the faith in God's Covenant with the people who chose to keep it.

Angels on the Walls

The pictures of angels on the walls of the missionary school had thrown us into confusion. Our vision of angels was too deep within us not to rebel against their externalization, no matter how attractive to the eye. We told the missionary teacher who pointed

them out on the walls that men have no wings and angels have no
bodies. We repeated to each other as if to re-enforce our view that
angels who come down to earth solely for good deeds would not
waste their time posing for a portrait, nor would they push aside
the thick cloud which hides them. That the Rambam would have
backed us in the mystery with which we enwrapped the angels, I
learned later when I studied him. He writes in the *Guide*: "Angels
have form but no substance." This means that they are beyond
human perception.

They were not less real to us in their invisibility. On Sabbaths
we would adorn ourselves in the finest clothes, decorate our hair
with a garland of the little yellow flowers, to greet them cheerfully
with *Shalom Alekhem*. It sounded as if they themselves were
answering *Alekhem Shalom*. Our eyes would be fixed on the
guests of the table, should they be messengers in disguise who
visited Abraham in his tent. When Avi would chant *Shalom
alekhem mal'akhei ha-Sharet, mal'akhe Elyon*—"Peace be with
you ministering Angels, Angels of the Most High"—our regard
would turn to the shadows of the candle light which could perhaps
reflect some token of them. In the silence of the night when the
Sabbath guests had departed, I would sometimes lie awake with
eyes closed, greeting these invisible companions, *"Shalem alekhem,*
beloved angels, how fortunate you are to be messengers of God."
On a clear night—the sky is uniquely brilliant in Jerusalem—
we would gaze at the stars as if some angels were hiding behind
them, tenderly watching over the world below. We thought that
the soothing and mysterious stars could be a fitting abode for our
friendly angels, always ready to carry some good messages. A
shooting star might bring an angel with it. But we mused, since
the destruction of the Temple, the tender angels who commiserate
with human beings are probably weeping all the time, like the
ancient Jews by the streams of Babylon. How could they come
down to earth and bring cheer, when they themselves are so
saddened?

Our conception of the stars was not far from that of the
Jewish medieval philosphers, who regarded them as pure mind,
which they termed Intelligibles. They leaned on this astronomic
misconception of the times, because it re-enforced their view of a
unified spirituality between heaven, earth and men. But the
dethronement of the heavenly bodies from Intelligibles to mere
planets does not carry with it the rejection of such an invigorating
spiritual belief.

The pictures on those walls which weighed heavily on our minds, led to speculations which otherwise might not have entered into the realm of our thinking. We wanted to probe into a mystery which we knew was fathomless, but the thoughts forced themselves upon us. What is the nature of those wonderful beings who travel invisibly from heaven to earth for the good of men? Do they have free will? How could they, if their task consists chiefly in transmitting messages? A messenger has no choice but to deliver. In between the deliveries do they utilize their time in studying the Torah? This, too, was answered in the negative.

"God gave the Torah for the people on earth and not for heaven," exclaimed a little girl. "I love angels and feel very sad that they have no Torah to study, am happy that I am a human being; even though I am a girl, there is much of the Torah that I can learn." "This is a sacrilegious thought," chorused the whole group. "Angels stand above all creatures; they sit at the throne of God and are nearest to Him." "No," said she, "no one is nearer nor farther away from God. He created heaven and earth, and we are all equally near to Him. We are estranged only when we violate His commandments." "Angels need no commandments. They have no temptation and perform God's will spontaneously," replied a young Hassidic boy. "But we have a choice of not obeying, and our obedience comes from our free will," was the retort. "What a desecration!" cried all. "No, it is not. The angels, kind, tender and full of sympathy for all, are perfect beings, but they are messengers and Israel is the king to whom the messages are delivered. With whom did God make the Covenant, with Israel or with the angels?" Frightened by her own thoughts, she tried to soothe herself and the group. "Let us not compare angels with other beings. Angels are angels; men are men. *Hodu la-Shem!* Thank God that He created angels in heaven and men on earth. We love them in any form; we shall always look forward to greet them with tenderness, and seek for their hidden selves everywhere, but not in concrete pictures on the walls. When our Temple will be rebuilt, they may come down to earth and rejoice with it. Then the people might be privileged to feel their presence in some sort of vision."

These philosophical discussions happened to have taken place on a Friday afternoon. Sabbath was drawing near. We rushed down the hill, picked some of the tiny flowers from the tree below, the boys curled their *peyot,* the girls pinned colored ribbons on their braids,—all of us anxious to appear before the angels in our very best, and hoping that we had not offended them. The earnest and tender tone of our *Shalom Alekhem* that night was like an apology for having sought to unveil their magnificent mystery.

Condolence to Job

When we reached our seventh year, the group of boys a little older than ourselves considered us mature enough to impart some of their knowledge and discuss on an equal level the mysteries of the universe. Once they surprised us with a dramatization of Job. Three of them represented his friends who came to comfort him; a talented Hassidic boy impersonated the suffering and protesting Job. I can still recall our emotional reactions and perplexities. We shared Job's indignation at the uncharitable attitude of his friends, especially since he was not aware of having committed a sin. Sharing vicariously Job's suffering, we, too, raised the question as to why God wanted to test one so righteous. Abraham had to be tested before being chosen the forefather of a people. Job had already attained old age, and his long past should have been sufficient testimony to his righteousness. Wealth and health could be restored, but how could one family take the place of another? Would he not miss them just as much with the substituted members? Our older boys swallowed their pride and acknowledged their ignorance in such weighty matters. Besides, they had to run back to the Talmud Torah, and they left us to our meditations.

After prolonged thinking, we tried to see whether we could not bring some comfort to Job—not along the lines of his narrow-minded friends. His sufferings were, of course, hard to bear, but he was singled out for his virtues and not for sins. Being the most righteous of his generation, God wanted to see whether he would remain so under adverse circumstances. By choosing the most righteous one, God could find out whether men, with the freedom He gave them, could reach the same height of perfection as angels who are not encumbered with the difficulty of choice. It was not easy to resign ourselves to the loss of his family, but eventually he would meet them in heaven and be with them *ad olam,* for all eternity. The greatest reward of all was that God appeared to him in a vision and he felt as if he saw Him.[25] Job being a righteous

---

[25]"But now mine eye seeth Thee" XLII, 5.

man on his own path, and not the creator of new ways for others, as were Abraham, Moses and the Prophets, he could not possibly have had this vision, were it not for his undeserved suffering. Did not Rabbi Akiba rejoice in his martyrdom because he could prove thereby his love for God? Much as we sympathized with Job, we felt that we could sincerely console him that he was a privileged character, that we hoped that he found much joy when he met his former family in heaven, and that the two families joined into one to give him double affection.

We were not perturbed that God's testing may denote a lack of universal foreknowledge or limitation of power. It is God's great will-power not to want to know man's choice ahead of time. He could have, if He had wanted to. He preferred to create intelligent beings who would know the difference between good and evil, and have the freedom of choice. Out of His supreme goodness and love He gave us commandments which are assisting our choice. Of course, evil must be punished either in this or in the next world. But there are so many Yom Kippurs between one's birth and one's last days, that by the time we reach the world to come, most of our sins may have been forgiven, unless one is as wicked as Pharaoh, Haman ha-Rasha, or Nebuchadnezzar. Our assumption of God's need for testing human character yielded many fruitful explanations. Why did God harden Pharaoh's heart? This was necessary to test Israel's persistence in the pursuit of freedom in face of obstacles. God had to know their strength of character before entrusting the Torah to them. Pharaoh was so wicked that the hardening of his heart did not add to his punishment, already enormous in itself.

With such naive outlook one could cut the Gordian knot. But a childlike attitude with its purity and accuracy of feelings may be nearer to mysterious truths than adult sophistication. We came out of our experience with Job with a sense of security as that of the seamen who have reached the shore. Our perplexities were left behind us, we stepped on solid ground. Both God and man came out triumphant in their relations with each other. We felt as if we had found the key to great mysteries by discovering—we thought it was our own discovery—the basis of the relationship: the harmony between God and man through the help of His commandments. Through them, men and God gravitate towards one another, both in the same direction. ("Gravitation" was not the expression we used, but I do not recall the wording which implied that very meaning.)

The moving face of that Hassidic young boy impersonating Job, so eloquently reciting the verse "Even if He slay me I trust in Him", came before me when I wrote an essay on a comparative conception of suffering in the Bible and in Greek literature.[26] This verse is sufficient unto itself for the contrast between Job's protestations and those of Greek tragedies, whose hostility towards their gods left no room for mutual relationship. The other half of that verse, "But I will maintain my own ways before Him", epitomizes the drama of the interrelationship between God and Job. On the one hand he would trust in Him even if He should slay him; on the other, he holds on to his ways unconditionally because his is the right path, but that unconditional path is *before God*. Therein, I think, lies the drama of the whole story. He trusts in God; he trusts in his own ways, too. The apparent conflict between the two trusts is solved with the inevitable climax that he will "maintain his own ways", but *before God,* and *not outside Him.* The relationship with God is clouded, but not lost for a moment. His very irritation against the self-righteous, unsympathetic friends, who came to comfort him, was for their strict arithmetic which almost seemed to leave God out of account.

The exciting drama of Job led us to further speculations on the moral structure of the world. As I now look back with the maturity of an adult, it seems that in our childish search for the ethical criterion, we unknowingly followed the path of Jewish philosophers and also of Immanuel Kant and John Dewey. The philosophical definition of a moral act is the proper choice between conflicting ends. "Proper" applies to an act harmonious with the complete personality and the social whole. It is easy, we said, to be good and follow the right course when there are no sharp rocks on the path. The test of man's goodness lies in the choice of the good in face of obstacles. If he does not turn away from it through alluring temptations or allow himself to be pulled down by difficulties, he is a virtuous man.

A little girl remarked: "You remember, while playing ball the other day counting each others' number of bounces, Sarah Bayla asked that we carry some food to the *Magrib* hall. We dropped the ball, lost our scores for the race, and ran towards her. This was good on our part." Said another, this denoted goodness, not

---

[26]It was a college paper, not meant for publication.

virtue; there was no hesitation, no conflict. Who would hesitate between playing ball and bringing food to old, hungry people! "What tests could we undergo to prove virtuousness?" "Should a Bar Mitzvah boy happen to be hungry some early morning, crave food, and yet put on his *tefillin* and pray before breakfast, his would be a virtuous act. He overcame temptation, conflict and even physical discomfort."

"I have an instance of real heroism which also embraces virtue," exclaimed the youngest of us "Hannah encouraged her sons to die rather than desert God." "This was, of course, supreme virtue, and such heroism would be greatly rewarded in heaven," uttered a young Hassidic boy. "It was not for reward, but for the love of God and her people that Hannah made her choice between her sons and the desecration of God," replied a little girl. "Picture her joy on Hanukah when she sees from afar the shimmering candle-lights and hears the song of *maoz tzur yeshuati*. How happy she must be with our celebration and with our affection for her and the Hasmonaim!" "Is not this a reward?" resumed the Hassidic boy. My cousin interrupted by jumping with joy, for her name, too, was Hannah.

Our speculations invariably ended on a joyous note. After all, we were children and not Jewish philosophers. If our line of thinking coincided with theirs, it is because Jewish thinking and Jewish living are one. The emotional and intellectual contents are blended into one organic whole. We lived Jewishness, that is why we could think it out in its entirety, in spite of our tender years. We were as intense in playing as in thinking. Coming down the hill we usually ended on Tzipra's terrace to relax from some serious absorbing thought. No wonder that our jumping and running made her tremble lest we break the square stones.

THE TERRACES

Like butterflies which suck from all flowers, we imbibed the spirit of the Hassidic and the Mitnaggedic camps by running back and forth from one to the other. The one was exhilarating, the other awe-inspiring. As we ascended the roof of the *Yeshivah,* there unfolded before us a panorama of the city, with the hills of the Psalms (that was our name for the Judean hills) far in the horizon. The inside which we peeped into through an upper window was also fascinating. We never tired of the rabbis, seated at a long row of tables, to watch their earnest faces bent over large thick volumes, as they intoned their contents with fervor. Suddenly there was a halt, all eyes turning towards Avi, who was then the head of the *Yeshivah*. We surmised the halt was due to an obstruction by a difficult passage. The foreheads would wrinkle, the eyes sink, the elbows rested on the table, when after a few moments Avi's face would light up: "I have it, I have it!" The sing-song intonations would be resumed, and the heads bent again over the pages. Sometimes we would see Avi running down the stairs, rushing to his library shelves, returning with a large tome, one finger in it, and opening the book beamingly: "The *Meharsha* (a great commentator) agrees with my interpretation." We stood motionless, as if glued to the window. In our phantasy we pictured it to be similar to the one in which Hillel was covered with snow while listening to the discussions inside. We no doubt must have wished that we, too, be covered with snow, which appears but rarely in Jerusalem. Our beloved *ger* was also at one of those tables. He was seated near Avi, who from time to time would glance at his page to see whether he could keep up with the pace. When he would ask him whether the passage was clear, his gentle "Yes, *barukh ha-Shem*" (Thank God), could be heard through the window, and it thrilled us. From the roof, walking on tiptoes, we would turn to the Hassidic terrace, and relieve our tension. The flow of words made up for our long hypnotic silence. A pertinent remark of ours I happen to remember: "The Hassid sings with a cup of wine in his hand; the *Parush* with a heavy book in front of him; but both are singing for their joy of Jewishness." The joy of Jewishness is no doubt at the bottom of what makes one a Jewish Jew.

With all its intense learning, our *Yeshivah* was not like a secluded monastery, losing sight of the life without. Questions of the town were brought to it and reviewed in the light of the *Halakhah* in all its ramifications. There came up the question of the *shemittah* (sabbatical fallow year) in the colonies. There was the agitation which shook Galician Jewry as to whether a prominent rabbi of theirs was right in deviating from the wonted Kabbalistic interpretation of the *sefirot*.[27] A Hassidic rabbi referred the matter to Jacob Mordecai, and also asked Avi, then fifteen years of age, to write a dissertation on the subject. He was known to be

---

[27]*Sefirot:* A Kabbalistic conception of the ten attributes or manifestations through which God makes His existence known.

versed in the Kabbalah. His first two books, which he wrote before the age of nineteen, were written in a Kabbalistic vein.

There were special sessions in our *Yeshivah* for storekeepers, carpenters, shoemakers. Colonists were given inducements to attend, and they did whenever possible, because Reb Jacob Mordecai, Sara Bayla and their sons took a keen interest in the welfare of the colonies. There were also a few doctors who would come for a while between office hours. Avi would collect for them the many medical references in the Talmud. Among those doctors was the well-known pious Dr. Moshe Wallach from the Bikkur Holim Hospital, who would never write a prescription on the Sabbath. He would call for the pharmacist at his home, go with him to the store, and watch that there be no mistake. When a patient was ordered by him not to fast on Yom Kippur, he knew that in his individual case fasting would be a sin.

An interesting visitor to the *Yeshivah* who would attend it a few times a week, was a Jewish attaché to the Russian Consulate. The wealthy Mr. Nabon, with access to the Sultan, who in his youth earned a livelihood by shoe-shining, found pleasure sitting at those tables whenever he could. He would bring the children a large bouquet of a variety of flowers from his own garden—the largest in Jerusalem. When he or any other Sephardi would come to the *Yeshivah*, the Yiddish sing-song would be changed into Hebrew with a Sephardic intonation, which Avi acquired from Hakham Bashi Elyashar. Pains were taken to clarify passages to those not so steeped in Talmudic study.

Much attention was given to impart some learning to laymen, so that their daily life be permeated with the Talmudic spirit. This idea was at the bottom of Avi's attempts to industrialize Jerusalem. He would not only make it economically independent, but also an ideal community without a strict division between men of affairs and men of learning. Both groups would interpenetrate, and Jewish learning would be inherent in the life of every Jew. That Jewish learning and Jewish life converge into one is at the very bottom of our philosophy. Learning without the Jewishness that flows from it would be empty and devoid of its aim; and Jewishness without learning would be chaotic. The organic union of the two is one of our fundamental principles.

The children would take an instinctive delight when on some afternoons the Hassidim, each with a volume of the Talmud under his arm, would go to our *Yeshivah* and stay there until they would

return for *Minhah* service in their own place.   Usually their visit
followed a lively discussion—an indication that they went to seek
an authoritative interpretation.   In their absence, in spite of
Tzipra's protests, we would indulge in noisier games and heavier
jumping on the terrace.

Dancing on the Terrace

Our dances were imaginative pantomimes of historical episodes.
One was around King Solomon. The handsomest boy was placed
in the center of a circle, each of us gracefully bending the head
to him, as a gesture of thankfulness for the glorious Temple. He
in turn would point towards heaven, indicating that thanks be
given to God, and not to him. The thoughts were translated into
rhythmic movements with songs of our own composition. Another
favorite dance represented the people's joy at the rebuilding of the
Second Temple. With hands clapping, heads moving up and down,
right and left, the body swinging with rhythmical movements, the
feet lifted a little towards the sky, and with a melody of our own,
the *hodu la-Shem* resounded through the terrace.

And then a sad and mute pantomine, as we sat on the edge of
the terrace pretending it was the river of Babylon, with a make-
believe lyre on our lap, that emitted no sound. How can you sing,
poor lyre, with Jerusalem destroyed? Then we would suddenly
arise with a melodious *nahamu, nahamu ammi*. In spite of my
poor singing, the honor of the solo was bestowed upon me, because
of my name *Nehamah*, derived from the association with the
haftorat nahamu, the week I was born. On account of my name I
felt a kind of kinship with the people who mourned by the waters
of Babylon. My solo was a string of comforting words, to which
the chorus would respond, *nahamu, nahamu ammi.* Some of our
dances were reproductions of the Hassidic ones, with all their
exuberance, as if invisible angels were attending and enjoying them.

Once in the midst of a joyous dance, the Hassidim came out
of the *Bet ha-Midrash* and joined us. A number of rabbis from
town happened to come to the courtyard for a conference on some
Sephardic-Ashkenazic argument. What happened that the Hassidim were dancing at such an odd hour? Out of curiosity the
rabbis came up to the terrace and stood in wonder at the imaginativeness of the children. Hakham Bashi Elyashar remarked with
his usual enthusiasm: "They bring with them a breeze from the

First Temple. Such must have been the dances in those times. How insignificant our disagreements become in face of such vision." Turning to us, "Blessed children, may God give that your vision of the Temple become a reality."

Composing verses was a favorite pastime with us. One would improvise the words, another the music, and almost unawares we would burst into song. Messiah was among our richest inspirations. Upon his arrival our eyes will be dazzled by the brilliance of the Temple, with a golden dome and a golden chandelier within. The Mosque of Omar, lifted by a heavy misty cloud, will be placed nearby where Arabs, too, could pray. Our dear Leah would add a chanting line in Arabic, "And we shall see each other through the golden panels of the emerald windows." The Wailing Wall, too, would be a subject for lyrics. The dark Arab alley with lines of Jewish *Magribim* and Arab beggars with outstretched hands into which was dropped a fraction of a penny[28], the massive stone wall, the prayers under the open sky, the touching intonations, the bitter tears shed by the supplicants with prayerful notes on slips of paper pushed into the crevices, the sobbing on *Tish'ah be-Ab,* the "arrogant Mosque of Omar" looking down upon us—such a composite picture had to melt in songs. The dark alley leading to the Wailing Wall will become illumined, the gloomy wall transformed into a resplendent arch more glittering than gold. It will shine with the spirit of David and Solomon.

The tall Arab who daily appeared on the terrace at four o'clock for his prayers was an impressive figure. The jug of water we brought for his ablutions was always greeted with a smile and with "May Allah bless you and the courtyard." The blessings, the tall stature, the solemn washing of the feet, the deep bow of the head with the hands stretching to the ground, and the prayer on his slowly moving lips, were of poetic inspiration: "The Arabs will lift their hands towards heaven instead of bending them to the ground when the voice of the Messiah will fill the earth. . . . Jews and Arabs will hold hands and turn their gaze to heaven."

A poem by a Hassidic boy with earlocks down to his shoulders, who would never pass between two women, dwelt upon the apportionment of the Leviathan. An artist in words, he expressed in poetical lines the hope that the people of our courtyard would be sitting near the Hassidim and be accorded equal treatment at

---

[28]This was a yellow round piece of tin made for the purpose. Twenty such pieces constituted a penny.

that gigantic banquet. This, in spite of our teasings. As soon as we would see him approach the stairs, the girls would form a row on each side, and the poor boy would go back and forth and never pass through, even though the stairs were wide. This teasing ceased with the composition of his poems. He would even come up our hill, join our projects, but always at a distance from girls. At his Bar Mitzvah—he was a number of years older than the rest of the group—we presented him with a colorful canvas on which we embroidered in ornate letters *Ba'Olam habba en peridah ben hassidim u-perushim. Ha-Shem ehad lekulanu*: "In the world to come there will be no division between Hassidim and Porushim. God is one for us all."

Little did we know that this adorned canvas of ours reflected the spirit of Jewish philosophy, which marks no division among those who faithfully adhere to the prescribed commandments. As long as the essence and form remain intact, the currents, whether that of the Gaon of Vilna or that of the Ba'al Shem Tov, merge into one in the flow of Jewishness. Hassidism was not a divergent movement but one converging upon the joyous streams in Jewish life. This joy of living was, however, dug out and not innovated by them. The Talmud enjoins upon us to take pleasure in living, and no Hassid could have given it more poetical intonations than did Jehudah Halevi. Nonetheless, the Hassidim put joy and cheer into relief. We loved them, their songs, their dancing with the Sefer Torah affectionately hugged in their arms; enjoyed their going around and around the many long tables at the *Bet ha-Midrash*. We would join them whenever they let us, and happily shared their care-free, jolly mood.

FIRST DONATION TO THE JEWISH NATIONAL FUND—ON A PURIM

We were gathered around the table for the *Purim se'udah* (banquet) with special dishes for the occasion and with merry songs, when there came an unexpected knock at the door. Frumke, an old widow, brought a dainty little tray with an envelope on it in the shape of a *haman-tash:* "Reb Hayyim, this is my *shalah manot* (Purim gift) to you. I want to offer my savings for the purchase of a piece of land to be deeded to the community, with you and Hakham Jacob Meir as trustee. (This was before the establishment of the Jewish National Fund). I came to Jerusalem to own but six feet for my peaceful rest. But the children of the courtyard

with their earnest planning for rebuilding the Temple, inspired
me with the desire of contributing a small brick to it." We shouted
hizki, hizki ve-tithazzaki—be strong and more power to you—
pious Frumke. (Frumke means "pious" in Yiddish.) "When we
grow up we shall tell our children of your *shalahmanot.*" The
following day we cut out a piece of paper in the shape of a *haman-
tash,* and asked Israel Shimeon to inscribe in calligraphic letters
"Keep this *haman-tash* and show it to the Messiah when he comes
to redeem us."

This *haman-tash* implied in its mute way our belief that striving for common ideals would be recognized by the Messiah as a
cardinal virtue. Jewish continuity owes much to the tendency of
the Jew to knit his personal happiness with that of his people, and
draw creative strength out of this organic relationship. This self-
identification with the larger whole is particularly pronounced in
our Jewish leaders.

The *shalahmanot* on Purim brought an additional income
to our Temple fund by our carrying gifts from one neighbor to
another. But when Sarah Bayla prepared a tray of delicacies
for Reb Shemuel Salant, *Hakham Bashi* Elyashar and the Brisker
Rav, she would honor a dignified young *Yeshivah* scholar with
those errands. We besought her to entrust them to us so as to
increase our fund: "Mordecai ha-Tzadik would rejoice with an
additional festival day on our calendar, that of *simhat bet ha-
mikdash* (the Joy of the Temple)." She yielded, and we took
turns. When Reb Shemuel Salant offered, in addition to the small
coin, a piece of honey-candied almond out of my tray, I declined to
accept, much as my mouth watered. For Sarah Bayla's gift would
have been less than she intended it to be. Touched by my abstinence, he gave me a full quarter, which I, of course, deposited in
our collective bank. We wrapped that quarter in a piece of paper
on which we wrote: "The great Reb Shemuel Salant has a share
in the building of the *Bet ha-Mikdash.*"

The gladness of Purim was ours, too. A group of amateur
players from the colonies would come to our courtyard, and enact
in Yiddish the story of Esther in all its details. Women from all
over the city, Talmud Torah boys, and even young *Yeshivah*
scholars attended the performance. The women reacted emotionally as if they had never known the fate of the wicked Haman, the
glorious end of Mordecai ha-Tzaddik, or the triumph of Queen
Esther over her fears and inhibitions. Our courtyard on Purim

was a rallying point for the colonists and the rabbinical families. Differences were drowned in the wine of Purim. The wine was prepared at home. Avi and his brother Yitzhak had spent hours after midnight, pressing bunches of grapes with rounded heavy sticks.

An old Arab from Shekhem would usually take advantage of peoples' liberality on Purim and bring to our yard a trained monkey which could dance at the beating of the drum, collect the pennies with his hands, put them in the owner's wooden box, jump on his shoulders and caress him. Another Arab exhibited a trained docile bear which also could dance. Our zoo was limited to these two wild animals. But we pictured Daniel's den with the lions, and increased their number with as many names of animals as we knew, especially those mentioned in the Bible. We felt assured that the day would come when even wild animals would be endowed with self-control, and the wolf and the lamb would pasture together. We also visualized the animals in Noah's ark, and were glad that they cheered him up on the lonely waters. They must have been as friendly as the colorful birds nested on the roof of the Hassidic *shul*. They would eat out of our hands, and we could almost recognize them by their distinctive feathers and by their age. Each tiny, still featherless one, hatched out of an egg, was greeted with *mazal tov* and *she-he-heyanu*. We should have liked to have given them Jewish names, since they were born on a Jewish terrace. But names are given at the synagogue. Naming a child means "welcome", we grant you a place in the Covenant with God, which you should follow at your earliest understanding, and become a full-fledged member in due time. On Purim we gave the birds crumbs from our *haman-tashen,* and they liked it. We also brought over *haman-tashen* and other delicacies to everyone in the Magrib hall. They would bless the boys to be as righteous as Mordecai ha-Tzaddik, and the girls to be as beautiful as Queen Esther.

My sister Esther, of jovial mood, subsequently known as the humorist of the courtyard, took herself very seriously on the Purim of her second year of birth—she, the queen, in whose honor the family assembled at a banquet of *hamantashen* and poppy-seed cakes. At the mention of Queen Esther her eyes brightened and her face lit up. On the Purim, when she had attained the ripe age of three and grasped the historical significance of the festival, she rose from the table, ran to the mirror, and looking at herself admiringly cried out, "Am I not as beautiful as Queen Esther?" When she boasted about it on our hill, an older little Hassidic boy commented with self-assurance that there is a sparkle of Queen Esther's soul in everyone named after her, but she alone is queen and most beautiful of all. Another young child gave a different version: "All Esthers need not necessarily be beautiful, but they have the *zekhut* (merit) of recalling the queen to our mind on all days and not on Purim alone."

The distance between our personal self and that of the people as a whole was almost obliterated in our tender minds. This also is a trait of Jewishness. Purim is a fitting illustration. The story of an isolated region, that of Shushan, has become part and parcel of the Jewish whole.

Revelation on Mount Sinai

My parents engaged me at the age of eight to a young boy five years older than myself. Avi took him into our household, because his grandfather who came with him from abroad was too old to give him the proper care. When Immi told me while combing my hair that I was being engaged to Elisha, I objected to his large nose, to his short stature, and expressed the fear that we might one day stop loving each other. It turned out that I developed a profound love and admiration for him. I wanted to think like him and envisage the world with his eyes. I imbibed every bit of information he gave me. He loomed so superior to me; he knew much, and I but little. With such deep feelings for one who was to become my husband when I reached fourteen,[20] it was not possible for me to conceive that he might be wrong in his thinking, or not properly informed.

One Friday afternoon, when boys return home early, he said to me in a tone which betrayed imminence, "I have something to tell you; let us go up on the hill and sit on our favorite rock." It was not like our usual carefree climbing with laughter and caresses in our voice. We were silent. I automatically reflected his agitation. He held my hand gently, but I could feel the throbbing of his heart. We finally reached that rock, usually so near, this time far away. We sat for a long time without speaking. Could it be possible that

---

[20]My parents preferred that we should get married in my 11th year. At our request they consented to a little postponement.

he wants to inform me that he loves me no more, that he does not wish to marry me? It did not feel that way; he sat so close to me. Besides, even if he loves me no more, we have to get married just the same, since the signatures of our parents and also ours had been affixed to the *Tenaim* (betrothal document) a year ago. How could one break it? If the engagement is to be broken, only our parents could do it. And yet they were so affectionate to him even today. This devastating thought I quickly dismissed. Another upsetting one: he may have been called back by his parents. But mail from abroad comes only once in two weeks, and there was none from them lately. A series of thoughts crossed my mind in these short, but to me long, moments. We would soon have to go home, prepare for the Sabbath, draw water from the deep cistern, bathe in the pail, and purify our thoughts with holy matters. The tailor had brought my new pink dress on Monday, and I waited impatiently to wear it for the first time *likhevod Shabbat* (in honor of the Sabbath). I was looking forward to his liking my dress and a ribbon in my hair to match it. For days, *"tithadshï"* (Wear it in good health!) sounded in my ears. I even dared hope that he would add, "You look nice in it and I like the ribbon in your hair." All this became totally insignificant. The outward peacefulness of that mild day was incompatible with our state of mind—mine reflecting his more and more. Finally there was an almost imperceptible motion on his lips. I could see that as soon as he would succeed in silencing the loud palpitations of his heart, words would come out.

"Could you listen calmly to something frightening? I can no longer keep it within my bosom, and yet I do not want to share it with you, no more than one wishes to transmit a contagious disease. The communication itself may be a sin. Perhaps I am not responsible for it and am merely the victim of a *gilgul* who wants to isolate me from the rest of the world. Yet I am fully conscious of my thoughts, and conscious that I reached them through my own logic." If a *gilgul* entered into him, I mused, it would have to enter into me, too, since I am supposed to share his life in full. But what if these are his own ideas? He interrupted my train of thought and continued: "Now I shall tell you of my aberration, but as I am talking to you, these frightening thoughts are becoming clearer and they no longer look to me as not my own." In a slow voice, measuring each word: "I suppose you have never asked yourself how Moses obtained the two tablets with the Ten Commandments. I raised that question in my mind and have come to a dreadful conclusion. For days I could neither eat nor sleep, and trembled at the clarification of my own thinking. Moses himself wrote those tablets and attributed them to God! Now that I have uttered it aloud, I fear no more." Yet these words were trembling on his lips. "I wanted," he said, "to speak to Avi, but when I was feverish I could not, and now that I am calmer I dare not."

As I could not gather my thoughts, fearing that the earth would swallow us as it did Korah, I tremblingly said in a faint voice, "Let us pray on this rock and make believe that this is the one on which Jacob saw angels ascending to heaven. Let us pray that God banish such thoughts from your mind, and if you have to be punished, half of that punishment should come upon me, too. Let us pray that in your dreams one night you may have a vision of Moses descending from the mountain with the tablets, as Jacob saw the angels ascending." I closed my eyes and asked God to forgive him, and to forgive me for loving him even with his sins, and that when we reach Paradise we should not be parted.

I almost wished to share his sin. But how could I? Denying Revelation is shrinking one's personality and diminishing in stature by lacking the wonderful faith of all those who have preceded us, and the newly-born ones. How could one bear parting with such company? It is like becoming an unsociable being, isolated from a chain of great men and from everyone, everywhere. As the thought of such isolation was crushing me, I suddenly saw the mountain as in flames, the Israelites bending their heads in awe, even the children exclaiming "God is in the cloud," and singing in chorus *"na'asseh ve-nishma"*—we shall do and obey.—(I was already sufficiently familiar with the Bible.) I felt as if I myself were among the generation who stood at the foot of Mount Sinai, trembling at the thunder and lightning, and that my heart almost stopped beating at the *kol demamah dakkah*—the still, small voice.

Calmed by that vision, I turned towards Elisha, speaking as if to myself: "Why should I ask such a treacherous question which carries sin in its very bosom, when the answer was given us before we were born? Does not the Bible say that Moses ascended the mountain, remained there for forty days, and that God gave him the tablets? Then, God appeared on Mount Sinai, and the whole people of Israel stood at the foot of it and witnessed the vision? I wish I had been among them, but I should rather be glad that

I was born later, so that they may know that their vision goes on unextinguished."

"I have believed all this throughout my years," said Elisha, "but doubt has crept into my mind and I cannot chase it away. My excitement has subsided, and I am wondering now whether or not I can be called a Jew. Would you still care to marry me, if the disbelief disqualifies me from being a Jew?"

What a dilemma, not to marry the one I love so much, and for whom I would sacrifice any form of happiness. Yet I felt as if eternities stood between us, that my history was no longer his, and that his *shema* was no longer like mine. How could I part from Avi, Immi, Sara Bayla, relatives as far back as Abraham, and with this, carry all our days the sin against Moses who risked his life to take us out of Egypt. I felt as if the rock trembled under my feet. Not even Elisha could tear Revelation out of me. Without it, the prayers, the *shema,* the scrolls, the seder, all are emptied of their very soul. These and a multitude of thoughts crossed my mind, but speak I could not. In that one moment a chasm was created between us. I felt as if I were hanging in mid-air, with the foundation cut from under me. We descended the hill in an even more profound silence than we had ascended it. Our tender companionship was at a halt, my delight in drinking every word of his was marred, as if suddenly a fresh drinking fountain ceased to be potable.

To tell it or not to tell it to Avi, was my problem for days and days. How could I cause such a blow to him who engaged me to Elisha and who hoped that he would send him one day to Hildesheimer's Seminary and thus help contribute towards bringing a closer relationship between Talmudic researches of Jerusalem and those from abroad? Such a blow might prevent him from writing for days on end. But would not keeping it from him be a sin in itself? Yet I ought to wait a little while. Should it be a *gilgul* it might jump out by itself, and Avi would be spared the agony. On the other hand, if it is a *gilgul,* Immi could take us to an *absprecherin* (exorcist). Meanwhile a delay cuts him away from God, from Moses, and from all from which we stem. What about Immi, whose father died lonely in Siberia in order to help perpetuate the teachings God gave to Moses? She must not be told; her strength would not bear it. She attributed my lack of appetite and my restlessness to oncoming malaria.

Soul-searching for sins as cause of this trouble and the keeping of such a dark secret to myself, increased my confusion. My thoughts could no longer be contained within me; I had to speak out. It was long after midnight. I slowly moved towards Avi and Immi's bedroom, retracing some steps, advancing a few, seeking the door in the darkness, as I had no candle. I spent the rest of the night in their bedroom in outward silence and inner feverishness. The sun was rising in the vivid colors of mountain regions. I said to myself, "Only God could have given us the Torah. Moses by himself could not, no more than man alone could create such sunrise." When Immi went to prepare breakfast I mustered my strength. Without a tear in my eyes and with a controlled voice I simply told Avi, "I cannot marry Elisha; yet I love him so much." "Why?" asked Avi. "Elisha does not believe in Revelation; how could I marry him?" My strength faltered. I dug my face into the soft feather-pillow, awaiting for Avi's reply. That moment looked like an endless one. I felt sorry that I missed reading Avi's reaction in his eyes and forehead. I regret now that I do not remember his full reply. I have, however, a clear recollection of some of it.

"Faith which conquers doubts has more strength in it than unscrutinized belief. Doubt is detrimental to the one who doubts, but does not touch the never-diminishing greatness of God." These words rang within me; they brought both comfort and perplexity. Elisha's doubting did not affect the nature and holiness of God, nor the greatness of Moses, but would it affect him? Would faith emerge in him and conquer his doubting? It was too painful for Elisha and me to approach the subject again. I shrank from the choice with which I was faced, of either parting with him, or with Jehudah Halevi, with Isaiah who brought God's message to us, or with any Jew from the time of Moses. I also heard Avi tell him one day that doubts creep into the mind like germs into the body. The greatest sage, the Rambam, was a doctor of both the body and the soul, and he knew how to lead one out of perplexities. I drew great comfort from the parallel with germs. If doubts are like germs, the mind could be cured, too. But I must hasten to cure his soul before the germs consume it and make it incurable. I learned years later that Avi consulted some rabbis both in Jerusalem and from abroad as to how to deal with such an unfortunate situation. One of them wrote, "God Himself will bring the cure."

Yom Kippur was approaching, and I waited for it impatiently, as it might be a test of Elisha's conquest either of the *gilgul* or of his own sinful thoughts. Would he fast on Yom Kippur? Elisha was the first one in the synagogue and remained there all day long until after *ma'ariv*. My prayers had been answered. I, too, fasted in spite of the family's protest that at the age of nine fasting was not required. I replied that I had too many sins to be forgiven. I meant that those of Elisha were mine, too. Men and women had already left the synagogue. Elisha descended slowly and came over to me. *"Ahubati,* (my love) you could marry me. I am freed from my hallucination. Avi has led me out from darkness into light. I am cleared of all doubts. I am now one with those who stood at the foot of Mount Sinai." At breaking the fast on *motza'e* (the end of) Yom Kippur, he and I sat near each other at the table. From Avi's beaming eyes we could see that he read our contentment and relief.

The day following Yom Kippur I climbed up the stepladder in Avi's library, took down one thick book after another, until I reached the one I was looking for, the *Moreh Nebukhim*. I brought it over to Elisha, and for days and days, after his return from the Talmud Torah, we would sit on that rock and read page after page. I doubt whether I understood much of it; he probably did, as he explained some passages to me. I said to him, "The search of the path is the beginning not only of wisdom but of salvation. Search the path and you will reach the peak."

When years later I read Maimonides in a more mature manner, I felt as though I were greeting an old friend. It is because he understood doubts sympathetically that he could transmit to others the genuine conviction of *ani ma'amin be'emunah shelemah*—"I believe with perfect faith."

Orphans of the Spirit

Yosef was born in Jerusalem, the only child of *Hakham* Tzevi, a close friend of *Hakham Bashi* Elyashar. His father transferred to him his own unfulfilled ambition of attaining the rank of *Hakham Bashi*. He was schooled for it: first, at the *heder,* then at the school of the Alliance Israélite Universelle for some secular knowledge, and private lessons in the Talmud. He joined in due time a Sephardic *yeshivah* and distinguished himself in studies. He lacked imaginativeness and creativity, but had a fine analytical and retentive mind, with the capacity of utilizing borrowed ideas with a thoroughness as if they were his own. He often came to our *yeshivah,* and when time permitted, he would chum with the older boys and even with those younger than himself. His questions on the *shiyur* (lesson of the day) were penetrating and pertinent. He usually followed Avi down the stairs to the dining room, and gratefully accepted the invitation to stay. The meals would then become a series of questions and answers. Sometimes Avi would push the soup aside, fetch a quill pen, ink and paper to make a note of an answer. Such notes were eventually incorporated in his various books containing responsa, in accord with the *Halakhah,* to questions arising from new situations. Avi was particularly anxious to exert some influence on Yosef, foreseeing from his questions a stage of fermentation which could lead him astray. He read with him passages from the Rambam's *Mishneh Torah* and *Moreh Nebukhim.* Yosef would come back after a while with numerous indentations, indicating passages to be explained. Bookmarks were not available, and scraps of paper between the annotated pages too expensive.

Avi lent him a copy of Saadia's *Emunot ve-Deot,*[30] for he became concerned about him long before Yosef's father confided the troubles: Yosef no longer enjoyed his *yeshivah,* went to it reluctantly, and rushed back to his own room, where the largest part of the night was spent in reading French books borrowed from Ben Yehudah's book shelves. They were the works of Voltaire, Helvetius, Diderot, Montesquieu, who extended their legitimate protest against social inequalities to an unbalanced rebellion against the whole universe itself. Change in itself became their panacea. Change in social philosophy, customs and tradition would not be sufficient to offset the oppression and collapse in which France found herself. There must also follow a change in the conception of nature, of God—a complete transformation. Against the none too profound arguments of the French extremists, Avi gathered for Yosef passages from Saadia, Maimonides, the Gaon of Vilna, from the Nineteen Letters of Ben Uziel by Samson Raphael Hirsch, from annotations by his own late father Reb Jacob Mordecai on the margins of the *Zohar,* and even a number of sayings from the Ba'al Shem Tov (1700-1760)—the founder of the Hassidic movement. Avi's book *Musge shav ve-ha-Emet* (False Con-

---

[30]*Emunot ve-Deot*—Opinions and Beliefs—Saadia lived ca. 882-942.

cepts and the Truth), published much later, originated from such endeavors.

One night, after a visit outside the Old City, Yosef brought home a pile of books, among them a French translation of Spinoza, whom he could not possibly have understood. For days he absented himself from his *yeshivah,* as these volumes had to be passed on promptly to other young men of the colonies. In despair the father called on Avi. "I have never believed in *gilgulim,* nor do I believe in them now, but a *gilgul* must have entered into my son." Yosef stopped coming to our courtyard; he wanted to fight out the battle by himself. Meanwhile, to his father's heartache, Ben Yehudah and Nissim Behar secured for him admission to the Teachers' Normal School of the Alliance Israélite in Paris, with paid traveling expenses. His father's cherished dream of his becoming *Hakham Bashi* was shattered. He would be limited to teaching French in elementary schools at any odd place assigned to him away from Jerusalem, even as far as Persia. The years of Talmudic study would sink into the background. Furthermore, his present rebellious state of mind would be nourished in a French environment, and there might remain no Jewish spark in his only offspring, descended from a long rabbinic line. Yosef must choose between his father and the *gilgul.* The choice was made and the father felt as if he had lost his son. He hated to cause pain and disappointment to his father, but young folks usually console themselves that elders do not understand. But Avi was young, understanding, and took pains to maintain the young man's equilibrium. Yosef had no courage to face him; not on account of his contemplated study in Paris, but for the motives that led him to it. He fled from Avi as he did from his own inner self, lost at the moment in a borrowed one. His temperament was such that he would become intoxicated with each new idea until replaced with another.

I was completely unaware of this spiritual turmoil until one day, as I was about to go down the stairs, I came face to face with Yosef. His eyes were sunken, his face haggard, and he hardly knew why he came up. He needed to bring his thoughts and agitation into the open. His emotional disturbance was beyond my comprehension at first. We went to sit under the lonely tree whose little yellow flowers, with a balmy scent, were like a cluster of stars on earth. He talked to me as if I were his age. I was nine, he was twenty. My memory of intense moments carries the words with them with a faithful record in my mind. After a short silence I

asked him why he was agitated at the prospect of taking a trip
abroad for study purposes, and what determined his choice of Paris
in preference to Germany, which I knew was the home of many
great Jews. "I am going to Paris because there is freedom of
thought. I want to throw off the yoke of a past which is enchaining
every waking moment. I want to rid myself of restrictions from a
past which is no more, and which is like a ghost among the living.
We need change, change, change."

The impact of Voltaire, Diderot, Helvetius and Montesquieu
blinded his usual analytical power. His excitement was not contagious. I was sober and he seemd to me as one inebriated with
false ideas. The pathetic tone of "change, change" recalled to my
mind a Hassid who once drank a little too much on Purim. He
came to our yard with rolling tears, repeating incessantly, "The
earth is turning around my head; children please move with me
and let us all go away from it." "Where should we move to?" we
gently retorted. "Change from what?" I asked Yosef.

The panorama of Jewish history unfolded itself before my eyes
with a vividness as if I were living through these thousands of
years in one single moment. I could not give up even a particle
of it. "Should we change the Ten Commandments God gave
Moses on Mount Sinai, change the teachings of the Prophets and
the songs of King David in the Psalms, change our prayers, overflowing with the praise of God, change the *Pirqe Avot* (Ethics
of the Fathers)? (I had just started to read it and memorized
some passages.) Or the Talmud, which our *Yeshivah* scholars
study day and night to undertand it better and apply it to our
times? Change the festivals, which are like flowers in a garden?
Or the Sabbath, our most precious day of the week, on which God
rests *with* us? Or eliminate the *mitzvot* (precepts), which are a
kind of communicating language between God and Israel, the
electric wires between the soul and the body?[31] Should we detach
ourselves from Abraham, who gave us the first knowledge of God;
Moses, who handed down His Laws; the Maccabeans, who gave

---

[31]At the age of about six I was taken to an exhibit in a little hall beyond
the Gates of Zion, to see an electric bulb lit on the mere pushing of a
button. Excitedly I exclaimed *va-yomer elokim yehi or, vayehi or*—("And
God said, Let there be light, and there was light"). Immediately I corrected
myself with a benediction *Barukh ha-Shem she-bara or ba-shamayim ve-or
ba-aretz.* (Blessed be God Who created light in the heavens and light on
earth.) The wonder of those magic wires remained with me, but the kerosene lamps were still extant in my time. I was told about the rejoicing
when they supplanted the candles.

their life for the sake of these; Rabbi Akiba, the last word on whose lips were *"Shema Yisrael"*; from Jehudah Halevi whose *Tzion halo tish'ali* the sword of the Mongol could not touch—it lives forever?

We had been told the legend that Jehudah Halevi was killed by a Mongol at the Gates of Zion while he was kissing the holy ground and reciting his ode, *Tzion halo tish'ali.* Paraphrasing Halevi's *Yefe nof mesos tevel* I exclaimed, "How I wish I had wings to fly far, far away into the distant past and bring it all back with me." "But the past," I added, "makes the journey on its own wings and it is always present with us. It is rolling; it never stands still. We and the past are wrapped together. If you had a beautiful garden of pomegranates, figs, almond trees, oranges, sweet lemons, would you be reluctant to enjoy them because they were planted before you were born? How could we have picked the juicy pomegranates in Leah's garden, were it not for her ancestors?"

Yosef's eyes wandered around—I doubt whether my words reached his ears—and he repeated as if to himself: "The present has to regain its own selfhood, and cease to be a reflection of the past." "Do you call it a self when torn from its past? Would even the Sabbath be sanctified if it were not connected with the week preceding it and the one to come? What value is there in an isolated day if it loses memory of yesterday and the expectation of a tomorrow? You want to become a torn human being, a *regai,* a momentarist." "What do you mean by 'momentarist'?" Yosef asked. "I coined that word to qualify your intoxication with the moment. Like a drunkard, you stumble, you lose hold of the past and you see not ahead of you." At that instant a bird on the twig flew to the roof across. "You want to become unconscious of your Jewish wholeness as the bird who lives and knows only the moment. He is not aware that another bird may have flown or will fly the same interval of space. He may not even remember that he himself has done it before. He is a momentary being, and that is what you want to be."

Yosef seemed to be a little impressed. "The whole past could not and should not be obliterated; we should select whatever may serve as a guide for present demands." "Demands are momentary ("relative" would have better expressed my thoughts, but the term was unknown to me), while God's laws are meant to be everlasting. In them we can find a guidance for all times." I remembered a passage from the prayers—I know now how many times it is being repeated—which I quoted: "The Law God gave He never will amend; nor ever by another law replace."

As Yosef became more attentive, I summoned my strength to seek for arguments that might awaken him. "If God's instructions were to be modified, it would imply that those He gave us were not perfect. How could anything coming from God be imperfect? He provided us with intelligence to apply the revealed Laws to changing conditions. Don't you think that God knew that each generation would encounter different situations; that the Temple would be built, the Temple destroyed, and with His help rebuilt again, we hope? Since God has provided us with intelligence, why could we not fashion laws as we see fit? Yosef, they have become our own through our application of them. When a child starts walking he needs his mother's hand. After a while he applies the laws of walking in all directions, in climbing rocks, going up and down the stairs, or on level ground. Had God thought that the Laws He gave needed to be changed, He would have revealed Himself to each generation. He regarded that *one* Revelation as sufficient for all time. His revelation to Abraham was a mere individual one, not to be compared to that at Mount Sinai, intended for the whole people of Israel, those who were present and those to be born. That is why our *Yeshivah* scholars study continually to get the full meaning of His revelation."

I reminded him of Avi's saying that the revealed laws could meet any condition, including such of which we are not yet aware. Yosef did not agree. He claimed that the laws have to be evolved out of needs, and not vice versa. "Needs should not be our masters; the laws have to regulate them. Look what happened to Esau when he allowed the want of the moment to determine his entire life. The whole world became to him a dish of lentils which at that instant wiped out his father Isaac, and the children he himself would beget." Yosef hardly looking at me, as if he were sounding out his own thoughts, retraced his steps a little. He was not an *apikores* (heretic); he did not lose his faith as did Elisha ben Abuya when he entered the *Pardes*.[32] He was still observing

---

[32]Elisha ben Abuya was the teacher of the famous Rabbi Meir, one of the architects of the Mishneh. It is said that he was one of four scholars who entered the *Pardes* (a luring garden of speculation for penetrating the mysteries of creation). While his three colleagues emerged with their faith unshaken, Elisha ben Abuya came out a heretic, and unfaithful to Jewish tradition.

the *mitzvot,* but without joy. They had become a yoke from which he wanted to escape by going to Paris. "You have lost your spiritual sense of taste, as I lose mine for food when I am seized with malaria, and actually dislike even dainty macaroons. Yours is a case of *kadahat ruhni*—spiritual malaria." He went on with his own trend of thought: "Why should ethical and religious teachings be overburdened with detailed injunctions from a faraway past, when our own application would be more pertinent and accommodating? The love of Zion, nationalism, historical heroes, the broad ethical teachings of monotheism, would be sufficient to constitute the spiritual heritage without carrying an extraneous load with it."

My piano lessons provided me with part of the answer: "It is no more extraneous than the sound is to the piano keys. Without the wires there would be no sound; also if you break one key the melody is gone."[33] From the pathetic figures of the few Karaites who occasionally came to our courtyard, I drew my arguments for the Talmudists. "Without the scholars who have devoted all their time to discover the meaning of the Torah and the path to progress pointed in its pages, we would have remained as ignorant of it as the Karaites. We should thank God for those teachers who explained what may have been too profound for the understanding of each individual by himself. More extensive learning may help you offset French doctrines which are meant for themselves and not for us." I had a feeling that the French philosophers of the eighteenth century whom I knew only from what Yosef had told me that afternoon, were like a winding plant that would stifle him. I saw such a plant in Leah's garden. "Yosef, your Voltaire and the rest of them create a wall between you and your ancestors. You are becoming an orphan of the spirit. You act as if you have lost your parents of the spirit and are wandering like an orphan without a home. Let Avi adopt you and you will find more peace of mind at his *Yeshivah* than at the Teachers' School in Paris. He may solve your perplexities and read with you Jewish philosophers instead of your French ones, who probably could not even understand your troubles."

---

[33]There was but one single piano in Jerusalem belonging to the wife of a Jewish attaché in the Russian Consulate. She offered to give me piano lessons in exchange for my teaching her Hebrew. I had to walk many miles to reach her house. I was six when we started. She made more progress in Hebrew than I with the piano, but the fault was mine.

"Your Avi moves in a circle, always within the Jewish Law, while I want to get out of it. Had Reform not blotted out Palestine, I would have joined it when I came to Paris."

Through our elders' concern with Reform, the children, too, were aware of its dangers. Besides, at nine one was Jewishly mature. The talks at the dinner table became comprehensible, and we even ventured to express thoughts of our own. "Reform," I told him, "wants to sever God from our land, while you and your friends would like to cut off the land from God. Both are like the distorted reflection we see in the small pool of our hill. Reform," I continued, "is a *qeriat yisrael*—a cutting of Israel. It split it up with an axe, and out of the fragments it picked up and gathered a few convenient ones. This is Reform. To re-form, one needs material for re-shaping. What was there left to remold with the largest part cut off? How we pity their children. They are orphans of the spirit, missing its caressing waves which come with observances. God planted stars in heaven and *mitzvot* in our hearts, to draw the sparks of joy from heaven to earth."

Long silence followed; we sat and sat under that tree. Out of the overcrowded thoughts there shot out one almost unaware to myself: "I would not give up my birthright for a mess of French porridge." A white silk handkerchief sticking out from my pocket attracted Yosef's attention. I happened to have it with me to put the last embroidery stitches on a present to a little boy entering *heder*. A party was to be given for him that evening. I showed Yosef the words embroidered on it, in red, golden, blue, yellow silk thread, the number of stitches equally divided among the children: "If studies are hard, remember you are a descendant of those who stood at the foot of Mount Sinai." Yosef looked shaken; I could almost hear his suppressed conflicting thoughts, and began to feel sorry for him. Avi just passed by and said *shalom* from a little distance. Yosef jumped up. "It is too late, I must go now. Good-bye." With pity and tenderness in my voice I replied: *"Shalom, tashuv bi-meherah elenu ve'el am yisrael"* (peace be with you, and may you return speedily to us and to the people of Israel).

I remained alone under that tree for some time. My Jewish consciousness had deepened that afternoon—the clearer thinking that emerges out of a crisis. It was but a few months since I had absorbed the shock of my fiancé's perplexities about Revelation. That was a shattering experience, but it had vested me with a shield to repel all sorts of arrows. The respective doubts of Elisha and of Yosef illumined my own beliefs. They generated a new stage in my Jewish development. I believed my beliefs. Believing and thinking merged into one. My thoughts reverted to the Rambam with whom I was familiar through the covers of his books, Avi's frequent handling them, also a tiny bit with some passages I read together with Elisha, who explained them to me. The *ani ma'amins* (Maimonides's thirteen basic beliefs) I knew by heart, and I found myself reciting them under the tree with special fervor on the *be'emunah shelemah* (perfect faith). Yosef's confusion would have strengthened my own convictions, were there need for re-enforcement.

Yosef did not depart on the day he intended to, but sailed on the following boat two weeks later. The day he left, his father spent the afternoon at our *Yeshivah* and joined in the *Ma'ariv* service. Avi did not let him say *kaddish* for a son who may still return and not remain dead for the Jewish people. He corresponded little with his father, who did not bid him good-bye. Sephardic men of those times were extremely severe in the rearing of offspring, as well as in their conduct with their wives, whom they regarded as immature children and dealt with them accordingly. Yosef did not write to Avi, either. Once he sent me an illustrated picture card of the Arc de Triomphe with but one sentence: "I realize now the meaning of real freedom." Avi read between the lines of this ambiguous statement. He remembered warning him when he saw his perplexities, that change does not necessarily carry freedom with it, nor does freedom require change; they are not convertible terms; the "real freedom of a Jew lies in performing the observances." This, I think, is an adequate concept of freedom. One has the choice not to observe, but in observing he *chooses* to become one with his people.

Philosophically, freedom could be defined as the capacity of the individual to fuse his partial tendencies with the wholeness of his personality. This seems to be Spinoza's definition of freedom, provided the individual whole embraces also that of the universe. It is also John Dewey's definition, if the individual encompass society also. It is a disciplined freedom. Such disciplined freedom, Avi would say, is given by the Torah and the Talmudic codes.

Yosef was deeply disappointed with the Teachers Normal School in Paris. "Change" which had been to him a philosophical idol for which he forsook an idyllic life of the spirit, confronted him in all its materialistic prosaism. The yoke of observance was completely thrown off by the students, out of mere materialistic motives, with no philosophy behind it except perhaps that of assimilation. With his capacity for thorough thinking, he finally wrote a long letter to Avi—an extensive analytical dissertation.

Years later Avi read excerpts from it at literary meeting of the *Ohole Shem Society* of New York, of which the late Dr. Bernard Drachman was chairman. The gist of it was that by thinking out his theories honestly and to their logical conclusion, he had but two alternatives: reject Revelation, or relinquish his ideas about adaptations, circumstances, conveniences, etc. They are incompatible. His choice was made. In full humility and thankfulness he accepted all that is inherent in Revelation with the Talmudic interpretation inseparable from it. "Voltaire misled me, but he sent me back to cultivate my own garden, and you have helped me more than anyone else to till our rich soil and come back to it."[34]

Yosef left the Teachers School to resume Talmudic studies at the Sephardic Rabbinical Seminary at Constantinople. Avi, acting head of the institution at the time of Yosef's graduation, was among his examiners. *Hakham* Tzevi did not tire thanking Avi again and again for the beneficial influence on his son. Shortly before his last days, when the end was in sight, he asked *Hakham Bashi* Jacob Meir to write to Reb Hayyim that God should bless him for having brought back his son to him and to our people.

Yosef's was an extreme case, but in its milder form not an isolated one. It reflected the tensions of the times, the challenge of the radicals. They were more fanatic than those accused of fanaticism. There was also a sharp division among the rabbis themselves regarding the establishment of secular schools. But the violent commotion was only a momentary outburst which gradually receded, leaving no resentment between those who fought against the schools and those who were attacked for favoring them. They were eventually attended by the grandchildren of the rabbinic families. The generation that was kept from receiving a secular training felt as if it were shut off from a refreshing breeze. Whenever some among them would quote an appealing thought picked up here and there through contact with newcomers, Avi would open the *shass* (Talmud) and promptly find the page containing the same idea in

---

[34]The best thought which emerges out of Voltaire's philosophical work *Candide,* is that of cultivating one's own garden. Candide is a modern Job, but as shallow as Job is profound.

a richer manner. "Refreshing breezes blow from within when one digs deep into its wells," was a favorite refrain of his. He set himself the double task—not an easy one—of convincing the young that radicalism is pseudo-knowledge, and the old that knowledge is not radicalism.

The secular schools in themselves were a complete failure. There was no vision, no understanding of the people, and no respect for the learning with which their life was identified. Nor were they successful in their attempt at spreading French or German culture. With memory as the sole instrument of knowledge, the boys of Jerusalem reared on "Men of the Spirit" could not find much interest in the detailed battles of Napoleon or the diplomatic successes of Bismarck. The graduates lacked a *point d'appui* (point of support) and found themselves strangers in one world as much as in the other.

The schools in Constantinople where Avi landed after he left Jerusalem, were equally faulty. He conceived the idea of creating a model school there, which might be adapted in Palestine and elsewhere. His was an elementary and high school, with Hebrew as the language, plus a solid foundation in the Talmud. He had to write the text of each subject himself, borrowing the contents from German ones, but in a Hebrew mold with his own pedagogical methods. Even the lyrics of the Hebrew songs were composed by him, who could not carry a single tune. My little sister Tamar, with pronounced personality, but with no musical training, assisted in the singing. I still remember a song with its refrain *Ivrim anahnu, Ivrim anahnu* (we are Hebrews, we are Hebrews) which rang through the school garden during recreation hours. It was a resumé of Jewish history, from the time of Jacob's arrival in Egypt, set in poetical rhymes. His book *Torat ha-hinukh ha-yisraeli* (Principles of Jewish Education) published much later, originated from that experience. His *Mosdot torah she-be'al pe* (Foundations of the Oral Law), written before that time, was used in the Talmud classes. It was also adopted as a text in Dr. Holzman's *Lehrerseminar* in Berlin, and by a number of advanced Talmud Torahs in the Orient, as far as Damascus and Aleppo. I am mentioning Avi's books, and those of his activities that I can recall, because they reflect the problems of that age.

Likewise credit should be given to Avi's intimate friend *Hakham* Jacob Mier, later *Hakham Bashi,* in whom Avi found great support for his activities in Jerusalem. They worked closely together. At each visit of the *Hakham,* Avi would read him some of his writings. Following his *shalom, Hakham* Jacob Mier would say, *Mah hidashta ha-yom?* (What new things did you write to-day?) With a twinkle in his eye, Avi would ask *Mah mahashavtekha al zot?* (What do you think of this), to which his frequent refrain was *nifla ad me'od* (most wonderful). Sometimes the children, in a teasing mood, would echo when he happened to be around, *nifla ad me'od, ad me'od nifla.*

Yosef's tale seems to me a recapitulation of inner Jewish history, from the times of the desert to our own days . . . some holding on fast within the circle; others trying to run out, run and run. The children of the courtyard would have asked, "Where are you running? If you are running away from yourself and leave that self behind you, who are you?"

BON VOYAGE

The "Bon Voyage" was a solemn communal event. The ceremony usually took place at our courtyard, with prayers for the success of the mission and the safe return of the traveler. Sarah Bayla would prepare for him some cold food neatly packed in two small flaxen bags, a "fleishige" and a "milchige." The scribe would carefully examine the *tefillin,* and the children managed to insert secretly, in the bag containing the *siddur,* a piece of paper on which was written *yevarekhekha Hashem ve-tashuv bimeherah* (May God bless you and may you return quickly). Some weeks before his departure, the traveler would usually join some sessions at our *Yeshivah.* If he chanced upon the approach of a *siyyum* (conclusion of a tractate), the date of departure, when possible, would be deferred till after the *siyyum.* The return home was celebrated with a *gomel* benediction (on deliverance from the perils of a hazardous journey), toasting with wine and cake, and with a number of tales varying in interest with the eloquence of the narrator. Yosef's departure for Paris was lonely. Nissim Behar and Ben Yehudah were the only ones at the Gates of Zion to bid him good-bye, as he sadly entered the coach.

The trips left their impressions with us. Of Paris we had heard little, but we knew of London, where my uncle Yitzhak had been invited by the *Meqitze Nirdamim* Society[35] to decipher

---

[35]An international society for "awakening the slumbering" books and manuscripts, i.e., to publish them.

manuscripts at the British Museum. Berlin and other cities of Germany were familiar through letters read at the dining table from Berliner, Hildesheimer, Hoffman, Gutmacher, Jacob Posen, Baron Rothchild of Frankfort, and others. Of Vilna we were reminded by the Yahrzeit lamp for the *Gaon*. We were not even far off from Australia and Yemen through the travels of Jacob Saphir, who was known to the older generation of the courtyard. We knew that Immi's father, Reb Saul Benjamin Ha-Cohen, sailed on a small boat to the United States where he remained for several months. Immi was very happy that the *Yeshivah Etz Hayyim* in New York was named after his own in Jerusalem.

Siberia clung to our ears and remained in our heart, the sad memory of a grave, that of Immi's father. On his last trip to Russia in 1877, he learned that a number of Jews had migrated to Siberia. He became concerned over their remoteness from outside Jewish contacts, especially in a center of anarchist exiles. Do they have sufficient *Sifre Torah, Tefillin, Taletim, Siddurim, Mahzorin, Tenakhs, Shass, Shofars, Shohtim, Melamdim,* synagogues, a rabbi, a *Sofer,* a *Bet Din?* If he went over there, he could gather a few young men to come to Jerusalem and be trained for spiritual leadership of their community. Family and friends besought him, but in vain, not to risk at his age of over sixty a trip which might cost his life. The cold was bitter, and he passed away, not in loneliness, though. The whole community escorted him to his peaceful rest. The children would ask Immi to repeat that story, and by way of consolation we would tell her that he may have saved the Jews of Siberia from becoming lost like the Ten Tribes.

Avi was in Russia at the time of his tragic death. He was visiting prominent rabbis from whom he obtained rabbinical *semikhah* (ordination). He cut his journey short when he learned from his mother-in-law that Immi cried incessantly over the loss of her father and the impossibility of visiting the grave.

Among Avi's papers I came across a touching letter in Yiddish appealing to Immi's sense of piety. She must remember that it was a sacred mission that led her father to that land of wilderness; that the promised resurrection would extend to the remotest corners of the world; that immortality is not just a concept, it is a basic Jewish belief, one of the Rambam's Thirteen Articles of Faith. Was it not the aim of her father throughout his active years to strengthen Jewish life? This he accomplished through his death also. Jews of Siberia visiting his grave would be reminded that he laid down his life so that they might continue in God's ways. Let not his monumental work be drowned in tears, and let us pray that his life and death be remembered by generations to come so that they, too, might consecrate themselves to our Jewish heritage.

With each *Yahrzeit* of his, which was observed in every synagogue of Jerusalem, even in the Hassidic one, we learned a little more about the very cold land of Siberia. In our younger days, around four or five, we asked Israel Shimeon, the letter-writer, to inquire from the Czar of Russia how we could send a *Sefer Torah* to the Jews of Siberia.

My first lesson in geography I learned at the age of two, with tantrums and daily cryings, "Avi, why did you go to Berlin? Come back quickly to study in your room." His subsequent trips were preceded by weeks of letter-writing late at night, and also by feverish operation of our printing machine by Sarah Bayla and Immi. We sensed the importance of his mission from talks at the table. They centered around establishing intellectual relationship with those great men of Germany. They urged Avi to come to Germany and study at Hildesheimer's Rabbinical Seminary. But how could he leave the *Yeshivah* and the Land of Israel in a state of transition? He wanted to help combat radicalism through its own fallacies, and replace them with clear thinking. Such was also the way of thought of those great German scholars who sought to preserve tradition. Reb Jacob Mordecai, Sarah Bayla, and their sons, Yitzhak and Hayyim, were in close contact with them. Through such intimate relationship Jerusalem ceased to be regarded by the outside world as a mere object of charity, but rather as a medium whereby Jewish life could be strengthened everywhere. It was this ideal that led Reb Jacob Mordecai and Sarah Bayla to forsake a comfortable life in Russia and move to Eretz Israel.

Leaving Jerusalem

I awoke at dawn, before anyone else, to kiss good-bye to the *mezuzah* on the doorpost of the women's synagogue. This particular one was like a secret, intimate companion. I knew that one prays to God only, but standing in front of the *mezuzah* by oneself was like pouring one's heart and soul into it. I never initiated something with the children before kissing the *mezuzah* and praying to God. Like a silent friend it helped me regain calmness at every inner agitation. There was reason every day for coming to it. There was need for praying for the reconstruction of the Temple, for the speedy coming of the Messiah so that all Jews since Abraham could gather in Jerusalem. We prayed for rapid progress and for understanding the Bible without assistance. In our prayers we also included, when we were younger, the request that grown-ups should join in our efforts to reconstruct the Temple. When we reached a more mature age we learned to reckon with facts, but the zest and fervor did not diminish.

The day of our departure, the *Heder* and *Talmud Torah* boys were given a few free hours. We gathered on that hill and each promised to speak but Hebrew and dedicate himself to the recovery of the Holy Land. Forming a circle and holding each others' hands, we exclaimed in unison with moist eyes, *Im eshkahekh yerushalayim tishkah yemini*—"If I forget thee, O Jerusalem, may my right hand forget its cunning." I suggested substituting *Bet ha-Mikdash,* since they remained in Jerusalem anyhow. Sad at our departure, they sought for some comforting words. "You will have an extra day on each festival,[36] of which we are deprived." We used to call these "our lost days" and felt awkward that days which are holy elsewhere should be *hol* (ordinary) with us. I in turn promised that in spite of those wonderful extra *yom tov* days which I would cherish, I would return to Jerusalem as soon as I could. I meant it, of course. The day passed in mutual promises and expressions of tender feelings. They promised to be doubly nice to Sarah Bayla and cheer her up when she looked lonesome.

As dusk was approaching—the coach traveled only at night to avoid dust and heat—I again found myself in front of the *mezuzah* and reciting the words addressed to God in the prayer book: "And to Jerusalem, Thy city, return in mercy and dwell within her, as Thou hast spoken." How could I leave the city wherein God promised to dwell?

"Shalom, shalom, nessiyah tovah, tashuvu bimehera"—(Good-bye! Good-bye! Happy journey! Return soon!)—filled my ears. It was time to go; the loaded donkeys were ready to take us up to the Gate of Zion, the starting point of the horse and

---

[36] As the festivals were announced in ancient times by messengers, an extra day was allotted for those in the Diaspora, in case the message should not reach them on time.

wagon. As we passed the gate, *Tzion halo tish'ali* resounded within me, and each verse plunged me into deeper emotion. The horses and the coach started moving away from the gate, from the Temple site, from the hill, from the *Yeshivah*, from the cheerful Hassidim, and from the beloved Sarah Bayla. There was one puffing and running behind the wheels and in a heartrending crying voice: *"Mein Schwester, Mein Schwester, meine einzige teuere Schwester, geh nicht aweg von dem heiligen Land, bleib hier."* (My sister, my sister, my dear, only sister, do not go away from the Holy Land; stay here.) With tears in my eyes and in my voice, I leaned out of the window and exclaimed, *"Dodati, libbi be-mizrah va'ani be-ma'arav."* (My beloved aunt, my heart is in the East, though in the West I dwell.)[37]

The wagon advanced. The passengers were taking an excursion trip to Jaffa; their cheerful songs filled the air. They were hilarious; I was sad. They looked at the scenery; I kept my eyes closed, to see once more the city I left behind me, with the *kotel ma'aravi* (Western Wall—the Wailing Wall) still in ruins. When at midnight we reached Ramleh, a short midway stop, I begged the driver that we remain there overnight, so as to postpone for a few hours more our parting with the Holy City. I offered him a *medjida* (a lot of money—one dollar) which my Grandmother Sarah Bayla had given me, but he went on. The memories crowded my mind, from the little yellow flower to our touching gatherings on the hill. I could not bear the thought that this was my last good-bye to that hill which shared our life. Perhaps it is this departure which has kept all those memories so fresh in my mind, that I can record them now with accuracy as if they happened yesterday.

On the Boat to Constantinople

A boat without cabins, everyone stretched on the deck, and the water splashing on all sides, the waves majestic, the stopovers fascinating; but the thoughts rolled within me, unaware even of the dampness and the intermittent thin showers from the waves. The children of our courtyard stood before me; my ten years' experiences unfolded themselves as if I tried to hold on to them. Our numerous improvised lines to the stars, the angels, to the Prophet Elijah and to whatever stirred us to lyrics, all

---

[37] A verse from Jehudah Halevi.

dangled before me. I was reciting them to myself, but not a single new rhyme came to my mind, even though I was among the leading bards of the courtyard. It was as with the Jews on the streams of Babylon who could no longer play on their harps. I visualized Jehudah Halevi in a little sailing boat on the way to Zion, but he towards it and I away from it. That image floating on the waves, with darkness all around, came back to me years later when I read a touching poem by Avi, written during a stormy voyage on the Atlantic Ocean. The poem entitled "Jehudah Halevi on the Sea" depicted an old man in a corner of the boat, praying for the winds to blow eastward and hasten the course towards his beloved Zion to which he would still give the best in him.

There was a mixture in my thoughts of poems, prayers, passages from Isaiah, readings from *Tze'enah u-re'ennah*[38] which Sarah Bayla had to translate for us into Hebrew (Yiddish was not tolerated); important matters and trifling ones, of great and humble figures, of games and serious discussions. But late at night, with the stars reflected in the water or wrapped in clouds, the deeper Jewish self was stirred within me. Like Molière's *Bourgeois Gentilhomme,* who spoke prose all his life without knowing it was prose, I was philosophizing without knowing it was philosophy. I communed with the Jewish being without realizing that I was reflecting it.

At night, Immi, my sister Esther and I would take turns in watching our younger sister Tamar. The baby, Tehillah, was well protected in Immi's arms. They were both attractive children, one with deep, dark eyes and the other with pure blue eyes and curly golden hair. The steward, a Greek, would wake us at every stop: *"Billete, Billete, meine Dame. Schlafen Sie, schlafen Sie."* (Tickets, tickets, my lady. Sleep, sleep.) Whether jokingly or in earnest, he offered to purchase Tamar for any number of *medjidas* that Immi would ask.

During these watching hours my mind wandered from Elisha's to Yosef's perplexities, with Avi as the moderator. His patient and conscientious way of answering troublesome questions had made philosophers of us all. He himself was regarded as the foremost authority in Jerusalem not only on Maimonides's *Guide,* but on other medieval classics as well.

---

[38] A paraphrase in Yiddish of the Pentateuch with legends and commentaries, especially written for women.

That night, as if by some miracle, the whole of Jewish life had opened itself before me. Yosef and Elisha were the pivots around whom my thoughts were turning, because I felt as if they were tearing Jewish life asunder, each in his own way. I asked myself what remains of a vessel if the bottom is taken out, or if a hole is bored in it. I revived their arguments and answered them to myself one by one: It was the revealed Commandments that shaped the slaves of Egypt into a Jewish people; they were fed the manna so that they might study the Torah without distraction and carry it into the Land which would become holy through it. God would not have revealed Himself for the mere glory of being beheld, without a purpose beyond it; such a unique splendor was bound to leave a palpable remembrance for endless generations to come. There is no doubt but that this very experience has kept the Jews united, whether in Jerusalem or in Constantinople, in Hillel's times, our times, and those to come.

In the midst of these overcrowding thoughts, not even in logical sequence, as if in a dream, Immi woke up with a start, fearing that she might have overslept. "Say your *shema, yeqirati* (darling), and get your rest." Usually the last words of the *shema* and my first moments of slumber coincided. I recited the *shema* with fervor, but the emotion which I poured into it brought further reflections instead of sleep. As the waves rocked the boat from one side to the other, the *shema* came back on my lips. It was not an amulet, nor even a prayer; it was the absorption into an experience far more real, even though vicarious, than that present living moment.

As I wanted to pluck the stars and bring them down to the boat, I wondered at Abraham who could see beyond their splendor. Maybe it was as a reward for that discovery that God revealed His meaning to his decendants. The Revelation of that meaning, in this consists God's choice. But through this addition of meaning it became the great spiritual discovery; the earth was clothed with a moral garment. God drew bread out of the earth, chose the stars to shine, and Israel to reveal His Law. (I suppose this implied that the natural and the supernatural belong to the same category.)

I recalled how our little Arab friends, Abdallah and Leah, to whom we would occasionally translate parts of our prayers, would ask why we are referred to as the Chosen People. A variety of replies poured in from every corner of the hill where the children were assembled. The final remark was that all those willing to comply with the demands inherent in that choice could readily be part of it. Leah said, "I shall never eat a fruit of my garden without a *bore peri ha-etz*—Who createst the fruit of the tree." Indeed, I thought, when we say *bore peri ha-etz* we sanctify that tree and we let it know that the fruit did not come from its own strength alone. Each benediction is a sort of talk between man, nature and God. It indicates understanding and love. By loving God, we love His whole creation; all is a constituent part of Him.

When Hillel was asked to epitomize the Law, he should have said, "Love God with all your heart and might." This would naturally embrace the same consideration for others as for oneself. But would the heathen who put that question have understood the proper relationship between God and man?

This dynamic way of loving God seems to me to differ from the static *Amor Dei* which is more like an absorption in Him than the Jewish functional expression of it. Even the *devequt ba-Shem* (cleaving to God) is another form of tenderly clasping all the precepts in one embrace.

These haphazard reflections on a child level, were like an echo of the voice of Jewishness which filled the courtyard, where life was one with the Law and the spirit of great men who reinforced it.

With these thoughts were intermingled figures whom in our childhood we identified with Hillel, Rashi, or the *Gaon* of Vilna. In the darkness of the night, as through a powerful searchlight, I saw them in their own perspectives—heroic soldiers defending the citadel, with children standing by their side. Their experiences were ours, too, in our own way. We were never in need of indoctrination.

In the chapter on "Sarah Bayla and Her Times" in *Jewish Leaders,* I tried to recapture that period in its various aspects. Dissensions were many, but magnified by those who viewed them from without. The Hebrew word *mahloqet* (division) would be a more apt qualification. With very few exceptions, passions were aroused not from selfish motives, but from divergent paths towards the same end—to hand down an integral Jewish life to generations to come. Differences were finally submerged in this common goal which united factions and a variety of temperaments.

Instead of rectifying distorted pictures by those who lacked a sympathetic understanding, I would try to photograph these dedicated people in the light of their normal Jewish mood. A faithful reproduction would be a monument to a period that "may have faded, but could never die."

Among many scurrilous tales, the following carry with them the dramatic force of the Jewish spirit.

THE HALUTZ

Baruch disappeared from Jerusalem before his young sister-in-law became a widow. A small fund which he inherited from his grandfather in Russia made possible his traveling and studying in Paris. In his search of secular knowledge, he jumped from one field to another as far apart as art, philology, and chemistry.

He became associated with an environment which loosened his Jewish ties. He even changed his name from Baruch to Benedict.

It was a Gentile friend who suggested a trip to Italy and from there to Jugoslavia.

Baruch's departure from Jerusalem was hardly noticed until after the death of his brother. A search, through correspondence, was launched in every part of the Jewish world. Appeals were made to rabbis, community leaders, but there was no Baruch who fitted the description. Open letters were published in Hebrew periodicals, but he had ceased to read Hebrew. Requests were made to affix notices to the doors of synagogues, but Baruch had detached himself from the synagogue, too. He wanted to shake off the yoke completely. But there was some residue left, and when Yom Kippur came, it drew him to the synagogue.

It was a tiny one in Dubrovnick, Jugoslavia. He learned that it was the oldest in Europe. The hard, wooden benches, the thick walls with hardly an opening for sun-rays, the narrow gallery upstairs for women, pointed to its antiquity. He spent the day at the synagogue, and unwittingly his thoughts turned from the oldest synagogue to the most ancient Jewish city, Jerusalem. Through the emotion of the day, memories forced themselves upon him, and doubts began to creep into his mind on the turn his life had taken. (I am repeating here the story as it was told to me by several of his contemporaries). While sitting on the hard bench with the prayer book in his hand, he asked himself: "Why tear oneself away from such rich and long past? What is there in the world at large that Jewish life cannot encompass? What folly to jump off a life one feels at home in, and wander as a stranger elsewhere."

While these thoughts crossed his mind, he suddenly heard a bang on the *bimah* requesting absolute silence. An appeal had come from Jerusalem signed not only by rabbis, but also by a great number of sympathizers, old and young, describing the lonesomeness of the beautiful, graceful, pious young woman, who did not complain and accepted her lot with piety. "Is there a young man with a human heart whose joys of life would not be marred by the awareness of such loneliness? Baruch, come back to Jerusalem, help us win the freedom of that beautiful young innocent being, who knows that each law is derived from some Commandment of God. You could return whenever you wish. Poor as our community is, each and everyone of us want to earn the *mitzvah* of contributing towards your full traveling expenses." This was the first notice that Baruch got about his brother. He came back to Jerusalem and went directly to Reb Shemuel Salant. He left behind him his "Benedict" and the chimeras associated with it. He remained in the Land and became a successful colonist—a pious one. Immediately after the *halitzah*,[39] a fine young man, silently in love without even a nod to her, asked his parents to propose marriage.

This story was told and retold to visitors, newcomers, with a little drama added each time, but the substance is documentary. Ben Yehudah, on his visit to the United States, related it to Dr. Enelow of Temple Emanuel. *"Ha-rabbanim be-yerushalayim kannaim ad me 'od, aval ha-sippur ha-zeh be 'emet davar nifla."* (The rabbis in Jerusalem are extreme zealots, but this story is really wonderful.) Fanaticism could not have gone hand in hand with such deep concern for the happiness of one single individual. These rabbis of old were watchmen of the Law, not with a pistol in their hands, but with humane sympathy and understanding.

THE KADDISHLESS COUPLE

Mordecai and Miriam were much in love and devoted companions to each other. On Sabbaths they would take a little walk together beyond the gates of the city. Evenings, before retiring, they would sit at the table over a glass of tea, exchanging their experiences. On each wedding anniversary he would add a piece of jewelry, and she would embroider a *talit kattan* (*tzitzit*) with

---

[39]The ceremony which releases a widow and her brother-in-law from the duty of uniting in a (levirate) marriage.

a new design. Trivial matters as the style of clothes were not to
be discussed between husband and wife, this being purely a woman's
domain. But Miriam sensed Mordecai's taste and was guided
accordingly in the purchase of dress materials and in the choice
of shawls for the hair. She ordered the carpenter to make a
specially carved book-case for his *shass* (Talmud), and he on a
special festival occasion presented her with a *"Tze' enah u-re 'enah"*
bound in deluxe leather covers with her name imprinted in silver.
The in-laws, Menahem and Esther, were especially kind to her
because she had been an orphan. She was not regarded as a *shnur*
(daughter-in-law) but as a *teuere tochter* (dear daughter) and
treated as such. On seder nights, at his father's home, a special
arm-chair with a cushion was also set for Mordecai, so that his
wife, too, might be a queen. During the years of "Kest" (upkeep)
she was spared the heavier part of the housework, for she might
at any time carry a grandchild for them. The thickest layer of
pioke (solidified top skin of boiled milk) was reserved for Miriam's
coffee, in spite of her genuine protests. Marketing was done together, so that she might pick the food she liked best. She would be
consulted whether the chicken soup be prepared with *mandeleh*
(egg beads), *lokshen* (noodles) or rice; also about the ingredients
for the *kugel* and the cereals for the *kashe*. The *mitzvah* of *hallah*-
taking[40] was equally shared between Esther and Miriam. When
Esther made a dress for herself, she would provide Miriam with a
still finer material. The father even tolerated the few thin curls
that would occasionally peep out from under her neatly tied shawl.
"It is to her husband that she wants to be attractive, not to anyone
else." He often presented her with some silk shawls of delicate
texture and rich colors. Miriam, not of an egotistic nature, repaid
these attentions with an abundance of love and devotion. The five
daughters were cheered with her companionship, and joined the
parents in prevailing upon the couple to prolong their stay with
them. The house would become too lonely without Miriam.

When they moved out, they were only a few blocks apart. The
father established Mordecai in a small business of kitchen utensils.
He himself had a grocery store on the Yiddishe Gass. The son
would close his shop a little earlier than the normal hour, and
attended our *Yeshivah* late afternoons and evenings. Miriam

---

[40]Hallah-Taking: A small portion of dough is thrown into the fire, in
commemoration of the offering of the first portion of dough which was
given to the priests.

offered to assist in the business, but the parents objected. She should concentrate on building up her health. Five years had already passed and yet no offspring. The mother-in-law joined in prayers at holy tombs. They went together a number of times to the graves of *Rachel immenu* (our mother Rachel), Shimeon ha-Tzadik, and of course to the *kotel ma'aravi*.

Immi, whose children were late in coming, advised a trip to Tiberias, hard as riding on donkeys would be. There were the tombs of the Rambam and of Rabbi Meir ba'al Ness.

Visiting the graves gave deep satisfaction because great men of the past were alive in the minds of the people. It was like communicating with a revered and cherished contemporary; more than that, it was like pouring out one's heart to a sympathetic listener at a time of crisis. Among the most endeared ones stands out the tomb of Rachel, on the way to Hebron. When in trouble, one's first thought was a visit to Rachel's tomb. The walls were plastered with written pleas from people in despair, who looked for solace to our Mother Rachel. Dr. Wallach encouraged those pilgrimages, as they were an effective source of relief. In Miriam's case, he offered no hope; so far as he knew medicine had no remedy for her sterility.

As the tenth year of their marriage was approaching, the worry weighed heavily on Mordecai's father. Menahem loved Miriam as much as he did his five daughters. He had a deep admiration for her dignified character, her capacity for love and self-sacrifice. That his only son would not leave behind him a *kaddish* of his own, was extremely hard to bear. The females outnumbered the males in the family, but there was hope that through Mordecai some grandsons would be born. Parting the couple, so attached to each other, is heartrending. Bitter as the separation would be, to have his son leave no trace behind him is profoundly saddening, too. Should they divorce, Miriam would not remain alone; she would be living with his family and treated with the same affection as hitherto. Mordecai could stay with his aunt until he remarried. He should not even call on them—they would visit him instead, and spare Miriam's feelings.

Menahem thought it best to approach Miriam first. She fully understood and sympathized; she would talk to Mordecai as soon as she mustered the strength. Day after day she lacked the courage. Tears were overflowing while he was away. Before his coming home, she would warm up some water to wash her face, and spread a little olive oil under her eyes to wipe off the stain of tears.

Children of my age-group had already entered the ninth year. We began to understand problems of grown-ups, and we sympathized. We had a vague concern about Miriam, and were anxiously awaiting the time when the boys would sing the *shir ha-ma'alot* at her bedside on the birth of a child. She was friendly, and we loved her. As we called on her one Friday, we saw through the open door that she was chopping gefillte fish with tears rolling down her face. "It is from the onions," said one. "No," said another, "these are not onion tears; these are tears from the heart." She quickly wiped them off as she saw us coming in. She greeted us with forced cheer, a smile, and with a piece of almond cake, a recipe of her own which Mordecai liked. We did not tell her that a shiny tear stuck to the corner of her left eye. On the spur of the moment one of us touchingly remarked, "Good deeds we leave behind us are children of the spirit. They unite in chorus to say *kaddish,* and it must sound as if the twinkling stars were chanting it." Miriam tried to hold back a tear, but it remained in the eyes, and it saddened us.

An inspiration came as we left her, that we proceed to the *kotel ma'aravi* and pray. We were already allowed to go there by ourselves, provided an older boy escorted us. *Talmud Torahs* and *heders* closing early on Fridays, the boys in the courtyard and the Hassidic ones joined in our mission. Time and again we had seen people, with a distressed look, pushing some scraps of paper into the crevices and pray. The faces softened, the eyes brightened, and they left the Wall relaxed. We shall do the same. Could God be addressed in written form? Why not? Is not the *siddur* a series of written prayers and the Psalms songs of praise? Of course, God could hear even unuttered prayers in the silence of the night, but the *kotel ma'aravi* is a holy medium, the only remnant of the Temple. The cruel Titus left the Wall standing because it was nothing but a wall to him. He would have destroyed this also, had he known that when we close our eyes in front of it, the splendors of Solomon's Temple roll before us.

We poured our feelings on a white piece of paper, written and rewritten until the strength of our emotion permeated the words. "*Ha-Shem Elokenu* (Oh Lord our God), You promised Abraham that his seed would be as numerous as the stars in heaven. How sad Miriam and Mordecai must be when the friendly

stars, crowding the firmament, remind them that they have no
share in Abraham's offspring. God of Abraham, Isaac and Jacob,
make us worthy to accept our prayers, and bless Miriam as you
blessed Sarah and Abraham with their son Isaac, Jacob with
twelve sons, and the pious, silently-suffering Hannah with a prophet
in Israel. Miriam is kind and pious. She will teach Thy Commandments to her children and grandchildren." With everyone's
signature affixed to it, this paper was carefully deposited in the
tiniest crevice and pushed way inside. We prayed, our hearts
lightened, and we silently left for home. On the way we met
Dr. Wallach, who was curious to know what brought children
to the *kotel ma'aravi* at such an odd hour, but he merely said,
"May God answer your prayer."

Miriam decided not to prolong the agony, and to speak to
Mordecai on the day following the Sabbath. Meanwhile she
rehearsed the words and solemnly promised herself to conceal the
inner agitation. As they were sitting at the table over a glass of
tea, she asked him with apparent calmness and without reference
to his father, to grant her a divorce. Mordecai emphatically rejected
her demand, borrowing Elkanah's words, "Am I not better to thee
than ten sons?" She gently replied, "Elkanah had children of his
own," and she would pray that he, too, be granted sons and
daughters. Every birth would be a source of joy to her. "After
a hundred years (the euphemistic expression for the end of life)
your *kaddish* will surely be willing to say *kaddish* for me, too."

Unable to talk her out of it, and fathoming the depths of her
self-sacrifice, Mordecai approched Avi, then the head of the
Yeshivah, in that perplexing situation. The father had already
talked it over with Avi, who warned him not to interfere with
destiny, which is in God's and not in human hands. He told the
couple what they knew themselves, that divorce is permissible
under such conditions, but not required. They were still young
and they should trust in God. The father was pressing, time offers
no solution: "Why wait and keep the unborn children from coming
into the world?" There was no halakhic question involved, since
Mordecai completely rejected the idea of a divorce. It was a
humane task, that of quieting the father, and of giving moral
support to this fine, harmonious couple with deep concern for
each other's happiness. The Chief Rabbi Samuel Salant[41] was consulted, and he called a conference of *Hakham Bashi* Elyashar,

[41] He succeeded Rabbi Auerbach as chief Rabbi in 1878.

some other rabbis, Avi, the parents, Sarah Bayla, and also Dr. Wallach. There was no lack of sympathy with the father's passionate anxiety for perpetuating his son's memory, but the Law and humaneness stood against him. Just as they were admonishing Menahem that such kind of piety leads to impiety, the door was pushed open and Dr. Wallach came in.

With his usual warmth and excited mode of speech, "The suggestion I am proposing looks to me providential. My meeting the children on their way back from the *kotel ma'aravi*—no one except him knew of our mission—must have been an act of Providence. The picture has been haunting me since, and I thought and thought until a Divine inspiration came to me." He told them that a famous gynecologist in Vienna, who was doctor to the nobility, had very recently discovered some means of curing Miriam's type of sterility. It might require a year's treatment. Should the plan be acceptable, he would make a small financial contribution towards the expenses and write to that doctor. Without a minute's hesitation, Menahem offered to sell the house he lived in, and his wife was equally willing to dispose of her jewelry. The great-grandmother *aleha ha-shalom* (may she rest in peace) would surely forgive the parting with the costly diamond broach for such a holy purpose. The Committee did not accept the sacrifice. Menahem needs the extra little income to supplement the grocery earnings, especially with the youngest daughters yet to be married. The jewelry, too, has to be handed down. Young folks need some ornament; it makes the Sabbath more glittering to them.

Sarah Bayla came up with a fruitful idea. Let the community lay out the funds, and she would approach the Hildesheimers and the Berliner families. Should they not respond favorably, she would take it upon herself to gather the expenses from other sources. The Hildesheimers and the Berliners stood the full cost, and wrote to her that they were glad that she gave them the opportunity for such a *mitzvah*. It was also decided that Mordecai should accompany her. "You could not let a *Yiddish Kind* (a Jewish daughter) travel alone."

Miriam wrote to us that Vienna was overwhelmingly magnificent, but in her eyes Jerusalem was the most beautiful city. Besides family and friends she was missing the *kotel ma'aravi* most. We should give her a thought whenever we go there. Little did she know how earnestly we prayed for her at the Wall.

About a year after we left Jerusalem, my eleven-year-old friend Batsheba wrote to us: A miracle from heaven—*ness min ha-shamayim*—a son was born to Miriam and Mordecai. They called him *Nissim* (miracles). The *shir ha-ma'alot* were sung with more zest than at other similar occasions. *Arbes* (cold boiled chick peas) were prepared in large barrels. Not only our children, but all the people from town came to sing the *shir ha-ma'alot*. The community felt as if he were everyone's child, so great was the rejoicing.

We may not have the capacity nowadays to be vicarious participants in this simple but poignant drama. Menahem, no doubt, had a curious sense of values, but there was pathos in the conflict between his genuine affection for Miriam, and the anxiety for his son. A spiritual heir, a *kaddish,* may have meant to him what an heir to the throne was to Napoleon, or the reputation of the family to Armand's father in the famous play, "Camille," by Alexander Dumas. Miriam's concealed tear shone before me once again when I read about Napoleon's separation from his heart-broken first wife Josephine, who could not give him an heir. Miriam, with her dignified, silent self-sacrifice could range among the classic heroines. But could Alexander Dumas or other dramatists grasp the inner life of a people, so often misunderstood when viewed from without?

There is drama also in the rabbinic attitude towards guarding the Law, and at the same time warning against exaggeration. There is no room for ultraism in the philosophy of Jewishness, which views the Laws as the setting for a balanced behavior. This safeguarding of the moral equilibrium has been at the basis of the Talmudic painstaking efforts to encompass minutest details. Talmudic laws, an all-embracing blend of duty, humane considerations even to animals, and spiritual uplift, have become all one in the collective Jewish mind. The object of this unified whole is to lead to a good life, not without taking into account human weakness as well as strength. According to the philosophy of Jewishness, keeping within the Law leads to that good life, and there is no need for exceeding its bounds. Overemphasis may interfere with the well-balanced setting.

ABRAHAM, OUR BELOVED GER

The Jewish attitude towards proselytism is a corrollary of the philosophy that to intensify one's being is a safer road to perpetuity than expanding it; and that the fructification of its own seed would carry with it the very roots out of which Jewishness springs. It is neither isolationism nor snobbishness. This attitude stems from the fear that the joy of the Law, the very essence of Jewish living, may turn into a yoke to those who have not been nurtured on it as far back as its Revelation. By not having entered into the Covenant, they are under no obligation to fulfill its terms, except for the observance of the Noahide Laws.[42] But should one choose to join our fellowship, he must show a capacity for carrying out with joy and serenity the required responsibilities.

Rabbi Akiba, the son of a *ger,* certainly gave proof of what the Law meant to him. Onkelos (Aquila in Latin), through his translation of the Pentateuch into Aramaic, accomplished a far greater task than Mendelssohn's German one. The Aramaic translation has remained a valuable reference for all time. The *Ger Tzedek* (Righteous Proselyte), a contemporary of the *Gaon* of Vilna, did much to uplift the oppressed spirit of the Jews in Poland. They could not have shown a greater affection than placing him for his peaceful rest in a grave adjacent to that of the *Gaon,* with the same tree spreading its branches over them both. The *Ger Tzedek* belonged to the influential Polish family of Count Potocki. His studies in theology led him to embrace the Jewish religion, and he went to Holland for his conversion. The Polish authorities executed him when they learned of it. The Catholic priest Aimé Pallière of our own times, also was led to Judaism through his theological studies. The king of the Khazars chose Judaism because he preferred to turn towards the original fountain of all religions—the mother religion.

Our Jerusalem *ger* entered the Jewish world from a unique approach—through the gates of Christianity, meaning to be a good Christian. Jesus said "If a man smite you on one cheek, turn to him also the other." How could he be a good Christian if he belonged to the class that smites? He would be a more consistent Christian if he were to join the helpless persecuted people, than by remaining with the large group of persecutors. When he passed the *Bet ha-Midrash* of his small town between Minsk and Dwinsk, he would stop at the door and listen to the discussions. He knew Yiddish, and would contrast the absorption in the minutest moral questions with the callousness of his priest, who

---

[42]These seven laws, conformity to which entitled the alien in Israel to the privileges of citizenship, were not part of the Jewish cult, but implied ethical conduct.

would stir the peasants to hatred and cruelty towards the Jews. They harmed no one, dealt equitably, and found solace in their learning. They looked serene with the books on the table. There must be a fountain of goodness within those pages, a shield against the outward attacks. As he watched those people, he regretted his own ignorance, an illiterate even in the Russian language. Even though unaware of his fertile and alert mind, he thought there was still time to acquire some education. But why study Russian culture, which has not wiped out oppression and tyranny? He would rather study the lore of a people who do not forsake their God, even at the cost of life.

These thoughts would have remained latent, were it not for a sudden onslaught on the people of the *Bet ha-Midrash* on an Easter day. A number of Russians returning from church services fell on them. Little by little they were joined by the whole populace of the town. His two daughters ran to the Jews' defense, and they were stabbed. He was a widower and he himself had brought up his children in righteousness and tolerance. He could no longer bear to be part of that heartless community. He pondered more and more on the abnormality of human behavior. These men were not applying the teachings of Jesus. He will turn to those who hold on to their Law and live in accordance with it.

After meeting the requirements, he became a Jew. He sold his little inn and other belongings, which yielded him enough for traveling expenses to "the holy city of Jerusalem, where God's *Shekhinah* dwelt in the Temple." There he would serve those who study the Law. Sarah Bayla gave him free rent, and he chose to be a water-carrier. This was a profitable business in a place where water had to be delivered from house to house in a leather jug tied to the back. The children befriended him. He never missed a day's visit on the hill to impart his experiences to us. He worked hard, and to the amazement of all, he spent less than the usual minimum.

One day he rushed up the hill: "Children, I have a wonderful surprise for you; come with me to Sarah Bayla." Slowly, with trembling hands, he took out a large, knotted red handkerchief; pennies, nickels, quarters, medjidas rolled on the table, as if a magic golden mine had opened itself. "Sarah Bayla, please count and tell me whether there is enough to order a *Sefer Torah* for your *Bet ha-Midrash,* dedicated to the immortal souls of the Jews massacred in Russia. Should more money be needed, some people owe me for window cleaning." We clapped our hands, we jumped, offered to embroider with golden threads a *magen David* on the mantle. Sarah Bayla selected the finest material. Avi started the *parashah bereshit* with his *Sefer Torah,* and the Bar Mitzvah boys of that year read the *parashah* from it. *Hakham Bashi* Elyashar presented a silver ornament. On *Simhat Torah* the Bar Mitzvah boys vied with each other to carry this particular scroll.

The joy of the Sefer Torah engendered in us some new hopes for our dear Abraham. We associated him with Hillel, also a water-carrier of humble origin, with Onkelos, the nephew of a Roman emperor. In the study of the Law, kings and water-carriers are equal. Why should not our beloved *ger* join the Yeshivah? Sarah Bayla thought it an excellent idea. She would maintain him and arrange to prepare him for the Yeshivah through some private tutoring. We could hardly wait for the sun to set, the time he would usually join us on the hill. As he approached, we shouted, "Abraham, you may grow to be like Onkelos or Hillel." "If only I could be at the level of the Yeshivah, study with them that great Law which teaches that each act be pleasing to God, I would feel that I, too, stood at the foot of Mt. Sinai, and that I, too, could help a little to enrich the world, which still has to learn how to apply such laws." "You will, Abraham, you will."

When Sarah Bayla offered to have him as a steady guest at her table, he replied, "Would it not be like being paid for studying?" Sarah Bayla understood, and arranged that he carry the water to the public *miqvah* which she subsidized, so that the water be changed frequently. This would take little time, and not interfere with learning. The rest of his chores he could turn over to the Yemenite who cleaned the *Bet ha-Midrash* and the yard, who needed an additional income for the support of his nine young children. The oldest, aged twelve, was under my family's care, preparing to occupy a rabbinical post in Yemen. He was endowed with a remarkable memory and linguistic ability, speaking Arabic, Hebrew, Yiddish and Sephardic. He could multiply and divide mentally a large number of digits, and had a propensity towards the study of Kabbalah. He also played moving tunes on the violin which Sarah Bayla, observing his love of music, had imported for him. The *ger,* too, was musical. On some evenings when the two would chant together Hebrew hymns, the talks among women would be stilled. The children would sit breathless around them.

Abraham became more and more versed in the Talmud, and even joined Avi in his studies of the Kabbalah on Mondays and Thursdays after midnight. Beneath the simplicity of the peasant there was an unusually keen mind, a fine combination of naiveté and high intelligence. His remarks were pertinent and appreciated by the Yeshivah scholars. On the margins of Avi's *shass*, as well as on that of my uncle Yitzhak, there were a number of annotations of the *ger's* questions and remarks. Avi asked his brother Yitzhak, who was good at editing, to collect Abraham's sayings into a volume entitled *Eleh Divre Ha-Ger* with introductions by both of them. Owing to Yitzhak's premature death the manuscript remained uncompleted. It might have revealed to us the refreshing approach to the Talmud by one suddenly brought in contact with it, without having imbibed particles of it previously. Coming as he did from a Russian milieu where superstition was rampant, where the ideals of religion were drowned in the Czar's fanaticism, he must have been impressed by the way the Talmud enshrines the physical life within the spiritual, and hallows them both.

On the anniversary of his conversion, Abraham would come on the hill with holiday clothes, lots of candy, nuts, and with as many tales of the *Midrash* he knew. We composed some lyrics for the occasion, for him and the Yemenite boy to sing. The *heder* boys were allowed to remain on the hill an extra hour before returning for the evening session. On the Yahrzeit of his family, he would pray that his two daughters be regarded as Jewish martyrs, to which the children would reply a solemn "Amen." "We shall tell about them to our children, and they to theirs, up to the time of the Messiah." We consoled him that in the world to come they would be together with him for all eternity.

A Lonely Figure

Eliezer was a newcomer from Russia, not from Minsk, Dwinsk or Brisk, but from St. Petersburg. This was not known, for he was non-communicative, and carefully evaded intimate questions. *Shaharit, Minhah* and *Ma'ariv* he prayed at the *Hurvah,* the oldest synagogue. He was the first to enter it and the last to leave. His days were spent in one *yeshivah* after another, listening attentively, with an aching look in his eyes. Because of his wanderings through the *yeshivot* and speaking to no one, he was referred to as the fleeting shadow. That he was wealthy was assumed from his generous contributions to the *gabbetes*,[43] and to communal appeals. What made it more apparent was his stopping at the Kamenitz Hotel beyond the Gates of Zion, the only one in the country catering solely to prominent rich visitors, and not for residents.

Besides Eliezer, there was one other resident guest, Herr Ephraim Cohen, the director of the Laemel Schule. But he, a young bachelor, got special rates because the hotel keeper had marriageable daughters who waited on the tables. Indeed, he selected the more attractive one, gave her lessons in German, and when she acquired a little knowledge of the language, they became engaged. He had left behind in Berlin a broken-hearted student whom he had promised to marry. Herr Cohen knew Yiddish and Hebrew, but would speak German only. With an education equivalent to that offered by a Teachers Normal School, he looked down upon the community as ignorant and old-fashioned—that community which could boast, besides its famous Talmudists, of geographers, historians, journalists, pioneers in distant travels, etc. Such was the attitude of the director whom the overseers of the Laemel Schule sent to Jerusalem to civilize the "uncivilized" people.

Mr. Cohen and Eliezer exchanged but nods, for the latter knew no German. Besides, he was wearing a beard and *peot* (side locks). Eliezer felt lonely in town, lonely at the hotel, lonely everywhere. He was tender to the children of the courtyard, and never missed coming up our hill when he attended the *Yeshivah*. The candy which he purchased at high cost from the German confectionery out of town catering to visitors, far surpassed in taste that of Zemah's stationery store. This was a real treat, and led to some companionship with him. One could detect pain and pleasure in his relations with us. To our amazement, his refrain would be, "Remain always good Jews and do not be swayed by evil influences." We would ask, "How could one born a Jew not remain a good Jew?" His face would sadden; after moments of silence he would sit on a rock at a little distance, gazing towards the east, at the Mosque of Omar. His presence was hardly noticed, absorbed as we were in speculations or games.

Once the sound of our words was loud enough to re-echo through the hill. There was excitement in town. A few *meshum-*

---

[43] A group of women who attended to the needs of the poor.

madim (apostates) posed as pious Jews and mingled with the crowd on the Yiddishe Gass. As usual, there were reverberations on our hill, with one voice on top of the other. We were trying to give our version of a *meshummad*. Finally, out of the mingled noise, a clear-cut voice silenced the others: "A *meshummad* is the most pitiful of human beings, and the loneliest. He ceases to be himself, and cannot be someone else, either. He is alone in his new world, and lonely within. He has stifled the life of his ancestors as far back as our father Abraham; broken the Covenant with God, and lost his fellowship with those who stood at the foot of Mount Sinai and promised to hand down God's teachings from generation to generation. In his being, the sacrifices of the Maccabees, of Akiba, of our medieval ancestors who preferred death to apostasy, are all negated. He has silenced the poetical voice of Deborah, Jehudah Halevi, and his own Talmudic singsong. How could he bear the bleeding of his ancestors, unless he stilled his own self. What remains of a self, if all this is cut out? Eating, drinking, sleeping, do not constitute the whole."

"Why should anyone give up the religion in which he was born? Would we ask our friends Leah and Abdallah to change theirs, even though Ishmael and Esau were their great-great-grandfathers? God wanted to give children to Esau, too; they should remain faithful to him, as we are to Jacob." "Of course," added another, "we would be glad to teach Leah and Abdullah all we have acquired from our ancestors if they so wish."

The little orator continued her interrupted speech: "Every Jew is like a soldier. He could no more leave his Jewish army honorably, than a soldier would desert his." "What if a *meshummad* repents?" "If he repents, that means his Jewish heart is still beating and that he is breathing Jewishness. He should be forgiven, led towards the right path and be helped as a sick patient by a doctor. Running away from himself carries punishment with it, like Cain's conscience that made him flee from place to place. Poor *meshummad,* how we pity him in his betrayal, and how bitter must be his awakening." "*Meshummad, meshummad,* we despise you and also pity you," we all cried out in one voice.

Emotionally exhausted, we looked around and saw Eliezer, his head in his hands, sitting on a rock at a little distance. Slowly and totteringly he approached us. In a voice hardly audible at first, growing in pitch with the inner agitation: "Children, despise me, but hate me not and listen. I am of a weak temperment and prone to yield. I gave in to my wife; I became a *meshummad*. I am repenting, but too weak a man to confess publicly and break the wall between me and those pious people who befriended me at their homes, at the *Yeshivah*, and honored me with *aliyot*. I cannot stand the shame, just as I could not bear my wife's naggings. God who reads human thoughts knows that I am good at heart, but weak as a reed. You are right. I am the loneliest man. My only relaxation is meeting you on the hill. Your prayer over the candy is a soothing moment for me."

Our excitement exceeded his. We trembled, we were seized with fear. That kind Eliezer could not be a *meshummad*. A *gilgul* must have entered into his throat in order to scare us. Why should the *gilgul* pick on us? Yes, Eliezer was a *meshummad*, repenting and suffering. He said that by opening his heart to us he felt lighter, like breathing the air after a long confinement; it was his first moment of freedom since he moved from Kiev to St. Petersburg. "In talking to you, I feel as if a new being were born in me. I am becoming a real person." The tears in his eyes moistened ours. "We are only young children, we may have opened the gates, crumbled the wall, but you have to commune with grown-ups. They will believe and sympathize if you unfold your life before them as you did before us. You will feel better; you will become one of them." "How could I, when I lack the courage?" "We shall pray God to give it to you. They will read deep into you and believe. You will cease to be lonely." "You give me strength, I shall do so as soon as I possibly can. Keep it a secret meanwhile. Shalom." "May God help you Eliezer, *shalom u-berakhah ve-hatzlahah* (peace, blessing and success)." He descended the hill while we remained motionless and dreadfully scared. *"Shema yisrael, ha-Shem Elokenu ha-Shem ehad"* came out spontaneously from us all as if with one voice. The *shema* absorbed some of our excitement; the further prayer that God forgive those who sincerely come back to their people, quieted us a little. We kept the secret.

The following day Eliezer went to the Yiddishe Gass, bought some figs, dates, carobs; some oranges at the "Finstere Kleiten," ordered a few sandwiches at the hotel, took the *tefillin* and *siddur*, and disappeared. A few days later Arabs who passed around the neighborhood of the *me'arat ha-makhpelah* (Cave of Makhpelah—the last resting place of the Patriarchs) gave him some water and offered to bring him back to town on their donkey. He was too exhausted not to accept.

As a result of silent meditation, he appeared the following day
at the *Hurvah* at *Minhah* time, in sack-cloth and ashes on his head.
"*Yehudim bene rahmanim* (merciful Jews), my sin is unforgivable.
I have deserted my persecuted people and accepted baptism in a
moment of cowardice. Remorsefully I left St. Petersburg to do
penance in the Holy City. It is from some children in this community that I have drawn strength to stand before you, asking to
be readmitted to my people and to become one with it. I have been
repenting privately; now I come to confess my sin in public and
unfold my life before you."

A *ba'al teshubah* (penitent) is always welcome. There was
reality in his repentance, and the people recognized it. He was not
only forgiven, but befriended and welcomed as a guest at tables on
Sabbaths and festivals. Eliezer was no longer lonely, nor uncom-
municative; he was reborn. In his will he bequeathed to the community the funds he brought with him; the money to be used to
repair the synagogues, to replace with new benches the broken ones
at the *Talmud Torahs* and *heders,* to provide as long as the estate
would permit, a *shass* for bridegrooms whose parents could not
afford that wedding gift, to supplement for several years the collections of the *gabbetes,* and to add a small amount to Dr. Wallach's
private fund for poor patients. He also remembered with some
gifts the Arabs who had declined remuneration when they brought
him back exhausted from his seclusion. Not more than a small
stone on his grave did he desire, but with the following epitaph:
"Eliezer was born a Jew and died a Jew. The intermediate years
the good people of Jerusalem and their children helped efface. May
God do so, too."

Eliezer's visits to our hill became more frequent, and we could
gather each time one more fragment of his tragic past. We eagerly
picked up the threads and spun them into a picture, not far from
the real one. I shall try to render my wording as faithfully as
possible to the spirit of this authentic story. It could be the story
of many others during the wave of baptism, of those who emotionally were not ripe for the onrush of the nineteenth century emancipation and could not foresee an harmonious coordination in a free
world.

Eliezer's father, a prominent lumber merchant in Kiev, left
him an immense fortune. The girl he married, a graduate of the
Gymnasium (equivalent to junior college), regarded herself as
superior to the Jewish environment. Through bribes and other

means she obtained permission to reside in St. Petersburg, a privilege granted to but few Jews. The income of their estate allowed for luxurious living in a large mansion. But what was the good of a mansion without entertaining prominent people? In school, sooner or later, the children, in spite of their Russian names, would still be singled out as Jews. Little Stephan's friend noticed that there were no sacred pictures on the walls. How long could they bear the stigma? What is more, Eliezer's wife would like to build up a literary salon on the style of the German ones of the eighteenth century, when Schleiermacher, Schlegel, Novales, Schelling, Lessing were the guests of Henrietta Hertz, Dorothea Mendelssohn, Rachel Lewin, and others. These brilliant women and even Mendelssohn's children became baptized; why not follow in their footsteps? It would be making good use of their wealth to be hosts to similar celebrities.

Day in and day out his wife nagged him about it. "What is the sense of continuing a narrow, harassing life, with all the fortune at our disposal, with a magnificent mansion and growing children? What pride is there in being a Jew? Must we continue to suffer because a handful of people left Egypt and sought a home for themselves? They got their reward; why do we have to be their appendage? Are not the cathedrals of St. Petersburg more imposing than the famous Temple of Solomon where no carved images were allowed?" When he spoke to her of spiritual strength, she scoffed at him. "Nothing is immortal in this world; why should we prolong artificially a dead life, a peculiar one, full of do's and don'ts, as if the Jews of today have to listen to those old-fashioned bearded men. Greece with its precious art, Rome with its mighty power, the Phoenicians, inventors of the alphabet, Egyptians with their astronomy and secret art of embalming, Babylonians with a sense for gardening, Assyrians, are all only memories. Is not a Jewish claim to immortality pretentious and of narrow vision?"

He reminded her of Jewish heroism, greatness, dignity, idealism, ethical strivings, deep religious beliefs, the discovery of the Creator of the universe who shaped man in His image, of the Jewish share in substituting the great moral God on whom we bestow endless praises, for the Greek fighting gods who envied the mortals and were cursed by them. Eliezer would also direct her attention to the miracles performed on behalf of Jewish survival, the unparalleled heritage of the Bible, the Talmud, the great medieval works, and the impetus of the Jew to continue and enrich that tradition. But how could realities appeal to one who, like the luminous insect, finds expression through shining in the eyes of others? Eliezer hoped, however, to ignite a spark of reality in her being, by appealing to the worthiness of life when guided by ideals rather than sham appearances. Neither her projected salon nor the children's school are worth the loss. He would not be a deserter and run away from a suffering, dignified people because his father happened to have amassed a fortune through hard and honest labor. He was a faithful Jew, and he could not possibly use the money to deny his father and himself. There is no disgrace in belonging to a minority; the opprobrium belongs to the intolerant majority who cannot bear differentiation. The day will still see the "wolf dwell with the lamb." "Meanwhile the wolf will devour the lamb!" "No," said he, "if it has dignity and courage it will remain unscathed like Daniel in the lions' den."

These discussions, at first on a philosophical level, would culminate in quarrels, fights and threats. She would take away the children whom he dearly loved. They had already become estranged, assuring their mother that when they grew up they would become good Christians; she should not mind their old-fashioned father. Eliezer, who could not even bear the change of his name to Peter and of Masha to Marcelle (a French name sounded better than the many Russian ones she was weighing), lacked the strength of character to resist his family. He was born with a slight heart-murmur, and verbal battles affected him badly.

In a moment of weakness, in order to hold on to the children, he yielded and they were all baptized. They went to church regularly, and the children joined the choir. When his wife would speak of the enchanting music, his thoughts would revert to the *hazan* of Kiev, with an operatic voice. Urged to train for the stage, he would reply, "Are Figaro, Rigoletto or the Walküre more entitled my voice than prayers of centuries?" Eliezer, now Peter, would beg to be excused from church attendance, but this would create an unfavorable impression. Often his little boy had to remind him to remove his hat at services. The figures of the martyrs who refused to bow before the Roman emperors, would pass before his eyes; his knees could not bend. Marcelle would slowly push him down, careful not to attract the worshippers' attention.

On his parents' *Yahrzeit* which he observed even after baptism, he had to hide the light in the little glass with oil behind a marble statue. "It is time you freed yourself from your old superstitions. Careful, you may stain the statue!" The many Russian ikons would cause disturbing dreams, as he could not chase out from his mind the Commandment: *"lo ta'aseh lekha possel vekhol temunah (—thou shalt not make unto thyself a graven image nor any likeness)."* The priest befriended them. On special occasions he would present them with some ikon, and in a patronizing tone, "Marcelle, yours is among the nicest and richest corners in town. You are a good Christian." "I am still a Jew," Eliezer murmured to himself, "but I am a coward, and Jews are not cowards." He was neither Jew nor non-Jew, a nonentity, a shadow, a ghost from another world who cannot touch this one. He was a stranger in his own house. There was left no point of contact with his wife, still less with the children who hardly took notice of him. They were happy with school and their friends, who would admire the sacred pictures on the walls and the ikons on the shelves, some of rare quality, bought at a high price. Marcelle was absorbed in her parties; the intelligentsia feasted at her table with French wine, vodka and caviar. Peter felt lonelier and lonelier, and the wall grew thicker daily. Like all weak characters who suddenly muster a moment of strength, Peter summoned his, and reached a heroic decision. A divorce she would not consider; it would create too great a sensation. He bestowed the largest part of his wealth on her and the family, sufficient to provide for generations of offspring, with the feeble hope that his children's children might rediscover their heritage, as did some of the Marranos, sadly mindful of the difference between the strength of the Marranos and his own cowardice. Jerusalem would be a most fitting place to do penance and allay his inner agitation.

In communing with a society where each one was his real self, Eliezer regained his own. The shadow was vested with flesh and substance and he became a living Jew. The duality between appearance and essence has been the concern of philosophers as far back as the Socratic era. For Immanuel Kant essence remains unknown. In the philosophy of Jewishness it is not hidden; it is identified with Jewish living itself. It is this palpability of the essence that brings Jews in communion with each other, beyond space and time. Being oneself is a chief constituent of society in its highest form. Appearances do not interpenetrate, but real selves can react upon one another, create a far better republic than Plato's, and bring about the kind of world for which we are now striving.

THE ROMANTIC YOUNG COUPLE

Freda and Shlomo Schreiber were known in town as the most romantic couple, loving and sentimental. She was his "Freidele" and he her "Shloimele." They would speak to each other even in the presence of company, ignoring the prevailing custom of silence between husband and wife until after the first child has been born. He always addressed her by the nickname, and never "du, du." Fridays she would come to our courtyard to pick the little yellow flowers to embellish the Sabbath table. On the silk napkin covering the *hallot*, she embroidered "Welcome, beloved Sabbath, and Good Shabbos, my beloved Shloimele." He would select the finest material from his father's dry goods store whenever she wanted to sew a garment for herself. She was the best dressed in the synagogue, and his was the finest *streimel* (a Sabbath headgear trimmed with fur tails). She replaced the one he got for a wedding present with precious sable fur, usually hard to obtain. Shlomo and his father would alternate between attendance at our *Yeshivah* and the care of the store. When he arrived home at noon from the *Yeshivah* and evenings from business, the table was pleasantly set with his favorite dishes. His father would spare him the trips to Beyrouth for the purchase of goods, lest his wife be too lonesome during his absence. Once when she complained of a slight sore throat, he left the shop in his mother's care and took her, not to Dr. Buffle in the vicinity, but to Dr. Wallach, whose office was a long distance from the house. Dr. Wallach seldom treated simple cases, but how could he say "No" to such a devoted couple?

One day her dear Shloimele had a touch of malaria, a disease so common that half the population would go around with it. In the morning he attended the *Yeshivah* as usual, in the afternoon he stayed home at her request. She gave him some quinine, hot tea with lemon and ginger jelly, especially prepared for him. It was not too late in the afternoon when the thought occurred to her that a fresh cup of boiled goat's milk—cow's milk was hardly available—would do him good.

Milk had to be fetched from some Arab farm, quite a distance from town. Jewish customers would bring their own pitchers; the farm boy, after washing his hands, would milk directly into them. The same water would be used again and again, unless he handled some meat. In that case the hands would be cleansed with earth-clods, used also for scrubbing pots. The cisterns being too shallow, there was greater scarcity of water on the farm than in town. The long walks to the dairies have remained fresh in my mind, as Immi took me with her a number of times. The fields had a desolate look: dry grass withered by the hot sun; here and there a lonely shepherd with a sombre look, far from reflecting the serenity of the sky and the poetry of the hills.

I can well imagine Freidele's disappointment at finding no milk at the farm, after traversing such arid fields. The peasant advised her to go a little further to the nearby farm where the goats had more to eat. With some shortcuts there would remain plenty of time for returning before sundown. The shortcuts meant climbing up and down hills. She reached the farm and got a full pitcher of milk. The sun was still at the center of the sky. She would surely have returned before *ma'ariv,* had she not lost the way coming back. The hills were gradually turning into purple red, with the sun behind them still shedding some rays of light. She finally noticed from afar the path leading to the fields. Running down the hill with breathless haste, she suddenly saw an Arab jumping out of the bushes. "Yes indeed, you are on the right path. I shall let you go home, but you will have to stop a little while here."

The folks at home knew where she had gone; it was not yet too dark to worry over her delay. Fetching milk required much time. When the first star pierced through the sky, Freidele, too, appeared, but with her dress torn into shreds, the petticoat missing, the stocking dropping, no shawl over her shoulders, not even the little silk shawl on her head, which her father-in-law had brought from Beyrouth. The little crops of hair, usually hidden, were disheveled and erect as if some had been plucked. Her lips were bleeding; the face scratched, and her eyes like a stream of water. No sooner did she pass the threshold of her house than she fainted. When she was brought back to life she became hysterical, crying and sobbing. Her eyes remained closed, with all the cold water sprinkled on them. She refused to open them, and one wondered whether the wetness of her face was from the sprinkled water or from the tears of her closed eyes.

Dr. Wallach was called. He surmised what happened as soon
as he saw her. The pious Dr. Wallach consulted my family, who advised him of the tolerant Talmudic attitude in face of such disaster.
Sara Bayla ran to call Reb Shemuel Salant, and Immi went to fetch
Hakham Bashi Elyashar. Reb Shemuel Salant brought with him
some members of the *Bet Din*. He needed assistance at such a
tragedy. After joint deliberations, the *Hakham Bashi* spoke first:
"My dear child, you suffer from hallucinations; you are sick. Follow Dr. Wallach's prescriptions and you will soon be well. Calm
yourself; you tore your clothes in the bushes. I could have torn
mine, too, and lost my turban, had I been caught by the thorns."
Reb Shemuel Salant and Reb Jacob Mordecai echoed his words,
each in his own gentle tone. They took her husband aside, and informed him of the Talmudic law. They enjoined upon him to take
care of her with the love and kindness she was accustomed to, and
expressed the hope that they would be blessed with a child as soon
as her strength would permit. They all retired outside for a while,
so that he might wipe away her tears with his caresses. As he
approached her with tender and loving kindness, her hysteria increased and her eyes remained shut. Dr. Wallach felt helpless. Her
eyes, he said, would not open as long as that picture is still impressed upon them. In the days that followed she hardly touched
the appetizing food placed before her. Everyone in town brought
some delicacies.

Immi went far out of the city limits to fetch for her some
chocolate cake from the German bakery. Nothing would tempt
her. The doctor advised that she must be made to take some
chicken soup. Tureens with *lokshan* (noodles) *mandelech* (egg-
beads), rice, barley, even with *kreplach* (chopped meat turn-overs)
reserved for holidays only, poured in from all sides. She took
some only after she was warned by Reb Shemuel Salant that
abstaining from food was an *averah* (transgression), but still
with her eyes closed. Reb Shemuel Salant and Reb Jacob Mordecai
urged her to hasten the recovery so that she and her husband
might pronounce the benediction of *gomel* at the earliest possible
moment. Immi, her closest and youngest friend, sat at her bedside
telling her stories to distract her from the devastating experience.
With tactful care not to arouse her suspicion, they were calculated
to put her at ease and help restore her equilibrium. Avi would
select for Immi appropriate Midrashic tales to relate to her. This
proved beneficial. She began to relax and even told Immi how

she got lost on top of the hills. At that point of the story Immi would divert her attention with some digressions, which kept her from continuing it.

Fifteen months later there was much rejoicing in town: A son was born to Freidele and Shloimele. Her husband, romantic as ever, gave her the privilege of naming him. She called him Nahmanke, derived from the Hebrew word for comfort and consolation. Reb Shemuel Salant was the *sandek* (godfather), *Hakham Bashi* Elyashar and Reb Jacob Mordecai were the *Gevatters* (godfathers). Nahmanke was a comfort to the whole community. He grew up to be among the most pious colonists. He assisted Sarah Bayla in her efforts to bring newcomers closer to Jerusalem, so that they, too, should lead an integral Jewish life.

This story was told me by Immi long after we had left Jerusalem. I could revive it as if I myself had been in Freidele's bedroom and had seen her twisted face and tortured heart. Knowing the rabbis, who were kind and patient with the children of the courtyard, familiar with the locality, with the people's attitude and habits of mind, I could easily picture the vicarious suffering of the whole community, as they poured into her room one after another.

Immi happened to recall the above story as I was talking to Avi in later years about Immanuel Kant's assertion that under no condition is suicide morally permissible, except in the case of a woman who has been violated. Life, says Kant, must be kept sacred; hers has been desecrated and immorality objectified in her person. With her disappearance, unholiness—of which she has become the bearer—would be equally effaced. The rabbis, too, wanted to eradicate that unholiness out of Freidele's inner being. But, like expert surgeons, they tried to remove the malignancy without causing injury to herself. They and Kant were aiming equally at erasing the stigma; Kant through her very existence, they by cutting the experience out of her life. They approached the situation with the same ethical standards, but from a more humane angle. Her moral personality could be reconstituted by helping her genuinely to efface that experience, as if it were detached from her real self. The soul of an innocent victim could not be touched by the sin of the guilty one. The rabbis' challenge to Kant would be that one wrong act does not make up for another. The suicide would not atone for the wrong committed by someone else.

Kant has another famous illustration in regard to the absoluteness of truth. Should a doctor know that telling the truth to a patient would cause his death, he still must choose the truth. It was not the practical approach to the problem that was of interest to Kant. The doctor could have explained that it was contrary to medical ethics to share views with patients. He was not really faced with a definitely clear-cut truth or untruth. But for Kant, Truth in itself is an absolute, standing apart and above life. The Talmud has no lesser respect for truth, but its attitude is derived from a proper perspective of a good and sacred life, and from the laws which make this good life possible. Kant, too, strongly upholds the sacredness of personality, but there is a distinct division in his mind between Truth and life, instead of the two permeating each other. His ethics is rigoristic, abstract and superimposed, while that of the Talmud is humane, concrete and interpenetrating with the forces of life. His *Critique of Practical Reason* is undoubtedly a supreme ethical system, but he concentrates on the "ought" and neglects the "how," the ways and means of attaining the "ought." Consequently his system remains largely theoretical, without sufficiently permeating everyday life. Through his rigorism he fails to take proper account of human nature.

The Talmud, on the other hand, is consistently seeking ways and means for raising man to the heights of moral standards. The precepts are to remind one that immoral acts obliterate the Divine image in him. The good life and the step-ladder to attain it are blended into one; they are not connections only. When life and morality are set one against the other, the connecting bridge may sometimes collapse. Plato's dualism had probably a share in the moral breakdown of medieval times, with high ethical principles within the enclosed walls of philosophy, and barbarism around it. The division in Kant between the *noumenon* (the real world) and the *phenomenon* (the world of appearance), between the "ought" and the natural impulses, may have loosened the bridge between the ideal built within a system of ethics and the human world when it chooses to abdicate it. For a Hitler, it was not difficult to cut the ropes and leave Kant's "ought" behind the bridge. In a philosophy of Jewishness one must regard the ends and the means as inseparable from each other.

The great German scholar Moritz Lazarus (1824-1903) vitiated his fine volumes on Jewish ethics by the predominant task he set himself to bring out the kinship with Immanuel Kant (1724-1804). Elsewhere[44] I have tried to point out that his work would have been far more fruitful had he brought out the specific differences, instead of his painstaking efforts in picking out similarities.

Spiritual Fellowship

To an outside observer, relations between husband and wife would have seemed at a minimum in our Jerusalem milieu. They talked little with each other. The first meeting carried no romance; it was arranged by parents. Avi would run away from the girl he occasionally met on the street, whom he had taken for his fiancée.

Conversation between husband and wife was indeed brief. The days were not long enough for household chores under rudimentary conditions. Men's time was even more precious, whether that of a tradesman who had to spare a few hours a day for study, or of the *Talmid Hakham* (scholar) engrossed in the *shass*. Those capable of making annotations on the margins of printed pages would spend hours by the kerosene lamp to perfect them. But the awareness of their spiritual partnership, added to the ties of parenthood, engendered touching and idyllic relations, with a division of labor in this world, and the expectation of a joint bliss in the next.

The *melammed* engaged by Sarah Bayla would say, "Give the pay to my wife. She is the one who feeds me and wakes me before the cock's crow for my morning *shiyur*." Each time the scribe at our courtyard completed the writing of a scroll, he would adorn his wife with a piece of jewelry. "It is thanks to your patience and silence that my copying the Torah turned out perfect. The stretch of the lonely hours when I could not utter a word must have been wearisome.[45] But what if I had made a mistake *hass ve-shalom* (God forbid)." "Tired? I felt as if I were touching heaven itself. I, the wife of a scribe who is entrusted with such a holy mission. I watched you quietly and my heart swelled with joy." Such intimate conversations passed around the neighbors, and the children had sharp ears. They would re-live each story.

[44]Journal of Philosophy, Vol. XIV, No. 17.
[45]The scribe's profession is exacting as well as sacred. If he makes an error, the whole section of the parchment must be removed; but it must not be thrown away, for it is holy. There is a special place in the synagogue where such discarded sections are kept.

As I was playing on the floor with Mikhele, the son of
Tzemah the candy store keeper, I overheard a little talk between
his parents. "Your *streimel* is too worn out; it is time that some
of the furs be replaced." "No, my Gittel, a dress *likhevod shabbat*
is more urgent." As their eyes wandered towards us, they noticed
that Mikhele's shoes were more torn than they had realized.
"Well, the shoemaker's *streimel* will be the one to be refreshed."
"No, Gittel, let his wife get material for a *yomtovdige* dress."

To take a young son to *heder* for the first time was a *mitzvah*
that each parent wanted the other to enjoy. "It is you who will
teach your son to follow in your footsteps *le-Torah ve-la'avodah*
(for study and worship); the *mitzvah* should be yours," said
Masha to her husband Feivel. "It is you, Masha, who went through
labor-pains, nursed him, taught him the *berakhot* (blessings) and
the *shema;* you should be earning that *mitzvah.*" "Why don't you
both take me?" said the little boy who overheard their conversation. They set a precedent that became a custom with all parents.

The tender relations between Avi and Immi were marked by
intellectual companionship also. As soon as they were married—
she was twelve and he eighteen—Avi engaged an instructor to
enlarge her Hebrew knowledge. She studied the weekly *parashah*
(portion of the Torah) assiduously, which gave her occasion to
exchange *divre Torah* (matters of learning) at Sabbath meals.
She had been taught by her father that talks on the Sabbath are
to be devoted to holy matters only. On Fridays, Sarah Bayla
would wake her early to complete the *parashah* and receive instructions on the *kugel.*

It was customary that cooking be learned from mothers-in-law,
so that young brides grow closer to them, and feel less lonesome
for their own family. Immi cherished Sarah Bayla's kindness in
allowing her, while still a novice at cooking, to prepare eggplants
when the great Alkalai—the precursor of political Zionism—was
a guest at the table.

Women were honored on every occasion. Whenever Sarah
Bayla came to see Reb Shemuel Salant, he and the *Bet Din* would
stand up to greet her. The followers of the Brisker Rav would
consult his wife on the marriage of their children and on other
matters. When Reb Jacob Mordecai happened to notice on his
way to the *Bet ha-Midrash* some women with bundles, he would
run up the stairs, deposit the books from under his arms, and
rush down to relieve them.

Special attention was given to the old widows who came to end their days in the Holy Land. On *selihot* (penitential) days, the first knock of the beadle was at their door, to allow them extra time to prepare for the midnight prayers. Each time Dr. Wallach visited our *Yeshivah,* they would get precedence for a free check-up. He carried with him quinine and other drugs, to spare them the expense and the long walk to the pharmacy. Women, he said, who had traveled to the Holy Land at such risk and parted with their loved ones, merit *olam hazeh* and *olam ha-ba* —this world and the one to come.

I, too, showed my respect and deep affection for the old Hayye Esther. I would enter her room with a small glass of cod-liver oil in my trembling hand, close my eyes and gulp it down as fast as I could: "Hayye Esther, I am drinking it for your sake, because you came to the Holy Land. You should ask your grand-children to come here, too." I had a dreadful dislike for that coarse, undistilled oil, poured once a day into every child's throat, up to the age of three. Neither force nor inducements could make me drink it, except as a mode of thankfulness to Hayye Esther.

The place of women in Avi's surroundings may have prompted his series of articles in the *ha-Misderonah* on *kibbud nashim* (respect for women) in the Talmud. He points out that certain unfavorable statements were subjective expressions not in con-formity with the genuine rabbinic spirit.

In a society sustained by high ideals, men and women, even with diversified strivings, are spiritually equal on the scales.

OUR ARAB NEIGHBORS

Relations between Jews and Arabs grew to be neighborly. They would have continued so, if the Arab masses had not been stirred to hatred by the small privileged class who lived on their hard labor. The difficulties were with Turkish or Arabic officials, not with the people themselves. When some of them were a little cross during the Ramadan period, we knew it was due to the double fatigue of fasting at daytime and overeating all night. My own family had very pleasant relations with their Arab neighbors. Sarah Bayla gained their affection and esteem, and many came to seek her counsel or pay social visits. She knew how to serve them Turkish coffee.

I recall these incidents: A poor Arab farmer met with disaster. An epidemic had wiped out his chickens, and he was threatened to be dispossessed by his Arab landlord. Sarah Bayla gave him a few of her live chickens plus a small contribution to provide his family of eleven children with some food. She requested the *gabbetes* to obtain a live chicken from every Jewish household that could afford it. In a short while his lost chickens were replaced, and he remained on the farm. A year later, a day before Yom Kippur, he brought to Sarah Bayla a large fat rooster for *kapparot*.[46] When she explained that for such purpose a price must be paid, he requested that it be donated to a poor Jewish family.

Two Arab houses were separated from one another by a large vacant lot, belonging jointly to the two owners. Each claimed the larger part of it. The arguments often ended in vehemence. They could not resort to the court of justice and quarrel in public, after having partaken of coffee in each others' house, and when their children played so nicely together. They chose Sarah Bayla as referee. How could she give a proper decision when she had no knowledge of the measurements and the specifications in the deeds? A happy thought crossed her mind. "Ibn Ibrahim, you have a boy fourteen years old, and you, Ibn Mousah, have a girl of ten. If they are congenial and if it is agreeable to you, they could wed one day, and let this piece of property be theirs. You each have enough land in town to endow your other children in due time." They both hailed the suggestion enthusiastically. "Allah be with you, Sarah Bayla. King Solomon could not have rendered a better judgment." "What about the customary price paid to the father for giving his daughter away in marriage?" To this the boy's father readily agreed. "You are fully entitled to it." Two years later everyone in the courtyard was invited to the wedding celebration. They would have wanted us to stay for the banquet, but they knew that it would be embarassing because of the dietary laws.

A well-to-do Arab planned to join the pilgrimage to Mecca during the Ramadan period. With no bank available, where could he leave his funds? He was known to be a very good husband, providing his wives with luxury and servants. He bedecked them with jewelry, gave them gilded sandals, fancy veils, and even let them choose the color. He showed no favoritism, though one had

---

[46]*Kapparot:* A custom of using a fowl as a scapegoat for the sinner.

a greater attraction for him. But to leave the money with them would breed too much familiarity between husband and wives. It is for a husband to decide what a wife's needs should be. He left them sufficient money for their upkeep, and took along some for his traveling expenses. The rest, together with his most precious jewelry, he entrusted to Sarah Bayla. The receipt she wrote out, he tore in her presence. "Allah forbid that I should have no faith in Sarah Bayla." She, too, asked no receipt when she handed it back to him. Upon his return he brought a highly priced necklace of tiny, indented narrow strips of gold. It was beautiful to behold. She declined the generous gift, as it would be equivalent to accepting payment for the service. He insisted that it was not payment, but "habib," an expression of affection and esteem. She took it for a wedding present for some poor bride. The lot would fall to the first one to wed. The lucky bride was an attractive young girl of fourteen, with large, dark eyes, deep-black hair, a rosy complexion, red lips, a Sephardic brunette. The necklace brought into relief the fine contour of her long neck. The Arab was invited to the wedding. So impressed was he with the radiant looks of the bride, that the following day he gave the husband a pair of earrings for her, matching the necklace. From then on, he was among the most generous contributors to collections for the jewelry of poor Jewish brides.

Lemi Attah Amel—For Whom Are You Toiling?

The introductory chapter of Avi's book *Berure ha-middot*[47] bears the above title. It reflects the hopes and cry of those who have faith in the self-conserving, regenerating Jewish dynamo, in spite of temporary discouragements.

Avi quotes a sceptic who asked him "For whom are you toiling? Will the next generation devote any time to Talmudic studies? The Talmud Torahs scratch but the surface of knowledge. The revival of Hebrew carries with it neither the sacredness inherent in the language, nor the studies it connotes. One could be an ignoramus in Hebrew, too. Our modern literature caters to crude, popular taste. The theological seminaries are graduating careerist rabbis who are undedicated to the Call. Even Orthodox rabbis have little time for Talmudic research. Oratory plays the

---

[47] An examination of the exegetical principles by which the Torah is interpreted.

greater role. For whom, then, are you toiling?" Avi replied: "I am toiling for the Torah which is my life, my way of living, and the source of life of our whole people. It is my belief that there are innumerable persons who cling to that life. Among them the Torah will not be forgotten, and for them my work will not be in vain." He paraphrases Isaiah LIX, 21 and Ezekiel XXXVII, 9: "As for Me, this is My covenant with them, says the Lord; My spirit that is upon thee and My words that I have put in thy mouth, shall not depart out of thy mouth"—and if they depart from thy mouth, they will not depart from the mouth of thy seed, and if they depart also from the mouth of thy seed, then a breath shall come from the four winds and will breathe into the dry bones of thy seed, and they will arise and live.

"Furthermore," continues Avi, "outstanding works on the Torah, from the *Mishnah* to the *Shulhan Arukh,* were composed by those who sought to establish fortifications for weaker generations. Numerous discoverers, from those of the speeding wheel to modern inventors, have been wiped out from human memory. But those who have helped clarify the meaning of the Torah have lived on with the people who came after them, for thousands of years. "I shall render grace to God, should it be my portion to add a little to our people's enlightenment. *For this I am toiling,*"[48] concludes Avi. And for this, I think, all Jewish leaders are toiling.

THE PHILOSOPHY OF JEWISH EXPERIENCE

There would be no need of recapturing the spirit of a remote corner in Jerusalem to discover the philosophy which permeates the whole rabbinic literature had it been comprehended in its own terms. I feel as if I touched the heart of Jewishness in that concentrative Jewish environment. It was so palpable that it led me in later years to induce Jewish philosophy out of Jewish experience, instead of following the abstract methods of modern historians who thereby lost sight of the inner being. The colorful continuum of the old and the young remained with me like a symphonic ensemble of a Jewish composition. Only those who have no ear for it would look upon that milieu as old fashioned, in a barbed-wire enclosure. The superficial division between a ghetto and an emancipated *Anschauung* could have no bearing on it. This was not a naive

---

[48]Italics mine.

group, unaware of forces working against centuries of self-preservation. They carried the momentum of generations against such
attacks. Jewishness had been tried and tested throughout the ages.
Like a rolling ball it rolled by all civilizations, Greek, Roman,
Islamic and modern. With such an open horizon, largness of vision
is inherent, whether in or out of the ghetto. Occasional blurs do
not obscure the view; they are washed away by the vitality of the
current. Maimonides has remained our guide in spite of unen-
lightened antagonism.

As my object is to draw philosophical inferences from characteristically Jewish experiences, metaphysical questions could be left
out of this picture. While the profound perplexities regarding
man's freedom versus God's omniscience and omnipotence,[49] man's
suffering and God's goodness, received their moral interpretation
through the Bible and the Talmud, they arise in every religious
mind, and are also instruments of attack by non-religious philosophies. Jewish and non-Jewish scholastics grappled with them in
the same manner, with answers along the same lines. But, unlike
the spiritual earthquake which rocked the Church with each
scientific discovery, Jewish philosophy was not shaken by vicissitudes of cosmological theories. Galileo would not have had to
recant his statement before a Talmudic court. Neither the pre-
Copernican nor the Copernican astronomy affected the Jewish
vision. The chanting praises of God by an all-embracing universe,
where the mountains skip like rams and the Jordan flows out of
reverence for Him, have little to do with the stability or motion
of the earth. It is the concern of what constitutes man's role
in carrying out God's laws that gives a distinctive feature to the
Jewish way of thinking. Out of the emotional character inherent
in such relationship, further Jewish reflections proceed.

Some may find it incongruous to root philosophy in an emotional content. But the whole history of thought, from the early
Greeks to our day, is a refutation of the obsolete view that philosophy has to be an abstraction, a kind of mathematics of pure thought,
free from empirical traces. There are abounding examples of the
intimate connection between the destiny of a people and its philosophy. Witness the fact that the various systems are designated
as either French, German, British or American philosophy. It
is true that philosophers try to free themselves from bias when

---

[49] See "Three Dilemmas about God and Man" by Leo Jung, in his *Harvest*.

searching for principles pertaining to all minds and to the universe at large. But there is an emotional residuum which tinges thought, and gives to the philosophy of each people an individuality of its own. Even Descartes (1596-1650) in his attempt to scrap everything around him in his search for the "I"—what am I, who am I, or am I existing at all—did not reach being through cognition alone. Pure abstract thought could be erected into a system more or less like a chess game, but not into a philosophy pulsating with life.

Kant (1724-1804) hoped to remedy the abstractness of his system with his *Critique of Practical Reason*. There remains, however, a chasm between his two *Critiques*. Heine, in a humorous vein, describes the distress of the faithful servant Lumpe when he learned that there was no room for immortality in his master's metaphysics. "Do not cry, Lumpe," says Kant, "whatever I have left out in my *Critique of Pure Reason,* I shall restore in the *Practical.*" There are no two *Critiques* in Jewish philosophy. It is one continuous process of thought and emotional content tied to history and tradition, which are what sense experience is to the empiricist, the primary stuff out of which thinking proceeds. After seeking in the Bible all the proofs that would bear favorably upon his theory, the medieval philosopher Gersonides would seal his chapter with the prayer, "The Lord be blessed, I have verified my theory through facts." Saadia declares that thanks to the laws of the Torah, the innate religious faculty can exercise its function and not be an abstract form. Jehudah Halevi writes that religion is not based on thought, but on feeling; that Jewish religion is a code regulating our life so as to adjust our behavior to the historic traditions. In Him we see how Jewish history and its philosophy merge into one.

The metaphysics of Johann Gottlieb Fichte (1762-1814) in his *Science of Knowledge,* and Hegel's *Phenomenology of Mind*, are also a blending of metaphysics with philosophy of history, but in a position reverse from the Jewish one. In Fichte the *ego* creates the *non-ego;* it is the creator of the world and of God. With Hegel, the German State is the ultimate embodiment of what he calls *Idea*. The philosophy of Jewish history may be traced to the profound concern of lifting oneself and the universe to the level of "God's image." The emotional content reflects the vital moral force at the bottom of its life and the conviction which creates it. Its philosophy engendered that emotion which in turn constitutes its philosophy. A firm belief in the close relationship between God and His creation is one of its fundamentals.

I am not confusing philosophy with theology, although one may lead to the other. There is a clear line of demarcation between philosophy which centers primarily around man within his environment, and theology, the object of which is to study the nature of God. Notwithstanding some scholastic and kabbalistic speculations, the Jewish search is less for the nature of God than for the laws through which He has revealed Himself. One need not go beyond them. God *is* what He *is—Eheye asher ehye,* "I am that I am." Maimonides' vigorous fight against anthropomorphism and his refrain "God's ways and our ways are not the same," indicate his belief that God should not be defined. This seems to be in line with Jewish thought. Mysteries upon which the Torah did not clearly express itself are not of great value to human perfection, declared Gersonides, the philosopher who searched to fathom the stars in heaven and matter on earth. He was one of the most famous astronomers and physicists of his time.

Jehudah Halevi posits God through the mutual relationship with our forefathers. When we do not mistake the outer garb for the inner essence, we see that with the Jewish scholastics the Law played a far greater role in their philosophizing than the conflict between faith and reason that they hoped to solve by logical methods. The truth of the Torah and of the scientific source of knowledge (termed the Active Intellect) are identical if both are properly interpreted. The laws of the Talmud would throw light on those of nature. Their problem centered upon finding an harmonious comprehension of the physical world, grasped through science and interpreted by Plato and Aristotle, versus the spiritual world *within the fence of the Law.* The attempt to interrelate the two, and the effort to keep the spiritual world intact—not at the expense of truth—form the dramatic struggle of Jewish scholasticism. Their impulse to philosophize in the vein of contemporaries was motivated by the desire to show that the totality of Jewish tradition could not be affected by the growing sciences of the rapidly changing world, and by the supreme wisdom of Aristotle. He should not be brushed aside; his arguments should be carefully weighed with pros and cons and with utmost objectivity. Wherever there is disparity, Aristotle's errors must be brought to light. Great as he was, he had no tradition to lean on. With such aim in view, it is not surprising that our scholastics borrowed from their environment the problems, the form, the technique and even the vocabulary; but underneath this outer surface runs the Jewish stream. Because the historians did not sense it, they failed to see original traits in Jewish scholasticism. The Jewish Encyclopedia does not have a special rubric for Jewish philosophy. It is listed under Arabic-Jewish philosophy.

In the course of its development, Jewish life has appropriated from other cultures what could harmonize with its own, only in so far as it did not infringe upon its personality which has been carefully guarded. The varied reaction to the Septuagint is an apt illustration. As long as Hellenism did not encroach upon the inner being, the translation of the Scriptures into Greek promoted friendly relations and intellectual companionship. The Greek language was studied in the schools, and a knowledge of it even became requisite for admission to membership in the Sanhedrin. But when attempts were made to explain the Jewish Law in the light of Greek ethics, the Septuagint was compared to the making of the golden calf, and the day of the translation was proclaimed a fast-day to mourn the national deterioration.

Preserving the essence is another Jewish fundamental. The fight against Maimonides was not for his enlightened views, but for the fear that his attempt at a synthesis of compatible Jewish and non-Jewish theories might cause some inner transformation. His halakhic works are sufficient testimony that he himself was guarding against it. That the purpose of the *Guide* was to strengthen Jewish existence, could be seen by its vogue and by the full acceptance of the *Mishneh Torah* as an authoritative source.

Even though our scholastics are the only ones who have organized Jewish thought into a system, it seems not to have been within their scope to give a full survey. They wanted mostly to solve perplexities arising from outward contacts. For a proper and complete view, one should dig into the halakhic works of those very philosophers, as well as into those who were not regarded as such because they did not specialize in the subject. In the halakhic works the genuine Jewish thought is not hidden under alien speculation.

Nahmanides, for instance, did not formulate a metaphysical *organon,* yet there is a profound philosophy in his writings. He took as his starting point the facts of Judaism, including even the historical narratives of the Talmud. He digressed from the too-much discussed problem of the relation of religion to reason, and turned his attention to the relation of religion to man. He tried to remove the antithesis between soul and body, and asserted that contempt for the flesh was inconsistent with religion. He upheld the doctrine of Judaism that men should rejoice on days of joy, and weep on days of sorrow. He feared the philosophers because their teachings might lead to a denial of the past and despair of the future. While history has upheld Maimonides against his antagonists, they are in a Jewish perspective nonetheless as important factors as his followers.

On the surface it may appear strange to claim a distinction between medieval Jewish philosophy and the philosophy of Jewishness, when Jewishness is at the very bottom of them both. The scholastic viewpoint, the modes of analysis, the solutions, the concern, were all of Jewish temper and they vibrated with its pulsations. The results, too, could not be far apart. But philosophically the difference is as between the *a priori* and experimental methods. The scholastics' approach is not from Jewishness to philosophy, but vice versa. The point of departure was not Jewishness as a subject unfolding itself of its own, but with alien thought superimposed upon it, one measured vis-a-vis the other. Perforce, the problems of the outside world had to be given first rank, since theirs was an answer to a challenge. Argumentations and speculations were a necessity, and so was the search in reason for the depths of the Jewish being. The philosophy of Jewishness is the reflection of that very being flowing from its own source, fearing no challenge, and growing a natural growth. It is the translation of its emotional self in terms of thought and conduct, and an intellectual crystalization of the deep-rooted emotional beliefs. It is a homogeneous philosophy. Reason is within its orbit, inherent in it, but not an outside measure versus which it should be evaluated.

Jewish scholastics, by the very act of seeking fortification through reason, have lent some supremacy to it. The medieval philosopher Gersonides (1288-1344) states and re-states that if the Torah did not coincide with reason, he would not feel obligated to accept it. But in the same breath he affirms that the Torah and reason could not possibly contradict each other. Maimonides (1136-1204) starts his *Guide for the Perplexed* with justifying our Laws in the eyes of reason, so as to give them double strength and a triple one, by paralleling our metaphysics,

on which the Laws are based, with that of Aristotle and his interpreter Ibn Sina. His *Yad ha-Hazaqah* which preceded the *Guide*
and the *Ani Ma'amin* (Thirteenth Articles of Faith) which crowned
it, were the cement which kept his philosophical edifice grounded
on the Jewish base. The *Ani Ma'amin* replaces outward verification
with inner strength drawn from the Jewish impetus. It is a kind
of declaration of Jewish independence from philosophies not its
own. In this declaration, the Jewish beliefs remain his beliefs,
whether or not they are fortified by the world view of his time,
for which he had a philosophical respect. Jehudah Halevi, the
supreme exponent of a pure philosophy of Jewishness, was rid of
all perplexities by tracing the course of the Jewish stream through
the stream itself. He took the self-evidence of Jewish existence
as the axiom out of which to derive further thinking. The assumption of a premise is legitimate with philosophers. To Halevi the
Law is the category by which the Jewish mind functions; hence
reason shaped by the Law could not be its cause.

These points of departure lead to one more differentiation, that
between reasoned-out faith and immediate experience. Faith, in
answering a challenge needs substantiation, demonstration and verification by what is outside of itself. Experience is ultimate; it
requires no further explanation. It is what it is. Jehudah Halevi,
who protested against scholasticism, begins his philosophy with
what he regards as irrefutable, the ultimate experience of the
Jewish people "testified to by the whole race, by the prophets, and
by the very presence of God in their midst." The scholastics have,
of course, not disregarded that profound *vicarious* experience, but
in their philosophizing it becomes a conclusion rather than a
premise. Maimonides does not start, but ends with, the *Ani
Ma'amin* (the Thirteen Articles of Faith).

Jewish philosophizing did not cease with the last scholastic,
around the 15th century, as is usually believed. There has been
a continuity of thought and similarity of nature. The change
was in method. The medieval conclusion has been reverted into
a premise out of which philosophical reflections were unfolded,
without being cast into a fixed mold. For the Germans, a system
was an emblem of philosophy. Schopenhauer received less recognition because his writings were unimpeded by technicalities. But
William James and John Dewey did not want to fence their
thoughts within a system. Would anyone deny that Albert
Schweitzer is a philosopher because his thoughts are not tech-

nically formulated? The "Great Leaders" in these two volumes could also be regarded as faithful exponents of Jewish philosophy, even if we excluded the *Gaon* of Vilna, the *Ba'al Shem Tov*, Israel Salanter, the modern exponent of our ancient ethics, Samson Raphael Hirsch, the vigorous adversary of Geiger's[50] imitative foreign doctrines, or Rabbi Isaac Reines, who developed a system of logic for the study of the Talmud.

If we were to construe out of their various writings a philosophy of Jewishness, it would consist in the manner of relationship with God which in turn hallows the network of all other relations: that with the Law, nature, forefathers, continuous past and infinite future. The study and interpretation of the Law would strengthen this kinship. The *She'elot u-teshuvot* (rabbinical Responsa) with the authors' painstaking efforts, even where encumbered with too much *pilpul* (casuistry), reflect perhaps the most fundamental philosophical principle without which Jewish life could not have sustained itself. It is the belief in the potential elasticity of the laws' inner growth, in as natural a manner as flowers grow from the seed. These authorities search in the seed itself for the constant and the variable. Through minute study of the roots from a historical, psychological, logical and even casuistic angle, they hope to discover the science of that growth: their criterion of growth is neither utilitarian nor pragmatic, even though the laws are pragmatic in themselves. To any outward transformation their challenge would be, at what point do you start and where would you stop? How would the line be drawn between essential and superficial if wholeness is at the basis of Jewish life? Their own test is through that very basis: would an elaboration or re-interpretation of a law affect the integralness of the tradition from which it has emanated? Hillel and Shammai of old did not depend solely on their logical deductions. They wanted a seal of approval from the past, a *bat kol min ha-shamayim*—a voice from Heaven. The *Gaon* of Vilna perused each law in its minutest details before deciding on the slightest innovation.

The philosophy of Jewishness may be no more than a restatement of Jewish experiences. But these are the contents of its philosophy, so closely knit that words, thoughts, actions, prayers, beliefs, commandments, form one continuous process wherein per-

---

[50]Abraham Geiger 1810-1874, among the foremost Reform rabbis in Germany.

sonal and vicarious experiences could hardly be distinguished from one another. If anyone in our courtyard, Hassid, Mitnagged, Sephardi, Yemenite, scholar, carpenter, water-carrier, were asked about his profoundest experience, his reply was bound to be the *Shema Yisrael.* The characters in this volume would, I think, have given the same answer. The *Shema* to the Jew is not just words or even ideas, but an evoking of a vicariously living experience on which he leans in moments of intensity, serenity, joy or distress, as if his own life had started with it, jointly with those who share it with him.

What may have been lost sight of in the daily repetitions of the *Shema* is the specific emphasis on "Hear, Israel" which is as significant as what follows. It indicates an intimate relation between Israel and God, and also throws light on the nature of the kinship. The love *"with all thy heart and all thy soul and all thy might"* has to be expressed in the teaching of His words to the children and the children's children. Israel, God, His laws, and continuity become the unified concept out of which Jewishness unfolds itself. Even the children in our courtyard grasped that such love must be understood in terms of fulfillment.

The vicarious experience of the *Shema* has translated itself as it were a sensuous one: emotionally poured into the channel of prayer, and intellectually as a basis of a philosophical structure. It has cemented prayer and philosophy into one. Philosophy has been vested thereby with an emotional content which has drawn it closer to Jewish reality. On the surface it may appear as a theological dogma, and not a legitimate philosophical premise. Yet the living experience which grew out of this initial stage makes it the reality of the Jewish consciousness, the starting point of its awareness, and the making of the Jewish mind to whom history and tradition have become the category of its thinking. One could no more question the validity of such a starting point for a specifically Jewish philosophy or philosophy of Jewish history, than one would question "situation experience" from which proceed the various empirical philosophies, including those of James and Dewey. A comprehensive view of Jewish philosophy has to take into account the nature of the prayers, which in turn are like a daily expression of it. The festivals, too, are an integral and inseparable expression of the innermost Jewish being. They are the converging system of thought and action, and thus the consummation of Jewish philosophy.

Another primordial category is that of the Chosen People. Misunderstanding of that concept comes from the inept parallel with the Christian scholastic notion of "grace" which is a rather static one. With them, grace is a divine distinction bestowed upon some individuals for the sake of their own salvation. The *atta behartanu* (Thou hast chosen us) has its counterpart in *vekiddashtanu bemitzvotekha* (and hast sanctified us with Thy commandments). Choice and the profound meaning it carries are one dynamic process. Together with the Covenant, they are for the Jewish conscience stronger than Kant's *Categorical Imperative,* because they are reenforced by the joint responsibilty of a people as a whole. That choice, which knits into one God, the love of God, and the translation of that love into action, underlies every move "when thou walkest on the way, when thou liest down and when thou risest up." It is the responsibility flowing from it which inflamed the righteous indignation of the prophets. It is the cornerstone of Jewish history, of its religion, and its thought. It reflects the passion to be a worthy instrument of a purposeful world, and help its growth through the application of the Law. It is not like Schopenhauer's world of "Will and Idea", because it is sanctified through partnership with God. Schopenhauer ends with pessimism and despair. The Jewish world blooms into joy—*sasson ve-simhah.*

"Deutschland ueber Alles" has somewhat increased the modern distaste for the idea of Election, even though the two are far apart: The German "Ueber Alles" has led to world-destruction. Out of the Jewish concept has evolved a will to live a moral life. It is this moral will that made Jewish history not only that of a people, but also that of God and the cosmos. The choice is both the impetus and the guarantee of the moral life. It is a merging of man's moral will with God's Law. "What the *Tzaddik* decrees, the Holy One, blessed be He, fulfills." The moral act consists in making this world one in which good intentions are brought to fruition, and brute forces to serve living ideals. The task Israel has set itself is that of overcoming the rift between the spiritual and the physical order, so that they should not form two irreconcilable entities, that of the spirit and that of the flesh. The life of the spirit is in our very actions, in the prosaic daily affairs; hence the multiplicity of precepts and laws whose function is to lend moral character and beauty. No matter how much our world progresses, it may always find some fruitful ideas in a philosophy which grasps life in its entirety, and makes no artificial abstraction of one phase from another.

To transform the concept of choice into a lifeless "Mission" of generalities, is to alter its very function and to misunderstand the origin and purpose. That choice has meaning only in the historical concreteness it has assumed, and no abstract form could fuse with it.

In this connection I cannot help thinking of Abraham, the *Ger* of our courtyard. I still remember his pithy sayings which reflected his dynamic response to Jewish teaching. To quote at random: "In the midst of the Torah, I am not like a reed shaken by the winds; friendly laws surround me, and they themselves come to life through me ... I am a spiritual messenger, and I bless God *she-natan Torah* (that He gave the Law), and made those who want to accept it a living embodiment of it ... I am not just a passive receptacle when I study the Torah; my whole being becomes a moral will striving to attain the supreme good in it." Nahmanides expressed the same in more intellectual terms when he wrote to his son,[51] "The moment you close the book (i.e., the *shass*), concentrate upon what you drew from that page and put it immediately into practice." Our *Ger* detected ethical points in most complicated Talmudic passages which required keen perception. I see now similarities[52] between his own thoughts, inspired by Jewish sources, and a masterly work on Ethics by Gersonides, entitled *Toaliot Middotiot*. Gersonides, the ardent Aristotelian, searched for moral lessons, not in Aristotle, but in the Biblical narratives. He drew from each narrative a practical guidance for a good life.

That laws should be studied not only by jurists, philosophers, moralists, but by the people as a whole, from the age of five on, is a distinctively Jewish phenomenon. When past and present mingle like this, enriching one another, informing one another, man's short span on earth assumes a profound meaning. Jewish philosophy views each individual act, qua Jewish, under the aspect of eternity, that is, in its relationship with the past which has engendered it, and with the future to which it is to be transmitted. Our *Ger*, in his simplicity, fathomed the spring of Jewishness when he said to himself while passing by the *Bet ha-Midrash* of his small town: "They look serene with their books on the table. There must be a fountain of goodness in those pages."

---

[51]This letter to his son in Spain was addressed from Acre, Palestine.
[52]It would be out of place here to draw parallels. I merely want to put the *Ger*, who so thoroughly absorbed the Jewish spirit, into a Jewish relief.

Indeed serenity, clear consciousness of purpose, wholesomeness —these are the indicatives of the genuine Jewish whole as could be seen by those who live it.

The obvious conclusion of the philosophy of Jewish experience is that only experiences inherently Jewish constitute the basis of Jewish philosophy.

HAYYIM JOSEPH DAVID AZULAI
(1724-1806)

By Elio Toaff

(translated by Mitzi Feuerstein, from the Italian)

HAYYIM JOSEPH DAVID AZULAI (HIDA)

By ELIO TOAFF

The Azulai family, originally of Fez, Morocco, moved to Palestine in 1644 and settled in Hebron, where it achieved great renown, chiefly through the merits of R. Abraham, profound scholar and Kabbalist.

In 1724, in Jerusalem, Hayyim Joseph David Azulai was born to Rabbi Raphael Itzhak Zakharya and to the daughter of Rabbi Joseph Bailer, the famous kabbalist who came to Jerusalem by following R. Yehuda he-Hassid.

HIDA's education was started by the family. He received his early instruction from his father and from his maternal grandfather, who initiated him into cabbalistic studies. His first teacher was Rabbi Jonah Nabon, Talmudist, ritualist and mystic, who died in 1760, in the prime of life. Among his other great teachers was R. Hayim Ben Attar, for whose sake HIDA moved to Jerusalem. But this great man, too, died after only two years.

The genius of Azulai revealed itself early: he had not yet reached his seventeenth birthday, when he had already compiled his first work of research, *E'lem Davar,* containing Talmudic fragments that had escaped the notice of preceding authors. At the age of seventeen, he composed his second treatise, *Shaar Joseph,* which demonstrates his wide and deep knowledge of the Talmud. It remained unpublished until 1757, when, during his sojourn in Leghorn as a greatly revered envoy (*Shaliah*) from Eretz Israel, a local Maecenas, the physician and Maskil, Dr. Michael Pereira de Leon, housed him in his palace and furnished him with the means for publishing his book. In gratitude, HIDA dedicated it to his patron.*

His whole life was dedicated to study and research, from his early years, to his favorite occupation—the interpretation of the Talmud, and Kabbalistic meditation. His tranquil, methodical life was disturbed first in 1753, when financial emergency compelled the rabbis of Hebron to send him to the West as a *Shaliah,* and a second time, in 1772. His first mission lasted five years, and the second one six. In 1753, when he travelled to Europe by way of Egypt, he was twice exposed to the gravest perils. From

---

*Cf. A. Toaff. "Hebrew Studies in Leghorn in the Eighteenth Century"—Livorno, Belforte 1909, p. 19.

Jerusalem he had gone with a caravan toward Hebron, but the inhabitants of Halhul attacked him and only by sheer miracle did he escape a violent death. His woes were not at an end. On his way from Hebron toward Gaza he was overtaken by the villagers of Sumson, terrible, cruel men, whom he describes as "not men, but serpents and scorpions." That danger overcome, he arrived safe and sound in Egypt, whence he proceeded to Europe. At that time such a trip would take from thirty to forty days, depending on the type of boat that was being used and the number of oarsmen. In the case of passengers coming from the Orient, another forty days had to be added for quarantine in a Lazaretto (hospital). However, these difficulties did not faze HIDA, who was barely 29 years old and desirous of putting to best advantage the time spent in his mission. Even though he felt reluctant to foresake the serene life of study, he was attracted by these journeys, which, besides bringing relief to the city and to the students of Hebron, all in dire circumstances, gave him the opportunity of visiting many lands where famous and prosperous Hebrew communities existed; where most eminent teachers, whose fame had reached even distant Palestine, lived; and where he, by visiting and consulting libraries rich in rare volumes and manuscripts, and by coming in contact with the most renowned personalities of the Western Hebrew literary world, was able to increase his culture and to widen his knowledge.

The reading of his most interesting book *Ma'agal Tov* which is a diary of his journeys, gives us a very clear idea of his personality and activities and furnishes us with precious information about Europe's contemporary luminaries; about the leading Hebrew communities and also about the libraries, museums, and public and private collections of manuscripts, rare Hebrew and non-Hebrew works, which to him were of equal importance. HIDA was not a man restricted to the world of Hebrew studies and unmoved by the progress which was ever changing the world about him. He shows interest in the museums of Paris as well as in the marvels of Venice and Amsterdam. His book is perhaps the most important document on the life of the Hebrew communities of Egypt, Italy, Germany, Holland, England, France, Turkey and Tunis of the 17th Century and a precious and lively chronicle of facts, events, and the peculiarities of these people whom he depicts in faithful detail in a pleasant narrative style— small workaday facts, all the manners and customs of that time.

He describes everything—he is impressed by everything: by the strange and rare animals which he saw at the Zoological Garden in Paris; by the carriages drawn by six horses traversing the main bridge which crossed the Seine, and by the prostitutes who, day and night, stationed themselves under it; by the legends at the basis of popular beliefs; by the great and small persons with whom he had dealings. Thus he relates that when, with some non-Jewish friends, he visited the Palace of Versailles, the King of France, coming out of his apartments with a large retinue, and noticing him in the hall, turned to a nobleman in the cortege and said, "From which country is this man an ambassador?" In Venice, when he had to go to the Ducal Palace to obtain permission to send to Hebron the amount he had collected, he was unlucky enough to bump into one of the governors, a notorious anti-Semite, who, on seeing him, said, "I consider this Oriental as one of those who killed Jesus." Nevertheless, permission was granted to export the collected monies. In his eagerness to see and to learn everything, he did not disdain visits to textile factories, paper mills, printing shops; also to cemeteries where his interest was aroused by ancient gravestones. But what attracted his attention the most, was the life of the various Hebrew groups. HIDA's views of the Italian, Dutch, German and other Hebrew communities make it possible to comprehend their solidity and power, as well as their economic and cultural level. One phrase, one brief allusion is sufficient to understand a community's circumstances. Typical is his description of Monte S. Savino, where the reception to the envoy from Eretz Israel was not so enthusiastic as it had been, for instance, in Ancona, or in France, at Avignon or Carpantras. In Leghorn the Massari of that community, upon learning that he was quarantined in the Lazaretto, brought him three baskets full of prepared food, sweets, fruit and wine. HIDA relates that on arriving toward evening in Monte S. Savino, he did not find a single soul to take care of him; upon leaving the *Bet ha-Knesset* (local synagogue), he was taken to an empty house with open windows, although it was mid-winter and the cold intense. He asked of the persons accompanying him, "Who is the *Parnas* here?" One of them answered, "I am!" "What a pity for the generation that has you for a *Parnas!*" he exclaimed.

This brief episode shows his ready wit. He perceived then already that this community was on the road to disintegration. Fifty years later, it was no more: "Of its ancient glories nothing

but an old abandoned cemetery remained, whereas in Florence
the ancient *Aron-Ha-Kodesh* of carved wood is exhibited to many
tourists as a relic of art of that ancient community."

In 1758, upon returning from his first European mission,
HIDA moved to Jerusalem, where he held the position of third
judge in the *Bet Din* of the Sephardic rabbinate. He was also
a member of the most renowned Kabbalistic circles, and was
asked to join the group called *Ahavat Shalom* (Love of Peace),
presided over by the eminent Rabbi Shalom Shar'abi, the celebrated
Ra-Sha-Sh. His fame spread rapidly and he was made one of the
seven governors of the Holy City, whose many decrees, regulating
its public life, bear his signature.

In 1764 he went on a mission to Egypt and there he was
appointed Chief Rabbi of Cairo. He had not sought such a post;
his great passion was study, research, not the authority that he
would gain from a rabbinic position. Already in 1761 the community of Amsterdam had offered him the Chief Rabbinate. But
he refused it, although he realized its importance spiritually, socially, and financially, as the most famous of all the Sephardic
communities. Only strong pressure made him accept the Chief
Rabbinate of Cairo, but his thoughts turned very often to his
beloved Hebron, and after only five years he left that post to
return home.

But even there he could remain only a short time. In 1772,
because of war between Russia and Turkey, the usual help from
the countries in the Diaspora did not come, and the city suffered
dire poverty. Her leaders, anxious about the future which loomed
ever darker, urged upon Rov HIDA a new mission to Europe,
which, due to the war and the revolution of Ali Bey, spelt a
voyage, whether by land or sea, fraught with danger.

Azulai traveled to Alexandria and from there embarked for
Tunis, the first stop of his trip. The political situation having
become graver, he was prevented from continuing his mission
to the various Hebrew centers of Europe, and much against his
will he had to sojourn in Tunis for fully eight months. That
community was certainly not the ideal place for a scholar. The
population was uneducated and very superstitious. In order to
be left in peace, he had to hide the fact that he was a Kabbalist
and a writer of works on such subjects. Had it been known who
he actually was, his life would have become unbearable because
of endless requests for interpretations which he was not willing

to offer, except to persons able to understand their true value. In Tunis at that time, Kabbalah was not considered a science—esoteric, traditional, serious—which required study and meditation, but rather something magical, which initiated its practitioners into sorcery and withcraft, giving them powers denied to all others. During his stay in that city, he was on guard not to reveal doctrines dealing with the various names of the Divinity, *Segulot,* and similar subjects, nor would he narrate *Agadot* that were not within the people's grasp.

In Tunis he received the sad report of the passing of his wife Rachel. He suffered great grief, but hid the news of the death and his feelings, to avoid being compelled by the Tunisians to remarry; for to them it was inconceivable and sinful for a sage to remain without a mate. In his own words: "There would not have been valid reasons to satisfy them; they would certainly have gone so far as to force me by order of the king himself." So he wept in secret over the loss of the sweet companion of his life, the virtuous mother of his sons.

Eventually, he left for Leghorn, the city so dear to him; here he remained for three months and proceeded on to France and Holland. Having completed his mission for Hebron, in 1778 he returned to Leghorn, where he established himself permanently.

Another great Leghorn philanthropist, Eliezer Hai Shealtiel Recanati, desirous of making it possible for HIDA to teach and study all he wanted and to write his books in peace, founded for him a *yeshivah* which before long became famous not only in Italy, but in all the countries of the Mediterranean basin.

HIDA never went out of his house, which was only a short distance from the magnificent Leghorn synagogue, nor would he accept the Chief Rabbinate of that community. Only once a year, attired in white vestments, did he go to preach his sermon at that sanctuary, on *Shabbat Shuvah* (the Sabbath of Penitence). Two rows of people—Jews and non-Jews—flanked his passage from the door of the house to the synagogue.

Many tales were circulated about him. Even today one can hear some of them repeated by the Leghorn Jews, especially when, on the day of his *Yahrzeit,* they convene at the synagogue to recite prayers in his memory. They say that an angel used to come down from heaven to teach him the secrets and interpretations of the Torah. Many wonders and miracles are attributed to him. HIDA remained in Leghorn until his death, which occurred on the night of *Shabbat Zakhor,* the 11th of Adar 5566-1806. Little by little, he has become a legendary figure. His second wife was Rachel of Pisa. Of his four children, Abraham, a *Shaliah,* died in Jerusalem, in 1779, Raphael was Rov in Ancona. His son Moshe wrote *Zikhron Mosheh* and *Lehem min ha-Shamayim.* Sarah married Rov Samuel Sanguinetti, also a *Shaliah.*

The news of his passing brought deep sorrow to the Jewries of Europe and Eretz Yisrael. The greatest masters of that period wrote about him, and two Italian poets, Rabbi Isaiah Norzi and Rabbi Joseph Eliezer Morpurgo, honored his memory with elegies which had a very wide distribution.

The magnificent epigraph on his tombstone was written by his affectionate disciple, Rabbi Eliezer Ha-Cohen. On the days of penitence, at the time of the new moon, and on every anniversary, the tomb of Rav Azulai is the goal of a devoted pilgrimage of people who go there to pray and to recite psalms.

II.

The literary work of Azulai plays an exceptionally important part in the history of Hebrew literature. He was not a scholar given to only one specialized branch of learning—his genius embraces the entire Hebrew lore. He did not limit himself to the Kabbalah or to Biblical or Talmudical interpretation, or to any special branch of Hebrew knowledge. Simultaneously, he dedicated himself to Midrashic, to Halakhic, as well as to ritualistic science, to Kabbalah, to history, and to bibliography; in every discipline he displayed deep erudition, painstaking effort and thoroughness of method. He mastered the enormous spiritual, philosophical and religious heritage of Judaism.

His contribution to Hebrew literature is immense. Starting at the age of seventeen, he continued his literary labors, according to the catalogue prepared by Hakham Eliakim Carmeli in his introduction to *Shem Ha-Gedolim* (Vilna-Edition 1854), well into his 71st year. The number of his publications, including sermons and some minor works, is reported to total about one hundred.

Besides rendering invaluable help in the interpretation of Talmudic texts, HIDA, through discovering new things in the works of little known ancient masters, or of others whose writings had remained in manuscript, saved from oblivion and destruction, pages from little known and unedited writers. To them he brought fame as he added to the knowledge of future generations of scholars. His work on the Talmudic tractate *Horayot,* which he entitled *Shaar Joseph,* is actually the fruit of his research and of his great experience in deciphering and interpreting ancient manuscripts. These two books alone, written at an early age, would have been enough to assure him fame as an eminent Talmudist.

His method and approach are utterly different from the "pilpul," then so widely practiced in central and eastern Europe. His style is traditional Sephardic, which had its most qualified exponents in Eretz Israel and which aimed at a clear and precise interpretation of the law (*Halakhah*). His major work on this subject is his *Birke Joseph,* published in Leghorn in 1774. It met with enormous success in all the Sephardic and Ashkenazic Jewish communities; it gives to each paragraph of the *Shulkhan Arukh* the relevant laws, pointing out their significance with unique depth and competence.

His travels greatly facilitated his studies. Knowing many languages, intelligent, young and full of enthusiasm, he undertook long and dangerous trips to visit libraries and collections of manuscripts; whenever he found something especially interesting, he managed to buy or copy it. Thus his studies multiplied in every branch of Jewish learning; he penetrated to sources which others could only partially approach. As Bible commentator, he is renowned for having written three works on the Torah and several treatises on the other books of the *Tanakh.* His method always remains the same: he examines ancient authors for original opinions, new interpretations, unusual teachings, then elaborates them and reports them in his works. In the comments of HIDA we discover in high splendor, the arguments on Biblical questions of R. Isaiah Di Trani or of Rabbenu Hananel bar Shemuel, together with the interpretations of an unknown scholar, which Azulai unearthed from ancient, half-destroyed manuscript notes.

His evaluation and salvaging of these ancient works deserve the deepest gratitude of all students because, but for his self-denial and deep sense of responsibility, a tremendous quantity of important and profound material from scholars of every century and country, experts in all fields of learning, might have remained unknown and irretrievably lost!

He made very copious notes, writing down everything he found so that he might not forget it. Eventually, he published that magnificent and fundamental pioneering work in Hebrew bibliography:

Shem Ha-Gedolim. This book is divided into two parts. The first dedicated to the authors and the second to their works, provide biographical and bibliographical knowledge of an extraordinary number of scholars, from the period of the Geonim up to HIDA's own; many of them, but for his book, would surely have been condemned to oblivion.

This work is arranged in alphabetical order. Under the name of an author in the first part of this volume one can find the complete list of his books, or, knowing the title of his work, one can easily find its author by looking into the second part. No one before him had ever attempted to accomplish this, hence Rav Azulai is rightfully considered the father of Hebrew bibliography.

He mentions more than one thousand three hundred authors, and the number of their works (which he catalogues with marvelous precision and briefly describes) is above two thousand two hundred. His comments on the various authors, whilst of necessity brief, yet are amazingly eloquent and concise. They have been the fountain for all students who, after the publication of the book, dedicated themselves to the study of Hebrew knowledge. Hence the extremely wide circulation which the book enjoyed in all the countries of the world.

During his travels and his stay in various communities he occupied himself with widely divergent problems: how to make peace between rival families and how to bring harmony into litigating communities. He adjudicated public and private cases, and above all, he responded to ritual questions which from time to time were addressed to him by various rabbis. He decided to edit and publish these responsa (*Hayyim Shaal*—Leghorn 1789) because they referred to questions so practical that they repeatedly arose in the life of various countries. Rav Azulai would describe, after a brief statement of the traditional responsum, the situation in which he found himself when he had to intervene to give his opinion: "About this question I wrote," he says, for example, "when I was a young man in Venice in 1754 during my mission on behalf of Hebron and, therefore, did not have at my disposal the necessary books." (Hayyim Sheal, Part I, C 18). These notations were not intended for the reader; they were personal notes to remind him of particular situations; they were retained in the publication because they are truly interesting.

In the community of Rome they were discussing, for example, whether in the *Kedushah* they should read *Nakdishakh ve-na 'aritzakh* or *Nakdishkha ve-na 'aritzkha*; in the dispute between those who defended the traditional pronunciation and those who insisted upon the exact grammatical form, his responsum held that they should continue the traditional usage in the recitation, while at the same time teaching the school children the correct grammatical form (cfr. Joseph Omez: Paragr. 10).

In 1796 when he had already definitely established himself in Leghorn, he read in a French journal, to his utmost indignation, a false report claiming that the Italian rabbis convened in Florence at a solemn assembly for the purpose of reforming the Jewish religion; that they had decided to abolish a number of prohibitions and to change completely the traditional codes. All the Italian rabbis rose up against this falsehood and even published a book to defend themselves against this accusation and to deny most vehemently this calumny (Leghorn 1796). HIDA was not fully satisfied with the protest by the Italian rabbis and he appointed himself as their defender by calling together the most famous emissaries from Eretz Israel in Italy, such as Haim Baruch Sasportas, Rabbi Ephraim Nabon and Rabbi Jehuda Leon—the latter already established in Rome as rabbi—solemnly to proclaim with all their universally recognized authority that the report was without foundation: "It is impossible for such a thing to happen in Italy."

The work which was published after his death and which is the principal source of information regarding our great Sage, his travels, his impressions of people and things that he saw in the countries he visited, is *Ma 'agal Tov*. In this volume, an inexhaustible fountain of interesting accounts, he recalls opinions he heard from illustrious men, the customs and practices of the various communities; he describes modest and imposing synagogues of small and large communities, their cantors, directors, and all the things he observed, whether beautiful or ugly, pleasant or unpleasant.

The first edition of *Ma 'agal Tov* saw the light of day only in 1934 in Jerusalem, through the efforts of the editor, Professor Aron Freimann, of blessed memory.

To describe fully all his works would truly be an arduous task, and it would take volumes to do justice to the personality, and to the qualities of Rov Azulai as writer and scientist!

These notes are meant only to whet the appetite of the student to learn more about the life and works of this great man, probably the last and most qualified representative of the Sephardic world and Sephardic Jewish learning.

They are a dutiful and modest tribute to HIDA's memory on the occasion of the 150th anniversary of his death.

NATHAN HACOHEN ADLER
(1741-1800)

By Josef Unna

NATHAN HACOHEN ADLER[1]

By Josef Unna

It is with good reason that in many places in our religious literature the town of Frankfurt a.M. is called *"Ir ve-Em be-Yisrael"* (A Mother City in Israel). As Ernst Simon points out,[2] the first Hebrew source to mention Jews in that city is Eliezer Ben Nathan's *"Harab'n"* (Mayence, at about the middle of the 12th century). In that book the town is mentioned twice: once, in connection with the meticulousness with which her Jews, who attended the fair of the Gentiles, observed the laws of the Torah. From the seventy-ninth chapter it appears that in the Jewish community of Frankfurt, owing to the wealth of its *Baale Battim* (prominent members), there was no need of a charitable institution. On the contrary, poor people from far away benefited from their generosity. As early as in the period preceding that of the author of *"Yoseph Ometz"* (at the beginning of the 17th century), it was resolved that a certain portion of their contributions was to be sent to the Jews of the Holy Land.[2a] From that time, the Frankfurt Jewish Community was characterized by a combination of Torah-learning and high worldly standing. At all times scholars, famous for their Torah learning, could be found among the *Baale Battim* who studied the Talmud in the Bet Hamidrash in the Jewish quarter.[3]

This explains why, when a new rabbi had to be chosen, great efforts were made to entrust the office to the very best men. Candidates were considered only if they belonged to the leaders of their generations. The community of Frankfort was never orphaned, even if the place of the rabbi became vacant. That is why its

---

[1]As sources were used:
  Rabbi B. H. Auerbach: Mishnat Rabbi Nathan, Frankfurt a/M, 1862.
  Rabbi M. Horovitz: Frankfurter Rabbinen, Vols. I-IV, Frankfurt a/M, 1882/5.
  Rabbi A. I. Schwartz: Derekh ha-Nesher, Torat Emet, Galanta 5688.
  Rabbi Moses Sofer: Drashot Hatam Sofer, ed. I. N. Stern, Sereth, 5689.
  Die Inschriften des alten Friedhofs der Israelitischen Gemeinde zu Frankfurt a/M. with an introduction by Rabbi M. Horovitz, Frankfurt a/M, 1901 ("Inschriften").
  Simon Unna: Gedenkbuch der Frankfurter Juden (based on notes of the Burial Society), first Volume 1624-1680, Frankfurt a/M, 1914; do. years 1680-1828 in Hebrew MS form.
[2]"Knesset," published by Mossad Bialik, Vol. VIII, pp. 132-144.
[2a]See the chapter on half-a-Shekel and Purim money.
[3]We find more than one proof of this in the "Frankfurter Rabbinen."

167

leaders were in no hurry to choose a new one. There were many men among its members who could, in the meantime, fill the functions of a rabbi. They were well qualified to deliver halakhic decisions and to guide the youth, the students of Yeshivot. In the time of Rabbi Adler this happened twice: after the death of R. Jacob Joshua Falk, the author of *"Pne Yehoshua"* (1755), and also after the death of R. Abraham Lissa (1769)[4]. An excellent description of the life in the Jewish quarter, after R. Abraham Lissa's death, may be found in the fourth volume of M. Horovitz's book, *"Die Frankfurter Rabbinen"*. It deals with the nomination of R. Nathan Mass as a substitute for the Rabbi and Head of Yeshivah[5].

To their spiritual and economic achievements, we may add the political weight of the Jews of Frankfort. This, too, contributed to the consolidation of their position. It hardly ever happened that they were driven out of Frankfort for a longer period. From the year 1580 onwards, the Jews, at an average, constituted ten per cent of the total population.[6] All these factors contributed to their self-assurance. It explains the intransigent attitude of their wealthy members towards their leaders. But the Jews of Frankfort asserted their opinions also against the government and insisted on their age-old rights and privileges. The rabbis of the community, to whose decision important questions were submitted from all over the world, too, announced their opinions firmly; nor did they yield to outside opposition, if they thought their view was based on the precepts of the Torah, though it brought them into sharp conflict with scholars all over Europe. Two characteristic examples of this spirit may be given here, taken from the period preceding the generation of R. Nathan: the long-drawn rivalry between the old-established Frankfort families of Kulp and Kann regarding the leadership of the community,[7] into which the whole Jewish quarter

---

[4]As to biographical notes on him and his works, cf. L. Lewin: Geschichte der Juden in Lissa (Pinne 1901), p. 185 ff.

In the years 1899/1900 his comments on the Masekhta "Megillah" appeared in the monthly *"Torah mi-Zion,"* Jerusalem.

[5]He was the author of the books *"Binyan Shlomo"* on the Tractates Sanhedrin and Avoda Zarah, based on his lectures as Rosh Yeshivah in his native town. (Offenbach 1784-96).

[6]Dr. Josef Unna: Statistik der Frankfurter Juden bis zum Jahre 1866. Frankfurt a/M, 1931, p. 10.

[7]Kracauer, I.: Die Kulp-Kannschen Wirren (Archiv fuer Frankfurter Geschichte und Kunst, 3. Folge, Vol. X).

was drawn, and as *"Get of Cleve"* which aroused rabbinical circles all over Europe.[8]

The Adler family, of priestly stock, was one of the oldest ones of Frankfort, which combined Torah-learning and social standing. R. Nathan speaks of himself as the descendant of R. Shimeon hadarshan, the author of *"Yalkut Shimeoni,"* who lived in Frankfort about 850 years ago. The family, for centuries before Nathan's birth one of the most influential ones,[9] adopted the name of Adler in the year 1616, during the time when the Jews of Frankfort returned after their expulsion during the Vinzenz Fettmilch riots. On that occasion, according to the family tradition, the head of that priestly family carried the flag of the town, which had an eagle ("Adler" in German) as its symbol. It is not clear whether this honor was bestowed on him because he was a Cohen who, according to the Torah, must be specially honored, or because he was one of the "Gabbaim."[10]

Nathan Hacohen Adler was born on the 10th of Tevet 5502 (17.12.1741) as the son of R. Shimeon Hacohen. That is his father's name as we find it mentioned in all the documents,[11] whereas he himself signed sometimes "Nathan ben *Yacov* Shimeon.[12] His mother was Tzerla, the daughter of R. Shemuel Windmuehl. She is mentioned in the "Gedenkbuch" as "a distinguished woman and venerable matron." She died about two years after the death of Nathan.[13] In addition to Nathan, Shimeon Adler had three sons and three daughters.[14]

When still a child, Nathan distinguished himself in his studies, by his piety and the qualities of his character. Many stories about him were told and handed down in the Jewish quarter of his native town, which was proud of her famous son. One of those stories runs like this: At the age of six, he was already well versed in the prescriptions relating to sacrifices. One of the men standing near

---

[8]Simon Kopenhagen: *Sefer Or Hayashar,* Amsterdam 1769, and Lipschitz, I.: *Sefer Or Israel,* Cleve 1770.

[9]"The Adler Family" by M. N. Adler (Reprint from "Jewish Chronical").

[10]Sefer *"Yosef Ometz"* of R. Yuspah Hahn, para. 709; he, too, was among the first who returned.

[11]See "Memorbuch of the Jewish Community of Frankfort" and "Inschriften": End of introduction.

[12]For instance "Responsa of Hatam Sofer, Yoreh Deah, 241, and in several letters which are printed in the Sefer *"Torat Emet."*

[13]See "Memorbuch of the Jewish Community of Frankfort."

[14]I owe this information to the courtesy of Dr. Ettlinger of Nahariya, who possesses a rich collection of documents on the Jews of Frankfort.

him in the synagogue saw him recite by heart with great fervor the chapter of *"Ezehu Mekoman."* Surprised, he said that he did not believe that such a small boy understood what he was saying. He asked him a question about the rules regarding sacrifices, and the little boy gave at once a clear and correct answer. Nathan Adler had a special predilection for the study of sacrifices and temple rites, for he cherished the hope that he would be privileged to serve as a priest in the Temple, if it were rebuilt in his lifetime. (In our days, too, the author of "Hafetz Hayyim" devoted himself to the study of the laws pertaining to priesthood and taught them to the Cohanim amongst his pupils). Nathan's great piety in his early youth is recorded in this story: When R. Hayyim Yosef David Azulai, on a visit to Frankfort, observed the child's intensive study beyond midnight, and his character, he said of him, "This is a man of God." Nathan Adler throughout his life adhered to this rule: He would never put down a word of Torah on a sheet of paper on which something secular had been written. He feared that if that sheet were eventually thrown away, it might lead to the desecration of the holy word.

From his earliest childhood, he received instruction from the great Talmud scholars of his native town, principally from the Gaon Rabbi Jacob Yoshua Falk, the author of *"Pne Yehoshua"*; from Rabbi Moshe Rapp, and Rabbi David Tebele Hacohen Schiff. Falk was Rabbi and Head of the Bet Din (Rabbinical Court) during Nathan's childhood. His thirst for knowledge and his brilliant mind enabled him to attend the daily *Shiurim* (courses) of that great scholar, who, in turn, enjoyed the thought that a young child of his community was capable of following the intricate discussions of the best of his students in his illustrious *yeshivah.* He was certain that "Nathan would become outstanding in piety and knowledge and his fame would reach distant countries."

R. Moshe Rapp, his second teacher, a native of Frankfort, served as the Head of the Bet Din after Rabbi Falk had left Frankfort in the wake of the twofold quarrel which raged in the Jewish community and split it into two camps: the one between the Kulp and Kann families, and the controversy touching the Gaon R. Jonatan Eibeschuetz. R. Moshe was known to have been the Gaon's friend. He took his side in the battle of the books about the amulets[14a] and was one of his chief supporters—whilst

---

[14a]See the chapter in "Jewish Leaders."

Rabbi Falk belonged to the opposite faction. It is probably for that reason that little is known about any public activity on the part of R. Moshe Rapp during the period when R. Jacob Yoshua functioned as Head of the Bet Din at Frankfort. In the struggle within the Jewish community R. Moshe sided with the opponents of the latter. For three years between the death of R. Jacob Falk and the election of his successor (1756-1759), R. Moshe was recognized by all the members of the community, without party distinction, as substitute rabbi and head of the Bet Din; ten eminent scholars served with him.[15] The "Memorbuch" of the community of Frankfort praises him as "the aged judge, who toiled most of his life with the holy Torah and taught many pupils."[16]

The most outstanding of R. Nathan's teachers was R. David Tebele Hacohen Schiff, who later became Rabbi of London. His sister's grandson published the book *"L'shon Hazahav"* (in two parts) from Schiff's manuscripts, and in the introduction proudly dwells on the close relationship between master and pupil.

We must not fail to mention another important personality among Frankfort's Jewry: the "saintly Gaon R. Meshullam Zalman," as he was called by his friends and followers. He was not a native of that town but "he dwelt there for forty years and pitched there his tent of the Torah," as the "Memorbuch" says of him. He was praised as "a Tzaddik who fasted frequently and excelled by the emphasis he laid on the aesthetic aspect in the fulfillment of the Mitzvot." We find all these qualities again in R. Nathan, who became his pupil and, later, his friend. R. Meshullam Zalman died in 1790.[17] One of the few T'shuvot (Responsa) from the pen of R. Nathan which are known to us, is addressed to him.[18]

R. Nathan drank the words of his teachers thirstily and was "like a cistern which does not lose a drop." Conscious of this quality, he never wrote down new interpretations (*Hiddushim,* novellae) which he heard from his teachers, nor his own. He contented himself with short annotations in his books, saying that it was only in order that the Torah may not be forgotten by the people that our sages allowed to write down our oral tradition.[19]

[15]"Frankfurter Rabbinen."
[16]"Frankfurter Rabbinen" III, pp. 88-89, and in a similar vein the inscription on his tombstone "Gaon and Rosh Bet Din" ("Inschriften" No. 3094).
[17]"Frankfurter Rabbinen" IV, p. 93 and "Inschriften," No. 5855. R. Meshullam died on the 5th of Sh'vat, 5551.
[18]Sefer "Torat Emet," p. 79.
[19]Sefer Sh'mot, 34, 27—Tractate Gittin, p. 60 b.

This explains why so little has been preserved from his pen. Most of his teaching has come down to us through his disciples, who at every opportunity mention him and his teaching, with unusual love and admiration. The greatest of them, the "Hatam Sofer," mentions R. Nathan's *Minhagim* (customs) and his teachings on innumerable occasions.[20] Rabbi B. H. Auerbach was the first to attempt a systematical publication of Rabbi Adler's teachings.[21] About fifty years after his death, Rabbi Auerbach, at Frankfort received the Mishnah volume which R. Nathan had used all his life and in which he had jotted down new interpretations in a unique way: by points on some words or allusions to some other passages in the Talmud. Auerbach undertook the task to decipher those allusions, but he published only the first part of his "Annotations" on "Zeraim" (*"Mishnat Rabbi Nathan"*—Frankfurt, 1862). How admirably Rabbi Auerbach had succeeded in reproducing the master's words was shown by Horovitz, who drew attention to the fact that some of the commentaries in the "Mishnah of R. Nathan" had already been published in *"L'shon Hazahav"*[22] by R. David T. Schiff. That book was very rare even at the time of R. Auerbach, and he did not have it before him when deciphering, with such insight, R. Nathan's annotations. This shows that not all the comments in the Mishnah of R. Nathan were his own. He evidently noted down also what he had heard from his teacher, R. Schiff. The other volumes of that Mishnah came into the possession of the son of his most outstanding pupil, the author of *Ktav Sofer*. In one of his responsa (*Orah Hayyim*, No. 48), the latter tells us how great his joy was when, on a visit to Frankfort, he received the Mishnah volumes of his father's teacher as a present. Only fifty years ago those volumes were still in the possession of the *Hatam Sofer's* grandsons; unfortunately, nobody knows where they are today.

R. Nathan wrote his annotations in the form of hints also in his copies of the Talmud and in other books he used.

From his disciple, the *Hatam Sofer,* we know that in all his studies he based the oral tradition on the Mishnah. From the

---

[20]Remarks of "Shaar Yoseph" on the Drashot of the "Hatam Sofer", Part II, p. 371.

[21]Biographical notes on him by R. Moses Auerbach in the volume "Rabbi Benjamin Hirsch," Jerusalem 1948, pp. 63-66.

[22]This book, in two parts, comprises commentaries by R. David T. Schiff on several tractates, responsa, and commentaries on Talmud and Poskim, arranged according to the weekly Torah portions, as well as a commentary on the six books of the Mishnah (London 1823).

second volume of *"L'shon Hazahav"* it appears that he had taken over this system from this great teacher. The *Hatam Sofer* also reports that R. Nathan taught him many Halakhot in this way on their journey from Frankfort to Boskowitz. Taking a Mishnah as his starting point, he would expound to his pupils the teachings of our sages, then go on the first Poskim (Decisors), the RIF, the RAMBAM and eventually the Shulhan Arukh, all of which he knew by heart, leading up to the later authorities who had dealt with the question.

R. Nathan's excellent memory is also mentioned by R. Auerbach in his preface to the *"Mishnat Rabbi Nathan."* There he tells a story he had heard from his father: once R. Nathan examined some of his young relatives on a subject he had studied during that week. While speaking, the pupil observed that R. Nathan sat with his eyes closed, and he wanted to find out whether he was really listening to him. He omitted one word of the "Tosaphot"; whereupon R. Nathan interrupted him at once and drew his attention to that omission, for he was just as thoroughly versed in the commentators as in the texts themselves.

He was not yet twenty years old when he already enjoyed the reputation of being outstanding in Torah learning and piety. Bahurim from near and far came streaming to learn the Torah from him. Their veneration for him may be compared to that enjoyed by the greatest Hassidic rabbis. The students felt for him not only the love of children for their spiritual father, it was an attachment of boundless enthusiasm: their "souls were bound up with his soul" so much that they were ready to serve him unconditionally. They knew him to be so pure of heart that all his deeds were dictated by holy motives only, even if he sometimes deviated from the ways of his native town. Three examples are offered, relating to *Minhagim* (rites) in the synagogue: (1) Nathan Adler did not want to miss the threefold blessing of the priests for even a single day. He felt that his love of God and his fellow-men were more important arguments than the reasons adduced by the Poskim for their prescription to have the priests pronounce their blessing only on the festivals. He mounted the dais every day and pronounced the blessing, as is done in Jerusalem, the Holy City. (2) He used in his prayers the Sephardic version of R. Isaac Luria (ARI)[23]; and (3) he prayed with the

---

[23] It is said that R. Pinhas Horovitz also secretly used to pray according to the ARI's version.

Sephardic pronunciation as used in the Holy Land. This habit shows how deep was his love of Eretz Israel, for this is assumed to have been its motivation.

He knew that the change from the Ashkenazic to the Sephardic pronunciation might lead to mistakes. R. Nathan therefore used the opportunity of a visit to Frankfort of a Sephardic *Hakham* from Jerusalem, R. Hayyim Modaï (the author of the Responsa *"Hayyim L'Olam"*). He took him into his house to learn from him the Sephardic pronunciation until he mastered it.[24]

Young Nathan did not content himself with the study of the Torah in its various forms, but he also devoted some of his time to the study of nature and of Hebrew and Aramaic philology. He was convinced that such knowledge would lead him to a better understanding of the Creator and of the written and oral tradition. He was also profoundly interested in philosophy, by which he gained a deeper insight into the teachings of the Kabbalah. This seems to have been due to the influence of R. Meshullam Zalman, and of the *Gaon* Pinehas Horovitz, the author of *"Haflaah,"* who came to Frankfort in the year 1772, and who conceived a deep friendship for the "Great Eagle" (Eagle=Adler), at that time still a young man. Like him, R. Horovitz endeavored to achieve mastery of the Talmud and Poskim, combined with pure piety and modest living. His famous books, especially *Panim Yafot,* a commentary on the Torah, bear testimony to this endeavor. The friendship between these two great men was destined to be of decisive influence on the community of Frankfort. Their friendship was rooted in both their deep veneration for the Torah and in their inclination towards Kabbalah and Hassidism.

R. Nathan, however, turned to "practical Kabbalah" as well. This was contrary to the spirit of the Jews of Frankfort. He himself wrote amulets (*"Kemeot"*) for the sick, as we are told by the *"Hatam Sofer."*[25]

The latter's son, the author of *"Ktav Sofer,"* tells us that his father was in possession of a booklet of "Practical Kabbalah and Amulets," now lost, which he had received from R. Nathan.

The Frankfort Jewish community was highly sensitive to any inclination among its members towards practical Kabbalah. This might still have been the reaction to the false Messiah, Shabbatai

---

[24] R. Maimon: *"Sare Hameah"*, Part I, p. 90.

[25] *"Derekh ha-Nesher,"* p. 35, note No. 118: letter by R. Shimeon Sofer, reprinted from the Sefer Igrot Sofrim, part III, p. 64/65.

Tzevi, though Marcus Horovitz holds that the difficulties R. Nathan and his pupils encountered correspond rather to the war waged by the *Gaon* of Vilna against the Hassidim of Poland, which fell into the same period. As a matter of fact, phenomena similar to those of the Hassidim of Poland could be observed among the pupils of R. Nathan, and the style of the leaflets that appeared against R. Nathan and his disciples was not unlike that in the pamphlets by the Mitnagdim against the Hassidim. But there was another reason why that conflict assumed such violent forms at Frankfort. According to the tradition as we find it in the book *"Divre Kehillot"* by R. Shlomo Zalman Geiger (1792-1878), Frankfort had been a centre of opposition to the Kabbalah since the time of Shabbatai Tzevi. Nathan Asati, who proclaimed himself a prophet, visited Frankfort on his way across Europe, but its notables treated him with contempt and drove him out of the town. They were afraid that he would find admirers who would believe in him. It was for that reason that the "Minhag of Frankfort" was adopted, introducing changes into prayers that were liable to be misunderstood by the people (cf. p. 167). They looked with suspicion upon a movement of any kind whose leader was revered with religious fervor. If we add to those reasons the other factor—strict adherence to the Frankfort tradition—it will be easily understood why the changes introduced by R. Nathan into some prayers caused such an uproar and why the Kabbalah he practised met with the disapproval of the leaders of the community. However, none of them dared to oppose him openly, for they all knew the purity of his heart and his endeavor to do everything for the glory of God. One of the reasons why the leaders of the community exercised such restraint was the realization that his greatness and saintliness was equalled by his modesty. Any secular ambition was foreign to him. Ample testimony of this quality is furnished by his pupils, particularly by Rabbis Sofer and Auerbach. From the time of his youth, he had renounced the pleasures of this world. This was chiefly due to the influence of his teacher and comrade, R. Meshulam. He did not allow his pupils to call him Rav Nathan, but insisted on being called "Rabbi Nathan" or simply "Nathan."

His love of his fellow-men knew no bounds. Once he happened to see somebody take wood from his own shed. He immediately declared all his belongings ownerless (*"hefker"*), so that the man might not have committed the sin of stealing. We are told that his door was open day and night, in order that people might be able to enter at any time. And in all his activities his wife, Rechla, of the Wetzlar family, proved to be his worthy partner. She was born at Giessen and died in the year 1805.[26] When she died, R. Pinehas Horovitz himself devoted an obituary to her, in which he praised her great qualities.

There is no need to stress R. Nathan's devotion to every single *Mitzvah*. But one in particular should be mentioned, that of *Sandeka-ut* (being the godfather of the child at the time of his circumcision). He went to any length in order to fulfill it. All who knew of his predilection, did their utmost to honor him—and themselves—by inviting him to accept this function at the circumcision-ceremony of their newborn sons. R. Nathan would spend whole nights on journeys, often undertaken under the most difficult conditions, in order to follow such invitations that reached him from villages around his home town. A number of stories are told about it by R. Maimon in his book *"Sare Hameah."*[27]

Because of R. Nathan's work and his great qualities, the Jews of Frankfort held him in profound regard. But his pupils' enthusiasm did not know any limits. Some of them exaggerated his saintliness and went so far as to tell stories of miracles wrought by him. They declared that, under the influence of their teacher, they themselves were able to work miracles, and they tried in that way to gain control of the Jewish quarter. They threatened one of the *Baale Battim,* whom they disliked, that if he did not do *T'shuvah* (repentance) in a way that had been made known to them in dreams, they would be compelled to proclaim the *"Herem"* (religious boycott) against him. When things had reached an impossible state, the leaders of the community could not contain themselves any longer. R. Nathan was summoned to appear before them to justify his behavior and that of his pupils. But R. Nathan did not appear! Whereupon it was decided to proclaim, on the 3rd of Elul 5539, in all the synagogues of the town, that R. Nathan Adler and his colleagues were strictly forbidden to hold a private

---

[26]See Appendix A4, copy of the inscription on her tombstone: "Inschriften" No. 4478. It is not known when R. Nathan married her. She bore him one son and one daughter. The daughter, Idel, died at the age of 12, when R. Nathan was Rabbi of Boskowitz. The *Hatam Sofer* speaks of this event in a letter which is reprinted in the preface to the *Sefer Yalkut Eliezer* on the Book of Psalms. The son was named Shimeon after R. Nathan's father. He died childless.

[27]Part I, p. 87.

Minyan of their own. The name of R. Eliezer Wallau, the spokesman of R. Nathan's group, was also specifically mentioned.[28]
R. Nathan did not heed that injunction either, and continued in
his saintly ways. He knew that there was no wrong thought in
his heart. Even his friend, R. Pinehas Horovitz, found it necessary to intervene and to voice a protest against his own friend.
In a second proclamation on the 10th of Elul, which was also
signed by the Head of the Bet Din, R. Nathan and all his followers were warned that if they did not discontinue their activities,
the "Herem" would be pronounced against them. But even then
R. Nathan did not disperse the *Minyan* in his *Bet Hamidrash,*
until the matter was brought before the government which decided
against him, although he protested twice. We can well understand the grief which this whole sad business caused R. Nathan,
who had no equal in sincerity of thought and goodness of heart
and whose only wish was to live a life of Torah and worship
in the midst of his people. We may assume, however, that that
state of affairs was no less disagreeable to the other side, and
above all to the Rav of the community, who was attached to
R. Nathan in personal friendship and admiration. It was like a
sign from Heaven when, towards the end of 5542-1782, an honorable solution presented itself through the election of R. Nathan
as rabbi of the community of Boskowitz in Moravia. That was
also the reason why R. Nathan accepted the offer, although he
had never before contemplated the idea of serving as a rabbi in
any community and of using the Torah "as a spade to dig with."

The hour of separation from Frankfort turned out to be a
compensation for all the suffering in the preceding years. He
realized that all that his adversaries had done had not been aimed
against him personally, but had been intended only to prevent the
penetration of the ways of the Hassidim and the ideology of the
adherents of Shabbatai Tsevi into the Jewish community. Nobody
had intended an affront against his personality, for not the slightest
suspicion had fallen upon him. The notables of the town accompanied him several miles outside the town to a point agreed upon
beforehand, as a sign of their admiration and as an expression of
their regret at the departure from his native town of that *Tzaddik*
who loved them as they loved him. For many of his pupils this

---

[28]He was the grandfather of R. Zalman Geiger, mentioned above. He
was born at Frankfort and died there on the 1st of Nissan 5581 ("Inschriften" No. 5063). In the later part of his life R. Zalman was Dayan of the
community.

was not enough; some among them did not wish to leave him altogether. They stayed on with him also at Boskowitz. Outstanding among them was Moshe Sofer, the famed author of *"Hatam Sofer."* It is touching to read of the attachment of this disciple to his teacher. On no account did R. Nathan want him to accompany him on the long and troublesome way to Boskowitz, for he was still young (only 19). Young Moshe walked for three days behind the coach in which his master travelled, and tried in every possible way to convince him to change his decision, until at last R. Nathan took him into the coach, exclaiming "My son, my son!"[29]

The *"Hatam Sofer"* remained faithful to his teacher throughout his life. He himself said with reverent pride that his hand did not leave the hand of his teacher throughout the fourteen years during which he served him. Even when R. Nathan left the rabbinate of Boskowitz, R. Sofer went with him, back to their home town.[30]

But when they reached Fuerth, R. Nathan demanded that he should return to Moravia, in order to settle at Prosnitz and to teach the Torah in that province, as he had noted how popular the "Bahur from Frankfort" had become there. Some letters of the "Hatam Sofer" to his master are preserved, and they are full of longing for him and his teaching. It appears that he turned to him for advice in small, as well as in important matters, and the contact between them was never severed. In his obituary on R. Nathan, the "Hatam Sofer" exclaimed: "We are disciples who have not done their full duty; there are many questions I ought to have asked and many problems that should have been raised, and through my own fault I have not been able to quench my thirst."[31]

All along his way Rabbi Adler encountered the same attitude of reverence as shown by the people of his town at the time of his departure. As the Jewish proverb says: he who flees greatness, greatness follows after him.[32] When they passed Prague, where the great R. Ezekiel Landau served as rabbi,[32a] he invited him to deliver a *Derashah* (discourse on a *Halakhic* subject) in the great synagogue of the town. For subject he chose the *Sugya* (theme)

---

[29]*Drashot* of the "Hatam Sofer," Part II, p. 744, and *"Shaar Josef,"* ibid.

[30]Of his fondness for Frankfort we learn from the fact that he signed each one of his responsa "Moshe Sofer of Frankfort on Main." In one of his letters to his master he writes of Frankfort: "She is unique, none is like her in the whole world." (*Derekh ha-Nesher*, p. 42).

[31]Drashot of the "Hatam Sofer," p. 743.

[32]Tractate "Eruwin," 43 b.

[32a]See his biography in "Jewish Leaders."

of *"Hatzitz M'ratzeh."*[33] It was reported that even many of the graduates of R. Landau's *Bet Hamidrash* were unable to grasp the deeper meaning of his words.

The new Rabbi of Boskowitz was received with great honor. Still, he could not stay there for long, for he soon found out that in this town, too, he was not to find peace and tranquillity. There were matters connected with questions of Tarfut in which R. Nathan was very strict, stricter perhaps than the other scholars of his generation. This embittered the *Baale Battim,* and in particular the butchers under his supervision. They brought complaints about him before the government, and, because of his decision, accused him of "squandering the funds of Israel." At the beginning of the year 5546 (1785), R. Nathan decided to leave the rabbinate of Boskowitz and to return to his native town. On his way home he passed the town of Fuerth and won the friendship of the great rabbi of that town, R. Meshullam Zalman Hacohen.[34]

Back at Frankfort, where his mother was still living, R. Nathan was again surrounded by the love of the friends of his youth and the admiration of the whole community. Not one of them dared to mention the *Herem* of 1779. However, a movement similar to that of 1779 arose again. Again a number of his pupils chose the same objectionable ways and instead of honoring their rabbi for his greatness of spirit and soul, they declared him able to work miracles and told stories of miracles they themselves had wrought. They did not shrink from reiterating stories of nightly visions and dreams which aimed at discrediting certain people. It was then that the leaders of the community proclaimed in all the synagogues that the old *Herem* was still valid and anybody who contravened against its provisions would be severely punished (1789). This time R. Nathan tried at once to curb these tendencies among his pupils and to induce them to heed his warnings. One of his pupils, not a native of Frankfort, was expelled for contraventions of this kind. Two of his greatest admirers refrained afterwards from all forbidden activity: R. Eliezer Wallau and R. Loeb Emerich, whose tombstone bears eloquent testimony to his high qualities. He continued in his Hassidic ways, but did so modestly within the walls of his *Bet Hamidrash,* and became one of the greatest *Mohalim* (performer of circumcisions) of his time in that district. After the death of his only son he is said to have fasted from one Shabbat to the other

---

[33]Tractate "Yoma," 72 a.
[34]L. Lewin: Zur Geschichte der Juden in Fuerth. Jahrbuch der Jued. Literarischen Gesellschaft, Vol. 6, pp. 203/9.

except on days where he introduced a child into the Covenant of our Father Abraham.[35]

Very soon a spirit of peace prevailed in the Jewish quarter of Frankfort around the revered figure of R. Nathan. The past was well-nigh forgotten. The community elders, however, were reluctant to revoke the Herem, in order not to cause a new conflagration. But, suddenly, on the 11th of Elul 5560 (1800), it was proclaimed in all the synagogues of Frankfort, in the name of the *Gabbaim* and the *Bet Din* that there was no substance in the *Herem* with which the followers of R. Nathan had been threatened, that everybody recognized him as a scholar and *Tzaddik* and that he was even above the slightest suspicion. That happened about a fortnight before R. Nathan's demise. They did not want to disturb his tranquillity. When it was felt that his sun was setting and that death was approaching, they wished to remove anything that could mar this great figure and therefore decided upon this step. The text of the two proclamations against the followers of R. Nathan and a detailed description of the phases of the conflict appeared in a small book called *"Maasse Ta'tuim,"* published anonymously in 1789. Only three generations later it became known that the author had been Loeb Wetzlar, a native of Frankfort.

After an illness of several weeks R. Nathan's pure soul returned to the Creator on the 27th of Elul 5560 (16.9.1800). Great honor was rendered him at his funeral, as is being told in the "Gedenkbuch." The members of the holy funeral brotherhood alternately carried the coffin[36] and the head of the Bet Din, together with its members, bestowed upon him the title of "Morenu."[37]

Two eulogies delivered by leaders of that generation have been preserved.[38] They show how great the love and admiration of

---

[35]"Inschriften" No. 4896. In the "Gedenkbuch" the following was added to the ordinary text: "and on his grave the crown of the Torah was conferred on him by the Rosh Yeshivah R. Zalman Trier who bestowed the title of 'Morenu' on him. Of him it may be said, 'He who induces to good deeds is greater than he who does them.'" (Tractate Baba Batra 15a).

[36]On the customs of the Hevra Kadisha at Frankfort see "Protocols of the Hevra" in the "Siddur Parshat Para," published by Eduard Feist in the year 1892.

[37]Up to our times it has remained a custom at Frankfort that only members of the Bet Din were called to the Torah by the title of "Morenu."

[38]The inscription on his tombstone was copied in the "Inschriften" at the end of the Introduction, and, again, in full in the book *"Derekh haNesher."* At the end of his book "Mishnat Rabbi Nathan" R. Auerbach reprinted only the first part. As to the inscription in the "Gedenkbuch" see Annex A No. 2, as well as Annex B in the Memorbuch of Frankfort. A photograph of the tombstone is reproduced at the end of the treatise by Julius Hulsen: Der alte Juden-Friedhof in Frankfurt a. M. (1931) Plate No. 12.

friends and pupils had been: one, by R. Pinehas Horovitz, is published in part in the preface to the book *"Mishnat Rabbi Nathan."* The other, by R. Moshe Sofer, though with some omissions, was published in his book *"Torat Moshe"* (Parshat Sh'mini), and again, in full, from the manuscript of the "Hatam Sofer" in the second part of his "Drashot." How close the spiritual ties between them had been is seen from the report that on the very day when R. Nathan passed away R. Moshe, in a dream, was shown a Torah Scroll wrapped in black, and was reminded of the custom prevailing in the Frankfort community to drape the Torah Scrolls in black on days of public fasting.[39] The meaning of this dream became clear to him only after one month, when the news of R. Nathan's death reached him. In his eulogy he dwelt at length of the saintly habits of his teacher and on the teaching he had received from him. In his great grief he could, however, not refrain from alluding to the pain which R. Nathan's adversaries had caused him at Boskowitz as well as at Frankfort. He enlarged on the words of our Sages:[40] "That student who died in the prime of life—his wife mourns him in the *Bet Hamidrash* and asks: This is the Torah: and is this the reward?[41] R. Nathan was only fifty-eight when he died."—Another passage from his eulogy: R. Moshe regrets that "he did not stand at the graveside of this holy man, for then some of his spirit would have been conferred upon him." That was not the opinion of the great R. Hayyim Halberstamm of Sandz, who attributes R. Moshe's saintly ways to the fact that "he was the devoted servant of the *Tzaddik* R. Nathan and learnt Torah from him."[42]

The "Hatam Sofer" did not content himself with eulogizing his beloved teacher on the day he received the sad news of his death— at that time he was still rabbi at Mattersdorf. Every year, on the 27th of Elul, he delivered a *Derashah,* and combined reminiscences of his master's saintly life with some of the teaching he had received from him. In the annotations *"Shaar Yosef"* to his first *Hesped* on the 27th of Tishri 5561, the publisher draws attention to all the passages where R. Moshe Sofer mentions the words he had heard from his teacher and his saintly conduct as he had observed it:

[39]This custom, too, was observed as long as the ancient Jewish Community of Frankfort existed.

[40]Tractate "Shabbat," 13a.

[41]As to Frankfurt, compare with the quotation under n. 30. Rabbi Sofer's criticism of this teacher's opponents is elaborated there.

[42]"Sare HaMeah" by R. Maimon, p. 90.

"Every word of his teaching is a true and authentic rendering by his pupil. This was not the case with others of his pupils and their followers, who told many legends and handed down often doubtful *Halakhic* decisions in R. Nathan's name."

The memory of the great scholar was also kept alive in Frankfort. Until the destruction of the ancient community of that town, there was a small *Minyan* in the house of the famous *Mohel*, R. Benjamin Niederhofheim, which met every day and preserved part of R. Nathan's *Minhagim* (ritual). This *Minyan* had existed from the time of R. Nathan and had taken over such *Minhagim* as the introduction of *"K'dushat Keter"* into the *Mussaf*. They also followed some of the Sephardic *Minhagim* on the High Festivals.[43]

An account of R. Nathan and his impact on his environment would not be complete without the names of his most important disciples, for it is through them that we know so much about him. It is from their enthusiasm for their teacher that we realize his greatness.

(a) His teaching and his Hassidic ways were carried on by R. Seckel Isak Wormser, known as the "Baal Shem of Michelstadt" (1788-1847), where, during most of his life, he resided. His piety and unselfishness were famous, and he was beloved and honored in his district by Jews and Gentile alike.

(b) R. Josef Meir Schneitach. He, too, derived his name from his last place of residence. He was a native of Fuerth and the author of *"Sheelot Ut'shuvot Riwam Schneitach."*

(c) R. Abraham Halevi Bing, the District Rabbi of Wuerzburg. His biography is to be found in R. Seckel Isaac Halevi Bamberger's preface to his *"Zikhron Avraham,"* which contains annotations to the *Shulhan Arukh, "Orah Hayyim"* (Pressburg 5652).

(d) R. Menachem Mendel Kargau, the author of the book *"Gidule Taharah al Hilkhot Mikvaot"*, which two of his pupils published from his manuscript (Fuerth 5605). His biography is contained in: L. Loewenstein: "Zur Geschichte der Juden in Fuerth," II, Jahrbuch der Juedisch-Literarischen Gesellschaft, Vol. VIII, p. 118, 119.

---

[43]See the pamphlet "Beth Haknesseth Niederhofheim," of which a 2nd edition appeared in 1930.

(e) R. Loeb Carlburg, known from the preface to the book *"Mishnat R. Nathan."* He died at Frankfort on the 7th of Adar 5599.

(f) R. Abraham Auerbach, the father of the author of *"Mishnat R. Nathan."* A description of his life is given in the essay published by R. Moshe Auerbach mentioned in note 21.

(g) Last and most important, is the "Hatam Sofer", R. Moshe Sofer, who did not "leave the tents of the Torah of his teacher during the fourteen years while he studied with him"[44].

R. Nathan exercised so deep an influence on his environment that even in later generations the pupils of his pupils liked to mention his name, both in connection with his decisions and as a luminous pattern to their disciples. A list of over ninety books, in which Torah and Mussar is quoted in the name of R. Nathan, is to be found in the initial part of the *"Torat Emet"*, the second part of the comprehensive biography *"Derekh HaNesher"*.

One of the latest additions to the literature on R. Nathan is to be found in the work by R. Maimon *"Sare HaMeah"*, in which the author used much of the legendary material on R. Nathan which he had collected while on a visit to Frankfort. The dialogue between him and R. Mordekhai Halevi Horovitz, the author of "Die Frankfurter Rabbinen", is characteristic and of special interest. The latter drew a parallel between R. Nathan and Rabbi Eliyahu, the Gaon of Vilna, both as regards their Jewish outlook, their way of life, and their influence. In many respects they resembled each other: R. Horovitz compared the influence of R. Nathan Adler on West European Jewry with that of the *Gaon* of Vilna on the Jewry of Eastern Europe. R. Maimon relates

---

[44]This close attachment between the teacher and his brilliant pupil is reflected in our historicial literature. The numerous biographies of the "Hatam Sofer" are full of reminiscences of events in the life of R. Nathan during the time when he was together with him. The most important ones are:

    1. The introductions to the works of the *"Hatam Sofer"*, published by his descendants and pupils.

    2. The Sefer *"Hut Hameshulash"* written by his grandson R. Shlomoh Sofer of Beregsass (Munkacs 1894).

    3. Vol. 6 in the series of books *"D'muyot B'zionut ub'toldot ha-Yishuv:* The "Hatam Sofer" and his disciples—their attitude towards Eretz Israel", by S. Weingarten, Jerusalem 1945.

    4. Schachnowitz S.: *Licht aus dem Westen,* 2nd edition. Keren Hatora Zuerich 1953. This last book is written in the well-known descriptive style characteristic of the author and gives a vivid picture of the life of Jewry at Frankfort and in Hungary.

that at the beginning this idea seemed very strange to him. But at the conclusion of the talk he, too, agreed with the Rabbi of Frankfort who was many years his senior. R. Horovitz succeeded in convincing him that there was no exaggeration in this view and that it was not local pride that had led him to this conclusion. Some of the points mentioned before, illustrate matters: both the *Gaon* of Vilna and R. Nathan were revered and honored by the whole people as *"Gaon"* and the pride of Judaism, although neither of them held a public post (except for the three years in which R. Nathan, almost against his will, served as Rabbi of Boskowitz); they were not heads of *yeshivot* nor the official leaders of their communities. As regards their way of "learning", they resembled each other in that they did not content themselves, as most of the other scholars of their time did, with the study of the holy scriptures; both felt the necessity of acquiring also worldly wisdom and those branches of science which one needs to know in order to draw nearer to his Creator and to deepen the reverence for God in his heart until he reaches the full understanding of our holy Torah in all its aspects. The subjects were: Hebrew and Aramaic philology, natural science, and philosophy. It was these which led both the *Gaon* of Vilna and R. Nathan on in their way to Kabbalah and pure Hassidism, free from all empty mysticism. Both the Gaon of Vilna and R. Nathan were well aware of their unusual gifts of mind and memory, but both stayed utterly humble. This consciousness of their own qualities led them to the same result: both of them jotted down their new ideas on the pages of their books only in the form of allusions, without going into details, and both refused to print them during their lifetime. This made it very difficult for later generations, for only few people were able to decipher those hints and to penetrate into the depth of their thought and the wealth of their knowledge. Both (and this is where they resemble each other most) gave the same reason for this habit of theirs, namely, that one may put the oral tradition into writing only insofar as it was absolutely necessary to prevent the Torah from being forgotten. He who need not fear that he might forget new interpretations should limit himself to mere points and short references.

There is one more detail, which shows how much these two men had in common: their attitude towards the priests' blessing in the present time. However, whereas R. Nathan succeeded, to a certain degree, in observing this *Mitzvah* as he wished it, the *Gaon* of Vilna was not granted the fulfillment of his endeavor. We have heard of the "holy war" waged against R. Nathan because of this question by the leaders of the Frankfort community. As regards the Gaon of Vilna, we find reminiscences by his pupils[45] to the effect that the Gaon, too, wanted to introduce that custom into his *Bet Haknesset,* but his plan could not be carried out.

This comparison with the Gaon of Vilna shows that the unusual admiration for R. Nathan, by the Jews of Frankfort, as well as by generation after generation of pupils, was not exaggerated. Up to our days, the name of the "Great Eagle" has been held higher than any other personality that grew out of the Frankfort community. Though the ancient Frankfort community and its customs have been destroyed in the great catastrophe that befell European Jewry, the memory of R. Nathan Adler will be cherished forever and will stay a blessing for future generations.

---

[45]In the Responsa *"Meshiv Davar",* by the Gaon Naphtali Tzevi Yehudah Berlin (Part II, No. 104).

RABBI HAYYIM OF VOLOZIN
(1749-1821)

By Walter S. Wurzburger

RABBI HAYYIM OF VOLOZIN

By Walter S. Wurzburger

It was during a very turbulent period in Jewish history that Rabbi Hayyim of Volozin made his significant contribution towards the preservation of classic Judaism, which accords the *Halakhah* (religious law) a pre-eminent position in the life of the Jew.

The emergence of the Hassidic movement hurled a formidable challenge against the rabbinic doctrine, which regarded strict observance of the *Halakhah* as the cornerstone of Judaism. Hassidism stressed the *subjective* religious experience of the individual. Weighed in the Hassidic scale of values, it seemed to be of relatively only minor importance whether or not a given religious act fully conformed to the rigid standards circumscribed by *objective Halakhic* norms. Especially during the early stages of Hassidism, there loomed the danger that the new movement might completely succumb to antinomian trends and, perhaps, break with the *Halakhah* altogether.

The gravity with which the leading rabbinic authorities of the time viewed the anti-legalistic orientation of Hassidism is attested by the fact that the *Gaon* of Vilna, who always scrupulously avoided any type of involvement in communal activity, temporarily abandoned his isolation and plunged into the forefront of the battle against the new sect. But in spite of the determined opposition of the *Mitnaggedim,* Hassidism made tremendous inroads into the rank and file of the Jewish masses. The tide could not be stopped by pronouncements or declarations charging Hassidism with deviations from accepted traditional forms. What was necessary was a vindication of the *Halakhic* approach to Judaism. It had to be established that meticulous adherence to the objective norms of Jewish law was not a matter of dry and barren legalism, but that it constituted the repository of a dynamic religious way of life.

The task of formulating a constructive program aiming at a renaissance of *Halakhic* Judaism fell upon the shoulders of Rabbi Hayyim of Volozin, who possessed in abundant measure the qualities of leadership called for in such a crisis. He was endowed with an unusual array of talents, combining intellectual

189

brilliance and profound erudition with a remarkable genius for practical affairs. He was as much at home in the intricacies of Talmudic law, the veiled regions of mystical speculation, as he was in the world, where his intuitive understanding of people and his skill in the solution of communal problems brought him great fame. Unlike his spiritual mentor, the renowned *Gaon* of Vilna, who withdrew from society and devoted himself to intellectual pursuits, Rabbi Hayyim eagerly accepted the burdens of communal responsibility. It was his passionate concern for the welfare of his fellow-man that impelled him to assert leadership in the Jewish community. Altruism was the keynote of his philosophy of life. As recorded by his son, Rabbi Hayyim's credo could be summed up in the words that "man was created not for his own sake, but to help others to the limit of his capacities."[1] A study of his life will show that it was due to his extraordinary sensitivity to the spiritual plight of his people that he emerged as the predominant figure of *Halakhic* Judaism of his time.

I.

Rabbi Hayyim was born in 1749 in Volozin and brought up in a prosperous, pious home, his father serving as "Parness" (lay leader) of the Jewish community. Hayyim received the traditional training, which emphasized the Bible, Talmud, and Codes. The extent of his brilliance can be gauged by the fact that at the age of twelve he was already studying under the illustrious Rabbi Rafael Hamburger. At the age of fifteen, he sat at the feet of Rabbi Aryeh Leib, the author of *"Shaagat Aryeh"* and one of the leading Talmudists of his time, distinguished for his independence of mind and self-reliance in the pursuit of truth.

But the decisive influence exerted upon his intellectual development was that of the *Gaon* of Vilna, the association with whom began when Rabbi Hayyim was nineteen years old. Three or four times a year, Hayyim would come to Vilna, for a month at a time, to submit questions and problems to the *Gaon;* from him he acquired his basic philosophy of life, as well as the methodology for the study of the Torah.

The close relationship between them, which lasted throughout the latter's lifetime, moulded Rabbi Hayyim's pattern of thought and activity to such an extent that one may be inclined to view him

---

[1]*Nefesh ha-Hayyim,* Preface.

as the executor of the spiritual legacy which the *Gaon* bequeathed to his people. Rabbi Hayyim popularized and promoted his teacher's philosophy of life, because he was convinced that the return to the authentic Judaism which was advocated by the methods of the *Gaon* held the answer to the spiritual crisis which confronted the Jewish people.

By his approach to the discovery of the original meaning of the classical sources of Judaism, such as Bible, Talmud, Midrash and Zohar, the *Gaon* had wrought a major intellectual revolution in Jewish thought. He was strongly averse to the method of the *pilpul* (a form of casuistry) which solved Talmudic difficulties by ingenious, though sometimes far-fetched, modes of analysis. Instead, he substituted scientifically sound methods of elucidation and interpretation, employing with special skill textual emendations and other forms of literary criticism. The student of the Talmud is often fascinated to observe how the *Gaon* of Vilna with one brief note or comment disposes of difficulties which had given rise to a vast body of literature.

The *Gaon's* methodology was inspired by the determination to discover authentic Judaism which, for him, was synonymous with the Judaism formulated in the classic texts. He firmly believed that a religious practice or observance could be regarded as genuinely Jewish only if it could be validated by some reference either in the Bible or the literature of the Talmudic period. In his search for authentic Judaism, he was willing to disregard or even set aside the opinions and rulings of well-established authorities, if he held that their views were incompatible with those of the Talmud. By the same token, he was most vehement in his opposition to the religious reformation advocated by the Hassidic movement, which emphasized the subjective religious experience at the expense of strict adherence to Talmudic law. Any departure from the norms of Talmudic Judaism was in the eyes of the *Gaon* an inexcusable defiance of the supreme religious authority of Israel.

The religious philosophy which the *Gaon* imparted to a circle of select disciples became the guide of large segments of the Jewish people, primarily because Rabbi Hayyim dedicated his almost unlimited energy to the dissemination of his master's teachings. He was so self-effacing that he looked upon himself primarily as a pupil and follower of the *Gaon*. But he protested vigorously when others would refer to him as a "disciple" of his illustrious teacher. In his humility, he felt that the intellectual superiority of his

teacher over him was so pronounced as to constitute a difference
not of degree but of kind. Hence, it would be a reflection upon the
Gaon's greatness, if he permitted himself to be called his disciple.[2]

But his humility must not mislead us into a false appraisal of
his historic importance. He was too much of a creative personality
in his own right to be relegated to the role of a blind follower of
his revered mentor. His independence of mind is attested to by
his divergence from the Gaon's position in a number of important
issues, ranging from such practical matters as the determination
of the policy toward Hassidism to such meta-physical problems
as the interpretation of the Kabbalistic notion of the *Tsimtsum*
(divine self-limitation to make room for the universe). He possessed a remarkably systematic mind, which enabled him to cull
from the vast Talmudic and Kabbalistic literature a succinctly
formulated philosophy of *Halakhic* Judaism, which he presented
in his *Nefesh Hayyim.* Because of his genius for practical
affairs, he succeeded in creating the instrumentalities for the implementation of a philosophy of life which, though it had sprung
from the matrix of the *Gaon,* still bore the stamp of his own
individuality.

At an early age Rabbi Hayyim was thrust into a position of
leadership in the Jewish community. He was only twenty-five
years old when he became Rabbi of Volozin, a community which
he served almost continuously until his death.

Financially independent, he refused to accept any remuneration for his services. His fortunate economic situation, later on,
enabled him to start his own *yeshivah* and, at the beginning, to
finance it exclusively from his personal funds.

At the age of forty he was called to Vilkomir, staying on as
rabbi of this community for only a year. Certain influential
Vilkomir businessmen were resentful of their rabbi's policy of supporting himself from income derived from his business enterprises
and refusing to accept a salary from the community. As a result
of strained relations with them, he returned to his native city and
resumed the spiritual leadership of Volozin.

Jewish folklore attributes his departure from Vilkomir to a
trivial incident. Rabbi Hayyim is supposed to have been asked
by one of the more prominent members of the Vilkomir community
to give him the time of the *Molod* (the exact time when the

---

[2]Rabbi Hayyim's introduction to the *Sifra Detzeniuta* by the Gaon of
Vilna.

new moon becomes visible). Since the rabbi did not have a Jewish calendar with him at the moment, he was unable to furnish the requested information, whereupon a whispering campaign, charging the rabbi with gross ignorance for not knowing such an elementary thing as the time of the *Molod,* swept through Vilkomir!

His bitter experience in Vilkomir prompted him years later to offer a unique admonition whenever he conferred *Semikhah* (traditional ordination) upon one of his disciples. He would invariably tell the young rabbi that in addition to mastering Jewish religious and civil law, it would also be necessary for him to know the time of the *Molod.* As this down-to-earth advice to his students would indicate, Rabbi Hayyim, notwithstanding his intellectual brilliance and profound scholarship, never became alienated from the needs of the common man. It may appear paradoxical that the advocate of a way of life which concentrated on an intellectual approach to God, should nevertheless find the key to the hearts of the people.

While he labored to create an intellectual and spiritual élite which would be committed to the study and analysis of *Halakhah,* his personality would not allow him to become estranged from the rank and file. A glimpse into his daily working routine furnishes a typical illustration. Nothing was permitted to interfere with the popular lectures which he delivered every evening in the *Bet Hamidrash* (the local synagogue), where he spoke to the worshippers on the portion of the week. Here was a pre-eminent Talmudic authority whom rabbis from all over Lithuania constantly consulted on important decisions, who did not begrudge his time and energy to the community at large on matters which others might have been inclined to view as of no great consequence.

His concern for the spiritual welfare of his fellow Jew is revealed by the order of priority which he assigned to the publication of his books. Rabbi Hayyim, in the course of the years, wrote numerous responses on intricate problems of Talmudic law. He was surely aware that, for his reputation as one of the outstanding contributors to *Halakhic* thought to be perpetuated, it was desirable for his contributions in this field to be printed. Yet, he never requested this of his son, although he did urge him to make every possible effort to have the *Nefesh ha-Hayyim* published after his death.[3] It is not difficult to find the reason for his preference

---

[3]Introduction to "Nefesh ha-Hayyim."

for the latter book. He felt that it could prove of tremendous practical value to the Jewish community, because it would promote a better understanding of what he regarded as authentic Judaism. He was convinced that, at a time when the vagaries of an unbridled emotionalism were rampant, an urgent need existed for a work which would emphasize the primacy of the study of the Torah and which would stress the importance of strict adherence to *Halakhic* norms, even though at times this might appear to curb spontaneous religious expression.

But Rabbi Hayyim's concern was not limited to the spiritual well-being of his people. He was especially perturbed by the plight of the unfortunate *Agunot* (Jewish women who could not remarry, because they could not furnish convincing evidence of the death of their husband). He brought his vast Talmudic erudition to bear upon the solution of numerous cases of Agunot. Many of his responses dealing with the *Agunah* problem reveal the tormenting inner conflicts and the tensions which he had to endure whenever he had to make a bold decision permitting the remarriage of an *Agunah* under conditions where other authorities would take exception to his ruling. But he felt that he had no moral right to shirk responsibility for rendering decisions on acute problems. His intellectual honesty outweighed all other considerations. He repeatedly emphasizes that he was admonished by the *Gaon* of Vilna that, when it came to the realm of Torah, "where truth is the sole criterion,"[4] never to bow to any other authority.

He was too multi-dimensional a personality to have his service to his fellow man confined to the sphere of intellectual labors. He was one of the moving spirits of the assembly of Jewish notables that met in Minsk in 1806 and decreed that a Jewish family which could afford more than two candles for Friday night had to contribute a certain amount of money for the relief of the struggling Jewish farmers in one of the impoverished districts of Lithuania. He undertook to become one of the two administrators of this relief fund. He was instrumental in reorganizing the *Kupat Ramban,* an old established charity for the support of scholars in Israel. Thanks largely to his efforts, that institution was able to regain its prestige and influence among all segments of Jewry, who submerged their internal divisions in order to forge a common link with Zion.

---

[4] *"Hut Hameshulash,"* responsae 8 and 9.

In his diverse philanthropic efforts Rabbi Hayyim was immeasurably aided by his reputation for practical wisdom. To the
common people, he epitomized common sense at its best. Numerous folk tales and legends sprang up, extolling his brilliant
handling of such situations. Whether it was advising a French
general on the outcome of the Napoleonic wars or persuading a
reluctant yeshivah supporter not to withdraw his subsidy, popular
fancy always wove a halo of infallibility around him.

His intuitive grasp and keen psychological insights are best
illustrated by an incident which made a tremendous impression
upon his contemporaries. With a great deal of pomp and fanfare
there came to Vilna a very impressive person, dressed in Oriental
attire. Upon arrival, he was received by officials of the Russian
Government. The story was circulated that he was an emissary of
a Jewish king in Africa who had sent him to bring the good tidings that the beginning of the redemption was at hand.

The man referred to himself merely as the "Crimean Jew."
While praying, he displayed extraordinary fervor and his entire
bearing was one of extreme religious devotion. He accepted an
invitation to one of the most pious and prominent homes in Vilna
only under the condition that he could personally slaughter the
chicken, which had to be cooked in new utensils. Moreover, he
requested that he have a private *Minyan* (quorum for public
worship) arranged at his home so that he could personally lead the
services. All these requests were gladly granted by his host, who
was overjoyed to have as his guest a man about whom it was
rumored that if he was not the Messiah himself, he was, at any
rate, his representative.

Thus the "Crimean Jew" obtained access to the most influential homes and was taken into the confidence of practically all the
leaders of the Jewish community. Only Rabbi Hayyim of Volozin
was suspicious. He sensed that there was some fraud perpetrated
and he advised extreme caution. His judgment was to be vindicated soon. For in a very short while it was discovered that the
"Crimean Jew," far from being a representative of the Messiah,
was in actuality a secret agent of the Czarist Government, who
who wanted to check on tax evasions by the Jewish population!

The rabbi's deft handling of affairs, his sound approach, as
well as his reputation, paved the way for success in the crowning
achievement of his life—the founding of the Yeshivah of Volozin.
It was a most difficult venture upon which he embarked with a

great deal of reluctance. He was fully convinced of the desperate need for the establishment of an institution which would spearhead the drive to win back the Jewish community to the ideal of Torah study. But Rabbi Hayyim was too modest to believe that he was the man for such a gigantic undertaking. The leading rabbis of Lithuania, however, regarded him as the logical choice to lead this all-important effort, and he eventually succumbed to their persistent pleas and agreed to start a *yeshivah* in Volozin.

Its beginnings were extremely humble. In 1803, he gathered ten disciples who were supported from his own private means and instructed by him personally. Although Rabbi Hayyim approached his task in a spirit, to use his own words, comparable to the "insignificant sexton who summons people for worship in the synagogue,"[5] the *yeshivah* from the very beginning reflected the personality of its founder. He made certain that its atmosphere would be conducive to the development of a spiritual élite. Nothing was allowed to detract from the dignity of the *yeshivah* student, who was never permitted to forget that the study of the Torah outranks all other occupations and activities. For this reason Rabbi Hayyim could not tolerate the practice employed at other *yeshivot,* where needy students received their stipends in the form of free meals provided on a rotating basis in the homes of public-minded individuals. He realized that this form of subsidy was wrought with serious psychological hazards, inasmuch as handouts received at private homes were apt to induce feelings of inferiority. He undertook the onerous burden of organizing ambitious campaigns for the support of his *yeshivah,* when owing to its phenomenal growth, he found it no longer possible to maintain it out of his personal funds.

It is difficult to present an adequate appraisal of the revolutionary impact which the Yeshivah of Volozin made upon the intellectual and spiritual life of Lithuanian Jewry. Prior to the founding of the yeshivah, the intensive study of Torah had fallen into neglect. This was due, in some measure, to the severe economic pressure to which Lithuanian Jewry was subjected. But the chief responsibility for the decline of Jewish learning must be pinned upon the inroads of the Hassidic movement, which accorded to scholarship only a secondary place in the Jewish scale of values. Since, as Hassidism holds, the presence of God is revealed every-

---

[5]His open letter, quoted by M. S. Schmuckler, *Toldot Rabbenu Hayyim Mivolozin,* P. 38.

where, knowledge of the Torah is not necessary to achieve close communication with Him. The Hassidic ideal is personified by the *Tzaddik* (the Saint) who need not be a *Talmid Hakham* (a scholar). Hassidism had shifted the center of gravity of Judaism from the study of the Torah to the cultivation of religious experience which reaches its climax in prayer. Knowledge of the Torah ceased to play the part of an intrinsic value.

This revolutionary conception dealt a devastating blow to the status of Jewish learning. Instead of occupying a pivotal place in the hierarchy of Jewish values, learning was relegated to the role of a handmaiden of sentimentalism. The ultimate objective of learning was not producing a deeper insight into the Torah, but to induce intense feelings of reverence and piety.

The immediate consequence of this upheaval was the neglect of Talmudic studies. Instead of concentrating upon the analysis of its intricate legal problems, people turned to the study of devotional literature, which seemed to offer a far richer return in the cultivation of religious emotions. Talmudic studies were abandoned to such an extent that in many synagogues one could not even find copies of the book which previously had occupied a commanding position in Jewish life.[6]

When Rabbi Hayyim founded the Yeshivah of Volozin, he provided a base of operations from which a counter-attack could be launched against the inroads of an excessive emotionalism. Lithuania did not possess any other academy of learning which could sustain an organized effort at restoring the primacy of Torah study. If that country subsequently gained renown for its network of *yeshivot,* it was due to Volozin, "the mother of *yeshivot*". Its pioneering efforts inspired the establishment of numerous other yeshivot throughout Lithuania.

The founding of the Yeshivah of Volozin, therefore, must be regarded as the birth, not merely of an institution, but of a movement which changed the entire complexion of Lithuanian Jewry and brought about a renaissance of learning. The resurgence of intellectualism was a triumph of Rabbi Hayyim's philosophy of life, which saw in the study of the Torah the most exalted form of divine worship. He utterly objected to the Hassidic contention that the study of the Torah possesses religious significance only to the extent that it is motivated by the intention of achieving communion with God.

---

[6]*Nefesh ha-Hayyim* IV; 1.

Drawing upon his mastery of rabbinic thought, he demonstrated that the proper motivation for the study of the Torah was *Lishmah* (for the sake of gaining a better insight into the Torah) and not for the purpose of intensifying religious emotions.[7] The cultivation of awe and reverence for God, according to Rabbi Hayyim, was only the *beginning* of all wisdom. Without the fear of the Lord, a human being could not serve as a receptacle for God's Torah. But a receptacle is only a means to an end. It does not make sense to concentrate all one's time and energies upon the building of a perfect container. One must acquire the treasures which are to be stored away in it. The perusal of devotional literature, therefore, must not be allowed to become the predominant intellectual concern of the Jew. For nothing can replace the real treasurer, i.e., the intensive study of the *Halakhah*.[8]

Since in his hierarchy of supreme values, intellectual virtues rank above practical ones, the study of the *Halakhah* must not be geared exclusively to the needs of religious observance. He emphatically objected to any attempt to by-pass the research of the original Talmudic sources by concentrating Jewish learning upon the mastering of the various codes of Jewish law (e.g. The *Shulhan Arukh*), extracted from the Talmud.

According to a popular saying, to study the codes of law without their original Talmudic sources is like "eating fish without spice." But Rabbi Hayyim went one step further and charged that it was like "eating spice without fish."[9]

Searching analysis of the classical *Halakhic* sources represented to him the highest form of divine service. Although he was so scrupulous about his daily prayers that he went at times to extreme efforts in order to worship with a *Minyan* (quorum for public worship), he nevertheless told his disciples that he would be willing to trade the value of all his prayers for the discovery of a single novel law which would derive from his Talmudic researches.[10]

He constantly admonished his students to be mindful of the hegemony of learning in the Jewish religious life. He warned them to be on guard lest exaggerated concern over their spiritual growth interfere with their pursuit of *Halakhic* studies. Even the

---

[7]*Nefesh ha-Hayyim* IV, 3.
[8]Ibidem, IV, 6-9.
[9]*Keter Rosh, Orhot Hayyim,* Sec. 49.
[10]Ibidem, Sec. 48.

Mishnah's recommendation to ponder "the proper way which man should choose for himself" does not apply to precious time which one could possibly devote to the study of the Torah. According to our rabbi, it is intended only for those periods which, anyway, could not be utilized for the acquisition of *Halakhic* knowledge.[11]

He gave dramatic expression to his conviction that Torah study had to provide the spiritual justification for the very existence of the universe. Since "the world might collapse if at any given moment it would be totally deprived of the spiritual support furnished by the pillar of Torah learning",[12] Rabbi Hayyim took steps to insure that in his *yeshivah* there would be at all times, day or night, at least one individual engaged in the study of Torah. At the conclusion of the fast on Yom Kippur, while the students went home to break the fast, he remained in the *yeshivah,* engaged in study, until one of the disciples finished his meal and was able to relieve him.

It was on the issue of the primacy of *Halakhic* studies that the vast theoretical differences between Rabbi Hayyim's philosophy and that of Hassidism revealed themselves. Because the latter assigned a secondary place to the study of Torah, Rabbi Hayyim was convinced that it represented a major departure from classic Judaism. But he nevertheless maintained cordial personal relations with the Hassidim, since he felt that they had no *intention* of making a radical break with the *Halakhah.*

His conciliatory attitude towards the new sect stands in striking contrast to the position of the *Gaon* of Vilna, who excommunicated them and even refused to enter into discussions with the leaders of the movement, who were anxious to convince him of their loyalty to *Halakhic* Judaism. The *Gaon's* unbending opposition was due to his suspicion that the new movement was another manifestation of the pseudo-Messianic tendencies which had played such havoc with traditional religion. Since Hassidism followed so closely upon the heels of the Frankist movement, there were ample grounds to fear that the relatively minor changes it had introduced into the order and timing of prayers foreshadowed the outbreak of a major anti-nomian revolt and the beginning of a new sect which ultimately would openly challenge the validity of the Halakhah. Hassidism's accent upon religious sentiment and its disparagement of learning represented to the *Gaon* further danger

---

[11]*Ruah Hayyim,* II, 9.
[12]*Nefesh ha-Hayyim,* IV, 25.

signals, warning that a complete break with the *Halakhah* might be in the offing.

Rabbi Hayyim did not share the apprehensions of his mentor. He was satisfied that the Hassidim had no desire of seceding from *Halakhic* Judaism. But while he conceded the nobility of their motives, he was convinced that the methods advocated by them reflected a misunderstanding of the unique nature of Judaism.

He felt that, without virtually abrogating the authority of the *Halakhah,* the new movement reduced it to a secondary place in the realm of religious values. What really mattered in the Hassidic scheme was not the adherence to the *Halakhah,* but the quality and intensity of the sentiments accompanying the performance of a religious act. The fulfillment of a *Mitzvah* to them possessed genuine significance only to the degree that it was suffused with *Kavanah* (the intention of achieving communion with God). By the same token, infringements on *Halakhic* precepts could, under special circumstances, be justified on the grounds that the technical violation of the law was necessary for the attainment of a spiritual end.

It can thus be easily recognized that Hassidism was walking a tightrope in attempting to adhere to the rigid pattern of the *Halakhah* while at the same time acknowledging the primacy of the subjective intention of the individual.

Although Hassidism wished to remain loyal to *Halakhic* Judaism, it nonetheless subordinated the specific *Halakhic* values to spiritual values which can be based upon an appeal to universal religious sentiments. In the final analysis, its approach stressed the elements of natural religion which are common to all of mankind, rather than the specific Jewish values which rest solely upon a specific divine revelation to Israel.

Rabbi Hayyim did not deny the validity of the universal religious values which were espoused by the Hassidim in their doctrine that God could be found everywhere and that every act can serve as the expression of man's desire to seek communion with God. But he demonstrated that, insofar as Judaism is concerned, the subjective factor in religion (the *Kavanah* of the individual) must be accommodated within the objective domain of the *Halakhah.*

A person may spend the entire night of Passover meditating upon the profound spiritual values which are to be expressed by the eating of the Matzah. Yet all this will be of no avail, if he fails to perform the prescribed physical act of eating the Matzah

On the other hand, an individual who eats the Matzah without being conscious of the *Kavanot*, which should be associated with this act, still has satisfied the requirements of the law.[13]

The subjective religious experience, according to Rabbi Hayyim, must never be allowed to overrule the objective *Halakhah*. He frowned upon any suggestions that under extraordinary circumstances deviations from the *Halakhah* might serve a genuine spiritual purpose. Hence, transgressions of the *Halakhah* cannot be justified on the ground that they are deemed necessary for the attainment of a sublime spiritual objective. Ever since the Torah was given, the *Halakhah* has remained the ultimate standard for the evaluation of any act performed by a Jew. Whatever favorable references to *Averah Lishmah* (violation of the law committed with a holy intent) are found in the Talmudic literature, they apply, according to him, either to the period before the Torah was given on Mount Sinai or to the non-Jew, who even today is not bound by the content of the Sinaitic revelation.[14]

Behind his ardent espousal of a strictly *Halakhic* approach to religion, there loomed a metaphysical view concerning the relation of God to the world, which differed radically from that of Hassidism. The latter doctrine stressed the nearness of God, whose glory fills the universe. Accordingly, reflections of the divine can be experienced everywhere. As Rabbi Shneyur Zalman of Liady put it, in a classic passage: "All that man sees—the heaven, the earth and all that fills it—all these things are the external garments of God, but by observing them, man recognizes the inner spirit, the divine vital force which permeates them."[15]

Rabbi Hayyim believed that the Hassidic position regarding God's immanence in the world was fraught with serious dangers to the integrity of Judaism. It was very likely that in the popular mind the doctrine might be confused with an outright pantheism. Moreover, if God's presence is equally revealed everywhere, then all the distinctions between the sacred and the profane would be obliterated. How then, he asks, could the *Halakhah* regard certain locations as disqualified for the act of prayer or for the study of the Torah?[16]

---

[13]*Nefesh ha-Hayyim*, Chapter IV.
[14]Ibid. Chapter 7. Cf. also *Orhot Hayyim, Keter Rosh*, Sec. 132.
[15]*Tanya*, Chapter 42.
[16]*Nefesh Ha-Hayyim*, III, 6.

He rejects the notion that man can directly encounter God's immanence in the world. God's presence in the world is a mystery beyond the ken of all human understanding. Insofar as the *Halakhah* is concerned, we must treat the world *as if* God's relation to His creation would be confined to the exercise of Divine Providence. While God is immanent in the world, He is concealed in such a manner that we cannot apprehend Him directly. The *Halakhically* prescribed way of life is based, not upon the ultimate metaphysical *reality,* but upon the *appearance* of the world to a finite human mind. "Though, in truth, from His side, all of existence is equally filled with this Being, without any separations, distinctions, or divisions, as if creation had not taken place at all, we are neither capable nor permitted to contemplate this fact at all."[17]

TSIMTSUM

However illusory the appearance of finite creatures be, the *Halakhic* approach disregards all questions regarding ultimate metaphysical realities. The *Halakhah* postulates individual finite beings existing in time and space. How the existence of a finite and composite world can be reconciled with the absolute infinity, simplicity, and unity of God, constitutes a serious metaphysical problem, which the Kabbalah attempted to solve by the notion of the *Tsimtsum* (God's self-limitation or contraction to make room for the world: "To make possible the existence of a finite world, God, as it were, withdrew, in some sense, from the universe"). It was on the interpretation of the *Tsimtsum* that Hassidism clashed with the staunch advocates of the *Halakhic* approach. Rabbi Shneyur Zalman of Liady contended that the notion of the *Tsimtsum* had to be invoked in order to account for the problem of how a transcendent God could be the cause of a finite, material world. The notion of *Tsimtsum* explained how the transcendent God through this self-limitation became the immanent God who is actually present in the universe.

To the *Gaon* of Vilna, this interpretation of God's relation to the world was extremely objectionable, since it certainly implied a blurring of the distinction between the Creator and His creatures. If, as Hassidism suggested, the verse *"the entire universe*

---

[17]Ibid.

is full of His glory" is to be taken in a literal sense, implying God's immanence is the universe, one might easily arrive at an outright pantheistic position. This is why the *Gaon* of Vilna insisted that the notion of the *Tsimtsum* be taken not as mere concealment, but as actual withdrawal, God limiting His presence in the universe to the exercise of Providence.

Rabbi Hayyim accepted in substance the position of the *Gaon,* although he adopted in certain details Rabbi Shneyur Zalman's exposition of the term *Tsimtsum.* Because of the superficial resemblance between the latter's interpretation and that of Rabbi Hayyim's, many writers have mistakenly assumed that the Gaon's favorite disciple forsook the metaphysical view of his own teacher to embrace that of Rabbi Shneyur Zalman.[18] There is, however, one fundamental difference which has escaped their attention. Although both interpret *Tsimtsum* not as withdrawal but as concealment, they apply it to two entirely different aspects of God. For Rabbi Hayyim, it is the *immanent* God who has concealed himself to make possible the appearance of an independent world. *Tsimtsum* supplies the answer to the question: How can there be any room for individual finite beings, if God's presence permeates all of reality? Accordingly, God's self-concealment makes it possible for the world to appear as if it possessed independent reality. While metaphysically speaking, God is immanent in the world, His presence is a mystery transcending the bounds of human cognition. Hence, insofar as our knowledge is concerned, we must treat the world as if it possessed independent reality, subject, of course, to Divine Providence.

For the author of the Tanya, *Tsimtsum* relates not to the immanence but to the transcendence, of God. The problem of God's relation in the world is encountered on a different level. The difficulty solved by *Tsimtsum* is how the existence of a world can be reconciled with the transcendence of an infinite God. In Rabbi Shneyur Zalman's scheme, it was the self-concealment of

---

[18]Thus Teitlebaum in *"Harav Miliady"* (Warsaw 1941) Vol. 2 p. 92 maintains that the differences between Rabbi Hayyim and Rabbi Shneyur are merely a matter of terminology. Rabbi Charles Chavel incorporated Teitlebaum's conclusions in his essay "Shneyur Zalman of Liady" in the Jewish Library, Vol. VI, p. 75. The interpretation set forth in this study, which obviates the need for the rather implausible assumption made by Teitlebaum, is based largely upon extremely helpful suggestions which I received from my revered teacher, Rabbi Joseph B. Soloveitchik, to whom I am also indebted for having drawn my attention to the implications on natural religion which follow from Rabbi Hayyim's and Rabbi Shneyur Zalman's views concerning the *Tsimtsum.*

the transcendent God, which made it possible for Him to become the Creator of the Universe, in which He is immanent and in which He can be apprehended, since the entire universe is literally filled with His presence.

Whether *Tsimtsum* applies only to God's transcendence or to His immanence in the world is far from being merely a purely theoretical, metaphysical issue. It is responsible for two complete divergent attitudes towards the entire domain of natural religion. Since Hassidism limited the self-concealment of God to His transcendence, God's presence can readily become manifest to the discerning mind which can penetrate beyond the outer surface to the inner essence of reality. We, therefore, need not rely on any special Divine revelation to find reflections of divinity. The human mind and the human heart can gain access to God without having recourse to the bridge established by His revelation in the Torah. Hence, natural religious impulses which are based upon universal human experience play a paramount role in the Hassidic structure of religious values.

In Rabbi Hayyim's system of thought, the situation is completely reversed. There prevails a rather negative attitude towards any form of natural religion. Since God's presence in the world is subject to His self-concealment, it is extremely difficult for the human intellect or emotion to encounter Him through any of His manifestations in reality. Instead, the revealed word of God becomes, for all practical purposes, the only means of reaching Him. Paradoxical though it may sound, man, according to Rabbi Hayyim, finds it easier to establish contact with the transcendent, than with the immanent, God. While God's immanence in reality is a mystery veiled from human understanding, the transcendent God has revealed Himself in the Torah. And it is through the study of the Torah that man can achieve communion with Him.

In Rabbi Hayyim's theology, the revealed work of God must bear the main burden of providing a link between man and God. Since God's presence in the world is completely concealed, our rational and emotional faculties are inadequate to the task of gaining any real insight into His nature or His relation to the universe. With natural religion shoved to the side lines, there is little to be gained from employment of the philosophical method. Whatever knowledge there is to be obtained on fundamental metaphysical issues has to be grounded upon His Divine revelation to select geniuses in the realm of the spirit. Small wonder, then, that in a slighting reference to the Jewish rationalistic philosophers, Rabbi Hayyim declared that "the wisdom of the Kabbalah begins at the point where all of philosophy ends."[19]

His own metaphysical views, which were intended to give a rationale for the meticulous adherence to every iota of Jewish law, were largely based upon Kabbalistic notions. Man is given a key position in the entire universe. Representing within himself a cross-section of all reality—from the lowest to the highest regions of being—he alone is capable of serving as a bridge between the various realms. It is up to man to determine whether the cosmic chain of being is to be brought closer to perfection or further away from it. The performance of a *Mitzvah,* though seemingly a trivial physical act, possesses, therefore, cosmic significance. For it sets into motion a series of events which have repercussion even in the most exalted realms of being.

In this anthropocentric universe, even God depends in some measure upon man. Just as food is necessary to enable the human body to be united with the soul, so does the world at large require the spiritual sustenance of the *Mitzvot* in order that God may be united with His creation.[20] Thus God is present in the world to the degree that man brings Him into it. The human task consists in the consecration of our deeds to the service of our Creator so that we may succeed in expanding and enlarging God's presence in the universe. Man's bearing the image of God implies for Rabbi Hayyim that he partakes, in some measure, of His creative powers. It is up to man to become a "builder" of the world by supplying the spiritual justification for its existence.[21]

Rabbi Hayyim carries the notion of the spiritual efficacy of man to the extreme of maintaining that man's immortality is the result of his own creativity. Man's part in the world to come is not just a reward bestowed upon him, it is the "natural" product of his own spiritual labors. Accordingly, our share in the world to come is not something ready-made, merely waiting for us to qualify for it by dint of our meritorious conduct. On the contrary, we ourselves must create our own portion of the world to come. It is through our loyalty to a God-given way of conduct that we build the spiritual worlds in which we remain even after our physical existence has come to an end.[22]

---

[19]*Orhot Hayyim, Keter Rosh,* sec. 61.
[20]*Nefesh ha-Hayyim* II, 6.
[21]Ibid. I, 3.
[22]Ibid. I, 12 *Ruah Hayyim* I, 1.

The dynamic role assigned to man in this world view provided an attractive setting for the thoroughly Halakhic approach advocated by Rabbi Hayyim. Rigid observance of all of the minutiae of Jewish Law was not a matter of conformity to a barren legalism but dictated by the cosmic significance of each Mitzvah. Yet even the scope of the Mitzvot is, relatively speaking, limited. Their influence is confined to certain aspects of reality. But the study of the Torah (linking man directly with the word of God), is the one method through which the total spiritual needs of the human personality can be satisfied. That is why Rabbi Hayyim's metaphysics lent itself especially to the revitalization and revival of Jewish learning, which was the paramount objective of his life.

To the modern mind, his system may appear somewhat narrow and excessively intellectual, leaving little place for the spontaneous elements which we may consider desirable in the religious life. But there can be no doubt that, historically speaking, his efforts were largely responsible for the renaissance of Torah learning which became the hallmark of Lithuanian Jewry.

When, in 1821, Rabbi Hayyim died, he left an impressive array of disciples. Inspired by their master, they carried on his work and labored for the preservation of Halakhic Judaism which regards "the four cubits of the Law as God's pre-eminent domain in the world."

BIBLIOGRAPHY

R. Hayyim of Volozin Nefesh ha-Hayyim, Vilna 1874 Ruah Hayyim

S. Maimon Sefer Hagro: Jerusalem 1954
Sare ha-Meah: Jerusalem 1952

M. S. Schmuckler Toldot Rabbenu Hayyim Mivolozin Vilna, 1909

Asher Ha Kohen Orhot Hayyim, Sheiltot Keter Rosh: Tel Aviv, 1955

TZEVI HIRSH KALISCHER

(1795-1874)

By Jacob Katz

(translated by Nathaniel Zelikow, from the Hebrew)

TZEVI HIRSH KALISCHER

By Jacob Katz

Rabbi Tzevi Hirsh Kalischer is generally considered the first of 19th Century Torah authorities to become possessed with the idea of resettling the Land of Israel. This group included such luminaries as Eliyahu Guttmacher, Samuel Mohilewer, Naftali Tzevi Berlin, Isaac Jacob Reines. It was Kalischer's creative thinking and dynamic action, however, which broke the ground upon which all the religious resettlement movements built.

Tzevi Hirsh was born in Nissan 5555 (1795) in the city of Lissa (Leszno) Poland, then a great center of Jewish learning. His ancestral lineage stems from the Maharal of Prague on the one side and from Rabbi Mordecai Jaffe of Grodno, Poland, on the other. His teachers were two of the great masters of the day —Rabbi Jacob Lissa and Rabbi Akiba Eger. Although, after his ordination, his services were sought by many communities, he refused to accept any rabbinical post but, instead, engaged in business to provide his livelihood. He settled in the city of Thorn at the age of 29 and the community, which recognized his true worth, seized upon the occasion to designate him their rabbi. He accepted and served without remuneration until his death in 1875.

Rabbi Kalischer was the author of many scholarly books on Torah, the Halakhic Codes and Jewish philosophy, but the work which expressed the consuming interest of his life was *Derishat Zion* (In Search of Zion). The ideas there expressed became the beacon which guided the religious to concrete activity on behalf of the resettlement of Israel. His main thesis was that "the beginning of redemption would take place in a natural way by the desire of Jews to settle in Palestine." The core of his thinking led Kalischer to conclude that

1. Salvation would come to the Jewish people through self-help in a normal manner;

2. Colonization in Palestine must commence at once; and

3. The re-introduction of Temple sacrifice in his own time was halakhically feasible.

209

He chose a novel way to publicize his ideas. It was in 1830 that he broached the idea of a return to Zion in correspondence with Rabbi Moshe Sofer of Pressburg, Hungary, and his son-in-law, Rabbi Akiba Eger. The specific question discussed was the restoration of sacrifice before the final redemption and rebuilding of the Temple. The implication of this correspondence was the possibility of a restoration of Jewish life in Israel, without awaiting a miracle.

In 1860, together with Rabbi Eliyahu Guttmacher, he summoned the first conference of the *Hibbat Zion* (Love of Zion) in Thorn. This movement later on became part of the organized Zionist movement. From this gathering emerged an appeal to the religious community to become active in the work of resettlement in Israel. A year later, he took an active part in the organization of the First Society for the Colonization of Palestine, while in 1864 Rabbi Kalischer founded in Berlin the Central Committee of Societies for the Settlement in Israel. He was also instrumental in influencing Sir Moses Montefiore to help settlement work in Israel, while through the Alliance Israélite Universelle he succeeded in persuading Karl Netter to found Mikveh Israel, the first agricultural training school in Palestine. Rabbi Kalischer advocated, too, the creation of a Jewish military guard to protect the new settlers. Among the Torah authorities he won over to his activities were Israel Salanter, Meir Lebush Malbim, and Hayim David Hazan, the Hakham Bashi of Jerusalem.

Rabbi Kalischer's life was completely dominated by his urge for the realization of the resettlement of Israel as an immediate religious goal, as well as an end of Jewish persecution everywhere. His all-enveloping belief was expressed by him in his favorite quote from the Prophet: *"But you, oh mountains of Israel, your branches shall blossom forth and yield your fruit for my people Israel, for they are at hand to come."* (Ezekiel XXXVI, 8).

The fame of Rabbi Zvi Hirsh Kalischer, as one of the personalities who heralded the advent of the *Hibbat Zion* Movement and of Zionism, is based upon his efforts on behalf of the agricultural settlements in Israel during the 1860's and 1870's, as well as on his later activities. It is buttressed by an analysis of the thinking of these heralds and of their functions in the course of the relevant events.[1]

---

[1]For a clarification of the concept of "Heralds of Zionism" see J. Katz "Return to Zion," 5710.

But this recognition of Kalischer's place in history is not sufficient for a clear understanding of his character. It has diverted the attention of the historian from seeing him through his own world and the conditions of his times. His biographers, rather than attempting to recreate the essence of his personality through careful research and from a study of his writings, portrayed him as if he had been solely one who, by twenty or thirty years, preceded Zionism, with its social diagnosis and its political interpretation. Actually, Kalischer, in his evaluation of the condition of the Jews of his days, was not above the standard of his generation. He did precede his successors by devotion to action, in accordance with the principle of later Zionism, but the motivations for his activities was different from those of Zionism. The connection between them, based on his role as a herald of a new era, derives not from identity of thought, but rather from the amalgamation of purposes and actions in the stream of history, in which different motives join in the creative process, yet which, to one viewing it from hindsight, appears as if created from single goals and ideas.

II.

The title "Forerunner of Zionism", bestowed upon Rabbi Kalischer, surely does not establish his place in the chronology of the nationalist movement, except in historical retrospect, for the purpose of "explaining a matter *ab initio*". On the scene of his era and in his generation, Kalischer established a place for himself among the remnant of leaders in Germany who were God-fearing men and in whose hearts burned the love of holiness. They were: the sage and chief of the Rabbinical Court of Wuerzburg, Rabbi Issac Dov Bamberger; the sage and chief of the Rabbinical Court of Altona, Rabbi Jacob Ettlinger; the sage and saint of Gratz, Rabbi Elihu Gutmacher; and the sage and chief of the Rabbinical Court of Eisenstadt, Rabbi Ezriel Hildesheimer. All these were giants of Torah and piety of the old German type, who were rightly considered remnants of prior generations. Their attachment to the world of tradition set them out as unique individuals in their own times.

By origin and education, Rabbi Kalischer does not belong to the German school. He was born in the Polish city of Lissa in 1795, which two years earlier had been annexed by Prussia, but was reincorporated into the territory of Poland between the years 1807

and 1815. His first teacher, Rabbi Jacob Lissa, the author of
Havat Daat, was a typical Polish rabbi of the end of the eighteenth century. Yet, in spite of his background, Kalischer's personality fits into the sphere of German Jewry, and one can venture the
guess that the days during which he studied in the yeshivah of
Rabbi Akiba Eger at Posen were decisive in this transformation.
Even though Rabbi Eger himself was isolated from the spirit of
his times, his sons and pupils came into actual contact with those
who were identified with the fermentation of the Western ideas of
equality and political change. Kalischer expressed himself on
emancipation and reform, not like the earlier generation of Torah-
authorities, who thrust aside everything new. He opposed them
after solid discussion, personal search, and evaluation. His abundant ties to the German Jewish scene are seen also in his view of
the great figures of the "enlightenment," such as Moses Mendelssohn and Naftali Herz Wessely, whose teachings he often quoted
with admiration and respect. This attitude is an indicator of his
personality, both as to type and character. The *toute ensemble* of
traditional life to which the "remnant" of religious leaders adhered,
is not their only characteristic as a historical phenomenon. If this
were the case, Rabbi Samson Raphael Hirsch would have to be
counted among them. But Rabbi Hirsch is in a class by himself.
The philosophical basis of his position sets him apart from the circle
of "remnant" leaders. The latter were observers of Torah and
Mitzvot because they dwelt in the world founded upon traditional
thought, explanations and expositions. Rabbi Hirsch, however, required a new set of concepts to establish the meaning of *Halakhah,*
the doctrines and the ethics of tradition; and that which is different
in this set of concepts distinguishes him from the religious leaders
of the older generation. From the typological standpoint, Samson
R. Hirsch fits into a later period, when the thinking of the "new
leaders," who had first shown their prowess in belittling the authority of the *Massorah,*[2] began to return to basic values. The remnants, however, submerged themselves in another world of tradition; they employed only the concepts of the past and its methods
of thinking.

Rabbi Kalischer's point of view is revealed first in the area
of *Halakhah.*[3] He employed the wealth of its concepts, not only
to clarify questions of religion and law (his book, *Moznayim*

---

[2]Chain of Jewish tradition.
[3]Traditional law.

Lemishpat, is a compilation for common use of latter-day authorities on questions of the *Hoshen Mishpat*).[4] He delved into *Halakhic* thinking to elucidate problems that touch upon national concepts: "The Right to Offer Sacrifices in our Times," the binding authority of "The Laws of Settling in Israel." He clarified them first through *Halakhic* thought. Only then do they become basic points for his philosophy of the State.

I do not want to create the impression that his *Halakhic* opinions were reached independently. One may contend that his concept of the Messiah or of Zionism were decisive in questions of sacrifices—to permit them, because in offering them he saw a means for hastening the redemption. As to the obligation to settle in the land of Israel—that he saw as a duty, because, as the fulfillment of a command of the Torah, it would strengthen his advocacy of public activity to that end. A study of his *Halakhic* discussions, as of his controversies with opponents, will reveal his conviction that as against all subjective viewpoints, his deductions were based on the objective proof from the sources of *Halakhah.* His ability to identify his thinking with the objective stream of *Halakhah,* is in itself the best evidence of his complete harmony with tradition.

In his philosophical speculation, too, Kalischer was tied to the world of the past. The names of thinkers like Spinoza, Mendelssohn and Kant, then currently acclaimed, were, in his judgment, bound to lead one astray. In his deliberations there is no grappling with their problems. The small number of new concepts incorporated in the storehouse of his language shows that his thinking does not vary much from that of the medieval scholars.

The role of "surviving leader"[5] fits Rabbi Kalischer by many tests. But it is not explained by saying that we have before us a type of person belonging to earlier times, who was projected into a period not his own. Even he did not escape the changing historical influences, and if he succeeded in keeping alive the world of concepts belonging to the past, he was also forced to reflect in his ideas the events of the present. Even though the strength of his concepts was not destroyed by their opposition to the new realities, yet they were put to new uses.

---

[4] The Fourth Part of the *Shulhan Arukh,* dealing with civil and criminal law.

[5] Elsewhere referred to as "remnant leader".

The generations that preceded Rabbi Kalischer, the preachers of the 17th and 18th Centuries, utilized time-hallowed concepts to interpret Biblical verses and sayings, not alone for the purpose of inspiring action, but to present them in different proportions. They do not intend to state the problems for which the concepts were originally created. This was suitable for conditions at the close of those centuries because then life progressed along well-trodden paths. Those who addressed themselves to the common intellect, both rabbis and preachers, served only to warn about loyalty to ideals which were observed without dissent. (In places where inner changes took place, as in Hassidism, new methods of inquiry were born.)

The homily[6] served a double purpose. It made room for intellectual activity, yet had as its main purpose the clarification for the common people of accepted ideals.

The homiletical approach reduced intellectual and moral power at a time when Haskalah and Emancipation shook the foundations of the community. The subjects with which they were now compelled to deal were open questions, which old-fashioned homiletics could neither grasp nor answer. Consequently, all who, from that time on, were obliged to explain problems of Judaism in the new milieu, avoided the use of homily. Only the religious "remnant" to some extent still clung to that method. They employed it whilst yet in the net of the categories of thought in which they were reared. They abandoned it as the spiritual crisis compelled them to struggle in the arena of contemporary ideas. Thus, most of Rabbi Kalischer's observations, in his commentary on Torah and the Passover Hagadah, were in the style of homily, and only occasionally does one find any apposite modern references to the burning questions of the day.

By contrast, in his book *Emunah Yeshara,* which was intended for the perplexed of his time, the systematic discussion of principle is primary, and the homiletical method secondary. And in his *Derishat Zion,* in which he deals with settling in Israel and urges action, he wrote everything in the systematic exposition, "fusing proof with proof," and intentionally abandoning the homiletical method. The author did not lack homiletical support, but felt that it would not be persuasive. He therefore relegated it to the footnotes. Kalischer desired to find his own way in his genera-

---

[6]In Hebrew *D'rush*—the method of preaching based upon interpretation of Biblical verse.

tion's perplexities of faith. He posed, and again and again returned
to, the central question of religious thinking of his time: Is
religion identified with its historical expression in Jewish tradition, or has it possibly an independent spiritual existence? But
his answers are framed in a way of thinking that generation
would not accept. But for Rabbi Kalischer's activities for "Zionism," in which he stood revealed, after a while, as one who was
in advance of his times, we would have considered him as one
straggling along, who seeks that which has already changed and
passed.

III.

This coupling in one person of "straggler" with "herald"
beclouds the ability to grasp him as one who perceived in his
own time that which others did not see until a later period. That
is the distinguishing characteristic of Kalischer in the historiography of Zionism. However, further research proves that his
acts as "herald" and the thinking forces that he set in motion
were well combined in his philosophy.

Rabbi Kalischer did not reveal the weak points of the Emancipation as a political solution of the Jewish question, nor did he
deprecate it because of the danger of assimilation that appeared
in its wake. Emancipation, in his eyes, had only one meaning—
direction in the history of the Jewish people according to the
divine pattern: "Not as in former years when Jacob was very
impoverished and could not raise his head. Now it can be said of
Jacob and of Israel, 'God has accomplished great good in giving
us freedom in the majority of countries.'" This concept of Providence is set forth in the two characteristics of the "remnant
leaders": their devotion to the methods of traditional thought on
the one hand, and contact with those stirred by their environment
on the other. The teachers of the "survivors", such as Akiba Eger
and Moshe Sofer, could react toward the developments of the new
era, among which was the Emancipation, by isolation and negation. But the new generation could not do so. They would attack
the breach of the religious fences, following in the wake of the
political and social changes (Rabbi Kalischer many times displayed his bitterness against the laxity of his generation in the
observance of Torah and *Mitzvot*), but they were not able to
seclude themselves from the new orientation in the lot of Israel
and they were compelled to discover its significance.

For a full understanding of the events of these days, Rabbi Kalischer lacked the pattern of historical and political thinking. Political liberation appeared to him in the light of the traditional battle of Israel among the nations. More than by the removal of conditions which had oppressed the Jewish communities in their respective lands, was he impressed by individual brethren who had ascended the ladder of Gentile society. He wrote: "From the time of the destruction of the Temple we have not had officials and noblemen as in this generation; everywhere in the world freedom has been given us. Jewry now numbers many officials and honored rulers."[7]

Kalischer looked upon the noblemen (he mentioned with high regard the names of Rothschild, Montefiore, Fuld and Crémieux) not only as important people for the completion of his program, but, above all, as chosen heroes of God, whose appearance was evidence that He remembered His people to restore the nation as of old. He was comforted by the "closeness to royalty" of certain individuals, through whom, even in the Diaspora, the fulfillment of Scriptures is realized, as it is written, *The sceptre shall not depart from Judah.*[7a] Upon Rabbi Kalischer's first meeting with the philanthropist, Anschel Rothschild, he refers to the comments of the "Shelah"[8] on this verse, a famous expression of the traditional approach.

Kalischer's view not only explained the events of Emancipation, but gave it historic authority. His generation wavered between the acknowledgment of the good of Emancipation and disillusionment because it had not brought forth the expected practical results. Indeed, those who fought for equal rights added to their real purposes the ideology of the Messiah, by identifying political and social freedom in their countries with the vision of the "end of days"; nevertheless, they judged the value of the historical event by the concrete achievements of their movement. Since they saw in the application of equal rights but the initial step for persons of equal status towards eventual absorption in the non-Jewish world, they looked upon discrimination still practiced in the non-Jewish society as a disillusionary repression. The signs of these restrictions (though not in the menacing fashion of the critical period of the 1880's) were apparent from the very

---

[7]Collected Writings of Rabbi Kalischer: p. 697.
[7a]Ber XLIX, 10.
[8]*Shelah* was a leader of 17th Century Jewry.

days of the granting of Emancipation and deepened the strained relationship between the emancipated and their emancipators.[9]

Rabbi Kalischer's appraisal of these matters was different from that of his contemporaries. He associated this turning point of Jewish history with Providence, hence was freed from feeling grateful to mere humans. But still less did he feel resentment for the social restrictions imposed by non-Jews, for he did not look upon social intercourse between Jews and non-Jews as the goal of equal rights. On the contrary, he censured all social intercourse between them as a danger to the uniqueness of the Jew living in accordance with Torah and tradition. On the other hand, he observed with pleasure the improved condition of his people and the strengthening of their security and in his innocence he fully believed, like his generation, that persecutions and oppression were at an end. Rabbi Kalischer did not see the crisis of the 1880's (he died in 1875). But the persecutions of the Jews in Rumania occurred while he was still alive and this brought forth from him the sole denunciatory utterance in his books.[10]

As against his optimism in the 1860's, one now senses in his words bitter disillusionment as to the status of Jews in the world; among other causes impelling settlement in the land of Israel in the 1870's was the fact that even in those days the yoke of persecution of Jews had not abated. However, his belief in Providential design visible in the Emancipation prevailed. The persecution of Jews in Rumania appeared to him an indication from Heaven that one should begin the return to Israel, the first step in God's plan of redemption. "In truth it is amazing that in these times where in all the world precious freedom is proclaimed for Israelites by granting them under the law equality with all the inhabitants of the land," this "small state is the one exception. Who knows if it was not for just such a time that these decrees were promulgated there . . . and that through the persecution it shall be proclaimed to the destroyed cities of Israel that our salvation will be achieved little by little, as it is abundantly clear from the Midrash and the holy Zohar."[11, 12]

---

[9]*Sefer Habrit,* commenting on Numbers Chap. 30, Sent. 3: "It is good to be friendly with the non-Jew, but one needn't be his constant companion."

[10]Kalischer "Collected Writings"—P. 440.

[11]Ibid., P. 441.

[12]Zohar—Ancient volume of mysticism, ascribed to the authorship of Rabbi Simon Bar Yohai.

IV.

To Rabbi Kalischer the turning point in his age appeared as the first rung in the ladder of redemption, after which the remaining rungs would be conquered, in accordance with the order which he found in the traditional literature, from the verses of *Tanakh* and the commentaries, to the words of the *Agadah*[13] and *Zohar*. His experience was that of previous generations who would fain foresee, if not bringing about, an early coming of the Messiah. From the turmoil of their day, they came to view the present as the threshold of a new era, and associated it with "the beginnings of the redemption" (*ahalta de-geulah*). From their understanding of the prophecies in the Tanakh, and the accounts of the redemption in the *Agadah,* or perhaps also from the thought-world of the Kabbalah, they formulated for themselves a complete Messianic concept and they awaited its revelation and realization. Rabbi Kalischer's conception of the Messiah saw that age as one of miraculous redemption and as its end-purpose, the revelation of prophecy and the holy spirit, as well as the sanctification of God's name upon all His creatures. The steps are: the ingathering of part of our people in the land of Israel by permission of the government in power; the restoration of sacrifices at the Temple site; and the transformation of the land into a "settled country." The succeeding step is the war of Gog and Magog.[14] In the end, the complete ingathering and the fulfillment of all the promises of the prophets, including the resurrection of the dead. This conception is comparable also to other conceptions of the Messiah, in that the first steps are to be the result of human efforts, as conditions of the revelation of the succeeding steps by the hand of Heaven—"through the awakening below will come the awakening above."[15]

In the concept of earlier generations, the conditions were the fulfillment of the *Mitzvot* or symbolic acts which are not part of the process of redemption. But in the Messianic concept of Rabbi Kalischer there appears, besides the restoration of sacrifices, in the class of symbolic conditions, the condition of a "resettled country" as the final step of the redemption, the attainment of which rests

---

[13] Agadah—non-preceptive portion of rabbinic literature.
[14] War which is destined to precede the final redemption.
[15] Kalischer, Collected Writings, P. 42ff.

in human hands, and is an essential condition for the succeeding steps, which are in God's province. This is Rabbi Kalischer's middle-of-the-road position. On one hand, he adhered to the traditional world of thought in all details, but on the other, he brought to bear its entire power for an answer in line with the spirit of the age, which pressed for action and disassociated itself from mere contemplative expectations. This tendency is found also in the philosophical development of Rabbi Kalischer himself. In the first draft of his exposition in 1836, the resumption of sacrifices was still considered by him the basic means for the realization of redemption, while the re-possession of the land, or at least the re-possession of Jerusalem, the achievement of which he imposes upon Asher Rothschild, is no more than a means to a means. As against this, in his book, *Derishat Zion,* twenty-four years later, "a resettled country" is the primary condition and the resumption of sacrifices is secondary. In the propaganda writings of the succeeding years, he progressively side-tracked the subject of sacrifices; and the theme of action for resettlement took its place.

Rabbi Kalischer knew that his conception of the Messiah was opposed to the popular belief that the Lord suddenly would descend from Heaven to earth, saying to his people: "Go forth." But the gradual process of the redemption: "That little by little the redemption of Israel will come to pass," was in his view a basic faith whose truth was beyond all doubt. It was but a correction of popular view, based on careful study of the sources of tradition. This conviction empowered him to characterize the opposing view as well-nigh a denial of the faith. When his beloved friend, Rabbi Elihu Gutmacher, impressed by the arguments of opponents, hesitated as to whether there was perhaps place also for the belief of redemption taking place all at one time, Rabbi Kalischer wrote: "Therefore, my beloved friend, please listen to a younger voice than yours. If a person comes to you with an oral or written statement, saying as in great piety: 'Wait for the Lord, because suddenly from Heaven Messiah will be sent,' rake burning coals on his head, saying, 'You deny prophecy.'" This personal certainty in his belief can be evidenced from his enthusiastic activity for reaching the rung of practical work in his Messianic concept—the transformation of the Land of Israel into an inhabited land. For this project, Rabbi Kalischer toiled throughout the last fifteen years of his life, even though the practical achievements were disappointing, and in spite of the opposition of men who were great and good in his eyes.

The Torah scholars of other lands were far from the historical
scene that had brought Rabbi Kalischer to this Messianic awareness. Rabbi Meir Auerbach of Jerusalem accused Rabbi Kalischer
of ignoring the burdens of the Jews in the majority of countries
of the dispersion, and concentrating his decisions on the emancipation of the Western Jews alone. Were not the Jews of North
Africa, East Asia, and in Eastern Europe, subject to the oppression
and degradation of the *Galut?* In the eyes of this resident of
Jerusalem, in those days still a weak and neglected city, but because
of its constant contact with all part of Jewry considering itself an
observatory from which one could view matters from a higher plane
that that of Thorn in East Germany, all the Messianic excitement
of Rabbi Kalischer lacked a real basis!

One who was not caught up in the Messianic experience of
Rabbi Kalischer and did not identify himself with his theories,
would not accept his testimonies. The sources upon which Rabbi
Kalischer relied could be interpreted otherwise; in any event it
was not an argument that could not be rebutted. Kalischer was in
the position of one who had the burden of proof. He sought to
arouse people to action in which no man had anticipated him, while
his opponents clung to the mystical approach with a faith which
relied on time-hallowed traditions. The very sources from which
Rabbi Kalischer drew his evidence also served the cause of his
adversaries. All the well-known sayings which make the redemption depend upon moral and religious virtues, but which exclude
it from the direct action by humans—such as "the matter rests only
with repentance"— were mobilized by the opposition. Kalischer
was not prevented from interpreting these quotations according to
his view, but there was nothing to move his opponents from their
opposition.

In his desire to persuade the community toward non-conven-
tional action through the means of traditional thought, Rabbi
Kalischer did not consider the weakness of his position. However,
the lack of an echo of his Messianic direction did not escape him
and, though his faith in the correctness of his belief was not
shaken, he became very careful in the choice of his arguments.
When the controversy in the wake of the appearance of his book
Derishat Zion calmed down, he reduced the Messianic emphasis
in his writings, through which he repeatedly exhorted the community to action on behalf of settlement in Israel. In the place of
the Messianic picture, he offered other ideas, some of which he

had advanced earlier in support of his view, and others, which he evolved later.

At times he would stress the practical aid that the agricultural settlements in Eretz Israel could offer to the unemployed in Israel, to immigrants from Serbia, Hungary, Morocco, and, in the end, from Rumania. The argument of immigration was a novel one which came to him through events following the time of his original inspiration. The importance of the commandment to dwell in Israel—that is to attempt actual settlement there— and the fulfillment of the laws which are bound up with the land,[16] is another argument mentioned in *Derishat Zion*. His later writings added new reasons to sustain it, such as the thought that all 613 commandments form one complete whole, and the non-fulfillment of any part of the *Mitzvot* interferes with the proper observance of the rest. Or take this theory: According to the Midrash, Jews were destined for exile only because of their sins against the commandments bound up with the Land; thus, the observance of these *Mitzvot* will become the first cause of their redemption. Rabbi Kalischer even indulged in the warning of *gilgool* (transmigration):[17] since the opportunity has been afforded to fulfill the commandments connected with the Land, at the very least through an agent (vicariously), anyone who abstains from such fulfillment, he argued, is liable to the punishment of *gilgool* in order to compensate for his dereliction.

During this period Rabbi Kalischer saw the prospect of realizing greater influence through the theories from the *Sefer Haharedim* and the *Shelah* than through the idea of preparation for redemption, which he almost concealed and mentioned but in correspondence with those very near to his views. His evaluation of public opinion was sound, at least in the negative aspect. Those who agreed with Rabbi Kalischer's Messianic theories were few. They were: Rabbi Elihu Gutmacher, Dr. Hayyim Lurie, Rabbi Nathan Friedland, who were either influenced by him, or themselves came to think as he did. Above all, there was Rabbi Judah Alkalai, who in his spiritual world view was a unique type and in the dynamics of this Messianic approach exceeded even Rabbi Kalischer. Others, like Rabbi Ezriel Hildesheimer or Dr. Marcus Lehmann, who were ready to support

---

[16]Biblical commandments whose observance is mandatory only on those residing in the Land of Israel.

[17]Cp. the Responsum of RLBH (Ralbah—R. Leviben Habib).

Rabbi Kalischer within the framework of The Society for Settlement in Israel, the social organization founded to advance his goal and that of his circle, or those who labored with the same purpose within the framework of other organizations, like Carl Netter through the *Alliance Israélite Universelle,* though influenced by Rabbi Kalischer's published writings, acted as they did, not on the strength of his argument, in any event, not because of his basic theory. Theirs was a rational activity, part of an isolated and limited purpose, such as relief to downtrodden brethren or assistance to those performing a *Mitzvah*—a purpose which could be deflected by certain known misgivings or because of other pressing activities. In vain did Rabbi Kalischer reprove Dr. Lehmann on his quick retreat because of practical and religious scruples, and Rabbi Hildesheimer, in that he saw his work for the settlement of Israel only as one of the many *Mitzvot* in which he was engaged. Between them lay a deep gulf, which separated a person possessed of a single vision, though irrational, perhaps, from people who perform their deeds upon a rational principle of values.

If Rabbi Kalischer did not succeed in arousing a movement among the religious, he was still less successful with the circles which had put themselves beyond the boundary of tradition. His words were received by the typical *Maskilim*[18] of those days as a voice coming from a lost world, whether they read them in the original or in German translations, which made their appearance somewhat later. Moses Hess was the only one of the *Maskilim* of the generation of whom we know that after reading his book he concurred with Rabbi Kalischer. However, Hess arrived at a conclusion similar to that of Rabbi Kalischer on the basis of entirely different data. This closeness of Hess and Kalischer contains a hint of future possibilities for an interlocking of the two branches of Zionism, after a period of drifting apart; the one which grew and blossomed from the soil of ancient Judaism and the other, the fruit of the new dialectic development, a kind of returning after a long period of estrangement. Hess himself sensed that the historical meaning of this meeting of the minds was proof for his idea that the day will come when "religious Jews will stretch forth a hand to the non-religious Jews on the basis of our nationalism, which we have in common."

---

[18]*Haskalah* was the Jewish counterpart of the enlightenment movement of the 18th century, which usually rejected traditional religious values.

V.

One who seeks to understand the source of the impulses of historical personalities does not discharge his duty by mere description of the line of thinking explicit in their words. He must inquire to find whether, perchance, behind explicit motives there were hidden aims and drives, which were not sufficiently known or entirely clear even to the persons themselves. An affirmative answer to this question is gathered from the views of the historians, who attributed to Rabbi Kalischer political perception in line with later Zionist formula, or saw in his words and deeds an expression of the new nationalism, to which he adhered because of its growing influence upon the European peoples of this period. Both of these ignored the powerful influence of the Messianic foundations in the thought-pattern of Rabbi Kalischer. His use of traditional values appeared to them as lacking a standard by which to understand the man and to explain his teachings.

One who sees Rabbi Kalischer as a political interpreter of the distress of the *Galut,* or he who considers his Messianic belief as but an ideological justification, has nothing, in fact, upon which to rely, except the simple sociological scheme, according to which the forces for any act derive from the material data of the situation, and the accompanying reasons offered are merely the reflection of the material forces in the mirror of the consciousness of those who project them.

In later Zionism, oversimplification gave rise to the belief that Zionism was developed to satisfy material needs. However, with respect to the forerunners of Zionism, among whom we include Rabbi Kalischer, such a theory does not contain even a particle of truth. It is sufficient to go back and observe the optimism of Rabbi Kalischer in his appraisal of the status of Jews in the 1860's. He saw no rule for the exodus of the Jews from the lands of the dispersion. To him it tended but to prove that there existed people who could go and do the work for preparing the redemption. In his letter to Rothschild in 1836, he foresaw that they would come "from all lands without hindrance, without onerous taxes, or enslavement by the ruler of the land." Here he points especially to residents of Poland "who are still in distress." In *Derishat Zion,* written in 1862, he applies the same rule to inhabitants of Russia, Poland and Germany: "From every place the poor shall come and the rich will help them."

The program, on its material side, rested principally on the potentialities and needs of the old—settlement in the land. Gradually, Rabbi Kalischer would use every report, from near and far, about the awakening of Jews to the idea of settling in the Land of Israel, to show that his plan had solid foundations. However, originally the program was not intended to serve an actual need, except for the Palestinian Jews alone, whose productivity problem had long concerned the Jewish people. On this point Rabbi Kalischer actually grasped the realistic data and he argued that his program would offer real cure for the ills of the *Halukah*.[19] This purpose fits in well into his general plan of making the land a "settled country," and everything that was accomplished in his day for the sake of the *Yishuv* he evaluated from this viewpoint, even though it served the ulterior purpose as well.

The second view, which sees in the nationalism of the European countries a source of inspiration for the awakening of Rabbi Kalischer, apparently finds support in his writings. In his call to the Jewish community he dwells specifically on the movements of his day and offers them as *ad majorem* plea to his own people: "Why do Italians and natives of other countries sacrifice their lives for their fatherlands?" he asks. "How much more should this be the case for a land which inhabitants of the entire world declare holy?"

The question is: What power and what weight has this in the general motivation of Rabbi Kalischer? The modern nationalistic historian, for whom Kalischer's other arguments have no moving power, transfers his motives to the rabbi and strives to find in nationalism the motivating force of his works. However, a study of the sources refutes this interpretation. First of all, the Providential explanation of Emancipation and the Messianic conclusion that Kalischer drew from it, had the primacy of all his other ideas. The matter is expounded in his letter to Rothschild in the year 1836, and serves as background for the *Halakhic* discussion with Rabbi Akiba Eger that year on the subject of the restoration of sacrifices. The Messianic view of the great turn in the history of the people of Israel formed the core of Rabbi Kalischer's philosophy; around that core were integrated the other ideas and they became the impulses of action and argument, each in its time. Apparently, it was precisely the nationalistic motive that remained a secondary idea

---

[19] A system of relief for supporting the Jewish poor in the Holy Land with funds collected from abroad.

in Rabbi Kalischer's view, nor did he grasp it to its depth. That argument did not appear except in publications designed for the masses, but in his private letters, which reveal his inner relation to things, there is no trace of it.

The place of nationalism in the philosophy of Rabbi Kalischer is nicely defined by the phrase of *Kal-va-homer* (inference *ad majorem*), which he employs in every place that he mentions it. The ideas of other peoples, he noted, should serve as a "reminder of guilt" to his own, who were indifferent to holy matters, when others were making the supreme sacrifice for even profane things. That differentiation between holy and profane stands out with emphasis. The thought process of Rabbi Kalischer, composed wholly from time-hallowed traditions, did not absorb even an iota of an idea from the tenets of the modern nationalism. The very word was missing from his Hebrew vocabulary. He clung to the foreign word "nationale." How much less did the auxiliary concepts of nationalism, such as history, the national feeling, the attachment to language and land, find place in his words. Their place was occupied by proof from the reasoning method of the Middle Ages, to which he clung consistently.

He did not properly evaluate the unifying power of nationalism for those absorbed within its bounds. He never felt the contradiction: that on one hand he himself praised the sense of belonging achieved by Jews within the ranks of the free citizens of a country, and on the other, he demanded action to hasten the redemption of Israel. His generation felt this inconsistency and it was a paramount cause in the express surrender of those who were renewing the hope of redemption. The Zionists of a later period grasped the problem very clearly in their logical consistency, even though their practical solutions tended toward an opposite purpose from that of the earlier Zionists. However, Rabbi Kalischer treated this problem lightly. He drew upon the analogy that princes and kings, too, acquire possessive property in lands not theirs. In another place he seeks to resolve this inconsistency through the projection of the spiritual character ascribed to the end of the redemption! "This is not a principle against the love of our land and government, since we desire Messiah, not in order to possess the land of our fathers, but only in order that it may cause the light of the Lord to shine on us, the holy spirit and prophecy." Here he follows his teachers, Rabbi Akiba Eger and Rabbi Moshe Sofer. They used this theory in their controversies with the leaders of the early reform movement. These words were uttered, no doubt, from subjective honesty, but they reflect lack of real contact with the basic problem. Those answers were perhaps sufficient in the past, when the citizenship of the Jew required of him loyalty only to the sovereign and nothing more. As regards national citizenship of the nineteenth century, this answer was no more satisfactory.

Nationalism as it concerns Rabbi Kalischer, is that of ancient Judaism, which views the continued existence of the people and its unity as a solid fact, and the relationship of individuals to the national body in their voluntary identification with the sum total of tradition also in its philosophic and practical meaning. In his view, those who threw off the yoke of tradition are the exception. In the controversy between those who introduce new concepts and those who guard the old, Rabbi Kalischer stood wholly with the latter. Yet he would not shun people who were not deed-perfect in observing *Mitzvot*, and even desired to persuade them as to the merit of his Palestine program.

Obviously, the actual settlement in the Land of Israel should be accomplished only through devoted observers of *Mitzvot*. He was severe with the leaders of the religious community of Germany, who declined to take part in his program, for fear that the settlers make light of observing *Shabbat* and the *Mitzvot* associated with dwelling in the land. Rabbi Kalischer discounted these fears which, he thought, came from erroneous comparison with the breaching of the religious fences in the West. In the Land of Israel he was prepared to guarantee their full observance of the precepts of the Torah. He considered compulsion an acceptable instrument to that end. He himself planned to migrate to Israel in his old age and to accept religious leadership in Mikveh Israel. Rabbi Kalischer declared specifically that if the danger to the observance of the *Mitzvot* could be foreseen because of the work of settlement, then the plan would be a failure from its inception and it would have been better not to start. All this is self-evident to Rabbi Kalischer and need not have been said, except to indicate the error of those who relate Rabbi Kalischer to "nationalism" in the modern sense. The hallmark of modern nationalistic ideology, including religious nationalist ideology, is the inclusion of tradition itself within the notion of national wealth or a similar one, whereas to Rabbi Kalischer the nationalist values were included in the concept of tradition.

The name "herald" does not fit Rabbi Kalischer because of any unity between his ideas and those of Zionism. The correctness of this title stems from another source. The accomplishments of Rabbi Kalischer are a sign of the renewal of the hope of redemption, to return and to work, after a period during the initial days of the emancipation that saw an abandonment of this hope. He established a solid historical bond between himself and those who came after him. There are clear traces which lead from Rabbi Kalischer to those in Russia who prepared the new national life, the most important of whom was David Gordon. Not the famous leaders in the West, but the common folk of Russia listened to Rabbi Kalischer. Touching partnership in the work for the settlement of Eretz Israel, he declared: "As to the basic problem, it is only in Russia that many of the right-hearted wait with all their might for the holy inheritance of our fathers. To them apply the words: *'It is in your mouth and your heart to accomplish'*,[20] but as to the German philanthropists (with all due respect), one can say: *'Why have I come and found no man and why did I call and there was no answer?'* "[21] The connection between Rabbi Kalischer and those who left the walls of the old city of Jerusalem, to settle outside, is also manifest. Rabbi Eleazer Raab, one of their leaders, came into contact with him while still in Hungary, where he worked for the association for settlement in Israel.

Even though Rabbi Kalischer's influence over those who followed after him is beyond doubt, his ideas were not accepted in their original form. They underwent various interpretations, as happens to other patterns in history. Those that follow accept the ideas of those who precede them, but with changes that alter their meaning.

It is the function of historiography to restore to our forebears their rightful role.

---

[20]Deb. XXX, 14.
[21]Is. L, 2.

RABBI JACOB ETTLINGER
(1798-1871)

By Akiba Posner and Ernest Freiman

(Translated by Rabbi Leonard Rosenfeld, from the Hebrew)

RABBI JACOB ETTLINGER

By Akiba Posner and Ernest Freiman

Historical perspective is the acid test of mortal man. Under its critical judgment, transient 'giants' crumble to dust and popular idols vanish into nothingness; even as the genuinely great assume a new stature and emerge with a more majestic grandeur.

History measures each person, weighs his actions and judges his ideology. In the light of truth, it may accept and immortalize him and his philosophy or entomb him forever in the dead and forgotten past.

The century which has elapsed since the passing of Rabbi Ettlinger has now rendered its unbiased historical judgment. It has assigned him to the illustrious circle of great leaders whose wisdom and courage has made them the architects of the Jewish future. Like many of his immortal colleagues, he always carried the torch of the Torah aloft and pushed back the frontiers of darkness, ignorance and evil, better to reveal the kingdom of God. He forged yet another link in the divine and endless chain of Jewish history.

A new world dawned over Europe even as the 18th Century faded into history, and nowhere did its sun shine more brightly than in Germany. The dark Middle Ages were disappearing everywhere. In principle, though not always in practice, the newly-found liberty bells pealed for all, Jew and non-Jew alike. Everywhere, the struggle for emancipation was being fought with marked success.

Social, political and economic discrimination against the Jews were yet quite prevalent. As a people and as a religious group they were singled out and subjected to periodic acts of oppression and aggression. But on the whole, freedom, equality and fraternity were on the march and commenced to embrace the Jews as well and endow them, too, with a share of their blessings.

The ghetto walls began to crumble. Cultural centers and academic institutions were opening their doors and Jewish students from varying social strata were finding their way in. Communal and housing restrictions were relaxed and the social and economic status of the Jews improved visibly.

Jewish religious and communal leaders faced new problems. Religions as traditions, beliefs and practices were suddenly caught up in a whirlpool of change and progress. Theirs was the responsibility of securing the fixity of the hallowed traditions of the past amid the flux of the present, even as they were bound to anticipate and plan for a future yet unborn. Theirs was the task of guarding the time-honored heritage, the national spiritual riches, and to transfer the divine faith and *mitzvot* intact to the new generation. Their prime concern was to prevent these treasures of Judaism from being dissipated in a strange environment and overwhelmed by foreign cultures.

The new circumstances demanded that the leaders leave their ivory towers and protected isolation. They must now enter into this new secular atmosphere, learn its language and its mores and introduce Torah-ethics into mundane social and amoral economic intercourse. Without minimizing the blessings of emancipation, they had to discover ways and means of sanctifying the new life with religious values and enriching it with Torah observances.

The great rabbis of the day recognized full well the dangers imminent on all sides and knew that Emancipation often went hand in hand with assimilation. They understood that secular education as well as commercial bonds with non-Jews may well undermine tradition and dilute religious faith and observances. The growing ranks of religious reformers with their attacks on synagogue architecture, on prayer and on *mitzvot,* underscored this fear.

In this period of tension, as revolutionary and evolutionary forces were reshaping the face and the soul of Europe in general and of the Jewish community in particular, Rabbi Jacob Ettlinger appeared on the Jewish scene in Germany. Intellectual giant that he was, he well understood the titanic forces at play. He recognized his own responsibility and gladly accepted the yoke of leadership.

I.

In Karlsruhe in the Grand Duchy of Baden, a few days before Purim 5558 (March 17, 1798), Yakov, the son of Rabbi Aaron Ettlinger, was born. The family had taken its name from the small town of Ettlingen, where for many generations it had resided.

His father, Rabbi Aaron (1769-1849), a scholar of renown, was rabbi at the "Klaus" (*Bet Hamidrash*), and was Yukov's (as he was also known affectionately in his youth) first teacher. It was he who not only introduced his son to formal learning but inspired him also with profound piety. Yakov's Talmudic and religious education was continued under the guidance of the local *Rov*, Rabbi Asher Wallerstein, son of Rabbi Arieh Leib ben Asher of Metz, the author of a celebrated volume of Responsa, *Sha'agat Aryeh*. By Rabbi Ettlinger's testimony in later years, it was he more than anyone else who was responsible for his academic attainments. Till the age of eighteen, Yakov sat at the feet of Rabbi Wallerstein and steeped himself in Torah and Talmudic learning.

He simultaneously acquired his training in general studies at the local Jewish School. So proficient was he in his secular education that he became one of the first Jewish students admitted to the University of Wurzburg.

Study at a university was common practice of many rabbis of his day. It was their custom to devote about three years to secular studies and then to return to Torah learning and to dedicate thereto the rest of their lives.

These were fruitful years in the life of Rabbi Ettlinger. New vistas of learning opened before him at the university. His brilliant mind absorbed and digested these newly-found ideas and synthesized them with his vast store of Jewish knowledge and religious philosophy. Even during his university career, he continued his Torah education at the *yeshivah* of the illustrious Rabbi Abraham Bing of Wurzburg.

Though he did not remain at the university for a formal degree, affidavits and certificates from his professors attest to his diligence and excellence.

His tenure at the university was terminated abruptly on August 2, 1819, when his lodgings were attacked by a mob of students shouting the infamous "Hep-Hep." This had been the traditional slogan of medieval Jew-baiters. It derives from the first letters of *Hierosolima Est Perdita* (Jerusalem is destroyed). He escaped bodily harm by following the advice of his Gentile landlady and jumping out of his window into a back yard.

As a result of this anti-Semitic outbreak, all Jews of Wurzburg were forced to abandon the city for several months.

Yakov moved on to Fuerth and for a period studied at the *yeshivah* of Rabbi Wolf Hamburger. Soon, however, he returned home to Karlsruhe and settled down to an intensive schedule of learning and teaching.

In 5585 (1825) he married Genendel (Nanette), daughter of his uncle, Kaufman Wormser, in Karlsruhe. The match gave him a degree of financial independence. This, plus a modest income from tutoring, provided him with the economic security needed to carry on his intellectual activities.

His approach to study was original, creative and productive of many *hiddushim* (novellae). Under his father's prodding, he began to reduce to writing the results of his study and research. After one period of intensive study of the tractate Sanhedrin, he had compiled sufficient material for his famous publication, the *Arukh La'Ner.* This was to be but the first of a rich literary library which he was to produce.

He was extremely modest and withdrawn. But the leaders of the community fully recognized his extraordinary talents and often invited him to preach in the Great Synagogue. His sermons and lectures were well received and these, too, were ultimately published.

The government of Baden was well disposed towards the Jews and in an edict published in 1809 had organized the Jewish communities into a Jewish Council and divided the country into district-rabbinates. Of these, Hadenburg in 1826 became the first domain of independent rabbinical activities for Rabbi Jacob Ettlinger. Since the Jewish population was small and scattered, he established his home in Mannheim and officiated at the "Klaus" (*Bet Hamidrash*) founded by the famous philanthropist Lemle M. Reinganum in 1708. His most illustrious pupil in his school at Mannheim was Samson Raphael Hirsch, later rabbi of Frankfurt-am-Main.

In 1827, when Rabbi Ettlinger was but 29 years old, the Jewish Council of Baden appointed him one of the three members of its "Religious Conference." This was the highest committee of the Council, which gave advice and direction to all Jewish communities in the province in religious and spiritual matters.

Though he lived in a small Jewish community, his name resounded throughout Germany. His opinions and decisions were sought from far and wide. His *Halakhic* correspondence was voluminous and left an impact on many Jewish communities.

He was often invited to distant cities when an occasion demanded a fine preacher and an inspirational speaker. He was constantly called to community functions at which non-Jews were to participate. Jews of Germany were not slow in recognizing him as a talented statesman among his brethren and as a gifted ambassador to their neighbors.

In 1829 the family Lebren of Amsterdam turned to him with two requests. They asked him to prepare a detailed curriculum for the Rabbinical Seminary in Amsterdam. They further sought to induce him to come to Holland, to head this famous academy and help train the rabbinic leadership for the entire country.

In his reply, Rabbi Ettlinger readily accedes to the first request. He explains that at the direction of the Duke of Baden, the local school was being converted into a rabbinical seminary and he was thus involved in the preparation of its course of studies. He points out, however, that varying conditions in Germany and Holland make it difficult to fit an identical curriculum to both communities. Educational factors, availability of proper faculty and previous training of students, must be considered in drawing up a curriculum.

Yet he outlines broadly the syllabus he projected for Baden. The subjects included were intensive and extensive courses in Talmud, Codes, Hebrew Language and Grammar, Bible and Prophets, Mussar, Medieval Jewish Philosophy and Homiletics. He strongly urged in-service-training for rabbis both in the area of practical *Halakhah* as well as in preaching and lecturing.

Concerning the second request, Rabbi Ettlinger admits that his income was then quite modest and he would not be averse to increasing it. Yet he felt that his unfamiliarity with the Dutch community and the whole social structure of Jewish life there, made it difficult for him to accept their invitation at that time.

This letter written in such a gracious manner reveals much of the character, the broad horizons, the awareness of current reality and its problems and the sense of personal responsibility on the part of the author.

Rabbi Ettlinger thus remained in his community for another seven years until he was called to serve in a distinguished, though distant, city.

After the death of Rabbi Akiva Wertheimer (1778-1835) in Altona, Denmark, the leaders of the congregation invited him to fill the place. This position placed the incumbent at the head of the local *Kehillah* as well as of neighboring Wandsbeck and the counties Schleswig and Holstein. He was also to become the presiding judge of the Jewish Court, which enjoyed official government recognition.

This invitation was extended on the basis of Rabbi Ettlinger's renown and did not involve any "trial" or probation. The contract was brought to Rabbi Ettlinger by an honored delegation from Altona. It took the form of "two tablets", each containing five paragraphs. Outlined therein were five items of duties and responsibilities of the rabbi to the community, and five items of duties and responsibilities of the *Kehillah* to its *Rov*.

Since the contract provided for only a three-year tenure, Rabbi Ettlinger returned it and asked for a revision of this point. The leaders of the *Kehillah* assured him that this should hardly cause him any apprehension. They pointed out that the three-year clause was based on a very ancient local custom which was also common in many prominent Polish communities. Yet, in deference to his wishes, they assured him that they were ready and anxious to extend the contract for life. They further offered to amend the local custom after he had settled in Altona, if he so desired.

On Lag B'Omer, 1836, Rabbi Ettlinger came to Altona and was welcomed with great honor and ceremony. A few days later, on Shabbat, the twentieth of Iyyar, he preached his first sermon, which was received with great enthusiasm. In appreciation and in commemoration, the *Kehillah* published this address.

Preaching played an important role in Altona and Rabbi Ettlinger placed considerable emphasis on it. Through his eloquence its role was further enhanced and in his talented hands it became a potent weapon.

His sermons and lectures show painstaking preparation, systematic organization, and a courageous modernity of form and content, quite novel to the Orthodox pulpit of his day. The problem addressed was carefully analyzed, facts and arguments properly marshalled and the message clearly presented. The sermons were often introduced and closed with special prayers related to the theme. Time and time again, popular acclaim prompted the publication of his oratorical masterpieces.

There were times when Rabbi Ettlinger composed special prayers to be recited during services or read from the pulpits of all synagogues throughout the country. One such instance was in response to a request by the government that special prayers be offered on *Succoth* for a bountiful harvest. This Rabbi Ettlinger prepared in Hebrew and in German and distributed throughout Schleswig-Holstein.

Almost to his dying day, he employed his homiletic talents as vehicles of education and inspiration to promote piety, knowledge, love of God and the worship of His Holy Name.

Rabbi Ettlinger was, indeed, the master of the spoken word. Yet the full scope of his activities and influence extended far beyond the range of the pulpit.

II.

Communal education claimed a major part of his time and energy. Already in his youth in Karlsruhe, he had dedicated himself to teaching. Private tutoring, *shiurim,* and public lectures were even then his major preoccupation. In Mannheim, he was not only concerned with the teaching of the young, but was the prime organizer of the Rabbinical Seminary for Baden.

It was his outstanding personality which attracted pupils from near and far. His own harmonious blending of modern education and worldly knowledge with traditional Jewish learning, left an indelible imprint on all his students. This, added to his charm and warmth, made for many close and intimate relationships. When he moved to Altona, his two favorite pupils, Getschlik Schlesinger and Shmaya Meyer, came with him.

In Altona, Rabbi Ettlinger involved himself immediately in the educational activities of the community. Three years after his arrival, he helped found a Jewish elementary school under the auspices of the *Kehillah.* By Danish law, he was recognized as its supervisor. This academy, which catered to a large student body, maintained high educational levels, both in its religious and general studies. Its faculties were staffed by highly qualified, Torah-true, teachers.

The school was opened in 1839 and already the next year it became the center of heated controversy. The law provided that any pupil completing elementary school and wishing to continue his studies on a secondary level must submit to an examination called confirmation. Upon successful completion of the tests, he was to receive a certificate of confirmation. Though this bore no resemblance to the religious confirmation sponsored by the Reform movement in Germany, it yet aroused a storm of protest. Rabbi Ettlinger found it necessary to make a public declaration emphasizing the Orthodox character of the school and the lack of any Reform implications in this examination.

Soon after his arrival in Altona, he also established a *yeshivah* and regularly delivered the *shiurim* (lessons). Similarly, he taught a number of classes geared to the adult Jewish population of the *Kehillah*.

But the audiences which benefited from his teaching were not limited to the boundaries of Altona, or even Denmark. Despite his numerous commitments and preoccupations, he published many books during his lifetime. Still others appeared posthumously and many manuscripts still remain. His writings comprise commentaries on many tractates of the Talmud, critical *Halakhic* analyses, responsa, commentaries on codes, lectures, and sermons.

The range of his *Halakhic* correspondence was, indeed, worldwide. All major Jewish communities and all outstanding rabbis exchanged letters with him. A list of his correspondents reads like a 19th Century rabbinic "Who's Who."

Even as his influence was not bounded by geography, it is not delimited in time. To this very day, his decisions, opinions, and interpretations are indispensible tools of rabbis and scholars.

Altona was one of the great European Jewish communities. Although only about 200 years old, it could boast of such outstanding rabbis as Rabbi Tzevi Ashkenazi and Rabbi Jonathan Eibschutz. Altona then was a part of the Kingdom of Denmark, which maintained a fairly liberal policy towards the Jews. The government, for various reasons, permitted them to maintain their own court of law. Rabbi Yoker—as he was affectionately called in Germany (though in the scholarly circles of the East he was better known by the name of his famous Talmudic commentaries, the *Arukh La'Ner*)—was its presiding judge. Altona's was the last of Jewish law courts in western Europe and many Jews preferred to settle their litigations there. Here they could anticipate a fair trial, which was often denied them in governmental courts. Here, too, much time was saved, for, in accordance with Jewish practice, disputes were often placed on the calendar on the very day that they were brought to court. Monetary savings were also considerable, as the court charged only nominal fees.

Management of the court taxed Rabbi Ettlinger's time and energy. Yet, through it, he was able to gain a valuable insight into all areas of community life. He acquired a more intimate knowledge of the social, economic, and family tensions and problems of his constituents and his guidance, therefore, became more real and pertinent. Through the medium of the court, he was able to project the wisdom, justice and general ethics of the Torah into all walks of community life. The *Bet-Din,* by its decision, arbitrations, and counselling, removed the Torah from its isolation in the Holy Ark and from the academic ivory towers in the *yeshivah* and *Bet Hamidrash* and made it again, in fact, the book of life.

Among his associate judges (*Dayanim*), were Rabbi Yehezkél Joelson (1789-1885), a pupil of Rabbi Akiva Eger, two pupils of Rabbi Moshe Schreiber (Hatam Sofer), Rabbi Yeshaya Hollander and Rabbi Yakov Katz, as well as Rabbi Elia Munk (1818-1899). These and many other learned members of his congregation helped the rabbi by representing him in outlying communities and by preparing his pupils for his *shiurim* in the *yeshivah*. One of his outstanding pupils in Altona was Rabbi Ezriel Hildesheimer, later rabbi and founder of the Rabbinical Seminary in Berlin.

In Kislev 1842, his wife passed away and her sister took over the responsibilty of caring for home and children. After eight years and much prodding by his in-laws, he married Bat-Sheva (Sophie) Meyer, of Wurzburg. This happy and fortunate settlement of his personal affairs freed him again for greater service to his community and people. Particularly did he now throw himself into the struggle against the rising Reform movement.

III.

In 1844, twenty-four Reform rabbis assembled in Braunschweig. Their purpose was not only to coordinate and strengthen Reform activities, but also to intensify their attacks against the Torah, the Siddur, the traditional synagogue, and Zion.

Rabbi Ettlinger mobilized seventy-seven Orthodox rabbis and launched a counter-attack. He published an ideological pamphlet called *Shlome Emune Israel* (The Faithful in Israel), wherein he systematically refuted the thesis of the Reform movement and vigorously defended the truth and eternity of the Divine law.

Three years later, he again came to grips with the leaders of Reform, when they sought to revise the ritual of circumcision.

In these struggles, he impressed all with his integrity, his scholarship, and his good judgment. His personality and his talents brought him not only a host of personal friendships, but also new allegiances to traditional Judaism.

The methods employed by Rabbi Ettlinger projected him into the forefront of community affairs.

Leaders of the *Haskalah* and Reform movements had long since recognized the value of periodicals as an instrument of mass education and persuasion. Though the subscribing public was relatively small, yet, in time, these various publications left their mark on the influential strata of the Jewish population.

Rabbi Ettlinger recognized the promise and the power of such a medium and with the assistance of Dr. Samuel Enoch, principal of the school in Altona, founded a bi-weekly "letter" which he called *Shomer Zion Hane'eman* (The Faithful Watchman of Zion). It was written in Hebrew and German and soon became an invaluable weapon in the arsenal of Orthodoxy in their struggle with the forces of reform Judaism. Its contents ranged from popular and timely articles to *Halakhic* responsa. Principles of Judaism and its ethical motif, holiday material, poetry and prose, were contributed by outstanding rabbis, scholars, and men of letters throughout Europe.

In this project, as in many others, Rabbi Ettlinger demonstrated that he was ever adept in enlisting the aid of the modern and the contemporary in the defense of the traditional.

In 1863, the Danish king decided to complete the equalization of the status of the Jews in Denmark by abolishing the Jewish Court, which had been in existence for almost two hundred years. The dissolution of this *Bet-Din* obliged the Jews to bring their litigations to the general governmental courts. This action was received with mixed feeling by the Jews. But for Rabbi Ettlinger it had at least one salutary effect. It afforded him freedom from a heavy and time-consuming responsibility.

In 1864, after the Danish-Prussian War, Altona and Schleswig-Holstein were ceded to Prussia. King Wilhelm, its new sovereign, visited Altona in 1865. Rabbi Ettlinger was received in audience and invited to the state dinner. He made a deep impression on the king, even as he had previously done in his meetings with state officials in Baden and Denmark. Fortunately, the rights which the Jewish community had acquired from the Danish king were continued under Prussian rule.

One of the high points of his career was on the occasion of the 25th anniversary of his election to the rabbinate of Altona. All his constituents wanted to do honor to their beloved leader. At the gala festivities, which started on Saturday night, *Lag B'Omer,* were present not only all Jewish residents of Altona, but also representatives from the many small neighboring communities, where Rabbi Ettlinger also served.

Many and varied were the gifts which he received. Among the many items of silver and jewelry was an album of pictures. His birthplace in Karlsruhe, his home, his *Bet Hamidrash* in Mannheim, and his present home in Altona were included in the vast pictorial array depicting the rich and colorful life of this spiritual giant.

On Sunday, a special program was arranged in the local *yeshivah*. Festivities were brought to a close with a banquet in his honor. Outstanding rabbis, community leaders, and governmental officials participated and paid homage to the beloved rabbi. A permanent endowment for the aid of needy students was created and named "The Rabbi Ettlinger Foundation".

He passed this milestone and continued on in ever-increasing service to his community. In all the years of his ministry, he faithfully discharged his many obligations and always to the complete satisfaction of all. He rose to his full grandeur in 1864, on the occasion of the 200th anniversary of the synagogue.

He reached his seventieth birthday in good health and in good strength. But then the disabilities of old age began to set in and suddenly he found himself unable to meet the heavy schedule which his commitments and duties required.

IV.

As he felt the approach of the dusk in his life, he prepared his last will and testament in detail. It is, indeed, a remarkable document, for it sheds light on his character and reveals the depth of his ethical and religious personality. In the will, Rabbi Ettlinger left specific instructions for his last rites. He requested that the word *Tzaddik* in the phrase *Zekher Tzaddik Livrakhah* (The memory of the righteous is a blessing), as well as all other praises, be scrupulously omitted from his tombstone. Only the names of his books were to be mentioned. He further asked that no eulogies be delivered at the funeral and suggested that his friends and pupils remember him instead by the study of the Mishnah and through charitable contributions.

Rabbi Ettlinger was called to his eternal reward on the 1st day of Hanukah, 5632 (December 7, 1871), at the age of 73. His funeral took place on Sunday morning and many from all parts of the country came to pay their last respects. Though he indicated his desire for no eulogies, yet his pupil-colleague, Rabbi Dr. Ezriel Hildesheimer, spoke briefly in evaluation of the departed saint. At the cemetery, his son-in-law, Rabbi Dr. Solomon Cohn, said a few words of farewell.

By special request of his family and by special permission of the city officials, the old Koenigstrasse cemetery in Altona was reopened and he was interred there.

Friends bought a house in Jerusalem after his death and named it Bet Yakov in his memory. It housed and supported many scholars, who sought to dedicate their life to learning and divine worship, free from the cares and demands of the mundane world.

With the passing of Rabbi Ettlinger, a whole generation of scholars was orphaned. He was the last of the *Geonim* (Talmudic luminaries) of Northern Germany, whose opinions were solicited and accepted by all rabbis and communities in Eastern and Western Europe. His deeds and achievements spread his name and fame throughout the world. From all corners of the Diaspora, people turned to him for guidance.

One looks back over the life of Rabbi Ettlinger and sees there a brilliant student, an outstanding preacher, an erudite scholar, a masterly teacher, and a fearless leader. Yet somehow, much of his many-faceted personality seems to defy reduction to paper and print.

How does one document and compress a lifetime of scrupulous personal ethics, an absorbing love for Eretz Israel, a genuine modesty, and the host of attributes which one finds only in genuine 'giants of the spirit'?

Is it sufficient to note that he was the godfather of Orthodoxy in Frankfort and the Hildesheimer Seminary in Berlin?

Is it sufficient to tabulate the monies which he raised for Palestine or to tell of the box of its holy soil on the roof of his house, in which, according to his wish, he was buried?

Is it sufficient to re-read his will, which forbade eulogies and words of praise on his tombstone?

Nouns, verbs, and adjectives can unfold a chronology and pinpoint highlights of his life, but hardly convey the complete personality or reveal the full genius of Rabbi Ettlinger.

Loved by young and old, admired by scholar and layman, a rabbi's rabbi and a teacher's teacher, Rabbi Ettlinger belonged to that small circle of rare individuals whom God sends to us at critical moments of our history to pioneer new paths, to discover new ways, and to help our people through difficult transitions. They belong not to a given time and place, but become the architects and the artisans of Israel's immortality.

Though called to their heavenly reward, they continue to live in a this-worldly eternity—even as Rabbi Ettlinger lives on in Frankfurt (Main), in Berlin, in Israel, in New York, and in every corner of the globe where a revitalized Orthodoxy is again gathering in our lost and straying brethren to a rededication to God and Torah.

ISAAC LEESER AND THE *OCCIDENT*

(1806-1868)

By Moses Legis Isaacs and Nancy I. Klein

ISAAC LEESER AND THE *OCCIDENT*

By Moses Legis Isaacs and Nancy I. Klein

The reader of a biography looks for, in addition to the usual recitation of dates and events, an analysis of the relations of the subject with his environment—that sort of equilibrium of action and reaction that makes up the life of a famous person. Often this is a difficult task, involving both research and interpretation, but in the case of Isaac Leeser, all this, including a picture of the environment itself, is laid before us in the *Occident*. This remarkable magazine, covering a whole generation of important American Jewish development, reflects in each page the thoughts and character of Isaac Leeser, while beyond the page we see the community and the problems surrounding him.

Isaac Leeser was born in Germany in 1806. When he was eight years old, his mother died and he and his brother Jacob were henceforth brought up by their father and grandparents. Isaac received a good education, both Jewish and secular. His mother's brother, a successful merchant in Richmond, Va., being childless, decided to adopt Isaac, and brought the young man to this country in 1824, when he was just eighteen years of age. He attended school for only a few weeks, and then for five years worked in his uncle's business. During this period, he helped the Rev. Isaac Seixas, the *Hazan* of the Richmond Sephardic synagogue, in his various duties, so that when an opening occurred for a *Hazan* in the Mikveh Israel Congregation in Philadelphia, he received a strong endorsement from people of prominence in Richmond. He applied for the position with some reluctance, being persuaded in the end by the urging of his uncle. He remained at Mikveh Israel until 1850, when he withdrew under circumstances to which we shall allude later. In 1834, he was stricken with smallpox; his brother Jacob came to his bedside, contracted the disease and subsequently died. This tragedy, together with the severity of the infection, required a long period of convalescence.

In 1857, friends of Leeser organized the Congregation Beth-El Emes and elected him minister. He held this position until his death, probably from cancer, on Saturday morning, February 1, 1868. His biographers make no mention of his ever having married.

247

The data of the preceding paragraphs are contained in one place or another in the *Occident,* a brief account of his coming to America being contained in the issue of April, 1852. What must have been an awkward and trying situation is presented. There is first printed a speech introducing Leeser to a gathering in his honor, in which the speaker orated, "In the year 1831 a poor, uneducated youth was toiling in the rugged path of mercantile life and earning a scanty subsistence by the sweat of his brow, etc., etc.," and by virtue of the opportunity that America affords, had made good. Leeser's response thanked the speaker and the audience, but made no corrections. These were given in a footnote which provides part of our biographical material.

The *Occident* was the first Anglo-Jewish paper published in America, and while it later had competitors, it was the only one during its existence that maintained a consistently Orthodox point of view. Isaac Leeser founded it in 1843, putting out twenty-five volumes, and even providing for the contents of the February, 1868 issue, which appeared after his death. It made its appearance monthly, except for the years 1860-61, when it was published as a weekly, usually having sixty pages bound between yellow covers and containing advertisements of Jewish interest. In the first issue, Leeser stated that the columns would be open to all sorts of discussion on Jewish religious topics, but that he, as editor, reserved the right to comment on any points which might require an answer from the traditional point of view.

Each issue usually began with an editorial, which, although written in excellent English, was generally long-winded and slow in getting to the point. We shall refer again to some of the opinions carried in his leading articles. After the editorial, which often was continued through several issues, there generally followed articles contributed by others, ranging from those of current interest (as in the case of the relics containing Hebrew writing said to have been found in the mound-builders' mounds in Ohio), to articles on Biblical topics. Then came reports on organizations such as the Philadelphia Foster Home for Children, which Leeser helped found, the Jewish Board of Delegates, of which Leeser was secretary and vice-president; followed by news items from various cities in this country and abroad. He often urged people to send in news of importance and decried the lack of initiative on the part of secretaries of organizations who neglected to forward items that should be known by the general public.

Although Leeser again and again stated the peaceful aims of the *Occident* and his desire never to create enemies, many numbers of the magazine bristle with polemical material, most of which can hardly be blamed on the editor. An example of this may be seen in an irate letter heaping abuse on Leeser for not publishing in full the writer's inaugural sermon. It is a letter typical of the times, full of bombast and replete with Hebrew quotations. Leeser published the letter, commenting only that it was just as received except that he was forced to correct the Hebrew in the quotations. Similar treatment was given on other occasions to correspondents of this sort, and so effectively that one finds no rebuttals.

From cover to cover, the personality of Leeser is impressed on every page and we can see depicted a one-man's eye-view of the expanding Jewish horizons in America. The peek that we get into Leeser's environment offers a fascinating picture of Jewish communities. In many respects the scene has an embarrassing similarity to our own.

In 1844 Leeser remarked on the suprising growth in the number of synagogues. Sixteen years before, there had been only one in New York; now there were two in Albany, one in Syracuse, one in Easton, Pa., one in New York City, one in Charleston, one in Savannah, and two in Philadelphia. By 1852 he was already aware of a curious phenomenon which had not appeared before in the two hundred years of American Jewish history, namely, the self-segregation of Jewish communities according to their country of origin. He decried this tendency of the Germans to form German congregations, the Poles Polish congregations, etc. He even argued that there was no reason for separate Sephardic and Ashkenazic synagogues. He particularly resented a pirating practice, which seemed common, of a new group coming into a congregation and then by majority vote ruling out the prevailing *Minhag* and substituting their own. This always resulted in the old group breaking off and starting a new service.

In other editorials we see Leeser inveighing against lack of decorum in the synagogue, and once he wrote sternly:

> "We regretted to observe in the place we attended, that many spent the Kippur day in running in and out; and we must pointedly condemn the practice of paying a round of visits to various places of worship on that solemn day; for such intrusion disturbs the devotion."

Public addresses by Bar Mitzvah celebrants were also in vogue in those days and some are printed *in extenso,* one, for example, starting with, "Allow me, dear parents, on this solemn occasion to express in a few words the heartfelt emotion of my youthful bosom," and then proceeding in more than a few words with all the thoughts and pledges with which the congregation is currently familiar.

One becomes impressed with the fact that the difference between the times of Leeser and our own is mainly a quantitative rather than a qualitative one. Perhaps the chief difference lay in the matter of food, since there were then practically no manufactured articles of food, save such basic staples as flour, and therefore the problems of *Hashgahah* were negligible, except in the matter of meat. In the latter case, Leeser found it necessary to organize for Philadelphia a Board of Jewish Minsters to supervise the *Shohetim.* The prototypes of the scoundrels whom we find today falsifying on *Kashrut* were not lacking, dear Reader. They were then busy with such things as the sale of cheap invalid *Tefillin,* claimed to be made by reputable scribes in Europe.

The publication of the *Occident* was no mean task, because it meant setting up not alone English type, but frequently Hebrew type for some correspondence and for quotations in articles and editorials. But Leeser's vision went beyond a periodical publication. He was ambitious to have for the American Jew a supply of books such as Bibles and *Siddurim,* as well as texts for Jewish schools, history books and books tending to stimulate the mind of the reader into thinking on Jewish affairs. He found the only available English translation of the Bible used in Jewish homes to be the King James version. He recast first the Pentateuch and then the rest of the Bible, correcting errors in the King James version and removing Christological references incorporated in parts, such as in the Song of Songs. There were two editions of Leeser's Bible during his lifetime and his text has been much used even up to the present. He brought out prayer books with English translations, both for the Ashkenazic as well as for the Sephardic services. His great hope was to have a strong Jewish publication society which could supply the people with an abundance of literature. He remarked once that if people would only read, the threat of Reform would be mitigated. He was able to put through the formation of such a society in 1845 with the publication of a number of works, but unfortunately, after only six years, the warehouse of the society burned down, destroying not only almost all the books which it had produced, but apparently all further interest on the part of the sponsors. During his lifetime, he was unable to reestablish the society, but as an incentive, he bequeathed in his will the plates of his edition of one of Grace Aguilar's works, to a "Jewish Publication Society," if one were formed within five years after his death. The present Jewish Publication Society, founded in 1871, resulted from this bequest.

Leeser made frequent trips to Jewish communities in different parts of the country to further the sale of his publications and he was perhaps the only individual in this period who saw all these groups and talked to their leaders.

For some years, until 1850, in addition to his work on the *Occident*, Leeser was still *Hazan* of Mikveh Israel Congregation. He had been engaged at a salary of $800 a year, and while the appointment was only that of *Hazan*, Leeser voluntarily assumed the duties of minister to the congregation. He introduced an English sermon before the *Mussaf* service and carried on the various activities ordinarily performed by the rabbi of a congregation.

Leeser seemed to have a faculty of incurring fast and lasting enmities, and practically from the start there was an opposition group of no small dimensions, which, from time to time, caused the pot to boil over. For instance, in 1834, a member of the congregation acted in a disorderly fashion during the services, and after a trial before the *Parnas* and the Board, was put in *Herem*. The *Hazan* was instructed to make the announcement of this *Herem* on three successive Sabbaths. Leeser not only refused to do this, but also refused to appear before the Board to explain his action. A vote of censure was passed against him for this. Again in 1849, when Leeser's contract came up for renewal, his enemies sought to embarrass him by insisting on the fulfillment of an early by-law that the *Hazan* post a bond of $800 (his salary was then $1200) for the "faithful" performance of his duties. Leeser had insisted that the new contract have an indefinite term, subject to good behavior, which was interpreted as a demand for a life contract. While the argument was going on, the *Occident* carried some statements that were considered contumacious by the Board, and again a vote of censure was passed. At a subsequent meeting of the congregation, it was said that the affair might have been dropped except for the ill-advised actions of Leeser's friends, whereupon the matter was put to a congregational vote.

Twenty endorsed the action of the Board, seven were opposed and there were two abstentions. Leeser was not permitted to present a defense of his position.

Out of fairness to Leeser, part of the above information, it must be stated, comes from an anonymous pamphlet, published in 1850, the general tone of which can be gathered from the following quotation, which tells how he "hurried through our beautiful ritual in a hurried and unimpressive manner, how unintelligibly he muttered the offerings, and what impatience he bore with anyone who he thought detained him too long with offerings. . . . Our business has been with him as a *Hazan* and it has been no part of our purpose to dilate upon the numerous objections to his personal deportment, they will readily occur to all who know him; and his best friends are always obliged to admit that he is an indiscreeet, imprudent man."

This was answered in the same year in a pamphlet just slightly less anonymous, the author being "An Israelite"—in which Leeser is well defended and the first author properly taken to task. Leeser from that point on fulfilled the few remaining months of his contract as *Hazan,* but discontinued his sermon and other work for the congregation. He described his withdrawal from the congregation as partly voluntary and partly compulsory.

The cause of Leeser's difficulties with the congregation stemmed from his determination to raise the dignity of the minister or rabbi. In the Mikveh Israel the minister was looked upon as an employee of the synagogue, bound to carry out the orders of the *Ajunta* or Board of Directors, and more directly those of the *Parnas.* Leeser challenged the right of the Board to bring him to trial for not obeying orders and he knew full well that the determination of whether or not his bond would be forfeit for failure to perform his duties faithfully would be a matter for the sole judgment of the *Parnas.*

Writing after his separation from the congregation, he puts the matter very clearly:

"It is therefore a great evil that in some places the affairs of the congregation have been put in the hands of men who, however expert in business and acquainted with the ways of the world and whose claims to be trustees of synagogues often depend solely upon their possession of superior pecuniary means or other fortuitous circumstance, have not the requisite religious information, nor a religious character superior to that of other persons to constitute them absolute judges of what is necessary to the advancement of the interests of Judaism in this extensive country."

His courageous stand, while full of painful consequences to him, made the path easier for all those who followed. Only a few years later, Leeser's successor, the famous Rabbi Sabato Morais, was given a life contract.

A matter not unconnected with the attempt to dignify the position of minister was Leeser's dislike of what we term today "shnoddering"—the public announcement of donations at the time of the reading of the Torah. We have seen how sputteringly angry it made the anonymous pamphleteer, and in the pages of the *Occident* itself we find plenty of evidence that Leeser's attitude was distasteful to synagogue officials, but Leeser repeatedly argued his point. In 1852 he wrote:

"Now tell some of our would-be righteous that they had better assist you in the abolition of the money offerings; and to introduce in their stead the reading of a passage of the Scriptures in the language of the country, or to finish the service with a sermon or a lecture, or even to recite one from the printed collection of some of those who have received the public approbation in the absence of any who could produce an original composition; and it is possible enough that you might be regarded as a heretic, as an innovator dangerous to the cause of Orthodoxy. But in the name of common sense, what has our religion got to do with ostentation? Is it necessary for the whole community to be informed that a certain gentleman or lady has had the will to appropriate, say fifty dollars toward the support of the charities or the general treasury of the congregation? Could not he or she send the voluntary gift to the collector or whoever the proper person be to receive the same, without proclaiming it in the midst of the multitude? And yet, more derogatory still to all propriety, is the making known to all, that Mr. So and So has made an offering, or so-called *Mattanah,* to the *Hazan* or *Shamas,* for which, of course, these officials must be duly grateful."

When Leeser came upon the scene of American Jewish affairs, he found hardly a synagogue which could boast of communal activities or an educational program. It was under his goading and leadership that most of these organizations, so vital to the life and smooth functioning of the community, were established. He was one of the leading spirits in the establishment of a foster home for children, although its beginnings were enveloped in an unpleasant controversy, centering upon Leeser's participation in the work. He was an early advocate of B'nai B'rith and of Jewish hospitals. Elsewhere we have mentioned the Jewish Board of Ministers of Philadelphia and his interest in educational institutions.

Perhaps more important than any of these was the Board of Delegates of American Israelites, which he was instrumental in founding and of which he was vice-president for many years. This was an organization of Orthodox congregations, not confined to Philadelphia, which elected a body of delegates who could speak in the name of American Jewry on matters of public importance. Its actual coming into being was precipitated by the famous Mortara case which shocked the Jewish communities of the whole world. One instance of its later activities is of particular interest. In 1862, the hospitals of Philadelphia were receiving more and more wounded Jewish soldiers, but there were no Jewish chaplains to serve their needs. The Board of Jewish Delegates petitioned Congress and there was ultimately passed a law not specifically providing for Jewish chaplains, but permitting the President to appoint, with Senate confirmation, chaplains for specific religious groups. John Hay, President Lincoln's secretary, wrote to the Board, saying that the President would name as chaplain any person designated by it. A Rev. Frankel was accordingly appointed and served with distinction. Parenthetically we may add, that the Senate ignored the appointment, making it lapse with the adjournment of the session, but Lincoln at once reappointed Frankel.

The influence of the Board of Delegates in obtaining the appointment of a chaplain aroused the jealous ire of a group of Reform leaders who openly proclaimed in the non-Jewish press of Philadelphia that the Board did not speak for American Jews. Tragically and characteristically, just a few years after Leeser's death, the Board fell into the hands of the organization of Reform congregations.

Of Leeser's many activities, education was perhaps to him his most important interest. Even his publications were instruments of teaching. He was most critical of congregations which provided handsome new buildings of worship, without making any provision for education. He aided in the establishment of Jewish schools in Philadelphia, and wrote and published "Catechisms" for their use. This book, published in 1839, and dedicated to Miss Rebecca Gratz, is an item of particular interest. If republished today, it would fill a want experienced by every teen-ager. It contains a list of succinct questions about Judaism, together with very well-put answers. In the introduction Leeser remarked that none of his publications had ever paid for itself, but his urge to supply the needs of the community carried him on.

In higher education he gave prominent publicity to the numerous proposals for liberal arts colleges under Jewish auspices—none of which, unfortunately, ever passed the planning stage. He lived to see the start of instruction in Maimonides College, which was planned to give the degrees of Bachelor of Divinity and Doctor of Divinity. Leeser served as the Provost, Professor of Homiletics, Belles Lettres and Comparative Theology. The college survived about six years. The prospectus promised training in *Hazanut* and *Shehitah* as well. The original plans called for a department of Natural Sciences but this was never implemented. How much actual service Leeser rendered to the college is problematical because he was already fatally ill when he assumed his duties.

Another aspect of contemporary Jewish life which engaged Leeser's attention was the growth of the Reform movement. His career was contemporaneous with the movement from its very beginning until it was fairly on its way as an established entity. The beginnings had occurred in Charleston, South Carolina, where something in the air seemed to inspire one leader after another to experiment with reforms in the service. The first was a Reverend Poznanski, who began to speak against the idea of a Messiah as well as attacking some of the other Principles of Faith. The congregation was resistant at that time to a point where Poznanski had to leave. He hied himself to New York to become a *Shohet*. On the way, he managed to obtain an endorsement from Leeser, who was wholly ignorant of what had happened. When Leeser discovered the facts, he published a long open letter of denunciation of the scoundrel.

Leeser could never bring himself to regard Reform as a movement; he considered reformers as individual sinners who nonetheless were Jews. Commenting on the views of a correspondent, he said,

> "He has a perfect right to say that we should not hate our reformer-brothers for their opinions, since we should tolerate

the sinner though we detest the sin; besides, errors have always existed and will do so yet longer; till the time when all mankind shall be converted to one faith and serve the Lord with one accord."

In the period of which we write, Jewish communities were springing up all over the country, usually too small to support a synagogue. The early settlers were generally woefully ignorant of Jewish learning and conducted themselves along traditional lines solely on the momentum of their early training before coming to America. For the most part they made no provision at all for the education of their children, a matter frequently dealt with in the *Occident.* In some there was even a spirit of rebellion against their past, described by someone to Leeser as "wanting to be a *goy* on principle."

In the communities which could boast of having a synagogue or regular services, Orthodox rabbis were few and far between. In the period covered by the *Occident,* there were perhaps only three names—Bernhard Illowy, a student of the Hatam Sofer, Morris Raphall and Sabato Morais—which could be listed as truly representative of the Orthodox rabbinate, but they were hardly a match for the forces arrayed against them. For the most part the leaders were *Hazanim* who seemed everywhere to be in ample supply.

If the Reform movement had started in clear-cut fashion, its effects might have been more quickly recognized and more easily combatted, but its beginnings were slow and erratic. Isaac M. Wise, for example, who put the Reform movement into successful operation, was, as rabbi of the B'nai Jeshurun in New York, irreproachably Orthodox. He was said never to have left his house without first studying a *Blatt* of Talmud. His "peculiarities", as Leeser calls them, developed one by one. In a letter written in 1858, four years after he had come to Cincinnati, he threatened to sue Leeser for publishing a letter which implied that he was not a Sabbath observer.

In this period Reform Judaism stood in much the same position as the right wing of Conservative Judaism does today *vis-à-vis* its direction and goal. To Leeser, a turn-about to Orthodoxy by Reform seemed as plausible and as short a step as some today consider the recapture of synagogues which have seceded to the Conservatives.

In 1855, a conference was called by Wise and others to meet in Cleveland to develop a *"Minhag* America." Leeser determined to attend this meeting with as many Orthodox friends as he could muster, in order to bring Wise and the others "to their senses" and persuade them to give up the aberrations which they had introduced into Jewish practice.

Without much preliminary organization, Wise introduced a resolution containing a series of basic principles, which declared that 1) the convention agreed that the Bible was divinely inspired, 2) all decisions to be made by the group must be based on Talmudic authority and 3) these principles must be the basic guides of all future synods. There was considerable quibbling about the exact wording, although no one challenged the content, so that the vote took place a day or so later. Leeser left after the first session, fully convinced that the gap between the new and the old was small, indeed, and the task of bringing about a return to the fold not as difficult as he had anticipated.

This resolution, in view of the results which followed, might be called in modern terminology a smoke-screen. Wise, for example, in his *Israelitish History,* published the year before, was already scoffing at the divine origin of the Bible. In one instance, quoted in later years in the *Occident,* he pictured Moses as either finding a store of hidden water at Meribah, or with some friends putting it there and covering it with a rock thin enough to be broken by Moses' rod the next day. Wise does not go into the procedure of how to handle water for six hundred thousand people by subreption.

Wise found easy pickings when he came to Cincinnati, for there existed a sizable group which was both profoundly ignorant, Jewishly speaking, and wealthy financially. The fly in the ointment was that his pupils were perhaps too apt. He freed them of the onus of the second day of *Yom Tov,* but on the first day of *Succot* in 1855 we learn that a surprised Dr. Wise rose to preach to an almost empty synagogue. He thundered at the empty seats to produce their owners, declaring that the festival of Succoth was just as important as Rosh Hashanah or Yom Kippur. The seats responded not at all, for their owners were enjoying for the first time in Cincinnati, business as usual on the initial day of a holiday.

Those who had already abandoned religion and those who took to Reform too easily turned out to be untrustworthy and generally

poor material for the movement. The established Orthodox synagogues appeared to be greener pastures, and there followed inva-
sions of these by tactics that would today be classed as fifth-column
techniques. Bitterly Leeser protested that if Reform had any justification at all it would be to take the place of no religion, and that
alone. As the movement continued to grow, poor Leeser states in
indignation that "the impious had never before aspired to the dignity of a party."

Although Leeser never abandoned the idea that Reform would
one day vanish and all of its adherents would return to Judaism,
he was nonetheless ever active in combatting the spirit of Reform
by publicizing any discomfiture within its ranks. As an interesting
example of this there is a long editorial in the issue of December
1865, in which he reported a meeting of the Board of Trustees of
the Emanuel Seminary of New York. A resolution had been introduced to allow election to the board of those who did not belong to
Temple Emanuel, on the ground that there was no fear of getting
Orthodox members. The resolution was vigorously opposed and
finally defeated by those who argued that the same thing could
happen to Emanuel as was purported to have happened to the Breslau Seminary in Germany. There, it was said, the school had been
established by an "out-and-out" reformer, but by sly and devious
means the Orthodox had gained control and had turned the institution into an Orthodox *yeshivah*. Furthermore, it was argued, there
were some synogogues in the South and West which had defected
from Orthodoxy in only a few minor points, and if representatives
of these ever were to get in, they would be "as dangerous as the
Orthodox." Leeser analysed these statements at length, going all
the way from denying that the Breslau Seminary was founded by
an "out-and-out" reformer, to the observation that Dr. Frankel, the
head put in by the Orthodox captors of the board, was not nearly
Orthodox enough for Samson Raphael Hirsch. Leeser titled the
editorial, "A New Case of Illiberality." He often used the word
"illiberal" as applied to the Reform attitude toward Orthodoxy.

An interesting evaluation of the effectiveness of Leeser's opposition to Reform may be found in Philipson's, *The Reform Movement in Judaism,* published in 1931.

"The city of Philadelphia was, in the fifth and sixth decades
the century (sic), the stronghold of orthodox Judaism, owing
largely to the prestige and influence of the Reverend Isaac
Leeser, minister of the Mikveh Israel Congregation of that city,

and the foremost representative of orthodox Judaism in the country. Any effort at reform in that community naturally met with the greatest obstacles, and the pages of the *Occident,* the organ of Mr. Leeser, present a vivid picture of the opposition superinduced by every step toward reform in the country."

It is a sad paradox that in spite of his wholehearted sincerity and his courageous fight against any type of Reform, there are today widely held beliefs that Leeser was something less than Orthodox or that he was the prototype of the present-day Conservative. It is true that some feathers are put in the canard by the fact that Leeser was a strong advocate of decorum in the synagogue, but in fairness to him, it must be pointed out, that, not being a prophet, he could not have foreseen that he was invading in this one respect a guarded precinct of the Conservative movement. But more directly contributing to this reputation are the two biographies most likely to be read by an inquirer today.

The first, in the *Jewish Encyclopedia* (New York 1904), states that in introducing the English sermon into the service, Leeser was influenced by the Reform rabbis of Germany. There is certainly no reason to assume this. The English sermon was in the nature of an innovation, it is true, but it was definitely not a reform. There was no *Halakhah* opposed to it nor was there any positive tradition against it, as there was, for example, against family pews. Leeser repeatedly stated that he was not a rabbi and that decisions on Jewish law must come from recognized authorities in England or on the Continent. To Leeser, the sermon was a most important educational tool, a synergist with the written word of the *Occident.* It was a positive force for Orthodoxy. The article in question concludes with the statement that in religious controversies Leeser took an active part on the "Conservative" side. The capitalization of the first letter of this adjective misleads the reader of today in an obvious way.

The other current biography, in the *Universal Jewish Encyclopedia* (New York 1939), states that although Leeser is described by later writers as Orthodox, he himself "rejected any label" and, further on in the same paragraph, "Leeser believed himself to be a staunch Jew who opposed departure from ancient tradition; he did not, however, oppose such adaptation as did not, in his belief, violate Mosaic and rabbinic practice. He rejected all parties in Judaism." As if such an attitude were unorthodox!

It might be appropriate here to quote an actual passage from Leeser on his rejection of "any label." It was written in 1867 during his final illness when he was trying literally with the last efforts of a dying man to get Maimonides College under way and we can see in his words the strain and exasperation which this struggle between the two parties had brought upon him. He wrote:

"Some may object at the moment, that it (Maimonides College) is not pledged to either Reform or Orthodoxy. These hateful words are always at hand when anything is to be done, from the election of a secretary of a society to printing a book or establishing a college. The illiberal always ask: 'To what party does he or it belong?' For our part we belong to no party, strange as it may sound, we commenced life with certain conditions and we have not swerved from them. We know only *Judaism,* and if you call it Orthodoxy, *you* do so not we, though we do not hesitate to state that as things are now we are with those who are called Orthodox. The advanced reformers in America received no other instruction, and it has not injured their progressive mind to progress to the great length that they have done. In truth there is no Reform literature existing except a few late works which may be authority among the extreme adherents of the new fashion but have outside of this as yet limited circle obtained no adhesion whatever. By a system of mutual admiration, these works have received the assent of the partisans of these authors, but this is literally all. No works excelling Rambam, Rashban, Rashi, Eben Ezra, Albo, Ralbag, Bechaye (Bahya) and their compeers have yet appeared, all Israel drink from their fountain, and therefore they will continue for a while longer, to be the standard which all have to follow. If we admit that they can be viewed differently by Reform and Orthodoxy, we only admit what is done to the Holy Scriptures themselves, which are not rarely distorted by those who want to carry their doctrines *into* them instead of being taught *by* them. No one of the faculty, we will venture to say, will teach with a special eye to his party views, but simply on the broad basis of Jewish science and life; and we do not see any reason why all should not be satisfied with such a combination. We are almost ashamed to say this little even. Do not our Orthodox and Reformers, both so-called, send their children to colleges and convents of gentiles, without any dread of having their religious views undermined; and shall they now fear to trust men of approved character, only because they have the odor of conservatism attached to them?"

If Leeser rejected parties in Israel it can hardly be concluded from the quotation that he rejected Orthodoxy. Paraphrasing his thinking in modern terminology, we see that there had grown up an opposition to every step of progress in Jewish life by the "illiberal", meaning here, as usual with Leeser, the unorthodox. There being no such thing as a second generation of Reform leaders, all of the rabbis must have had an Orthodox upbringing. Since this had not thwarted their "development", why should they now have grown so excited about an institution which would be Orthodox or whose teachers would be Orthodox?

The notion that the literature of Judaism constitutes a neutral ground for all parties in the training of rabbis, is a curious one and not a little difficult for us to understand, certainly from a practical point of view. It reminds one of the non-denominational school for priests in the story by Daudet, the head of the school being "le vieux diable." It is interesting to note that the same sort of thinking kept Sabato Morais in the hope that the Hebrew Union College could be made to serve both the Orthodox and Reform rabbinate. He abandoned this idea in 1885, of course, after the famous Pittsburgh Conference. Something of the same philosophy of education is still to be found today in some schools for the training of Hebrew teachers and in a recently created organization of *Hazanim*. Evidently what is rational to one man can be irreconcilable to the next.

And now, having recounted the trials and tribulations of Isaac Leeser, his successes and failures, his strength and weakness, we must come to the inevitable question of his place in the history of American Judaism. What answer can we draw from the long list of "firsts" in which he participated? Is his place a permanent one or is it one of ever fading historical interest?

If we look at his tangible achievements, we are sorry to report a picture of tragedy. The *Occident* ceased publication a year after his death. A few years later, Maimonides College closed its doors and not so long after that the Board of Delegates of American Israelites became part of the organization of the Reform congregations. Many more bitter endings of his works could be added to this list, perhaps the saddest of all being the fate of the Shearith Israel Congregation of Cincinnati. This was organized with Leeser's hearty encouragement. He spoke at its dedication. Its purpose was to provide a firm anchor for Orthodoxy in the very midst of Reform. It was generally known as the "Frum Shul." Eventually, however, it became part of the Isaac M. Wise Temple. And lastly one may ask, where are the descendants of the generation of Jews with whom Leeser worked and lived? Only a remnant stays in Orthodoxy.

And yet, in spite of the gloomy and negative picture which we have just painted, we, today, owe a great and lasting debt to Isaac Leeser. If it were only the record of his times which he has left for us in the *Occident* we might say, "Sufficient." We owe him, however, much more than that. When he came upon the scene, American Jewry was almost two hundred years old, but it was sterile and stagnant. Aside from a very small number of synagogues, there was absolutely nothing of scholarly achievement, nothing in the way of publications, very little of Jewish education even on an elementary level, and the barest minimum of communal activity. In all these realms Leeser, often single-handed and frequently in the face of fierce opposition, created Orthodox institutions of the highest standards and character. He showed for all time the compatibilty and harmony of Orthodoxy and American life. But for him, the later immigrations of European Jews might have found only a vacuum of Reform to greet them. Truly, in the words of the 1850 pamphlet published in his defense, "he should be the pride, as he is the ornament, of the nation."

SAMSON RAPHAEL HIRSCH

(1808-1888)

BY MORDECAI BREUER

SAMSON RAPHAEL HIRSCH

By Mordecai Breuer

I. Hamburg

In 1690, Menahem Mendel Shapiro left the city of his birth, Frankfort-on-Main, and went to Hamburg. There he was given the surname of "Frankfurter."

His son and namesake was born in 1742 and studied at the academy of Rabbi Jonathan Eibschuetz. Ever anxious to spread knowledge of the Torah among his people, he published many Talmudic works. An intimate friend of Moses Mendelssohn, he was influenced by his ideas on the enlightenment of the Jews of Germany, for, in 1812, while serving as *Dayan* and Chief of the Rabbinical Court in Altona, he founded the Talmud Torah School, the first of its kind in Germany.

One son of the *Dayan,* Raphael, changed his name to Hirsch, after his grandfather, Tzevi-Hirsch. Throughout his life, he was singularly devoted to the study of the Bible. At the end of a business day, he would spend hours reading Sacred Script and pondering its commentators.

The second son, Moses, assumed the name Mendelssohn, after his father, and because of his admiration for the philosopher. He was engaged in literature and was a great lover of Hebrew.

Thus did the *Gaon* Jonathan Eibschuetz, on one side, and the philosopher Moses Mendelssohn, on the other, stand by the cradle of Samson, the son of Raphael Hirsch, who was born on the 24th of Sivan, 5568 (June 19, 1808).

It was a period of revolution and war. The armies of Napoleon were bringing the ideas of the Great Revolution all over Europe. Hamburg itself was joined to France. With the defeat of Napoleon, his hosts left behind them a great ferment which made its mark also in the *Judengasse,* where, ever since the days of Moses Mendelssohn and the Berlin "Enlightenment," new winds had begun to blow. When Samson was ten years old, the first Reform Jewish temple was opened in Hamburg, and the grandson of the Altona *dayan* was "eye-and-ear witness to all activity connected with this thing and to the war of the Lord's faithful against it."

265

The year he became Bar Mitzvah, the Orthodox elements
of Hamburg succeeded in installing in the rabbinate a man great
in Torah and secular learning, who up to that time, had stubbornly refused to accept upon himself that burden: Rabbi Isaac
Bernays. The directors of the community hoped that this scholar
would succeed, by means of modern weapons, in mending the
breach of Reform and in drawing the heart of youth to the Torah.
Rabbi Bernays entered upon his role with full energy and enthusiasm. He changed the title "Rabbi" to "Hakham," not only
to distinguish between the traditional, and the Reform, rabbi, but
also to symbolize a new type of spiritual leader in Israel. He
donned a modern rabbinic vestment and preached his renowned
sermons in purest German. Through philosophic approach he
conveyed to his spell-bound audience the light of true Judaism
and paved an original way in Biblical exegesis.

Hakham Bernays had a decisive influence on young Samson,
who pursued sacred lore with him while completing general studies
in the *gymnasium* (the local high school). His parents had entered him as an apprentice in business before he had finished his
studies at the institute. But, in less than a year, the young man
left Hamburg, turned his back on trade, and set out in the direction
of the *yeshivah*. He journeyed to Rabbi Jacob Ettlinger in
Mannheim. In his old age, Hirsch remarked, "It was no external need that impelled me to choose the path of a rabbi in
Israel, but an inner plan of life." This plan had matured in his
heart at the time when he interrupted his studies to try himself
in commerce. It had been a year of inner struggle. The "big
world" opened before him. Which road should he choose? When
the year ended, he traveled to the *yeshivah*.

II. Mannheim

When Hirsch, in his twentieth year, journeyed to the academy
of Rabbi Jacob Ettlinger, his life-plan was already clear and
ordered in his heart. He was convinced that he had been designated "to fight the war of the Lord and to restore the crown
to its pristine glory". He sat at the feet of Rabbi Ettlinger for
but one year. Whence, then, did he derive his preeminence in
Torah, in Talmud and Codes? Suffice the testimony of Rabbi
Abraham Samuel Benjamin Sofer, author of *Ktab-Sofer*, who,
in 1848, after his first meeting with Rabbi Hirsch, wrote: "We

conversed in a lengthy, learned Torah discussion with the new Chief Rabbi (Samson Raphael Hirsch). He was versed in whatever we touched upon, both in Talmud and Codes. We are, indeed, fortunate. He considers us more learned than himself. If he realized what a scholar he is, we could have no peace from him." Samson Raphael Hirsch acquired most of his knowledge in the manner characteristic of a genius: he was self-taught.

On his way to Mannheim, Hirsch stopped for a short while in Frankfort-on-Main, one of the centers of Reform in German Jewry; there he sought to study at close range the convulsive state of the community. He visited the linguist and famous liturgist, Wolf Heidenheim, in nearby Roedelheim; he met Baron Anselm of the house of Rothschild and was invited to dine with him.

Jacob Ettlinger was a renowned Torah scholar. He had studied at the school of Rabbi Abraham Bing in Wuerzburg, where Rabbi Isaac Bernays was his fellow-student and comrade. Together with him, he also attended lectures at the University of Wuerzburg, but it is told that when he was accepted as Chief Rabbi of Altona, he did not look with favor upon his students attending the philosophic lectures of Hakham Bernays in neighboring Hamburg. To summarize Ettlinger's stand on Reform and his influence over Hirsch's way of life, it is sufficient to quote his words (*Minhat Ani,* on *Parashat Pinehas*): "Let not him who is engaged in the war of the Lord against the heretics, be held back by the false argument that great is peace, and that it is better to maintain the unity of all designated as Jews than to bring about disruption."

Among the other students at the academy, Rabbi Hirsch associated particularly with Gershon Jehoshaphat, who later become *dayan* in Halberstadt. A firm friendship developed between them, the mark of which we shall recognize at a decisive moment in Hirsch's life.

III. BONN

In 1829, Rabbi Hirsch spent a year at the University of Bonn on the Rhine. Historians and writers err when they invest him with the doctorate; this man, who later served as the archetype of the new genus, "Rabbi-Doctor," did not acquire a Doctor's degree, nor did he even complete his academic studies. But a savoring of the spiritual life of the Gentile sages was essential for him before implementing his "inner plan of life."

The only information available to us of his activity during this year touches upon the first lecture he gave before the Orators' Club he had founded among the Jewish students at Bonn (most of whom were preparing to be rabbis in Israel).

One of his fellow-students noted in his diary at the time: "Hirsch has great influence over me; he has made life very sweet for me here at Bonn. . . . I already knew him at Heidelburg. . . . One evening both of us bemoaned the loneliness of the Jewish students of theology and we decided to found an orators' club. This club has exercised a distinct influence over me and has led to the formation of the strongest ties of friendship between Hirsch and myself. After his first lecture, we talked at very great length, and I learned to admire his exceptional eloquence, the keenness of his intellect, and his quick and lucid grasp. This debate, however, did not draw us close to each other, since we touched at times upon the religious aspect as well. . . . That winter and the following summer we studied the tractate *Zabahim* together. Gradually, there resulted mutual love and esteem. I respected his lofty qualities of spirit, his rigorously moral deportment, and I loved the goodness of his heart. His comradeship brought me great benefit and pleasure."

But the author of this diary was one destined to become Hirsch's opponent and most bitter disparager: Abraham Geiger, the central pillar of extreme Reform.

IV. OLDENBURG

In 1830, Dr. Nathan Adler, Chief Rabbi of the German principality of Oldenburg, left his post to become Chief Rabbi of Hanover, and later of London. He recommended as his successor the twenty-two-year-old Samson Raphael Hirsch, whose fame had already spread among the Orthodox rabbis of Germany. The government of Oldenburg consulted also Baron Anselm Rothschild, with whom it had commercial relations, and he, too, spoke with favor about "that precocious young man." Rabbi Hirsch immediately accepted, for he saw in this proposal the initial implementation of his "inner plan of life."

The religious state of the Jews of Oldenburg was then a gloomy one. Reformist aspirations, ignorance, and assimilation prevailed in all the small communities of the province which were headed not by rabbis but by teachers, cantors, and *Shohetim* (ritual slaughterers). In the city of Oldenburg itself, there were only fifteen Jewish families and in order to maintain a *minyan,* Doctor Adler had been compelled to impose fines on members of the community who did not appear at least on Sabbaths, festivals, and fast days.

Hirsch was not discouraged by these conditions. He viewed them as a first test in his struggle to restore the ancient glory of the Torah. He was convinced that it was only alienation from Jewish sources which had brought about the low level of Judaism among the people. Were they but to see the light that is in the Torah, they would return to the good way!

He therefore began to translate sections of the Mishnah, which he sent to the teachers of the communities, sheet by sheet, copied in his own hand.

In 1831, he married Hanne, of the house of Judel, an esteemed family from a small city in northern Germany, a noble woman versed in the Bible no less than in the works of Schiller. His wife was truly a *"helpmeet to him."* She understood his aspirations and shared them, heart and soul.

His position in Oldenburg did not burden him too much. He found time to continue his studies and to build his home and family. (During the eleven years of his residence in that city they were blessed with five children.) At the time, Hirsch was investing all his energy in the preparation of a volume in which he addressed himself for the first time to the Jewish public of Germany. In his preface to this book, *Horeb,* on *The Commandments of Israel,* he underscores with great emphasis the duty of every Jew, first of all, to have a thorough knowledge of the *mitzvot* of the Torah for the purpose of fulfilling them, "for they are in the will of the Creator—and this fact is the sole and sufficient reason for every Jew to keep them." But the commandment to meditate on the Torah includes also the obligation to speculate on the reasons for the *mitzvot,* and if the *Halakhah* in all its ramifications—the Law, written and oral, the enactments and decrees of the Sages— is the word of God, directly and indirectly, then, pondering the rationale of the commands allows room for every thinker, loyal to the words of the rabbis, to express the thoughts of his heart. Hirsch's noteworthy contribution in the *Horeb* lies precisely in his theory of the commandments. By this he infers the rational basis of the commandment from consideration of the details of the laws involved. This was in accord with the principle, preeminent in all his writings, "to understand Judaism out of its own sources."

Hirsch fully recognized that he was setting forth a fresh formulation of Judaism and the commands. He was certain that "the thinking youths and maidens of Israel" for whom he had written his book and who had ceased to understand the language of the older generation, would understand and once again reveal the truth of the Torah and the reason for its commandments. On the title-page he inscribed the words of the prophet: *"Because they have called thee an outcast: She is Zion, there is none that careth for her"* (Jeremiah XXX, 17). He dedicated his work, the first fruits of his thought, to his parents, "who watched over me in the days of my childhood, guided me in the days of my youth, my friends in the days of maturity." And to his friend Gershom Jehoshaphat he writes: "Only one thing can prevent my publication (of *Horeb*): If I became convinced that it will do more harm than good to the sacred theme for the sake of which it was written." In the opening of the book he sets forth the theme: *"Not thine is the work to finish; neither art thou free to neglect it"* (Abot, II). He emphasizes that it is not its purpose to make final pronouncements on Jewish Law. In his humility, the author never expected that three generations of the Orthodox laity of Germany would take *Horeb* out of the bookcase even when it was necessary to obtain a clarification of some point of *Halakhah*.

After Hirsch had completed his manuscript, he turned to a publisher. The latter, however, was reluctant to invest money in a large book which had a doubtful future. The author chose a characteristic way of proving to the publisher that there was a public to read and buy his book. He quickly wrote a brochure in which he raised all the burning questions which confronted the younger generation of German Jews. He offered his answers in a brilliant warm style. This brochure is well known as the *Nineteen Letters on Judaism*. When the publisher printed this modest pamphlet, its success was so great that, after a year, he brought out *Horeb* as well.

None of Rabbi Hirsch's works captivated the hearts of the readers or evoked at once so great an echo as this little book, which, in a few pages, contained in essence all his teachings, his system of Biblical exegesis, his views on contemporary events, and his method of polemic for the purpose of restoring the Torah to its former state of honor. To the *Nineteen Letters* (*or Epistles*) one may apply the famous words: "This is the entire Torah of Rabbi Samson Raphael Hirsch and as for the remainder, go thou and study."

In the first epistle, dealing with the confusion of the new generation, he shows his understanding of the spiritual forces that led to youth's assimilatory ambition. Hirsch's attitude was utterly new: This young spokesman for ancient Judaism, waging the battle of the Torah in the public gate, seeks, first of all, to penetrate to the depths of the soul of the reader. He does not threaten him with excommunication or ostracism, but seeks to speak the *"word in due season"*, *"the word that is heeded"*, and to *train a child in the way he should go."* This approach, basically pedagogic, is characteristic of Hirsch in all his undertakings.

The *Nineteen Epistles* made a mighty impression upon the Jews of Germany of all shades of opinion. Previously there was only one man in the circle of Orthodox Judaism who knew how to lash back in their own tongue at the defamers of his religion: Hakham Bernays. It was no wonder, then, that at first he was considered the writer of the book, for Rabbi Hirsch had employed the pseudonym "Ben Uziel." When the real author was revealed, the loyal adherents of the Torah knew that a bold champion had arisen who would fight the battle of the Lord on their behalf. Thus, a new period began in the struggle for the future of Judaism.

An example of the powerful impression the book made on the troubled Jewish youth of the times is furnished by Heinrich Graetz, the historian, who, in his nineteenth year, after reading *Nineteen Epistles,* wrote to Rabbi Hirsch, asking him to be received as a student in his home. The latter agreed, and for three years Graetz served as disciple and assistant in the house of the Rabbi of Oldenburg, specializing in Jewish studies and general sciences. In his diary, Graetz draws a vivid picture of Samson Raphael Hirsch. His way of life later removed him far from his master. But, without doubt, it was Hirsch who saved the effervescent young man from assimilation.

Among his other literary labors in Oldenburg one must mention polemical articles against those leaders of Reform who had completely negated the hallowed things of Israel, especially all the commands of the Torah which served to set Israel apart from the nations. Their purpose was to make a pact with the new *Wissenschaft des Judentums* and to reform Judaism by means of a modern exegesis of its literary sources. Against this aim the pen of Rabbi Hirsch now entered to do battle. In 1838 he published

a brochure entitled *The Wrestlings of Naphtali,* the beginning
of an enterprise which was to engage the fighting rabbi until his
last day. In this work, which reveals his moral strength and
scientific honesty, one may see at once the impassioned preacher
who couples his expressions of grief and anger with words of
kindness, hope, and faith. With exceeding rigor did Rabbi Hirsch
guard "literary ethics". Anonymous polemic was alien to his purity
of soul, and when he went out for the first time to assail the exponents of Reform on a particular matter, he explicitly signed his
name to the preface.

In Oldenburg he achieved another deep satisfaction. In nearby
Bremen, a pamphlet had been issued in which the Old Testament
was attacked in a distinctly anti-Semitic tone. Rabbi Hirsch immediately published "annotations" to this pamphlet, disproving the
charges. The Duke of Oldenburg is reported to have sent his
captain to the rabbi's house to thank him for saving the honor of
the Bible, sacred to Jews and Christians. This was "the public
hallowing of the Sacred Name (*Kiddush ha-Shem be-rabbim*)".

But Hirsch did not derive much comfort from his small community in Oldenburg. This handful, a prayer-quorum of Jews,
could not satisfy him. The epidemic of Reform had spread and
when Rabbi Hirsch left his post, the Jews of Oldenburg elected
a Reform rabbi to succeed him.   There were also instances of
moral recession in the commercial relationships of Jews and Gentiles. Rabbi Hirsch had delivered to the Duke a detailed and
very original proposal on the "Statute of the Oath of the Jews"
in order to remove the practice of perjury. If rumors and the
diary of Graetz are to be credited, then Rabbi Hirsch at one time
ruled that *Kol Nidre* was not to be recited in the synagogue of
Oldenburg. Was this a compromise on the part of the stout-hearted
fighter? Certainly not. When he saw that the members of his
community, in their reliance upon the reciting of *Kol Nidre,* were
not keeping their oaths, he did not hesitate, in a *hora'at sha'ah*
(an emergency decree), to repair the breach to stop the violation
of the Torah's law of honesty.

V. Emden

In 1841, he was offered the position of Chief Rabbi of the
Districts of Aurich and Osnabrueck in the province of Hanover.
He accepted and moved to his new place of residence, Emden.

The conditions and duties that awaited him there brought more contentment than his work in Oldenburg. He invested many fruitful efforts in the administration of the communities, in education, and in social work. He founded a free loan fund, the first in Germany, which was maintained for many years. He raised the Boys' Talmud Torah to a very high level and also opened corresponding classes for girls, in which effort he was greatly aided by his wife.

But the great work, begun in Oldenburg in his *Nineteen Epistles* and in *Horeb,* he could not now continue, for leisure time was lacking. His pen, however, did not rest. In 1844 he published a second brochure against Reform. On its title-page he used a slogan which again and again was to be his battle-cry: "Truth stands; falsehood does not stand!"

In that year, the Jewish periodical most widely disseminated in Germany wrote of him: "It is impossible not to mention the vigor and consistency Rabbi Hirsch demonstrates in all his writings. He is not a performer of mental sleight-of-hand. Seriously, stubbornly heedless of the uproar of the masses, he goes his way as an honored teacher of the people in Israel, and we know of no other rabbi in Germany who reaches the measure of his height." In that periodical he is awarded the designation "Leader of the Orthodox wing". It is no wonder, then, that rabbis and laymen from all over Germany and Western Europe had begun to turn to him when in need of an opinion or official proclamation.

Rabbi Solomon Trier, the venerable rabbi of Frankfort, included Hirsch's responsum on the fundamental meaning of circumcision in Judaism among other responsa of great authorities in a compilation issued in the wake of an episode of lawlessness in his city.

When the Reform rabbis convened their first assembly in Brunswick, the heads of the *Pekidim ve-Amarkalim* (Overseers and Stewards) in Amsterdam besought the opinion of the leading rabbis on the subject. Hirsch's manifesto denounced the assembly and its revolutionary objectives and recommended steps for the repair of the breach in the House of Israel. Turning to "the children of my people, whose assembly has caused all this", he wrote: "Would that you pay heed and open your eyes on your ways! Do you not know that they will bring us to a bitter end? Do you not understand that were your doings to bear fruit, the House of Israel would be rent asunder, for a derision among our enemies, and the loss of our greatness? If your followers will heed your words to secede from the authority of the Talmud, what with forbidden foods and marriages made permissible for them, the covenant between us shall no longer stand and broken-heartedly we shall part, one from the other."

To Rabbi Hirsch it was clear already at that time that with the spread of Reform, those who revered the word of the Lord would have no choice but to set up a division between themselves and the "lawless ones". In another area, too, this manifesto pointed to the crystallization of his plans. Here, for the first time, he used the rallying-call he was destined to inscribe on his banner: *Torah im Derekh Eretz* (Torah together with the norms of society, social harmonization). Speaking of the sad state of Torah education for the youth, he says: "Let us, therefore, build anew houses for Torah and fear of God, so that true Jews learn to know the Torah for its own sake and become as full of *mitzvot* as a pomegranate (is of seeds). Be not afraid for the Torah because of modern science, when you see those wise in their own eyes who have become estranged from the Torah. For true science loves Torah and collaborates with it.

"We must build seminaries for teachers to instruct the children of Israel in Torah and *Derekh Eretz,* which, if acquired together, will bring healing to all our plagues. Above all, we need schools for Torah and *Derekh Eretz* for the education of our youth, for we know most assuredly that any city or settlement which is without such school, shall not be saved from the strife of the times."

Hirsch revealed himself as a fighter in the ceaseless conflict over the emancipation of the Jews, which at this time was raging throughout the German states. In 1843, reacting to the defamatory statements in a German daily, he publicly emerged for the first time in favor of the Emancipation. He showed that it was precisely the Jew faithful to the religion of his fathers who could not be suspected of lack of loyalty to the state (country) in which he lived. "The accomplishment of emanicipation we can greet with blessing and joy as but a humane deed of justice welling forth from fear of God." Nevertheless, Hirsch saw the concrete danger of assimilation in the wake of the Emancipation.

In the same year, the heads of the community of Nikolsburg, in the province of Moravia (of the Austrian Empire), offered him the rabbinate of the city and province. Many obstacles and misunderstandings on both sides had as yet to be overcome, technical and formal questions had to be settled, but in the end the stubborn efforts of the Moravian authorities were crowned with success and Rabbi Hirsch prepared to occupy the rabbinate which in the past had boasted of such incumbents as Maharal of Prague and Rabbi Mordecai Banet.

There was great sorrow in Emden, both among Jews and Christians, who sent him a delegation, urging him to remain in their city. In his six years of residence in Emden, Hirsch had endeared himself to all the people in every strata of society, in the city and in the province, in the main because of his efforts to organize the communities and their institutions. But he saw in Nikolsburg a larger field of activity, in which he could develop his energies to the full and so he set his face to the east.

VI. NIKOLSBURG

The Jewish communities of the district of Moravia, old and well established, resembled in many aspects the "Council of the Four Lands" in Poland. The district rabbinate, the central governing body, exercised authoritative powers that influenced nomination and confirmation of rabbis, the supervision of communal activities, and the presentation of Jewry's problems before the secular authorities.

The appointment of the Chief Rabbi was subject to the confirmation of the central government in Vienna and his activities were under its jurisdiction.

During the period of Rabbi Nehemiah Trebitsch, his predecessor, the demands for "modernization" of Jewish life, with special emphasis on the introduction of the German language into the synagogue and house of study, had multiplied and became more insistent, both on the part of the government, as well as on the part of Jewish *maskilic* circles, close to Reform. Here the aims of Reform coincided with the aim of the government of the Empire, for the Germanization of all the lands under its protection. Rabbi Trebitsch was unwilling to agree to any compromise and died grief-stricken, while the tension between the "enlightened" and the steadfast, traditional Jews continued to grow.

The election of Samson Raphael Hirsch to this rabbinate took place against this chain of events. The Orthodox circles understood that they would not succeed in obtaining the appointment of a Chief Rabbi of the "old school." They therefore hoped that the author of the *Nineteen Epistles* and *Horeb* would know how to stand firmly on the basis of traditional Judaism and perhaps even attract to the Torah the younger element, disillusioned by the current rivalry. The *maskilim* (the "enlightened") agreed to the designation of Samson Raphael Hirsch out of a feeling of assurance that his outlook approximated theirs more than that of the Orthodox. There is no doubt that Rabbi Hirsch was well aware of these pressures, and if, nevertheless, he accepted upon himself this difficult post, it was only out of his sense of mission: to open up a road for the Torah in the new state of things, as it were, and this precisely in an area where Torah and reverence for God still prevailed. All Jewish circles in Moravia received him as their rabbi with great expectation. All rabbis and persons of eminence of the state journeyed to meet him and brought him to Nikolsburg as one of their own. The *maskilim* sent the preacher, Dr. Mannheimer, and the cantor, Sulzer (both representing the "progressive" element of Vienna), to beautify the ceremony of the reception.

This was, indeed, a handsome, though superficial, proclamation of the unity of Israel. So far as Hirsch was concerned, neither will nor effort were lacking to save, together with Israel's Torah, also unity in the Jewish camp. His brief experience in Nikolsburg, however, convinced Rabbi Hirsch that in matters of Judaism, whenever truth and peace are wrestling with each other, truth always has the primacy. His way was strewn with handicaps! When, during the installation ceremony, he made an address in polished German and left out the customary *halakhic* and *agadic* adumbrations, the Orthodox were disappointed. When his first demand was the founding of a *yeshivah* in Nikolsburg, the *maskilim* were disappointed. When he ruled that the wedding canopy be set up within the walls of the synagogues, the *maskilim* rejoiced and his older colleagues were scandalized; but when he opposed any change in prayer services and the study of Torah, the Orthodox took heart and the *maskilim* became alarmed. No wonder, then, that on both sides the attitude towards him was: "*Kabdehu vehashdehu* (Esteem him and suspect him)."

In one respect, however, all who came in contact with him were in accord: in admiration of his ethical personality and his dedicated leadership, the charm of his conversation and the brilliance of his oratory. Before his purity of heart they all bowed their heads.

Concerning Rabbi Hirsch's organizational and educational work, we learn in his own writings: "In the province of Moravia the organization of Torah-study was most excellently developed. There each community was obliged to retain a rabbi, charged with the advancement of the Talmud Torah and with the material sustenance of students of a Torah academy (*yeshivah*), corresponding to the number of its members. If the number of members of the community was too small to support an academy, they were obliged to participate appropriately in the support of students of the nearby academy. At the head of this entire system stood the Chief Rabbi of the province, who not only instructed a large number of the students of his own academy but directed Torah studies in the entire province as well. Every year or semester, he had to fix the tractate that was to be studied by rabbis and students in each particular place, and provide an adequate number of copies of the German text, or, when the need arose, to have a tractate acquired or printed, through the general fund for the provincial communities."

In Nikolsburg itself, Rabbi Hirsch maintained a *yeshivah* to which students flowed from all parts of the province. He taught them according to the principles laid down in *Nineteen Epistles* and in *Horeb*: "To understand Judaism and the Torah 'out of themselves' and to utilize the general sciences as auxiliary studies for the understanding of the Torah."

The year 1848 brought waves of national and social revolutions to almost all the countries of Western and Central Europe. The peoples of the Austrian empire rose up and demanded their independence. The general unrest also penetrated to the *Judengasse,* and many Jews participated in these movements, for they envisioned the dawn of their liberation from discrimination and subjection.

Samson Raphael Hirsch was among the leaders of Moravian Jewry who would link the emancipation of the Jews to the other national and social demands. He was more active in connection with the parliament of Moravia which was established as part of the democratic movement in this part of the empire. In the preparatory assembly at Kremsier he spoke out vigorously for an end to the humiliation of his people. His endeavors bore fruit; upon his return to Nikolsburg he brought with him the tidings of the emancipation of the Jews of Moravia. The fighter against Jewish assimilation to the Gentiles and their culture won a brilliant victory in the struggle for human and civic rights of his people.

This was his point of view: On the one hand, he viewed emancipation as the gift of Providence that should give the Jews inalienable human rights and a broader opportunity of observing the Torah. On the other hand, he saw it as a trial of his people in *Galut*. He revealed his attitude in two incisive announcements to the Jews of Moravia, in connection with the struggle for emancipation in 1848: He called for preparedness to meet eventualities calmly, with trust in the Lord, and abstention from rash words and actions. When the first success had been attained—the special taxes imposed upon the Jews were abolished—he called for unity of all the Jews in their communities, and summoned them to continue loyally and voluntarily the support of the Jewish institutions; "Our strength is in unity, division shall vanquish us!" He called for increased attachment to the dignity to Jewish tradition so "that we may emerge as Jews from this struggle! For what value will there be to our attainment if we shall be emancipated Jews, but no more Jews!"

When the political war ended, Hirsch issued another call which shows how well he discerned the damage which the long exile had inflicted upon Jewish society: In 1849 he called on all councils of the communities to establish a stipend-fund for the Jewish youth who should henceforth be directed more and more towards agriculture and physical labor.

Henceforth, Rabbi Hirsch was held universally in highest regard throughout the province. He returned with full vigor to the work of organizing and educating. But the difficulties which he had encountered in the first years of his life in Moravia did not decrease; and to them were added disquieting signs, in the wake of the political events, of the dissolution of the communities. All his political achievements notwithstanding, Rabbi Hirsch saw as his major role the strengthening of traditional Judaism within the communities. He knew that the future of the Eternal People depended not on its political status but on its spiritual power. He understood that the Torah could be firmly established only by means of far-reaching organizational changes and by his acquisition of larger authoritative powers. The establishment of a central seminary for rabbis and teachers who, in the midst of a changing world, would know how to imbue the youth and the masses of the people with love of Torah and observance of the *mitzvot*, seemed to him vital if all his work as Chief Rabbi of the province were not to be in vain. But he encountered throughout the communities stubborn opposition to his plans. In these days of his crisis, the representatives of one hundred members of an Orthodox Jewish society in Frankfort-on-Main urged the spiritual head of 60,000 Jews in Moravia to become their rabbi.

VII. FRANKFORT

The decline of Frankfort in the first half of the 19th Century is truly amazing. The city of two great luminaries, the sainted authors of *Sh'ne Luhot Hab'rit* and of *P'ne Y'hoshu'a* respectively, early in the century was still filled with Torah and piety.* The Berlin "Enlightenment" and the French Revolution together broke down the walls of the Frankfort ghetto and with them the foundations of the ancient community. "Enlightened" circles, with the help of the civil government, erected a Jewish school, the "Philantropin", the reform aim of which was conspicuous from the outset. The opposition and the excommunications by the rabbis of the city were of no avail. The tendency of the Napoleonic order towards centralization of rule bore rather heavily upon the Torah-true leaders of the ancient community as they attempted to conserve its distinctive character and traditional rights even as it facilitated the destructive work of the men of Reform. The characteristic feature of this development in Frankfort was that, from the start, all steps taken to alter the face of the community and its religious life were effected under the protection of the civil government and through its power of coercion. In 1818, public instruction in Torah was forbidden and its abolition enforced by the municipal police. The students of Torah literally concealed themselves in underground tunnels; religious teachers were driven from the city and any one supporting a Talmud Torah was fined fifty gulden. Upon official orders a council was appointed for the community, composed mainly of representatives of Reform. This council abolished the religious burial society and intentionally neglected the making of repairs on the Orthodox synagogues. The Torah-true women of

---

*Three witnesses of unimpeachable character attest to this fact: Rabbi Horovitz, the author of *Haflaah,* Rabbi Nathan Adler, and Rabbi Moses Sofer, author of *Hatam Sofer.*

Frankfort were compelled to visit ritualaria in the suburbs of the city, since the ritual pools of the city had been wrecked and sealed up.

The House of Rothschild, loyal to ancestral tradition, donated a large sum for the erection of an Orthodox synagogue on condition that the community appoint a second rabbi, to minister together with the aged Rabbi Solomon Trier, and with his consent. When the council designated a Reform rabbi and thus lost the donation of the Rothschilds, the old rabbi resigned, at the age of eighty-seven. That same year saw the uprisings of 1848, which brought redemption to the Orthodox elements of Frankfort, for now they began to find an attentive ear for their claim on the municipal authorities against both the tyranny of the directors of the community, who had never been chosen in a democratic manner, and the systematic coercion of conscience practised there.

After his arrival in Frankfort, Rabbi Hirsch summarized in these words the essence of their complaints: "They say we are the few. But by what law does the majority, which has turned its back on the faith of its fathers, have the right to force the minority, and even the last pauper among them, to join equally in this turning of the back?"

A small group of eleven loyalists, among them Emanuel Schwarzschild, who testified that in his time he was the only one of the Jewish boys of Frankfort who donned phylacteries every day, finally received permission from the heads of the city to organize a private religious society (Religionsgesellschaft) within the framework of the community. They rented rooms in a private dwelling for prayer services in accordance with the accepted traditional form. The number of affiliates of the society increased rapidly and by 1851 had reached one hundred. The Barons Wilhelm and Anselm Rothschild were also counted among its members, and a large sum of money for building an Orthodox synagogue was placed by the House of Rothschild in the possession of the society.

The Orthodox community in Frankfort was set up, then, by "heads of households." Early in 1850 they directed themselves to the governmental authorities and sought permission to select a rabbi with utmost freedom of choice. The letter of application of the founders to the head of the city in this matter, is interesting chiefly because its text has a simplicity and clarity of expression which is generally attributed to the pen of Samson Raphael Hirsch—and this, at a time when no one, and least of all Rabbi

Hirsch himself, could as yet foresee that Rabbi Hirsch, the rabbi of the principality in Nikolsburg, would be the rabbi of this dwarf-community. "The undersigned," so the letter opens, "believers in the Mosaic faith, have separated from the local Jewish community and have erected a new religious community." The municipal statute established that the rabbis of the community were to examine each new rabbi before his appointment. But, the founders of the new community emphasize, the Reform rabbi is not qualified to serve as an examiner, "since it is precisely his views and activity which lead to the separation ('*Austritt*') of the undersigned."

After permission had been granted, the Frankfort group offered the post to Rabbi Michael Sachs in Berlin, but after protracted negotiation, the latter rejected the offer. Only then did they turn to Rabbi Hirsch in Nikolsburg, apparently on the recommendation of his loyal friend, Rabbi Gershon Jehoshaphat, who was then stopping in Frankfort. Rabbi Hirsch responded in the affirmative. What moved the Chief Rabbi of a province inhabited by a large Jewish population to accept the office of rabbi in a small, private society? In his letter of resignation to the Minister on Religious Matters in Austria, we read: "Nevertheless (in spite of his dissatisfaction with his work as Chief Rabbi, a position which in actuality had only nominal power), I should perhaps have remained in my post, had there not reached me this call from Frankfort: to come to the aid of a group, small indeed, but the very fact of whose founding constitutes for me the most gladdening event in Israel in decades. For now, for the first time, a Jewish community has been knit together about a sacred principle, openly and proudly, the very one to which I had determined to dictate my life, to spread it and firmly to establish it."

Here, once more, the sense of mission! The path of Rabbi Hirsch led him from Moravia, where light and darkness served in confusion, to benighted Frankfort, where he might be able to shape a "creatio ex nihilo." His resignation caused great commotion among all the Jews who had settled in Moravia. At once, delegations from all over the country appealed to him to stay, and the councils of the communities endorsed declarations assuring him the fulfillment of all his demands. Rabbi Hirsch struggled with himself and finally dispatched a long letter to Frankfort in which he requested that he be freed from his commitment in light of the promises now given him in Moravia. The men of Frankfort, however, did not agree to free him from his previous commitment, and thereby decided his struggle. "On the way in which a man wishes to go, he is led," said the Sages.

Thus Samson Raphael Hirsch journeyed to Frankfort, the city of his father's father. His restless creative power, dormant in Nikolsburg, where he was occupied with thousands of petty little matters of administration and organization, now reasserted itself; he began once more to write, to preach, to encourage, and to defend. As soon as he entered into his new role, he initiated projects for matters pertaining to prayer, to the laws of *kashrut,* and especially to study of Torah. Within a year, the cornerstone for the building of the new synagogue was laid. On that occasion the rabbi called upon the members of his community to make every effort to put up, alongside of the synagogue, a school for their sons and daughters, which should imbue them with Torah and *Derekh Eretz.* The erection of the synagogue evoked a faint echo in Reform circles, but the establishment of the school, which opened its doors even before the building of the synagogue was completed, aroused their sharp opposition. In the speeches defending his school, we read words which reveal Hirsch's serious, deliberate, and clear approach in public debate: "From the first moment, when 'the small flock' summoned me to come here and poured out upon me an unstinting trust, I became aware of my single mission: to hold aloft the principles of the faith of our fathers, without the least reservation, in the midst of this small circle. It is these principles for the sake of which this circle joined together with earnestness so great and with self-sacrifice so strong. I had no intention to go out in offensive warfare against the opposing current and thereby to enlarge still further the grievous breach in the souls of men."

But the breach was large enough. The partisans of Reform thought that the old community of the Talmud Torah and the *Shulhan Arukh* had been definitively and finally interred. And behold, the "antiquated" Judaism rose up resurrected! This fact alone was not likely to irritate and disturb the men of the Reform very much. Had the rabbi of the small community been superior only in Torah and piety, and had his organization been modelled precisely after the plan of the Frankfort community at the beginning of the century, the "progressive" people could have calmly rested and looked forward with confidence to nipping in the bud of the new creation. But this was not to be. Rabbi Hirsch knew well that a faithful implementation of the *Shulhan Arukh* and a genuine grasp of the principles of Judaism assured improvement in the religious life of both the community and the individual. Moreover, he emphasized, in accord with the rabbis' postulate: *"Beautify thyself before Him with commandments,"* the esthetic aspect of all the ways of the life of the community and introduced *"the beauty of Japhet (Greece) into the tents of Shem."* The synagogue edifice was built on the highest level of modern architecture; its furnishings and lighting enchanted the eye. *Shehitah* and the slaughterhouses themselves were planned in accordance with hygienic principles; and this was also true for the ritualaria. In the synagogue services a men's choir took part, under the leadership of Mr. Japhet, whose musical works aroused the attention of renowned composers. With such a revival of the old community the partisans of Reform could not make peace, hence their seething anger and the bitterness of their battle against Rabbi Hirsch's accomplishments. For they appeared to them in the nature of a revolution; obviously it bore within itself, from the very beginning, the healing drug of life and growth.

Hirsch was not "merely another scholar of the Torah". That he was also learned in secular studies, a scientist, an artist of the German language, a divinely gifted orator, leader, and teacher—brought consternation to his opponents. But just as the opposition grew stronger, so did the adoration of the members of his community become more profound and intensified. His *Kehillah* grew larger from year to year. However, only few who joined the original one hundred members were natives of Frankfort. This period was one of economic expansion for Frankfort; it had developed into an important commercial mercantile center, and there was a great migration from towns near and far to the metropolis. In the course of time, the Jews who had settled in Frankfort constituted the majority of the members of the Orthodox community. In 1874, after twenty-five years of existence, it numbered 325 heads of families. The synagogue had been enlarged and now contained 1,000 seats. (When Rabbi Hirsch from the pulpit announced a campaign for a building fund, within three days 50,000 gulden were collected!) His community possessed a handsome ritualarium, three slaughterhouses, high schools (including technical curricula) for boys and girls, with 408 pupils; and various philanthropic funds. It is said that Rabbi Hirsch, whose home was on the bank of the River Main, would view with deep satisfaction each year the ever-growing number of Orthodox Jews who went to fulfill the custom of *tashlikh* at the river.

It was natural that this brilliant development should awaken dormant forces in other cities. Autonomous Orthodox communities arose, mainly in those places which succeeded in drawing to them a rabbi of the type of Frankfort, for example, Mainz (Rabbi Lehmann), Darmstadt (Rabbi Marx), Berlin (Rabbi Ezriel Hildesheimer).

It was then that the designation "German-Jewish Orthodoxy" came into vogue.

VIII. Autonomy of the Orthodox Community

Samson Raphael Hirsch was the leader of those who fought for the principle of autonomy of the Orthodox community and the separation of its members from the local Jewish community, which had ceased to conduct itself in accordance with the Torah and the Tradition. To this controversy, almost from the day of his arrival in Frankfort, he devoted an ever greater proportion of his energy, and it is fitting that we follow its progress closely.

But it is necessary, too, that we present Hirsch's concept of the Jewish community. He does not conceive it to be a sectarian religious organization. This is what he said: "Every Jewish resident in this city is obliged by law of the Torah . . . to be a member of the Assembly of Jeschurun (i.e., of the Orthodox community) as the sole Jewish community established in this city. He must fulfill only two conditions: he must have been circumcised and married according to Jewish law. Thus does it become possible for him to affiliate with the Jewish community. Disqualified from membership in the council is he who publicly violates the Sabbath and eats forbidden foods, but even he does not lose his right of membership in the community."

Hirsch's community is "religious" not because all its members are "religious", in the full sense of the word, but because the religion of Israel is the established common basis of his community. This "religious" basis does not stand in contra-distinction to any "nationalistic" basis but is identical with it and covers it, as long as the religion of Israel is the religion of the traditional Torah. A Jewish religion which is not the religion of the traditional Torah cannot constitute a Jewish community; neither the beliefs and opinions, nor the religious conduct of the individual, but the stabilizing base of the public is the sole determining factor. The Hirsch community is not a religious organization of conformist affiliates, but a national union of the entirety of Israel. Individual Jewish transgressors, "though they sin, they are still Israelites", but a Jewish community characterized by denial of the Torah no longer represents the entirety of Israel. For this reason Rabbi Hirsch begins his talk at the presentation of the constitution of his community with these trenchant words: "The assembly of Jeschurun which exists in this city under the name of Israelitish Religious Society is none other than the ancient Jewish community of Frankfort as it has existed for hundreds of years."

In the communities which Rabbi Hirsch had served before coming to Frankfort, there were members who had left the Orthodox camp and had followed Reform; in Oldenburg these even constituted a perceptible percentage in the community. However, in these communities leadership was in the hands of a rabbi of uncompromising loyalty to the Torah. This was not the case in Frankfort. There the leadership of the community was in the hands of Reform rabbis, who ruled with an iron hand and persecuted the adherents of the Torah, and this by virtue of the authority of the municipal government. The humiliation of the Torah in Frankfort was due to two factors: to the rule of the Reform religion, and to a community council that operated with the cooperation of the non-Jewish authority. Rabbi Hirsch saw in the rule of directors of a community supported by civil authorities and able to govern by the coercive force of the civil government a grave thrust at the democratic foundations of the Jewish community, as laid down by the Sages. So long as this coercive power were not removed, the danger of extermination continued to face his Orthodox community. Under the status quo, only full autonomy of the Orthodox community would guarantee its own permanence and that of its institutions. The state at that time made it obligatory for the Jewish citizen to belong to a recognized Jewish community. The struggle for independence of the Orthodox community, therefore, assumed the form of a struggle for the abolition of state-enforced affiliation and the granting of legal guarantees for religious living and for the maintenance of religious institutions, also outside the frame of the established community. This struggle was eventually successful because it had begun simultaneously with the historic process of separation of church and state which had then been initiated in Western Europe. The con-

flict of Bismark with the Catholic Church is what finally brought
to Rabbi Hirsch and to his loyal adherents the "statute of redemption", abolishing compulsory affiliation with the recognized Jewish
community.

Among the reasons for independence which Rabbi Hirsch
claimed for his Orthodox community, two stand out prominently:
the principle of partnership and self-rule of the members of the
community, and the argument that the difference in religion and
outlook between Orthodox and Reform Judaism is far greater than
the difference between the Catholic and the Protestant Church.

It should be noted that after publication of the statute of separation, the heads of Rabbi Hirsch's community, with their rabbi's
consent, informed the council of the established community that
they were interested in continuing social ties (*Gemeinschaft*) with
all the Jews in the city and prepared to do so, even if ties of
membership in the community (*Gemeinde*) would be sundered.
For this purpose they proposed that welfare institutions, such as
the hospital and the cemetery, for example, be administered by
both communities in common. The community council rejected
the outstretched hand, but Rabbi Hirsch had never intended to
sever the last ties uniting the entire House of Israel.

His triumph was complete. By the power of the state, in the
period of reaction following the fall of Napoleon, the adherents
of Reform had altered the face of the Jewish community; by the
power of the state, in the period of the ascendancy of liberalism,
Rabbi Hirsch broke the chains of the Reform community. Success was complete, however, only vis-à-vis the outside. Within
the Orthodox community dissension broke out, and only a portion
of its membership were in favor of this separation from the established community, Rabbi Hirsch's firm legal decision notwithstanding. When the statute of separation from the community
had been attained, there were not available to the Orthodox community all the necessary community institutions. Particularly,
the cemetery still belonged to the Reform community only, and
one may understand the hesitation of old established families in
the city to separate not only from the living but also from the dead.

The second matter was even more important. When it became
apparent that the Prussian Government would grant the statute
of separation to the Orthodox community, the council of the
Reform community announced that it was henceforth prepared to
give the Orthodox Jews services and definite religious institutions

as well, in accordance with their spirit. Rabbi Hirsch at once declared that this readiness on the part of the Reformists would change nothing in regard to the demand of the Orthodox community, but would give even stronger impetus to the demand. For precisely now the religious Jew belonging to the Reform community would be compelled to admit that there existed, so to speak, equality of rights between the Reform religion and the religion of the Torah. But now something tragic occurred, from an unexpected direction. Rabbi Isaac Dob (Seligman) Bamberger of Wuerzburg, one of the celebrated Orthodox rabbis in Germany, issued a statement to the effect that since the community council was ready to satisfy the demands of the Orthodox, and to the extent that it was prepared for such, an Orthodox Jew was no longer obliged to separate from the Reform community.

This statement was a grievous blow for Rabbi Hirsch. Bamberger did not find it necessary to discuss the matter with Hirsch before publishing his opinion, which was contradicted by the declaration of 389 rabbis, who, in 1872, under circumstances similar to those obtaining in Frankfort, made the secession of the Orthodox from the Reform community in Vienna mandatory.* In the open letters of Rabbi Hirsch to Rabbi Bamberger, we hear echoes of the pain and grief of the fighting rabbi, the fruit of whose prolonged battle was plucked from him, virtually in the hour of the awaited victory, by a "stab in the back" from a man whose loyalty to the Torah was not subject to doubt. Nevertheless, most of the rabbis of the Orthodox communities remained loyal to him who had guided their way. It is fitting to quote from the letter of Ezriel Hildesheimer to Hirsch: "Yesterday I received the pamphlet (the reference is to the reply of Hirsch to Bamberger) which I had been anxiously awaiting. I cannot express in words how pleased I was with the exhaustive and irrefutable arguments, in spite of the deep pain over the distressing circumstances."

But an expression of fidelity and identification such as this offered but slight consolation. That which had been done could not be undone. It is true that even before Rabbi Bamberger's

*This declaration had been signed by, besides Rabbis Hirsch and Bamberger, Rabbis S. Freund of Prague, the Hassidic Tzaddik of Czortkov. J. Gesundheit of Warsaw, A. Glasner of Klausenburg, A. Gutmacher of Graetz, the Hassidic Tzaddik of Vishnitz, Tzevi Hirsch Kalischer of Thorn, Ameisel of Lomza, B. Schreiber (the author of *K'tab Sofer*) of Pressburg, and A. Hildesheimer of Berlin.

utterance, all the Orthodox elements of Germany were not in entire agreement with Rabbi Hirsch. Among some of them, many of his practices, and his progressive system of education (of which more later) aroused wonderment. Rabbi Bamberger's view, however, deepened, sharpened, and perpetuated the rent among the Orthodox, a situation which Rabbi Hirsch saw in all its tragic implications. Rabbi Bamberger passed away a year after the incident, but in his name, the opponents of Rabbi Hirsch within the Orthodox group continued their battle. It is proper to emphasize that the former explicitly wrote that also for the future was it forbidden for the Torah-true members of the Reform community to look upon its council as the council of a Jewish community, and it was their duty to establish their own community council.

IX. "TORAH WITH DEREKH ERETZ"

Already in 1844 Hirsch proclaimed an educational system, the essence of which he summed up in the maxim of the Fathers: *"Torah with Derekh Eretz."* The insistence upon the study of general sciences was no innovation among the Orthodox of Germany; Samson Raphael Hirsch's two most distinguished teachers, Rabbi Jacob Ettlinger and, particularly, Rabbi Isaac Bernays, had earlier affirmed it.

Samson Raphael Hirsch's innovation consisted in his establishment of the Orthodox school in Frankfort in which he concretized the system of education embodied in that dictum. In the achievement of this school he saw his life's accomplishment, no less than in his communal and literary achievements. To his qualities of leader and fighter which had been shown up to now, there was now added another one: that of the great teacher, adored and never forgotten by the thousands of his disciples, boys and girls. His community he served as rabbi and preacher, clear-purposed and inspiring enthusiasm, but to the school he was founder, teacher, principal, organizer, and supporter, all in one. From the day of its founding in 1853, to 1877, Hirsch himself directed the institution, together with all his other tasks and duties. He designed and implemented himself all educational and organizational tasks in the school, which has served as model to all others, combining Torah with *Derekh Eretz*. He had to do so much of the work himself because of a lack of teachers "who had a true under-

standing of Torah and secular studies", for there was no seminary
to train such men.

The school project had to struggle at the outset not only against
the wrath of the Reformists, but also against the lack of faith of
the members of the Orthodox community, which prevented their
sending their sons and daughters to his school. Hirsch had to
gather the donations for the support of the institution, going from
house to house; often was he obliged to plead with parents to
entrust their children to him. He wrote expository and polemic
articles, many writings on pedagogical subjects astonishingly in
accord with the educational ideas of the Twentieth Century. He
worked devotedly and ceaselessly to perfect the institution, eventually overcoming the lack of faith and frequent disparagement.

In his testament he wrote concerning his followers: *"which
I took out of the hand of the seducers of the time with my sword
and with my bow"*—this applies to thousands of his pupils, boys
and girls.

One of them writes: "He conversed with us in our own
language, took interest in every blow dealt us by pupils of the
Philantropin, checked on the class of the stamps we exchanged,
gave a rigorous examination to our footballs—in brief, he was
our intimate." Another one relates: "He never raised his voice
to a pupil. If he traveled to another city, he would say to him,
'Behave so that they will see you are a pupil of Rabbi Hirsch.'
He influenced them by his personality; the look of his burning eyes
was engraved deep in the memory of those he had educated."

His personal influence reached very far. A certain youth society
that sent him its constitution, he urged to have its members participate in regular sessions of Torah-study as the main part of
its program of activities; and to consult the local rabbi regarding
any doubt that might arise. A certain rabbi he counseled to suffer
imprisonment for the purpose of exerting an influence against
violating the conscience of Jewish children in a Gentile school.

The meaning of the slogan "Torah with *Derekh Eretz*" in
Hirsch's system was not confined to the "principle of enlightenment" alone. In his statement against Reform, he wrote in 1854:
"Judaism is not a mere religion, the synagogue is not a church,
and the rabbi is not a clergyman (priest). Judaism is not an
appurtenance to life, and to be a Jew is not part of the mission
of life. Judaism encompasses life in its entirety. To be a Jew is
a sum of our life's mission—in synagogue and in kitchen; in field

and in counting-house; in the office and on the speaker's platform; like father, like mother, like son, like daughter; like servant, like master; as man, as citizen, in thought and in feeling, in word and in deed, in times of pleasure, in hours of abstinence; with needle as with chisel or with pen. To be a Jew—in a life which in its totality is borne on the word of the Lord and is perfected in harmony with the will of God—this is the scope and goal of Judaism. Since Judaism encompasses the whole of man and in keeping with its explicit mission, proclaims the happiness of the whole of mankind, it is improper to confine its teachings within the "four ells" of the house of study or of the home of the Jew. Insofar as the Jew is a Jew, his views and objectives become universal. He will not be a stranger to anything which is good, true and beautiful in art and in science, in civilization and in learning. He will greet with blessing and joy everything of truth, justice, peace, and the ennobling of man, wherever it be revealed. He will hold firmly to this breadth of view in order to fulfill his mission as a Jew and to live up to the function of his Judaism in areas never imagined by his father. He shall dedicate himself with joy to every true advance in civilization and enlightenment. But all this on condition that he be never obliged to sacrifice his Judaism at any new level but rather fulfill it with even greater perfection."

To this model of the Jewish man, God-fearing and punctilious in observing the *mitzvot,* who engages all his energies to deepen his religious consciousness, and to find the correct relationship between his Judaism and the universe and all that it contains, Hirsch applied the name *"Israel-Man"*. The Torah is the fount of God's revelation, but also in nature, as in history, the will of God is revealed to the eyes of *"Israel-Man"*. The *"Israel-Man"* must know God's Torah and dedicate himself to its study and observance. But he also must open his eyes and look at the wonders of the Lord in nature and the mighty deeds of the Lord in history. The study of nature and history, with all their ramifications, in the view of Samson Raphael Hirsch, is not a requirement of "enlightenment" alone but a requisite flowing from its concept of the *"Israel-Man"*.

"Torah with *Derekh Eretz"* as a "principle of enlightenment" served him only in the category of a "temporary (emergency) ruling" (*horaat shaah*); "Torah with *Derekh Eretz"* as a system in the apprehension of Judaism, belonged, for him, to the category of instruction throughout the generations. King David, peace be upon him, was not bound to the need for nature and history studies; a Jew of 19th Century Germany was so bound. In his letter to Rabbi Bamberger, Hirsch wrote: "'Torah with *Derekh Eretz*' is the sole true principle which will lead our generation from the sickness and confusion of the present to truth, peace, and cure."

His approach to nature is well illustrated by his famous remark after his visit to Switzerland: "I shall now be able to give the proper answer if they will ask me in the True World, 'Have you seen my Switzerland?'" There was not a trace of dual values or double aim in his grasp of "Torah with *Derekh Eretz*".

Rabbi Hirsch quotes a saying of the Rabbis: "Any one who associates the Name of Heaven with the unseemly thing (idolatry) shall be uprooted from the world." "Torah with *Derekh Eretz*" is not "the Name of Heaven joined to the unseemly thing" but a unitary and all-inclusive concept of Judaism, all of which is devoted to the cause of Heaven. "Before heaven and earth we openly confess," he continues, "that were our Torah to demand that we abstain from everything going under the name of civilization and enlightenment, then, without vacillation should we honor this demand, since our Torah is our faith, the word of the living God, and besides His words there is neither counsel nor understanding."

He was not unaware that his conception of the principle "Torah with *Derekh Eretz*" carried, hidden within it, some dangers, and he admitted explicitly in his letter to Rabbi Bamberger that this aphorism of the Sages served as a subject for debate and dispute. When the close friend of his youth, Gershon Jehoshaphat, informed him that he had begun to study in the university, he wrote to him: ". . . I desire greatly to know what kind of university life you had, what was your main pursuit, and whether your scientific work became for you a supplement required by the time, a supplement which was only a burden. Or did it give you, as it should have given you, an illumination of the spirit in which your own wisdom should become united with that wisdom which is the heritage of the assembly of Jacob? Because of this it is highly important that you choose with caution the branches of science with which you will occupy yourself, and that you decide for what objective you will devote yourself to them."

The program of studies which Rabbi Hirsch marked out in
Horeb many years before the founding of the school in Frankfort,
shows clearly the nature of his conception:

1. The Hebrew language

2. The mother tongue (German)

3. Bible

and as fields auxiliary to Bible study

4. Science of nature and man

5. History

6. Science of living (*mitzvot* based on written and
   oral Law)

7. Writing and arithmetic

There is here no division between "sacred studies" and "secular
studies" but all studies are directed to working out a unitary,
Jewish personality: *"Israel-Man"*.

An added characteristic feature in Hirsch's teaching should
be underscored: Judaism as a message from all humanity. *"Israel-
man"*, who derives the recognition of his Creator from Torah,
nature and history, looks forward to the acceptance of the Kingdom of Heaven by all the world and exemplifies this kingdom
in his own life, private and public. The Torah was given to Israel,
but it was destined to be universal, in the end of days, like nature
and history. *"Israel-Man"* brings about not only the redemption
of Israel but also the redemption of all mankind: "to set the world
aright by the Kingdom of the Almighty."

In the eyes of superficial critics a contradiction seems revealed
in Rabbi Hirsch's system: "On the one hand, an extremeness"
in demanding autonomy for the Orthodox community, and on
the other, a "spirit of compromise" on the question of enlightenment. The truth of the matter is that there is here neither extremeness nor readiness to compromise, but a consistency in grasping Judaism as the presentation of the Kingdom of God on earth
and the likeness of the Jew as *"Israel-Man"*. Hirsch viewed an
Orthodox community, subservient to a Reformist community structure, as a forcible dethronement of God's Kingdom, just as he saw
it in the restriction of the Torah-Jew to the walls of the synagogue
or the house of study—both an unbearable limitation of the rule
of Torah in life.

X. Research and Polemic

With his coming to Frankfort, Rabbi Hirsch continued his literary work which had been temporarily interrupted in Nikolsburg, in consequence of his being taken up with the small matters of the provincial rabbinate and the large issue of the emancipation. Now there was assured to him again a fixed circle of readers, a small but faithful group which avidly imbibed every word written by his hand. Another circle of readers, too, awaited his writings: the Reformists, who had knowledge of his sharp pen, from the time of *Nineteen Epistles* and *The Wrestlings of Naphtali*.

First, Rabbi Hirsch set up for himself a permanent literary platform: the monthly *Jeschurun* ("A monthly to advance the Spirit of Israel and the life of Israel at home, in the community, and in school"), which appeared under his editorship from the year 1854 to 1870. *Jeschurun* made an important contribution to the shaping of Orthodox Judaism in Germany. In this organ, Rabbi Hirsch published hundreds of articles, his ideas on Torah and Judaism, and continued therein what he had begun in *Horeb* and *Epistles of the Undisclosed*.

In Frankfort he wrote the most important among his literary creations: the commentary on the Pentateuch and its translation into German. While still in his youth, he had begun to note down novellae in explaining difficult verses in Scripture; many of these novel interpretations bear upon them the seal of the influence of his first teacher, Hakham Bernays. His system in Scriptural exegesis Hirsch defines in his preface to the first edition of his commentary on the Book of Genesis: "To explain the verses of the Torah out of their own content; to derive this explanation from the verbal expression in all its shades; to draw the meaning of the words out of the linguistic storehouse of the Sacred Scriptures; and to derive and describe by means of these linguistic investigations and out of *halakhic* and *agadic* traditions transmitted to us from our national past together with the text of the Bible, those truths upon which is based the Jewish outlook on the world and life, and which are the foundations of Israel's life for ever and ever." In these words three aims stand out. The first is to penetrate to an understanding of Scripture without leaning for support on alien text-books and auxiliary science. Word and passages reach their correct interpretation by means of comparing the content and meaning of various places of the Bible. For this purpose the science of phonetic relationship (approximation) serves him as an immanent accessory. In this Hirsch saw a genuine "Jewish science", and he rejected the utilization of Semitic philology as a method antagonistic to his ambition "to explain the verses of the Torah out of their own content."

The second goal is to prove that the source of the Written Torah and Oral Torah is one, that the Written Torah cannot be understood without the Oral Torah, and that the Oral Torah is determining the Scriptural exegesis.

The third aim is to construct upon the content of Scripture, the foundations of Judaism, its dogmas and doctrines, so that they may serve as guideposts for an authoritative, Jewish evaluation of man, nature, and history, from generation to generation.

These purposes faithfully reflect the best part of Samson Raphael Hirsch's system. The primary axiom in this system is to grasp the unity in Judaism: unity between word and verse; between what was written down and oral tradition; between the sources of Judaism and its eternal world view. Well did Rabbi Isaac Elhanan Spector summarize these teachings in his written approbation (of the first Hebrew translation to a portion of the commentary to the Book of Genesis, issued in the year 1898 by Rabbi Moses Zalman Aaronson of Kovno): "Value cannot be set on the many novellae introduced by the *Gaon* and Sage, great in knowledge as in conveying understanding, lucid and conforming to reason, unifying Torah and tradition. Wondrously did he do also in this field, wherein there are contained all chief aspects and contents of the Torah; how deep his thoughts, revealing hidden wisdom from the Torah of the Lord, removing all doubts, and showing how the Torah of the Lord is perfect, the word of our God stands forever."

Samson Raphael Hirsch did not consider himself at liberty to deal with Biblical exegesis on the basis of "scientific freedom" but strove to perfect legitimate Jewish science "to understand Judaism out of its own content." Another guiding principle in his work reflected the Talmudic maxim: "Study is great, since it leads to action." One must occupy oneself with the Torah out of desire to observe it in deed and thought. This pedagogic approach found full expression in his system of explaining the rationale of the *mitzvot*. He projects everywhere their content and symbolic-educational value, herein following the lead of Rabbi Aaron Halevi in the *Hinnukh* (Book of Education); however,

Rabbi Hirsch went farther on this road to elucidate the minute details of the commands on the basis of the general ideas underlying them. Already in *Horeb* he laid down the bases of the system of his, and in the commentary on the Pentateuch he devoted himself precisely to explaining the details of disciplinary *mitzvot* such as sacrifices, the work of the tabernacle, forbidden foods, the laws touching Levitical purity and impurity.

Some people see in Hirsch's explanation of the motivation for the laws an exaggerated rationalism. The opposite is true. When he entered deeply into the minute details of the procedure of the sacrifices, it was done out of dread and awe before the word of God, Who speaks to the Jew out of each and every letter in the Torah. It is exactly in this aspect of his doctrine that Hirsch reveals a spiritual kinship to esoteric wisdom (mysticism, Kabbalah). In his annotations, in preparation of the exegesis, we come often across quotations from the *Zohar,* and in his annotations on the portion *Terumah*, we find these words in the sacred tongue: "Behold, the content of the truths, intimated in the form of the candlestick, its ornamentation, and the measure of all its parts, is very deep. Even the vain interpretations, due to bateyes, of the candlestick, breathe a whisper of the meaning! But His mighty deeds who can understand?"

Are these the words of a rationalist?

The commentary was published, book by book of the Pentateuch, between the years 5627 and 5638 (1867-1878), the first draft being taken by the audience at his weekly lecture in the community's *Bet ha-Midrash*. This monumental creation aroused great enthusiasm even among his opponents, but since Rabbi Hirsch was very sparing in quotation, he was also accused of lack of scientific attitude and even of plagiarism. He replied: "My commentary is related to what I studied under Bernays only in the sense that he served me as an encouraging example to enter the palace of the Torah to draw from it awareness and outlook. For every word of wisdom or folly which I discovered in this manner and hazarded to note down in my work, without indicating the name of its author, the responsibility rests before God and man upon myself alone."

Rabbi Hirsch completed in his old age two more exegetical works, one on the Book of Psalms, the other on the *Siddur* (Prayer Book). The first was published in the year 5642 (1882), the second posthumously. Among the many polemic works which he wrote in Frankfort, one should include his dispute with "moderate Reform" in German Jewry. In the middle of the 19th Century the debate with the Reform had closed and there was almost nothing to add to what had already been said and written in Oldenburg and Emden. A new peril, however, lay in wait for Judaism. When Zacharias Frankel, in 5614 (1854) in Breslau, opened the Jewish Theological Seminary to prepare rabbis, Hirsch turned to him with a public request to clarify the principles of Judaism on which the institution was based, its position on dogmas and doctrines as Revelation, the divine origin of the Torah, faith in the Rabbis, the binding force of rabbinic legislation and the traditional practices of Israel. When Frankel and his associates would not condescend to reply to the "Prayer Book scholars (*Siddur lomdim*) from Frankfort", Rabbi Hirsch declared: "We now know where we stand. Hoary Israel has nothing to expect from you. Relief and deliverance will arise to us from another place."

When, in 5619 (1859), Frankel published his book, *Darke ha-Mishnah* (Ways of the Mishnah), and Hirsch demonstrated in *Jeschurun* that he had deviated from the fundamentals of the faith in a matter so basic as *"Halakhah* taught to Moses at Sinai," then many of those who at first had been astonished at the boldness of the great warrior in attacking a personality so renowned as Frankel, admitted that Hirsch was justified in erecting a partition between pure Judaism and Judaism that was "conservative" but was not firmly based on the faith of Israel, as sanctified from generations of yore.

After a number of years, when Heinrich Graetz, who meanwhile had become one of the central pillars of the Breslau seminary, published the first part of his "History of the Jews", there no longer remained any doubt about the skepticism and the undermining of the foundations of the faith by the spirit of that institution and its new goals in Judaism. Hirsch, through scholarly work unique in acumen and comprehensiveness, revealed this aim to the public view. The fact that Graetz had once been his disciple and enthusiastic adherent only added to the sorrow with which the aggressive words of the teacher were written.

But here again: Rarely, in his polemic articles, did Hirsch attack the personality of the disputant, but remained within the boundary of the thematic debate, as against his many opponents, who never tired of mocking at the "absence of his scientificity".

XI. Public Need

In the last decade of his life, upon his approaching the "age of strength" (four-score years), Rabbi Hirsch bestowed increasing attention upon the needs of the Jewish people beyond the borders of his community. Postal and other ties brought the scattered Jewish communities closer together; an ever stronger stream of migration began to change the map of Jewish demography on the face of the world, the rebuilding of Palestine was transformed from dream to reality, and the problem of organizing Jewry began to shift from the local community to national and world unions. These new directions found the venerable leader prepared to search for new solutions.

In ever increasing measure, rabbis, famous Torah-scholars, and laymen, from all Jewish settlements in the world, turned to him with questions, proposals, and petitions. Particularly, strong ties bound him to the greatest of the Russian rabbis, Rabbi Isaac Elhanan Spector of Kovno. In 1882, the year of the oppressive Czarist edicts, Hirsch, in cooperation with Rabbi Spector, achieved an immense amelioration of Russian Jewry's burdens and aided thousands of their immigrants. Especially did he labor to nullify the evil decree to prohibit the study of Torah, for which purpose he composed a special booklet, *On the Attitude of the Talmud towards Judaism and towards the Social Status of its Adherents.* A rabbi who brought him a letter from Rabbi Isaac Elhanan, related that he sought information on the condition of the Jews in Russia and Poland. "When I described their sufferings to him, tears flowed from his eyes."

When no one in Germany as yet dreamt of the possibility of the growing power of anti-Semitism, Rabbi Hirsch once remarked in a conversation: "Just as mischievous children are pulled by the ears, so will they deal with us. The Jews are the school-books of the nations, a disorderly pupil tears them. And they point to the high level of Gentile culture!"

In Hirsch's attitude to national and world Jewish organizations, which had developed during the second half of the 19th Century (such as *Alliance Israélite Universelle* and the order of B'nai B'rith), two fundamentals stand out: the guarding of the authority of the local rabbi and non-acceptance of "neutrality" of different organizations as respects questions on the nature of Judaism. Therein he out-distanced many of his colleagues, who were in accord with him on the question of the Orthodox Jewish community, among them Ezriel Hildesheimer. Hirsch saw in the activity of the "neutral" Jewish organizations, with all their social achievements, a danger to the clear character of Judaism.

For this reason, in 5645 (1885), he founded a union that should accept upon itself the fulfillment of the religious and spiritual roles of Orthodox Jewry on a world level, and whose ultimate purpose should be to unite all Orthodox Jews of the world into one organization—The Free Union for the Interest of Orthodox Judaism (*Freie Vereinigung fuer die Interessen des Orthodoxen Judentums*). This union, his last organizational creation, in existence until the destruction of German Jewry by Hitler, supplied the religious needs of Orthodox Jewry in Germany and in other lands. The means, possibilities, and political influence of "The Free Union" were limited, but its main importance is to be seen precisely in that it paved the way for the organizing of the Orthodox in the generations after Hirsch. It is of great significance that the matter of the settlement of Palestine was one of the world problems which occupied Samson Raphael Hirsch in his last years. An intimate of the "Overseers and Stewards in Amsterdam", Rabbi Hirsch was always engaged in the gathering of monies for the needy Jews in the Holy Land. However, from a private letter of the year 5642 (1882), we learn that he had thought of the national, religious, and social significance of the migration to Palestine and its colonization, and he did not see therein any ideologic problem but only a practical question. From that time he published many open calls for the support of the Jewish colonies in the Land of Israel. A short time before his death there arose for the first time the question of the Sabbatical year in these colonies. Whilst joining those who took a rigorous view, he appealed for liberal donations on behalf of those who kept the seventh year. It was his life's last request to the public.

On the 27th day of Tebeth, 5649 (1888), Samson Raphael Hirsch died. Great masses swept on to Frankfort to participate in the funeral and stood about the rabbi's house, where his five sons and four daughters were mourning. All walked in the way of their father and remained believers and punctilious in observance of the *mitzvot* until the end of their days. The family life of Rabbi Hirsch was exemplary, and this, in no small measure, was due to his wife, who had died six years before him. In his eulogy over her grave, he said: "What Sarah was to Abraham, this she was to me." If his mission was *"to call upon the name of the Lord,"* she helped him by training the children and by the care she took of their home. He dedicated to her the second part of his commentary on the Book of Psalms with these words: "Loyal companion of my life, faithful comrade in my aspirations, my staff and trusted counselor in my home and my labors, who educated, molded, and is the beloved and loyal friend, of her children and grandchildren."

This man, who in his public demands at times apppeared to be "as severe as Shammai" in his consistency and in his non-compromising attitude, was possessed of a soft heart, as seen in his personal letters and in his home attitude. His wife was accustomed to scatter bread crumbs every morning among the birds on her window sill. After her death, it was discovered one morning that the rabbi continued with this duty and in his dying hour he even begged those standing about him not to forget to feed the birds! Rabbi Hirsch, as he was gathered to his people, could have said about himself that he had fulfilled the mission for which Providence had placed him on earth. The sense of this mission found expression in the pseudonym he assumed as rabbi of "Assembly" of the Congregation of Jeschurun: "Keeper of the Sacred Charge." As such he was remembered by his pupils and by the members of his community who listened to the flaming words of his sermons. A visitor of his synagogue, who did not understand German, said after he had heard the address: "I did not understand even a word, but I imagined that I was seeing before me the prophet Isaiah, and that I was hearing the voice of one of the prophets of Israel." And a student wrote in his memoirs: "No artist can picture the fire in his eyes, a blend of calm wisdom, burning energy, and strength which penetrates. I was compelled to look into his eyes. I felt that he was searching the chambers of my soul, and that he sees all that I have done and knows all my thoughts."

The organizational and literary creations of Rabbi Samson Raphael Hirsch have left their imprint on Jewish history and Jewish thought, and as a "legitimate revolutionary," one who succeeded in shaping his generation so that it might conform with the eternal Torah of God, his people shall remember and venerate him to the end of days.

ISAAC ELHANAN SPECTOR

(1817-1896)

By Samuel K. Mirsky

ISAAC ELHANAN SPECTOR

By Samuel K. Mirsky

Among the outstanding rabbinic scholars of the past century, Rabbi Isaac Elhanan occupies a unique position. The city of Kovno became famous in rabbinic circles mostly because of him, who, for more than three decades (1864-1896) was its spiritual leader. Although he did not speak nor understand Russian, the Russian Government recognized him as the spokesman of religious Jewry in Russia. World Jewry saw in him the expounder of Rabbinic Law *par excellence*. His authority was almost beyond question. His life story was told in a little book called *Toldot Yitzhak*,[1] written by his secretary Jacob Halevi Lifshitz and published in Warsaw 1896. In 1946, which marked the fiftieth anniversary of his death, the writer of this article dedicated to his memory the first half of volume III of *Talpioth* published by the Rabbi Isaac Elhanan Theological Seminary of America,[2] in which evaluations of Rabbi Isaac Elhanan, and newly discovered letters written by him, were printed. The following is a study of his life and works.

I. Ancestry and Early Life

In the small town Rosh in the Gubernatorial district of Grodno, in the year 1817, a son was born to R. Israel Isser, the son of Elhanan, and his wife Rachel, the daughter of R. Isaac.[3] The newborn child was named after both his grandparents, Isaac Elhanan. He was his parents' third son.[4]

R. Israel Isser was the rabbi of the town Rosh and the teacher of his own sons. When Isaac Elhanan was ten years old, his

---

[1] The book was translated into Yiddish by Nota Lifshitz, the son of the author, and published in Brooklyn, New York, in 1929.

[2] The Rabbi Isaac Elhanan Theological Seminary was founded in the year 1896 in New York to commemorate the name of this outstanding rabbinical scholar and leader.

[3] The exact day of his birth was unknown even to himself (*Toldot Yitzhak* p. 4).

[4] The first two sons were called Moshe Yoseph and Abraham Aaron. Very little is known about them except that the latter died young and heirless and was often mentioned with pity by his brother. After Isaac Elhanan another son was born, and was named Moshe David. Towards the end of his life he settled in the land of Israel, where he died.

mother died and his father assumed the role of both parents. At the age of thirteen, he became engaged to, and after a short time married, the daughter of R. Leizer Yezersky from Wolkowysk near Rosh. A year later, his father passed away. To conquer his grief, Isaac Elhanan threw himself with all his zeal and energy into his books. For seven consecutive years he studied with extraordinary diligence under his teacher, the rabbi of Wolkowysk, R. Benjamin Diskin. A fellow student was his intimate friend, the rabbi's son, Moshe Joshua Leib Diskin, who later became the rabbi of Brisk and spent the last years of his life in Jerusalem.[5]

In 1837, while not yet twenty years old, Isaac Elhanan became the rabbi of the nearby town Isabelin.[6] His weekly salary was seventy-five kopeks, in American money about one dollar. The poverty of the small Jewish town and of his own home left its imprints upon Isaac Elhanan. He used to relate the pathetic story of his wife and children asking for food which he could not provide for them. Many a time he may have wept in deep pain and sympathy because of the sufferings of his loved ones. "But greatness in learning can be achieved only through a self-imposed ruthlessness against one's self and one's own. The love of Torah must suppress all other loves." However, though suppressed, these loves are not destroyed, but surge up constantly, creating an inner unrest. Through this friction between the love of Torah and personal attachments, a spark is struck which illumines, and thus broadens and enlarges, the circle of one's interests. A person caught between these two forces finds himself increasingly driven to ever higher attainments.

Fortunately, a letter in his own handwriting in the first year of his service as rabbi of Isabelin, addressed to his teacher Rabbi Benjamin Diskin, came to my hand.[7] The young rabbi, later on renowned as the greatest responsa-writer in his time, expresses deep gratitude to his former teacher. Written on Monday, the fifth of the month Tamuz in the year 5597 (1837) in Isabelin, it reads: "I received your honored letter before the Holy Sabbath and derived great joy from reading your replies to my questions. I wish that the heart of my great teacher should always be with

---

[5] R. Moshe Joshua Leib Diskin, known as the Rabbi of Brisk, is the founder of an orphanage known as *Bet Yetomim Diskin* and the *Yeshivah Ohel Moshe* in Jerusalem.

[6] He was ordained as rabbi by R. Benjamin Diskin of Grodno and R. Isaac of Tiktin, cf. *Toldot Yitzhak* p. 6.

[7] I published it in *Talpioth*, Vol. III, 3-4, pp. 321-325.

me to answer all the problems that I will submit to him." He proceeds with a few *halakhic* expositions which he offers to his master's judgment. This epistle sheds light upon the first steps taken by a spiritual giant groping his way in his early life.[8]

To improve his economic conditions, he left for the first time his small town and went to Karlin to meet the rabbi of that town, R. Jacob, the author of *Mishkenot Yaakob*. They had become acquainted through correspondence in *halakhic* matters,[9] but the personal impression was much greater and led to permanent friendship. When, in 1839, the rabbinate of Beresa became vacant, R. Jacob recommended Isaac Elhanan and he was chosen. In that town his reputation as an authority grew speedily. He became involved in a controversial matter with R. Isaac of Shavel[10] referring to the writings of a bill of divorce in which his opinion finally prevailed.[11] In connection with another responsum, too, his decision was accepted and praised.[12]

In 1846 he became rabbi of Nieshvez. The communal leaders of Beresa were sorry, indeed, to see their rabbi leave, but the town of Nieshvez offered larger opportunities. Thence his fame spread to all neighboring cities. Questions on matters of Jewish law came to him from all parts of the country and even from abroad. The thoroughness with which he treated them served as an invitation for more, so that before long he became the central authority for applied *Halakhah*. The great R. Nahum Jaffe of Grodno, who was revered not only for his learning but even more so for his noble character, turned to him again and again with his problems.

In 1851 he became the rabbi of Novogrodek.[13] There he published his first book, *Be'er Yitzhak*. In the introduction he writes: "I know my limited value compared to the greatness of those who corresponded with me, and yet, great scholars have made a peg upon which to hang their weapons. With the help of God, my words found favor in the eyes of the leaders of this

---

[8]The subject matter discussed in that letter is quoted in his first book *Be'er Yitzhak*. Yoreh Deah, 23. The contents of the letter given there is interwoven in a larger *halakhic* exposition, and at the end it is stated: "And I offered these matters to the great and elder rabbis of our time, may their souls rest in paradise, and they have agreed with me with the help of God."

[9]*Ibid.* 25.

[10]Shavel, a town near Kovno, Lithuania.

[11]See *Be'er Yitzhak*, Eben Ahezer 1415.

[12]*Ibid.* 8-9. It had to do with the spelling of a name in a *Get*.

[13]There are various spellings of Jewish towns in Russia and the common spelling of this town is Navahradok.

generation. They turned to me, and my answers appeared correct in their eyes. I, therefore, have written down all the proceedings of our correspondence to serve as an eternal memory before God."[14] These words, repeated in various forms in the introductions to his later books, contain the very essence of his life's work and the main feature of his spiritual physiognomy. He was accepted as the greatest authority on Jewish Law in his generation. From near and far, scholars and common people corresponded with him or came personally to him with their problems. He always dealt with each of them, both thoroughly and profoundly.

II. His Literary Legacy

His main works are his books of responsa: *Be'er Yitzhak* (1858) *Nahal Yitzhak* (two parts, 1872-1884)[15] and *En Yitzhak* (two parts, 1889-1895). They contain answers to questions, in the order of the *Shulhan Arukh,* dealing with innumerable problems. To present his method of treatment, I shall offer an outline of one of his typical responsa.

He was asked whether a young divorcee who was pregnant at the time of her divorce and gave birth to a child is allowed to remarry after making arrangements for the nursing of the child. The question could easily be answered yes or no, depending on the opinion of R. Samson and his opponent Rabbenu Tam, as quoted by the Tossaphists on *Yebamot* 42a and *Ketubot* 60b, further discussed in Alfasi and R. Asher ad loc. and finally incorporated in *Shulhan Arukh Eben Haezer,* XVII. Moreover, the same question was already discussed in another book, *Tzemah Tzedek,* by R. Menachem Mendel of Lubavitch, sec. *Eben Haezer,* 45. This latter book is quoted by R. Isaac Elhanan in his responsum to *Eben Haezer En Yitzhak,* 17.[16] However, R. Isaac Elhanan traces the opinions of the two Tossaphists not only to their original source but to the reasons which could have prompted their opinions. He then tries to establish Maimonides' opinion in this matter. On surface judgment, Maimonides, in the eleventh chapter in the laws of divorce, paragr. 25, seems to side with Rabbenu Tam. Thus did all the commentators to Maimonides

---

[14]Introduction to *Be'er Yitzhak*, Koenigsberg 1858.

[15]See *Talpioth,* Vol. IV, 3-4 pp. 873-881, where notes on his book, *Nahal Yitzhak,* in his own handwriting, are published.

[16]Due to an obvious printed error the number of the responsum in *Zemah Zedek* is given as 55 instead of 45.

assume. However, R. Bezalel Ashkenazi, in his *Shittah Mekubetzet* to *Ketubot* 59b, states that Maimonides follows R. Samson's opinion. Although R. Isaac Elhanan seems to be inclined
to adopt the latter opinion and to allow the divorcee to remarry,
without waiting the period prescribed by the law for the nursing
of the child, he is not overlooking a possibility that there might
be an error in the text of *Shittah Mekubetzet*, and instead of
Rambam (Maimonides) it may read Ramban (Nahmanides). By
an independent study of both texts, Rambam and Ramban, R.
Isaac Elhanan comes, however, to the conclusion that the present
reading in *Shittah Mekubetzet* is correct. "And this will serve
as a strong foundation for a lenient attitude."

R. Isaac Elhanan never lost sight of his inclination to leniency,
but neither was he blinded by it from considering all other opinions.

There are two methods of answering a question. One is to
reply simply, almost curtly and directly, to the question asked.
This was the way of the Babylonian *Geonim* and the early rabbis.
The second method takes the question as a point of departure for
a thorough discussion of the particular matter involved. R. Isaac
Elhanan adopted the second method, digressing where necessary
in order to deal comprehensively with the question. Since most
of his replies were directed to rabbis, he dealt with every problem as a subject for a *halakhic* treatise. However, he constantly
sought to reply specifically to the question asked, and in his conclusions he was always clear and direct without being afraid,
as is the case with some authors of responsa, of making an express
commitment or taking a definite stand.

The general tendency of *Halakhah*, in the language of our
Sages of old, is to spread and develop like an organic plant. So
did R. Isaac Elhanan divide his responsa into various parts, which
he termed branches. The genius of his mind allowed him to recognize the relation of many different laws and decisions in *Halakhah*,
which, superficially, seem completely unconnected, and to show
how they are really one, and how they shed light on the central
point in question. Through his deep and wide knowledge, every
question was referred to the core of the principle involved, and
all associated and affiliated principles, scattered in the far-flung
laws of the Torah, were seen to fit themselves into a definite
pattern, as proofs, references, guiding lines and substantive points.

Questions relating to *Agunot* (forsaken wives) are extensively
dealt with in his books. These are treated by him not only from

a legal, but also from a social and humanitarian viewpoint. In his *halakhic* discussions he seeks ways to rebuild the shattered lives of families, always trying to insure that no new tragedy would arise from his decision. Many principles laid down and expounded by him have been adopted, later, by rabbinic authorities on *Agunah* matters.[16a] The word "Agunah" became, for him, a synonym for the people of Israel. He used it as a code word in his letters to influential persons outside of Russia, to keep them informed of the sufferings of his people.

Most of his correspondence on *halakhic* matters was incorporated in his books. Some remained unpublished. For instance, a responsum written by him to R. Mordecai Rosenblatt of Osmene, which dealt with birth control, remained unpublished during his lifetime. For he had written: "I request that you do not give it publicity in my name, lest people, in applying it, become lax." Since, in the meantime, much has been written on this topic, I felt that the time has come to make his opinion known, published it in full.[17]

In accord with a widespread custom, to preface rabbinic writings on *Halakhah* with *agadic* expositions, he wrote lengthy *agadic* discourses in two of his books. They seem to embody some of his semi-annual homilies on *Shabbat Shuvah* (between New Year and the Day of Atonement) and on *Shabbat ha-Gadol* (preceding Passover).

III. His Function as Arbitrator

Even before he became the rabbi of Kovno, he was invited to arbitrate in disputes of national concern. In 1858, while rabbi of Novogrodek,[18] he, together with R. David Tevl of Minsk, R.

[16a]Like *Tre Rube* and similar rules of evidence.

[17]See *Talpioth*, Vol. III, 1-2. On R. Mordecai Rosenblatt, who was also known as R. Mordecai Weitzel (the name Rosenblatt is derived from the name of a book, *Aleh Havatzelet*, published by the author), see his biography by Ch. Lunsky (grandson of the author), Vilna 1917.

[18]R. Meir Berlin in his book, *Rabban Shel Israel* (biography of his father), New York, 1943, p. 28, writes that R. Isaac Elhanan, at the time he was called to arbitrate in the Volozin dispute, was rabbi of Nisvez. This must be an error on his part, for on the document containing the terms of settlement written down and signed by the arbitrators, R. Isaac Elhanan signed as rabbi of Novogrodek. See my article on the Volozin Yeshivah, Jewish Institutions of Higher Learning in Europe, New York, 1956, p. 41; Lifshitz, *Toldot Yitzhak*, Warsaw, 1896, p. 61, writes that R. Naftali Tzevi Yehudah Berlin, the head of the Volozin Yeshivah, came personally to Novogrodek to invite R. Isaac Elhanan as an arbitrator and urged him to accept the invitation.

Joseph Peimer of Slutzk, and R. Z'ev Wolf of Vilna, was called upon to make peace in a controversy between the students and teachers of the Yeshivah of Volozin. R. Isaac Elhanan, the youngest of the arbitrators, was asked to deliver a lecture at the Yeshivah. This was considered a distinct honor, since only visitors of the highest caliber who happened to come to Volozin were asked to do so.[19] It seems that the decison which for a long time restored peace to the famed academy was written by him.[20]

In 1864 he became the rabbi of Kovno, a position he held to the end of his life. In 1866 a controversy arose which threatened the existence of the Yeshivah of Mir, and again he was instrumental in settling it to the satisfaction of all.[21] The confidence placed in him by all parties was due not merely to his clear mind and great learning, but also to his warm heart and unlimited love for Torah. His interest in the Yeshivah did not stop with the rendering of the decision, but he continued to help it to sustain itself. A letter he wrote to R. Isaac Blaser of Petersburg about the collection of money in that city for the benefit of the Yeshivah of Mir, throws light upon his continued fatherly love for the institution whose spiritual upbuilding he had promoted.[22]

Even communities outside of Russia referred disputes between synagogues and rabbis to R. Isaac Elhanan, and his opinion was decisive. One outstanding case is described in detail in a recent book.[23] When, in 1891, Rabbi Herman Adler became Chief Rabbi of England, a society, *Mahzike Hadat,* was organized in London, with the intention of forming a separate community, not subject to his authority. The newly organized synagogue ap-

---

[19]See the collected writings of Zalman Epstein, Petersburg 1908, pp. 121-123, where a description of such a lecture by the Rabbi of Russein is described. The topic of the lecture would be announced in advance, so that the sharpest minds among the senior students would be able to challenge the lecturer to defend his thesis. See also Isaac Rivkind, *Sefer Turof,* Boston 1938, p. 233.

[20]On the text of the document see *Toldot Yitzhak* by Lifschitz pp. 62-63; *Zikhron Yaacob* by the same author II ch. 13, and cf. *Mekor Barukh* by Baruch Epstein IV p. 1692 ff., Jewish Institutions pp. 40-41.

[21]See the letters written by R. Berish Maislish of Warsaw to R. Isaac Elhanan of Kovno, Jewish Institutions pp. 90-91.

[22]Published from the Archives of R. Isaac Blaser in *Talpioth* Vol. V, 1-2, pp. 138-139.

[23]"A Fortress in Anglo-Jewry, the Story of the *Mahzike Hadat*", by Bernard Homa, London 1953.

pointed as its rabbi, R. Abraham Abba Werner,[24] formerly *Dayyan* in Telsi (Lithuania) and rabbi in Helsingfors (Finland). R. Isaac Elhanan, faithful to his policy of peace and unity, threw his authoritative decision on the side of the Chief Rabbi of England, and all the efforts of the new community to turn the controversy into a battle between Jews of Russian descent in England and Anglo-Jewry, and thus to gain the support of the great Russian rabbi, could not move him.[25].

IV. His Social and Political Activities

Constant economic and political distress troubled Russian Jewry at this time. Laws aiming at the impoverishment of our people in Russia who lived in compact masses, the pogroms and other persecutions, intended to frighten them away from the land in which they had lived for generations and maintained their religious and cultural way of life, eventually achieved their purpose. A mass emigration from Russia was the order of the day. The question was: "Whither?" With the aid of philanthropists and other influential persons in political life, committees were organized to guide the masses at the crossroads. The Russian Jews were still under the influence of their spiritual leaders.

Russian Jewry, in the days of R. Isaac Elhanan, knew many stars in the firmament of Jewish learning, who drew their light from hundreds of years of tradition. It was as if the heavens, before the sunset, were suffused with a glorious multi-colored brilliance. Every town and hamlet could boast of a great *lamdan*. Above these scholars stood the official rabbis, and towering above them were the great teachers in the central *yeshivot* and *Hassidic* rabbis. Only extraordinary knowledge, mental power, and true piety, would cause one to be considered an outstanding spiritual leader. Among them, R. Isaac Elhanan stood forth as one of

---

[24]The surname Werner was adopted by the son of the rabbi, who lived in England, before his father came to join him. The rabbi's earlier surname was Hyma (from the name Hayyim) and hence the family name Homa, by which his descendants are known. The author of the book "Fortress in Anglo-Jewry," Bernard Homa, is a grandson of R. Abraham Abba Werner.

[25]Among the letters by R. Isaac Elhanan and his opponents which appear in a photostatic reproduction in the book above mentioned, there is a postcard written by R. Joseph Rosen, known as the Rogatchover, who sided with R. Abraham Abba Werner, in which he said: "The whole world follows blindly the Old Gaon of Kovno (i.e. R. Isaac Elhanan)."

the greatest. In many a gathering of rabbinic and lay leaders held in Petersburg, he worked hand in hand with Baron Guinzburg and others to call off a pending Czarist decree.

He consistently opposed mass emigration from Russia. The tide, however, could not be halted. Organized immigration to new lands (North and South America) and to the Holy Land was a providential imperative. He kept in close contact with leading Jews in London, urging them to voice their protest and enlist the help of liberal governments against the massacres of the Jews in Russia.[26] At the same time he gave his moral support to *Hoveve Zion,* the movement for the resettlement of the Land of Israel.

In his memoirs about the beginnings of that movement, Judah Appel[27] writes: "The city of Kovno was always a metropolis in Israel, containing a multitude of important and famous people. It was therefore essential that a society of *Hoveve Zion* be established there. From all larger Jewish centers, like Vilna, Warsaw, Bialystok and Moscow, they turned to Kovno with an urgent appeal to become active in this holy matter. . . . Moreover, there lived the *Gaon* R. Isaac Elhanan Spector, who was most highly respected, both in Russia and abroad, and whose words were greatly heeded. All that was necessary was that the *Gaon* lend his hand to them and sanction their activities. Indeed, R. Isaac Elhanan gave his both hands to *Hoveve Zion* and to all their activities."[28]

He worked tirelessly for the abolition of the Czarist decree to control the curriculum of the elementary and higher Jewish schools (*hedarim* and *yeshivot*). To that end, he mobilized all forces of influence in Petersburg and convened there many a meeting. Some of his letters to Jacob Poliakov and others in which his innermost feelings of deep concern are poured forth, were published by R. Jacob Halevi Lifshitz,[29] and by Leon Rabino-

---

[26] A society for the collection of information about the pogroms and persecutions, *Hayeh im Pifiyot* (Be with the mouths of thy people Israel), was headed by R. Isaac Elhanan. The society published what might be called a Black Book, exposing all the Czarist activities against the Jews. See about this society *Zikhron Yaacob* III, chapt. 13.

[27] Judah Appel, *Betokh Reishit Hatehiyah* (In the Beginning of the Rennaissance) p. 375.

[28] See *Ketabim* to the History of the *Hoveve Zion Movement,* I p. 262, 363 and II p. 232; cf Aaron B. Z. Shurin, "R. Isaac Elhanan's Attitudes to the New Settlement in the Land of Israel," *Talpioth,* III, 1-2, pp. 58-72.

[29] *Toldot Yitzhak* pp. 87-89.

witz.[30] An unpublished message to Moshe Aryeh Leib Friedland reveals not only his soul trembling for the fate of the *heder* and *yeshivah* but also his anxiety for the unity of Israel and for the cooperation of all classes, religious and non-religious alike. He writes: "Current events have brought our people and our holy Torah into a terrible perplexity because of decrees regarding the study of Talmud, of a type not issued for many generations against our people, and now freezing the blood of our brethren in this land, where *rov binyan u-minyan,* the majority by structure and numbers of Jewry, live. Our people—may God have mercy upon them—whose material and spiritual destruction came only through separation of our hearts from our heads, should never forget, even after a thousand generations, the sin of causeless hatred, which has destroyed Temple and driven us into exile. Therefore, when due to our iniquities, Jewry and the holy Torah reached again a crisis through these terrible decrees, everyone of us in whose heart lives a spark of Judaism and who is not counted among the Karaites, is duty bound to help in this matter with all his power; to put aside his private feelings and opinions, and come to the protection of the holy Talmud . . . I well know my honorable and dear friend, the exalted Baron Guinsburg. His heart is perfect with God and Judaism, he works wholeheartedly for the saving of our holy Torah. Now, in this moment of danger, we must unite, go hand in hand and arm in arm, forget our private views and bend our efforts together for the saving of the Torah. By no means let us feel secure at this moment of danger, so that we may deem it sufficient to act individually. We must maintain joint efforts, and increase them to the greatest extent. If we shall now slack them, God forbid, then we shall be challenged, even by the coming generations, who would say that we, too, through separation of hearts and causeless hatred, have left our holy religion unaided against the terrible decree which has befallen us and is threatening the Torah to be forgotten from amongst the children of our people, May God have mercy upon them."[31]

The letter is meant to persuade Mr. Friedland who, because of religious scruples, was unwilling to work together with irreligious people, even in this cause.

---

[30]*Hamelitz* vol. 36, No. 67.
[31]A. R. Malachi, *Talpioth* Vol. III, 1-2 pp. 73-80.

V. The Ideal Rabbi

A deep melancholy seemed to shine from R. Isaac Elhanan's eyes, as is evident from his picture, and even more so from the description by the few survivors who had the privilege of knowing him personally. It is not due to the Czarist oppressions, which he constantly fought and which made a deep impression upon his delicate soul. It was rather the melancholy which encompasses and involves a person as he stands at twilight, watching a sinking sun. Such sentiments are expressed in his proclamation, *Et la'assot la-Shem* (It Is Time To Act For The Lord), which he issued in 1879 and in a pamphlet, *Etz Peri,* which was published in 1881, containing, in addition to his own, also articles by R. Israel Salanter, R. Alexander Moshe Lapidut, and others. R. Isaac Elhanan writes: "As little as thirty years ago, there were among us great *Geonim,* pillars of scholarship, who with their knowledge nurtured our people, and to whom all looked for Torah. The remaining few are already old, may the Almighty lengthen their years. The coming generation, Heaven forbid, may be orphaned of all scholarship! Everyone familiar with the ways of Torah and its teaching, understands that the continuation of learning is impossible without strong and indefatigable fighters in its cause, who can bring to light the hidden pearls of the sea of the Talmud."

This was his call for the establishment of what might be called a post-graduate *yeshivah* and which in the language current among rabbinic circles, is called a *Kollel.*

A man, named Ovadiah Lachman, residing in Germany and having large possessions in Poland, had become interested in rabbinical learning and turned for advice and guidance to R. Israel Salanter. The latter, on hearing of his readiness to donate 10,000 marks to establish a foundation, first considered using the money for the issuing of his magazine, *Tevunah,* but, after deliberation, decided that it better be used for an Institute of Graduate Rabbinic Studies. R. Alexander Moshe Lapidut of Rossein was suggested to head it, but he recommended R. Isaac Elhanan of Kovno, since the latter was considered the greatest rabbinic authority of his time.[32] R. Isaac Elhanan at first hesitated, but after his son R. Tzevi Hirsh, at that time engaged in business, agreed to assist him in the administration of the *Kollel,*

---

[32]*Zikhron Yaacob* III p. 223.

he agreed.[33] After R. Tzevi Hirsh accepted a rabbinic position in Mittau, Latvia, R. Isaac Blaser of Petersburg was called to take charge of the *Kollel* under the spiritual leadership of R. Isaac Elhanan. From a group of ten young men, the *Kollel* grew to a center of higher Jewish learning. The students, all married, received a stipend which enabled them to support their families and devote all their time to study. The *Kollel* became a model for other institutions of the same kind in various cities.

The comparison of the ideal rabbi to an angel of heaven, made by our Sages, on the basis of the verses in Malakhi: *"The law of truth was in his mouth, and iniquity was not found in his lips; he walked with me in peace and equity, and did turn many away from iniquity; for the priest's lips should keep knowledge, and they should seek the law at his mouth: for he is the messenger of the Lord of hosts,"* was literally fulfilled in R. Isaac Elhanan. "To me," said R. Isaac Salanter, "the main quality of a rabbi is greatness in Torah and the fear of God, and vast knowledge in practical law, so that he should possess the power to be liberal in the interpretation of the Law (*Koha dehetera*), even as the rabbi, the *Gaon* of Kovono."[34]

VI. The End

The beginning of R. Isaac Elhanan's life was not much different from that of many other rabbis and scholars of that time and place, which, historically speaking, is not too unlike our own, but psychologically, very far removed from us. His development was rather unique—that of a spiritual giant whose ideal it was to merge, and to be gathered in at the end of his life, with his people. He started with a short trip from the little town Isabelin, where he first served as rabbi, to Karlin, whence he came back with forty rubles in his pocket to improve the economic conditions of his own family. He continued with countless trips through small and large cities throughout Russia, and with copious correspondence with barons, diplomats, and ministers of all countries, collecting millions of rubles to improve the condition of his

---

[33]About the *Kollel* see Samuel Rosenfeld, R. Israel Salanter, Warsaw, 1911, pp. 53 ff.; Eliezer Eliyahu Friedman, *Le Toldot Kat Hamussaryyim,* Jerusalem, 1926, p. 131; R. Dov Katz, *Tenuat Hammussar,* Tel-Aviv, 1946, i pp. 170 ff.; Dr. Menahem G. Glenn, *Israel Salanter,* New York, 1953, pp. 78 ff.

[34]See R. Dov Katz, *Tenuat Hammussar* 1 p. 335.

brethren exposed to pogroms and every form of persecution. He ended with bidding farewell to his family and people, leaving for his family a total inheritance of 38 rubles and for his people a priceless heritage, which will last forever!

On the twenty-first day of the month of Adar in the year 5656 (1896), after a sickness of sixteen days, R. Isaac Elhanan passed away, and the entire Jewish world felt a personal loss. In spite of the shortness of time for the preparation of his funeral,[35] tens of thousands of people participated.[36] His son and successor in the Rabbinate of Kovno, R. Tzevi Hirsh Rabinowitz[37] and R. Isaac Blaser eulogized him at the cemetery.

Sixty years after his death, his granddaughter, Bluma Solomonson, the only survivor of his grandchildren, records: "From my memory at the age of six or seven: Grandfather and Grandmother used to go out for the summer months to a resort on a mountain near Kovno. Later this place was fully built up and became almost part of the city, but in those days, 1888-1889, it was surrounded by gardens and served as a summer resort for the residents of Kovno. For a number of years, Grandfather used to take me out there for rest and recreation. One summer, his other granddaughter, Esther, the daughter of R. Tzevi Hirsh, may the memory of the righteous be blessed, was with us. She was later exterminated together with all the Jews of Rovno (Vohlyn) . . . In the resort I was greatly impressed by his cordial relations with the domestic animals. The cat, for instance, was sitting on a chair behind the back of Grandfather and was eating directly from his hand. . . ."[38]

This little episode, told as a child's impression, seems to reveal one of the main features in R. Isaac Elhanan's character. One can see in it the fulfillment of the Talmudic dictum: "It is forbidden for a person to eat before he provides food for an animal, as it is written: 'And I will give grass in thy field for thy cattle and thou shalt eat and be satisfied—Thou shalt first provide thy animals with food and then eat thyself.' "[39] "His love for nature," Bluma writes, "was limitless: He greatly enjoyed flowers and would become intoxicated by the beauty of a tree and the grand view of a sunset. A couple of weeks before Purim he became ill. One

[35]He died on Thursday late at night and was buried on Friday.
[36]See *Hamelitz* of the 24th of Adar of 5656, No. 47.
[37]See about him M. S. Shapiro, Talpiot vol. III, 1-2 pp. 81-85.
[38]*Hatsofeh*, Tel-Aviv, 21 of Adar 1956.
[39]Deut. 11:15.

of the well-known physicians of Kovno in those days was
Dr. I. Feinberg, holding the rank of general in the Russian Army.[40]
Grandfather had a great deal of respect for him. But he did not
rely on his own opinion, and decided to invite Prof. Jaffe from
Koenigsberg and Dr. I. Dembo and Prof. Dobroklonsky from
Petersburg.[41] At his bedside, scholars including his son, R. Tzevi
Hirsh, were constantly present and Grandfather kept on talking
about a Talmudic matter to the point of utter exhaustion."

All over the world, Jews mourned the death of "The Rabbi
of All the Diaspora."[42] "The name Rabbi Isaac Elhanan," wrote
one of the eulogizers in a booklet, *Kol Nehi,* is no longer a proper
name, it has become an adjective."

In various parts of the world plans were made for fitting
memorials. Samuel Rosenfeld, in writing about the various projects
for the perpetuation of R. Isaac Elhanan's name, stated that the
most fitting memorial would be a *yeshivah.* "The name R. Isaac
Elhanan," he wrote in that article, *Sheat Ha-kosher,*[43] "is the
best guarantee for a synthesis of spiritual and worldly matters and
for a spirit of harmony and tolerance in such an institution."

The author of that article did not know that in New York City
a small group of people, immediately after hearing of R. Isaac
Elhanan's being called to the Academy of Heaven, had decided to
establish a *yeshivah* perpetuating his name. Even if he had known
thereof, he probably would not have been much impressed, for
the center of Jewry was still in East European countries, and one
could hardly foresee that the New York *yeshivah* would become a
central institution of learning for world Jewry. The city of
Kovno, like all other cities of Lithuania as well as other European
Jewish centers, is now a matter of the past, but the name R. Isaac
Elhanan is very potent today and will stay so for generations
to come.

---

[40]Dr. Isaac Feinberg, referred by Bluma Solomonson, was a disciple
of Abraham Mapo. He used to send daily telegrams to *Hatzefirah* on the
condition of R. Isaac Elhanan. He also participated with a Hebrew oration
at the funeral.

[41]Dr. Dembo and Prof Dobroklonsky issued a bulletin describing the
condition of R. Isaac Elhanan. See *Hamelitz,* 17 Adar 1896.

[42]Many books containing eulogies on R. Isaac Elhanan appeared in various
countries. See the list in the article by A. R. Malachi in *Hasped Al R.
Isaac Elhanan, Bitzaron* Vol. XXXIV, No. 8, p. 184, note 12a. See also Rav
T. Zair *Pirkey Hayyim,* New York, 1954, pp. 159 ff.

[43]*Luah Ahiasaf,* 5659 (1899).

SIMHA ZISSEL BROIDA (ZIFF)

(1823-1897)

By Eliezer Ebner

SIMHA ZISSEL BROIDA (ZIFF)

By Eliezer Ebner

The story is current that during a meeting of German university teachers some seventy years ago, when the question of curricula was discussed, one professor remarked: "There is one subject that is taught in no other place on earth but in a small Russian town by the name of Kelm. The subject is the perfection of man."

The man who brought this distinction to Kelm was Rabbi Simha Zissel Broida. He is not widely known today because he concentrated his efforts on the education of the élite few rather than of the many. His writings, contained chiefly in his many letters to his disciples, have as yet not been published in book form. But wherever *Mussar* is studied, his name is mentioned with reverence.

The *Mussar* movement, launched by Rabbi Israel Lipkin-Salanter (1810-1883), had set as its aim the systematic study and application of the ethics of the Torah. It was R. Simha Zissel, his most prominent disciple, who developed it into an integrated educational program of self-perfection. More than the study of the *Mussar* texts, however, it was his own example that taught his students how perfect a man may become.

I

The Man

Rabbi Simha Zissel was born in 1823 in Kelm, which, politically, belonged to Russia, but, from a Jewish-cultural point of view, was part of Lithuania. His background was similar to that of other great Russian rabbis: a home where learning and piety were traditional. He possessed a very keen mind and from early age engaged in intensive study of *Humash* and Talmud.

IIis father, Rabbi Israel, first a merchant and then a *Dayan*—religious judge—was one of the leading scholars of his time. His mother, too, was highly educated and renowned for her ability to render legal decisions. Her life was dedicated to the needy. When

319

her only daughter died, she solicited money for the poor during the funeral. People asked her to desist, but she replied: "Because I am mourning, shall the poor suffer?"

Simha Zissel was fond of sports and games, and the leader in boys' pranks. Yet even then he would occasionally disappear from his games, to be discovered in the synagogue pouring over the work of the Rambam and Bahya's *Hovot Ha'levavot* (Duties of the Heart). At his Bar Mitzvah he offered an original discourse on one division of the Talmud, a unique feat at his age.

In accordance with contemporary custom he married young, and Sarah Leah, his wife, undertook to provide their livelihood. (She ran a grocery.) He could, thus, devote himself undisturbed to Torah. Rabbi Simha Zissel never accepted remuneration from his students, even though at times his family were well nigh penniless. Yet when the rabbinate of St. Petersburg was offered him, he declined out of consideration for his friend, Rabbi Isaac Blaser.

He had three children, a son and two daughters, all loyal to the pattern of their parents. He was rather strict with his children, criticizing them for even slight infractions. In a letter to his brother he explained: "The more I love a person, the stricter will I be with him. If I notice in my child any wrong, I reprimand him sharply. I have no pity upon him. Though it may cause him pain now, it is better so. It spares him pain in the future. My children know my attitude and accept my strictures in this spirit."*

After his marriage, he decided to go to Kovno, chiefly to oppose the study of *Mussar* as then taught by Rabbi Israel Salanter. Those who opposed it argued that it interfered with the study of the Talmud. But when he listened to a *Mussar* talk by Rabbi Israel, he was so inspired that he decided to remain in the latter's *Bet Hamidrash*. The meeting of these great minds was of abiding importance: For one entire year, Rabbi Simha Zissel studied nothing but the books on *Mussar*. In the course of time he became its outstanding exponent. Students used to say: "If you seek perfection in the fear of sin, follow Rabbi Isaac Blaser (another disciple of Rabbi Israel), but if you wish to learn the meaning of faith, go to Rabbi Simha Zissel." Rabbi Israel had advised him to train himself in self-criticism. "That," he would say, "I am still trying to do." (The father of the Mussar movement, who measured his words carefully, characterized his pupil with this

---

*The quotations from his letters are taken from Dov Katz's *Tenuat Hamussar*, Vol. II, Tel Aviv, 1950.

verse: "Your beauty is perfect, my beloved, there is no blemish on you" (Song of Songs IV, 7).

He was too humble to permit his picture to be taken, but we have this eye-witness report from E. E. Friedman,* a writer and native of Kelm: "He was of striking appearance; always dressed in modern garb. The curls of his hair went down to his neck and his beard was long. His shirt collar was ever fresh, his shoes always polished. He spoke to people calmly, with tact and friendliness; every word was chosen. His eyes seemed to penetrate deep into your heart." Those who saw him only once would never forget his neatness and his pervading serenity.

In 1856 Rabbi Salanter left Kovno and Rabbi Simha Zissel, now thirty-four years old, returned to Kelm. He withdrew almost entirely to his studies, and adopted as his own regimen that of the *Gaon* of Vilna: He would sleep no more than two and a half hours in half hour periods during the day; at night would study uninterruptedly for twelve hours. Nothing could interfere with his schedule. It is reported that some very important persons tried to see him during his morning periods of study, insistently but without success. They resented his refusal to receive them but he would cite supreme authority in his defense. He followed the same rule throughout his life even in later years, when his heart began to trouble him.

He sought to elucidate the *Halakhah* in its practical application. He proceeded from the source of the law in the Torah, through its exposition in the Talmud, the commentaries and codes. Rabbi Eliezer Gordon, the founder of Yeshivat Telz, said of him, that he knew three of the six divisions of the Talmud by heart, together with the commentaries of Rashi and Tosafot; that he could recite by heart each law of the four divisions of the *Shulhan Arukh*. His saintliness, however, overshadowed his erudition.

Before settling permanently in Kelm, he spent, at the behest of Rabbi Israel, some time in the city of Zager, to head the local Talmud Torah. There he met Kalman Z. Visotzky, one of the greatest Jewish philanthropists of his day. At the advice of his teacher, Rabbi Zissel accompanied him, a former student of Rabbi Israel, to Moscow for two years to be his mentor. The city attracted him because of its cleanliness, which permitted him to concentrate on Torah subjects while walking on its streets, and

*Eliezer E. Friedman: *Letoldot Kitat Hamussarim*, Jerusalem, 1926. See also Jacob Mark, *Gedolim Fun Unser Zeit*, p. 249, New York, 1927.

because of its noise, which enabled him to study *Mussar* aloud
without being noticed.

Upon his return to Kelm, he accepted the position of *Maggid*
(preacher). He spoke every Sabbath, but though he was highly
gifted, both content and style of his preaching were too philosophical
and profound for the average Jew. He soon discovered the
fact that it is almost impossible to change in a short period of time
the character of the average person. He encountered the current
antagonism to the *Mussar* approach, and so he set for himself one
task: to influence and educate the chosen few: These, in turn
would—as indeed many of them did—become the future leaders
and teachers of communities and *yeshivot*.

Gradually he attracted to his home a group of learned laymen.
They visited him every Sabbath and to them he conveyed his
thoughts on Torah and *Mussar*. The members of this group became
known as *"Mussarnikes,"* they accepted his as their spiritual guide
and aided his educational work with the youth.

The perfection which Rabbi Simha Zissel urged on those near
to him, he demanded first of himself. He was so honest in self-
examination that occasionally he would postpone criticism of
others until a later time, when he himself felt free of that which
he saw to be wrong in others.

It is perfection, rather than greatness, which describes his personality. For in calling someone "great", we have in mind one or
two outstanding traits, such as his intellect or a moral virtue. In
his case, however, we are at a loss to single out the virtue by
which he is best known. There is, however, one aspect of his personality that does stand out—his sense of order, planning and
consistency, his capacity to relate and integrate all thoughts and·
actions into that consistent harmony which makes perfection
possible.

Not only in the rigorous regimen in the study of the Torah
imposed upon himself, but in all his educational enterprises, order
and planning prevailed to an unusual degree. They pervaded all
his conduct with near-scientific precision. Even his thoughts, the
most uncontrollable of man's activities, he had disciplined to obey
his will.

Both his ability to concentrate and the depth of his emotions
are illustrated in these incidents: Once Rabbi Naftali Amsterdam,
a close friend, accompanied him on a trip. At night, in the hotel
room, he reports overhearing Rabbi Simha Zissel learning *Mussar*:

"Since I slept only lightly I heard almost all night how again and again he chanted these verses: *'Open to me the gates of righteousness, I will enter into them and give thanks to God. This is the gate of the Lord, the righteous shall enter into it.'* (Psalm CXVIII, 19-20) "He was singing these verses," Rabbi Naftali continued, "with so much pleading as to touch the very heart." Once, sitting in the Sukkah, he intoned in his own haunting melody: *"Remember thy Creator in the days of thy youth, before the evil days come and the years draw nigh when thou shall say: I have no pleasure in them."* (Ecclesiastes: XII, 1) He kept on chanting the verse for six successive hours, for its message to become rooted in his mind.

Flowing directly from his sense of order, was his appreciation of cleanliness. The eye-witness reports how immaculately he was attired. Even after years of wear, his clothes looked like new and shortly before he died he had them all cleaned because he knew that they would be given to the poor. His books, too, although he used them extensively, were in perfect condition, even after many years. In his youth he had learned the art of book-binding for his livelihood.

He was a master of self-control. The more he understood the intricacy of the human mind, the power and subtlety of temptation, the more he desired to keep his reason ever alert and strong. He imposed upon himself special exercises and resolutions in self-control. He had a special garment which he would put on before reacting in anger against anyone. To overcome laziness, he would get up from his bed as fast as he could. He had the habit of breaking a fast with a dish of small fish: the tedious necessity of removing the many bones helped him to discipline his appetite for food. To thwart any smugness or pride, he would occasionally go to neighboring villages where he was unknown, dressed as a beggar, or playing a cripple. For the same reason he did not permit his students to rise before him, or to call him Rabbi. One of his important resolutions, adopted also by a few of his disciples, was that "the tenth day shall be holy." While this quotation originally refers to Yom Kippur, the tenth of Tishri, he expanded it to apply to every tenth day of the year, when he would conduct himself with particular care and saintliness.

He usually made such resolutions on Yom Kippur. The extent to which he lived up to them is evident in this incident: He was determined not to say his prayers by heart, but to read them from his prayer book. Once in the midst of the morning service at the *yeshivah,* he suddenly did a most unusual thing. He left his place, walked to the back of the hall, picked up a prayer book, looked into it for a moment and then returned to his place to continue with his prayers. Only later on did the students understand what had happened. One word in his own prayer book had become illegible and although he knew it by heart, he did not want to deviate from his resolution, even to this extent.

During the last thirteen years of his life, as the result of a heart attack, he was a very sick man. The doctors had given up all hope. A noted specialist declared that only his spiritual resources kept him alive. Yet, during all these years no one heard any expression of pain from his lips, for he did not permit his own suffering to cause anguish and grief to others. For the same reason he continued to give his *Mussar* talks, speaking for an hour or two at a time. It happened occasionally that he was near total exhaustion and his voice became inaudible. Once blood flowed from his mouth and his listeners began to withdraw in order to give him the rest he needed. But he motioned to them to come back and after a little while he resumed. When the physician would forbid his public speaking lest he endanger his very life, he replied that the danger to his own life was less than that to the spiritual life of his students, were he to cease addressing them. (Referring to his illness he said: "I know that it is but a punishment for my many sins. However, my pain is so great because I cannot labor either in prayer or in Torah.")

In a letter to his students in the Bet Hatalmud of Garubin, he revealed his humility: "At first, I ask of you something of a personal nature. Self-aggrandizement destroys body and soul. It is a disgrace for me to be addressed 'our master and teacher,' because I am neither. In the interest of the institution I have not protested in the past. But now I ask of you not to use this title when referring to me. Do merely write: 'Our friend who seeks our welfare, Reb Simha Zissel.' Or simply: 'Our friend who seeks our welfare.' I think this may be the truth." Once, when someone called him God-fearing, he protested and explained that this was the title given to Abraham, only after he had passed all his tests in faith to God. The title commonly used, when speaking of him was "Der Alte (the Old One)". This name conveyed the respect and affection in which Rabbi Simha Zissel was held.

Because he was humble, he did not react with anger to any insult of a personal nature. Although he was on occasion called upon to defend his educational ideas and methods, he did not reprimand anyone for accusing him personally. He welcomed having his "faults" made public. Once a dismissed teacher, in his anger, insulted him publicly, calling him wicked and one who had no share in the world to come. Those present, in fury, tried to stop the man, but Rabbi Simha Zissel bade them forbear because "my accuser is speaking the truth."

To love one's fellow man is commanded by the Torah and Rabbi Simha Zissel considered it basic in the quest for self-perfection. He devoted much time and effort to train himself and others in the art of dealing kindly with people. Amongst his Yom Kippur resolutions we find the following: "In every prayer remember the law to love your neighbor as yourself. Set aside at least one period to arouse oneself to deeds of loving kindness! Think occasionally about this law of neighborly love with a view to discovering the virtues of the fellow man. This will be conducive to you to love him. Be particularly mindful to observe this law on the holy Sabbath." He practiced steadily what he preached.

Since he was poor, he could not give much charity and he feared that he would fail in the observance of this *mitzvah*. Hence, he turned to his brother, Rabbi Leib Broida, both wealthy and learned, and asked for financial aid, which he used to help the poor.

When once there was a fire in Kelm, he hastened to the scene and helped to extinguish the fire, although, according to Jewish Law, a man of his position was not required to do so.

When he walked on the road and chanced to meet a horse-drawn carriage with passengers, he would walk alongside it for a considerable distance to observe the *mitzvah* of accompanying a person on the road. On Friday nights, on returning from the synagogue, he would stop at the entrance of his home and look with joyous attention at the Sabbath setting of the room. It was one of his ways of showing his wife the appreciation due to her devoted work.

The same *mitzvah* motivated his interest in communal matters. "Every one," he writes, "should attach himself to the community and worry about its welfare." One may serve the community best, he said, by strengthening the faith, for that means strengthening the whole Jewish people. He gave freely of his counsel to the community, and it was always eagerly sought.

He had the right word and the kind attitude for any person. His knowledge of the human mind enabled him to predict the future development of a new student. It was said that he could discern the character and personality of a writer from his handwriting.

In 1865 he became the head of the Talmud Torah of Kelm, which under his leadership grew into a *yeshivah* that attracted gifted students from other institutions of learning. The administrative duties were relegated to the group 'of laymen devoted to him. One of the most active among them was Nathan Tzevi Finkel, who, in later years, became the spiritual leader of the well-known Slobodka Yeshivah. As Rabbi Simha Zissel insisted upon spacious and comfortable accommodations for his students, the annual budget of the Talmud Torah reached the sum of 15,000 rubles, a very considerable sum in those days and not easy to raise. At times, Rabbi Simha Zissel himself was forced to approach individual benefactors and because of the universal respect he commanded, they responded generously.

Seven years later, the Talmud Torah moved into a large and well-equipped building of its own, modelled after a modern Russian high school. A room in the attic was set aside for Rabbi Simha Zissel. There he stayed during the weekdays, coming home only for the Sabbaths and festivals.

In the year 1875, the suspicious Czarist government charged the school with inciting resistance to the government. The police confiscated its books and documents and it was only after some time that Rabbi Simha Zissel was vindicated.

He decided to transfer the *yeshivah* to a more desirable location, the small town of Garubin in Latvia, not far from the Baltic Sea. A rich friend, Rabbi Eliezer Dessler, donated a large estate for this purpose.

The Bet Hatalmud, as it was now called, existed for ten years. Because of his failing health, Rabbi Simha Zissel gradually withdrew from active leadership. He consulted his revered teacher, Rabbi Israel Salanter, about discontinuing the school in Garubin. The latter emphatically advised against it, comparing the closing of the Bet Hatalmud to the destruction of the Holy Temple. However, five years later, Rabbi Simha Zissel found himself unable to continue its existence for reasons of both health and finance and the school closed its doors.

While he conducted the Garubin institution, he did not lose contact with his education work in Kelm, his native town. In fact, in the year 1880, he returned there permanently and hence-

forth directed the affairs of the Garubin school through communica-
tions and occasional visits. In that year there flourished in Kelm
an élite group of ten young men in whom he took great pride.
They were scholars of a high order and followed closely the directives of their teacher in the study and application of *Mussar*. With
the closing of the Garubin school, some of its best students went to
Kelm. In addition, students from other *yeshivot* came there to
absorb the spirit of " *Der Alte fun Kelm*," especially in the month
of Ellul, when many of his former students, now leading rabbis,
would make their pilgrimage to this citadel of Torah and *Mussar*.

In his last years he was helped to establish an outpost of his
type of *yeshivah* in the Holy Land. Two of his disciples, Rabbi
Baruch Marcus (later Chief Rabbi of Haifa) and Rabbi Samuel
Shenker, founded the Yeshivah Or Hadash in Jerusalem. He
advised them with respect to its conduct but he also helped it financially. At his influence Samuel Strauss, a noted philanthropist,
built a number of apartments in Jerusalem for the accommodation
of poor rabbis and students. His love and yearning for the Holy
Land was revealed in the letter which he sent to his students: "O,
inhabitants of the Holy City, who dwell at the gateway to heaven
near the holy mountain, hail to you, hail to you that you have been
so rewarded! Would that I had the wings of the dove! I would
fly to dwell with you in your midst, in the midst of all Israel, as
all her children are gathered within her in joy. If I were but well
enough, I would travel to your holy dwelling place and bind myself
to you."

However, Providence decreed otherwise. On August 6, 1897,
the eve of Tisha BeAb, at the age of 74 years, Rabbi Simha Zissel
passed away. He died as he had lived. While his strength was
leaving him, he got up to recite his morning prayers. As soon as
he finished he returned to bed and breathed his last.

II

His Teachings

The subject matter of *Mussar* is Torah-ethics. Its aim is the
perfection of man. To reach this objective one must have a knowledge of psychology in general and of one's own character in
particular. Rabbi Simha Zissel would put it this way: "Just as it
is impossible for a man to be a surgeon without a consummate

knowledge of the art of surgery, so it is impossible to cure the
soul without knowledge of the soul. One has to recognize the
opportunities for self-education which flow from the evil dispo-
sitions rooted in man. He who lacks such knowledge is bound
to become the prey of such temptation."

To arrive at self-knowledge and to advance from there to
perfection, one must be able to think. This ability is the very
key to progress, not only in the sciences but also in morality and
ethics. It is the most God-like capacity in man and yet, he would
complain, most people do not guard and cultivate it. They let it
run wild. "The beginning of man's fall is lack of thought." And
putting it still stronger, he said: "He who neglects the capacity
of thinking commits suicide."

Hence the attention he gave to the development of the art
of thinking. He imposed upon his disciples the rule not to let
one day pass without exercise in the art of clear thinking. He
was cautious, however, in not insisting on too much at first. It
would not do to force it, he counselled, do it, "rather slowly and
easily, start with a few minutes and increase gradually," the first
step being the ability to concentrate on one subject for five minutes.
(In prayer, too, he asked his students to train themselves at first
in paying undivided attention to the words of the first blessing
of the *Amidah*.)

The habit of sustained concentrated thought conditions a
person to the primacy of his intellect over his appetites. He will
think and examine before acting at the urge of his emotions and
senses. Reason alone, unless constantly used, will not be able
to withstand the powerful sensual impulses. It is like an efficient
tool used by unskilled hands. On the contrary, reason will become
subservient to the senses adding its gift of imagination to the
stimulation produced by direct contact.

This is why youth is more prone to follow emotions despite
the fact that it may have the same intelligence as older persons.
But having failed over a long period of time to exercise the
intellect, the young person lacks the maturity necessary to control
emotion.

Another detriment to spiritual development is a closed mind.
Most people follow cherished notions adopted during their youth
and do not permit their concepts to grow and change. Thus, for
instance, at an early age, the notion of "mine is mine" was rooted

in us. In later life it impedes conformity with the laws of the Torah which involve inconvenience and sacrifice. Again, from infancy we have taken nature for granted. We do not ask: Who made it, for whom and for what purpose? The same holds true with the miracles related in the Bible. Rabbi Simha Zissel advises, therefore, that a man who begins the study of *Mussar* should look at himself as if he were born today and came face to face with Torah and a world filled with many marvels. That, he felt, was the meaning of the words in the Torah: "Which I command you today," as explained in *Sifre:* "They shall be as new in your eyes,* as if you heard them today for the first time."

This is the reason for the many benedictions as well as for the admonitions in the Torah to remember things of the past. We should feel appreciation as warmly as if it came through a sensual perception and not take things for granted. Constant reflection and an impressionistic attitude towards every subject of study, every object of observation and every *Mitzvah* we fulfill, will eventually lead to a harmony of knowing and doing.

The failure to re-think basic concepts leads to a lack of faith in God, all knowledge and proofs about His existence notwithstanding. Theoretical knowledge remains abstract, because it is not rooted in vivid consciousness. *"And you shall know today and lay it to your heart, that the Lord, He is God."* (Deut. IV, 39) It is not enough to know, one must lay this knowledge to the heart—the center of one's emotions.

To arrive at a more perfect faith, it is necessary to study and observe everything with this aim in mind. There is nothing that cannot serve as a reminder or lesson in faith. He used to say: "All the world is an institution for *Mussar* and every human being is a *Mussar*-book." When studying nature we should try to discover nature's Creator. We should learn to see in all occurrences "the hand of God" and not blind natural causes. To this end he cites many examples from the Talmud which explains simple natural happenings as the result of underlying moral causes.

Self-analytical, serious, sincere, meditative and philosophical, was the way in which *Mussar* was studied at Kelm. Yet, it was not merely an intellectual approach. The study of *Mussar* and its demands were charged with the fervor of an emotional involvement, for only a combination of intellect and emotion will produce

---

Sifre ad loc. Deut. 11, 13.

lasting results. Rabbi Simha Zissel held that the study of *Mussar* must proceed amidst self-arousal. The student must respond with his own emotional reaction to the subject matter, be it with joy or sadness. He was wont to quote from his favorite *Mussar* book— *Tomar Devorah,* by Rabbi Moses Cordovero: "For such is its nature, that external stimulation, whether through joy or sadness, creates gradually a deep-seated inner response." Hence the peculiar way in which *Mussar* is to be studied: A *Mussar* book, such as *Hovot Hal'vavot, Sha'are Teshuva, Messilat Yesharim* or *Orhot Hayyim,* serves as text. The student reads a few words and then repeats them in a sing-song fashion several times till he feels that their meaning have become imbedded in his mind. In a group setting, each student is further aroused by the general fervor that rises from many voices. Once dissatisfied with the lack of intensity of the learning, he interrupted the students and said: "Is this the way you defend yourselves against a robber?" By "robber" he meant man's evil inclination.

In three rules, which he called "high principles for coming closer to God," Rabbi Simha Zissel set forth his formula for success in the study not only of *Mussar,* but of Torah and general knowledge as well:

(1) All study should proceed from emotional arousal, whether joy or sorrow.

(2) All study should be tested by asking oneself: What did I think before and what do I know now?

(3) One should abstract ideas from illustrations and apply them to new situations.

To these rules must be added the profound impact of his frequent *Mussar* talks, his insistence upon constant practical application of theory, and the device of progressively designed exercises for the control of will and instinct.

The mastery over one's will and the ability to react thoughtfully to any experience should lead to equanimity and serenity. As opposed to distraction and disorder in thinking and action, serenity to him is not merely a means to acquiring other virtues, but an end in itself. The chief reason why the rabbis bid the worshipper eliminate from his mind foreign thoughts while praying, is to attain this serenity. Yom Kippur, completely removed from material thoughts, serves as such opportunity to reach it.

The following rules pertaining to thinking, speech and action were followed in his Bet Hatalmud, both in Kelm and in Garubin:

(1) When you close a door, test it whether it is closed well. Before you sit down, make sure that nothing lies on the chair.

When you walk in a crowd, do not push.

Do not look into windows when not necessary.

Do not look up from your study when someone enters the study room.

(2) When you have something new to tell, wait at least fifteen minutes.

When you are asked for advice, do not answer immediately.

Watch your speech closely, lest you inject any scoffing, gossiping or swearing.

When you wish to speak to someone, ask yourself first if it is necessary.

(3) Order your thoughts and style of speaking before you begin to talk.

Do not do anything unless you think first of its purpose.

Closely related to equanimity, he emphasized, is orderliness. Hence his insistence upon external and technical things, such as punctuality, cleanliness and strict adherence to schedules. It was a reflection of a mind that knew that the best results are achieved by precise planning and execution. He pointed to the wide range of precise measurements of time and objects in ritual law as proof of the Torah's insistence upon orderliness.

The following item may illustrate to what extent punctuality was practiced in his *yeshivah*. Towards the end of the Sabbath there was little light in the auditorium and it was not possible to read the time on the clock of the wall. Yet the *Ma'ariv* service had to begin exactly at a set moment. The problem was solved by having a student "read" the clock with his fingers probing the dial.

The greatest obstacle in the path of self-perfection is the love of the self. It accounts for the greed and pride of possession, for the sake of which man will become immoral and criminal. Hence the Tenth Commandment—*"Thou shalt not covet"*—upon which all the others are based. Furthermore, he taught, "to the same degree that a man loves himself, will he be estranged from God."

The first step is to be fully aware of its presence. A man ought to say to himself: "I know that I am inclined to coveteousness; I must therefore purify and strengthen myself not to transgress any law of the Torah that touches upon these sins."

The next step is a rather subtle one. "Unless it be unavoidable," he said, "it is better not to oppose temptation in a head-on collision, but to evade it, to minimize in one's mind its urgency; to forget it altogether, if possible, or to side-track it. It is best not to think so much about a particular desire . . . it is more important to pay it as little attention as possible than to devise even the best counter-measures to overcome it."

However, the most effective method is to offset selfish desires by intellectual delights. He who has once experienced such joy in his study of the Torah or of general knowledge, will cherish its superiority over material delights. To seek spiritual joys will automatically reduce the power of the others.

The antidote for the love of one's ego is to love others. This is not merely a lofty ethical principle but a practical attitude as well. For the society of men is based upon social interdependence. Moreover, by doing good to others a man benefits himself, too. An application of this conviction was the usual custom in his *yeshivot* that all janitorial labor be carried out by the students themselves. Indeed, not every student was deemed worthy of such work! The story is told of a rich woman who visited her son unexpectedly in the *yeshivah,* and found him sweeping the floor. In her indignation she went to complain to Rabbi Simha Zissel. But he replied: *"Ver es kert do, kert die welt."* (He who cleans here, cleans the world.)

The love of fellow men leads to understanding and love of God. Man comes closer to God by emulating His example—*"As He is gracious, so you be gracious."* Since God loves man, we come nearer to Him by doing the same. *"Thou shalt love they neighbor as thyself"* is considered a fundamental principle in the Torah, because it contains both the love of man and the love of God. To help people and to participate in their burdens ought not to be stressed because it is a *Mitzvah,* but rather because your neighbor is "as thyself." It should be done naturally, as one loves his own self, without any particular motive.

Another way that leads to God is the pursuit of truth. Because truth is the seal of God, it follows that he who strives after truth strives after God. Most people interpret facts in their favor and engage in wishful thinking. This may go so far as to completely change falsehood into "truth," without becoming aware of the error. He explained Rabban Gamaliel's dictum: "Make His will your will" (Abot II, 4) to mean that we should bring ourselves to see the logic and truth of a matter and act accordingly, so that our own will merges with the will of God, Who is the highest reality and source of truth. To reach the truth, "everything must be clear and pure without any admixture of falsehood, self-love, pride or desire." The pursuit and attainment of truth, it follows, is predicated upon character perfection. Indeed, one is impossible without the other.

The cause of errors or half-truths is twofold—wishful thinking and superficiality. Of the two, the latter provides the opening wedge for desire to take hold of us. Gradually, reason and intellect become subservient to our desire and facts and truths are bent to fit our wish. The way out of this confusion is a sincere self-analysis and the deliberate practice of truth, beginning with relatively unimportant matters, until one becomes habitually disposed towards truthfulness.

Dedication to truth is of crucial significance in the education of the young. If the teaching of children is not motivated by idealistic reasons, the teacher will fail to implant the virtue of truth in the child. Parents must be guided by the ideal of truth in relations to their children. Rabbi Simha Zissel traced the heresy of the brilliant Tanna Elisha ben Abuya to the fact that his education was not motivated by idealistic reasons but by the desire to attain honor and vain-glory. The moral and spiritual weakness of his own generation, too, he sees in this lack of devotion to truth and selflessness.

His great accomplishments in education were due not only to his own genius, but resulted also from the high standards governing admittance of students to his *yeshivah*. Being a perfectionist, his aim was for quality above quantity. In defense of his restrictive choice of students he cites from *Hovot Hal'vavot*: *"A little of the pure is a lot."* Of those whom he did accept he writes: "I am bound to them by nature with true love, to help them in their material and spiritual needs. For the sake of such persons I find it right to interrupt my own studies and to attend to them as much as is necessary." In *Mussar* circles it was wittily said: "If Rabbi

Simha Zissel gets hold of someone, he will take him completely apart to make him over anew."

Another radical departure from the practices of the standard *yeshivah* was instruction in secular subjects, in the Bet Hatalmud of both Kelm and Garubin. For three hours a day the students were taught the Russian language, history, arithmetic and geography. He was aware of the argument that "secular learning detracts from the study of Torah and Talmud and may even lead the student away from traditional observances." He permitted, nevertheless, the teaching of secular subjects because "general knowledge helped men to understand nature, God's own handiwork. It is an act of *Kiddush Hashem* (the sanctification of God's name) to demonstrate in this age of *Haskalah* ("enlightment") that a Jew may be modern in manners, dress, speech and general education, and yet be a scholar of Torah with a high ethical and pious disposition. The background of Torah and *Mussar* would offset any possible detrimental influence arising from the study of secular subjects."

He changed the slogan of the *Haskalah*, "Be a Jew in your house and a man outside," to read: "Be a Jew and a man in your house and a Jew and a man outside."

In one of his letters he outlined his educational program as embracing four points:

(1) Study of Torah: Lessons in the Talmud for beginners and advanced students, until they are able to "learn" independently with clarity and profundity.

(2) Instruction in the acquisition of virtues for the improvement of human society.

(3) Acquisition of polite manners in keeping with the spirit of the time, to be able to get along with people in conversation and action. All these studies are based on deep piety, skillfully woven into the subject matter. The reading and writing of the Russian language, arithmetic and geography are taught in this house under our supervision.

(4) In this curriculum some time is regularly set aside for the study of *Mussar*. This is done with much insight into the character of the boy and the spirit of the time in a manner that is pleasant and acceptable to him, so that he will joyously take upon himself the "yoke of Torah and *Mussar*."

He admitted that this ambitious program was not easy to carry out. "But you must know," he continued, "that to administer such a program in the spirit of faith and reason demands constant search and examination."

How well he succeeded is seen from the testimony of competent judges who visited his institutions. They were deeply impressed with its modern facilities, the carefully planned and meticulously carried out curricula for all classes, the devotion and skill of the teachers, and the conduct and knowledge of the students.* Among the teeming millions of last century's Russian Jewry, there was no similar school in which the spirit of learning, piety, moral perfection and general knowledge blossomed in such harmony and degree.

The Bet Hatalmud continued after the death of Rabbi Simha Zissel for some forty-five years.** It was destroyed by the Germans during World War II.

---

*See "Lebanon" Journal, 1873, Vol. XXVI, 1875, Vol. XLVI,—Cf. also Lebanon, 1873; Vols. VII and XIX, 1874, Vol. XXXII, 1875, Vol. XXXIII, 1876. About the school in Garubin see, *Hatzefirah,* 1881, 1882, and 1885.

**Those who followed him in its leadership were his brother, Rabbi Leib, and his nephew, son-in-law, and outstanding disciple, Rabbi Tzevi Broida, who led the institution for 13 years. He was followed by Rabbi Simha Zissel's son, Rabbi Nachum Ze'ev—a rare combination of businessman and saintly scholar, who in turn was succeeded by Rabbi Reuben Dessler, Rabbi Daniel Mofshowitz and Rabbi Gershon Miadnik.

JOSEPH TZEVI HALEVI DUENNER
(1833-1912)

By Benjamin de Vries

(translated by Dr. Herman Axelrod, from the Hebrew;
adapted by Vivienne H. Siegel)

JOSEPH TZEVI HALEVI DUENNER

By Benjamin de Vries

The personality of Rabbi Duenner poses many a paradox. Though he played a very prominent role in the West European Jewish community of the late 19th and early 20th Century, he has not until now been singled out either for a comprehensive biography or even for a more casual evaluation.

Yet this is not so amazing as it might at first appear. To begin with, he lived in Holland, at a time when the Jewish community there, suffering from a severe case of spiritual anemia, had only the most tenuous bonds with *Klal Yisrael*. But a more decisive factor was Duenner's character. The ivory tower he inhabited was doubly isolated, spiritually even more than geographically. He was, indeed, so sensitive to criticism as to feel wounded when no offense was intended.

The contrasting qualities that he bore within himself would in another man have been incompatibilities. A gentle ingenuousness went hand in hand with a haughty assumption of authority, strongly reminiscent of some great rabbis of former generations; abstract thinking with practicality; extreme piety with a critical temper, an affinity for *Klal Yisrael* with Dutch separatism, a love of Zion with a staunch *Galut* patriotism, and strangest of all, a strain of Galician "enlightenment" (*Haskalah*), flirting tentatively with West European Orthodoxy.

His contemporaries in Holland held him in profound regard, even while they could not fully comprehend him, for his penetrating look was so awesome as to keep most people at a distance. Nor was it their inadequate knowledge of Torah alone which created the gap between him and his countrymen. More erudition, by itself, could not have bridged the gap, for Rabbi Duenner towered above them all in more than an intellectual sense.

They were content, therefore, to exalt him as a man of unusual moral stature, who in a specific way was the savior of Dutch Jewry. He embodied for them the crucial quality that had been lacking in their former leaders—the grandeur of the rabbinate. Their feelings towards him were essentially those of the *Hassidim* for their *rebbe,* and their hero worship inspired them to imitate his speech and behavior. Sensing his uniqueness by sheer intuition, they obeyed him in a pure act of faith, rather than from conscious understanding.

Had they been able to penetrate his forbidding exterior, they would have discovered a warm-hearted and soft-spoken man, for that is how he revealed himself in his rare moments of relaxation, when not hard-pressed by official business. Then, indeed, they would have loved him. But the wall of reserve lasted to the end.

That is why his life, in retrospect, strikes us as essentially a tragic one. Here was a gifted teacher who left many disciples but failed to found a school. Nor was there even one among his pupils worthy to be his successor, either in knowledge or authority. He has been dead only forty-five years, but already all recollection of his accomplishments has been buried deep in the recesses of historic memory.

This is an attempt to rescue him from undeserved oblivion before it is too late.

Joseph Tzevi, the son of Leiser Duenner, a poor innkeeper, was born in one of the suburbs of Cracow on the 13th day of Tebet, 5693 (1833). There may have been a *Hassidic* tradition in the family, for it is said that Joseph's mother, all of whose other children had died before reaching maturity, sought the help of a *Wunderrabbiner* (miracle man) some months before his birth.

The boy was sent to *heder* at the age of four, and though hampered by physical weakness, he was soon recognized as an intellectual prodigy. At thirteen, he went to study with Rabbi Dembitzer, then a young *maskil* of twenty-six. The two became friends, and this relationship continued even after Joseph received his religious ordination and gained prominence in his own right.

As an eligible bachelor, Joseph was naturally offered many a fine match, but in vain, for at that time he was entirely preoccupied with his studies. The world of *Haskalah* attracted him, and much to the displeasure of the pietists, he joined a circle of *Maskilim* in Galicia. One night, as he was leaving the *Bet Hamidrash,* some zealot stabbed him in the back, and while the wound eventually healed completely, leaving but a small scar, the incident provided the *Maskilim* with useful propaganda. As for Joseph Tzevi, the experience convinced him that emigration to Germany was the wisest course.

His first way-station was Wurzburg, where his brother Wolf had preceded him. But upon his arrival there, Joseph was advised by Rabbi Bamberger, the leader of the community, to go on to Minstreifel in the Rhineland. A warm letter of recommendation from the rabbi secured him a position as teacher in the home of Baruch Levi, one of the outstanding men of the city. Fortunately, his duties allowed him time to prepare for entrance, in 1859, to the University of Bonn. Three years later, having majored in philosophy and philology, he was awarded his doctorate for a dissertation on Ibn Ezra.

His social contacts were limited almost entirely to Orthodox circles, but he acknowledged no limits to the range of his thought. He maintained close association with Moses Hess, who, though a much older man, regarded him very highly.

Even as a student, Duenner betrayed a dichotomy of view which was to become intensified as time went on: a strong attachment to Western Orthodoxy, coupled with intellectual liberalism; loyalty to the *Galut,* together with a love of Zion. Although these qualities were not precisely contradictory, the synthesis was a rare one at the time.

Events were taking place in Amsterdam which were to affect his career. The Dutch community, lacking effective spiritual leadership, had reached a point of crisis. The death of Rabbi S. Bernstein left the Yeshivah Saadat Bahurim, the official rabbinical seminary in Amsterdam, without a principal, and the leaders of the community had not been able to find a candidate who could satisfy all the factions.

In 1858, on one of his visits to Germany, Meir Lehren, a director of the rabbinical seminary in Amsterdam, met the young Duenner at Cologne, and being favorably impressed, invited him to Amsterdam for the holidays. There his scholarship and personality made a strong impression upon his brothers, Akiba and Hirsch Lehren. At Meir's request, he examined the members of the senior class, and Meir thereupon hinted that at some future time, he would like Joseph to direct the institution. Since then, Joseph had heard nothing more. In 1861, however, he got word of the death of Meir Lehren, and of Rabbi Abraham Shushan, the Chief Rabbi of the city. A delegation was sent to ask Duenner if he would be interested in becoming principal of the seminary. He agreed, on condition that he would get authority for a complete reorganization of the institution. In 1862, after much debate, his appointment was made official, although the Orthodox group had reservations about this modern young man who was "tainted" with secular philosophy, while the non-religious thought him too Orthodox.

The worldliness of the Dutch community stood in strong contrast to the intellectual German milieu, which Duenner had just left, for the Jewish intelligentsia of Holland, like their compatriots, were more preoccupied with law and medicine than with abstract philosophy. But while the adjustment was not easy, he threw himself enthusiastically into his work, and so successful were his efforts that in 1874 he was offered the Chief Rabbinate of Amsterdam, a position which had not been occupied for forty years.

He accepted this post, but retained also his leadership of the seminary. He now became so engrossed with his rabbinic duties that he gradually allowed most of his contact with the outside world to lapse. He held himself aloof also from the local community, partly from a natural reserve, as well as from a lack of awareness of the importance of social relations. But by the force of his personality, he raised the rabbinate to a new peak of distinction and authority, and earned for himself a measure of reverence unique in the history of the Jews of Holland. He married Sarah Landauer, the daughter of a prominent Munich family, and of their fifteen children, five sons and five daughters survived. Rabbi Duenner died in 1912, at the age of 79.

In 1862, in a memorandum to the curators of the seminary, he had set forth his views regarding the role of the spiritual leader. He felt that the modern rabbi, in order effectively to promote the cause of traditional Judaism, should have a broad secular and classical background, as well as a thorough grounding in Talmud. The curriculum at the seminary was thereupon drawn up in accordance with his convictions.

On his arrival, Dr. Duenner discovered an appallingly low standard of Jewish scholarship, for Amsterdam had never been particularly Torah-minded. As time went on, he strove to create a new type of *Talmid Hakham,* unknown up to this time either in Eastern or Western Europe: a scholar who could study the *Gemara* with the commentaries, who possessed a good grasp of *Halakhah,* was fluent in Hebrew and also at home in research literature.

As a teacher, Duenner had few equals. His style was lucid and forceful. A man of profound thought, he was patient with his disciples, persevering until he was certain that he had made himself thoroughly understood. From his advanced students he demanded a great deal of preparation, seeking to develop in them the capacity for independent thought.

The members of the community were often divided in their evaluation of their Chief Rabbi. While they marvelled at his erudition, they were unable to understand the many facets of his nature. Some were disgruntled at his "modernism" and his "foreign birth." Others resented his firm stand on *Halakhah* and his refusal to compromise even the most minor custom. However, as his students began to secure positions of prominence all over the country, his personal position became more secure, and he was given an altogether free hand.

Seeking to restore to the rabbinate its former glory, he emphasized the importance of outward appearance, clarity of speech, and uncompromising ethics, as well as a measure of reserve between the rabbinate and the people. The authority of the *psak,* the religious decision, was final, and he considered the Torah the exclusive province of the rabbis.

Duenner understood and approved the prophetic role of demand and reprimand, and so had no patience with the technique of appeasement, for he felt it accomplished nothing. He preferred to devote himself to a picked group, a scholarly élite, rather than to the indoctrination of the general community. Nevertheless, he had a great attraction for some of the non-religious members of the community, for they understood that his attitude was not based, as with other rabbis, upon unreasoning opposition to *Haskalah,* nor on unworldliness, but rather on conviction and principle. Through his dynamic personality, he was able to achieve results beyond the power of others; some of his disciples tried the same methods but to no avail.

He stood firm in his loyalty to Zionism, even though this was a very unpopular stand at the time, for even his admirers were anti-Zionists. The irreligious character of the secular Zionists did, indeed, disturb him, but he remained a member of Mizrachi to the very end.

Toward the end of his life, his activities were limited almost entirely to his rabbinic duties and to his studies. Though he derived some satisfaction from the fact that the Reform movement had weakened, and presented no great danger to the Dutch community, at the same time he perceived clearly the accelerating drift away from traditional Judaism. His attitude towards the influx of Russian Jews in the 1880's was ambivalent. Though he disapproved of their occasional lack of polish, he respected their scholarship.

In comparing him with Rabbi Samson Raphael Hirsch and Rabbi Ezriel Hildesheimer, two other outstanding rabbis of the day, it must be admitted that he lacked the former's administrative talent and the latter's devotion to public service, though he was at least their equal in the field of Jewish scholarship and especially of the Talmud. It is unfortunate that his responsa were destroyed during the Nazi invasion, for a study of them would doubtless have been very revealing of his approach to the history of Jewish law.

The isolation of the Dutch community in which he spent the significant years of his life, as well as his austere temperament, have combined to dim the memory of his extraordinary accomplishments. Yet he is a man who deserves to be remembered. His teachings and his high academic efforts will not be forgotten.

His Works

His scholarly efforts embrace the whole panaroma of Torah learning. The commentaries on the Talmud reveal extraordinary *bekiut* (expert knowledge), *harifut* (ingenious argument), free from pilpulistic extravagancies. His articles on *Shemot* and Ezekiel are contributions of high value and, last but not least, his comments on Saadia's magnum opus ensure him the lasting grateful respect of the scholarly world. East European savants called him "the *Gaon* of Amsterdam." He composed a historical and critical commentary on fourteen tractates of the Talmud—pioneering, bold and reverent.

His other works include an important research on *Wesen und Ursprung der* (Character and Origin of the) *Tosefta;* a significant commentary on the second chapter of Saadia's *Emunot ve-Deot,* and many articles in learned reviews, such as the *Monatsschrift, Joodsch Letterkundige Bijdragen,* and *Israelitische Letterbode.*

ABRAHAM JACOB GERSHON LESSER

(1834-1925)

By Judah M. Isaacs

ABRAHAM JACOB GERSHON LESSER

By Judah M. Isaacs

In response to the *Haskalah* movement, the so-called enlightenment which confronted Orthodox Jewry in the latter half of the nineteenth century, individuals reacted in one of three ways. Some embraced the movement whole-heartedly and took its teachings as a disproof of all religion. Others closed their minds to the principles involved and forbade the study of "philosophie" by their children. A third group felt that the discoveries of science were not in conflict with religious teachings, that, in fact, such teachings were exemplified and buttressed by the new science. In general, this is the attitude of the educated Orthodox Jew of to-day.

Rabbi Abraham Jacob Gershon Lesser was one of those who felt that a knowledge of science was not inimical to the practice of religion. In his book, *Ohel Moed,* written in 1897, he expressed the view that those who as a result of their philosophic studies rejected religion, were "victims of philosophy" and had succumbed to it because they had not delved deeply enough. In support of his opinion, he recalls the English poet, Alexander Pope, who said: "A little learning is a dangerous thing; Drink deep or taste not of the Pierian spring." He also mentions that Saadya Gaon concurred in this view.

Rabbi Lesser's approach to the problem of the new knowledge is all the more remarkable in that he was expected to be, and was, an old-fashioned Orthodox rabbi. In fact, there were probably very few of his contemporary colleagues with whom he could have discussed his views because he was a scholar long ahead of his time. In his works he refers to or quotes Pythagoras, Socrates, Plato and Aristotle. Among others, he includes lengthy Talmudic-type discussions about Jesus, the apostles and the New Testament, in general. He was acquainted with the medieval church writers, referring to Eusebius and others. He was also familiar with the writings of later philosophers. At the same time, he felt it to be a high purpose to pass on *she'elot* (questions relating to ritual) that housewives brought him, settling quarrels, performing the

347

humdrum requirements of his flock without complaint, with great humility and as if this work were the most important part of his life.

Rabbi Lesser was born in the town of Mir in Lithuania in 1834 (23rd of Kislev 5594). He was the son of Ariel Meir ben Gershon (Lisa) who died in 1843 (15 of Shevat 5603), when Abraham was only nine years of age. He was also the grandson of Rabbi Samuel Avigdor of Karlin, author of *Tanna Tosfaa* and Responsa *Sheilat Shemuel*. His mother was Deborah Bilah, daughter of Jacob, who survived her husband until 1889 (8 of Adar II 5649) and who managed to rear and provide for the education of her son.

He received his early education at the Yeshivah of Mir and at that of Rabbi Geshon Tanhum of Minsk; subsequently from Rabbi Samuel Avigdor, his grandfather, and from his father-in-law, Rabbi Joseph of Kletsk. *Semikhah* was conferred on him by Rabbi Joseph Reisin of Slonim, author of *Edut Beyoseph,* Rabbi Jehiel Heller, author of *Amude Or,* Rabbi Samuel Avigdor, Rabbi Isaac Elhanan Spector of Kovno and Rabbi Isaac Eisik Shapira of Slonim, author of *Noam Yerushalmi.*

In 1861, Rabbi Lesser was called to the rabbinate of Amstibovo, Grodno District. Later he served as rabbi of Holinka, Suwalki District, of Horodok, Vilna District and Ludwinow, Suwalki District. While still a comparatively young man, he engaged in disputation with the leading rabbis and teachers of Europe, including the rabbis of Dvinsk and of Bilsk.

His fame had reached the United States and in 1880 he was invited to come to Chicago to become the rabbi of the *Bet Hamedrash Hagadol u-Bnai Jacob.* This was one of the leading congregations of that city and was the result of the combination, in 1867, of Bnai Jacob (founded in 1862) and Bet Hamedrash Hagadol (founded in 1866).

Some of the problems of the early communities are reflected in a proclamation inserted in a local paper by the congregation on the appointment of Rabbi Lesser:

"It is well known to all that many disruptions and troubles were caused between families and quarrels in some congregations by men who call themselves rabbis, who for the sake of a few dollars will divorce a husband who is in America from a wife in Poland, which brings ruination and misfortune to helpless and innocent children. And these self-styled rabbis, for the sake of a few dollars, will give Cabala (authorization to act as a *Shohet*) or authorize men to be *Shohetim* who know nothing of *Shehitah* (slaughtering). And for the purpose of abrogating these shameful deeds, and save the name of Judaism from disgrace, we, the Polish Congregation, Bet Hamedrash Hagadol and others of our brethren in Chicago have brought Rabbi Lesser from Poland . . . a man who, besides the salary that he receives, does not want to take anything from any parties. . . . If a man is capable and worthy to be a *Shohet* he gives Cabala gratis and the same in case of *Gittin* (divorces)."

At this time Chicago was rebuilding after the Great Fire of 1871. Immigrants were pouring into the city and the city was entering the lusty growth it developed in the latter part of the nineteenth century. The Russian and Polish Jews who had come were crowded in the district bounded by Canal, Halsted, Polk and Fourteenth Streets, especially around Canal Street. There were also many Irish and Italian immigrants crowded in this area but the gangsters of their period, perhaps more religious than their modern descendants, learned to respect Rabbi Lesser and considering him a holy man, invariably stepped aside to let him pass. This was all the more remarkable because, as Bernard Horwich recalls in his book, "My First Eighty Years", after mentioning that fruit, vegetable and junk peddlers who had horses and wagons could escape the street hoodlums, says (page 126): "Those who peddled on foot, however, were never safe from attack, and so bad was the situation that a good many of the Jews of that neighborhood stayed only long enough to save sufficient money to pay for their steamship tickets, and returned to Europe."

When Rabbi Lesser arrived in Chicago, he found Jewish education in a deplorable condition. Some congregations conducted *hedarim*. There were some thirty private schools or *hedarim* conducted, occasionally by persons who had failed at all other occupations. Finally, there were also the itinerant teachers who went from house to house and in many cases taught the minimum required to enable a boy to recite the *Haftorah* on becoming Bar Mitzvah. On the basis of comments of contemporary observers, it would be difficult to determine which of the three systems was the most inefficient.

One of the first things to which Rabbi Lesser addressed himself when he became rabbi of his congregation was to organize an efficient Talmud Torah. Since his congregation was financially unable to sponsor the project, he persuaded the Congregation Ohave Shalom Marianpol (now called Anshe Sholom) and Congregation Anshe Keneseth Israel to join him. As a result, one Talmud Torah was established on the west side and one on the south side.

Another important contribution of Rabbi Lesser to the community life was the organization, with others, of the Marks Nathan Jewish Orphan Home, of which he was the first president. It was established with funds left by Marks Nathan and was a courageous and successful experiment, combining strict Orthodoxy with modern institutional methods.

In 1898, Rabbi Lesser was invited to become the rabbi of the K. K. Beth Tephila Congregation, the largest Orthodox congregation in Cincininati. He was also appointed rabbi of the Bet Hamedrash Hagadol.

In coming to Cincinnati, he entered into the midst of the hotbed of an agressive reform movement. Feelings were running high and the modern spirit of indifference or at least of live and let live had not yet developed. It is an interesting commentary on the tact and understanding that he displayed that no overt clash occurred during his tenure.

To appreciate the position that Rabbi Lesser filled during the years of 1898 to 1925, it is necessary to consider briefly the origin and growth of the Jewish community in Cincinnati. The earliest congregations in the city were, of course, Orthodox. The first was composed of English settlers and the first of these was Joseph Jonas, who was born in Plymouth, England, and arrived in Cincinnati in March 1817, filled with the idea of carrying Judaism into the western wilderness. Jonas, whose brother later became one of the closest friends of Abraham Lincoln, was warned against settling in the wilds of America and amongst the gentiles, by his friends in Philadelphia, who assured him that in the new country he would forget his religion. In 1819, he was joined by three other English Jews, Lewis Cohen of London, Barnet Levi of Liverpool, and Jonas Levy of Exeter. These four and David Israel Johnson, who lived in Indiana but subsequently moved to

Cincinnati, conducted during the autumn of 1819 the first Jewish religious services held in the midwestern part of the United States.

On January 18, 1824, this group, then numbering twenty, founded the Bene Israel Congregation, which was chartered by the General Assembly of Ohio on January 8, 1830.

In the 1840's a large number of Jews came to this country from Germany, fleeing in part from the political disturbances of the time. Those who settled in Cincinnati decided to organize their own synagogue and on September 19, 1841, the Congregation Bene Yeshurun was organized. In April 1854, it appointed Rabbi Isaac Mayer Wise, who was officiating in Albany, New York, as its rabbi. He had been a rabbi in Radnitz, Hungary but finding some difficulty in working with the government, decided to emigrate to America. In 1875, he organized the Hebrew Union College in Cincinnati and from it organized reform spread throughout the United States.

It is also of interest that among the early congregations was a Polish Shul organized in 1847 which later became a conservative congregation. The following year another group of German immigrants organized Ahavat Ahim.

The Congregation Bene Israel elected Rabbi Max Lilienthal in 1855 but the orthodox element about forty in number broke away in September 1855 and established a new congregation, Shearit Israel. By 1866, Shakhne Isaacs, who subsequently publicly burned the Reform *siddur* when it was presented to him, detected a weakening in the Orthodoxy of Shearit Israel, principally evidenced by the elimination of a *mikvah* in the plans for a new building. With a few others he formed a new congregation, K. K. Bet Tephila Congregation, still known as Reb Shakhne's Shul. A small building was secured on Lodge Street with subsequent moves to Eighth Street and Central Avenue, to Carlisle Avenue and finally, in 1907, to the building at Eighth and Mound Streets. This building, interestingly enough, was purchased from Bene Israel, the first congregation formed in the city.

Reb Shakhne's Shul, with which Rabbi Lesser spent his entire career in Cincinnati, has never deviated from strict Orthodoxy and although located in a section of the city largely deserted by

Jews, still exists with many members under the jurisdiction of Rabbi Eliezer Silver, president of the Agudat Harabbonim.

In the early history of the Jewish community, the prominent families were the wealthy German Jewish families. Having arrived during the era of great industrial expansion, they amassed considerable wealth. Many of the sons of these families attended Harvard University and President Eliot once expressed the view to Professor Nathan Isaacs of Harvard, himself a grandson of Shakhne Isaacs and a follower of strict Orthodoxy, that these boys constituted one of the finest groups that ever attended Harvard. Julius Freiberg and his brother-in-law, Levi J. Workum, established in 1853 the largest distillery. In 1867, Abraham Kuhn and Solomon Loeb, clothiers in Cincinnati, left for New York to establish Kuhn, Loeb & Company. The Fleischmans of Fleischman's Yeast fame contributed a mayor to the city. Other mayors from this group were Frederick Spiegel in 1904 to 1906 and Murray Seasongood in 1926 to 1930. The Ransohoffs, Freibergs, Kuhns, Fechheimers, Seasongoods, Stix, Bettmans and Wolfsteins and others too numerous to mention contributed lawyers, doctors, bankers and business men not only to the city's life but also to the national life.

Not as important as the Reform community, the Orthodox group took more time to find itself. A few, the Manischewitz in matzoh baking and the Oscherowitz in kosher meat packing, achieved national prominence rather early in predominantly Jewish activities. In later years, the Moskowitz family in steel, the Schiff family in the manufacture of shoes, and the Harris family in real estate, built up national organizations. The Isaacs family, which was among the early settlers in the city, became known in educational circles. However, for some time the Orthodox community formed a self-contained, self-centered group biding its time until its sons could take a place in the medical, legal and business life of the city, with many achieving national prominence. It is of interest that Rabbi Lesser never learned to talk English and the only words in English that he could write comprised his name. As a result, he did not take part in the civic life of the community and left much of this type of activity to Reform Jews. His influence was primarily that of a humble pastor of his flock.

One of his important outside activities and interests was the organization in 1902, with three other Orthodox rabbis in the

Middle West, Rabbi Sander Lifshitz, Rabbi Asher L. Zarchy and
Rabbi Isaac Neustadt, of the Union of Orthodox Rabbis of the
United States and Canada (Agudat Harabbanim) which, interestingly enough, urged as the prerequisite of an active Orthodoxy
the training of ordained rabbis, teachers and preachers who had
mastered the English language and who would be able to combat
the forces of Reform.

Rabbi Lesser's principal writings are embraced in two volumes,
Beaharit Hayamin (In the Last Days) published in 1896, and
Ohel Moed (The Tent of the Meeting) published in 1897.[1]

In the preface to *Beaharit Hayamim,* Rabbi Lesser described
the circumstances that led him to write the book.   In 1892, a
Christian clergyman who had traveled through the Holy Land
and had been impressed with the agricultural accomplishments of
the scattered Jews, became convinced that the time had come for
the return of the Children of Israel. To contribute his share to
the cause, he proposed to petition the President of the United
States and other high officials of the government to lay his proposal before the rulers of the world. "It is your duty," he told
Rabbi Lesser, "to support me with whatever you can." He, therefore, requested that a treatise be written in Hebrew to set forth
the hope of Israel for the future according to the tradition. He
proposed to have it translated and published at his own expense
and in this way he hoped to carry out his proposed undertaking.

Rabbi Lesser was very reluctant to undertake the task. He
was quite friendly with the minister but it did not seem that
such a person was the man to bring salvation to Israel. In addition, he was afraid that the work might cause a misunderstanding of the attitude of the Jews toward this country. However,
as the minister urged him day after day to proceed, he became
afraid that his reluctance might be construed to mean that he
was trying to hide something. To overcome such an impression,
he invited the minister to sit through a Seder from beginning
to end. Or again, the minister might think that the refusal to
prepare the manuscript was a sign that the people were ignorant
of the things that concerned them so greatly. Finally, with reluctance, Rabbi Lesser proceeded to write the treatise and delivered it to the minister. But nothing happened. Months and

---

[1]Other contributions were items published in *Bet Va'ad Lehakhamim,*
a monthly publication edited by Rabbi B. Abramowitz, New York, 1903.

years went by and still nothing. Rabbi Lesser finally became fearful that while the minister would not edit the manuscript, some stranger might undertake to alter it. So to indicate what he had really written, he decided to publish the manuscript himself.

The book is cast in the form of a dialogue between a father and son. The son asks a question usually very learned in form, with many appropriate quotations and the father answers at length with more quotations. The father occasionally begins his questions somewhat as follows:

> "Well, my son, I will again repeat what I told you before: incline your ear to listen and devote your mind to the acceptance of good instruction."

In other words, the treatise is somewhat medieval in character and one cannot but wonder at the dilemma faced by the minister on receipt of the manuscript. His problem can be appreciated when we examine some of the discussions in the book. In answer to the question of the son as to whether the Messiah must be anointed by the special oil of ointment to establish his legal title, the father answers:

> "Exactly so, my son! And for this reason the Apostle Matthew was mistaken when he wrote (Matthew I, 1): 'Jesus the Messiah (annointed), son of David.' It is not recorded that Jesus was ever properly anointed with the sacred unction as a sign of his elevation to the royal dignity to be king over Israel and he was, therefore, by no means entitled to the name of 'Messiah.' "

Again in answer to the question of the son:

> "Father! Will the Messianic king send missionaries among the nations to proclaim the name of the Lord . . ."

> "My son! Far be it from him to do such a thing! In the first place the very act of sending out missionaries to catch souls and to persuade people to forsake the faith of their fathers, is in itself unworthy, corrupt and despicable . . ."

It is not to be wondered that nothing happened.

In spite of its style, the book has great dignity and maturity and even though written before modern scholarship had unearthed many recent discoveries, contains perhaps most of what can be said from the traditional standpoint for the return of the exiles.

In the introduction to *Beaharit Hayamim,* Rabbi Lesser discusses the reason why the Temples were destroyed. In a series of Discourses (of which there are thirteen as indicated by the following numbers), he establishes that a Messiah is to be expected *beaharit hayamim* (in the latter days) and that belief in such coming is essential to the faithful believer (I), that Israel will no longer be despoiled by the nations (II), in fact, the nations will restore Israel to the Holy Land (III). The redemption from the Babylonian captivity did not fulfill the prophecies about the latter days (IV) and even the original settlement in Palestine did not exhaust the promise of the land to be given to Israel (V).

Rabbi Lesser was troubled about possible claims of dual allegiance and sought to refute them (VI). He also answers the possible critiscism that, if redemption were intended, the roster of tribes would have been accurately kept by pointing out that the lack of such identification prevented many false Messiahs (VII). He also discusses the form of government: whether in the latter days it would be republican or monarchial (VIII) and whether if monarchial, the king must be anointed to be legally established explaining in this connection that Jesus was not legally anointed (IX). The general qualifications of the true Messiah are indicated (X). The Messiah will be king over the whole earth (XI) and the people will follow the Jews but not through the missionary efforts on the part of the Jews (XII) and all the peoples of the earth will be under the sovereignty of the Lord, with Israel his peculiar treasure, as teacher and instructor in the Law (XIII).

A second work published by Rabbi Lesser, a volume of sermons and *halakhic* dissertations on the Jewish holidays, was published in 1897. This volume, called *Ohel Moed* (The Tent of the Meeting), takes its name from the covers of the book, which as a tent encompasses the *Moadim,* the holidays. It is doubtful whether these sermons were ever delivered but they were of great importance at the time. They were aimed at a special group of readers who in the nineties of the last century were called the *Maskilim* or enlightened ones, those who, in searching for truth and knowledge, often exalted the philosophy and wisdom of other peoples above their own and frequently ceased having faith in their own religion.

Throughout the sermons, Rabbi Lesser attempts to show that Judaism is a religion that is largely based on reason; that there is no basic conflict between philosophy and religious faith and that many of the philosophic concepts attributed to other nations were really borrowed from Judaism. For example, in one of the sermons on *Shavuot,* the author tells us that Judaism is in reality a combination of religion and philosophy. This view is in accord with the opinions of some of our Sages who said that Moses received at Sinai the basic essentials of all wisdom and science. In the same sermon the view is advanced that the intellectual giants of the world, many of whom were venerated by the *Maskilim,* had derived their philosophic ideas and concepts from Judaism or else taught knowledge that was previously known to the Jewish people. He quotes the early Christian scholar, Origen, as having said that Pythagoras received much of his wisdom from the Jews and their literature and incorporated it into his own writings.

Then, too, Rabbi Lesser offers the testimony of Josephus, who wrote in his book, *Against Apion,* that many of the nations have taken from the Jews the best part of Jewish teachings. Specifically he cites among these, the concepts of reward and punishment and of the immortality of the soul, which were taken from Jewish ideas which preceded the times in which these men lived. Even the Greek scholar, Simonides, who is credited with the discovery of the laws of association as part of the memory process, was in reality not the discoverer of the theory. The rabbis in the Mishnah in *Peah,* who determined whether a forgotten sheaf in a field might be considered *shik-hah* on the basis of its proximity to some other stationary object which could serve to recall to the mind of the owner that he had forgotten the sheaf, were really the discoverers of the "law of association." This corroboration of the wisdom and truth of the Torah is not limited to the ancients. Even today, scholars and scientists, we are told, are finding scientific reasons for *milah,* the dietary laws, the *mikvah* and other *mitzvot.*

Having thus brought forth these many proofs that the world is indebted to Judaism for much of its greatest teachings and having attempted to raise the prestige of the Torah and faith in the eyes of the *Maskil,* Rabbi Lesser proceeds to interpret the Biblical passage in Deut. IV, 5, *"Behold, I have taught you statutes and judgments. . . . Keep therefore and do them, for this is your wisdom and understanding in the sight of the nations, which shall hear all these statutes and say, Surely this great nation is a wise and understanding people."* This passage is explained to mean that the Torah is more than a mere collection of religious rituals for the Jewish people. Rather the Torah is "your wisdom and understanding." This is so even "in the sight of the nations" whose great philosophers and teachers have borrowed from the Torah's teachings. The Jewish religion is based on reason to such an extent that many of the nations of the world refer to us as a "nation of wise and understanding people" rather than a people whose religion is predicated upon faith and dogma.

In similar fashion the author treats of many subjects of interest to the intelligent Jewish reader of his day. He illustrates his thought with apt examples and quotations and sheds light on many Biblical and Midrashic passages.

In his person, Rabbi Lesser was short and stocky in build. But one was not conscious of his size because his head was leonine in appearance, his eyes were flashing and piercing and his snow white hair and patriarchal beard made him a perfect model for a Rembrandt or a Tissot. Probably one would say that his outstanding characteristics were gentleness and understanding of human nature but he was capable of quick anger when, for example, he felt that some irreligious action was being perpetrated. His observations were keen and penetrating and sometimes unexpected. One time he astonished a study group by saying that baseball was very important for the Jews in America. He explained that whenever two or three Americans foregathered, they generally discussed baseball, especially during the World Series season. In Lithuania where he served, whenever the natives met together, they had discussed the Jews. Baseball, he felt, furnished a release for the energies of the people.

His home life was ideal with the wife of his youth, Bayle Bluma (1837-1916), whose whole world he comprised. Perhaps one of the finest tributes to a wife to be found anywhere is in his *Ohel Moed,* where he discusses how a woman may acquire merit:

"Bayle Bluma, the daughter of my teacher and father-in-law, the famous Rabbi Joseph . . . gave me permission in my youth to go and study Torah many years until I was ordained, while she and her son remained alone and in want and need, without bread or clothes, and she did not complain of the bitter-

ness of her lot. In all the years that I officiated, the preoccupations and work of the house rested on her shoulders and
she did not permit me to do a thing against the honor of the
Torah. She spurred me on to rise early and to go to bed
late in order to study Torah day and night and it was her
principle to clothe me always with garments of honor as well
as she was able."

Rabbi Lesser had one son, Hyman Joseph Lesser, who became supervisor of the kosher department of Swift & Co. in
Chicago. Hyman Joseph had twelve children, the eldest of whom
was Meyer Lesser, an advertising executive, head of Blaine,
Thompson & Co. He pioneered the national advertising campaign
for sound in connection with the moving picture, "The Jazz
Singer."

On Yom Kippur, 5685 (October 7, 1925), Rabbi Lesser died
quietly, as he had lived. His age was 91 years. He always remained in the midst of his people in humble surroundings on
a drab but respectable street in the basin of the city. During
his last illness, his family had gathered around him. He lay in
his bed quietly, his eyes closed, serene and at peace with the
world, his beautiful white hair surrounding his face and a
yarmulki on his head. His even sculptured features gave him
great dignity. He was a great and humble man in his time.

BIBLIOGRAPHY

Brickner, Barnett R. The Jewish Community of Cincinnati, Historical and Descriptive, 1817-1933. Cincinnati, 1935. (Type-
written).

Bet Va'ad Lehahamim (monthly periodical) Edited by B. Abramowitz, New York, 1903. Contains contributions by Rabbi Lesser.

Bregstone, Philip P. Chicago and its Jews. Chicago, 1933.

Deinard, Ephraim. Siphrat Yisrael Be'amerika. Jaffa, 1920. pp.
2, 11.

Deinard, Ephraim. Kohelet America. St. Louis, 1926. Part 2,
pp. 7, 19.

Encyclopaedica Judaica. Berlin, 1934. Vol. X, p. 807.

Finkelstein, Louis. The Jews, their History, Culture and Religion. New York, 1949. Vol. 1, p. 406.

Friedberg, B. Bet Eked Sepharim, Tel Aviv, 1951, p. 34, no. 798.

Gottlieb, A. N. Ohole Shem. Pinsk, 1912. p. 309.

Grosse Judische National-Biographie. Edited by Solomon Winiger, Cernowitz, 1925. Vol. 4, p. 35.

Gutstein, Morris A. A Priceless Heritage. New York, 1953. p. 126.

Heller, James G. As Yesterday when it is Past (Kehilah Kodesh Bene Yeshurun) 1942.

Horwich, Bernard. My First Eighty Years. Chicago, 1939. pp. 139-142.

History of the Jews in Chicago. Edited by Hyman L. Meites, Jewish Historical Society of Illinois. Chicago, 1924. p. 213.

Isaacs, Moses Legis. Ad Meyah Shonah. Orthodox Jewish Life, Vol. 20 May-June 1953, p. 34.

Sefer Hayobhel shel Agudat Harabbanim Haorthodoksim d'arzot habrit vekanada.

(The Jubilee Volume of the Union of Orthodox Rabbis of the United States and Canada). New York, 1928, pp. 34-36, 137.

Lesser, A. J. G. Beaharit Hayamim, translated by H. Eliassof, Chicago, 1896.

Lesser, A. J. G. Ohel Moed. Chicago, 1897.

Otzar Yisrael. Edited by J. D. Eisenstein. New York, 1951. Vol. VI, pp. 62-63.

Philipson, David. The Oldest Congregation in the West (Bene Israel) Cincinnati, 1894.

Philipson, David. Publications of the American Jewish Historical Society, No. 8, pp. 43-57.

The Universal Jewish Encyclopedia. Edited by Isaac Landman. New York, 1941. Vol. 3, p. 205.

Toledot Anshe Shem. Edited by Oscar Z. Rand. New York, 1950. Vol. 1, p. 80.

DAVID HOFFMANN

(1843-1921)

By Yeshayahu Aviad-Wolfsberg

DAVID HOFFMANN

By Yeshayahu Aviad-Wolfsberg

Preface

It is a great privilege to write a biography of the sainted Rabbi David Tzevi Hoffmann, without doubt one of the greatest scholars of this century. Our age never saw a man so highly qualified, both as a *lamdan* (rabbinic scholar) of classical quality and of unusual standing in the *Wissenschaft* (science) of Judaism. The first and most famous personality in Torah-true Judaism, he was a link between two worlds, not hostile to one another, but for a long time kept apart. He never left his old *Bet ha-Midrash* and never deserted his comrades in modern research. But he fertilized Jewish traditional learning by the introduction of scientific methods and scholarly efforts into the field of *lamdanut*.

Some appreciations were written after his death. His son-in-law, Alexander Marx,[1] the world-famous Louis Ginzburg[2] his pupil and colleague, Josef Wohlgemuth,[3] A. A. Kaplan,[4] and Chaim Tschernowitz[5] (Rav Tsair) have paid tribute to him. They approached him with love, in admiration of his singular capacities, his unusual piety and righteousness. But they all confined themselves to essays. It is strange that nobody wrote a biography on a larger scale.

Now that I have been invited to fill this gap,[6] there is much hesitation in my heart. To write on David Hoffmann requires much preparation, wide scholarship, and profound familiarity with all he achieved and knew.[7] I hope to be forgiven for being arrogant enough to undertake it. My only apology is my love for him and my ardent desire to contribute to his fame.

---

[1]In "Studies in Jewish History," 1944, and in "Essays in Jewish Biography," 1947.
[2]In "Scholars and Saints."
[3]In the Jeschurun, 1921.
[4]Ibidem.
[5]E. M. Lipschitz, *Hator*, 5682, reprinted in *Ketabim* III, 252-266.
[6]*Masekhet Zikronot*, 244-264.
[7]In 1943, on the occasion of the 100th anniversary of Hoffmann's birth, I wrote an essay in "Sinai," edited by Rabbi J. L. Maimon.

Univ. of Tulsa Library
Tulsa, Oklahoma

His Life

The life of David Hoffmann is typical of a man whose ideals are not conditioned by personal interests. From his very early years he knew only one cherished aim: perfection in the field of Judaism. In accord with the time-hallowed concept of our people, perfection for him meant the combination of assiduous and uninterrupted study of the Torah with the most precise practice of its law. This undivided and indivisible wholeness was the cornerstone of his model life; laid in his youth in the humble decency of his native place and his parental home, it remained the unchanging basis throughout his years.

He was born on the first of Kislev 5604 (1843), in Verbo (a small town of Neutra, then part of Hungary, now of Slovakia), to his father Moshe Yehudah, the local *dayyan* (literally ecclesiastical judge, often assistant or second rabbi). A precocious child, he started studying Torah very early. At the age of five he was thoroughly acquainted with the Pentateuch and Rashi's commentary thereon. I was told that once, when Rector of the Rabbinical Seminary at Berlin, he lost his patience with one of the students who did not remember Rashi's commentary on a verse, and exclaimed: "When I was a child of five years, I knew it!"

Soon he entered the world of the Oral Law and became a student of the ocean of the Talmud. After his primary education at home and in the *heder* of his native town, he deepened his knowledge in the Torah academies of his country. His distinguished teacher and main guide was Rabbi Moshe Schueck, Rabbi of Huszt, one of Rabbi Moshe Sofer's foremost disciples, a famous *Possek* (decisor), whose responsa Hoffmann very often mentioned. The years spent at the feet of Rabbi Schueck were of high importance for the young *illuy* (prodigy). They tied him to the famous school of Pressburg, founded by Rabbi Moshe Sofer[8] and led by his illustrious son, Abraham Samuel Benjamin. At Huszt and Pressburg, Hoffmann acquired the Hungarian method of Talmudic study.

It was in Pressburg that he took his first steps towards a new path. There are no autobiographical notes and one can but

---

[8]See "Jewish Leaders," ed. by Leo Jung, p. 115.

imagine what impelled him towards secular education. He was one of the many *yeshivah* students who were fired by the ambition to be at home in the realm of traditional erudition and to adjust himself to the modern scientific world, the vast territory of modern culture. In every period of our history there arose great minds who were opposed to the neglect of science and philosophy. Let us mention only Saadia Gaon, Maimonides, and Rabbi Elia, the *Gaon* of Vilna, among countless others. Young Hoffmann realized the necessity of such studies very early and devoted to them his great talents and all his energy. In Pressburg and Vienna he developed into a man of broad knowledge, of great theoretical insight, supported by an admirable memory. His interest embraced both philology and mathematics. At the universities of Vienna and Berlin, he widened and deepened the excellent training he had received in both classical and oriental languages. These efforts enabled him, in later years, to make important contributions to the lexicography of Mishnah and Talmud, and served him well in his exegetic work. His prowess in mathematics benefited his activity as a decisor in problems of the Jewish calendar. His German was pure, his style lucid and simple (in the positive sense of the word). The works of the great poets, too, attracted him and promoted his spiritual structure.

His studies brought him to Germany. He graduated at the University of Tuebingen. More important is the fact that he came under the influence of the famous circle of Wuerzburg, headed by Rabbi Seligmann Baer Bamberger,[9] a most impressive leader of contemporary Torah-Judaism. Bamberger was old-fashioned, but he had an understanding of the changing world around him and knew how to react to its needs and how to create suitable conditions for the education of his community. He was impressed neither by academic methods, nor by exaggerated concepts of modern civilization, nor by the criteria of high *bourgeoisie*. The milieu of a medium-size town and its many small Jewish nuclei in lower Franconia called for more modest ways of adaptation to the new life. Rabbi Bamberger did his best by founding a seminary to train teachers for the numerous towns and villages which needed them. Beyond that, he succeeded in rally-

---

[9] See "Jewish Leaders," edited by Leo Jung, p. 179.

ing around himself a group of men enthusiastic about Talmud Torah and thirsting for exhaustive knowledge in the *Halakhah*. His ideal was simplicity, clarity and study that would explain and conform with, the traditional practice of Judaism. He and his circle were distinguished by piety, expressed in simplicity, clarity and decency.

Hoffmann entered this circle and realized how great was his affinity to this atmosphere. He came somewhat prepared for it. In Hungary he had frequented the new type of *Bet Hamidrash,* inaugurated and headed by Rabbi Ezriel Hildesheimer[10] in Eisenstadt. This revered scholar, a native of Germany, who chose his university studies out of love for science but also with a view to combining it with rabbinical training, had a powerful influence on Hoffmann, as on many other gifted young men; he was the first, most eminent and successful teacher of a new generation of rabbis whom he instructed to be real spiritual leaders of their flock: skilled to enable them to remain faithful to the original Jewish approach in theory and practice without denying or ignoring the best aspects of modern culture. It is Hildesheimer's merit to have paved the way of implementing such program. His scientific rank was well established; he worked in steady and full contact with his contemporaries, not only in Western, but also in Eastern Europe. He did not yield to any form of assimilation; because of his complete, vital and pure Jewishness, he contributed more than anybody in his time to the creation of able leaders, well versed both in the field of rabbinical learning and in modern science. His great achievement, not limited to his time but enduring for generations, was the establishment of a scientific institute with outstanding men to promote a new trend of research. His astonishing instinct enabled him to find the famous, never to be forgotten group: Abraham Berliner, Jakob Barth, and David Hoffman. The merits of Barth and Berliner are undisputed.

If I stress Hoffmann's role and am inclined to look at him as the leading personality, it is because of his primary function of instructor and scientist in the Talmudical area. For many years he was not only the official head of Hildesheimer's seminary, but *the* authority to whom most German and other rabbis

---

10See "Jewish Leaders," p. 213.

would bring their problems and doubts for his decision. They trusted his all-encompassing erudition, his skill in solving questions and aiding them in their perplexities. He presented an unusual example of religious integrity and of the ability to render a true and definitive judgment. He not only safeguarded the values of tradition against any violation, but had also the courage and power to issue and maintain a more lenient opinion, according to the Talmudic principle that "the power of a more lenient opinion is preferred"[11] to the inclination to more rigid ones that are neither necessary nor essential. Last but not least, he was a man whose piety was attractive and convincing: "The Name of the Lord was beloved by reason of his conduct."

To complete his biography: After having finished his studies, he became a teacher, first in Hoechberg near Wuerzburg, afterwards in Frankfort (Main) in the secondary school of the *Israelitische Religionsgesellschaft,* the community that represented the Orthodoxy of Separatism, founded in 1851 as an answer to Reform. Under the leadership of Rabbi S. R. Hirsch, that community had established a school to foster a strong religious conviction and to assure its steadfast continuity for generations. It was a providential event when in 1873 Rabbi Hildesheimer invited Hoffmann to join the faculty of the rabbinical seminary in Berlin he had just inaugurated. With this appointment Hoffmann started his real career and kept studying and teaching with unparalleled intensity until the day of his death, in 1921.

He married the daughter of a great *Talmid Hakham,* Rabbi Jonah Rosenbaum of Zell in Franconia, a disciple of Rabbi Mendel Kargau and friend of Rabbi S. B. Bamberger. Hoffmann had a great veneration for his father-in-law and quoted him often in his responsa. (It was from him that he obtained responsa of Rabbi M. Kargau and *halakhic* material written by Rabbi E. Bergmann, one of the early immigrants of German origin to Eretz Israel.) Hoffmann was happy enough to see his family growing. He had five learned sons and two daughters, one of whom became the wife of the great historian Alexander Marx, Hoffmann's favorite disciple, later professor at the Jewish Theological Seminary of America.

---

[11] B. Betzah 2b.

There are very few sensational facts in his life. His days were crowded with spiritual and religious service. When Rabbi Ezriel Hildesheimer grew older and weaker after a life of extremely hard work and overwhelming activities, Hoffmann took upon himself most of the rector's duties in the seminary. After Hildesheimer's death, by unanimous choice, he became rector. The burden of that high office remained on his shoulders to the very last day, when, physically but not mentally exhausted, he collapsed.[12]

Besides teaching, being in charge of the institute, and doing much research, Hoffmann, during all these decades, was the head of the rabbinical court (*Ab Bet Din*) of the Orthodox community *Adath Israel,* created and led by Rabbi Ezriel Hildesheimer. He was the permanent rabbi of the *Hebrah Shass* in Berlin, where he used to give a daily lecture in Talmud. All Orthodox rabbis, except some followers of the Hirsch group, Frankfurt a. M., looked upon him as their great master and leader. He guided and advised them in his mild and fatherly manner that never knew despotism and rigorism. Only rarely, when the vital interests of traditional Judaism required it, did he speak out strongly and sharply, surprising his contemporaries by his vigorous method. His vast erudition gave him the weapons, but he added to them the art of fighting and the elegance of his spirit. Thus did he rebuke the attacks of Gentiles on the Shulhan Arukh and the ethics of the Jewish religion, and their assaults on the dietary laws. In the period of the Reform *Richtlinien*[13] he spoke in the accents of authority and powerful condemnation about that aberration.

His work reached its climax in his efforts to counteract Biblical criticism. Although everything he did in his life, even with regard to practical problems, was based on scientific work and methods and found its expression in articles, pamphlets and books, it is in the field of theoretical controversies that Hoffmann's contributions were most creative and were received with utmost respect even by adversaries.

---

[12]In 1913, on the occasion of the 70th anniversary of his birthday, he was honored by friends, colleagues, and disciples with a Jubilee Volume that gave expression to the high esteem he enjoyed.

[13]Cp. the index in "Jewish Leaders."

When he passed away, the loss of this champion of integral Judaism was felt very deeply in widest circles. It was not only the group of traditional Jews, faithful to the Torah, inspired and shaped by Rabbi Ezriel Hildesheimer and himself, that mourned his death; so did all Jews, aware of the interests of Judaism and familiar with greatness within our ranks. Nobody, truly attached to the theory and the practice of our "tree of life," could ignore Hoffmann's achievements and their blessings. He found many admirers and followers. In silence he lived and quiet was the road of his research work, hence he evoked calm disciples rather than fervid partisans. But, on the other hand, he never aroused furious antipathy. He was universally respected. Only people who despised scientific efforts had no esteem for Hoffmann. He did not suffer from such attitude. A wise man, he did not long for applause and met human vanity with a smile; envy, lack of sympathy or of recognition never hurt him.

He lived in utter simplicity, almost in austerity. He voiced no requests for greater salary, his exacting work and academic fame notwithstanding. He was a man wanting nothing of material comforts, like most of our illustrious Sages in antiquity and the Middle Ages.

I mention all this not only to emphasize his perfect and harmonious personality, his indifference to exterior conditions as they touched his work. I wonder whether those responsible for the institution which he headed, who had the benefit of his manifold merits and enjoyed the riches of his spiritual harvest, were doing their duty by this unique man, during his life and after his death.

Men of lesser importance and achievement were honored by the edition of their publications, articles and essays, dispersed and scattered in many journals, special volumes, and yearbooks. Nothing of this kind has been done in the case of Hoffmann. There are many praiseworthy contributions from his pen in the *Magazin fuer die Wissenschaft des Judentums,* edited by him and his colleague Berliner; in the *Israelitische Monatschrift* (supplement to the *Juedische Presse*) and the *Litteraturblatt* of the same weekly, as well as in the *Jahrbuch der Juedisch-Literarischen Gesellschaft;* many others in other learned reviews and during the last years of his life in Wohlgemuth's *Jeschurun,* today almost inaccessible. They were never collected. It is still not too late to pay this tribute to the great teacher whose work added so much to the glory of our people.

Only the Jubilee Volume on the occasion of his 70th birthday marks the appreciation of his importance.

II. THE SCHOLAR

Hoffmann in many respects recalls great Jewish authors and polyhistors among other nations. The scope of his studies and publications is amazing. But in all his vast literary work there is evident a common denominator and a distinct orientation. The secret of his productivity was his mastery of the Talmud, his major interest, and the sovereignty of his knowledge of the Oral Law. He was first of all a great *baki* (expert). So he devoted himself especially to research work in the *Mishnah* and the *Halakhic Midrashim.* He was no less active in practical *Halakhah.* But the impact of the then fashionable Biblical Criticism on the religious condition of Orthodox Jewry, particularly in Germany and West European countries, caused him to engage in extensive and intensive occupation with the Written Law. In spite of his astonishing familiarity with the *Humash* (Pentateuch) and all the books of the Bible, the real source of his success, even in this field, was his authority in post-Biblical literature. As we study his scholarly work, it is most impressive to realize how closely his essays on *Halakhah* are connected with his writings on exegetic and apologetic subjects. They are dependent on the progress and the clarification of his views on Midrashic literature.

He gave his attention to many branches of Jewish learning. His are a multitude of short yet comprehensive publications touching all kinds of problems. The richness and vigor of his spirit enabled him to produce incessantly; in the course of his laborious life many fruits ripened. This would have been impossible but for his expert acquaintance with auxiliary sciences. He had respect for them without overestimating them. For him, Torah and tradition remained always the center, not only of his interest, but of Jewish life and thought. Other branches of human activity belonged to what Maimonides had termed ancillary functions like that of "cooks and perfumers." But no derogation of, or hostility towards, science may ever appeal to the authority of either Rabbi Moshe ben Maimon nor of Rabbi David Hoffmann. Deep respect to serious research was always paid by our great teachers, in accord with the teaching of Maimonides, the "great eagle." Even a superficial look at his *Guide for the Perplexed"* will indicate how deeply rooted was his recognition of the great thinkers and scholars. It is only when they went beyond the limits of exact solid and careful research to advance their subjective view that he refuted their statements. His basic attitude endorsed the reliability of the scientific method. That may sound too optimistic, but since it applies only to the most assured methods, principles and axiom indispensable to any attempt at factual knowledge, one can hardly oppose it.

It was one of Hoffmann's strongest convictions that to reach worthwhile results, one must proceed on lines that will make it difficult for anybody to resist. In his preface to his standard work on "Leviticus", he declared expressly that he endeavored to prove the traditional conception of the Torah, as given by God and not written by anyone but Moses, not by merely repeating the dogmatic approach but by arguments in themselves powerful enough to convince everybody except those who adhere fanatically and blindly to prejudices, created by modern unbelief and criticism of the Bible.

A. MISHNAH

Since his studies in Mishnah and Midrash are accepted by almost all experts, I should like to start with a short survey of this work, his earliest scientific enterprise. (His biography of Mar Samuel, the famous Amora, is of special interest and will be dealt with later.) Though he published his *Abhandlungen ueber die Pentateuchischen Gesetze* (Treatises on the Laws of the Pentateuch) prior to his books on the above topics, yet some of his investigations were made and published before he became concerned with Biblical problems. Again and again let us emphasize that Biblical items in Hoffmann's research work are based on his post-Biblical studies.

In the *Magazin fuer die Wissenschaft des Judentums*[14] of 1876 and 1877, we find Hoffmann dealing with Mishnah and Midrash, preceding any other work. This research occupied him for a long period. In 1881 appeared his famous studies on *Zur Mishna-Kritik (Criticism of the Mishnah)*. Preparatory labors enabled him to summarize his studies in a book, small but very important: *Die erste Mischna und die Controversen der Tannaim,* Berlin (1882). It is, indeed, much more than a summary, being full of new data and of profound insights. As the title indicates, the problem of the first, the earliest, Mishnah is the main item. Hoffmann traces all lines towards the exploration and discovery of the very earliest roots of the outstanding code of the Oral Law.

At the outset, it is vital to stress that all his efforts in the field of the Oral Law, be it Mishnah or Midrash, are so intensively tied to one another that one may not separate the various sectors. His *The First Mishnah* (1882) and *Zuer Einleitung in die Halachischen Midrashim* (An Introduction to the Halakhic Midrashim) (1887), as all his discoveries in the wide range of specific Midrashim (*Mekhilta d' R. Shimeon b. Yohai, Midrash Tannaim, Midrash Ha-Gadol,* etc.) form a unity and show how amazing and admirable was his scholarship. His ergography (the amount of work accomplished) is no less impressive than his biography. (I introduce this remark here not in order to give expression to his greatness, but to explain the interdependence of the various topics of his research.)

Dealing with Mishnah and Midrash, he touched upon most important problems: How the Oral Law was shaped and how it attained literary form. It is not a question of its age. For Hoffmann, as for any Jew faithful to the genuine Jewish attitude, the Oral Law is not younger than the Bible. He begins his study on the Mishnah by emphasizing the unity of both fundamental documents of Judaism. But the Oral Law, although, as far as it contains *Halakhot* given from Sinai and the principles of interpretation is, exactly as the Written Law, of divine origin, it assumed its final shape no earlier than in the time of the

---

[14]Founded by Abraham Berliner in 1874 and edited by him in collaboration with David Hoffmann from 1876-1893. They published also a Hebrew supplement, *Otzar Tov.*

Tannaites. During all the generations from Mosheh to the teachers of the Mishnah there was no final physiognomy and every authorized transmitter of the tradition used the style which seemed best to him.

Mishnah is the term of a group of *Halakhot* or a single *Halakhah* deriving from Tannaites. Sometimes the term is more comprehensive, but we confine ourselves to the Mishnah of Rabbi Judah ha-Nassi, who did not offer any new *Mishnayot* of his own but a collection of the *Mishnayot* of his predecessors. His Mishnah has become authoritative, not those attributed to Rabbi Akiba, Rabbi Meir, Rabbi Hiyyah, Rabbi Oshaya and Bar Kappara, although the collections of Rabbi Akiba and Rabbi Meir[15] (an anonymous teaching in our Mishnah represents the view of R. Meir) (*Stam Matnitan*—Rabbi Meir) have been of highest value to the ultimate work of Rabbi Judah. Rabbi Sherira Gaon does not stop as he comes to Rabbi Akiba but derives his Mishnah from his "previous teachers" (*rabotav ha-rishonim*) and in the Mishnah, Sanhedrin III, 4 in the name of Rabbi Jose it is said: "This is the Mishnah of R. Akiba, but our Mishnah reads. . . ." There is no doubt that already in the days of the Second Temple there existed a well-defined Mishnah and parts which were incorporated in *our* Mishnah.

It seems to be well established that the Midrashic form of the Oral Law preceded the Mishnaic one. The (*halakhic*) Midrash accompanies the verses (*pessukim*) of the books of Moshe and attaches to them its interpretations. The Mishnah is the attempt to systematize the oral legislation. So it does not surprise us that there is no compulsion always to quote the Biblical source.

Nevertheless, the Mishnah, too, is very old and Hoffmann offers examples thereof. There are *Mishnayot* preserving material from the past, not more actual in later days. He calls them historical *Mishnayot* because they deal with laws that were valid in the time of the Temple and its cult. Thus, in the last chapter of the Tractate *Pesahim,* where among the questions asked by

---

[15]Sanhedrin 86a. There we read as follows: Any anonymous teaching in the Tosefta represents the opinion of R. Nehemiah; in the Sifra—it is the view of R. Judah, in the Sifre that of R. Simeon, and all of them accord with R. Akiba's reading.

the son one refers to the paschal-sacrifice, it would be foolish
to think that a Mishnah, composed after the destruction of the
Temple, would combine actual facts with obsolete ones. (This
argument is characteristic of Hoffmann. We meet it again in his
polemics against authors who assume that the Bible has been
written over a long run of time. Some of them claim that Leviticus was composed as late as the days of Ezra. Here he argues
very strongly and convincingly that all that is written in the
Torah regarding the Tent of Meeting (*Ohel Moed*) would sound
very strange if we were to follow the view of the critics. For, you
may agree that some episodes and laws are sometimes attributed to
the distant past, though they are the work of a much more recent
time; but that is understandable only if a decree applies to the
present circumstances but by no means if its practice is out of date!)

Hoffmann endeavors to disclose the traces of the First Mishnah in the Mishnah of Rabbi Judah, which in the Babylonian
Talmud is called *Matnitan*. According to the *Geonim* (heads of
the Academies, from the 6th to the 10th centuries, C. E.), Hillel
was the first to reduce and organize the overwhelming material
of the Oral Law that existed before him. The very fact of the
adoption of the six orders of the Mishnah may be considered
as the beginning of the final redaction.

The parts of the Mishnah concerned with *halakhic* problems
and facts which belong to the ceremonies of the Temple supply
the material for dating the text. Hoffmann's inquiries are very
subtle and exhaustive.[16] There is no doubt that the king mentioned here is Agrippa I. Rabbi Judah in Mishnah 6, does not
offer an additional remark, but engages in controversy with "our
rabbis." His version is a very old one, as shown in Mishnah in
Pesahim mentioned above. In this tractate (X6) we can recognize the early Mishnah, as we become aware that the Tannaim,
Rabbi Tarfon and Rabbi Akiba, though they belong to a relatively old generation, discuss the phrase: *"vehotem bigeulah*
(and he concludes with the blessing of redemption)"—an old
formula variously interpreted by these teachers. Hoffmann finds
traces of the First Mishnah in *Shekalim* V, and attributed

16We quote only one example, the Mishnah, *Bikurim* III, 2-6: "When
they reached the Temple mount, even King Agrippa would put the basket
(containing the offering of first fruits) on his shoulder."

this chapter to the time of Agrippa I. Here he establishes the fact that the Mishnah and the Tosefta were not fixed simultaneously. In a similar way, the description of the cult for the Day of Atonement in Yoma II, 3, III, 1, and IV, 3 is to be regarded as of early date and the comparison of this text with the Mishnah in Tamid I, 4; III, 1-2, indicates that they are well-nigh contemporaneous.

It is worthwhile to draw the attention to Hoffmann's important remarks on names and authors in the Mishnah. He confirms Rabbi Sherira's opinion that they are *Mishnayot* having the stamp of the academies of Hillel and Shammai (like Sanhedrin V, 2). The fact that Ben Zakkai is mentioned without his full name and without his title: *Rabbi* or *Rabban Yohanan ben Zakkai* is sufficient proof that this passage alludes to an early period of his life and was formulated then; for later, nobody would have dared to deprive the revered Sage of his high title. Only on the assumption that it remained as a token of the time before Rabbi Yohanan was given the appellation "Rabban" (our Teacher), does that omission make sense. Even with regard to one of the most outstanding rabbis, there was neither an obligation nor an inclination to change the name or title already adopted. Both content and form of the Mishnah were sacred and neither needed nor permitted revision. This faithfulness to a crystallized literary coining not only demonstrates the holiness of every spiritual creation in our nation in that early time (and for many generations) but affords scholars the opportunity to discover facts and classify historical processes and literary development that otherwise would have remained obscure.

I am not in a position to go step by step wtih Hoffmann in the light he throws on the Mishnah in its earliest stages. I want only to illustrate the problem we are faced with, by taking into consideration a special chapter Hoffmann wrote on critical research in the tractate *Abot*. He stresses some strange phenomena in the present text: (1) the gap of three generations between Hillel and Shammai, in Mishnah 15 and Rabban Gamliel in Mishnah 16; (2) it is strange that the son of Rabban Gamliel I in Mishnah 17 is called Shimeon without the title "Rabbi"; (3) after Rabban Gamliel III (Rabbi Judah ha-Nassi's son) again Hillel appears, and the question arises: Why were the quotations from Hillel divided and separated? (4) In the third chapter already there is neither a chronological nor a systematical order. (5) The fifth chapter does not show any continuity with the preceding one and hardly mentions an author. Hence it may be asked why it was integrated into a tractate which is supposed to be a specific memorial to the Fathers of the Mishnah.

The only answer to all these difficulties is that this tractate was subjected to many changes from the first generations or, to speak in the language of Hoffmann's perspective, from the times of the First Mishnah to a later period when the last redaction was made. Here the Tosefta of this tractate helps our understanding. There is another Tosefta, called *Abot de Rabbi Natan*. Hoffmann concludes that those texts which both Toseftas have in common and that are cited in the same style and order, represent the original and primary Mishnah.

It is fascinating to follow his bold, but well-established theory on the structure of Mishnah *Abot*. He distinguished three versions: *Abot* of Rabbi Akiba, *Abot* of Rabbi Meir, and *Abot* of Rabbi Judah the Prince. But what is much more important is the assumption that Rabbi Akiba was not the initiator of the collection but was preceded by a redactor who concluded quotations from previous generations with some from Shammai and particularly Hillel. This would explain the large number of Hillel's sayings, whereas Rabbi Akiba, in his edition, confined most of the other authors to three characteristic maxims. There existed an older tractate *Mile d'Abot* (Words of the Fathers) and Rabbi Judah, in finally moulding it, gave perceptive attention to the construction of the various parts.

The second part of the study is devoted to the controversies. It has often been said that polemics are characteristic of later times, whereas nothing like them is found in the early Mishnah. This is not true. Hoffmann emphasizes that perfect unanimous opinion, without controversy, is to be found only in the Midrash. As far as the Mishnah is concerned, he refers to the famous Tosefta, Sanhedrin VII, the somewhat differing parallels in Yerushalmi Sanhedrin I, 19c and Babli Sanh. 88b and compares them with Maimonides, *Hilkhot Mamrim* I, 4 and his introduction to the Mishnah. He shows that before Bet Shammai and Bet Hillel there were only four controversies, but, as early as the time of these schools, disputes became frequent. There were political reasons and causes which weakened the authority of the Sanhedrin and prevented it from taking decisions binding upon everybody. Forty years before the destruction of the Temple, which was the seat of the supreme court, marks the beginning of the deterioration of the full activity and authority of the Sanhedrin and the abolition of their power to try capital cases. This is exactly the time when disciples of Hillel and Shammai, "who had not attended their teachers sufficiently," increased in number and, therefore, multiplied "the controversies in Israel, so that two Torahs came into being."

Many other studies in the Mishnah were made by David Hoffmann, both preceding the small volume we dealt with and following it. He did not confine his investigations to the structural character of the process of shaping the works of the Oral Law. There is a great deal of research concerning lexicography, history (Antoninus and Rabbi Judah ha-Nassi), liturgy (*Amidah*), and other matters. All I can do in this context is to allude to his polymorphic work and to the multifaceted information he conveyed.

Nor can I dwell fully on the two Orders of the Mishnah (*Nezikim* and *Taharot*), translated and annotated by him, an immense effort and achievement. How Hoffmann approached and supplemented this gigantic task will be appreciated by a careful study of the Mishnah in the light of his commentary. After an examination of all the classical works (that of Maimonides, Obadya of Bertinoro, Tosefot Yom-Tob, Tiferet Israel), one will find in his notes on the Mishnah (exactly as in his commentary on the Pentateuch) a unique interpreter, full of knowledge and wisdom, who utilized everything said by the rabbis of old and was equipped richly wtih the best methods of modern science. The old and the new are combined and synthesized in that rich and exact commentary that will remain a glorious document both of his author's creative power and of his epoch.

B. Midrasii

It is difficult to decide in which branch David Hoffmann excelled most. The unity of his scientific work is really extraordinary. One can classify his books and essays according to the topics; the subjects are different, but there remains not only one author, but his authority is always the same, for he treats them all with the same dignity and his knowledge suffices to nourish all the territories of the research. Being master in the vast ocean of Torah and Talmud, possessed of all instruments of modern research and having the charisma of a fine brain, a wide and clear view and a constructive spirit, it is no wonder that he succeeded whenever and wherever he applied his talent to a problem.

His research in Midrash has been the most fruitful one of his academic endeavors. But let me repeat that his studies in Mishnah and in Midrash are interdependent; one is not conceivable without the other. So we are not surprised to find that some years after "The First Mishnah" his *Zur Einleitung in die halachischen Midrashim* (Introduction to the Halakhic Midrashim) was published, a second station on his scientific road.

I can deal only with some important points. Again we realize how Hoffmann judges the relations between Mishnah and Midrash (the Tannaitic and first of all the *halakhic* one). This branch of the Oral Law, in its fundamental structure, is older than the Mishnah. The Midrash interprets the verse of the Bible and remains connected with it, depends on it, and quotes it. The Mishnah is often remote from the Biblical source and is built on a systematic scheme. The strong ties between the written and oral Torah in its Midrashic form are evident and are stressed by the fact that the interpretation, the exegesis of the Midrash is derived by means of rules, e.g. of the *Middot* of Rabbi Ismael.

The Midrashic form of *Torah She-be-al-Peh* has led to a special literature, of which the *Mekhilta, Sifra* and *Sifre* are the outstanding examples. But Hoffmann shows that in the Talmud there is a plenty of Midrashic material, at times identical with the content of the collections known to us, and at others missing in the books which we know. Rabbinical literature in the Middle Ages cited passages that are not found in our Midrashim.

To clarify the structure of the Midrashim and the authorship of the various collections, Hoffmann, in a chapter of utmost importance, establishes the different attitudes, respectively, of Rabbi Akiba and Rabbi Ismael and their ways of interpretation; *K'lall u-p'rat* (interpretation based on a general proposition followed by the enumeration of particulars already comprehended in the general proposition) and *Ribbuy u-Miut* (amplification and narrowing qualification). Rabbi Akiba and his school were very fond of every chance given by the wording of the Torah for the purpose of broad exegesis (*"Kol hekhi de-ikka lemidrash darshinan"*), whereas Rabbi Ismael and his adherents limited the abundance of possibilities, saying: *"Orha de-kra le-ishtuye hakhi"* (It is the custom of the Torah to speak in this way)—without intending to suggest a definite meaning or conclusion. Rabbi Ismael preferred a simple explanation; Rabbi Akiba succeeded by a more profound and ingenious exegesis to fix *Halakhot* which, before his time, were mere traditions without roots in the text of the Bible.

Hoffmann realized very early how important was the famous letter of Rav Sherira Gaon (10th Century, C. E.) for the history of literary traditions. The development and evolution of Midrashic literature, especially the question of its final redaction, is less clear than that of the Mishnah. For example: the words *Tanna* (*a teacher*) *de be Rav* or, more usual, *Sifra* (the book) *de be Rav,* were explained in various ways. Many scholars assume that Rabbi Abba Arikha, the famous Amora of Sura, is meant by *'de be Rav.'* Hoffman rejects this opinion, preferring the view that "Rav" here is a general expression, a *nomen appellationis,* teacher, and that *be* means *Bet Midrash* (the school). He adopts the theory of Rav Sherira that Rabbi Hiyya was the redactor of the Sifra, yet does not exclude the possibility of later additions. Rabbi Hiyya was by no means the author of the *Sifra;* he only edited it.[17]

A careful study of the *halakhic* Midrashim shows how complicated their structure is. We are not only confronted with the famous controversies of Rabbi Akiba and Rabbi Ismael. The overwhelming weight of Rabbi Akiba, as the common source of Mishnah, Tosefta, Sifra and Sifre, has found its classical definition in the Talmud, where Rabbi Ismael is not mentioned. But the latter is the author of the *Mekhilta.* We know the difference

---

[17]But even conceding that *Sifra de be Rav* owes its final redaction to Rabbi Hiyya, Hoffmann sticks to his theory that this Midrash belongs to Rabbi Akiba and his school. It was Israel Lewy who affirmed that the great Amora, Rav, was the author of Sifra.

in methodology between Rabbi Akiba and Rabbi Ismael, of which the tension between *Ribbuy ve-Miut* and *K'lall u'P'rat* is characteristic. But we ought not to forget that in the long run other elements entered both Rabbi Akiba's and Rabbi Ismael's Midrashic collections, and there is no doubt that during the long periods of our history much material has been lost. On the other hand, much has been added and annexed and transferred from one source to the other.

Very important is another point stressed by Hoffmann. The school of Rabbi Akiba did not neglect the book of *Shemot,* nor did the school of Rabbi Ismael neglect the other books of the Pentateuch. There was a *Sifre* to *Shemot* and a *Mekhilta* to the other books. Hoffmann gives a very lucid and striking explanation of the whole situation. It was in Babylon that the academy of Rabbi Akiba attained highest authority and priority, whereas in Eretz Israel his primary significance was recognized only in connection with the Sifra (*Torat Cohanim*), but as regards the Biblical books, Rabbi Ismael was granted the same authority.

Another very remarkable result is the critical appreciation of the *Sifre.* It comprehends *Bamidbar* and *Debarim,* but it is evident that *Sifre,* as far as *Bamidbar* is concerned, belongs to the school of Rabbi Ismael, whereas the *Debarim* chapters resemble the style of *Vayikra.*

There are symptoms that facilitate the diagnosis to what kind of Midrash and to whom a specal passage may be attributed. The terminology of introduction gives a hint. Among others, the academy of Rabbi Ismael likes to use: "*shomea ani* (I understand)", instead of "*yakhol* (one might assume)"; and "*ha-din noten* (it is a legitimate conclusion *ad maius*)", instead of "*vehalo din hu* (Is not this an analogy especially from minor to major?)". We very often find "*eno tzarikh* (this reference to a Biblical verse is unnecessary)", a phrase in *Sifra.*

The *Mekhilta* of Rabbi Simeon ben Yohai, of the school of Rabbi Akiba, one of the favorite objects in Hoffmann's scholarly endeavors, which will be dealt with later, may be considered a *Sifra* to *Shemot.*

The fact that our *Sifre* to *Bamidbar* must be considered as belonging to the school of Rabbi Ismael, does not deny the existence of Midrashim, belonging to the fourth book of the Bible, which are of '*de be Rav*' origin, i.e., the product of the academy of Rabbi Akiba.

To complete this chapter, let me briefly refer to the lengthy investigation of Hoffmann (dealing with the *Mekhilta* of Rabbi Ismael) as to whether there existed exegetic material regarding *Vayikra* and *Debarim*. He quotes Maimonides ("Introduction to Mishnah") : "Rabbi Ismael expounded from the beginning of *Shemot* to the end of the Torah. That is called '*Mekhilta*'." Although we do not find a quotation of *Mekhilta* to *Vayikra* in the writings of Rambam and particularly in the *Sefer ha-Mitzvot,* where he brings Midrashic explanations in abundance. there existed, without doubt, such tradition, which is verified by Talmudical sources.

The small volume that contains these results based on Hoffmann's profound knowledge and analytical ability, is his first classical contribution to this branch of Jewish science (*Juedische Wissenschaft—Hokhmat Israel*). There are some other scholars who participated in this research work, especially Israel Lewy and M. Friedmann (*Meir Ish Shalom*). But it was Hoffmann who fostered these studies decisively and his part therein cannot be overestimated. He was an outstanding *lamdan*, devoted to studies on structural problems of the Oral Law in all its species, a scholar of painstaking, scrupulous care, gifted with a sense of subtlety. He never forgot or overlooked the literature of Middle Ages or of modern science. He enlightened several generations and suggested an approach which does not alienate traditional circles from the old and sacred *lumdanut* (Torah learning), but widens and broadens their outlook. There is no field of study where his results became so positive and generally accepted as in the research on the Midrashim.

Thereafter, for many years, Hoffmann kept studying this literature. His most important publications in this respect are the *Mekhilta de Rabbi Simeon ben Yohai to Shemot* (1905), the *Midrash Tannaim to Debarim* (1908, 1909), and the *Midrash Ha-Gadol to Shemot* (1913). He was greatly stimulated by the manuscript of the Midrash *Ha-Gadol* in the Berlin library from which he also extracted those parts which together formed the so-called *Midrash Tannaim*. The manuscript of *Midrash Ha-Gadol,* as the Midrash itself, is relatively young; it came from

Yemen and was written after Maimonides, whom it quotes. The title, *Midrash Tannaim,* is due to Hoffmann, who was convinced that the principal nucleus of it has Tannaitic origin. He discusses at length the question whether there existed a special collection or whether we are dealing with the work of a compilator of later times. Both the school of Rabbi Akiba and that of Rabbi Ismael are represented here and it is peculiar that at times parts of *Sifre* are missing and at others, the *Mekhilta of Rabbi Ismael.* The impression prevails that the author of *Midrash Ha-Gadol* did not have before him all that we possess of the works of either school and, on the other hand, he knew Midrashim unknown to us. At times his material differs from that in our texts and (what complicates the situation) he likes to restore Midrashic texts by the corresponding passages in Mishnah and Talmud, thus making harder a scientific evaluation of the earlier manuscript.

It is not difficult to realize that the *Leitmotif* of Hoffmann's studies as we know it from his first publication, has been preserved in this new book. Incidentally, it was a masterpiece of pedagogy to compare the material from the *Midrash Ha-Gadol* with *Sifre,* with *Mekhilta de Rabbi Ismael,* with that of Rabbi Simeon, the Talmudical parallels with Maimonides. It shows the great scholar in his self-critical righteousness, abandoning previous teaching and theses in recognition of the contribution of other authors, e.g., Prof. Solomon Schechter; it also manifests his great talent to explain concisely obscure or obsolete words, his explanation often leading to very interesting and far-reaching results. One example: *megillat harissim.* According to Hoffmann, who derives it from an Arabic root, the meaning of *harissim* is *"tsofim* or *shomrim* (observers or watchers)". He suggests that we have before us a literary reminiscence of Essenes and refers to Josephus (Bell. Jud. II, 85), where a religious rite is mentioned that reminds him of a Talmudic source: *"hitpallalti im dimdume hammah"* (I prayed in the morning and the evening, when the sun seems to stand still, i.e., at dawn and sunset) (Sabb. 118b).

It is noteworthy that all his annotations as well as all his prefaces are of utmost concentration. He does not omit anything of importance, but is never expansive. He consistently follows the rabbinic counsel to use *lashon katzerah* (brief speech) and so his books and articles are always *"miut ha-mahazik et hamerubbah"* (a little that contains much). In many respects he seems

to be a successor of our Sages of old who knew neither pride
nor vanity, but because of their greatness and piety became truly
humble men. Their spiritual effort eliminated all negative trends
which at times affect scholars and writers. Hoffmann never tried
to be brilliant—though he possessed even this faculty—but
only deepened his knowledge and fructified his moral qualities.
In his writing there is no sign of self-conceit. A man of profound
learning and wisdom, he offers the results of his indefatigable
efforts in the most unobtrusive way, in utter simplicity.

The *Midrash Ha-Gadol* became for David Hoffmann an unfailing source of information; he discovered a great deal in this
manuscript. He had published the *Mekhilta de Rabbi Simeon*
in 1905. It was his intention to achieve a reconstruction of this
old Midrash, well known to the *Rishonim* (scholars before 1500),
whereas the *Midrash Tannaim* is a construction of Hoffmann.

But he extended his efforts and edited the *Midrash Ha-Gadol*
to *Shemot*. So we become aware of multifold activity: editorial
work, accompanied by annotations, and an extractive-construc-
tive-reconstructive endeavor, built on deep understanding of, and
penetration into, the structure of our Midrashic literature. Israel
Lewy was the other investigator in the field of the *Mekhilta de
Rabbi Simeon,* whereas Solomon Schechter was his companion
in the research work on the *Midrash Ha-Gadol.* Much has been
done since those days (by Albeck, Ginsberg, Lieberman and Mar-
golis), but the pioneering merits of these three scholars are beyond dispute.

There are other publications by David Hoffmann concerning
Midrash research, e.g., *Ueber eine Mekhilta zu Deuteronomium*
and *Likkute Mekhilta* (Collections of Mekhilta material), both
in the Jubilee Volume Ezriel Hildesheimer (1890) and the *Likkute batar Likkute* (Further Collections) (1892); there is the
Midrash Shlosh Essreh Middot (Of the Thirteen Exegetical
Principles) in the Jubilee Volume dedicated to Abraham Berliner (1903).

Hoffmann wrote special articles in addition to his prefaces
and notes, to demonstrate the significance of these Midrashic
works, and to allot them their proper place in the totality of our
basic literature.

C. Biblical Exegesis

He gave to the study of the Written Torah no less than to that of the Oral Law. In previous times many scholars could devote their interest to everything. In our time, the study of every branch requires a great deal of additional knowledge. Particularly in exegetic work of the Bible, it does not suffice to know the commentators of earlier periods and the literature of the Talmudic epoch. Even the grammatical approach of the Spanish scholars does not provide the modern student with all that he needs.

Special dilemma of our century derives from Bible Criticism, an academic attempt commenced hundreds of years ago by Astruc and Spinoza and developed by modern scholars. Many rabbis of the liberal or Reform type submitted to it. Orthodox rabbis reacted, but not in a homogeneous way. Some did not take it into consideration at all and behaved as if it did not exist. Others studied its literature without achieving a clear point of view. They ignored the situation and kept on teaching as usual. A small group wrote new commentaries of homiletic or edifying character: they were pious men who did not fail to attract religious readers. Others, again, were successful because they knew how to adjust their philosophical erudition to the profound riches of the Bible that will give every generation an opportunity of raising new treasures. Well was it said: "*hafakh bah*" (Turn the Torah and turn it over again, for everything is in it) *Abot* V, 25.

But all that was no answer to the challenge of Biblical Criticism. Its results were destructive.

In other branches of research some scholars preceded Hoffmann. But he was the first Jew to devote his vast knowledge, his unique capacity, and the strong will to a scientific exegesis of the Torah on a traditional basis. To our days he has remained the only one. There are other men who contributed something to this effort. Rabbi Chaim Heller, the famous *Gaon,* opened a new path, exploiting the possibilities offered by the *Targumim.* The late Jacob Neubauer deserves laudable mention and may perhaps, be viewed, in a sense, as a successor of Hoffmann. Jacob Sperber, who died so young, did considerable work, especially in the books of the Prophets. B. Jacob and U. Cassuto inaugurated new aspects, utilizing the results of the history of religions and of archeology. But these two scholars, though conservative and rejecting destructive tendencies, did not share Hoffmann's unshakable conviction of the unity and authenticity of the Torah. He never abandoned full faith in the divine origin of our Torah. He has become the matchless commentator of traditional Judaism in modern times. There are others worthy of fame: Rabbi Z. Mecklenburg, author of *Ha-Ketab ve-Ha'Kabbalah,* Rabbi M. L. Malbim, celebrated for his great work, *Ha-Torah ve-HaMitzvah,* and especially Rabbi S. R. Hirsch. But Hoffmann worked in utterly different manner. His commentary was accorded the maximum of scientific character without any sacrifice of the old Jewish conception. One of the most eminent scholars of the last generation, Josef Halevy, in his review of Hoffmann's *Leviticus,* did not hesitate to say that "since Rashi, rabbinic Judaism has not produced a similar commentary."

When Hoffmann undertook his immense task, the apologetic motive was not primary. Certainly, he did cherish the chance to foster the old faith and to safeguard the integrity of the Bible. He did everything he could to strengthen the foundations of the religious doctrines. But his commentaries were not written only, or first of all, for an apologetic purpose. Exactly as Maimonides did not write his *Guide for the Perplexed* in defensive tendency, though he did not avoid the opportunity to confirm and to assert the traditional concept of Judaism, so was the deepest root of Hoffmann's exegetic work the ardent desire to write an adequate commentary based on the solid ground of all literary and scientific data at his disposal. It is really the old rabbinic way in the renewed shape that Hoffmann gave it. We may compare the progress and the new aspects of his exegetic work with that of Rabbi Abraham ibn Ezra, not because they resemble one another, but because of the courage manifested in their commentaries. The erudition of Hoffmann's work is characteristic of the *Geonim* (great authorities of old); his astonishing sovereignty in every aspect of the Torah (as wide as the earth, as deep as the sea) bear the stamp of *lamdanut.*

In his literary work Hoffmann reduced the homiletic approach to a minimum. His is not a popular book, written for the sake of satisfying sentiment. He aims to spread knowledge and exact understanding of the Torah. For this purpose the Torah *She-be-al-Peh* is exhaustively consulted. Nobody before Hoffmann used Midrashim, above all, the *halakhic* Midrashim, in so systematic a way. His masterly familiarity with them and especially his own contributions to their elucidation, enabled him to build his commentary on these bases. He took into consideration the *Targumim,* the renowned commentators of all times, especially those who stressed the *halakhic* aspect and those who did not neglect linguistic and grammatical problems.

It is a pity that the framework of an individual's lifetime did not suffice for finishing his immense program. We deplore most of all the fact that his *perush* (commentary) remained a torso. In full, we have only *Vayikra* and a considerable part of *Debarim;* the second part of the latter was published only after his death and it does not contain the last two *Sidrot: Haazinu* and *Vezot ha-Berakhah.* Anyone who knows the problems and difficulties involved in these chapters can imagine what a loss it means not to have their interpretation by Hoffmann. Perhaps even more do we miss his promised introduction to *Debarim.* An evaluation of this book and its position among the other books of the Pentateuch, by a man so well acquainted with the whole literature, both Jewish and Christian, both ancient and modern, and so qualified to compare and decide, would have become a turning point of Bible exegesis and of incomparable aid to the traditional doctrine.

No less do we miss the interpretation of the other books. In his eighties, Hoffmann prepared a full commentary of *Shemot*— I imagine for his lectures in the seminary. I once saw the manuscript in Israel (in the possession of one of his grandchildren). I suppose that manuscripts perhaps exist or existed, covering other books. They may have been written with a view to publishing them one day, but as *Bibelarssenschaft* (the science of the Bible) progressed very quickly, it was necessary, in the light of new results, to improve and change his commentary again and again. There was always lack of time and so it was not granted to Hoffmann to give us a final composition!

The same condition applies to *Bereshith* and *Bamidbar.* How rich and lucky would we have been had he succeeded in composing a complete commentary of the Torah! For many cen-

turies it would have been one of the highlights of exegesis and
in many respects an incomparable work.

A series of his papers, preparatory of the commentary to
Bereshith and *Shemot,* appeared between 1914 and 1921 in
Wohlgemuth's *Jeschurun.* In these articles, Hoffmann confines himself to the discussion of a large number of problems,
but does not offer a continuous interpretation.

No full analysis of Hoffmann's exegetic system can be given
here. Those who, even to a limited degree, know his *Leviticus*
and *Deuteronomium* will be happy to use these books for wise
treatment of every problem, however minute. To the interpreter,
there is "no thing too great or small." He who wants to study
this commentary and to understand the master's work will act
wisely if he reads these books again and again. They are most
weighty, because very concise and condensed.

Hoffmann never seduces his readers by eloquence. Even his
prefaces and introductions are written in very simple and lucid
manner. He stresses in both books his insistence on the authenticity of the Bible, on the unity of the Oral and Written Law and
on their interdependence.

I want to draw attention to the subtlety of his exegetic work.
How excellent is his architecture, e.g., of the book of *Debarim!*
He divides it into three chief parts followed by two appendixes.
The main segment consists of three *speeches:* the first one (I,
6-IV, 10) gives the historical background; the second one may
be called the speech on the Law (V, 1-XXVI, 19) ; the third
one the speech on the covenant (XXVII, 9-XXXI, 13).[18]

The scheme of Leviticus likewise is presented by Hoffmann
in brilliant fashion. He shows his great erudition in the discussion of the chapters dealing with the sacrifices, rejecting the
numerous controversial hypotheses pronounced by the "critics"
and coming to the conclusion—against their claims—that this

-----

[18]Rabbi Elijah of Vilna was aware of these implications when stating
that we may observe a repetition of the books *Shemot, Vayikra,* and
Bamidbar in *Debarim,* which in *Debarim* starts in with *Elleh* (These are)
corresponding to *Shemot;* with V, 1 corresponding to *Vayikra;* with XVII,
9 corresponding to *Bamidbar.* The appendixes are represented by the song
of Moses corresponding to the song of *Haazinu* (XXXI, 14-XXXII, 47)
and by the report on Moses' death preceded by his blessings (c. XXXII,
48-XXXIV, 12).

legislation is utterly consistent. He does not evade any difficulty, but dedicates profound investigation to the tensions between the Biblical text and the Midrashic and Talmudic interpretation. This problem has been actual ever since the days of Rabbi Saadia Gaon and even earlier. Philosophers deal with such complications more easily than philologists. Hoffmann declines to offer unsatisfactory answers and resorts to other literatures; especially such as legal character, like the Corpus Juris (codification of the Roman Law), where, too, there are discrepancies between the Digests, Institutions, and Codes, which call for interpretation to eradicate conflicts. Justinian (6th century codifier of the Roman Law) says that people will detect in his words a silent tendency to harmonize divergent trends if they study *"subtili animo"* (with a subtle mind). That is exactly our old approach and the meaning of the principle of Rabbi Ishmael's famous statement: *"Ve-khen shne Ketubim"* (When two passages are in contradiction to each other, the explanation can be determined only when a third text is found, capable of harmonizing the two).

Hoffmann refers to ancient oral traditions which precede the written law and are repeated in the valid *Halakhah.* Thus there is no clash between Deb. XXV, 3 *"Arbaim yakenu, lo yossif"* (Forty stripes he may give him, he shall not exceed) and the maximum of thirty-nine stipulated by the Mishnah. We have two examples which strengthen the traditional view and refute modern criticism. The same figure of thirty-nine we meet again in the law of *Shabbat*: "There are thirty-nine kinds of work prohibited on the *Shabbat.*" This is the parallel to our Mishnah, but not to a correspondent figure in the Torah. But it is not difficult to realize the close relation between both cases, the third example being a strong proof. The Bible itself brings both figures in close connection and there is no possibility of constructing a "conflict between the Oral and the Written Law" and "two different sources in the Biblical text." For *one* sentence (*Vayikra* XXII, 15-16): *"Sheva shabbatot temimot tihyena . . . tisperu hamishim yom"* (Seven weeks shall there be complete . . . and ye shall number fifty days), illustrates in an excellent way that it is not fair to speak always of divergence.

According to his conception—and it is a traditional one—the Biblical law of *malkot* (stripes) contains a reference to an older oral one and the phrase *"Im bin hakot ha-rasha"* (If the wicked man deserves to be beaten), confirms it. This is a general principle and in the many passages that are "short and hidden" we are allowed to recognize the hint in those phrases. Thus many questions are solved.

Our Sages often base a *Halakhah* on a passage in the Bible and their method seems to be arbitrary and occasionally to oppose or contradict the wording of the text. But the *Halakhah* in such cases is not the product of the text in the Bible. The rabbis were good teachers, always interested in an effort to fit a law into a Biblical verse, and therefore they were in search of an *asmakhta* (intimation, textual support). Hence they would choose a phrase that had some resemblance, or stimulated an association, or permitted an assonance.[19] It is for mnemotechnical or pedagogic reasons that they anchored a statement of oral law in a text. There is no basis for the argument that a gap often exists between the Bible and the tradition. Is is begging the question to maintain a negative attitude towards the traditional conception.

A telling illustration of his workmanship is offered in a famous example: *"Lo tevashel geddi behalev immo"* (Thou shalt not seethe the kid in its mother's milk). He shows how the three-fold repetition of this verse in the Torah *echoes* the statement of the tradition in its three-fold verdict: *"Issur bishul, issur akhilah, issur hanaah"* (the prohibition to seethe meat in milk; to eat meat and milk; to use meat in milk). The prohibitions are not derived from the text; it is the text which reflects an existing *Halakhah le-Moshe Mi-Sinai* (Sinaitic tradition); that is why the Torah repeated the prohibition three times.

To characterize Hoffmann's classical method of exegesis, combining both ancient and modern assets, I quote a passage from his book on *Debarim* (I, 10-11 and 12). In verse 10, Moses, in his retrospective report, says: *"Hashem hirba etkhem"* (the Lord, your God, hath multiplied you and, behold, ye are this day as the stars of heaven for multitude). In verse 12 he complains: *"Ekha essa levadi"* (How can I myself alone bear your cumbrance, and your burden and your strife?), a consequence of the increase of the people. Now because of this complaint, we have the interpolation—the benediction of Moses: *"Hashem Eloke Avokekhem . . ."* (The Lord, the God of your fathers, make

---

[19]See Israel Frankel, PESHAT, Toronto, 1956—Editor.

*you a thousand times so many more as you are and bless you
as He hath promised you).* But for this intermediate verse,
the audience and later on the reader might have thought that
the great leader regretted that his nation had grown and caused
him so much pain and burden. So he blesses them in order to
stress that the increase remains a positive fact and shall continue.

Here is a token of penetrating interpretation, without any
deviation from, or violation of, the text. But the master's additional remark reveals his genius. "For," says he, "this verse 11,
interrupting the course of action, excludes the possibility of another author, such as the Critics of the Torah postulated. These
can be attributed only to Moses, the devoted father of his people,
the *'raya mehemna'* (faithful shepherd). An author in a later
period, who would have assumed the role of Moses and spoken
in his name, is unlikely to have interrupted his speech. This can
be understood only out of the actual and real situation of an
address delivered under these specific conditions of a unique leader
who bids farewell to his flock and summarizes everything: the
legislation, the events, and his exhortations!"

There are countless precious instructions in Hoffmann's great
commentary, which secured him a place of honor in the history
of exegesis. Among the most important chapters are the following: *Vayikra,* XVIII and XIX, dealing with *Kedushah* (holiness); *Debarim* XVII-XIX, expounding legislation concerning
the king, the places of asylum, Sanhedrin, and the witnesses in
court. In these vital issues, he displays extraordinary skill and
wisdom.

Wherever there is a chance, the commentary leaves the narrow
framework of one verse and proceeds towards a larger scope.
Thus one finds prefaces embracing the problem as a whole. Because of his sovereignty in the realm of all our literature, Hoffmann knows how to clarify a matter of very complex character.
He compares texts in all books of the Bible. How important the
Book of Ezekiel has become in this respect! We realize how far-
reaching is the coincidence of this prophetic work with *Vayikra*
and *Debarim.*[20]

---

[20]Hoffmann, for argument's sake, accepts the hypothesis of Biblical
Criticism and compares the *Sefer Kedushah* (Book of Holiness), the second
part of *Vayikra,* with the first one, the fundamental part of the Priestly

Though he refutes everywhere the attacks of the Critics, he does not neglect other exegetic tasks. He not only forges weapons against destructive tendencies. He interprets Scripture. He translates and explains every verse and term, so that nothing stays unclarified. He overlooks no difficulties in text, vocabulary, or grammar; some arising from chronological data, others from problems of facts presented. But the major problem, engaging his constant attention, was that of understanding the Oral Law in combination with the written one. Chapter XXIII of *Vayikra*, dealing with the holidays and containing one hundred and twenty pages, may serve as an example. Among many others, it is the controversy concerning the date of the "Waving of the *Omer*" (ib. v. 11), and of Pentecost (*Shabuot*) which gives the Master much concern. He mentions every dissenting opinion, from that of the first century's Boethusians to those of the Karaites, and of all authors of Biblical Criticism. Against them, in the broadest manner, he presents the traditional point of view, rejecting all arguments maintained against it, strengthening it by conquering all doubt and explaining every difficulty in the text. That chapter is a document of spiritual and intellectual power. There is no parallel in Biblical literature to this penetrating inquiry.

Where there is no need for expansion, Hoffmann's remarks arc brief. IIis method is always adapted to the object. Fundamental questions require exhaustive treatment. In the case of the Omer, he mobilizes all his amazing learning in order to solve a problem and one item becomes so important that one becomes aware of a disproportion—though only a formal one—in the composition of the whole book. The student is rewarded by the thorough discussion of a weighty problem. The lack of proportion

---

Code, then the latter with Ezekiel, and at times *Debarim, Shemot* and Jeremiah, with Ezekiel. Comparisons are arranged between other Biblical books, too. In larger measure, this method is introduced in the *Wichtigste Instanzen gegen die Graf Wellhausensche Hypothese (The Most Important Judgments against the Graf-Wellhausen Theory)* (of Biblical Criticism), with the impressive proof that it is uttcrly wrong to place the priestly code in the time of Ezra or even later; that the interrelations and interdependence of the first and second part of *Vayikra* are manifest; that one cannot separate the Torah according to the ideas of the critics without hopeless corffusion and self-contradiction. Doctor Hoffmann fought a very energetic battle against his adversaries, particularly as to their unwillingness to take into consideration the important role of Ezekiel for the final decision of the unity and very early origin of the Pentateuch.

is due to the exegetic character of the matter, not to the author. It is a source of high enjoyment and profit to realize how the cautious, modest Hoffmann in this instance forgets his usual way and becomes, almost unwittingly, a gripping writer.

Here one becomes aware of all his special capacities. He is master of every line in the Bible. In all early translations (from Septuaginta to Targum Jerushalmi, Targum Onkelos, Peshitta, and Vulgate) he is well versed. This implies, besides other attainments, considerable linguistic knowledge. In all Midrashic literature he is one of the fathers of research and evaluation. His mastery of Mishnah and Talmud is generally taken for granted. But all this is only the basis of his exegetic work. He studied and knew the vast territory of commentaries to the Bible, from the Middle Ages to modern times: Rashi and Rashbam, Ibn Ezra and Ramban, Abravanel no less than the *Biur* of Mendelssohn and his school, Mecklenburg, Malbim and S. R. Hirsch. The books of Christian commentators, too, were open to him and particularly the efforts of modern scholars, with their critical and hypercritical trend. His absorptive capacity seems supernatural, yet was only part of his creative power. No less overwhelming is his masterly combination of every fruitful result, his circumspection, his prudence, and his abiding originality. He never yields to the authority of a scholar, no matter how famous, remaining always—not obstinate and stubborn—but firm and unshakable. Last but not least, he never surrenders to a dull eclecticism which so often traps men of vast knowledge. Hoffmann's greatness in Biblical exegesis reveals itself in this: that the attention he gave to great problems he granted also to those that seem unessential. It is the main feature of true exegesis that it views nothing as without importance!

His commentaries represent fifty years of effort. Even a giant like him was forced by the magnitude of the task to work very hard. There were also other obligations which did not permit him to devote himself exclusively to Biblical exegesis. Hence he was unable to write a commentary to the whole Bible. But what remained undone notwithstanding, every honest man must bow his head in humble reverence before a man of Hoffmann's stature. His service to our venerable faith is unparalleled and cannot be overestimated. But no less important is his contribution to research work of the Torah. Many of his arguments and discoveries will remain the lasting assets of true scholars.

His *Leviticus* and *Deuteronomium* and many preliminary studies in the Bible may be considered the unsurpassed standard works of his life. The last century has produced a very small group of men who may be compared with him—S. O. Rappaport, Meir Ish Shalom, I. H. Weiss, Israel Lewy and F. Is. Duenner— but even among them he occupies a special place of honor. None of them was so courageous and capable as to take upon himself the additional burden of Biblical exegesis along the lines of old *lamdanut* combined wtih modern science, and with a view to preserving and fostering both the Jewish tradition and the pulse of religious life.

Hoffmann was always very modest, eschewing talk. He behaved according to the motto of Bacon of Verulam: *"De nobis ipsis silemus"* (About ourselves we are silent). That is why he never referred to his emotions or to the *motifs* of his work. But I would fain interpret his inner tendencies. Master of Talmud and Midrash, one of the ablest and noblest products of the Hungarian *yeshivot* and the old way of Jewish scholarly attitude, it was neither by his teachers, nor even by the scientifically well-equipped Rabbi Ezriel Hildesheimer that he was trained to become an outstanding authority on the Hebrew Bible. That was his own merit and achievement. What immense effort it must have spelled for a man whose world and whose foundations were essentially Talmudic to become so thoroughly master of the Written Law; to acquire such knowledge and skill as made him the author of books and essays of highest academic level!

The psychological process that led him to this enterprise must have been very exciting and revolutionary. He may be assumed to have perceived that all endeavors of traditional Judaism to fortify its position were condemned to failure so long as only the Talmud and rabbinical literature are considered as fundamental, for both religious practice and study. If there is no regard for the Bible as the eternal source of religious impulse and learned effort, if there is no possibility of deepening the relations between the Written and Oral Law and of making a successful attempt, even in observant and pious circles, to apply scientific methods

to the study of the Bible, a dangerous gap will result! The unity
of the Torah was at stake.

Thus a disciple of the *yeshivah,* in whose soul Talmudism
never ceased to be a mighty factor, became a pioneer of Biblical
studies, unique and without a successor of high standing! And
this, too, should be stressed: his studies in the field of Mishnah
seem to prepare his commentaries to *Vayikra* and *Debarim.* Although the former are important in themselves, Hoffmann only
alludes to the connection between them.

It is amazing how he succeeded in building his great projects
in both fields. The transition from preoccupation with Talmudic
and Midrashic problems to research work of Biblical character
is very difficult and presupposes a very broad-minded scholar who
is able to go back to the Bible in an attitude unaffected by Talmudic ways of thinking. I want not to be misunderstood. Far
be it from me to deprecate the study of the Talmud and its very
high value and significance. But the two ways of thinking differ
greatly. Hoffmann approaches the study of the Torah unprejudiced, as though he had not been, for long years, devoted
to Talmudic investigation. To be sure, he does stay occupied
with the relation of the Bible to post-Biblical literature, and the
harvest of his work is very rich. But he succeeded in giving
much attention to the text of the Pentateuch as an "independent"
book—on its own merits, and in discussions with scholars, both
Jewish and Gentile, he did his utmost to convince his adversaries
without resorting to the interpretations and deductions borrowed
from Talmudic literature, but out of argumentation that the text
of the Bible itself suggests. It is true he did find in the books
on the Oral Law much confirmation of Biblical statements and
he crowned his work by emphasizing the true coherence between
both sectors. But his devotion to the written Torah remains remarkable. It moves all who follow his path and know how
imperative was his attachment to post-Biblical literature!

It was not only a matter of ability. The return to the oldest
documents fits a master of *Juedische Wissenschaft* (the science
of Judaism) and of universal understanding. It is always the
earliest and basic stratum that requires the most minute consideration. Jeremiah's words, *"Is not my word like as fire, saith
the Lord, and like a hammer that breaketh the rock in pieces"*

have remained ever true. The attacks of the Critics have enabled
a scholar of Hoffmann's standing to deepen the understanding
of the Bible!

Among his many great merits, that of having restored the
full dignity of Bible-study in Torah-true circles is not the least.
It would be wrong to believe that only apologetic motives led
to these efforts. They were inspired by his love of the Torah.

Hoffmann seemed to have had a presentiment of what is perceptible today, and particularly in Israel: that the vitality of
the *Tanakh* (the Hebrew Bible) is extraordinary. In anticipation of this new epoch he worked during many years and gave
the young Torah-true generation a chance to withstand the attacks against the Sacred Books, fortified by knowledge that would
enable them to enjoy them, all scientific problems notwithstanding.

D. RESPONSA

At all times, there were only very few great scholars, at home
and fruitful in both theoretical and practical *Halakhah*. In our
century there is nobody like David Hoffmann, who deepened the
study of the structure and history of Mishnah and Midrash and
excelled also in the field of responsa literature.

He reached a very high level of mastery of the Talmud and
the great codices, not only in literary attainment and research,
but also in using their importance for all aspects of the religious
life. His knowledge was not restricted to a multitude of data, nor
based only on an excellent memory. It was rather an amazingly
wide and deep comprehension of the ocean of the Talmud and
the literature based thereon. Fortunately, his childhood and youth
were spent almost exclusively on this study. In his hunger for
knowledge and passion for Torah he did not neglect anything,
but stayed profoundly interested in the vast territory of responsa
no less than in the standard codes, commentaries and novellae.

Ability is only one condition of perfection. In rabbinic studies
and circles, too, mental capacity precedes any effort. But not less
decisive is the moral qualification. In ancient times, when piety
and humility were guiding factors, it was not astonishing to observe flourishing study in the realm of responsa of practical
Halakhah. But in our modern world matters have changed so

much that we are greatly impressed on meeting men who are at home in the traditional sources and methods.

It is due to Hoffmann's unparalleled religious and ethical standards that his general erudition did not weaken his attachment to religious practice established by the Law and kept valid and fresh by both minute analysis of special cases and scrupulous casuistic discussions. He is almost unique in his equilibrium between the dual approaches without preference to either of them and without neglecting anything. That made him so precious to those who looked at Hildesheimer's Seminary with highest appreciation. There is no contradiction between Hoffmann, the conserver of the rabbinical tradition, and Hoffmann, the master of scientific studies. The unity of his personality is natural, consistent, unchanging. He was really great in all respects. It is a token of the essential importance and relevance of the Berlin School that it became the framework and climate for his development and astonishing opus. There is no other *Bet Midrash* that produced such miracle. He gave of his glory to his institution.

What follows is but a concise evaluation of Hoffmann as *possek* (decisor).

He laid down his decisions in a work containing three volumes that include also some novellae. The book bears the title *"Melammed Le-hoil"* (Teacher for Benefit). The title suggests the author's purpose: to be helpful to those who turned to him.

Hoffmann wrote most of his responsa not in order to solve problems removed from reality, nor to deal with synthetic questions which are sometimes made up by scholars for theoretical reasons. As the recognized religious leader, the teacher of many rabbis, and well-nigh the arbiter of German Jewry, he very often was approached for a decision in acute matters; most of the *She-elot* (questions) were urgent and that would not brook protracted consideration. He was compelled to trust his rich knowledge, his vast memory and his amazing sense of discernment. His interrogators were not all "great scholars, whose questions were half an answer," as our Sages put it. He had to adjust his *"Teshuvot"* (Responsa) to the capacity of those who believed in him but were not able to follow the exuberant animadversions of his tremendous erudition.

Despite all those complications, his responsa are not casual nor abrupt. The serious student will find many important references and valuable discussions. Hoffmann dispatched his decisions without any intention of publishing them as they were written. He thought of making them eventually available to the public, but not without a careful revision of the text. Unfortunately, his many imperative tasks prevented him from doing so. His responsa appeared only after his death, incomplete and unrevised by him. With the exception of a small part, the edition of which was supervised and briefly annotated by Rabbi A. E. Kaplan, who because of his untimely death could not continue this work, they were published as found. It is most regrettable that one volume of the copies was lost during the *Shivah* (the week of mourning). This volume was reported to have contained very important and courageous decisions towards the solutions of most pressing problems.

Thus, in this aspect of his work, for causes as tragic as unavoidable, perfection was not achieved. Hoffmann was very well acquainted with rabbinical parlance. But since his responsa were written hastily, connoisseurs of pure Hebrew occasionally demur. The same applies to the structure and composition of some responsa. They reveal the hurry in which they were written. Some may complain of too much attention given to *aharonim* (more recent authorities) and especially to such of Hungarian origin.

But all this does not touch the importance of his role in this branch. For this work, too, done almost *en passant,* remains a monument of rabbinical authority and capacity. Hoffmann's *Teshuvot* were manifold, numerous and influential and the spectrum of his decisions was very broad. His merits are exceedingly great.

He deals with many questions that belong to the four sections of the *Shulhan Arukh.* Reading *Melammed Le-hoil,* one is impressed by a scholar who, though not born in western Europe, handled with remarkable competence matters specific to Jews in Germany and neighboring countries; though he never forgot, neglected or underestimated classical problems of practical *Halakhah* dealt with in centers of Jewish life elsewhere. He reveals his qualities in answering questions connected with modern technique, food industry, astronomy, or the calendar, as far as they belong to the realm of religious practice.

Some of his responsa will remain of basic importance for an understanding of his time. A very long one deals with problems of the *Orgel* (the organ), so passionately discussed in the past. Questions of highest significance are included here, such as *hukkat ha-goyyim* (imitation in Jewish life of non-Jewish religious attitudes, customs or rituals) and the meaning of *abodah zarah* (idolatry). He takes into consideration all that was uttered in this connection and adds his own point of view. Without exaggeration or fanaticism, he takes a firm stand, his conclusions know no compromise. His modesty makes him consult some of his great colleagues in Germany, to learn whether or not they consent. In his arguments concerning the problems of the organ, he stresses the element of the imitation, not only of Gentiles, but also of Jews who left the ways of their fathers. He also dwells on historical data, e.g., musical instruments in the Temple, and the organ in one of the synagogues of Prague, thus combining events and facts with deductions of theoretical character.

The organ had become in Europe one of the decisive symptoms of Reform, hence Orthodoxy's spirited rejection of this innovation. The Rabbinical School of Hildesheimer imposed upon its pupils a holy duty to decline a call to such deviating congregation or synagogue and cancelled the *Semikhah* (rabbinic diploma or authorization) originally granted to a rabbi who now violated the tenets of Torah-true Judaism. Hoffmann did not apply this rigorous standpoint to every change in the religious life. He restricted it only to destructive measures endangering the foundations of the Jewish tradition, such as the abolition of Messianic belief, the introduction of an organ, and the participation of women in synagogual choir. A rabbi who asked him how to behave in case of minor matters—whether to abandon his office or not—received his decision not to quit and leave his post to a successor who may keep on reforming and changing the time-hallowed laws of the the synagogue.

In this responsum, Hoffmann proves not only his *bekiut* (wide knowledge of the whole relevant literature), but also his great sense of responsibility. He knows that his decision will be accepted both by his numerous disciples, the rabbis in many communities, and also by his colleagues, men of high standing in matters of the Law. As subsitute of Rabbi Ezriel Hildesheimer, who then was still alive (old and tired and heartily approving of Hoffmann's responsum), he had become the undisputed leader of Torah-true Jewry. He knew that the structure of religious life in the traditional *Kehillot* would depend on him and so he weighed his words carefully, realizing that a restrictive *psak* (*humra*) must be well founded and removed from thoughtlessness and fanaticism. This is the classical type of a teacher of Jewish Law (*moreh hora'ah*).

Let us turn to two responsa of highest interest which help characterize the master. This fifty-first paragraph of the third part of *Melamed Le-hoil* contains his answer to a question of great actuality:

"Is it possible to arrange that all *Kiddushin* (marriages) be made on condition that if the husband dies without any child so that his wife becomes dependent on the brother-in-law (to marry or reject her), the marriage become retroactively invalid?"

After an exhaustive discussion, at the close of his reply, Hoffmann makes this statement:

"This is the end result: If the great rabbis of our time will join to issue an ordinance to the effect that if one desires to arrange a marriage on condition that if the husband should die without surviving issue (*zera kayyam*) and his brother will not, within one year, grant *halitzah* (lit.: "the taking off of his shoe," symbolically freeing her for marriage to an outsider) and the local *Rov* or another *Rov* testify in writing to his wife to the effect that he was unable, up to this date, to persuade the brother-in-law to grant the *halitzah*, that then the marriage shall be cancelled. (This condition to be made in accord with the decision of the Hatam Sofer [R. Moses Sofer] in chapter CXI of his Responsa, with some modifications as necessitated by contemporary situations.) Then, thanks to these great rabbis and to their power—for being considerate to the daughters of Israel! Thereby they will also strengthen and preserve the *mitzvah* of *halitzah*. For no brother-in-law will refuse to perform it, knowing that he could not force his sister-in-law to pay him money; for, if he were to refuse her, she would be free to marry without any *halitzah*. It would be *he* who canceled retroactively his dead brother's marriage. The guilt would be on his head, his brother and all of us being without guilt. And although we have not thereby removed all the scruples I mentioned in the second paragraph of this responsum, it is still better to be considerate about settling the problems of the daughters of

Israel. Compare Resp. XXX in *Or Ne-elam* and my own brief to the French rabbis, in which I decided that under no circumstances may *all* marriages be made conditional and that only rarely is it permitted to arrange for one to be so."

It would be most attractive to comment at length on this responsum, the attention given by him both to *Halakhah* (always imperative to him and never misunderstood nor misinterpreted), to the claims of life and to values as high as the welfare of the Jewish women (*takanot b'not Israel*). He who has the right approach to this problem and is deeply rooted in *Halakhah* will seek and find solutions never detected by men whose knowledge is defective or whose humanitarian qualities are not fully developed. It is of utmost importance to stay aware of the wisdom which reveals itself equally in his care for the daughters of Israel and in safeguarding the behests of *Halakhah*.

A different discussion is involved in another question that has no practical significance today but concerns our understanding of matters which cause astonishment at, resistance to, and defiance of our Law. A request was addressed to David Hoffmann: Would he please offer a rational explanation of the laws governing the case of *"edim zomemim* (the plotting witnesses)."[21]

Here is an exact quotation of the first part of his extended reply:

"The law concerning witnesses plotting (perjury) seems strange to us for two reasons:

"(1) Why are they punished only if other witnesses prove their perjury (as to time and place concerning which the plotters had testified) by asserting: 'You were with us' (at that time in a different place, and hence could not have observed the deed concerning which you testified)? Why are the plotting witnesses not punished, if those refuting them say 'the person killed or the killer was with us?'

---

[21]Deb. XIX, 16-19: *If an unrighteous witness rise up against any man to bear perverted witness against him . . . and the judges shall inquire diligently, and, behold, if the witness be a false witness, and hath testified falsely against his brother; then shall ye do unto him as he had purposed to do unto his brother; and thou shalt put away the evil from the midst of thee."*
Rashi comments: "As he had purposed (to do), but not as he (actually) did, hence they (our Sages) said: 'If they put him (the defendant) to death, the first witnesses are not put to death'" (Mak. 5a) Further: Wherever the text reads "a witness, the Torah speaks of two."

"(2) Why are the plotting witnesses subject to capital punishment only if the accused had not yet been executed, but not if he had already suffered the supreme punishment?

"Both ancient and modern sages have warned us to find a motivation (for the law) which will commend itself to our intellect. Let me, therefore, too, offer my bit:

"It is well known that there is almost no man on earth who has not both friends and enemies, and if two witnesses testify that e.g. Reuben had killed a person, and afterwards, two others come to refute them by testifying that the killer or the person killed 'was with us' in a different place, then we do not know which set of witnesses has told the truth and which has lied. For it is possible that the first set testified falsely because of their hatred for Reuben and it is also possible that the first two told the truth and the second two lied because of their friendship for Reuben and their effort to save him from execution. Since there is equal (even balanced) doubt, one may not punish either Reuben or the witnesses.

"However, if the second set of witnesses are not at all endeavoring to save Reuben, for they offer no testimony at all about either the killer or the killed, but say to the first witnesses: 'You were with us,' then it seems reasonable to assume that the second two witnesses tell the truth. For why would they lie? If it were due to their friendship for Reuben, it is quite possible that by refuting the first witnesses they may not save Reuben at all. For, if it be true that he killed (the person involved), it is possible that other witnesses will come to testify to that effect (with the result that) he, as well as the first witnesses, will be executed.

"And if the witnesses refuting (the first perjuring set) were anxious to save Reuben, would it not have been better (for their purpose) to say that Reuben or the victim had been with them, for then, even if one hundred witnesses came, they could not make Reuben (be convicted as) guilty, for 'two witnesses (until refuted) are as valid as one hundred.' Therefore, we must surely assume that since they did testify thus, it is evident that their thought (intention) is not at all to save Reuben, hence they are not (to be presumed to be) friends of Reuben. Why then should they lie? Of necessity, therefore, the (second set) later witnesses are telling the truth.

"But perchance (you may argue) the refuting witnesses are lying because of their enmity for the (first set of) witnesses. This is wrong for the following reasons:

"First, for even if it be clear that every man has enemies, yet it rarely happens that the enemies of the one (witness) are also the enemies of the second (of the first set). Then also, if the refuting witnesses lie and refute because of their hatred for the first set, why do they need the folly of such refutation? By such refuting testimony they commit two wicked deeds: they declare a wicked man innocent and an innocent man wicked. They could (instead) come and testify that the witnesses desecrated the Sabbath or slew a person, then they would commit only *one* wrong. And since there appears no logical motive, why should the refuting witnesses lie? Hence we may assume that they are telling the truth, and therefore the refuting witnesses are believed and the refuted ones punished.

"That, however, is right only as long as Reuben, the defendant, is alive. But if he had been executed already, on the testimony of the (first) witnesses, and the refuting witnesses came afterwards, then one may say: Still, the refuting witnesses lie because they are friends of Reuben. And if that seems contradictory because (as his friends) they should have saved Reuben by refuting (the first set), one may argue: 'Perhaps they did not know of the matter until after he had been executed and they may have said: "Since we were unable to save our friend, let us (at least) have our revenge on the witnesses who brought about his death." Thus all witnesses in cases of capital punishment will live all their days in fear of friends of the defendant who might want to avenge his death on them, and (as a result) no man will want to testify because of fear for his own life.'

"That is why the Torah said: 'If they (the judges) have already had him executed, the perjuring witnesses are not to be slain.'

"Thus no man will be afraid to testify, for even if the defendant had wicked friends who might offer perjured testimony on his behalf (for his benefit) they would surely endeavor first to save their friend and refute them, and their testimony will not harm them."

I have quoted the first part of this long responsum so that the reader himself might recognize the depth of Hoffmann's conception, his psychological insight and his convincing mental power. It it also worthwhile to pay attention to his style. His explanation is too lucid for any additional remark. The whole paragraph demonstrates his unusual ability and his productive and constructive way of thinking.

In the field of *Hilkhot Gittin* (the Laws of Divorce) he has contributed very greatly to religious practice. He took into consideration the classics of *Halakhah,* as well as of later authorities, the German school of the last century and his teachers in Hungary.[22]

Since the days of *Gaon* Rabbi Jacob Ettlinger,[23] whose authority was deeply respected in the whole rabbinical world, there was, outside Russia and Galicia, no *possek* (decisor) and *meshiv* (author of responsa) like Hoffmann. As a matter of fact, the former's way of study and decision influenced the latter. Both extended their activity to almost every branch of Jewish Law, without giving preference to one of the four *Turim* (Orders of the *Shulhan Arukh*). Both enjoyed the confidence of wide circles. Hoffmann was the most overworked one of all the rabbis. Many rabbis, though able and entitled to issue decisions, did not choose to enrich the literature of responsa and to promote the practical religious life according to the time-hallowed rule of our old sources. It was the great scholar in the theoretical field who took upon himself the heavy task of day-by-day problems and gave the exciting example of an *ish ha-eshkolot* (a man of universal knowledge) who did not disdain any burden and who acquitted himself of day-by-day duties with the devotion he gave to scientific efforts. This is an additional trait of his greatness—ascribed in our history to the Sages of old, who, in their dedication, did not discern between "major and minor" things.

---

[22]There are most precious notes on *P'sik Resheh* (a dialectical term for the unavoidable consequence of an act—Sabb. 75a) and definitions of *"Lo tahmod* and *Lo Tit'aveh* (*"Thou shalt not covet"* in Shem. XX, 17 and Debarim V, 18) respectively, which I commend to the study of anyone who wants to get acquainted with Hoffmann's way of research, to understand the complicated world of our Torah, and to listen to a *Gaon's* attempt at solution.

[23]See p. 229 in this book.

E. Apologetic Work

Hoffmann, because of his theoretical studies, will occupy a place of honor for all posterity. But he was far from being indifferent to the problems of his time and to the sorrows of traditional Jewry. He was really the father of his coreligionists, the guide, magister, and arbiter of his time. All this he became not because of his ambition or love of authority. On the contrary, this role was imposed on him and he hesitated, like the elect of any period; even as the true prophet, in the very beginning of his career, would rather not assume his mission.

But notwithstanding his modesty and in spite of his inclination to dwell in the tent of Torah in splendid isolation, his profound sense of responsibility made him accept the yoke. He served his brethren with all his mental and moral greatness whenever his intervention was required, and especially also in defense of his faith or people. Throughout the ages, both have been despised and attacked. These assaults never ceased, only the methods and the arguments changed. Emancipation and assimilation did not bring a remedy; aversion and enmity even increased. The manifold aggressions of anti-Semites had to be resisted. Let us leave aside, for the present, the question as to whether these efforts were vital and successful or whether other ways of Jewish activity would not have brought more honor and respect. A full Jewish life of Torah and creative national consciousness might have been more persuasive and productive. Jews and Gentiles would have profited from such an unbroken, full-hearted, Jewishness. But the spirit of the time stressed "confessionalism" and almost all features of specific national character and Jewish originality were submerged or driven out. Instead of tracing the comprehensiveness and universality of Judaism within its own borders, spokesmen were eager to divest it of all its own assets and to "reconstruct" its skeleton in accord with a fashionable, flabby universalism. But disintegration has never helped any religion or any other historic phenomenon.

What inspired Hoffmann was the eternal Torah and the eternal Jewish people. But he participated in the tasks of his generation and his contributions were excellent. His book, *Der Schulchan Aruch und die Rabbinen ueber des Verhaeltnis der Juden zu An-*

dersglaeubigen (The *Shulhan Arukh* and the Views of the Rabbis about the Relation of Jews to Adherents of Other Creeds) was at first published as a series of twenty-seven articles in the *Juedische Presse* (1884), a weekly edited by Hirsch Hildesheimer in Berlin. In 1885 it appeared in book form, a second edition, revised and enlarged, in 1894. The attacks directed against the famous code by Gentiles and by Jewish apostates had reached a new climax when Dr. Justus, with the aid of a convert, A. Brimann, wrote his *Judenspiegel* and Dr. Ecker submitted an expertise to the court, supporting that libelous pamphlet. For a new trial, one year later, a new expert, Prof. Gildemeister, was invited by the court.

Hoffmann, in his refutation, succeeded in rebuking calumnies, removing mistakes and clarifying misunderstandings. He explains that decisions, laws and customs which may appear strange to us, are quite natural in the light of time and conditions that once prevailed. At times, they are only a reaction to the attitude of Gentiles towards Jews. The relation of Jews to Gentiles will be different when heathen, Christians or Moslems, respectively, are concerned. It is not our fault that in rabbinical literature the term *nokhri* (alien) often applies to all Gentiles. The Church's censorship is guilty of many misinterpretations through the term *akum,* coined and used indiscriminately (for heathen, idolator, alien, foreigner) by ignorant officials of the Inquisition.

Fundamental principles, like Jeremiah's precept, *"Seek the welfare of the city whither I exile you and pray for it,"* and Samuel's doctrine in the Talmud, *"The law of the government (in civil affairs) is the law,"* suspend many decisions which seem to discriminate against Gentiles.

But Hoffmann's book is much more than a successful attempt to refute attack on the Jewish code. It is full of positive content, rich in instruction and enlightenment. It ought to be studied even today by Jews and non-Jews alike, for the light it sheds on the development of *Halakhah* and its representative books. The real authority of Rabbi Joseph Caro and his standard work are described therein, the relations between him and Rabbi Moshe Isserles, his co-author of the final issue of the Code; the limits of personal authority, the practice of religious life, and how decisions ought to be made only after consulting the sources whence the *Shulkhan Arukh* and other codes are derived. The Talmud and the literature based thereon, the *Geonim* and the works of Rabbi

Isaac Alfasi, Maimonides, Rabbi Asher ben Jehiel, remain authoritative. Hoffmann defines exactly Rabbi Caro's codes: Only in the framework and context of preceding codes and commentaries of other authors discussing, analyzing, and, at times, opposing him, is he authoritative. For illustration, he quotes the book called *Gidule Taharah,* written by Rabbi Mendel Kargau, who (in Chapter CCI of *Yoreh Deah*) reveals three paragraphs as not being in accordance with the Talmud and Codes preceding the *Shulhan Arukh.* Hoffmann concludes: "As long as Rabbi Kargau will not be refuted, Rabbi Joseph Caro's decision will not be valid."

Special attention is given to the *Ger Toshab* (an alien who, to acquire citizenship in Palestine, renounces idolatry), to the legislation concerning the foreigner, to the terms *Kiddush ha-Shem* (the supreme duty of sanctifying God's name) and to laws dealing with *mipne darke shalom* (for the promotion of human peace and welfare). In each case Hoffmann shows the high level of the ethical principles involved, especially consistent love of mankind, irrespective of race, creed, or nationality. Likewise, *Hillul ha-Shem* (the supreme crime of causing a desecration of God's Name) is dealt with in a long chapter.

This book, written when Jews were menaced and accused, is not only a powerful refutation; it is an excellent sketch of the ethical standards of *Halakhah* and Jewish practice and a scholarly survey of many centuries: the work of a highly talented and versatile teacher who knows how to present defense; never a coward, nor a coarse fighter, but as noble as learned, as constructive as courageous! The number of rabbis and laymen who based their fight against adversaries of all sorts on Hoffmann's arguments must be enormous.

In 1910 he issued a revised edition of twelve articles, which had appeared in 1895 in the *Juedische Presse* under the title *Die Ueberlieferung der Vaeter und die Speisegesetze* (The Tradition of the Fathers and the Dietary Laws), in answer to an attack by a reform rabbi, Dr. Wiener. Again Hoffmann does not stay within the narrow framework of controversy, but, from the very first lines, offers a constructive study. Even more than in his book on the *Shulhan Arukh,* he strikes the adversary only by the way, though very efficiently, but without the sadism that so often in polemic essays diminish their value. His essays, more than sixty years later, are still attractive because of their rich, legitimate interpretation of the Torah. Essentially, we have before us a penetrating study on the relations between the written and oral Torah. Hoffmann shows that no real understanding of the Bible is possible unless we follow the old rabbinical conception. The simplicity of his method is extraordinary. He does not blind our eyes nor bewilder our ears by dithyrambic phrases. A master of the Torah has no need of special pleading. He discloses the roots of the Oral Law preceding the written one; he stresses that even after the death of Moshe, the Torah for most of the Jews remained a book known to them only orally, through the medium of teachers who, by word of mouth, taught and interpreted it. He demonstrates the need of interpretation and the impossibility of full understanding of Biblical verses without such additional explanation. Many passages are shaped in a way which requires an accompanying explanation to establish the basic meaning. As a famous example may serve *"Lo tevashel gedi bahalev immo"* (Thou shalt not seethe the kid in its mother's milk). But there are others: *"Le mohrat ha-Shabbat"* (on the morrow of the *Shabbat*) (concerning the waving of the Omer)[24] *Vay.* XXIII, 11 or *pri etz hadar* (a goodly fruit) *Vay* XXIII, 40.

Hoffmann's study is built on the tradition; but there was nobody before him so able to clarify the problem, to convince his readers, and to satisfy a skeptic. After explaining the special wording, he deepens the enquiry, as he includes *"bassar be-halav"* among the laws of sanctity.[25]

---

[24]He wrote a special treatise, published in 1874, by the Rabbinical Seminary on *Die Zeit der Omerschwingung und des Wochenfestes* (The Time of the Waving of the *Omer* and of the Feast of Weeks).

[25]Among other passages in the Torah which cannot be understood unless we accept his thesis—which is the traditional one—that in the text of the Torah there are distinct allusions to an Oral Law, are these: *Shemot* XXI, 9; *Kemishpat ha-banot yaasseh lah* (He shall deal with her after the manner of the daughters); Onkelos translates: *Kehilkhat benat yissrael yaabed lah,* and Ezra X, 3 has the same phrasing; *Kemohar ha-betulot* (according to the dowry of virgins) *Shem.* XXII, 16; *Ka-asher tzivitikha* (as I have commanded thee) XXIII, 15, without any indication of any such detail in the text; *levad mimikarav al ha-avot* (besides that which is due according to his father's houses) *Deb.* XVIII, 8 without any such detail in the text; *"Ve-khatorah yeasseh"* (And let it be done according to the law). The last quotation proves, according to Hoffmann, that oral laws are likewise called "Torah."

In this study, too, there is much of instructive teaching, valuable in itself and by no means only of apologetic importance. It reveals a great deal of the true meaning of the Torah. We are indebted to him for not rejecting Wiener the way many rabbis would have done, by showing vehemently that his adversary is an *am ha-aretz* (ignoramus) who does not know the Talmud. Instead, Hoffmann analyzed and explained the Biblical text and defined, in a convincing manner, the inner coherence and the organic ties between the Torah and the tradition that had begun in earliest time and left its traces in the text. His remarks are not only full of *esprit,* revealing his brilliant mind, but shine by solid reliability.

When repeated attempts were made to introduce reforms into religious practice and especially into the prayer-book, Hoffmann would warn his contemporaries. Thus he published his *Sendschreiben* (Epistle) to the Jewish communities in Baden. His voice is milder than that of many other authors. This is due to his noble, wise character, the harmony of his mind and soul, and to his vast knowledge. He has arguments instead of emotion, wisdom instead of passion, and deep piety instead of fanaticism. To the realm of liturgy, too, he brings his large historic erudition, the astonishing control of details, the masterly comprehension of our prayers, as of rites.

In Wohlgemuth's *Jeschurun* we find his essay on the "Oath in Israel" and other studies, originally an expert's statement which had to be submitted to a court. Wohlgemuth reports semewhere how Hoffmann wrote his opinion in the defense of Jewish Law *(Halakhah)* that became an expertise of remarkable comprehensiveness. During many weeks Hoffmann would sleep only for very few hours in order to finish it in time. He arose early because he was busy during the days, lecturing and performing his many other tasks.

Affluent German Orthodoxy did not grant sufficient facilities to its greatest exponent and representative. His salary was not too great and his burdens very heavy. But he did day by day what was imposed upon him and accomplished all the tasks for which he was destined.

He was well trained in Talmudics and in scientific investigation. But he did not specialize from the beginning in the many branches in which he achieved such marked success during his life. His con-

tributions to apologetics, polemics and defense, are the result of his
uninterrupted activities: *Thou shalt meditate therein day and night*
(Josh. I, 8). But his devotion was aided by unusual ability. As one
becomes aware of the scope of his interests and of his numerous
and precious publications, belonging to a great variety of scientific
territories, his record appears truly miraculous.

His systematic studies are to be found in his commentaries on
the Pentateuch, but some others deserve earnest attention, especially
his *Abhandlungen ueber die Pentateuchischen Gesetze* (Essays
on the Laws of the Pentateuch) and *Die Wichtigsten Instanzen
gegen die Graaf-Wellhausenschen Hypothese* (I, II) (The Main
Arguments against the Hypothesis of Graf and Wellhausen)
(Berlin, 1904 and 1916), wherein he offered the results of his
studies and his criticism of modern Biblical Criticism. These contributions may be considered preparatory preliminary and intermediate work, leading to the publication of his commentaries on
"Leviticus" and "Deuteronomium."

Another valuable investigation worthy of respectful consideration is *Der oberste Gerichtshof in der Stadt des Heiligtums* (The
Supreme Court in the City of the Sanctuary) (1878), published in
the annual reports of the Rabbinical Seminary, an important contribution to the history of Jewish laws and its institutions.

F. THE PERSONALITY

A summary of his scientific work will disclose the inner recesses of that great man's personality.

Anyone experienced in biographic work knows the handicaps
of an author in this field. Some persons will disclose everything
about their life, even if they tell much and incline to "coquetry".
Others are very taciturn and do not like to report much. Others
again, as they "reveal one handbreadth, cover another one". But
even those who are talkative do not enable the biographer to
comprehend them fully. "Every addition is a subtraction," says
the Talmud. Nor are a man's "confessions" always trustworthy.
At times there is a considerable element of fiction and phantasy
or lack of capacity to recognize oneself; at others, there is wishful
thinking or even the tendency to change, *corriger la fortune,* to
appear better than one has been.

To return to our special problem: We are concerned with one of the noblest types and of the most renowned scholars of Jewry. He belongs to those precious persons who lived within the "four cubits of *Halakhah*." Like our Sages, he devoted his life to study and teaching and forgot himself in doing so. Judaism, Torah, the Jewish people were his concern and in this service he, too, found all satisfaction. Like the pious men of old, he did not care for his own glory. This tradition is recorded in the Mishnah, where Rabban Gamliel said: "God knows that I did not act (so severely) either for my glory or that of my family . . . but to avoid *mahloket* (strife) in Israel." This is why we generally have so little autobiography from our Sages, why even biographies are not too frequent in our literature of old.

Hoffmann belongs to the classic type. His immense spiritual forces and his amazing learning recall the ingenious teachers whom we revere and who attained immortality. It is the astonishing combination of naiveté and grandeur that makes him lovable. I stress his intellectual perfectionism because none has ever been acknowledged as great among our people who did not shine by great knowledge, uninterrupted love of research work, and supreme skill in the mastery of detail. Like many of his predecessors, he did not specialize in a narrow field. The Torah, all the books of the Bible, and the whole of Talmudic and rabbinic literature, were his domain. He absorbed the exegetic writings of all centuries. All this he had in common with many others, though not all great rabbis were interested in every branch of literary creation. The scope of his work is a privilege he shares with a special group of learned fellow-Jews. Through the combination of all this with a vast scientific endowment and with unusual ability for methodical work in the Talmudic area, cultivated by only a few, he achieved well-nigh unique levels. Had he confined himself only to the old paths of study, he would have been, doubtless, equal to the greatest masters. He himself, although modest, was aware of his capacity. It is reported that he once said, "If I had time enough to prepare a *Shiur* (Talmudic lesson) as it ought to be done, I should be in a position to deliver my lecture no worse than the Hatam Sofer."

People would praise Hoffmann for his marvelous memory and rare assiduity. Indeed, he was endowed with both. But this does not explain much. (My great teacher, R. Zalman Barukh Rabinkow, used to maintain that memory is not a faculty bestowed from above, but a *zekhut* (merit) that we acquire: "It is powerful devotion to, and love of, Torah that establishes and strengthens our memory.")

He could not have succeeded in reaching such height and produced so much, especially in the field of the Oral Law, but for his infinite attachment to it. Even his inclination to modern ways of research is but the result of his love of Torah according to the classical pattern. He may be considered in this respect as a follower of Rabbi Elijah, the *Gaon* of Vilna, who once said that the lack of knowledge in auxiliary sciences diminishes our efforts in the study of Torah *esser yadot* (to a considerable degree). Hoffmann is one of the very few men of the old style who demonstrated how much we may gain when we mobilize scientific methods for the study of the Bible. More than anybody else did he illustrate the efficiency of traditional *limmud* (learning) combined with scientific approach. This synthesis was not an artificial amalgamation; it was based on unified and consistent method. Whenever scientific thinking had not stopped and the study of Talmud had been in search of the *peshat* (simple meaning of the text) by careful investigation, no real contradiction had come forth. An excellent representative of this approach, he used scientific methods not only in order to promote philological and historical interests, as when he wrote his great essays on Mishnah and Midrash. Scientific endeavors have their significance in themselves but they do not usually add much to the specific interest of the *Halakhah*. But his books and articles contributed to better understanding of the meaning and tendency of the Oral Law. It is true he did not disdain the scientific results and it may be said that his published investigations are most valuable discoveries in the realm of the history and structure of literature. But his effort throughout was based on exact knowledge and widest familiarity with the sources, on cautious analysis and profound respect for the sacred tradition, which he safeguarded not by pathos and emphasis, but by the earnestness and righteousness of his scientific attitude. Confidence in our old literature, its own statement and evaluation, rose greatly by virtue of a scholar who did not deny that the Mishnah was not born in one day but underwent development. But in accordance with this opinion (never derogated by our authorities, but not important enough, and perhaps somewhat distasteful, to many teachers), he always opposed uncontrolled, unlimited, and irresponsible criticism which destroyed every foundation. As against such tendency, Hoffmann succeeded in securing to tradition its proper position. He stressed the earliest stages of the Mishnah that are to be traced back much farther than critics were prepared to do. The acceptance of high antiquity and stability for its major elements, of a *mishnah rishonah* (original, first Mishnah) and of traditions reaching back to earlier ages and preceding our Mishnah even in its primordial shape—all these results of his studies seem to have been attained by the way and are not emphasized by him; but they are of utmost value because they are accepted for their solid foundations even by many readers who are far from being Orthodox.

Perhaps Hoffmann's main accomplishment was his contribution to exegesis in his *Leviticus* and *Deuteronomium*. Here he demonstrates the essential unity of the Oral and the Written Law. These standard works, revealing the importance and fertility of his studies in the Midrash, seem of only structural interest; but they have great weight for the conception of true Judaism. Though new problems have appeared since then and new answers are expected to be offered, nevertheless one result will last forever: *The Written and Oral Law are interdependent and can be neither segregated nor separated from one another.* Only ignorant or prejudiced persons can ignore what has been established by Hoffmann. He only confirmed what has been the point of view adopted throughout all epochs. But none before him was able to make it evident. His scientific productivity demonstrated his doctrine which corresponds to the unity of integral Judaism. *"Ahat dibber Elokim shtayim zu shamati"* (God hath spoken once (even though) I heard it in two ways) Tehil. LXII, 12—the truth of these Biblical words and of that other phrase: *"Kullam me'raeh ehad nitnu"* (All are given by One Shepherd) (Koh. XII, 11) are verified in his strenuous work.

He combined, in a natural and normal way, theoretical and practical activity, devotion to knowledge and to strengthening religious observance. No doubt, he was primarily a scholar, a *lamdan* and an enthusiastic student. But without any outside pressure, he gave a great deal of his time and ability to problems of the practical needs of our religion, in great service to our people.

Two generations had the privilege and advantage of possessing in David Hoffmann a teacher and leader. We are now in a position to complete his portrait and to appreciate his personality.

Hoffmann was the heir of our great Sages of all times. He was Hungarian by origin and an intimate analysis will find traces and trends specific to that group. But he rose above the boundaries of a special type of a *Landsmanschaft*. He belongs to the whole nation, exactly as he is a Jew not only of his time but of the stream of generations, although his appearance and actions are conditioned by the epoch in which he lived. A great man requires a framework broader than the present; past and future have a claim on him. His roots, too, go back to earlier ages, whilst his aspirations, expectations and his efficacy stay valid for times to come.

Hoffmann was the *praeceptor Germaniae* and, with the exception of small circles, every one faithful to our tradition acknowledged his leadership. All were proud of him and boasted of this powerful asset to Torah-true Judaism. Even Liberal Jews paid him tribute and wherever great men are mentioned, his name is called. I remember an event that impressed me greatly. Some time in the fall of 1914, at a memorial meeting in honor of the famous scholar Jakob Barth, in the Synagogue of the Adass Israel in Berlin, two great Jews happened to meet and shake hands: David Hoffmann and Hermann Cohen, who had come to attend this gathering. Two giants, perhaps the strongest brains that then lived and worked in the German metropolis and guided the Jewish population spiritually, demonstrated, by their friendly attitude and mutual respect and recognition, a symbolic unity, notwithstanding all the deep differences between Orthodoxy and Liberalism. Nobody but Hoffmann could have approached a man of utterly different orientation with such mild understanding, without abandoning anything of traditional Jewish values or of the full creed of a Jew. But his firm, inflexible, and unchangeable attitude did not prevent him from appreciating the high rank of his antagonist and from paying respect to the purity of Cohen's purpose and to his adherence to our spiritual work. It is an eloquent expression of Hoffmann's tolerance. He belonged really to the whole of the Jewish people, both by the nobility of his heart and by his work, both entitling him to the highest regard. He enjoyed the respect also of Russian Jewry. In accord with the Hildesheimer tradition, he kept in touch with the great rabbis of Eastern Europe, whom he at times consulted.[26] He enjoyed the high esteem of the great Russian scholars. The prodigious Louis Ginzberg was among his admirers and the very able Rabbi H. Tchernowitz, 'Rav Tzair', in moving eulogies gave expression to their adoration of Hoffmann. Tchernowitz, perchance, may be considered an enthusiast, but not Ginzberg. Yet his memorial address is a lyrical panegyric. These two men of Russian origin, both disciples of Russian *yeshivot*, trained in Kovno and afterwards in western universities, quite different from him in character and temperament, are united in their unrestrained veneration of the master.

What makes David Hoffmann unique, beyond his greatness as author, teacher and scholar, beyond all his achievements? He differs from his contemporaries, predecessors and successors. He was pious and learned like the venerated rabbis of old; he was at home in modern science like his colleagues of other schools. He was able to compete with both groups. But it was his outstanding piety that gave him superiority over all Jewish scholars who abandoned the old paths, as it makes him the equal of the old type who were not familiar with modern methods of Talmudic research. But fully to understand the mystery of Hoffmann, one must conceive of piety in a very deep sense. Even his piety is the expression of a very pure, noble and lofty personality, whose ethical level is sublime. This level is the very cause of Hoffmann's grandeur and secures him highest rank among his colleagues. His moral qualities, especially his integrity, enabled him to employ his intellectual ability in the service he rendered to Jewish learning and research.

Nothing he achieved was spurred by ambition. He knew no envy. That he had neither aggressiveness nor hostility becomes obvious as we compare contemporary scholars who are active in the same field of scientific work. Strange as it may sound, aggressiveness does not always depend upon real contrast and objective

---

[26]Though from youth his authorities and models were Hungarians (especially Rabbi Moshe Schuck but also other decisors of fame, Hatam Sofer and Rabbi Judah Assod, author of *Yehudah Yaaleh*), he paid respectful attention to outstanding Lithuanian rabbis, like Rabbi Isaac Elhanan and his son, to Rabbi Hirsch Rabinowitz, Rabbi J. M. Epstein (author of *Arukh ha-Shulhan*), Rabbi N. Ts. J. Berlin (the *"Netziv"*), not to speak of the *Gaon* of Vilna and Rabbi Hayyim of Volozhin. He quotes the Galician rabbis, Rabbi Sh. J. Natansohn (author of *Shoel u-Meshiv*) and Rabbi J. Shmelkes (author of *Bet Yitzhak*), and the great scholars of the Torah everywhere.

discrepancy; at times differences are not relevant and only com-
petitiveness explains scholarly vehemence. There is too much
resentment in too many authors. Hoffmann attacked only when
his adversary violated or abused sacred religious institutions or
opinions. He hated an ignoramus who presumed to play the role
of an expert. Even in such cases he gave priority to valid arguments but on occasion would not eschew sarcasm and derogatory
remarks. Herein he was a *talmid hakham* (disciple of the wise;
a wise disciple) of high standing. His being wise gave him a
superiority which at times had no other outlet but a smile or a
sense of sorrow. He possessed much wit and humor; he was kind-
hearted and ready to pardon. But when that great scholar was
confronted by a student's ignorance or stupidity, he would lose
his equilibrium and his temper and would show, unintentionally,
his sheer impatience. In polemics, it was the attitude of an aris-
tocrat who was wounded by the appearance of dwarfs of the
plebeian type who provoked his unfriendly remarks. But whilst
others usually wrote in terms of irony and contempt, he did so
only in moments of sheer despair.

Hoffmann wrote in the language of a wise and learned man:
very distinct and transparent. His phrases are clear and short.
He does not omit anything of importance but avoids the irrelevant.
There is no word that has no significance, but his text is free from
reiteration and verbosity. His Hebrew, as his German, is modest
and simple. One may perchance find fault with the imperfect
esthetic grace of his Hebrew, but it represents his personal mental
cleanness and his exact way of argumentation. His German style
is worthy of every praise; it indicates also his culture and his
familiarity with literature, which he had read with a penetrative
and adaptive mind. Hoffmann knew music and had fine musical
qualities. He was a *ba'al Keriah* (reader of the Torah) of high
level, and a *ba'al Tefillah* (chanter of the prayers—non-profes-
sional cantor) of taste.

When necessary, he could be belligerent, but he excelled in his
constructive functions and actions. Behind all he did and achieved,
taught and wrote, stood the man who lived according to the
prophetic rule: *"to walk humbly with thy God."* Was wisdom
or religious devotion his primary and stronger factor? His wisdom
was imbued with piety and his faith was fortified and fed by
wisdom. His life was not long enough to settle all the problems

he posed for himself and which he could have solved. But more than anybody else in the Torah-true field, did he succeed in strengthening the bastion of religious Jewry and of Judaism. Even when we allude to his limits (set to everyone on earth), we are impressed by an almost taciturn, unpretentious, unobtrusive man who was greater than his great work because he did not claim honors and official recognition and loved to walk along by-paths, far from the limelight. The highest level of personality is attained only by a man of great naiveté who does not know *"that the skin of his face was shining."* It is the aversion to publicity and cheap honor that bestows real glory.

Hoffmann's scientific work was not only intended to foster religious life and theory. It was in itself a religious service. It had nothing to do with methods in vogue in his time and afterwards, but derived from an extraordinary brain, guided and controlled by the heart. He was a *maskil* (a bright, wise person), not in the modern sense, but in the original definition: *The path of life leads the wise man upwards.* There are passages in his writings where his *thinking* becomes *thought* and philosophy; like those dealing with the 'qualities' of God, not so much with the theological doctrine of attributes, as with His ethical qualities. They were his reply to the calumnies of our adversaries.

We must not forget the loneliness of his later years. He carried a heavy burden of teaching and performed many functions of administrative character. He was never free enough from these chores to do his scholarly work as he wanted to do. What he did was achieved by super-human effort.

All the honor bestowed on him notwithstanding, the group of his real admirers and of those who knew and appreciated him was small. Only a few understood him and his marvelous way. Here we touch the tragedy of a man who did so much and procured for his time and his coreligionists so many valuable tools and gave them so much pride and respect in the eyes of others—and, nevertheless, others were crowned leaders and religious authorities! Hoffmann accepted this fact philosophically. But his fame, limited to a narrow circle of experts and connoisseurs and achieved only late and gradually, will endure, for no generation, really interested in the most precious of our spiritual assets, will forget this grand man.

He lived in the sempiternity of Jewish history and the eternity of faith and obedience to God and His Torah. A contemporary, endowed with the faculty to recognize human greatness, could not but be impressed by this scholar and saint, who made his way so quietly but assiduously and did not lose one moment of his days. He knew the necessity of keeping aloof from time-robbing mass affairs, as he understood his special place in the field of Jewish things, but this knowledge never led him towards self-conceit or arrogance. There was in him not an ounce of vanity or the "foot of pride." Any one who ever saw him—his small figure, his beautiful head, his open and deep eyes, his steady and searching look that was never hard or cruel but expressed the harmony of his thinking and acting, could never forget this man.

Everything within him was moderate: his relations to man, his love, his criticism. His was a steady and deep love of God, of Torah, and of mankind. He walked in the spirit of the great leaders and thinkers of our people. Hoffmann was not under the influence of Hassidism. His masters were rabbis who were totally immersed in the world of *Halakhah*. His lucidity guided him always. His apprenticeship with Rabbi Ezriel Hildesheimer reinforced his intellectual power and removed him from all sentimentalism. He is, in western form, a typical *mitnaged* (opponent of Hassidism), but without any fanaticism. His harmonious soul protected him from unbalanced reactions and from conflicts which overtake the passionate. He and his school, his works and his attitude, met with resistance in some quarters. The Seminary of Hildesheimer was suspected by diverse men, even before its inauguration. It is a token of Hoffmann's and his colleagues' character that they responded to unfriendly utterances with equanimity and endeavored to avoid polemics; they kept silent, answering attacks by productive scientific labor that required much more effort than the sterile aversion of their adversaries, and procured for our people and our Torah infinitely more strength and glory. Never was he intimidated by the negative attitude of his opponents, nor could anything ever cause him to deviate, in however slight a fashion, from the Jewish way. This man whose spiritual world was so wide and who was so open-minded, remained during all periods a protagonist of strict Orthodox observance, never misguided towards blind narrowness. He is one of the rare men who, by their personal appearance and behavior, cause Orthodoxy to be understood and held in high esteem. In his character and bearing Orthodoxy became believable and respected. His equilibrium and nobility as an expression of traditional Judaism have proved a strong justification of an attitude that to some people seems inconceivable, suspect and unwelcome. Thus Hoffmann himself became an asset to Orthodoxy; he conquered no less territory than his great books. He obtained highest credit for our people and its values, our religion and culture that have their roots and center in the marvelous documents which ever revive us.

At times the question arises: What is more impressive and greater: the highly qualified man or his immortal spiritual work? But the question is not exact and adequate and, therefore, no proper answer can be given. The greater mystery in my eyes is the fact that his lofty scientific level and his lifelong struggle with exciting problems which have alienated so many Jews from the path of faith, never prevented him from being pious and devoted to a true adherence to '*Judaismus perennius*' (Eternal Judaism) and enabled him to become a luminous example of a Jew of the highest standard, higher than most Orthodox men who never dealt with such dangerous topics as he did. Jewish pedagogy may yet refer to him to educate generations towards an ideal type.

It is difficult to characterize David Hoffmann. Perhaps this statement may sound strange. He was a man of perfection in every respect and so his portrait ought to be uncomplicated, harmonious and clear. But this very perfection is an obstacle to the attempt to procure a colorful picture that reflects his life in its riches and its glamor. Quiet and equilibrated as he appears, there is no doubt that he was full of facets. There is absent the romanticism so often connected with modern conceptions of personal greatness. Modern art of biographical advertising has developed a technique that gives impressive expression to a world of make-believe, but is unable to depict a sublime and true humanity.

He belongs to the small group of men whose importance and greatness do not depend on time and conditions, who would have adorned any period.

He achieved in his lifetime more than most of his contemporaries. He succeeded in approximating the great and outstanding personalities in spiritual height, creative power, moral standing, religious purity and harmony of thought and practice. God's compassion and the merits of his fathers rendered possible this astonishing life. He transferred highest values from the past to the future through the medium of his genius and by virtue of his exemplary life.

Perhaps the last words written by him in the second volume of his commentary on *Debarim* (XXX, 30) refer to the verse (XXXI, 30) : *"And Moses spoke in the ears of all the assembly of Israel the words of this song."* To explain the construction, the author quotes *"And David spoke the words of his song,"* from II. Samuel 2, XXII, i. This passage has become an unconscious testimony, a full stop set by himself to his life's deepest meaning. The work of this David, too, may be called a song. His life sang it to its very end.

His great efforts and achievements form, indeed, a song, sung in honor of the God of Israel, whose obedient servant he was in all stages of his life. He brought this song in valiant service to a glorious end.

HIRSCH HILDESHEIMER

(1855-1910)

By David Strumpf

HIRSCH HILDESHEIMER

By David Strumpf

A hundred years ago Hirsch Hildesheimer saw the light of the world. In our grateful memory he is enshrined, at once, as thinker, fighter, and messenger of peace, a powerful personality excellent in foreground and background. We cherish his slogan: "In our battle for the rights of the Jewish people we should use no weapon but that of humanity, no pride but that of human dignity." To Torah he dedicated his powers and with the pathos of his faith and his righteous indignation he did face the slanderers of the Jewish name. He was unshakable in his convictions, yet gentle in form. His whole life spelled indescribable heroism of love and kindness. Silent about his own achievement, a genuine pioneer of the spirit, he saw himself always only at the first stage of his work. He discovered profound associations unsuspected by anyone else, and his interpretations of time and event amazed by their boldness. Joseph Wohlgemuth said of him: "We shall never forget his role in the desperate years of the Russian pogroms. We met their victims, whose children had been tortured to death before their eyes, who, in their flight from terror, fear in their feverish eyes, were lost in the metropolis. They had come from great distances, from the deepest part of Russia, unaware of central relief organizations. When we asked them, "Where do you come from, wither are you bound?" only one word came from their trembling lips. On a piece of paper his blessed name was inscribed in Hebrew letters. In their home they had heard, "Upon the son of the great Israel Hildesheimer now rested the spirit of the All merciful God." There were many helpers, but these lost souls looked but for one: Hirsch Hildesheimer.

The imprint of that memory upon his students has been ever strong. We recall with what vigor he espoused the cause of the victims. He answered the call by immediate attention. He knew where to turn. His appeal was resistless. His blissful intercession was due not to his high position, the magic of his name, the dignity of his appearance, his noble personality and his fearless approach. Ultimately it was the marvel of his good heart that was decisive. When he spoke about the misery of the persecuted, his words pene-

trated every heart. Since Montefiore, Jewry knew no nobler nor
more eloquent spokesman than Hirsch Hildesheimer. Where his
brethren suffered because of their faith, where any human knew
misery because of poverty or tyranny, he would rush to aid and to
battle until the pressure was removed or the yoke smashed. He
headed every charity institution of his city and established and maintained many more in ceaseless activity. What gave him unique
significance was a sublimation in his character of two polar elements: a supremely endowed mind cleaving with every fiber of his
heart to our holy traditions and also profoundly identified with the
spiritual climate of his time. In Hildesheimer, Jewish tradition and
western culture were profoundly wedded: "The Jewish tradition is
anchored in the very depth of our soul. They who would destroy
the tradition destroy the soul's integrity."

The first Reform Jews hated that tradition and were bent on
destroying it. When David Friedlander and his followers offered
to join the Protestant church, providing some concessions were
made as to Christian dogma and ritual, he took a stand that was
both unforgettable and unforgivable. In their time the reformers, as
persuasive as ruthless, were most powerful. Their attacks on
Torah-true Judaism shook the Jewish community, because Reform
denied the revelation at Mount Sinai, the idea of the Messiah, the
Oral Torah. In Berlin, Friedlander and his consorts were anxious
to write the last chapter of the Jewish tradition. It was then that
Hildesheimer proclaimed, *"Let him who is for the Lord come to
me."* He rallied around him the faithful and rebuilt stone by stone
the temple of the Lord. Jewish history from the beginning of the
19th century moves under the impact of the clash between Judaism
and western culture which followed upon the Emancipation a few
decades earlier. This conflict produced assimilation and reform,
but it also brought about a seminal harmony between Torah and
Derekh Eretz (contemporary culture). Hirsch Hildesheimer expressed the values of the holy tradition in the categories of modern
thought, offering it to the people as a new goal, and helped it survive in integrity. Samson Raphael Hirsch, Ezriel Hildesheimer,
and Hirsch Hildesheimer are the three decisive shapers of this
synthesis.

It has been said that talent is sufficient to formulate new thoughts
but it takes a genius to reshape ever anew the eternal old verities

of man. Hirsch Hildesheimer possessed not only unique empathy for the postulates of his time, but also ability to restate great questions in their timeless essence. The phenomenal achievements of the two Hildesheimers have all the hallmarks of genius. That explains their overwhelming effect on very wide Jewish circles, both East and West. Both exemplified a deep understanding of the millions of persecuted souls in their tender care for their physical maintenance and for the perpetuation of traditional Judaism which the Emancipation and assimilation were now menacing. Hirsch's inexhaustible work, his optimism, sense of Jewish dignity and awe for the greatness of our faith would brook neither misinterpretation nor false humility. His hundreds of essays in the *Juedische Presse* reveal at once wisdom and power, intelligence and goodness.

I.

Born in Eisenstadt, Hungary, February 2, 1855, he was his father's third son, the fifth child among ten. He studied at his *yeshivah* and from early youth was noted for profound human sympathy. Soon he distinguished himself through his extraordinary memory, rapid perception and insatiable passion for research. This *Illuy* (prodigy) was pious, modest and humane. In 1869 his father was called to Berlin, as rabbi of the Torah-true community, *Adath Israel*. From Berlin, Hirsch went to Halberstadt, whence his forebears had come, to study Talmud with Rabbi H. A. Auerbach and secular subjects from private tutors. Since the middle of the 19th century, that city had been a center of Torah-true Judaism. Through the Hirsches—heads of a world-renowned firm, celebrated for its integrity and religious leadership—Halberstadt had become a commercial center of the first rank. Its rabbi was Benjamin Zvi Auerbach, renowned as Talmudic scholar and one of the first Torah-true rabbis to preach in classic German.[1]

In 1872, Hirsch was Dr. Auerbach's favorite student. After his death, he returned to Berlin to complete studies at the "Sophiengymnasium", then entered Berlin University to specialize in history, classical philosophy and geography. The following year, his

---

[1]His battle of the books in connection with Z. Frankel's *Darke ha-Mishnah,* and his edition of the *Sefer ha-Eshkol,* challenged by Albeck and vindicated by later research, are well known.

father, Rabbi Ezriel, after very great difficulties, succeeded in establishing the rabbinical seminary bearing his name. Torah-true Jewry
looked upon him as a veritable redeemer, for he carried the principle of *Torah im Derekh Eretz* into the wide world, and armed a
whole doughty generation for the battle of the revitalized faith.
Through the rabbinical seminary, he helped them escape the laby-
rinth of a confused *Zeitgeist* towards a clear comprehension of
the Jewish *Weltanschauung;* he saved many small communities
which had been languishing for lack of religious leadership. The
seminary's graduates, anchored in the faith and loyal to its traditions, brought about a renaissance of Judaism. Inspired by their
great master, they fostered his spirit both in the Jewish community
of Germany and far beyond its borders. An eager student at the
seminary, Hirsch acquitted himself successfully of his avocation
as teacher in the preparatory classes. His studies in the classic disciplines trained him on an academic level which was to benefit his
future research.

Free from financial worry, he dedicated himself to Torah and
the service of God. His parents' loving sensitiveness, their tolerance of other people's views, their contempt for any meanness,
helped him mature towards serene self-possession.

In Halberstadt he met his cousin Roeschen Hirsch who, for
thirty years of devoted partnership, promoted his happiness and his
work. Like Rabbi Akiba, he felt that most that he had achieved
was due to his wife's grace and kindness.

In 1879 he received his doctorate from Leipzig.[2]

Soon after his marriage, he was appointed lecturer at the Rabbiner Seminar on Jewish History and Geography of Palestine. The
fruit of his research, his book, *Beitraege zur Geography Palestinas,* has remained to this day a volume of great significance.

Beyond academic circles, his efforts for the colonization of the
Holy Land evoked a new spirit of hopefulness and responsibility.
It was the time of the frightful Russian pogroms. Whilst influential
groups would direct the stream of immigration to North America
and Argentina, he sponsored Palestine as a haven for the refugees.

---

[2]The great Theodore Mommsen looked upon Hirsch Hildeseimer as one
of his greatest students and begged him to decide upon an academic career.
When his thesis on Aurelius Victor was published, the head of the department at Koenigsberg University visited him and brought him his notes,
observing that Hildesheimer's book made his own unnecessary.

Predestined for the life of research, he was summoned, by the tide of violent anti-Semitism, to the arena, to fight for Israel. Like his classic prototype, he held the trowel in one hand, for the building of our faith, and the sword of the spirit in the other, to ward off attacks. He developed simultaneously in two polar fields, in scholarly pursuit and in communal work. A powerful figure, the advocate of the oppressed, a prince of peace, he invested his indefatigable intelligence, overcoming one handicap after the other and granting himself no rest. He would brook no quest for comfort; he would accept no rebuff; the more hopeless a situation, the more determined did he become, his conscientiousness impelling him on and on. In his time one may discern the first intimations of a world in transition, with religion and law losing ground. It was a period of a hundred problems and struggles. The theory of evolution and the Darwinian emphasis on the survival of the fittest was increasingly dominating the thinking of western Europe and undermining the faith in the eternal verities of the Bible. Only rock-like characters, rooted in the Divine, could point the way over a disintegrating present into the future of a full, uncribbed life.

HILDESHEIMER AS EDITOR

Carlyle defined the essence of a genius as an inexhaustible capacity for painstaking, detailed work. On that definition, Hildesheimer surely was a genius. The driving force of his life was duty. It was duty that made him give up his studies in history. It was out of a sense of duty that in 1883 he undertook the editorship of the *Juedische Presse*. Fully conscious of the adverse effect the new task would have on his plans for research, he accepted it because he understood that Stocker and Ahlwardt had poisoned public opinion with their hate-sheets and their deliberate falsifications of rabbinic texts. He proved himself a master in the defense of truth, emerging from the study into the open forum with all the tensions and noise it implied: the substitution of the champion's dynamics for the quiet hours of the scholar, the editor's ceaseless preoccupation with problems of the moment. He proved himself a man of truly historical import. He eschewed demagogy even in its most alluring form. He would have nothing to do with headline hunting; his quest was truth. He remained its pioneer throughout the vicissitudes of newspaper work. His mastery of the material, his lucidity and his ethical pathos broke down barriers and evoked in various groups a sustained struggle on behalf of the sanctuaries of humanity.

Die Juedische Presse became a platform for the exposition of religious attitude, for genuine academic enterprise and for the highest level of social endeavor.

With all fibers of his heart he clung to classic Judaism, without even a hair's-breadth deviation in theory and practice. Tradition for him was something absolute, congenital, unchangeable, immanent in every Jew. He could not comprehend a change in religious conviction. The story of some young people from Torah-true homes who had gone back on the traditions of their faith, he could neither comprehend nor forgive. How could anyone deliberately withdraw from the blissful influence of the old Torah and its holy laws? Nevertheless, he strove for tolerance in his social relations. A critic long ago felt tolerance to be an illusion, for "the most tolerant person would never accept reaction and Orthodoxy nor would the latter bear with disloyalty to the Torah, or with free thought." Hirsch Hildesheimer fought anti-Semitism and defended the Jews' civil rights because of his demand for tolerance. But his own tolerance was of a different nature. It was not due to lack of firm convictions which would yield to the fashions of the day; which merely suffers but never acts, which is anvil but never hammer. Hildesheimer possessed the tolerance which is indispensable to a leader in Israel. It was based on the power of a rich, creative person, yielding out of a fullness of power, stopping only where suffering wrong would be out of accord with the creative forces of his personality. Where tolerance of alien principles would have led to an intolerance towards his own, he would say "no" out of an inner assurance.

From his early youth, Hirsch Hildeshiemer had suffered from the baneful, intramural strife among the Torah-true. The great rabbis who had opposed his father's rabbinical seminary in Eisenstadt were masters of the Talmud, men of noble character and profound piety, but because of their aloofness from the culture of the day, they had lost contact with the youth, had no voice in the discussions of the educated; their influence diminished more and more. It was in those troubled times that Ezriel Hildesheimer proclaimed the paramount duty of the rabbis to study the culture of the time so that they might repel, with the best weapons of the period, the attacks on our holy Torah. His disciples looked upon him as a fiery messenger of God, whose contribution to Talmudic scholarship and whose dynamic activity were blessed by extraordinary success.

It was Hildesheimer's open-mindedness that dictated his attitude toward the *"Austrittsgesetz."*[3] This law achieved what Edward Lasker had prophecized: a new attitude on the part of the powerful leaders of the community. The new law gave all those who felt their conscience had been violated, the right to secede from the main congregation. This right had a wholesome effect on the masters of the community, who hitherto had been ruthless in their reformist tendencies. They could no more terrorize the faithful and force upon them a synagogue service violative of the traditions. Now such tyranny would cause secession, the weakening of the community. Their relations originally were not at all pacific. But for men like Hildesheimer or Samson Raphael Hirsch, the traditional Jews would have been coerced. It was a problem of coexistence or separate existence. The leaders of Torah-true Judaism chose separate existence. As a result, the communities began to be more considerate of the religious needs and sentiments of the Torah-true, in order to enable them to remain within the community.

Hirsch Hildesheimer has shown that in the battle against an outer enemy who wanted to destroy our civil and social existence, inner contrast ought not to be exacerbated. Ever larger circles became convinced that the sources of inner conflict, due to divided attitudes as to ritual and worship, could be removed through a forceful composition of the fundamental differences. Through the achievement of such wholesome peace without compromise, which became possible only because of the 1876 law of secession, the contending parties found a way to cooperative labor in the field of communal and humanitarian activities.

Throughout his life, he remained loyal to this program. Once the majority in the community protected the conscience of the Torah-true minority, Hirsch Hildesheimer would promote unity

---

[3]Legislation concerning the separation of Orthodox groups from Reform organizations.

notwithstanding all pressures of those who believed in secession (*Austritt*) *à tout prix*. There had not been a uniform attitude among the Torah-true about the law of secession. Marcus Horovitz, a first-rank Talmudic authority (author of the Responsa *Matte Levi*) opposed the *Austritt* on principle and accepted the position of rabbi of the united Jewish community in Frankfurt, although Ezriel Hildesheimer had originally dissuaded him. Samson Raphael Hirsch, on the other hand, considered it prohibited to belong to a community which had also non-traditional institutions. But both Horovitz and the famous Wuerzburger Rov, S. B. Bamberger, opposed Rabbi Hirsch on *halakhic* grounds. With all appreciation of the latter's tremendous achievements, they preferred a law which would oblige every community to consider the wishes of the Torah-true minority. Hildesheimer said about Horovitz: "This tremendous spirit mastered the ocean of Talmudic literature like one of the great *Geonim* of the past. My father looked upon Horovitz as the one among the thousands of his disciples who in all his utterances and actions would translate into reality the teachings of his masters."[4]

Hirsch Hildesheimer had the ease and the humor of a well-balanced scholar, profound loyalty wedded to a capacity for infinite tolerance—the emanation of extraordinary spiritual and moral power.

THE "JUEDISCHE PRESSE"

Hildesheimer would not permit the Jewish people " to duck until the storm was over." There were some who opposed defense, but he knew how many unspoiled souls were affected by the *"Stormtruppe"* of Biblical Criticism and their fellow travellers. Through the twenty-eight years of his editorship of the *Juedische Presse,* he raised his mighty voice against this pseudo-science.

His leading articles occasionally reached heroic qualities; they also proved invaluable for the exposition and defense of Judaism. We must not forget against what filth and low passions this man

---

[4]In *Yad Shaul* is published, for the first time, a most important letter, written by Hildesheimer to Mr. Schwarzschild, which throws vital light on the whole subject of *Austritt* in general and S. R. Hirsch in particular.

of the spirit had to battle. There were the lies about the *Kol Nidre* prayer, the slander against *Shehitah,* the horrid blood-libels connected with the towns of Xanten, Konitz and Polna. Of what have these preachers of hatred not accused us! How shamelessly have they libelled Talmud and *Shulhan Arukh!* It is here that the *Juedische Presse* performed a cultural task of the first rank, arousing mankind's conscience, enlisting the noblest spirits of western culture. It is due to that organ that the celebrated Gentile professors, Strack and Noeldecke, commenced to block these incendiaries, to drag the slanderers of the Talmud before a court of justice, to proclaim their *"J'accuse"* against the scoundrelly blood-libel. "We have witnessed," said Dr. Wohlgemuth in his famous memorial address, "how sleep fled his eyes, how he rushed without rest through the cities of Germany, here to stop the arsonist in his nefarious handiwork, there to prevent another fire."

Hildesheimer, throughout this heart-rending work, never despaired of humanity, never descended to bitter contempt. He would fight any unrighteousness. His plea was based upon God-inspired conviction, his heart elated by absolute confidence in the victory of truth. Even those who disagreed with him could not withhold their admiration and respect.

Against the enemy without, he battled for civil equality of the Jew. No less determined was his battle against those who would achieve emancipation by the surrender of Jewish principles: "There is no need to achieve civil rights at the price of disloyalty to the Torah. Reform spells the depression of Judaism to a superficial, soulless religion."

The chief causes of his struggle against the organ and other synagogue reforms were a deep sense of history, devotion to the traditional ideas, and indignation with needless radicalism. Yet he always knew both how to preserve contact with world Jewry and how to avoid the game of small politics.

He was eloquent in his demand that a Jewish journal undertake the fight against the indifference of the Jewish masses, which he called the deadly enemy of all religious effort. "Lack of knowledge," he said, "leads with inexorable necessity to lack of faith. This vacuum must be filled by the Jewish press. The treasures of our literature must be enlisted from the luminaries of the past. Thorough discussions of contemporary problems would show how, all changes of his social position notwithstanding, a Jew must remain Jewish in attitude and action and convey that loyalty to his children as the heirloom of his people. The press must promote Jewish ideals, the spirit of belonging, to kindle, feed and strengthen our global consciousness of unity. Teaching the essence of Judaism implies resistance to impious destructiveness and reformism.

"Jewish journalism must aim to be an organ for the integration of all members of our faith. Loyal to its own principles, it should continue the struggle for the preservation of the purity of our religious sanctuaries, continually assailed by slanderers and blackmailers. We must continue to fight for our civil rights, which the brutal chauvinism of our days strives to undermine." This is how he formulated the principles of the *Juedische Presse*. At the 25th anniversary of his editorship, an élite assembled to express its gratitude. Among them was the editor of a liberal newspaper who long ago had turned his back upon Judaism. Now he rose and declared: "In my youth I knew neither my religion nor my people. I was a man full of doubts and of resentment against the traditions of Israel. Then I met Hirsch Hildesheimer. My *Weltanschauung* collapsed; I had to revise all the foundations of my view of life, for I had met the power of Judaism, the moral greatness of those who avow it." The guest of honor responded: "You owe me no thanks for whatever I may have been able to do for the people and the Torah of Israel. To work for them is not only the highest, holiest duty, it is the only happiness that a human being is heir to."

It was in the *Juedische Presse,* with its universal Jewish interest, that Dr. Meir Tzevi Jung, then Rabbi of Ung. Brod in Moravia (later Chief Rabbi of the Federation of Synagogues of London), suggested a universal organization of Jews. "The mass misery," he said, "can be overcome only through a mass organization. We must create such an organization embracing Jewry with all shades of opinions. Its purpose: to establish colonies in Israel, industrial institutions and schools in the land of the *Golah,* all of them conducted in the spirit of the *Shulhan Arukh.* The Zionists, too, would gradually join such an organization. It would represent a unifying bond for all Jews in the Diaspora." This article appeared one year after Hildesheimer's death. He surely would have been its most eloquent champion. Unfortunately, it found no contemporary echo. Had it been acted upon, world Jewry would have been spared much tragedy.

AGAINST BIBLICAL CRITICISM

Friedrich Delitzsch won the Kaiser's plaudits, and headlines all over the world, through his series of lectures on "Babel and Bible." Its theatrical get-up and purple style procured popular interest, and established his claim as to the "Babylonian origin of the Hebrew Bible." Hildesheimer showed in many essays how Delitzsch's superficiality had degraded Biblical scholarship, how unjustified were his attacks and how utterly baseless his theories. Delitzsch had offered as *pièce de résistance* three tablets which allegedly bore the four-lettered name of God (Tetragammaton). Hence he claimed to have proved that the origin of Biblical monotheism was Babylonian. Hildesheimer, in his rebuttal, quotes exhaustively the code of Hammurabi with its large list of Babylonian deities and asks, "Does one need to add a single word? Hammurabi summons a whole army of his multiformed world of gods. Could he have had even a breath of a monotheistic point of view? How much less could he have taught it! And, above all: in this Pantheon, whose whole population is made to parade, the alleged main god is missing—even the very mysterious four-lettered deity whom the "Babylonian Monotheist" was supposed to have worshipped. How on earth could one explain that Hammurabi excludes the mightiest of gods, if not the only God, when citing his imprecations?!"

The famous Assyriologist, Professor Hilprecht of Philadelphia, in appreciation of Hildesheimer's scholarly impeccability, offered this final judgment: "The whole Babylonian nation went to sleep with this confession on their dying lips, 'Our gods are dead!' From this charnelhouse, malodorous with mildew and ruins, Israel should have derived its pure monotheistic concept of God! On the basis of my fourteen years' labor in the ruins of Babylon, I feel impelled to avow a view vitally different from Delitzsch's. My conviction is: 'Hear, oh Israel, the Lord thy God is the only God.'"

Another curious Delitzsch theory had to do with the Sabbath, which he claimed Israel had borrowed from Babylonia. The sainted Dr. Jacob Horovitz showed in a thorough dissertation that the Sabbath among the Babylonians was a day of mourning and contrition, a day of misfortune. In the Babylonian Sabbath, if ever there was one, one may not find the slightest trace of the blissful Sabbath of

Judaism. The Biblical Sabbath is a central institution without any atom of similarity to the Assyrian *Shabatu*.

HILDESHEIMER AS HISTORIAN

The early 20th century added to both the number and the gravity of the problems of the preceding period. The national states increased their power, expanding beyond their frontiers and becoming world states. Continental economy increasingly becomes global. It is the period of imperialism. Germany became an industrial commonwealth. The fourth estate emerges. As the big cities become bigger, as factories increase, so does socialism grow, in sharpest opposition to the then governments. The rise of capitalism drives the proletariat and the propertied classes further apart. The spiritual attitude of this restless epoch, all its imminent greatness notwithstanding, indicates a growing insecurity at its basis, a confusion of tendencies, polar in attitude and claim. There is determined optimism, looking forward to a roseate future; there is return to the pure sources of religion, to the simplicity of the hearts, together with mankind's grievous problems; there is a painful search for the meaning of individual life. It is a time of transition, the emergence of a new world with its feverish tensions, ending in the catastrophe of the First World War. At its end, there remains a completely changed mankind, spasmodically out of gear.

With the great thinkers of the past, Hirsch Hildesheimer agreed that any concept of Judaism that surrenders its traditions will eventually lead to its abandonment. It is fatal to look upon history as a matter of the past and to wrap it in a veil of the long ago. His holiest task was to teach, to work for the comprehension of Judaism. Jewish history never became to him merely a field of archeological research. It was his living source of abiding inspiration.

He was a man of optimistic strength, in steady touch with the rhythm of contemporary life. His style had a vitality and originality, as enchanting as it was convincing. His lectures and essays show that, full of pride and dedicated love for his people, he relived Jewish history in all its phases. No matter what period he describes, he holds the reader enraptured by his empathy and sympathy. This pregnant passage is quoted from *The Fate of*

Jewry in Ancient Rome: "Among the blood-drenched pages of Israel's history none emphasizes the wonderful survival of our people more incisively than the chapter of 'Israel in Rome.' Should you be asked where your God resides, counsels Rabbi Joshua ben Levi in the Talmud, then answer, 'In the City of Rome.' If the throes of disaster compel the anxious quest: 'Where art Thou, my God?' then consider this: Israel is still alive, unbroken in its power, but the proud, nation-devouring Rome has sunk into the dust. From that city emanated all the slander and persecution of our people. Again and again Israel was thrown down in bloody struggle; torn from holy Palestine, flung into a world alien and cruel, our people had to dwell with this deadly enemy, Rome." Hildesheimer offers a colorful description of the fate of Jewry in that city: "More than two millennia have passed," he says, "since the descendants of Jacob settled on the banks of the Tiber. They endured from generation to generation, keeping aloof from Romans and Barbarians. They lived to see the old Roman republic, the Roman emperors, Rome, the unimaginable city of marble, a second Frankish empire and a proud rule of the Popes, all sink in the dust. But they still pray in the streets of the Tiber to the God of their fathers; burst open are the gates of the Ghetto, this mark of infamy has been wiped off the face of the earth. Where the hatred of the people and church coercion have menaced the Jews for 2000 years, even there the sun of humanity has risen for them in all its glory."

To the assimilated Jew, with his faddist rationalism, historical Judaism may have been an exploded point of view, which he faced with indifference or antagonism and whose tremendous material of tradition he could neither comprehend nor revive. But Hildesheimer taught it as at once a living organism and most precious heirloom. The splintering of Judaism he fought tooth and nail. His articles in the *Juedische Presse* saved the tremendous spiritual achievements of the millennial past from oblivion and associated them, dynamically, with contemporary events and trends. Through the memory of the steadfast cultural work of the ancestors, he bestowed upon the Jewish youth strength and dignity, as he raised the position of Jewry in the world. Through assiduous study of the press, he kept in touch with everything from anti-Semitic attacks to debates in Parliament, to any speeches or writings which affected the civil rights of the Jews or their honor.

Contemptuous of all clichés and slogans, he approached all problems with directness and, because of his incisive mind, solved them without apparent effort. He looked upon Theodore Mommsen as his master who had taught him how to view world problems and perspectives. At his death in 1903 he wrote: "One of the great geniuses of mankind universally revered, a bold pioneer of scholarship, is no more. His was the record of life on the highest level, blessed by extraordinary achievement for the sacred assets of mankind. All denominational animus was muted before him. Jewry, too, benefited from his gigantic spirit. Our scholars know how his indefatigable search shed light on unknown aspects of our history. Mommsen was not only *the* great authority on political and social history of the Jews in the Roman Empire. He was also one of the great academicians to assail the shameless anti-Semitism of his time. To the very last days of his life he availed himself of every opportunity to express, in his own inimitable eloquence, his moral contempt for that mad movement. It was due to his initiative that seventy-nine notables signed a declaration against Jew-baiting and its loud-mouthed champion, Herr von Treitschke. Anti-Semitism suffered a momentary eclipse, but the filthy tide rose again early in the nineties. Its new henchmen outdid their predecessors in lowness of character and vulgarity of expression. This is what Mommsen had to say about them in 1895: 'You err when you think that where these people are concerned you can get anywhere with reason. I used to think so. Again and again I would protest against the horrible shame called anti-Semitism. But it is all in vain. *No anti-Semite pays attention to logical or ethical arguments.* He listens only to his own hatred, to his own envy, to his own abominable instincts. They are deaf to reason, right, or morality. There is no protection against the mob, be it the mob of the street or of the drawing room. Scum remains scum. Anti-Semitism is the creed of the scum, almost like a horrible epidemic.' " Hildesheimer ever retained profound reverence for the memory of Theodore Mommsen whom he called: "Master of Knowledge, champion of Liberty and Right . . . also of our liberty and our right."

ISRAEL

He set Israel above his chiefest joy. To sing her glory to his brethren was his sacred goal. He pioneered in new ways of settlement, striving to offer a maximum opportunity for independent work, for creative purpose. He aimed at promoting an industrious population, whose life would be tied up with the land of our parents. Too many generations had sinned against that wondrous land, excluding it from their calendar of duties. One day he proclaimed: "Had I not wife and child, I would walk barefoot up to Zion." Throughout his life Hildesheimer remained her noblest friend.

It was due to him that the school system of the *Hilfsverein der deutschen Juden* (German Jewry's Aid Association) in all its work remained based on Torah-true Judaism. It was his achievement that every new school answered a local need, that religious education remained the major interest. He recognized the Hebrew language as an important factor in the new life in Israel. It was his merit that the pupils received a thorough secular education. Throughout Palestine it was understood that only the *"Hilfsverein"* would convey to the pupils the benefits of modern culture without jeopardizing their religious assets. Like his father, he recognized the needs of the time and endorsed scientific training. To raise teachers and students, loyal to the tradition and at home in the problems of the day—that was the aim of both father and son, and realized by both. He was a pioneer in the combination of Torah and *Derekh Eretz*. In the introduction to his book *Beitraege zur Geographie Palestinas* (Contributions to the Geography of Palestine), Hildesheimer said: "To understand the laws related to life in the Holy Land, one must have engaged in a profound study of the country and its frontiers. In the oral Torah the borders of the land play a great role."[5] The fourteenth century physician Estori Parhi, in his work *Kaphtor va-Perah,* two Christian scholars in the 17th and 18th centuries, the geographer Joseph Schwarz in Jerusalem, and Adolph Neubauer in 1868, had written about the

---

[5]He singled out the *Tosephta Sheviit,* Talmud Jerusalem, *Sheviit, Sifre Ekeb* and *Yalkut Ekeb* as of particular significance, because they include a complete statement of all the borders of Palestine encompassing the land west and east of the Jordan. This list, because of its detailed thoroughness, has become one of the most important documents of antiquity but hitherto it had not been properly recognized nor subjected to special study.

geography of Palestine. In his lectures and publications Hildesheimer pointed up the vital significance of a scientific study of that
subject, especially also to counter the scholars of Biblical Criticism
who, for lack of such knowledge, permit themselves emendations of
the Biblical text whenever they fail to understand a passage. The
result of much of his detailed study was highly appraised also by
non-Jewish scholars. To him it was a sacred task to convey every
aspect of the emerging Jewish people. He deplored the small share,
in comparison with the great achievements of non-Jewish scholars,
the Jewish people had in the exploration of Palestine. In his
lectures, Hildesheimer made the arid material alive, showing how
to give it artistic expression, how to evoke from geographical
descriptions of local points historical nuances, how to use apparently
insignificant details for the light they could throw upon the ancient
past. The involved prosaic material, through his insight, became
fraught with meaning and the combination of the painstakingly
selected minutiae emanated a spirit which his students found
fascinating. It was due to Hildesheimer that the paramount significance of rabbinical literature for the topographical study of the
Holy Land is now generally recognized. The late Dr. Samuel
Klein, who taught geography at the Hebrew University, refers to
him as his teacher—a man of extraordinary scientific qualifications.
His practical labors for the Holy Land were related to the *Hoveve
Zion* circles of German Jewry, who aimed at the resettlement of
Israel as a command of the Torah for every God-fearing Jew.
Among their leaders was Hirsch Kalischer, Rabbi of Thorn, who in
his book, *Derishat Zion,* postulated the agricultural resettlement
of the Holy Land through Jews.[6] He was aided by Rabbi Elijah
Gutmacher, Rabbi Nathan Friedlaender, and Dr. Ch. Lurie, who
in 1861, in Frankfurt on the Oder, established the first society
Hoveve Zion, later joined by branches in other cities.

In 1883, with the cooperation of Ezriel Hildesheimer, there
was established in Berlin the society *Ezra,* for the purpose of
aiding Jews engaged in agriculture both in Palestine and Syria.
Its limited funds notwithstanding, it achieved considerable success.
Hirsch devoted himself with characteristic energy to the promotion
of its ideals.

---

[6]See his biography in the present volume.

The *Juedische Rundschau* reported Hildesheimer's encounter with Theodore Herzl which was meant to lead to the former's reporting on Palestine at the first Basel congress. But he did not attend that congress. Herzl's Zionism, rebuffed by Reform Jews, met with considerable reserve also from Torah-true circles. Perchance that was due to their fear that young people, swept off their feet by the nationalist zeal in the Zionist camp, might look upon the latter as a substitute for Torah-true life. S. R. Hirsch, in his *Horeb*[7] stated: "Our religious and spiritual task obliges us only to sentiments of mourning, hope and to prayerful wishes in connection with the faraway land. It prohibits us to seek any outward means for the reunion or the possession of the land." In the *Juedische Presse* this view is opposed with a statement of Rashi, who holds that only conquest by arms is forbidden, that the whole context of the Talmud refutes Hirsch's view. We do not know why Hirsch Hildesheimer did not join the official Zionist organization, although it moved him profoundly. When Theodore Herzl died, Hildesheimer offered his nephew, Lazarus Barth, an opportunity to eulogize Herzl in an extraordinarily warm article. Possibly, Hildesheimer felt obliged to attend to immediate purposes and tasks, feeling that the establishment of the homeland could come about only as a result of slow agricultural and industrial advance. Hence his ceaseless efforts to promote the purposes of the *Ezra*, whose flourishing was due to his ceaseless, dedicated endeavor. His energy was amazing. He had so many tasks, every one of which taxed his whole power, but he was a genius of hard work and of amazing spiritual many-sidedness. He worked sixteen hours a day, moving rapidly and achieving in minutes what would have occupied many hours. His was the richness of the genius—inexhaustibility, originality, ease and superiority. He had infinite memory; whatever he had read or experienced was always at his disposal.

His Battle Against the Blood-Libel

On June 29, 1891, in a barn in the town of Xanten on the lower Rhine, the corpse of a five-year-old boy was found with a gaping gash on his throat.

---

[7]456.

The anti-Semitic press pounced upon it with a claim that ritual murder had been committed for the purpose of obtaining blood. Suspicion was directed towards the former *Shohet* of the local synagogue. This was a germ of the so-called Buschoff trial, a dark page in German history, which ruined a family and started a movement encompassing all Germany and exploited for the purpose of vilification and slander of her one hundred thousand Jewish citizens. Buschoff was arrested and after a year in prison the trial commenced. Hildesheimer came to the rescue. His work preceded the date of the trial. He labored to assure that the government appointed judicial and scientific authorities of the very first rank, among them Professors Herrmann Strack and Theodor Noeldecke, to reveal the baselessness and the anti-Semitic motives of the accusation. Day and night he labored to achieve the clarification of the true facts, to obtain interviews, to arouse influential personages from their passivity and indifference and to enlist their interest in the establishment of the truth. Money had to be secured to pay for fees and travels. Opinions had to be scrupulously examined. Hildesheimer suspended his teaching in the single pursuit of this cause. He went to Xanten, followed the trial with greatest attention, offered valuable hints and produced the precious brief of the famous Professor Noeldecke of Strassbourg which stated that in the whole Jewish literature there was not one line of reference to ritual murder, how much less of sanction.

In many other trials Hildesheimer worked similarly. Whosoever needed relevant material turned to him and obtained it in an amazingly short time. The story of the ritual-murder libels belongs to chapters of human history which one opens with reluctance. To the non-Jewish world this is a local, temporal item which one may shrug off. In truth it has been a monster of horrible dimension which for centuries has cast a shadow on western history, bringing fear and terror into the Jewish world, destroying confidence and brotherly love, and ravaging truth!

These libels have always been outside the realm of reason, a matter of mass-madness, cancelling the normal outlook of the individual, vanquishing his reason and his personal values. A suggestion which would appear insane to the isolated individual will, as soon as it has become a mass madness, destroy his personality and conquer him, as a hypnotizer conquers his medium. Soon, everywhere the danger lurks of mass-insanity conjuring mad mass-action. The fate of a nation depends on its possession of men who recognize the danger early enough and possess ethical power enough to battle and stop instigators of that madness before it is too late. The whole history of the ritual murder libel is a single piercing shriek of human beings senselessly tortured. Dr. Hildesheimer's victory came from his sweeping power of persuasion. It was given to this indefatigable man to ward off the Damocles sword over the head of mid-European Jewry, to brand the blood libel as the monster of raving insanity.

Once more was Hildesheimer compelled to appear in such trial. In the city of Konitz, the high-school boy Winter was found dead and again a violent incitement against the Jews resulted. The Catholic clergy in the district received hate literature, especially the libelous pamphlets of Rohling. Again Hildesheimer came to the rescue. The Jews were acquitted but the real murderers were not discovered. The anti-Semites exploited that. They cast suspicion upon the Government and the scientist, Professor W. von Bergman, of having been bribed by the Jews.[8]

A curious accident brought to Hildesheimer a manuscript from the Vatican's secret library about the Trial of Trient which gave him an insight into the entanglement and ineffable tragedy of that trial in which all the accused to the last moment avowed their innocence. The apostolic brief is dated October 10, 1475, when the trial of Trient long ago had ended. It not only prohibits by penalty of excommunication the cult of the boy of Trient which the people had indulged in, but states expressly: *"Hitherto nothing is assured or endorsed by either our judgment or otherwise confirms the alleged murder of Simon of Trient by the Jews."*

The Pope indicated clearly enough that he condemned the whole trial and that he attached no significance to the confessions extorted from the tortured Jews, the single "evidence" of their guilt. In that brief, Pope Sixtus had promised an investigation through a legate appointed for that purpose. It was carried on by the Bishop of Ventinillia in 1476, both in Trient and Roverado, and established the innocence of the Jews, for Angelinus, citizen of

---

[8]This was in conformity with an ancient pattern, for in 1475 in connection with the blood libel of Trient, the very Pope Sixtus IV and his nuncios were similarly accused.

Trient, accused the Swiss Zanasius, a resident of that city and a Jew-hater, as murderer of the boy. Furthermore, it was established that the "confessions" of the Jews were obtained through the most cruel tortures. The papal legate established the fact that most of the so-called miracles of Trient were baseless lies, and that all the notaries of the Bishop of Trient were forgers who had written their copies in utter faithlessness. Thus the verdict was against the Bishop Hindebach of Trient and his henchmen who had brought about the execution of the Jews! Hirsch Hildesheimer arranged for a new revised and improved edition of the work *Das Blut im Glauben und Aberglauben der Menschheit* (Blood in the faith and superstition of Mankind), which Professor Herrmann Strack of Berlin had written, as well as a translation into German of Professor Chwolson's "The Blood-libel against the Jews"; both of these volumes exerted profound influence. The slanderers of Konitz were sentenced to penal servitude for many years.

The Battle for Shehitah

The last years of Hirsch Hildesheimer's life were devoted to the defense of *Shehitah* against persistent, ruthless attacks. It represents the hardest, most exacting, most fruitful enterprise of his life. It not only called forth his capacity for indefatigable work, but imposed upon him the obligation of acquiring detailed knowledge for his dauntless militancy against determined opposition. Switzerland and Saxony had already prohibited *Shehitah*. The anti-Semitic press aimed, by hook and crook, to bring about such prohibition in Prussia and all the federated states of Germany. Hildesheimer procured 300 briefs from veterinaries and from professors of physiology and anatomy, all declaring *Shehitah* the best method of slaughtering. In characteristic self-effacement, he published this first collection anonymously. When hate-mongering journalists declared this book a forgery, Hildesheimer sued them in order to establish its veracity before the court: Organized anti-Semitism arranged for a ruthless country-wide agitation. It succeeded in arousing Hildesheimer's depth of indignation and tremendous powers to ward it off.

The whole depth of this literary rowdyism was revealed in a pamphlet by a Dr. von Schwartz, which actually proclaimed the Jews' loyalty to *Shehitah* to be based not on religious scruples but on the large income the Jewish community derived from the *Shehitah*-fees. Hildesheimer answered: "It takes anti-Semitism to invent such low motivation, to interpret religious inspiration in terms of vulgar profits. These haters are utterly unaware of the fact that we Jews look upon the forcible suppression of our holy religious laws as an invasion of our constitutional rights, as a violation of freedom of conscience, as a deliberate curtailment of our civil liberties. The defense of *Shehitah* is for us not only an imperative for survival, but imposed by a sense of our dignity. We rely on cultured people everywhere to join us in our contempt for that unworthy insinuation. Christians would resent any Jewish judgment about the contents or the obligatory character of their laws or doctrines, especially if such Jews expect such judgment to have a decisive influence on the toleration or oppression of bases of Christianity which its clergy would describe as inviolable. All Jews would join the rejection of any such effort as irreverent. They would state that in intra-Christian problems the outsider had best preserve silence because that division of opinion between Christian science and precepts is a matter of intra-faith discussions and decision. In 1894, all 259 rabbis of Germany, of all shades of religious opinion, signed the following declaration: 'To remove wrong impression and false reports, we unanimously state that *Shehitah* (the ritual method of slaughtering animals) is a religious law of Judaism based on its Biblical and post-Biblical literature. In accordance therewith, an animal may be slaughtered only when none of his vital organs has been injured. Stunning by blows on the head, above or below a protective mask, would result in violation of the law of slaughter and would force hundreds of thousands of adherents of Judaism to do without this essential food in order to avoid burdening their conscience with this violation of religious law.'

"This declaration was endorsed, with enthusiastic unanimity, by all the rabbis of Austria and of other countries wherever the need for such a statement arose. There is not a single rabbi in Germany, even of the extreme Reform group, who would deny the obligatory quality of *Shehitah* and its eminently religious nature. Beyond the shadow of a doubt, this has been the historic position of Judaism in all countries and climes."

This collection of opinions in favor of *Shehitah* is a tremendous achievement and represents a genuine *Kiddush Hashem*. Henceforth, Hirsch Hildesheimer was regarded as the first authority on such problems, to whom questions and appeals were addressed from all over the world. Of crucial importance was the session on *Shehitah* of the Reichstag (German Parliament) on May 18, 1887. His *Gutachten ueber das rituelle Schaechten* (Briefs on Ritual Slaughter) evoked this statement from Rudolf Virchow, director of the of the Pathological Institute of Berlin: "My knowledge of *Shehitah* justifies these briefs. Its purposes is to avoid unnecessary cruelty to the animal, and through complete removal of the blood, it renders the meat most wholesome for human consumption. Whenever this ritual is observed in all its detail, both purposes are achieved in a manner infinitely safer than any other method of killing. There is not a ghost of justification in the statement that *Shehitah* represents cruelty to animals." Two hundred fifty-three *Gutachten,* written by luminaries of academies and expert veterinarians, express themselves in like manner.

On April 25, 1899, Baron von Tiedeman, government chief executive, declared, "I witnessed *Shehitah* today and I must say I am convinced that if practiced by a skillful *Shohet,* it represents the least cruel and most efficient method imaginable. My own opinion is buttressed by countless views of experts." What tremendous work was accomplished in so brief a time, how many conferences and consultations with government authorities, with officers of societies for the prevention of cruelty to animals, with parliamentarians and members of the clergy, how many statements of enlightenment, how many refutations of attacks!

Hildesheimer was no longer alive when the law prohibiting *Shehitah* represents cruelty to animals." Two hundred fifty-three monument to his glory. His own booklet on *Shehitah* together with the Briefs, formed the arsenal of defense for our religious tradition whenever it was assailed.

HILDESHEIMER THE MAN

He possessed a precious sense of humor, ingenious, kindly, which conquered the hearts of men and created around him an atmosphere of happy fellowship and serenity. In the highest sense of the word, he was the life of any party.

His personality was a harmonius combination of moral aristocracy and intellectual greatness, yet simple, tender, and of bewitching charm. Such superlatives may create an inner opposition in the reader. All light has shadows, but the shadows in Hildesheimer represented but his profound sympathy, his prophetic indignation at oppression, his restless quest to comfort the mourner, and strengthen the weak. There was no organization, cultural or charitable, that could not count on his cooperation. He led many such enterprises, from the Society for Jewish History and Literature to the *Hilfsverein der Deutschen Juden.* The minutes contain amazing documentation of his dedicated work. On the very day of his death, two letters arrived in the office of the *Hilfsverein,* pleading for two hard-pressed families in Russia. These last messages of his life might well serve as testament of his great heart. On December 5th of 1910 he died suddenly. A young rabbi had submitted a scholarly article which he was discussing with his usual eagerness when he was suddenly stricken. A verse from the Torah was the last breath of his lips.

Friends and disciples and a host of poor people followed the hearse, their hearts ravished, their eyes wet. He is buried in the heart of the Jewish people whom he defended, whose Torah he taught, whose dignity he upheld. The monument of his scholarship and philanthropy will be *aere peraennius,* untouched by time.

SAMUEL HIRSCH MARGULIES

(1858-1922)

By Dario Disegni

(translated by Mitzi Feuerstein, from the Italian)

SAMUEL HIRSCH MARGULIES

By Dario Disegni

Many years have passed since the death of Rabbi Samuel Hirsch Margulies, yet his portrait has stayed with his flock as a noble symbol and luminous example. He was a spiritual leader who guided them, aroused their hearts, and never failed to comfort those who mourned. The rabbis said: "It is not necessary to build monuments for the righteous; their words are their memorial."

He gave thirty-two years of dedicated work to Italian Jewry: a labor for the sake of Heaven, with no reward beyond the satisfaction which comes from fulfilling one's duty; of having benefited the institutions charged with guarding the spirit of Israel and arousing it to new life; of having spread knowledge of the ideas for which countless generations suffered and dreamt. He devoted himself to his role with a determination which did not recoil before any handicap, with a courage that gathered strength from the very difficulties against which it stumbled. He discharged his obligations without distinction between "major" and "minor", for to him they were all major; greater all the more, when they seemed minor; all the more important when they seemed of little consequence. A rigorous observer of the *Din Torah,* he proclaimed its principles according to the tradition of the Sages in uncribbed completeness.

I.

What were the conditions of life of the Jews of Italy, and particularly, of the community of Florence, when Rabbi Margulies appeared on the scene? Jewish Florence boasted a glorious past, particularly in the Middle Ages. At the end of the 19th Century, a religious crisis broke out. Assimilation was rampant. All services related to religion were abandoned. This was partly due to the fact that Rabbi Maroni, much advanced in age and failing in strength, lacked the energy to oppose the decadence. When he passed away, every one realized that it was difficult to find a replacement for him. Apart from the renowned Rabbi Elijah Benamozegh of Livorno, there were no rabbis of stature fit to accept this post, which demanded firm will, great spiritual power, and extraordinary wisdom.

The attorney, Moses Finzi, of blessed memory, was one of the important representatives of the Florentine community. In the course of his many journeys throughout Europe, he came to know Samuel Hirsch Margulies, a young rabbi of a distinguished family of Polish Jewry and trained in the Breslau Rabbinical Seminary, and thought him a fitting successor to Rabbi Maroni. His training prepared him for a life-program, progressive in method and loyal to the Jewish tradition. Rabbi Margulies accepted the invitation. The Jews of Florence at first received the news of his selection without great enthusiasm. The very conservative elements were afraid of the innovations which a rabbi who had studied philosophy in a modern institution would introduce. Many worried about the differences between Italian and Polish Jews, and that the new rabbi might not be able to adapt himself to the Italian language. But he had already been living in Ancona and there acquired a thorough knowledge of Italian. Within less than a hundred days, Rabbi Margulies appeared for the first time in the Great Synagogue of Florence and surprised the audience by his pure Italian speech and his almost Tuscan accent.

His first labors were devoted to organizing the religious services of the community, in particular to *Kashrut* and *Taharat ha-Mishpahah* (the institution of family purity). But he viewed education as his most cherished task. He opened an elementary school, *Talmud Torah,* in one of the modest streets of Florence, which he would attend every afternoon, in all seasons of the year, as teacher of the primary grades.

II.

That little school he developed later on into a rabbinical seminary. In that modest street was created the institution that was the dynamo which lit the lamp that spread the light of Samuel David Luzzatto. The seminary of Rabbi Margulies became so famous in Italy that Raphael Prato of Florence, then the President of the Italian Rabbinical Seminary, decided to move this institution from Rome to Florence. The new seminary grew to a high scholarly level because of the work of great scholars who assisted

Rabbi Margulies, such as Elbogen, Chius, Vogelmann, and finally the disciple beloved of the master, M. D. Cassuto.

We learned from our exalted teacher the responsibilities of a spiritual leader. He caused the thought to penetrate our heart that the rabbi of the community is responsible for all that is done within it. Oft-quoted by him was the dictum of the Sages: "If a rabbinical scholar is present in the city, all matters of the city depend upon him." He taught us that the rabbi, whilst a strict observer of *Halakhah,* should be mild in spirit, the guide who points out the way to God. He counseled us to establish an abiding contact with individuals and to engage in the spiritual training of families; dedicate to them the best of our power, to comfort the weary, uphold those in despair; to steady those in doubt and particularly those who hide their grief; to bring sinners back to His way of life. He brought to his pulpit learning, wisdom, and his rich human experience. Judaism's central position, he insisted, was occupied by the Prophets, whose messages contain all the light-spreading sparks, all the spiritual forces, holiness and purity as an eternal foundation of life. He taught us a sense of the prestige and glory of the rabbinate, its influence and indispensability, whether in contacts with scholars or with the masses of the people, the latter often prone to ignore its loftiness and to be aware only of the imperfections of some of its minor members. From the rabbi we learned to comport ourselves with tolerance as we view the circumstances which render it difficult for individuals to conform with the discipline of the Torah. But he would not tolerate any compromise, for that would diminish the authority of the Torah and deny its divine nature and origin.

III.

Between the rabbi and his disciples prevailed love and brotherhood, notwithstanding the great difference in wisdom and experience. He brought personal sacrifices for their sake so that they should not lack spiritual or material sustenance. He would undertake prolonged, wearisome travels all over Italy to gather money for the needs of the seminary. His students will never forget the burdens he assumed—how he would rise in the cold winter to teach Talmud and Midrash in the early hours of morning because the students were compelled to attend to their secular education during most of the hours of the day. Every Sabbath morning he would join in the prayer-service of the students, which began while it was still night. (The Jews of Florence nicknamed it "the prayer-service of the builders" (phonetically in Hebrew, "sons"). And when one of us, after having reached the end of his studies, left the seminary, our rabbi and mentor would accompany him in his thought, watch over his steps, counsel him in every case of doubt. The light of the seminary spread beyond its walls. It became a lighthouse to all Italian Jews. Besides the students intending to become rabbis, other young men attended classes in the seminary. They, too, were the rabbi's spiritual children. To his enterprise, Italian Jewry owes the founding and publication of a periodical, *The Israelite Week*. He taught that Israel could not survive without constant study of his sources in literature and history. The Jews of Italy, who had received various cultural influences, needed someone who could teach them to know and esteem their own. They were in need of a tie between them and the other members of their people in the four corners of the earth. *The Israelite Week,* under the editorship of Rabbi Margulies, served this purpose for many years.

Somewhat earlier, the rabbi had commenced publishing a scientific periodical, *Rivista Israelitica,* for scholars and researchers in the science of Judaism.

IV.

Rabbi Margulies attributed great importance to the renaissance of the people of Israel in the Land of Israel. Judaism, he said, from the days of the destruction of the Temple to our own days, has been a national-religious phenomenon. Because they were conscious of this fact, the Jews demanded that there be raised up anew the Jewish State. T. Herzl heard this voice and gave expression to this great idea. In a marvelous Passover sermon, the rabbi emphasized that in the national life of Israel in its own land, its springtime had been renewed as in the days of the Exodus from Egypt. He pointed out that in our days, by will of the Supreme Understanding, a new leader had risen, a genius, who, with his powerful and courageous voice, had sounded the call to renaissance;

he also pointed out that the best among Jewish youth had responded to this voice; awakened forgotten voices of the past and restored love for the national homeland. The movement of the revival was advancing with ever growing strength and was beginning to bring forth new branches from the old stock of Israel. He concluded with the prediction that the noble among the youth of our people, bold of heart and strong, were going to till the soil of Palestine.

About the year 1906 the cause of the Falashas stirred Italy. Professor Faitlowich, of blessed memory, after journeying to Abyssinia and living for a year among those abandoned Jews, directed the attention of the Italian government to the problem. The Falashas declared that they were Jews and sought help against the contrivances of the Christian missionaries. They vowed determination to remain loyal to the Torah and asked for text-books and teachers. Faitlowich turned to Rabbi Margulies, who at once organized a standing committee and after some time transferred a number of young Falashas to Italy. We remember, in particular, our comrade, Emanuel Timrath, who pursued sacred and secular studies in Italy and afterwards returned to his country and directed a school of teachers.

V.

When Italy conquered Tripoli, the heads of that community turned to Rabbi Margulies and proclaimed him the *Gaon* of the land of Lybia. He sailed to Tripoli, where he was received with great emotion. Although, because of his responsibilities in Italy, he could not remain there permanently, he promised his support to those movements introducing order into the Jewry of Lybia and to raise its moral and religious level.

Rabbi Margulies suffered greatly (and perhaps his suffering hastened the day of his sudden death) because of slanderous attacks by fellow Jews against him. During the days of the First World War, he was in danger of being exiled to one of the cast-off isles. He was delivered from his peril through the strong efforts of an important political personage, who vouched for his integrity.

I mention here a personal detail. Some months after the rabbi arrived at Florence, my mother, of blessed memory, was stricken with a fatal disease. The rabbi came often to fulfil the *mitzvah* of *bikkur holim* (visiting the sick). Sensing her inarticulate thoughts, he promised her, a few days before her death, that he would do his utmost for her son to study Torah until he reached ordination. He had no children of his own, but he loved his students as a father loves his children.

So much did he love his community, that he turned down the many invitations extended to him to greater and more comfortable posts.

To this day we still seem to hear his voice chanting the *Kol Nidre* prayer in the synagogue; the *Neilah* with its traditional melody; the words of his sublime sermons, wherein were mingled in marvelous blend the universal ideas of the teachings of Torah with those which welled from the soul of the "peculiar people", separated from all the others. In particular, we still hear the echo of his voice in his final sermon, a few minutes before he was taken from us. In all his addresses there was a kind of synthesis of hoary Israel and the life of our days.

A special majesty was added to him by his handsomeness and his manner of walk. In Florence all knew him and would look upon him with profound esteem as he passed along the streets of the city on his way to school, to the home for the aged, the orphan asylum, or to visit the sick. He participated in funerals and never failed to appear if the deceased belonged to the poorer class.

His pure soul was taken to the Eternal World without his having suffered the pangs of disease. He went up to Heaven as he was speaking words of encouragement and love to the school-children. Providence above had mercy upon him and spared him the sorrow of the years of persecution and murder and annihilation that were to follow. His memory, a source of blessing, has ever brought us nearer to our Father in heaven and has proved a source of dynamic Jewishness to all who share in its blessing.

JOSEPH LEIB BLOCH

(1860-1920)

BY JUDA ARI WOHLGEMUTH

JOSEPH LEIB BLOCH

By Juda Ari Wohlgemuth

In Western culture we admire the man who has put himself over. We call a leader him who has achieved fulfilment over all personal and collective handicaps. In truth, such people are neither leaders nor models. There are many successful men, free from egoistic drive, bereft of opportunity or of favorable milieu, or of ruthlessness, who have achieved the realization of their ambition, notwithstanding the fact that they are unrecognized, unappreciated, unknown to the common herd.

The powerful thinkers, the pure in heart to whom the weal of the Jewish people stands committed, the heroes of our religion who attracted the attention of their contemporaries in all climes, are distinguished by the fact that on closer view, one does not find a basic contrast between the champions and the mass of their followers. They are, rather, fortunate representatives of a whole group of men equally endowed as thinkers, equally inspired disciples of the "Word", equally unique in soul-strength.

Eastern European Jewry achieved its extraordinary religious and spiritual level through the élite of a goodly number of such men. The leader's personality is uniquely aided by his sharing in a free collectivity of men of similar qualities. Ultimately, he is *"optimus inter pares"* (the best among equals).

Rabbi J. L. Bloch was not only a *Gaon* (great luminary) of the Talmud, an integrated personality of the Jewish spirit, and a model of moral life. What set him above a host of comrades and colleagues is the fact, "alive and dead", he appears a singular, yet humble exponent of Torah, ever conscious of responsibility, a farsighted leader, ever purposive, indeed a pioneer of abiding spirituality.

I.

He lived in Telshe, a town in the western part of Lithuania, counting several thousand souls, mostly Jews, and blessed by a railroad station just a generation ago, when it was almost unaware of life beyond its environs. As against Germany, its western neighbor, its population was conspicuously poor. Near Telshe was the frontier of East Prussia. It separated not only states and nationalities, but cultures and modes of living.

The Jews of Telshe lived in modest frame dwellings and derived their meager livelihood from petty trades and crafts. They were well aware of their financial inferiority and always wondered how a German student, who normally enjoyed an incomparably higher standard of living, could ever adjust himself to the primitiveness of that little town.

But, in spite of all that, the Jews of Telshe had a healthy self-consciousness. This apparently forlorn community was ever pulsating with amazing vitality. The Yiddish newspaper coming from Kovno, the capital, kept them in constant touch with the cultural progress of mankind and the fortunes of Jewry everywhere.

The alertness of Lithuanian Jewry, trained by the Talmud, could not brook any self-confinement to the Ghetto. The Jewish "Litvak" had stability and serenity enough not to be downed by the troubles of life.

Rabbi Bloch became rabbi of Telshe a few years before the First World War. He succeeded Rabbi Eliezer Gordon, the famous founder of the *yeshivah*. The city had just been rebuilt by foreign help after one of the too frequent conflagrations had well-nigh ruined it.

Rabbi Bloch was not only a *Gaon* of the Torah, but thoroughly democratic, tenderhearted and most beloved. He enjoyed the respect due to a leader and the authority of a prince of the Torah. The latter meant that there was one court to decide all litigation, all suits, religious or secular: It was the *Rov* that one consulted in matters of business; the *Rov* who was the supreme interpreter of the Torah in the synagogue and in the houses of learning.

There were learned laymen or advanced students of the *yeshivah* who presided over lecture courses in Talmud or Bible. The *Rov* did not need to superintend them, since they were competent enough for those courses. But the *Rov* was ever alert, the city always submitted to his judgment and would never countermand his view. Even before World War I, life in Telshe was no more compact, the spiritual unity of the community had been adversely affected. Whereas the general picture of Jewishness conformed to the classic pattern—genuine Sabbath observance, unbroken passion for learning, the scope of Jewish life in pristine strength—yet there were breaches in the fortress of Jewish life. There were the so-called "enlightened Jews", mostly rich men who travelled to Russia, who would rather speak Russian than Yiddish, who publicly respected the Jewish tradition, only to avoid the enmity of the religious folks. There were some freethinking Zionists, socialistically inclined, not too numerous but not to be ignored. These two groups were in overt or covert opposition to the "Court of the Rabbi". Whilst the Jewish community in Telshe respected the concept of genuine Jewishness and what its leadership spelled, nevertheless the reading of anti-religious literature, of a press hostile to the Jewish religion and its often satirical reference to the rabbinate, had its repercussions. The towering personality of Rabbi Bloch, in spite of all the criticism of his authoritarian bearing, achieved full recognition by friend and foe alike. He was a disciple of the famous Torah Academy of Kelm, led by R. S. Siev, whose disciples created an élite of men imbued by the teaching of *Mussar* and trained to assume leadership of Torah-true Judaism. Rabbi Bloch acquired the spiritual skill to adjust the discipline of Talmudic thought to the sphere of piety. The disciples of Kelm, who won golden opinions as rabbis and directors of academies of the Talmud, have been of paramount significance for the preservation and promotion of our ancestral faith. But they differed greatly as to personality. All of them share the discipline of self-control, clarity of judgment, balance between intellectual effort and spiritual enrichment.

Yet none of them represented the essence of the Jewish prince of the spirit in its harmonious relation of intellect and emotion in as glorious a pattern as Rabbi Bloch of Telshe.

II.

The school of Kelm succeeded in training men who were unique in the combination of thinking and emotional power, based on deep commitment to the faith. In Kelm everything was rigidly organized: form as well as detail of curriculum, the mode of study no less than the fulfillment of religious duty. The real élan of mediation and action was led through *Mussar* based on imagination and striving for truth and self-perfection. If, e.g., the principal of the Talmud Torah would notice that the rubbers of a student were flung carelessly about the room, he might use the occasion to deliver a long discourse on the absolute need for order in one's public appearance; for a man's outer attitude but mirrors his inner being and one who is careless about matters of the spirit might be exposed to unbridled passions and therefore to sin. Such discourses often moved the listeners to tears, often to special prayers seeking atonement. Thence Joseph Bloch derived his phenomenal self-discipline, thence his daily Torah curriculum which would brook no outside influence, thence the abiding judicious attitude towards individual and collective needs. Even outwardly he looked like an aristocratic scholar, his dress perfectly neat, his face ever friendly and yet dignified, his eyes brilliant behind the protection of his glasses. When the Telsher *Rov,* usually accompanied by a member of his family, would appear at the end of a street, the students would nudge each other: "Look— the *Rov,*" with mingled awe and admiration. The *Rov* occupied one of the few stone houses of the town. To the Jewish people it was a palace. Rabbi Bloch was not always available for interviews. He insisted upon rigid etiquette. No wonder that some of this "distance and rigidity" appeared to some as arrogance and provoked the satirical animadversions of freethinkers. On *Simhat Torah,* the *Rov* would be carried in a chair—by a train of attendants and with loud chanting—into the great room of the *yeshivah,* apparently perfectly pleased to receive the adulation of his followers. Even friends might be excused from thinking that he enjoyed such trappings of authority. In truth, however, it was altogether different. His attitude was in complete conformity with the Torah and the spirit of *Mussar.* He held that the *Rov* of such a community and the head of such an academy was obliged to assume the symbols of outward authority, since the respect due to a prince of the Torah had in modern times suffered too much to permit dispensing with these externalities. The more thorough observer could not fail to see that Rabbi Bloch took all this with a sense of humor. Everybody in Telshe would remain standing in the presence of the rabbi, even as a servant of old in the presence of his master; but during his *shiur* (lecture) in the great hall of the *yeshivah*—and he spoke from a cathedra surrounded by a wooden fence—he would be assailed by ruthless questions of students of all ages, whose intellectual passion would "menace" him, as they gesticulated before him as if he were an ordinary combatant. His inner happiness with his opponents' keen arguments was revealed in his face.

None of us will forget the sight of the rabbi during divine service, when the priests blessed the congregation. He would move from his place to the midst of the synagogue and stand next to the beadle, a wretched figure of a man, praying out of one *siddur* with him and chanting the prayers in warm fellowship. The present writer cherishes the memory of the Law of the Torah cancelling differences of class or position.

Joseph Bloch, in another sense, too, was a pioneer: in the consistent attitude of the Torah-Jew towards the changing fashion of contemporary cultural patterns. This consistency does not mean the deplorable shutting out of the events of history, to which many otherwise fine types of leaders escape. Cultural development requires the assertion of one's position, the development of a program for the preservation of the tradition and for a spiritual future.

III.

The First World War afflicted Telshe bitterly. Part of the populace escaped into Russia, the rest suffered under the German occupation, although the latter, with all its brutality, was sheer paradise in comparison with the Nazi regime in the Second World War. It had been a tradition of Berlin's Torah-true Jews to support the Lithuanian *yeshivot*. When Rabbi Bloch during that war visited that metropolis on their behalf, he received sufficient help to carry on their academic work. War brought economic distress and considerable dependence to these aristocrats of the spirit, but it could not modify their steady purpose. The authority of the Torah and the precious quality of our tradition rendered him deeply resentful of any opposition to its ancient ways out of consideration for the opinion of the non-Jewish world. A German rabbi, venturing to criticize his attitude, found himself rebuked without any consideration of the fact that his high position with the occupation authorities might have rendered his displeasure a source of much danger to the *yeshivah*. In the light of the timidity of some modern leaders and their eagerness to compromise the dignity of the Torah, Rabbi Bloch's conduct appears the more admirable. This attitude he maintained in the difficult times after the war. Even before the establishment of the independent state of Lithuania, the need had arisen for taking a stand, for rejecting, for the Jewish population, the curriculum of state schools in which a small niche was reserved for the disciplines of religion, the total program dedicated to secular study. After the establishment, the situation worsened. Jewry was divided into various parties, contending with each other both within the Jewish camp and in their relation with their non-Jewish neighbors. This conflict was most pronounced in the field of education. There were passioned battles of the books, the magazines, and the newspapers about schools, especially the Yiddishist and Hebrew schools maintained by Bundists and Zionists, in which the children received an education often diametrically opposed to the *Weltanschauung* of Judaism. In that battle the youth organizations played a great role. Even cities like Telshe, with its compact loyalty to Jewish life and law, were exposed to the revolutionary energies of the youth. Men like Leo Deutschlander brought the best of West European methods of education to the leaders of Lithuanian Orthodoxy. But its effects were not too obvious. The elections to community leadership, as well as to the Jewish faction in the Lithuanian Parliament, were very upsetting. Rabbi Bloch stood up to fight for his point of view. An orator by the grace of God, he would charge his flock to engage in the political battle and to assure the continuation of Jewish education in the light of the Torah. Those who were present will never forget his interpretation of the meaning of the Jewish community. "Whether its tendency is towards the right or the left, is a problem in itself. But," said Rabbi Bloch, "I am the *Rov* in town and Jews obey their *Rov*," whereupon he burst into tears.

Thus he regretted the need to emphasize his authority. He humbly acknowledged his "failure" to fill in truth the position that God and his people had bestowed upon him, so that his word be taken for granted, so that his community would accept his guidance without the need of his introducing any personal remarks. He presented a rare combination of the courage to fight and the integrity of self-criticism!

Even towards his colleagues the Rabbi of Telshe displayed courage. There were some who could not decide on creative action in the light of the corroding effects of anti-traditional education in non-Orthodox institutions. But he built in Telshe a compact system of Torah education which gradually was recognized by all shades of opinion. He conformed with the demands of the state where they were unavoidable. He introduced secular education in the elementary schools and Hebrew as a language of instruction for some disciplines. Himself an anti-Zionist, he met the demand for Hebrew because it served as a preparation for entering his *yeshivah*. He knew how to attract to educational work those of his students who showed special aptness for this task. He had his reservations about Western education. He recognized the need to train the youth in some trade or craft in order to provide a livelihood for them and a social position, with the Torah remaining primary. He had deep philosophical interest but he would not recognize the relevancy of West European Orthodoxy's preoccupation with the problem of "Torah and Modern Education". He recognized the value of science and technical skill. To secure a Torah-true life, he looked upon the provisions of such disciplines as necessary and, therefore, acceptable. He made no point about the *Bachurim* studying non-Jewish books or foreign languages in their free periods. As long as these avocations were held within bounds and the piety of the youth was cultivated through intensive *Mussar* self-discipline and assiduous study of the Torah, he could see no danger in these tangential occupations with other mental interests.

His point of view did not meet with the approval of other rabbinic authorities, neither did his establishment in Telshe of a Girls' High School, with Hebrew as a language of instruction. But nobody dared assail the pure intention and the religious ethos of this leader, especially since the educational results in all his institutions were most satisfactory. Telshe and its *Rov* had become a symbol of creative far-sighted Judaism in the Jewish camp and beyond.

Rabbi Bloch was distinguished by self-discipline, a happy balance between the will to lead and inner humility, a far-sighted plan of a system of Torah education in which he recognized the needs of the time and yet knew how to fit them into the framework of the Torah. All this was crowned by his exceptional pedagogical qualities.

His genius revealed itself especially in the management of the *yeshivah* which the great *Gaon* Rabbi Hayyim shared with him. These two men differed widely in appearance and in attitude. Rabbi Hayyim was a small man, his face encased in a mighty beard and rendered most vivid by a pair of eyes as dynamic as they were benign. His whole life was his *"lernen"*, his study of the Talmud. He lived that *"lernen"*, he was passionately dedicated to it. The movement of his hand even in the hour of prayer betrayed his ceaseless preoccupation with his problems. Against his own will, it invaded his prayerful moments.

The students loved Rabbi Hayyim profoundly. They felt closer to him than to Rabbi Joseph Leib; with the latter they were always aware of a distance. Nevertheless, these two men cooperated in harmony and the students appreciated their different personalities. Rabbi Hayyim was more democratic, he conveyed his teaching through his strikingly expressive gesticulation. He is reported once to have explained: "My *shiur* (lecture) one cannot write down, because it is impossible to include the movement of my hands." The reader would miss both its force and the nuances of the argument.

The student who had completed the preparatory classes was admitted to the *yeshivah* and was then obliged to take the order of the *shiurim*. The young men studied together in a large study hall, either alone or with a colleague. Several times a week Rabbi Hayyim gave his first and second *shiur,* for beginners and for more advanced students. The third *shiur* was offered by Rabbi Bloch both for his best students and for the whole *yeshivah*. To this was added a *Kollel* (a postgraduate institution of young married or unmarried rabbis) which enjoyed independence of the Yeshivah. Rabbi Bloch's choice of subject and his manner of dealing with the Talmudic raw material were unique: his occasional publications and especially his literary legacy testify to that. He would commence with a difficult passage in the *Gemara,* a problem that impressed itself at once on the student of the text; to render the question more profound and for the purpose of preliminary answers, other passages of the Talmud or relevant opinions, that of Maimonides or other classic authorities, would be added. In this manner Rabbi Bloch arrived at a *Hakirah,* at a confrontation of two legitimate interpretations of concepts, at the presentation of two alternatives which appeared from behind the original question and which were being clarified through adducing of material of similar validity.

He buttressed the importance of that "either-or" situation through new passages and demonstrated occasionally the importance of this ambiguity for practical problems of Jewish law. At the end, he would sum up both the problem and the solutions.

This treatment of Talmudical problems finds its parallel in other tendencies of Lithuanian *yeshivot*. Whilst they did not altogether reject the brilliant *pilpul* (rabbinical dialectics), the rapid succession of various argumentations in the frame of a specialized problem, one can penetrate the character of that method of study only as one clearly understands that its abiding purpose is the clarification of a basic question. The exercise of analysis and combination are being consciously limited in the interest of a truth that is to be elicited. Rabbi Bloch's special quality in the frame of Lithuanian Jewish "learning" was definitely pedagogical. On the one hand he recognized personally an ever new insight achieved in the study of the unlimited territory of the Talmud. The study of the Talmud spelled both a fulfillment of a basic Torah-duty and the spiritual satisfaction achieved in the effort. But the student is subjected to a discipline: he may not lose himself in insubstantial speculations, no matter how ingenious. Since every problem is related to a difficult passage in the Talmud, the scholar assumes the status of one who serves, who attempts to qualify a definite passage in the ocean of the Talmud. He is both subservient to the text and cooperator in the timeless creative enterprises of the Torah spirit. A simple observation will help to distinguish this method from that of western students of the spirit. The latter aims at a survey to be achieved through criticism, analysis and synthesis. But this endeavor to systematize any specialized intellectual material implied a menace to the achievement of truth, for as we endeavor to classify and survey, we accept a point of view or a category of thought outside the subject matter that engages us; whereas he who studies the Talmud "on its page" (*al ha-daf*), will obtain his cognitions from the text itself.

Rabbi Bloch's directive had its profound pedagogic results. Without special emphasis, he trained his disciples to look upon themselves as subservient to the truths of the Torah. The ever fresh elucidation of research was their abiding purpose. This

Hakirah (search) raises the text-bound Talmudic problem (which arose once in time and from a definite position) into the sphere of general thought. The student is shown that behind the particular subject matter to which he devotes himself there is a philosophical and psychological complex of ideas which, in however infinitesimal measure, reveals the profound thought of the masters of the Torah and the motive of the Divine Lawgiver. The student recognizes that his specialized share of Talmud study is an important document of a universal world of the spirit. This awareness raises his interest and lends wings to his ambition to have part in the clarification of the Torah. He is made to see that his study of the Torah is an important part of the task of spreading it into wider spheres. Thus, above and beyond the intellectual, it is the didactic purposes of the Torah, the inculcation of its religious and moral teachings, which are promoted and increased. At the same time, a bridge is built, through *Hakirah,* for the moral and religious purposes of all Talmudic study, a view is obtained for the deeper *a prioris* of which the rationalist is not always aware. A man who studies without being conscious of the bridge and the shore and the concentric sphere of learning, subjects himself to the moral hazard of becoming lost in sterile pursuits.

Through a definitive survey of the results, through the necessity of accounting clearly for the divergencies of various opinions, the student is being trained not to accept any patchwork, but to aim at an integrated understanding, to be satisfied with nothing but a genuine illumination of a totality. This is a truly scientific facet in the matter of study initiated by Rabbi Joseph Bloch.

His *Hagadic,* non-preceptive, discussions, which complemented the *Halakhic,* or preceptive, lectures, also had a distinction of their own. All over Lithuania, the curriculum of the *yeshivot* was prepared in accord with the views of Rabbi Israel Salanter, who considered the study of the Talmud as insufficient for integrative Torah education that would be prepared for all the attacks of modernism. There was a cleavage between the *Mussar,* the preoccupation with *"Weltanschauung",* and the guidance towards self-training of a Torah-true Jew. But Telshe would not allow a *Mashgiah* (the special moral mentor of the *yeshivah* student) to function. The duties of the *Rov,* head of the *yeshivah,* included also this important aspect of education. It was a matter of principle with Rabbi Bloch, who would not recognize any independent region of the educational enterprise, outside the all-embracing world of Torah and Talmud. The *yeshivah* youth should receive all the guidance for thinking and living from one central source.

It is for that reason that he called his *Agadistic* and moral lesson, *"Lectures on Understanding"*. What was involved was recognition of "Being" and "Duty" as Torah-Jew. Matters of the Jewish spirit, always within the sphere of the Talmud, were the subject. That does not mean, however, that the emotional values were dealt with only on rational level. The world of *Hagadah,* all its gnomic wisdom, which appealed to the Jewish soul, all the admonitions meant to develop the good endowment of the Jew, may not be subjected to sober, critical analysis. Such method is perfectly in place where the intellectual aspects of the Talmud are involved. Indeed, the empathy, as well as the description which Rabbi Bloch gave to these themes, were thoroughly emotional; not, perhaps, in the spirit of the *Maggid* (popular moral preacher) of Eastern European Jewry; nor in the spirit of the leaders of Hassidism who impressed their followers through changing doses of short maxims, or fiery appreciations of spiritual values. This Lithuanian *Rov* recalled both types of moral preachers and more than once one discovers affinity with the teachings of the *Tanya* (the classic text of Rabbi Schneyur Zalman). But Rabbi Bloch retained his individuality even here. He approached his themes in a purely philosophic attitude. He felt urged to express in mature description any matter arising either from the stuff of the Talmud or from a single sentence which challenged him as a matter of theory or of practical recognition. It always came out of the totality of the text, never as accidental cognition, never from a desire to be original, or a craving to illuminate some isolated item.

There was the added, somewhat enigmatic, combination of stubbornness, allied to pious humility, derivable from the combination at the school in Kelm of aristocratic judiciousness, carefulness, sense of proportion and resolute self-criticism. Anybody who paid but superficial attention to his moral lectures might think he heard opinions that were revolutionary, that contradicted traditional ways of thought. But these idiosyncracies were articulated only in the initial point of his thinking and searching. His "queer" statements aimed at shocking the student, through some exaggeration and underscoring, into closer vision of the essential. Whatever he said had solid foundation, was underpinned by express reference to similar thought of Talmudic thinkers. Here he showed great accuracy and reverence towards the smallest nuance of the expression of great teachers.

For the future of the Jewish spirit, Rabbi Bloch contributed the pioneering achievement of a happy medium between a profound excitement with the question as such and the deep faith in the Jewish giants of the past as bearers of the divine revelation.

Today nothing is more urgent than leaders who deal in utter seriousness with the problems of our day in the light of eternal moral values, without stumbling in undisciplined egotism, in the lack of a humble integration of one's ego in the totality of our Torah-tradition, both rich in value and ever summoning to duty.

Finally, Joseph Bloch excelled in the rare ability to reveal the greatest ideas through minute details. The lingering occupation with detail, be it never so brilliant and so eloquently presented, cannot approach the pedagogical effect achieved by a thought, a motive simple and unexpected, suddenly thrust upon our consciousness when it is intellectually clear, emotionally attractive, eloquent —like a red thread, as the essence of the whole problem. It was here that Rabbi Bloch showed mastery which re-shaped many a soul.

The abiding harvest of his life seems to be the recognition that because of his genius in shaping human personality, he was a pathfinder for the future of the Jewish spirit. He knew how to impress his stamp upon his disciples as a group, as well as upon each individually, their different background and foreground notwithstanding. He knew how to give the student body a direction, disciplined through comprehension of the Torah and a consistent conformity with its laws. What distinguished the philosophy of the Yeshivah of Telshe from other *yeshivot,* with particular relevancy to our own days, is this training of a student to a sense of responsibility to the Jewish people and its spiritual future in accord with the tradition of the Torah. In other words, it is the rejection of a concept of Torah-true Judaism that would allow the individual Jew to worry only about the salvation of his own soul and—in a wrong kind of self-sufficiency or self-restriction—to ignore his responsibility for the whole Jewish people.

Rabbi Bloch strove to train his students in a militant concern for the traditions of Israel. Nor would he ever hesitate to take a definite stand on Jewish political questions. He made his disciples look upon the Jewish people as an indivisible holy entity. He impressed upon them the duty to work for its spiritual and material welfare as the abiding heritage of the Yeshivah of Telshe.

At all times he remained true to his vision of the élite. Again and again he emphasized the aim of Telshe to train *Gedolim* (authorities), who impose great service upon themselves and refuse to remain in the lower strata of selfishness and comfort. He was always anxious to let every student reach his potential, hence his judicious praise for one, a long admonition for the other, a censure by a gesture, a carefully thought-out strategy to help still another improve a fault or divert his energies towards an improved way of life.

It was his synthesis of immense Torah knowledge, unrevealed but tremendous love for the maturing disciple, and an extraordinary sense of responsibility as an exponent of Judaism, that evoked a maximum from the students. When thwarted in that effort, Rabbi Bloch would send the young man elsewhere to achieve the same goals for himself and for Judaism.

With all his emphasis on training *Gedolim*, he would never give up any man in whom he could discern Jewish values. His aloofness notwithstanding, his students forever remained loyal to him, although a warm personal attachment was not easy.

What happened to Telshe? After the death of his father, Rabbi A. I. Bloch presided over that academy for many blessed years. A new generation emerged of scholars of the Talmud and model personalities which assured Telshe its high position in Torah-Judaism. Then came the Nazi hellhounds. On the 20th of Tamuz, in one short day they destroyed that fortress of the Lord with its disciples—one of the bloody signatures of their bestiality and the end of the glorious history of that Torah center.

In Cleveland, Ohio, his sainted son, Rabbi E. M. Bloch (he died there in 1954), and his son-in-law, Rabbi Moshe Katz, reestablished that center, in spirit and method loyal to the traditions of its past. Its significance in American Jewry, its powerful contribution to both learning and living, are universally recognized. Its graduates have already made their mark in countless synagogues and *yeshivot* and in the many mansions of Torah-true Judaism in the U. S. and beyond its borders. Rabbi Bloch blazed the trail for

Torah-true Jewry to achieve a future, intellectually mature, emotionally sincere, organizationally united, attractive and benign. His was steadfastness together with an open mind for all imperative action; genuine self-criticism wedded to courageous initiative; academic industry together with an almost lyrical religious sentiment, wedded to eager action in the crises of the Jewish people. This creative leader on the height of Lithuanian Judaism is one of the peaks in the world of high mountains before which every Jew and all Israel stand in reverence, echoing the sentiments of the Psalmist: *"I lift up mine eyes to the mountains whence comes my help."* I need but close my eyes to see the *Rov* in the light of the *Havdalah* candle, gazing upon his cup and in sweet melody, word by word, thanking his Lord *"Who makes a distinction between holy and profane, between light and darkness."*

At the moment I have an awesome feeling this great *Rov* fulfilled every implication of his name: like Joseph of old, he was ever fruitful, like Judah he thanked the Lord and proclaimed him; *"with the strength of a lion"* he battled for his people.

RABBI TOBIAS LEWENSTEIN

(1863-1953)

By Moses Lewenstein and Salomon Ehrmann

(translated by Moses Jung, from the German)

RABBI TOBIAS LEWENSTEIN

By Moses Lewenstein and Salomon Ehrmann

In 1863 Moses Lewenstein, a former resident of Holland, was the rabbi in charge of the important Jewish community of Paramaribo (Dutch West Indies). It was here that Tobias was born on October 27th.

The father died soon thereafter and his mother took the three-year-old boy to Utrecht in Holland, where, until Bar Mitzvah, he received his education from Rabbi Jacob de Leon, a teacher widely respected for his erudition and his saintly way of life. Later he attended the Rabbinical Seminary in Amsterdam, headed by Chief Rabbi Duenner, the Hildesheimer Seminary, and studied Oriental languages at the University of Berlin. Here he received his doctorate in philosophy, with a thesis on Ibn Ezra. His first rabbinical post was in Leewarden, his second in The Hague, where he arrived in 1899. In 1903, barely 40 years old but widely known for his scholarship and his communal activities, he accepted a call to the position in Copenhagen of Chief Rabbi of Denmark. In that city, so he was informed, all synagogues and communal institutions conformed to traditional Judaism. But soon after his arrival a serious disagreement arose between him and the leaders of the community. The percentage of mixed marriages in Copenhagen was very high. Before his arrival it had become customary to receive into the faith non-Jews who wanted to marry Jews, even when there was no certainty that these "proselytes" were ready to conform to Jewish law in the future. Also, children born of mixed marriages were recognized as Jewish by the community, on the parents' mere agreement at their marriage that children born to them would be Jews. Such marriages and adoptions of children into the Jewish community, which contravened religious law, were strongly opposed by Dr. Lewenstein and finally interdicted. The leaders of the community tried to change his attitude and when they failed, they appointed in 1909 a second "liberal" rabbi, Dr. Schornstein, who they knew would approve of the former practice. But Dr. Lewenstein had been appointed for life and in his contract

473

he was recognized as the supreme authority in all matters of religious law.

When Dr. Schornstein, in agreement with the leaders of the community, proceeded to receive non-Jews into Judaism, Rabbi Lewenstein announced in the daily press that he would not recognize such conversions. Thereupon the board dismissed Dr. Lewenstein from his office. He brought suit in the Supreme Court, which resulted in the decision in 1912 that the board's notice had been illegal; that the court was unable to compel the board to re-instate Dr. Lewenstein, but that high damages were to be paid to him in compensation. It is interesting to note that the board paid that large sum not out of the community treasury (a considerable segment of the community having disagreed with its board's procedure), but from their private funds.

The members of the community had been carefully informed by Dr. Lewenstein, in an open letter in February 1910, about the background of these incidents. The statement is still relevant today and is therefore offered here in translation from the Danish original:

"The Board of Directors of the local Jewish community has publicly announced my dismissal as Communal Rabbi for two reasons: (1) because of my opposition to the manner in which the confirmations of children of local Jewish parents were conducted and (2) because of my protest against the fact that such confirmations were performed by the second rabbi with the approval of the Board of Directors of the community. Further, the Board of Directors has requested all paying members of our Community to declare forthwith, that they agreed with the proceedings of the Board against me. I feel compelled to submit an explanation of my point of view so that each member of the community may find it possible to form a proper opinion in this regrettable and unprecedented controversy between the Board of Directors and their religious leader.

"The core of the dispute is the question of the acceptance of non-Jews into Judaism. This matter is of basic importance for Jewry in general and the Copenhagen Jewish community in particular.

"Statistics show that the number of Jews in Denmark has been seriously reduced as the result of mixed marriages. Between 1880-1905 there were 395 purely Jewish and 272 mixed marriages. Of the children born of these mixed marriages, sixty-one are members of the Jewish community and 285 of the Christian Church.

"Before entry on my present position, I made it perfectly clear to the representatives of the Board, that this danger of further shrinkage of the Jewish community could be avoided only through proper Jewish education in school and home.

"During the last seven years of my incumbency as Chief Rabbi of the community, engaged couples have repeatedly applied to me concerning the admission of Christian brides into Judaism. I was compelled to refuse such admissions on the basis of our religious laws, since the intended conversion was prompted not by conviction but by ulterior motives. As a result of my attitude, the number of conversions has been essentially reduced.

"In regard to the admission of children of mixed marriages, it is, indeed, true that the Board of Directors failed to draw my attention, before my acceptance of the position, to the law of April 13, 1850. However, I made it clear before first confirmation that there was no doubt that the Jewish community would as little recognize as Jewish a child born of a mixed marriage, as would the Christian Church regard a child as Christian without baptism. The parents' intention alone in both cases is regarded as irrelevant. A child born of a non-Jewish mother cannot be recognized as Jewish, as long as the ritual conditions for admission into the faith have not been fulfilled. I was, therefore, unable to perform the Confirmation ceremony (Bar Mitzvah) of a Jewish boy who had not fulfilled the conditions for a factual admission to Judaism, though the parents had declared their intention that he become Jewish.

"Because of the importance of this issue, I append herewith the literal translation of a decision (1848) of one of the leading authorities of our age, Rabbi Jacob Ettlinger, of blessed memory, who was Danish Rabbi in Altona between 1836-1872:

'1. The Jewish religious law recognizes as permissible and legal only such marriages as are contracted between a Jewish man and a Jewish woman or a non-Jewish man with a non-Jewish woman. All marriages between Jews and non-Jews are illegal and, in a Jewish religious sense, invalid.

'2. According to Jewish law, the religion of children of mixed marriages is determined by the mother; hence, children born of a Jewish mother are considered Jewish even though the father himself be not Jewish. No agreement among the parents can change that.

'But children born of a non-Jewish mother are considered non-Jews, even though the father is Jewish. Boys do not enter the Jewish community, even if circumcised, unless religious requirements for the admission of non-Jews into Judaism have been complied with.'

"Further, Professor Wolf, in his capacity as president of the Jewish religious court, has shown that before the admission of any would-be proselyte, he must be warned that religious conviction alone and no other reason can form the basis of conversion:

'Withdraw, unless your conversion be the result of free conviction, with all your heart and soul. As long as you do not profess Judaism, its prescriptions are not incumbent upon you. Once you have joined Judaism, no salvation can be hoped for if you leave it again: you have broken the covenant which you had concluded forever.'

"I have consulted four recognized leaders in this matter: Chief Rabbi J. M. Duenner, Rector of the Rabbinical Seminary in Amsterdam, Dr. D. Hoffmann, Rector of the Rabbinical Seminary in Berlin; Rabbi Rabinowitz, Chief Rabbi of Kovno, and Chief Rabbi A. Hirsch of Hamburg.

"On the basis of the unanimous opinion of the four gentlemen, I submitted to the Board of Directors concrete suggestions. They informed me that in the future, without consultation with me in specific cases, Dr. Schornstein had been authorized to admit proselytes into Judaism, both adults and children. I regarded it as my duty to inform the members of my community that admissions into Judaism, without my cooperation, were not valid according to Jewish religious law. Further, I applied on January 13th to the Ministry of Public Worship and Instruction (*Kultusministerium*) for a decision as to whether I was obliged, in contradiction to my contract of service, to permit a "liberal" rabbi in my community to make religious decisions which were opposed to my own. I requested the Board to postpone admissions into Judaism by Dr. Schornstein until the Ministry had rendered its decision. The Board refused to do so. I never had any other difficulty with the Board except when a matter infringed upon the laws of our religion, in whose name I serve. Here, too, I sought a peaceful solution. It was refused and thus each one of you may judge on which side equity lies."

The controversy came to an end in that the Board, indeed, relieved Dr. Lewenstein of his office but the Supreme Court, as mentioned above, stigmatized the dismissal as illegal and sentenced the Board to the payment of a substantial compensation.

This Copenhagen case, in which the Danish government sided with the rabbi, focused the attention of the Jewish community at large on the fearless protagonist of Jewish tradition. The Jewish Religious Community (*Israelitische Religionsgesellschaft*) of Zurich needed an assistant to Rabbi Kornfein (whose energy was totally absorbed by the Religious School). Dr. Lewenstein received a call and on *Shabbat Shoftim* (August 17, 1912) he delivered his first sermon. For twenty-eight blessed years he worked in full harmony with Rabbi Kornfein in the spiritual development and enlargement of the congregation. The results of his efforts were soon apparent. The facilities for worship and religious instruction became inadequate, since the congregation grew markedly. In 1923 the foundation stone was laid for a new synagogue, to be erected, as Dr. Lewenstein put it, "to the honor of God, the glory of the Jewish community, and the well-being of all mankind." These words were symbolic, indeed, also of his own service.

The quality of Rabbi Lewenstein's personality was revealed in the fact that he did not stay satisfied merely with developing his congregation into a leading community in Switzerland, but that he strove to place his manifold capacities at the service of *Klal Yissrael,* the entire Jewish people. He became a Jewish statesman. To him Torah was both goal and way. Each of his political acts had for its exclusive objective the realization in public life of Jewish religious principles. Hence each political action became a *Mitzvah*-task. He spent an enormous amount of attention and care on every particular item and thus provided, as it were, the germ of its success. Thus did he prepare his political writings—crystal clear and utterly consistent in their fidelity to Jewish religious principles.

A good illustration is his "Circular Letter" of the Jewish Committee in Opposition to Calendar Reform. When in 1925, by agitation for calendar reform, the observance of the Sabbath was seriously endangered and the League of Nations established a special committee ad hoc, Lewenstein plunged into feverish activity. He succeeded in uniting the leading rabbis of France, England, Austria, and Holland in a committee whose executive secretary he became and who sent a delegation to the League of Nations. He collected hundreds of thousands of Jewish signatures opposing calendar reform; composed a number of pamphlets which illustrated the danger to the Sabbath of the proposal, as well as a Memorandum to the League of Nations; he obtained statements and finally he succeeded, at that moment, in averting the danger. It was to this preliminary activity that contemporary efforts at UN against calendar reform are greatly indebted.

In 1927, on the authority of the Mandatory Power, an effort was made in Palestine to organize all Jewish inhabitants into "compulsory communities" under a religiously-neutral supreme office. Dr. Lewenstein appeared before the Mandate Commission in Geneva as representative of the Torah-true communities, particularly the *Va'ad Ha-Ir Ha-Ashkenazi* in Jerusalem, which, under the leadership of Rabbi Hayyim Sonnenfeld, of blessed memory, insisted on full religious autonomy, unrestricted by any compulsion on the part of non-religious authority. Rabbi Lewenstein spent many weeks in Geneva and finally, with the help of Mr. Van Rees, one of the presidents of the Mandate Commission, achieved not only a weakening of the compulsory character of the community law, but also the agreement to an independent type of community on the basis of Torah. This regulation has had important consequences to the present day.

Rabbi Lewenstein's political successes, with Jew and non-Jew alike, were due to the fact that both friends and foes immediately perceived his utter sincerity. In touching but firm modesty, he shunned any sort of personal publicity. It was, indeed, this humility, in contrast to the determination and inflexibility with which he represented his cause, which won him the love and respect of all he came in contact with.

Much more comprehensive than these efforts in the larger world, was Rabbi Lewenstein's work within the Jewish community, transcending the congregations and countries in which he served as rabbi. Already in 1891, when still a student at the Rabbinical Seminary at Berlin, he delivered a lecture on the need of a union of all Torah-true Jews with exclusive orientation towards Torah and without any concession to Jewish organizations otherwise oriented. Without his knowledge, this lecture was published by his friends and colleagues (Pinchas Kohn, Eduard Biberfeld, Ernst Weill, Meier Hildesheimer, Gerson Lange). In his old age, he would proudly point to this pamphlet whenever he was asked why he had welcomed so warmly the foundation of Agudat Israel as a realization of his two-decades-old ideal. In this lecture, the author rejected, in an unusually decisive manner, a secular, a-religious Judaism, but at the same time he emphasized with even determination the need of upbuilding of Eretz Israel on a religious basis. At a public discussion with Max Nordau in The Hague, about the turn of the century, he demonstrated, from the texts of Jewish history and its source material, the impossibility of establishing in Israel a separation between Church and State, without at the same time facilitating a most hazardous collective assimilation. When, about a decade later, Agudat Israel was founded, he became one of the foremost representatives of a dynamic current within the organization, which knew how to apply the timeless criteria of the Torah to the changing tasks of the day. His constant thought revolved around the happenings in Israel after the establishment of the *Medinah*. In a postscript to his lecture on "The Messiah", published posthumously, he said, "These remarks were made in 5701/1941. In the meantime, the All-Merciful has granted me to witness the events which are an infallible omen of the eventual appearance of the Messiah.

"After 2000 years the State of Israel has again come into existence. After 2000 years the dispersed Children of Israel are returning, from near and far, into the old homeland. This wonderful event has occurred in an apparently natural way.

"There are two points of view struggling for mastery in present-day Israel. The first holds that the state came into being as the result of divine intervention, in accordance with the pronouncements of the prophets of old; the second, that it represents a natural phenomenon. Around these two poles gather the differing philosophies of life and ambitions of the Jewish citizens now living in the State of Israel. The State of Israel exists and never will disappear. It will achieve the gathering of the exiles (*Kibbutz Galuyot*). Eventually, it will build the Sanctuary (*Bet Hamikdash*),

which will express its international character, as Isaiah proclaimed:
'My House shall be a House of Prayer for all the nations'.'

Rabbi Lewenstein was not only the ideologist of Agudat Israel.
In a time fraught with great decisions, he also put his great organizational gifts at its disposal. The First World War prevented the
calling of the Agudah's *Kenessiyah Gedolah* (World Conference)
and kept the various countries apart. Contact between Agudah
branches in Europe, Eretz Israel, and the U. S. A. could not be
maintained because the central office in Frankfurt was totally cut
off from non-Axis territory. Dr. Lewenstein stepped into the
breach. Together with Dr. Nathan Birnbaum, Ch. J. Eiss, and
others, he established at Zurich a branch of the central office, whose
chairman he became. He undertook successful journeys to France,
England, Holland, and Denmark for the purpose of winning new
friends for the Agudah. After the war, in 1919, with intense effort,
he convened in Zurich a conference of Torah-true Jewish organizations, which was attended by delegates from almost all European
countries. Between 1919-1923, Dr. Lewenstein filled the position
of President of Agudat Israel. Hostile sentiment towards Germany
among the victorious allies (as also among French and English
Jews against German Jews) had impeded the work by the Central
Committee in Frankfurt. It remains Dr. Lewenstein's historic feat
that at the time of the peace conference in Versailles he staked
everything on the establishment of a united Jewish front for the
demands of world Jewry, specifically in regard to Eretz Israel.

The Agudah office in Zurich approached the office of the Zionist Organization in Copenhagen with a proposal for cooperation in
the political and economic area, with the proviso that public institutions in Israel be conducted according to the laws of the Torah.
The reply from Copenhagen was unsatisfactory. It referred to formal resolutions of the Zionist Congress, which recognized fundamental religious principles. Dr. Lewenstein thereupon went to
Paris in an attempt to obtain better results through personal negotiations with the Jewish Peace Delegation. It was Nahum Sokolow,
who, after several conferences, defeated that effort!

In the following years Rabbi Lewenstein worked primarily on
the task of convoking the first *Kenessiyah Gedolah* in 1923 in
Vienna, where he was elected to the Supreme Executive Committee
of the world organization.

A situation similar to the one in 1912, yet more acute, developed during the Second World War. When the large stream of refugees from many countries reached Switzerland, Dr. Lewenstein was among the first to assist them. He established homes for the children, obtained funds for their physical and spiritual needs, frequently visited the camps and, in particular, cared for the refugees from Holland, who adored him like a father. Now, again, with a few co-workers, Dr. Lewenstein established a second office of the World Agudah in Zurich. This activity in the area of philanthropy, politics, and religion brought him in touch with the religious authorities of the East, some of whom had found asylum in Switzerland.

At the end of the Second World War, again Dr. Lewenstein took the initiative in convoking conferences of representatives of Jewish world organizations, which had their offices in Switzerland, in order to cooperate with them concerning Jewish demands in regard to Eretz Israel and other lands. It is noteworthy that on these occasions Dr. Lewenstein and his Agudist colleagues intervened most emphatically in favor of an autonomous Jewish State. The representatives of the other organizations showed a far greater understanding for the scruples of the Torah-true than had the Zionist central office in Copenhagen previously.

The firm structure of the Agudah group in Switzerland, too, is the work of Dr. Lewenstein. He was not only the Chairman of the Rabbinical Council of Switzerland and member of the World Rabbinical Council, but his presence and addresses at the Agudah meetings imparted to those deliberations dignity and constructiveness. He shunned no exertions in his ambition to participate in the meetings of youth groups, both in cities or mountain resorts. His words always enthused and inspired them.

The duty of every Jew to work for the welfare of mankind was no empty phrase for him. The scores of manuscripts which he left testify to his well-trained mind, steeped in the science and lore of the West, yet ever aware of the Messianic promise. He would await, often with bated breath, a sign, however small, of growing God-consciousness among non-Jewish circles. Every moral progress in mankind became a cornerstone for the strengthening of the Torah. He never ceased to work for the souls of those who remained at the periphery of Judaism.

When in 1940, in his seventy-seventh year, he became Rabbi Emeritus, his community had grown to the fourth largest in Switzerland. Even then he felt the urge of serving with his undimmed fervor for the divine purposes. Until the last weeks of his life he welcomed in his home study circles for both adults and youths (*Shiurim*).

The leaders of his one-time community at The Hague implored him to visit them. He spent several months there in order to bring order into Jewish communal life in Holland, which had greatly suffered during the war, and to supervise preparations for the induction into office of a younger colleague. He returned to Zurich and by the grace of God celebrated with his beloved community the *Simhat Torah* festival, 29 Tishri 5713, at which, in full vigor, he delivered his last sermon, his last will and testament.

Zekher Tzaddik livrakhah.

AVRAHAM YITZHAK HACOHEN KOOK
(1865-1935)

By I. Epstein

AVRAHAM YITZHAK HACOHEN KOOK

By I. Epstein

Avraham Yitzhak Kook, the first Chief Rabbi of the Holy Land, was one of those spiritual sovereigns vouchsafed by God to Israel, whose eminence the process of years has only served to enhance. Like a mountain obscured at first by its foothills, Rabbi Kook rises as he recedes. Whatever denigration he had to endure from contemporaries who lacked the ability to follow his high-soaring vision, has by now been obliterated, and today it is safe to say that the name Kook holds a highly honoured and loved position among Israel's foremost saints, teachers and religious guides.

His Youth

While it is true that a great soul has little need of ancestors, Rabbi Kook had a family tradition which conduced to the development of his manifold powers. He came, alike on his father's and mother's side, of a long line of saintly men and women, in whom the love of God, Torah and Israel formed the inspirational fount of their lives. He was born in Greiva, a little Latvian townlet near Dvinsk, on the 16th Ellul, 1865. From his tenderest age he began to attract attention as a wonder-child, and exhibited marks of greatness. In his home none but the holy tongue was heard on the holy day of rest.

He received his early instruction at the hands of his father—a *Talmid Hakham* of great repute—who introduced him to the study of Bible and Talmud. At the age of ten, the boy was able to study the latter unaided. During his formative years, he came under the influence of some of the greatest Lithuanian rabbis of the time, including the *Neziv* (Naftali Zevi Berlin, the father of the late Rabbi Meir Bar Ilan), whose *yeshivah* in Volozhin he joined at the age of sixteen years. There his diligence knew no bounds. He is said to have studied eighteen hours at a stretch, covering in the process sixty folios of the Talmud! At the age of twenty, he married the daughter of Rabbi Eliyahu David Rabinowitz-Thumin of Mir, who subsequently became *Rov* of the Ashkenazi Community in Jerusalem.

485

About three years later, Rabbi Kook took up his first position as *Rov* in the small Lithuanian community of Zaumel. He soon proved his outstanding gifts for rabbinic leadership. He showed the deepest concern for the material, no less than the spiritual, welfare of his flock. Particularly impressive was his religious courage. Typical of this trait in his character was the dramatic scene enacted by him on the Yom Kippur in the synagogue at Greiva. It was during a raging plague when fasting was fraught with a measure of danger. Taking his stand at the reading desk with some food in his hand, the young rabbi, who was then about twenty, recited the appropriate benediction, and in the presence of the awestruck and astounded worshippers, ate and bade them go and do likewise.

His Early Rabbinate

In 1895 he became *Rov* of Bausk, a position formerly occupied by Rabbi Mordechai Eliasberg, one of the foremost pioneers of religious Zionism. For nine years Rabbi Kook laboured in his new community, striving to make it a veritable center of Jewish learning and piety; "and the purpose of the Lord prospered in his hand." Yet he felt a sense of incompleteness. From his earliest days he was in love with the Holy Land. Already as a child he expressed it by drilling his *heder* playmates to march to the rallying call "Towards Jerusalem." He could find no rest until this love was satisfied, in 1904, when he was invited to become rabbi in Jaffa.

His Arrival in the Holy Land

With his arrival in the Holy Land to take up his position, he experienced a real fulfilment. It is told that when Rabbi Kook first stepped on the soil of the Holy Land, he kissed, in his *hithlahabuth,* the first cow he encountered, exclaiming, *"Oi, ein Eretz Yisroel-dicke Kuh!"* Whether or not the story is apocryphal, it certainly fits in with the whole attachment of Rabbi Kook to the Holy Land, whose plants, stones and very dust he loved and venerated.

Soon he began to exercise a benignant sway over the whole of the Holy Land. He watched the *Yishuv* with a fatherly care; and the *Yishuv* loved him dearly, not only for his brilliant gifts and attainments, but for his ardor, courage and tenderness. They loved him for his championship of all who were poor, exploited or oppressed. Perhaps they loved him best when they saw him riding a mount—ass or horse—and touring the villages and settlements, asking after the welfare of his brethren, speaking to them words of encouragement and hope, and seeking to draw their hearts with bonds of love to God and the Torah. He did all he could to strengthen the economic life of the *Yishuv,* and to this end he did not hesitate to enter the lists against the most renowned rabbis of the age, both in the Holy Land and outside.

With the approach of the *Shemittah* year 5670 (1909-10), he became the central figure of a bitter controversy in which he found ranged in opposition to him some of the greatest rabbinic authorities of the age, including the redoubtable *Ridbaz* (Rabbi Yaakob David Willowsky) of Safad. The controversy concerned the operation of the law of *Shemittah,* as it affected the Jewish colonies in the Holy Land. The strict observance of the law prohibiting all manner of work during the *Shemittah* year was fraught with the greatest danger for the economic future of the *Yishuv.* This was no new problem. Already a generation earlier, it had agitated the rabbinic world, and in 1888 Rabbi Israel Elchanan Spector of Kovno sanctioned as a measure the nominal sale of land to a non-Jew during the *Shemittah* year. This measure was, however, hedged about by two reservations, which rendered it both impractical and inadequate for the changed conditions which faced Rabbi Kook.

In the first place, there was a proviso that the labor employed was to be exclusively non-Jewish, quite an unthinkable proposition under the new conditions; and secondly, the measure was restricted to orchards, and did not cover cornfields. It is here that Rabbi Kook exhibited his ranging greatness as a *Halakhist,* as well as his remarkable courage and strength of character. He maintained that the nominal sale could be made effective to apply also to cornfields; and, furthermore, to make possible the employment of Jewish labor. In exposition and defense of his views, he wrote a work under the title of *"Shabbat ha-Aretz";* and it is thanks to Rabbi Kook's tireless efforts and guidance in this important problem that religious settlements in Israel today are able to tend their fields in *Shemittah* years.

There were other religious problems affecting grievously the economy of the *Yishuv*—such as the observance of the laws of *Terumot* and *Maasserot*—for which Rabbi Kook found satisfactory solutions, within the framework of the *Halakhah*. It was his great concern for the economic life of the *Yishuv* which led him to forbid the use of Corfu *etrogim,* on the ground that they were raised on grafted trees, notwithstanding the preference shown for them by many rabbinical authorities, because they were more "goodly" in shape (*Hadar*) than those that were grown in Eretz Israel. Referring to a certain rabbi who sought to justify their use, Rabbi Kook exclaimed: "This scholar imagines that the question of *etrogim* can be settled by mere *pilpul.* He does not realize that it is a question of life and death for those who toil our Holy ground that their brethren should buy from them the products they themselves have raised."

THE WAR YEARS IN ENGLAND

The outbreak of the First World War found Rabbi Kook in Germany, where he was due to attend a conference of the *Agudat Israel.* Unable to go back to his beloved home-land, he made his way to St. Gallen in Switzerland, where he stayed till the year 1916, when he came to London, to act as rabbi to the Spitalfields Great Synagogue, *Machzike Hadath.*

These were days of great expectations. The air was filled with rumours of an impending declaration by the British Government asserting and vindicating the historic rights of the Jewish people to the Holy Land; and the decision to be close to the scene of this unfolding epoch-making event was the principal reason that attracted Rabbi Kook to these shores.

The effect of his arrival and presence in London was electric. His home in Princelet Street attracted rabbis, saints and scholars, as well as ordinary folk, who came to him for counsel, instruction and edification.

During the crucial months in 1917, when the negotiations between the Zionist leaders and the British Government were reaching their climax, Rabbi Kook threw himself life and soul into the battle of Zionism. The letter which appeared in *The Times* on May 24th of that year, under the signatures of the presidents of the

Conjoint Committee, denouncing Zionism as incompatible with the Jewish religion, brought from him a scathing reply in the form of a manifesto entitled "A National Treachery", which was read in many synagogues, and which created so profound an impression, even in non-Jewish circles, that reference was made to it in the House of Commons.

The publication of the Balfour Declaration was greeted by him as an act of divine deliverance on behalf of his people, and the day on which it was issued was to him a day of indescribable joy and intense happiness. At the end of the war he returned to Palestine as Chief Rabbi Elect of Jerusalem.

ASSUMPTION OF HIS CHIEF RABBINATE

His entry into Jerusalem on the 3rd Ellul, 1919, to assume the Chief Rabbinate, was to him the greatest moment in his career. Though hesitant at first, he accepted the charge not so much in fulfilment of a life-long ambition, but as a unique opportunity for utilizing all his God-given faculties on behalf of the ideals to which he had dedicated his life.

Three years later he was appointed as Ashkenazi Chief Rabbi of the Holy Land, and his achievements during his resplendent spiritual leadership are written large across the history of the Holy Land.

The news of his death on Ellul 3rd 5695 (1935), exactly 17 years to the day he had ascended his high office, plunged the whole of Jewry into mourning. The report of the proclamation of *Medinat Yisrael,* on the 5th Iyar, 5708 (1948), must have brought to not a few thankful and joyous hearts a feeling of sadness that Rabbi Kook was not spared to witness this most momentous day in Jewish history. How he would have thrilled to the miraculous rebirth of Israel! How his genius would have responded in hymn and praise of God for His salvation of His People! Israel has, indeed, been orphaned by his death. At no time was his prescience of greater need than today. He could have inspired in our people a religious revival keeping pace with Israel's national resurgence. He would have had the competence, the power and the vision to approach the problems of adjustment in conformity with the tremendous historic manifestations of our time. Just as he had succeeded in dealing with the question of *Shemittah* and *Terumot* and other religious problems that confronted the *Yishuv,* so would he doubtless have found solutions to many other religious problems which face reborn Israel. He has, however, left us a rich and imperishable legacy in his voluminous writings, which will prove an inexhaustible source of inspiration and teaching for generations to come.

THE QUALITY OF HIS LITERARY LEGACY

Rabbi Kook was a most prolific and voluminous writer. Several of his works were published during his lifetime. More have appeared since his passing; and the world is still awaiting a complete disclosure of his rich literary legacy.

Among the earliest of his publications was the religious periodical in Hebrew, *Ittur Soferim,* which he edited and of which two volumes appeared: in 1888 and 1898. To the same period belongs also his Hebrew *Hebesh Peër,* on the significance of *Tefillin.* Since then there has been incessant outflow from his pen of books, publications, essays, addresses, each of which is in its own way a classic and a gem.

His writings cover an astonishing range of subjects—*Halakhah* (including Responsa), *Agadah, Kabbalah, Hassidut, Mussar,* Philosophy, and comprising much that is of practical and worldly interest.

Everyone can find in his works matter to suit his own taste and bent of mind. The *Halakhist* is afforded choice specimens of delightful *pilpul* as well as practical guidance in matters of Jewish law. The *Agadist* is treated with fascinating homilies. The Moralist will be edified by ethical teaching, and the *Kabbalist* by profound esoteric thought.

His Literary Style

Mention must particularly be made of two wonderful volumes of his letters which are replete with things instructive and illuminating. In them are treated subjects of specific Jewish character; they abound also in reflections and observations relating to all kinds of problems—social, political and economic. Well might Rabbi Kook have declared: *"Homo sum: humani nihil a me alienum puto."* ("I am a man: nothing that is human do I think unbecoming of me.") Nor is the challenge ignored which modern thought presents to the Jewish religion. Perhaps Rabbi Kook stands alone among Jewish religious teachers in his persistent refusal to leave any difficulty unfaced. Hence the enormous value of his letters to which perplexed souls can turn for guidance.

Another point in the quality of Rabbi Kook's literary legacy is the majestic flow of his style—cataracts of ecstasy and floods of picturesque imagery, resulting in rich and original similes and metaphors. The words seem to burn upon the page and the reader is left dazed and enchanted. He was a veritable word magician. He enriched and illumined our Holy Tongue beyond measure. Even Bialik, that great master of Hebrew language, declared that for generations people will turn to the writings of Rabbi Kook as a fruitful source of Hebrew literary expression.

His writings are magnificent pieces of prose blazed forth through a poetic trumpet exalting the feelings and touching the imagination. The themes on which he discourses—God, Torah, Eretz Israel and the people of Israel—seem to transport him into ethereal worlds of rhythm, harmony and music, from which he brings down celestial messages in a flashing beauty of imagery that works like magic on our minds, shining words that set our souls aglow, a majestic flow of language that rushes on swiftly and carries the reader beyond the confines of space and time into the "upper regions" whence came the message.

THE MYSTIC ELEMENTS IN HIS WRITINGS

Yet notwithstanding the amplitude of his literary legacy, the knowledge of Rabbi Kook's teachings is still confined to a small circle of disciples. One reason for this is the difficulty of style and language.[1] His works involve hard reading. The mysticism that breathes from his writings, the transcendentalism of the concepts and the long sonorous sentences that would have delighted Milton, at times perplex the reader. In reading his works one may, now and then, not be able to see the wood for the trees. Rabbi Kook, with all his prolific output, wrote no systematic treatise, not because he was no systematic thinker, but because of his in-

---

[1]*Letters* II p. 267 (1909).

ability to control the almost torrential outflow of what seemed
the inexhaustible resources of a richly endowed soul. Much of
what he wrote was not specifically composed with an eye on publication. He wrote as he talked; he rarely conversed and his
talking was remarkably voluble. It was musing aloud. His writing
was thinking rapidly on paper. He wrote at first heat, seldom
correcting, putting down on paper when urged by an irrestible
impulse, and only then, the voluminous outpourings of his soul,
as they came forth from his ever active and fertile brain, in thought,
feeling and expression. I had the privilege of sitting at his feet,
while he was acting as *Rov* of the London Mahzike Hadath during
the first World War, and I well remember his having composed
that most difficult book, *Rosh Millin* (containing the essence of his
mysticism, pegged on to the Alphabet and Accents, and which is
understood by so few), in three days—*without correction*.

The only systematic presentation of Rabbi Kook's thought is
to be found in that classic, *Orot ha-Kodesh,* planned in 5 volumes,
but of which only two volumes have so far been published
(Jerusalem, 1938). This work, compiled under his guidance by
David Kohn, one of Rabbi Kook's closest disciples, is described
by Gerhard Scholem, in his *Major Trends of Jewish Mysticism,*
as "a veritable *theologica mystica* of Judaism, clearly distinguished
by its originality and the richness of its author's mind." "It is,"
he continues, "the best example of productive cabbalistic thought
of which I know." But the work itself is most difficult to study,
and in the absence of an adequate commentary, must remain a
sealed book for all except a very small number of experts. For the
general reader, the best introduction to Rabbi Kook's thought is to
be found in his letters, of which two volumes covering the years
1888-1920, have so far appeared under the title *"Igrot ha-Rayah".*
Whilst many of them are admittedly hard reading, there is on
the whole little mystifying about them; and, given close attention,
the letters cannot fail to make an impact upon the reader, enlarging his sympathies and enriching his mind with elevated
thoughts and a sense sublime. It is principally on the basis of
these letters, supplemented by some personal reminiscences, that
an assessment of Rabbi Kook's personality and teaching is attempted in the pages that follow.

THE MAN AND HIS TEACHING

It is impossible within the natural limits of this publication to do even the scantiest justice to one who was the most gigantic spirit of Judaism of his generation; nor is it easy for myself, admitted to his gracious friendship in my early years, to speak of him in measured terms. I have known many great teachers in my life, but never one who was so richly endowed with all the gifts of mind and soul which the Holy One, blessed be He, bestows on his "loving ones." A *Gaon*, mystic, and philosopher, he was a veritable religious genius, ravishing even the poetic genius of a man like Bialik, who declared that his first meeting with Rabbi Kook was one of the happiest of his experiences. He would have been great even if he had not read a single book, for his greatness came not from his books, but from the inner welling forth of a richly endowed soul. His personality had something ethereal about it. His large tender eyes, inscrutable and dreamy, gazing, as it were, into eternity, lent mystery to his aspect. He was gifted with extraordinary eloquence. Under the spell of his talks one often felt that beauty was returning on earth and peace to the tortured human soul.

His Personal Qualities

Rabbi Kook exuded love. Love held for him the key of Redemption. "The First Temple," he used to say, "was destroyed, according to our Sages, because of *Sineat Hinnam* (groundless hate), and it is only through *Ahavat Hinnam* (groundless love) that it can be rebuilt." In his presence one felt at home, free, and happy, warmed by an atmosphere of affection. Although conscious of his powers, he was free from any trace of egotism and vanity. In his discourse with all, he had a sweet courtesy and gentle repose. His humility was truly Hillelian. I recall how he once humbled himself in apologies before a workman for having used in the course of a talk a common figure of speech which, as it subsequently dawned on him, carried with it some disparagement of that man's particular trade, and thus might have hurt his feelings.

Conspicuous, too, was his courage in grappling with problems of Jewish law. It was grounded in the fear of God, which with him was as profound as it was sublime. "We do not say: *'Fear not, My servant Jacob,'* save to him who fears God with all his might," is a dictum from the *Tanna debe Elijahu,* which Rabbi Kook was wont to quote when making veiled allusions to his boldness of approach.

His native qualities he enriched by stores of knowledge gathered from many and varying fields. His erudition covered the whole vast domain of Jewish lore, *Halakhah, Agadah, Kabbalah, Hassidut, Haskalah* and *Mussar,* and comprising much of modern philosophic and scientific thought. Nor did the differences in conceptions and attitudes which inhere varying branches of learning, shut them off from one another, or involve him in a conflict. His penetrating intellect was able to discern a unity underlying all this diversity, and to create, out of all their very dissonances, a most beautiful harmony, which permeated all his writings. His *Halakhah,* notwithstanding its hard logic, was tinged with *Agadic,* and at times even mystic, elements. Any discerning student of his responsa, *Mishpat Cohen,* will discover a sweep and beauty all of its own. It was this power to infuse *Halakhah* with lighter strains that led the late *Ridbaz,* Rabbi Yaakov David of Safad, to remark to Rabbi Kook, at the time of the *Shemittah* controversy, "Your mind is wider than the *Halakhah.*" Rabbi Kook retorted: "No *Halakhah* which the mind outstrips, can be true *Halakhah.*"

HIS PHILOSOPHICAL SYSTEM IN CONTRAST WITH BERGSON'S

Rabbi Kook's marvelous synthesis was grounded in his philosophy, which is distinguished alike by its originality and profundity. Abraham Kaminka who, in 1912, met Rabbi Kook, at the time *Rov* of Jaffa, in an article in *Die Welt* hailed him as a second Bergson. And, indeed, there is much affinity between Rabbi Kook's system of thought and that of Bergson's theory of Creative Evolution, except that Rabbi Kook's system, having its source in traditional Jewish speculation, is richer in moral and spiritual results than Bergson's.

According to Bergson, the whole process of evolution is conceived as though there were somewhere a center from which worlds, life and matter, are thrown off like fireworks in a vast illumination. Rejecting the materialistic conception which assumes that everything, including life itself, could be explained in terms of mechanics and chemistry, Bergson postulates the existence of an impulse which acts as the thrusting force behind the whole evolutionary process, giving rise to ever and ever higher forms of life.

This principle, which he calls *élan vital,* or *life force,* interacts with and animates the stuff of the physical universe, using it and moulding it to its purpose, as the fingers of a skilled pianist uses the keys of his instrument to produce the great symphonies which are the marvels of the world.

Initially unconscious, a mere blind instinctive urge, the life-force, in the course of its development, gradually acquired consciousness, and as part of consciousness, purposiveness. To facilitate its development, in pursuance of its purpose, it created the various species of living organisms, which, by exercising their inborn capacities, refining their faculties, and acquiring knowledge and accomplishments, can advance to a higher and higher level of life.

While Bergson's theory imparts to evolution an ethical quality, absent in materialistic conceptions, the inherent weakness in his position lies in the absence of a standard of life by which the term higher can be measured. One cannot measure the length of a roll of cloth, unless there is a tape measure, marked out in yards and feet, by reference to which measurement can be made. Similarly the notion of advance to higher levels of life is meaningless, unless there is postulated the presence in the universe of some standards of value which are outside the evolutionary process which advances towards them. But if there is nothing behind the scheme of things beyond unconscious life, by what standard is man's advance towards a moral goal measured? From this insufficiency in the Bergsonian theory, Rabbi Kook's system is singularly free. He finds no horrors in the evolutionary theory for the sturdy faith of the Jew. "While as a whole," he writes, "there is no need for us to be extreme devotees of the theory of evolution, this theory contains many sparks of truth. Gradual evolution is one of the tens of thousands of illimitable ways through which the 'Life of the Universe' reveals Himself."[2] This accords with his conception of God. The relation of God to the universe, according to Rabbi Kook, is not that of an

---

[2]*Letters* II p. 147 (1908).

external creator to the object created by Him, but as that of an infinite force to its infinite manifestations. Thus divine force is constantly realizing itself in the infinite phenomena of Nature and history. "The all-embracing name of God," he writes, "is the all-active force in the whole existence and all its details, it is the center whence streams forth the light of which the phenomena are the reflections, and the bond of all forces in the universe whether material, spiritual, moral or social."[3]

NATIONHOOD AND GODLINESS

He perceived the whole of Nature, inanimate no less than animate, as throbbing with divine energy, moulding and directing towards the development of life at that higher level of holiness of which God has set the pattern and towards which the whole creation is being guided. This divine energy, working for holiness, reveals itself in humanity as a whole, and notwithstanding the errors and failures and sins of man, the human race is continually being driven on and approaching the holiness which is elemental in the universe. The whole historical process serves to confirm this view. According to Rabbi Kook, the life of the human race as a whole expresses itself in two ways. On the one hand it involves the ability to lead a social life; on the other, the aptitude for spiritual growth and development. The former he calls the idea of Nationhood, the latter the idea of Godliness. Nationhood embraces all the manifestations of a well-ordered society, while Godliness includes all forms of spiritual life. Of the idea of Godliness none is bereft. The spiritual is found to a greater or lesser degree in all peoples. From it issue all religions, whether true or false, which affect the course of history and character of civilizations. A perfect unity between the two ideas, whereby the national life becomes permeated with Godliness, would constitute the ideal state of society. Human sinfulness, however, has introduced a rift between the two, giving rise to that type of Godless nationalism, with all its comcomitants—discord, hatred, strife and war—that have throughout history ravaged human society.[4]

---

[3]*Letters* I p. 25.
[4]*Letters* I pp. 75 ff; See M. Waxman; *History of Jewish Literature* pp. 923 ff.

But notwithstanding the setbacks which humanity has had to experience, the trend is more and more towards Godliness. This striving towards it is the motive underlying the progress of humanity as a whole. "The very striving for righteousness," Rabbi Kook writes, "whatever form it may assume, is but the result of an illumination which has its source in the Divine; in every human endeavour to establish some equilibrium in social life and a tranquility of heart, we can trace the effect of some spiritual force working upon the mind of man."[5] Individuals and even nations may stray from the right path, but the human race is constantly approaching the good which is the impelling force behind the whole of the natural and historical process.

These views coloured Rabbi Kook's own attitude to life. He loved every manifestation of natural life. His love extended even to animals and birds, and embraced, it might be said, the rest of creation. To him might well apply the lines:

"Spirit form, shadow, light and flame—
The urn of the whole world is poured into his soul."

He saw the whole of Nature constantly rising towards that Godliness which will find its consummation in the Divine Messianic regeneration, the signs of which he clearly perceived in the resurgence of the *Yishuv*.

His Belief in Human Progress

This conception led Rabbi Kook to his belief in the inevitability of human progress. In every generation there is to be found a number of men who strive whole-heartedly towards the divine good in the world and thereby indirectly raise even the weaker members of the race to a higher level. Moreover there is still another factor which contributes to progress—the deeds and thoughts of the great men of the past. The good which these men acquired during their lives does not disappear after their death. They add to the sum total of the spiritual, moral and intellectual, and influence the lives of later generations.[6]

---

[5]*Letters* II pp. 75-6 (1907).
[6]*Letters* II pp. 320-321 (1910).

Rabbi Kook regarded the unbelief of our times as less accursed than the heresies of the past. Modern unbelievers, he held, were actuated in their view, though erroneously, by ideals of morality and righteousness. Modern moralists and scientists assail religion on the ground of morals. "The current religions of the day," writes Wynwood Reade in his *Martyrdom of Man,* "are directly adverse to morals" (which, by the way, may be aptly contrasted by the saying of Benjamin Franklin, "If man is wicked with religion, what would he be without it?" But to advocate moral laws is to fall in with a divine world scheme. Even the great world-conquerers are not bereft of high ideals. They work for what in their view is a better world, a better order and a better state of society, and in so far as this is their motive, can be said to be contributing towards the realization of divine goodness, which is ultimately to reign supreme. Whilst sparks of Godliness are to be found in all human beings, it is in Israel that it inheres in a most concentrated form. "There is no people," he declares, "among the nations of the world, in whose innermost soul there lies hidden that precious goodness emanating from the transcendent light, except Israel. Individual saints and sages exist everywhere, but there is no 'righteous nation' on earth but Israel."[7] Israel has been selected by providence as the bearer of the idea of Godliness wedded to Nationhood, to establish that ideal state of society, in which Godliness and Nationhood are fused in one complete harmony.

His Philosophy of Jewish History

From the very beginning of their history, the Jewish people have proved their special aptitude for this charge, in that they were the first to strive for the realization of a divine social order founded on righteousness for all nations of the earth. It is this worldwide outlook that made the Jewish people a fitting instrument to be chosen by God not for themselves alone, but for the sake of humanity, upon whom they were to exert influence towards the development of Godliness. But this function the Jewish people could fulfil only when they lived in their own land, which alone could provide them with the requisite social, economic and political conditions for the development of those ideals for the uplift and advancement of

---

[7]*Letters* II p. 178 (1908).

all people of the world. In contradistinction to other Jewish thinkers, Rabbi Kook is of the opinion that the early period in the history of the Jewish people, namely that of the First Commonwealth, was of a high quality. The nation as a whole was suffused with Godliness, a Godliness which found expression in the lofty literature, the *Tanakh*, it then inspired. It was the aberrations of individuals which ultimately caused the rupture between Godliness and Nationhood, leading to the downfall of the First Commonwealth.

The period of the Second Commonwealth, on the other hand, marked a rise in the state of the spirituality of individuals, but not of the Nation. The knowledge of the Torah had increased and correspondingly the observance of the precepts, but all these affected the individuals and not the social structure of the state. Religion in organized form took the place of the idea of Godliness in its widest connotation. This divorce of Godliness from Nationhood brought the downfall of the Second Commonwealth.

In the exile there occurred again the rupture between the ideas of Godliness and Nationhood. They continued to exist, but not in their unity, nor in their primitive form. Godliness was narrowed down to Torah study, to the observance of the *Mitzvot,* and to the Synagogue, while the National idea realized itself in the struggle for existence. Occasionally the Godliness of the Jews broke through its confines and contributed directly to the rise of humanity, but such moments were rare in Jewish history. The real perfection of Jewish life will be attained only when the people will be restored once more to its ancestral land.[8]

Rabbi Kook therefore saw in the National Movement an approach to the ideal era in the life of Israel. He believed that the restoration of Jews to the Holy Land would bring about the union of the two ideas of Nationhood and Godliness, filling the life of the group and of the individual with intensive spirituality.

The Religious Character of Jewish Nationalism

His hopes about the effects of the national restoration rested on the conviction that, in the final analysis, the National Movement was religious at heart, and sprang from the peculiar gift for Godli-

---

[8]*Letters* I pp. 75 ff. (1912) ; See Waxman, *loc. cit.*

ness with which the Jewish people were endowed. In his view, there were two factors which conduce to the holiness of the Jewish people and their attachment to the idea of Godliness. One was their heritage, the inner spirituality which was transmitted to them by heredity from their ancestors, and which could never disappear entirely. The second factor is the good deeds of the individuals. There are times in Jewish history when one force attains ascendancy, and other times when the other comes into its own. The Messianic fervour with which the National movement is charged and the universal ideals of justice and righteousness which animate it, can only be accounted by the spirit of the heritage of the nation which informs the Jewish masses. This makes the National movement one of redemption, notwithstanding the fact that the religious conduct of the individuals is not much in evidence.[9]

The prevalent irreligion among the young *Halutzim* in particular, was not to be compared with the infidelities of the past. The young today are singularly free from all superstitious and idolatrous cults which are the real enemies of Godliness and spirituality. Theirs is but a loss of sensitiveness to things divine, through a lack of understanding and perception. Outwardly evil, inwardly they are good—holy—the true representatives of the pre-Messianic generation which according to the Zohar was to be "good within and evil without."[10] Moreover, he went so far as to blame the religious elements for the attitude of the non-religious youth. Their estrangement from Judaism, he declared, is motivated in most cases by ideals of social justice, which they are led to imagine find no response in our midst, in view of our failure to participate actively in the affairs of the world; whilst they do not appreciate the limitations imposed upon us by the absence of the necessary geographical and political factors of which we have been deprived by our loss of country and kingdom.[10a] But this very quest for social righteousness is in itself the "way of the Lord," which Abraham our Father had commanded his children and his household "that they may do righteousness and justice." All the errors of the young generation thus consist merely in that they do not realize that in order to attain the good goals they are desiring, the

---

[9]*Letters* I pp. 92 ff. (1912) ; See Waxman, *loc. cit.*
[10]*Letters* II pp. 369-70 (1908).
[10a]*Letters* II pp. 178 (1908).

children of Israel must honour the Torah and cleave to the faith which is the light of the whole world and its life. There was thus every reason to hope that with clearer insight and enlightenment, they would be touched by the spirit of Godliness and realize in them and through their own lives, the divine qualities inherent in God's chosen people.

HOLINESS AS A BOND BETWEEN ISRAEL AND ITS LAND

It was this belief which determined Rabbi Kook's relations with the non-observant Jews in the *Yishuv*. He continuously preached and practised tolerance towards them and showed them every friendship. To the critics of his attitude he would reply by referring to the law of the firstling of an ass. Of all unclean animals, the ass was singled out to have its first-born sanctified, notwithstanding the fact that it lacked both the inward and outward characteristics that distinguish "unclean" from "clean" beasts. And the reason given by our Sages, was that the ass had helped to carry the baggage of the Israelites when they departed from the Egyptian house of bondage, and made their way to the Holy Land. Surely, he would rejoin, even assuming that these irreligious *Halutzim* are, as is maintained, bereft of all Jewish piety, both internal and external, their endeavours in assisting the Jewish people out of the *Galut,* and in rebuilding the Holy Land, stamped them with the distinction of holiness. Every endeavour must be made to draw them by bands of love and kindliness to the path of Torah and *Mitzvot.* To this end, however, there was for him one royal road— nationalism. "For there was," as he expressed it, "the closest connection between the national idea in Israel and the holiness that stemmed from Israel's faith and the observance of Torah and *Mitzvot.*"[11] And it was for the sake of the Torah and the Godliness which it engendered that all Jews had to work in harmony and unity for the rebuilding of the Holy Land, and for the restoration of this union between Nationhood and Godliness, which formed the quintessence of Israel's selection. To hold back from participating in this work of restoration is a sin. Moreover, to refuse to recognize in the happenings of the day the finger of God working out Israel's deliverance through historical forces,

---

[11]*Letters* II p. 143 (1908).

political combinations and diplomatic channels, and to sit with arms folded waiting for supernatural phenomena and miraculous transformations, as if God's salvation of our people could not be effected otherwise, meant, in his opinion, to limit the power of God, and was a sign not of deep piety, but of little faith.[12] True, there were many God-fearing and saintly men who were opposed to the national idea, but, with all the veneration and affection he had for them, he refused to accept their attitude in this matter. "Already in the days of Ezra," he writes, "many great men did not desire the establishment of a *Yishuv* in Israel, but preferred to remain in Babylon. Ezra was thus obliged to take with him the least desirable elements of the Jewish people, who were far from attractive and who desecrated the Sabbath even in Eretz Israel. Yet the result was that from these very people sprang forth salvation. The second Temple was built, and from it there proceeded the dissemination of the Oral Law and the spread of Torah in Israel. And so it will be in our days. By strengthening the *Yishuv* and increasing the number of our brethren in the Holy Land, we shall ensure the shining forth of the light of redemption and salvation".[13] Nor can this be otherwise. As the scene of the highest manifestations of divine holiness, the Holy Land could not fail to exert its influence even over transgressors and sinners, who in the end will turn to God with a ready heart and with joy. Moreover, out of these transgressors and sinners in Israel there shall one day arise a movement for the return to God which is destined to embrace the whole world. In the light of these tremendous implications, Israel's restoration becomes a necessity for the world no less than for the Jewish people themselves. "Israel," he used to say, "exerts holy influences by her very existence. Many hate her, many persecute her, but none can deny her existence, and her existence will never cease influencing human thought and cleansing humanity from its dross."[13a] But this influence Israel can make most effective only from the Holy Land. Indeed, the fact that many ideas of Judaism have already become part of the culture of humanity, should make it much easier for the Jews, once they return to the Holy Land, to exert spiritual influences upon

---

[12]*Letters* II p. 142 (1908).

[13]*Letters* II p. 348 (1910).

[13a]Quoted by E. Zoref, *Hayye ha-Rav Kook* p. 190.

other nations. "We stand," he writes, "now near the shore and may well raise our banner on high. The holy spirit of Israel has already made moral conquests throughout the world, and there is no longer any need for us to refrain from proclaiming our victory. But no heed will be given by the world to our proclamation unless it emanates from the place whence it was first heard—from the source whence the light shone forth—from Zion."[14]

This conviction in the ultimate reconciliation of the whole of humanity to God, through a restored Israel, is a recurrent theme in Rabbi Kook's writings, and one to which he devoted a special classic, *Orot ha-Teshubah*. It was his last conscious thought on earth. Visited by Professor Zondek, the famous surgeon, a few moments before he breathed his last, Rabbi Kook greeted him with the words "I am confident that one day the great physicians will become true God-fearing men."

THE SPIRITUAL POWER OF THE HOLY LAND

This spiritual power which the Holy Land exerts on all formed part of his credo. He asserted that Eretz Israel was the only propitious soil for the flowering of the Jewish religious genius at its best. The Talmudic saying that "The air of Eretz Israel makes one wise" (*Baba Batra* 158b) was for him more than a mere poetic fancy. It represented actual reality, enforced by common experience. "I have scarcely seen," he writes, "an 'idiotic' child among all our children of our Holy Land. All who are born there are by nature sharp-witted and clever. All the terrible poverty and hardships they have to endure, as a result of the crushing and distressing conditions, have not been able to dim the light of their intelligence; they all are full of knowledge and good understanding."[15]

Likewise, the saying "There is no Torah like the Torah of Eretz Israel" (Genesis *Rabbah* 16, 7), was a truth which he had confirmed in his own experience. In this connection the observation he made to me regarding his little book, *Rosh Millin,* is revealing. I noticed that Rabbi Kook continued to read it intently after its publication. He explained that when he had composed

---

[14]*Letters* II p. 48 (1907).
[15]*Letters* II p. 138 (1908).

the work he was transported in spirit to the Holy Land and he was seeking to recapture that experience by studying the contents of this work.

He indeed detected some differences in the quality of the Torah as studied in Eretz Israel from that pursued in *Hutz Laaretz*. In Eretz Israel, thanks to the *Shefa,* the holy flow of inspiration, the disciple of the Torah is able to grasp intuitively the general principles of the law, and proceeding from them penetrate into the details thereof. In *Hutz Laaretz* the process is in the reverse: the disciple has first to struggle with the details and is only then able to ascertain the underlying principles. It is that which accounts for the conciseness of the Jerusalem Talmud (Yerushalmi) as compared with the elaborate and complicated dialectics of the Babylonian Talmud (Babli) which led Palestinian scholars to describe those in Babylon as "the keen-witted who are able to get an elephant through the eye of a needle."[16]

RESPONSIBILITY OF RELIGION

All this placed a special responsibility upon all those who loved the Torah. They had it in their power to bring the youth of the *Yishuv* nearer to Jewish religious life and observance, provided they behaved towards them with gentleness and kindliness, and showed that they were truly concerned for them and ready to identify themselves with their problems and struggles.[16a] For this reason it was essential for the Jewish religious leaders in the Holy Land to be equipped with a knowledge of life and the world, without which they could make little appeal to the heart of the irreligious youth. "I see," he writes, "that the principal reason for our lack of success in whatever we do to strengthen Judaism . . . is that the light of God has been shut out from heart and mind. The main concern of all at present is the fostering of *proste frumkeit* (common religiosity), as if it were possible to keep the world alive by a body without a soul." And he goes on to plead for a more systematic pursuit of Torah studies, attended by a "breadth of mind and clarity of spirit," as well as for an active participation in the rehabilitation of the *Yishuv,* and in the fostering of its trade and

---

[16]*Letters* II p. 123 ff.
[16a]*Letters* II p. 348 (1910).

commerce.[17] He realized that this involved a complete reorienta-
tion in their educational methods, and would find no favor in the
eyes of the majority of the religious leaders of the *Yishuv,* "who
wish to walk only along the old paths and keep far away from all
progressive movements in life." But their attitude was, he insists,
altogether contrary to the way of the Torah, and greatly to be
deplored, as it gave a pretext to the irresponsible elements of the
Yishuv to break loose and strengthened the hands of the evil-doers.
"Alas," he continues, "for the simple piety of these people, although
their intention is good. I can do no other than strengthen the educational system, which gives its due share to the knowledge of life
and of the world, and which at the same time trains our children in
an appreciation of the joy of life in all its beauty and orderliness.
Such a training when combined with a training in Torah and the
true fear of Heaven can only serve to add to its attractiveness and
power."[18] There was no denying, he maintained, that those who
were trained by the old method were unfit by virtue either of their
knowledge or their general conduct and demeanour to take their
place in the battle of life, with the result that they grow up as weak-
lings, timid of spirit, and dependent upon others.[19] No wonder that
a great part of the new *Yishuv,* even of its more worthy elements,
cannot tolerate the whole trend and outlook of life of the old
Yishuv. "The quickened tempo of the new *Yishuv,* its joy of life,
courage of heart, breadth of outlook, is unable to endure the bent
back, the shrunken and sad countenance, expressive of fear and
timidity, the dejected gaze, expressive of despair, the hatred of life,
the strange oriental garb, the effects of which the attendant strain
of grinding poverty only serves to aggravate and to make recoil
who is accustomed to European life."[20]

And not only in the new *Yishuv.* The failure of Jewish religious
leadership in general, Rabbi Kook ascribes to this very lack of
knowledge of life on the part of religious leaders. He accordingly
attaches little value to the proposal made to him by a correspondent
to convene a conference of rabbis. "Your hopes regarding a conference of rabbis," Rabbi Kook writes, "are to me always mere
dreams, which to the distress of our heart do not possess the charm

---

[17]*Letters* II p. 100-1 ff. (1908).
[18]*Letters* II p. 310-11 (1910).
[19]*Letters* II p. 170 (1908).
[20]*Letters* II p. 185 (1908).

or beauty which envelops anything imaginative. The shepherds of our people are in deep sleep, not out of an evil heart, but through the lassitude of a soul which has not tasted for days and years, nay, whole periods, any real enlivening and sustaining food. When they will come together at the conference, they will certainly adorn the table with some *Halakhic* problem, very minute as far as its inner content is concerned, though it may appear great and important, judged by the complicated devices resorted to for solving it, 'even as one sets up a machine at the cost of many thousands of talents of gold in order to manufacture one single steel needle.' They may further adorn it by some *Agadic* theme, embellished with some pietistic exhortation void of life, some dessicated mystic thought, or antiquated philosophy, only to add to the suffocation in the atmosphere and increase the pain of *Knesset* Israel."[21]

HIS IDEA OF A MODERN YESHIVAH

In order to remedy the situation, Rabbi Kook advocated, from the earliest days of his rabbinate in Jaffa, the establishment of a modern *yeshivah* in the Holy Land. The *yeshivah* as he envisaged it, and to which he devoted many of his letters,[22] was to be founded on a broad comprehensive basis so as to embrace all the treasures of the Torah, Written and Oral—The Bible, the two Talmudim and Midrashim—*Halakhic* and *Agadic*—with a recognition of all that ancient and modern research has contributed. To the study of the Bible was to be brought all the aid that philology supplied, so that the innermost spirit of the sacred books might be revealed. History, particularly that of the Jewish people, and Jewish thought, were to occupy a prominent feature in the curriculum, and were to include a study from first sources of the great men of the Jewish people—what they had thought and done and suffered. The land of Palestine itself, what it held of material wealth, its geographical position, and all the sacred associations that had gathered round town or village, hill, valley or rivulet, was to receive from teachers and disciples the attention it deserved. And what the Jews have done in philosophy and science was not to be neglected. Such works as the *Emunot Vedeot,* the *Kuzari,* the

[21]*Letters* II p. 240 (1909).
[22]*Letters* II pp. 313 ff; 270 ff; 192 ff; 186 ff; 118; 93 ff.

Hovot Halevavot, the *Moreh Nebukhim,* the *Ikkarim,* and other
ethical books, were to be studied so as to draw from them "all that
leads to purity of heart, the peace of the soul and the fulness of life
and beauty." Nor was the free spirit of enquiry to be suppressed.
Hokmat Yisrael, he insisted, must not be allowed to remain the
monopoly of those who are bent on destroying the Torah and faith
in God, but must become, in the words of the eloquent prophet,
*"the gain of those that sit before the Lord for eating to satiety and
stately clothing* (Isaiah 23, 19)."[23]

The language of instruction was to be Hebrew, and attention
was also to be given to the study of general sciences, including
philosophy and economics. The students, moreover, would not
be encouraged to be pedants, but to be active, ever ready exponents
in the living world of the thoughts that are in them. From such a
yeshivah, he claimed, would emanate the wisdom, the knowledge
and the fear of God, the requisites for a skilful, judicious, cautious
and withal a satisfactory solution of the problems of the times on the
lines of tradition without endangering the integrity and unity of the
Kelal Yisrael.

With his assumption of the office of Chief Rabbi in Jerusalem,
the *yeshivah* dream which he cherished for many years, not only
began to assume the shape of reality, but became richer in scope
and content; and from the idea of a modern *yeshivah,* in the Holy
Land, serving the needs of the *Yishuv,* grew his project for a universal *yeshivah* at Jerusalem for the entire Jewish people. Founded
in 1924 by Rabbi Kook, the *Yeshivah* has ever since sought to
attract students from all parts of the Diaspora, with the object of
making them into really great men in Israel, veritable pillars of the
Torah, so that they might carry with them to their native land,
on the completion of their studies, the light of redemption and
truth which, as has been foreshown by our prophets, was to go
forth out of Zion and of Jerusalem.

TEACHING AND AUTHORITY

Teaching, however, had to go hand in hand with authority;
and although Rabbi Kook did not consider the time ripe for the

---

[23]*Letters* II p. 148 (1908). See also his letters to Isaac Halevi: p. 88.

convening of a Sanhedrin,[24] he gave expression to the hope that such an authority would ultimately be evolved, to which would be drawn the most prominent rabbis of the age. From this Sanhedrin might be expected authoritative pronouncements on all matters affecting Judaism. But for such a purpose he considered the universal *Yeshivah* to be a necessary adjunct. Past authority could only be restored by grafting it as a piece of living matter on the present and future. It must not be the product of the past alone, it must be a living organism of today, capable of making the future for God and humanity.

When we consider the breadth of vision of this great teacher in Israel, we begin to appreciate the significance of his resplendent leadership for the development of the spiritual and religious life of the *Yishuv*. Reference has already been made to his mighty strivings, in face of formidable opposition, in devising measures for overcoming the hardships involved in the operation of the *Shemittah* which threatened the economic existence of the struggling colonists. To one of the rigorist rabbis who insisted on the strict observance of the *Shemittah,* Rabbi Kook retorted, "You stand in fear of the punishment that may await you in the Hereafter for sanctioning a breach of the law, whilst you feel no concern for the whole *Yishuv,* which might become engulfed in complete economic ruin. It behooves each one of us to shoulder the responsibility, since we all aim at the rebuilding of the Holy Land."[25]

Characteristic, too, was his rejoinder to his formidable opponent, the *Ridbaz,* who discerned in the outbreak of some epidemics in the Holy Land, in 1910, a mark of divine displeasure, because of the *Yishuv's* laxity in the observance of the *Shemittah* in accordance with the measures sanctioned by Rabbi Kook. To this Rabbi Kook replied, "As to the cause which is responsible for the visitations experienced in the Holy Land, there is none greater than the *Sinëat Hinnam* (groundless hate) in which we are steeped here more than elsewhere. It is not the way of the Torah to allow the fear of punishment to guide us in establishing a point of law. We have to clarify from the Torah itself, whether or not a certain measure is permissible, and once we succeed in doing so, we dare not ascribe any visitation to our interpretation of the law, for God

---

[24]*Letters* II p. 341 (1910).
[25]See E. Zoref, *Chayye ha-Rav Kook* p. 75.

would not falsify in His own Torah. It behooves us to investigate our actions in other directions, in particular attitudes and failings, which unfortunately disfigure our times."

It is said that Schopenhauer would begin his lectures on Kant by saying: "Let no-one *tell* what is contained in the *Critique of Pure Reason.*" Likewise there was no intention in these pages to *tell* that which is contained in the manifold writings of Rabbi Kook. The only way to understand and appreciate Rabbi Kook's teaching is to turn to his works, and to study and ponder them. Yet it is hoped that what has been attempted here, is sufficient to provide a glimpse into the life and thought of a great teacher in Israel, who was a tower of strength, a treasure of learning, a master in saintliness, a personality whose gigantic spirit has imprinted immortality on much of his work and his achievements.

ERNEST WEILL

(1865-1947)

By Joseph Bloch and Simon Langer

ERNEST WEILL

By Joseph Bloch and Simon Langer

The historian of Torah-true Judaism in contemporary France will assign a prominent place to one of its outstanding exponents, the late Grand Rabbi Ernest Weill.

Born on the 25th of October, 1865, in Reguisheim, a picturesque Alsatian village near Colmar, he belonged to a well-known family whose reputation transcended its district.

His parents, proud and uncompromising Jews, considered it as their life's task to bring up their son in full respect of our faith. The mother, particularly, seems to have exercised a profound and lasting influence upon his spiritual growth, for in his articles and sermons he speaks tenderly of her as the builder of his character.

Reguisheim, at the time of his childhood, had still a Jewish population of approximately two hundred and fifty souls, deeply rooted in the Jewish tradition. Ernest received his first Jewish and secular education in the Jewish and Public School of the village, both established and maintained by the State.

The Franco-Prussian War of 1870-1871 was just over, with France defeated and Alsace-Lorraine ceded to the German Reich. The languages used in the public schools were thus French and German, and Ernest Weill learned to know both. Soon thereafter, his parents settled in Neuf-Brisach, a small town situated near the River Rhine, where he eventually attended the high school.

When in 1880 the Consistoires of Strasbourg, Colmar and Metz (the governing body of the Jews in Alsace-Lorraine) established, in Colmar, a preparatory school for the training of rabbis, Ernest Weill became one of its first and foremost students. He continued, at the same time, his general studies at the Lycée of Colmar, whose graduates attained the equivalent of an American B.A. or a B.S. When the dean of this Preparatory Seminary, Dr. Bloch, died, he was succeeded by Rabbi Zacharias Wolff of Pfungstadt (Germany), one of the best disciples of Rabbi Ezriel Hildesheimer of Eisenstadt (Hungary), later rector of the Rabbinical Seminary of Berlin. Dr. Wolff exercised a profound influence upon his students, more than a score of whom became rabbis in Alsace-Lorraine and stayed abidingly attached to their teacher.

After the liquidation of the Colmar school, Rabbi Wolff accepted the rabbinate of Bischeim, one of the suburbs of Strasbourg. In the fall of 1886, Weill graduated with honors from the Lyceum in Colmar and decided to become a rabbi. The training of rabbis being one of the major concerns of the Consistoire, they thought it sufficient, when the seminary in Colmar closed its doors, for the students to combine lectures at the University of Strasbourg with classes in the Talmud under the leadership of local rabbis. Yet the results were not in accord with expectations.

The students could continue their studies either in Breslau or in Berlin. The seminaries in both cities were known all over Europe, yet the one in Berlin was strictly Orthodox. Ernest Weill and his lifelong friends, Armand Bloch, (Strasbourg) and Joseph Zivi, (Biesheim) as the first rabbinic students of Alsatian origin, chose Berlin, not because that city, as the capital of Germany, offered greater opportunities than Breslau, the capital of a province, but because at the helm of the Berlin seminary stood Ezriel Hildesheimer, himself the teacher of Dr. Wolff, their former master in Colmar, and celebrated all over the Jewish world because of his great Talmudic knowledge and for his piety.

Their choice was of great importance for their spiritual future. Other students followed their example. The great majority of the Alsatian rabbis in the first half of our century received their training in Berlin at the feet of those giants of Jewish lore, Ezriel and Hirsch Hildesheimer, David Hoffmann, Jacob Barth, Abraham Berliner, and Joseph Wohlgemuth.

There were times when the seminary in Berlin counted over more than a *minyan* of students from Alsace-Lorraine. They constituted the strongest and the most cohesive *Landsmanschaft* among the young scholars coming from all European countries, and their influence upon the religious life in their homeland was very great.

The devastating effects of the two World Wars brought great changes in this respect, yet the spirit of the rabbis trained in the seminary of Berlin is still potent in Alsatian Jewry.

The students of Berlin were deeply impressed by the spirit of Ezriel Hildesheimer, by his joyous piety, and his steady readiness to make sacrifices. Ernest Weill soon became one of his preferred disciples.

Twenty-five years later he wrote of Ezriel Hildesheimer: "The great men who are our patterns of 'Talmud Torah Im Derekh Eretz' (Torah and Modern Culture) have devoted their whole life to helping us become strong representatives of traditional Judaism in modern society. To be modern and yet traditional at the same time—how audacious an effort to reconcile two seemingly irreconcilable goals! Yet they succeeded in achieving this synthesis. Our unforgettable master, Dr. Hildesheimer, dedicated his strength and love to the furtherance of this great cause. In him were harmoniously blended knowledge of Torah and broad secular education. But his rare human qualities, his great character, his whole personality, remained even more deeply engraved in our souls than his teachings." Ernest Weill's friendship with many a colleague, dating back to the time of their studies at the Seminary, resulted, among others, in the publication in 1910, of *Das Juedische Blatt*.

In 1891 Weill obtained the degree of Ph.D. at the University of Strasbourg from the famous Orientalist, Theodore Noeldeke, a great friend of the Jews. His doctorate thesis dealt with the Mishnah Commentary of Maimonides on the treatise of *Berakhot*. In the same year he received *Semikhah* from Ezriel Hildesheimer.

Soon he was offered important pulpits in Germany, but preferred the rabbinate in an Alsatian village to the great centers of religious activities on the other side of the Rhine. Indeed, throughout his life, he felt completely integrated with his native soil and with Alsatian Jewry, whose dialect he always liked to speak.

In 1891 the rabbinic position in Brumath became vacant. Of the three candidates invited to deliver the trial sermon in the presence of the members of the Consistoire in Strasbourg, it was Ernest Weill who carried the vote of the community, yet the Consistoire, the over-all governing body of Alsatian Jewry, refused the approval on the ground that for reasons of seniority the position should go to Rabbi Isidore Dreyfuss, Rabbi of Fegersheim, one of the three candidates and somewhat older than Ernest Weill. The latter was finally named Rabbi of Fegersheim as a successor to Isidore Dreyfuss. That rabbinate included the communities of Benfeld and Erstein, at that time still important, each of which numbered approximately three hundred Jews, and had a Jewish Public School of its own. The young rabbi had thus a welcome opportunity for showing his great pedagogic ability.

His first task in Fegersheim was to search for boys who were able to study and who would strive, eventually, to become rabbis. Dr. Arthur Weill, who after almost fifty years of service, retired, in 1955, as Rabbi of Basel, gave a vivid picture of that time: "As a boy of thirteen, I spent six months with Dr. Ernest Weill in Fegerheim, since it was my parent's wish that I should become a rabbi. He was still single and we boarded with the same family. He taught me every day. I am indebted to him, not only for this but also for my first hike into the mountains. We covered the ten miles from Obernai to the Hohwald (a resort, about 2400 feet high) in a pouring rain. Like other boys of my age, I liked to stroll around in my spare time. Sometimes I shot at the birds in our garden with a rubber sling. When once a neighbor denounced me to Rabbi Ernest Weill for this crime, he jokingly answered, 'There is no danger for the birds, for he will, anyway, never be able to hit one'."[1]

In 1897 he became the Rabbi of Bouxwiller. The high school of that town was attended by an impressive number of Jewish boys from all the neighboring villages and towns. This gave him a chance to extend his sphere of teaching. The closing of the Preparatory Seminary in Colmar in 1898 increased the number of his students who sought the spiritual guidance of this rabbi, already well known as an outstanding teacher.[2]

Ernest Weill outlived most of his pupils. All revered him and Arthur Weill once wrote: "The shining example of my revered teacher, Dr. Ernest Weill, a man of uncompromising religious principles, yet open-minded and selfless and of great understanding for the problems of others, has left an indelible mark in my heart." Lucien Dreyfus, writing in 1929 about Ernest Weill in the *Univers*

---

[1]Rashi gave once a similar answer to one of his pupils: See Pardes, 16 D. and Berliner on Rashi's Character, Breslau, 1900, page XVI.)

[2]Among his students were: Arthur Weill (Rabbi in Basel); Lucien Dreyfus (who become a high school teacher in Strasbourg and in 1942 was deported by the Germans); Henry Dreyfus (rabbi of Guebwiller); Benjamin May (rabbi in Frankfort, AM.); Anselme Debré (at first rabbi of Ribeauville, who left the rabbinate to become a physician); Moise Debré (rabbi of Sarreunion); Jerome Levi (rabbi of Obernai); Julien Weill (rabbi of Bollwiller, and after World War I rabbi of Dijon).

Israélite (a French-Jewish weekly), speaks of him in the same glowing terms.

It is in the modest town of Bouxwiller that Ernest Weill realized his greatest ambition, to inspire his students with love and respect for the teachings of Torah. He had the ability to communicate to all of them his enthusiasm for, and his ardent faith in, Judaism.

Not all his students became rabbis, yet not a single one has ever doubted that he owes the best of his Jewish education to the fruitful teachings of the master. One of his admirers, today a Professor of Physics in a college in Paris, writes: "It was in 1919, one year after the return of Alsace-Lorraine to France, that I met, for the first time, Ernest Weill, who had just become the Grand Rabbi of Colmar. At the school he was my teacher of religion, and I and a few other boys had just celebrated our Bar Mitzvah. Due to the war years and its difficulties, our knowledge in Hebrew was very small. As for general matters, we had to learn French as quickly as possible and to adapt ourselves to the French school methods. Though we were very enthusiastic about everything, we had, nevertheless, the tendency to consider Hebrew as of secondary importance. Ernest Weill, imperceptibly but rapidly, succeeded in changing our way of thinking in this matter, for he knew how to convey, in an almost casual, yet highly interesting manner, the essentials of Judaism. In his teachings, from which emanated so much warmth, he made it clear that Judaism was the religion which one had to live in order to understand it fully. Those among us who came from homes where religious obervances had still more or less their place, less of conviction than out of habit, were now able to understand the full meaning of these observances because of the explanations given by our teacher; while those who did not observe, could, at least, see the beauty of Jewish life in its diverse manifestations and its profound influence upon the spiritual development of the Jew." Another of his students, who attended the High School in Bouxwiller and eventually became a very prominent lawyer and an exponent of Orthodoxy in France, was once asked how it happened that there was so great a difference between him and his brother as far as Jewishness is concerned. "Well," he replied, "I was trained by Ernest Weill, while my brother was deprived of this opportunity."

The explanations given by Ernest Weill were always clear and appropriate to the age of his pupils. He never evaded any question, not even the most daring ones, and was never embarrassed about an answer. He was always searching for students susceptible to his religious teachings and capable of living up to them. He was ever looking for contact with youths and tried to impress them in the course of an *en passant* conversation or at the occasion of a walk or a hike. He never missed an opportunity to give advice even in questions which might have been considered pretty delicate for an adolescent. Ernest Weill showed them that religious life, and life in general, formed one unit. He was also interested in the general studies of his students, who were amazed by his knowledge in every domain. As they listened to him, they felt that Judaism was in no way in contradiction with modern science. It is a strange, yet remarkable fact that it was Grand Rabbi Weill, more than the teacher in science at the college, who aroused our interest in questions of a scientific and philosophical order. He liked to mention Bergson and Einstein and endeavored to translate, in words easily understood, certain philosophical concepts about time and space. He fashioned their spirit, always trying to stimulate interest in a text, rather than merely teach it. He succeeded in showing the profound meaning of Jewish doctrines and how to choose a way of life which spells ultimate blessing.

Four years before Ernest Weill became Rabbi of Bouxwiller, he married his cousin, Clementine Weill, with whom he shared more than fifty years of a happy life. Two sons and two daughters were born unto them. The former, Eli and Joseph, are well-known physicians in Strasbourg. The latter is also a leader in Jewish affairs and President of the Consistoire of Strasbourg. One daughter, Sara (Mrs. Joseph Rothschild of Zurich), is a leading Torah-true woman of that city. The other daughter (Mrs. Lucy Samuel), married Judge Samuel; he died some fifteen years ago.

Mrs. Ernest Weill was a highly intelligent and cultured lady, who backed to the fullest extent her husband's aspirations and endeavors. Into the volume of the translation into French of the *Kitzur Shulhan Arukh,* which she presented to Rabbi Joseph Bloch of Hagnenau, she wrote: "To the devoted friend and co-worker of my husband, as a token of affection and appreciation, by the one who had the happiness to share the author's life. May his memory be a blessing."

The congregational work in Fegersheim and later in Bouxwiller left Ernest Weill sufficient time to pursue his own studies and to teach. Gifted with a phenomenal memory and animated by a burning love for learning, his unusual will-power and tremendous capacity for work made of him in time a master of Talmudic knowledge, a rare phenomenon in Western Europe. The great scholars of Eastern Europe had high regard for him. The Sage of Lublin, Rabbi Meir Shapiro, of blessed memory, was greatly surprised to find in France a rabbi of such stature, so great a Talmudic scholar and so eager to fight for Torah and faith. He was at home in *Yam Shel Talmud*—(the sea of the Talmud). He knew its breadth and its depth without ever being lost. Under his leadership, in 1909, the monthly meetings of some Alsatian rabbis, for the special purpose of studying the Talmud, were re-instituted. Initiated in 1895, they had previously functioned under the chairmanship of Rabbis Bamberger (Cernay), Schuler (Boll-willer), Wolf (Colmar), and Cohn (Basel). Young colleagues were particularly welcomed, the participants dealing with special themes of the Talmud (*Sugyot*). These monthly meetings are held to this day.

No wonder that the reputation of Ernest Weill as a great youth builder transcended the frontiers of his Alsatian homeland. Thus, in 1904, he was invited to the vacant position of rabbi of an important Orthodox congregation in Cologne, combined with the Directorship of the Teachers' Seminary in that city, one of the outstanding institutions in Jewish Germany. Yet, most probably for sentimental reasons and never looking for honors, Ernest Weill declined the call. He preferred to remain in his little Bouxwiller, on native soil, considering deep down in his heart Alsace-Lorraine as part of France, rather than of Germany. The defeat of Germany after World War I brought Alsace-Lorraine back into the French fold. Those who have lived through the days of the Armistice will forever remember the explosion of happiness with which Alsatian Jewry greeted this event.

WEILL AS AUTHOR

Until 1910 nothing was known about any publication of Ernest Weill, except his Ph.D. thesis. It is thus the more surprising that a man who, until the age of forty-five never wrote an article, became, all of a sudden, a well-known and able writer. It was not the prospect of glory that attracted him into this field, but the call to duty.

The only then existing Alsatian Jewish newspaper, a weekly, was received in almost every Jewish home. Its openly Reform-tinged policy constituted a threat to traditional Judaism, to which the majority of Jews adhered. The tendency of that newspaper showed great disdain for the Torah and its representatives; even Jews who were not tradition-minded, felt hurt. The publication of a Torah-true newspaper was widely urged and Ernest Weill was solicited to take the lead. At first he hesitated, afraid of eventual financial difficulties. On the occasion of a visit to Strasbourg in 1910, of Mr. Jacob Rosenheim, the President of the Agudat Israel World Organization, the problem of an Orthodox newspaper for Alsace-Lorraine was discussed at great length. Mr. Rosenheim was ready to make available important financial help. Yet Ernest Weill refused, afraid to lose his spiritual independence, which he always considered man's most precious possession.

The problem was finally solved. In Bavaria, inhabited by a great number of Jews, a new religious constitution for them was planned by the State. Rabbi Pinchos Kohn of Ansbach, one of the leading rabbis in that country, considered that constitution highly detrimental to traditional Judaism and desired an organ for his views. There resulted an agreement between the two former students of Hildesheimer: each would try to find one half of the costs for financing the new weekly and each would have complete freedom to write, and to choose the editorial staff, in his respective country. Ernest Weill appointed Armand Bloch, Camille Bloch, Joseph Bloch, Moise Debré, Henry Dreyfuss, Max Guggenheim, S. H. Schuler, Solomon Schuler, Emil Schwartz, Arthur Weill, Joseph Zivi as members of the editorial board. With a few exceptions, it was the same rabbis who helped him provide for the publication of the newspaper. It was decided that the editorial be of a religious character, and have, if possible, the weekly portion of the Torah as its topic. Each member of the staff worked without any payment, and lent his best effort to the paper.

Yet, in spite of such propaganda, its beginnings were rather difficult, since the older newspaper was far ahead in the number of subscribers, and notwithstanding the fact that the annual subscription of the new weekly was only three marks (75 American cents), and included a nice calendar containing various informations related to the Jewish year. But Ernest Weill would always find a philanthropist to cover the deficit. The new weekly proved a great blessing and filled a long felt need. It was printed at first in Ansbach then in Strasbourg.

Pinchos Kohn and Ernest Weill were the Editors-in-Chief. The copies destined for Alsace-Lorraine bore the name Strasbourg, whilst in those destined for Germany, Ansbach figured as publication place. A supplement in French was eventually added for the readers of Alsace-Lorraine with Major Armand Lipman, Alexander Klein, a lawyer, and Fernand Weill, in charge.

The leading article in the first number reflects the ideology, the methods and the purpose of its editors. Here are some excerpts:

"Our goal can be expressed in one sentence: We want to preserve and to spread traditional Judaism. To realize it, we want to use the most modern means, a newspaper. It is not ambition which has prompted us to act. God alone knows how reluctant we were to undertake the difficult task. Duty alone has called us to put our limited strength at the service of our religion.

"Firm in principle, gentle in form, we shall endeavor to win adherents to its teachings. No personal motive will ever enter. We want to serve our sacred cause, accepted at Sinai by our ancestors and binding upon us, their descendants. We know that we shall uphold thereby also the chain of tradition transmitted to us here in Alsace by our fathers, which they wanted us to continue. Though part of our precious heritage may have been lost in our present age, the radical Reform movement, which has plagued Germany, cannot take roots in our country. The Jews in our country have a strong feeling of solidarity. Our efforts will be directed to maintaining, with the cooperation of all, our religious institutions in the spirit of our Holy Torah. Our newspaper has primarily in view the situation of Judaism in Alsace-Lorraine. We have secured the cooperation of able and reliable men in our midst, and hope that our organ, rich in content and refined in language, will become popular, inspiring and instructive."

For almost four years *Das Juedische Blatt,* faithful to these principles, rendered great service to the Jewish population of Alsace. From week to week it was eagerly expected by its readers, also by the youth, for which there was a special corner; its editorials, written with competence and good state, deserve to be read still today. The poetic pen of Pinchos Kohn, the ardor of Ernest Weill, the philosophic calm of Emil Schwartz, the satirical finesse of Moise Debré, each one writing according to his own temper, gave the newspaper its colorful nuances. Ernest Weill wrote about questions of the day, like the constitutional setup of the Consistoire, the Alliance Israélite, "Liberal" Judaism, and the battle against the directives of radical Reform (*Richtlinien*). Pinchos Kohn, in his brilliant "Rural Letters" (*Briefe vom Land*) tried to deal with the opponents of Torah-true Judaism.

Das Juedische Blatt slowly increased the number of its readers; subscribers came from beyond the borders of Alsace-Lorraine and Bavaria.

But the outbreak of World War I destroyed everything—*Das Juedische Blatt,* as well at its opponent. The last number bears the date of July 31, 1914. With a melancholic presentiment of the future, Ernest Weill, in his editorial on the political situation remarks:

"Fathers and mothers, as well as all civilized nations, would well do to pray that the Almighty, in whose hands are the hearts of the kings, inspire them with a desire for peace."

Is it sheer concidence that his first editorial, published in September, 1910, sounds like a prophetic vision of what eventually happened: " 'What matters an individual, when the existence of thousands is at stake?' This concept of the value of human life, inherited from ancient heathenism, we have considered self-evident. We have taken it for granted that war must tear up the most sacred bonds of marriage, that the young husband, brokenhearted, must leave behind his young wife, transforming her happiness into despair; that the sancity of the family must yield to the so-called higher reasons of the State. . . . But the words of this week's *Sidrah* sound like a revelation from another world. *'And what man is there that hath betrothed a wife and hath not taken her: Let her go and return to his house lest he die in the battle and another man marry her.'* (Deut. XX, 7)

"How old fashioned does this appear to us and yet how humane! The sanctity of the family takes precedence over the fear of the enemy! All the feverish preparations for war must leave nascent domestic happiness immune. The love of a young married woman has a stronger claim upon her husband than the call to arms of the State!"

Without doubt, the four years of general sufferings during the war found a painful echo in the house of the Rabbi of Bouxwiller. Alsace-Lorraine was considered a war zone and sometimes it was a battlefield. The secret sympathies of many were with those on the other side of the blue mountain chain called the Vosges. Caution in speech, and even more so in writing, was of utmost importance.

The folios of the Talmud offered Ernest Weill diversion and comfort, and he could silently prepare for the future. The victory of France was for Alsace-Lorraine like balm upon an open wound. The Jews, in particular, greeted the return to the Motherland as the happiest event of their time.

The task now was to rebuild Jewish life within the new framework. For rabbis and teachers who had received their education in German schools and who had to assume new responsibilities in French public life, the problem of the language was to some extent a handicap, but not for Ernest Weill. When, in November, 1918, a Tree of Liberation was planted in the public square of Bouxwiller, he was asked to deliver the official address. In order to be understood by everyone, he spoke in Alsatian dialect, but his sermon in the Great Synagogue of Strasbourg, on French Army Day, showed his mastery of all the refinements of classic French. It proved a sensation and brought tears to all eyes. In the peroration, he reached extraordinary heights both as to form and content. This is how he concluded: "France, thou hast never forsaken thy children whom thou wert forced to turn over to a foreign master. We languished, yet our heart remained awake. We felt hurt by thy misfortunes. We are comforted by thy success. When compelled to abandon us, thou didst leave us in the care of Guardian Angels, never remiss in their duty. When we were hesitating, they seemed to exhort us like the prophet of old, whispering into our ears:

'Strengthen ye the weak hands and make firm the tottering knees. Say to them that are of a fearful heart: Be strong, fear not. Behold your God will come with retribution, with divine

*recompense. He will come and save you. Then the eyes of the
blind shall be open and the ears of the deaf shall be unstopped.'*[3]

These faithful servants of thy cause were our mothers and our
wives, the widows and the brides of France. And now, goodbye,
fond memories, goodbye forever. How sweet thou wert, yet how
much more beautiful is the reality! Blessed be the day of thy
arrival! The mother takes once more possession of her children
and never again shall we separate. May the Lord bless France,
our Mother."

Weill had always been a French patriot. As such, he was
decorated with the Cross of the Legion of Honor on July 14th,
1929, on French Independence Day. The fundamental change in
the political situation in Alsace was followed by a period of great
and fruitful activity in his life. The Central Consistoire, which
had its headquarters in Paris, would have liked to see him at
the head of the Rabbinical Seminary of France, since he was considered the most suitable person for this position. However, he
refused because he considered the religious principles that governed this institution as not in agreement with his own. For
similar reasons he declined the Chief Rabbinate of Strasbourg;
the synagogue there had an organ. After having turned down
the offer of the Orthodox congregation of Strasbourg to become
the successor of Rabbi Buttenwieser, he accepted, soon afterwards,
the call to the Chief Rabbinate of Colmar. The Consistoire of
Colmar, indeed, had accepted his condition to cease playing on
Sabbath and Holy Days, the little organ, which up to then, had been
an integral part of the synagogue services.

In accepting that post, which put about twenty congregations
under his indirect influence, he hoped to develop a more fruitful
activity than as the rabbi of the Orthodox congregation of Strasbourg, which had been established along the lines of the *Austritts-
Gemeinden* (separatist congregations) in Germany.

In his inaugural sermon (Sept. 14, 1919), he insisted particularly on his intention to be not only one of the successors of
Solomon Wolf Klein, a contemporary of Samson Raphael Hirsch,
but also his follower. Rabbi Klein had not always had an easy
life in Colmar. When, in 1869, he was installed as a Chief Rabbi
of that city, the then President of the Consistoire, Mr. A. C. See,

---

[3] (Isaiah, XXV, 32)

in his address, said: "I do not hesitate to declare that we expect much of you, particularly since we have had as our spiritual leader, the outstanding Chief Rabbi of France (Lazare Isidor), who, according to his pastoral letters just published, seems determined to reconcile the needs of our time with the immutable principles of our sacred religion."

Mr. See did not mean *Talmud Torah im derekh eretz,* but surrendering loyalty to the fashion of the time.

In 1924, five years after his nomination in Colmar, he was again invited to become the rabbi of one of the leading Orthodox congregations in Paris, which had played an important role in the Jewish life of that city. In Paris, Ernest Weill would have found the finest field for rabbinic work and influence. Had he accepted the post, he might have become the recognized leader of Orthodoxy in the capital. Yet he could not see his way to give up the position in Colmar, which, by virtue of the concordat, was an official position.

THE CONSISTOIRE

The Consistoire was established by Napoleon I in 1808, for the purpose of organizing the Jewish congregations in the French Empire on a legal basis, and to place them under the supervision of the State. His avowed aim was to promote the moral and economic status of the Jews, but secretly he wanted to assimilate them as quickly as possible. Each province or department that numbered at least 2000 Jews was by law compelled to establish a Consistoire, composed of twenty-five persons elected by the Jews of the province. They, in turn, nominated the Grand Rabbi, who became the chief of all congregations of the province and had under his jurisdiction all the rabbis of his district. The Consistoire had primarily the following duties: to administer Jewish congregational life in accordance with the decisions of the Grand Sanhedrin; to improve the social conditions of the Jews; to direct them towards useful professions; to prepare for the French administration the exact list of the Jews of military age, for their draft into the army; to create Jewish elementary and Jewish professional schools and to authorize the creation of new congregations. The budget had to be approved by the State, though the State did not in any way participate in the expenses.

The Consistoires of the various provinces were governed by a central body—The Consistoire Central—composed of three rabbis and two laymen. For the first time in history, Judaism was thus recognized as one of the major religions. It implied for the Jews freedom of religion, yet, due to secret efforts of the church, they were excluded from holding public office. What Napoleon had in mind with the establishment of the Consistoires was "The Modernization of Judaism". Thus, no congregation could be established without the approval of the Consistoire, just as wedding ceremonies could be performed only in the synagogue. Not all proposed innovations can be mentioned here, nor were the rabbis willing to introduce them.

Since the practical results were contrary to those anticipated by public authorities, who expected the rapid assimilation of the Jews, the prefects, the administrators of the provinces, complained to the Minister of Religion. They accused the rabbis of being backward, "abiding by their ancient laws instead of following the requirements of the modern age." They reproached them particularly for their adherence to the Talmud, for delivering their sermons in German dialect, and for not making any effort to speak French correctly.

The Revolution of 1830 did not recognize Catholicism any longer as the religion of the State. The new Constitution proclaimed the equality of all major creeds. From that moment on, all the rabbis were paid by the State and their nominations had to be approved by the Minister. This explains why sometimes even small congregations with only twenty or thirty famlies, particularly in Alsace-Lorraine, could afford a rabbi.

When, in 1870, Alsace-Lorraine, as a consequence of the Franco-German War was incorporated into the German Reich, nothing was altered in the status of the Consistoires; they continued to function as before. A drastic change took place, however, in 1904. As an aftermath to the famous Dreyfus affair, the French Parliament voted overwhelmingly the separation of the Church and State. An entirely new situation came into being. The Consistoires became private organizations, no longer subject to the control of the State, thus losing much of their power and prestige. The rabbis, of course, together with all the members of the clergy, were no longer paid by the State.

When, in 1919, after World War I, Alsace-Lorraine returned to the French motherland, France maintained the concordat in these provinces with all its privileges and duties. Thus the French State, as it was the case under the German domination, continued to pay the salaries of the rabbis and even of the cantors, while in the rest of France the Jewish congregations remained on their own, as is still the situation today.

Ernest Weill remained in Colmar. Did the positive results of his activity there justify his expectations? It is always hard to realize an ideal. Some of his remarks to intimate friends indicate his disappointment.

He never craved popularity, nor did he care to obtain congregational approval of his concept of rabbinic standards. He was a man of energy, independent, revered by some, respected by many, yet misunderstood by others who did not think like him and who could not appreciate his religious point of view. One may venture to say that being too religious for Colmar, he lived above the congregation, rather than within it. The situation may be best summed up by his wife's casual remark: "My husband may not have changed Colmar, yet neither could Colmar change him." This statement, however, is correct only to a certain point. For many a young man or girl admired his spirit and religious integrity and became his faithful follower. Eventually, the relationship between him and his congregation grew much smoother. Though not following his line of religious thinking and practice, they all respected him greatly. They recognized that he was more than a name, that he represented a program of Jewish life which increased Colmar's standing as a congregation to an extent unknown since the days of the late Solomon Wolf Klein, one of his illustrious predecessors. They were very proud of the fact that his decision in religious questions was sought by many of his colleagues, who voluntarily and spontaneously considered him their "Chief Rabbi". Thus Ernest Weill's twenty years of activity in that city (from 1919 to 1939) were of the greatest fruitfulness for French Jewry. He became the standard-bearer of Orthodoxy. He founded the Association of France for Traditional Judaism (A. T. J.) which afforded him the possibility of spreading thoughts far beyond the confines of his rabbinic district. The charter of the Association indicates as its ultimate goal "to preserve the Jewish doctrine and to facilitate its observance among the Jews in France."

In the two yearbooks published, he wrote scholarly and popular articles about Judaism. In the first appeared his essay on "The Method of Judaism", a treatise on its theology. A study about Ramban (Nahmanides), which appeared in the second volume, shows a certain predilection for Jewish mysticism. The yearbooks also contained the translation in French of "Rabbi Akiba", a historical novel written by the late Rabbi M. Lehman, Mainz, and his commentary on "The Ethics of the Fathers" (*Pirke Abot*).

THE TRANSLATION OF THE "KITZUR"

Yet Ernest Weill's most important contribution to French-Jewish literature was the publication of the *Kitzur Shulhan Arukh,* published in instalments, of which the first four or five appeared before, while the whole was completed during the terrible years of the 2nd World War, in the various cities where he had taken refuge. His first task after the war was to issue the whole volume. Though being already over eighty years old, he worked on this publication with a zeal and steadfastness which many a young man might have envied. He repeatedly wrote from Aix-Les-Bains to Rabbi Joseph Bloch, his intimate collaborator in this enterprise: "At my age, I have to hurry. I would like to finish the *Kitzur Shulhan Arukh. . . ."* Unfortunately, his wish remained unfulfilled. Sudden tragic death ended his activity. It was his son, Dr. Elie Weill, together with Rabbi Bloch, who finished the work.

The *Kitzur Shulhan Arukh* has found well-deserved recognition and praise in all sections of French-speaking Jews. It remains a living testimonial to the profound erudition and wisdom, as well as to the energy and working power, of its author. It is much more than a mere translation into French of the Jewish Code for laymen. Most of the chapters are prefaced by an exposition of the ethical principles of the Torah's laws.

The finest and most important chapters of our *Mussar* were incorporated into the volume. What concrete Judaism, the fulfillment of the *mitzvot,* meant to him, found its expression in the following words at the end of his introduction to the *"Kitzur"*: "The practical precepts which embrace the whole life of the Jew, are equally binding upon everyone and know of no dispensation. No human power has a right to challenge their validity since they are the emanation of God's majesty and will, to which the greatest scholar as well as the most humble Jew must bow. These laws have forged and maintained the unity of Israel with the oneness of God." The *"Kitzur"* will forever remain a treasure of French Jewish literature.

Yet he considered as the crown of both his rabbinic activity and his life, the establishment of a *yeshivah*. The project haunted him since the days when Alsace became French, and he considered its realization as his most compelling task.

Indeed, with the exception of a seminary for rabbis, France had no institution where Talmud was studied solely for the sake of learning and not for eventual professional purposes. The country of Rashi and of the Tossafists had so far no place for the cultivation of the spiritual treasures which these giants of the spirit have left us. Within the framework of the *Keren Hatorah* of the Agudat Israel, Ernest Weill had worked for the spreading of Torah knowledge. Yet he writes: "We should fulfill our duty much more fully, if, shaking off our lethargy, we could establish in our own country, which has so little Jewish vitality, an institution capable of fostering among our youth the knowledge of Torah! What a great tribute of gratitude to our country it would be if we could bring to fruition those vital but hidden forces we possess and permeate French Jewry with their influence. Could there be a more legitimate ambition than to enrich the spiritual heritage bequeathed to us by Rashi?" It was granted to Ernest Weill to realize this dream. In 1932 he established, on the outskirts of Strasbourg, the Yeshivah of France. Many Jews greeted the new venture with outright skepticism, thinking that it had no place in western European Jewish life, or that it would serve only as a school for Talmud studies for boys who had nothing to do or who had failed elsewhere. They soon were convinced of the contrary. In his report on the first four years of the existence of the Yeshivah, published in 1937, after having paid a tribute to the Talmud scholars of France and Alsace of previous centuries, Ernest Weill writes: "The establishment in Strasbourg of the Yeshivah of France only revived an old tradition: The Torah, say our Sages, has a tendency to come back to its former home."

At that time the Yeshivah had thirty students and two teachers, one of whom was the scholarly son of a famous *Rosh Yeshivah* of

Lithuania (Elhanan Wasserman). During the four years of its existence (1932 to 1936), the Yeshivah counted a total of seventy-seven students, eight of whom continued their studies in other *yeshivot* while others went to the École Rabbinique in Paris. The Yeshivah was engulfed by World War II, yet by the burning enthusiasm and boundless energy of Ernest Weill, it was, after the war, restarted in Aix-les-Bains on a much broader basis than before, all the hardships of the moment notwithstanding. France was disorganized and food was scarce. The Jews had suffered enormously through deportation. Now that the horrible nightmare was over, their primary concern was to return as quickly as possible to their former homes, many of which had been destroyed or looted by the Nazis. The Yeshivah did not loom large in their view. Ernest Weill, as octogenarian, had to face one difficulty after the other, yet he overcame them all. Supported by a few whom he had won for his sacred cause, he started the work and gave the Yeshivah the significant name Yeshivat Hakhme Tsorfat (The Yeshivah of the Sages of France).

Only three months after it had reopened its doors, it could boast of more than forty students. Attracted by his great prestige, they came from many quarters, from France and Belgium, from Switzerland, and even from Africa, and, of course, from the concentration camps in Germany. Rabbi Weill, the Dean, took his mission most seriously. Once a week he examined each of the students in order to check on his progress. Aix-les-Bains became quickly known, even in Israel and in the United States, as a center for Torah learning. The credit for this goes primarily to Dr. Weill, but also to the *Rosh Yeshivah*, Rabbi Chajkin, a pupil of the sainted Hafetz Hayyim. One of its foremost students, Rabbi Roger Cahen, at present in charge of its administrative and financial affairs, said about his teacher: "For us, his students, Grand Rabbi Weill was a guide who had a lucid understanding of all the problems that confronted us after the war. Whilst tolerating no compromise in religious matters, he never went to extremes. He was a living example of Judaism to all who approached him. His personality has left an indelible impression in us. We, his students, aspired to reach his degree of concentration (*Kavanah*) at prayer, as well as his ardor of study. In his eyes we could see his burning zeal for Judaism."

During his whole life, Ernest Weill was a staunch defender of our traditions and an able spokesman for the honor of Judaism.

The outbreak of World War II had been a particular calamity
for the population of Alsace. This section of France, protected by
the famous Maginot Line, yet within easy reach of the German
guns on the other side of the Rhine, was declared war zone.
As in World War I, Alsace was again in danger of becoming a
battlefield. By order of the government, a great part of the population was evacuated to central France. Whole communities were
thus uprooted and their members scattered everywhere. Rabbi
Weill took refuge in Saumur, a little town not far from the Atlantic
Ocean, and settled there on a farm, with a *minyan* of other Jews.
The invasion of France and its subsequent defeat spelled disaster
for the Frenchmen in general, and for the Jews in particular.
Among the five million Frenchmen who fled southward to escape
the invader, there were approximately three hundred thousand
Jews, an immediate target of the Hitlerite hordes. While Jewish
congregations in Northern France ceased to exist overnight, those
in unoccupied France, through the influx of refugees, increased
tremendously in number. Marseille, for instance, the gateway to
overseas countries, which normally counted about ten thousand
Jews, had now over forty thousand, many of them in frantic search
of a visa to foreign countries. Jews could be found now, all of a
sudden, even in the smallest and most remote villages, which might
never have seen one of them before. Religious life was disorganized, the problems which Orthodox Jews faced were particularly
difficult. Food was scarce for every Frenchman, much more so
for an observant Jew. Kosher meat became a rarity. Kitchen
utensils, as well as anything else, had disappeared from the stores
and could not even be bought for good money. There were no
Siddurim or other religious objects. The problems became even
more acute with the approach of *Pessach*. Where could one bake
matzoh, what could one eat, what about dishes? These were
daily questions. Traditional Jews looked more than ever for
counsel and guidance to Rabbi Weill, who, with part of his family,
established himself in Nimes, one of the oldest cities in France.
It was in these trying times that he gave proof of his profound
knowledge of Jewish law and at the same time, showed a broad-
mindedness which astonished those who knew him but superficially. A council hastily formed by some rabbis of the region,
refugees like himself (among them Joseph Bloch, Haguenau;
Simon Langer, Paris; the late Abraham Bloch, Saverne; and

Jerome Levy, Obernai), with Ernest Weill as their leader, met regularly either in Nimes or in Marseilles to discuss problems of religious Jewry.

A practical guide for "Religious Observances in Times of Hardship and Duress" was printed, of utmost help to those who, in spite of all difficulties, endeavored to remain faithful to Jewish law; a *Hagaddah shel Pessach,* for which the Vichy government had to give its stamp of approval, was published. Jewish life continued as best as it could until Nov. 11, 1942. On that fateful day, Hitler crossed the demarcation line and occupied the whole of France. The hunt of the Jews by the dreadful Gestapo, with or without the consent of Pétain's government, was on. It spelled the destruction of every form of congregational life, for everyone went into hiding to escape arrest and deportation. Ernest Weill was fortunate enough to escape with his family to Switzerland, where, until after the war, he established his home in Zurich in the house of his son-in-law, Joseph Rothschild.

The defeat of Germany and subsequent liberation of France were for him the signal, in spite of his eighty years, to continue his life work—the re-establishment of the Yeshivah. One may imagine the difficulties he faced in a country which had so greatly suffered and of whose Jewish population almost two thirds had been exterminated, while those who were lucky enough to have escaped death were impoverished. Yet the word "impossible" did not exist for Ernest Weill, and in a short time he re-opened his Yeshivah at Aix-les-Bains. He succeeded beyond all expectations, and if this institution today counts among the foremost academies of Torah learning, French Jewry owes it to him.

Such was the man whose fruitful activity ended suddenly in the middle of March, 1947, when he became the victim of a motor accident, which three weeks later took his life. On the 12th of Nissan, 5707 (April 2, 1947), Ernest Weill rendered his soul to his Maker. It was a black day for French Jewry, now bereft of its greatest leader, who was unflinching in his faith, one in thought and deed.

Yet his name will remain enshrined in their grateful memory.

JOSEPH WOHLGEMUTH

(1867-1932)

By Juda Ari Wohlgemuth

JOSEPH WOHLGEMUTH

By Juda Ari Wohlgemuth

A scholar may not limit his interests to the operations of his own mind or to his special subject matter. He must have an appreciation of the problems of the larger world.

Nevertheless, for a successful achievement of his academic pursuits, it is essential that he stay free from the exacting demands on time and energy of the problems of his age. Indeed, the life of many a man of research would have been richer, more effective, had it been freed from the troubles of his community.

For the *Talmid Hakham* (scholar) who is a leader, Judaism prescribes a unity between intellectual enterprise and labor for social welfare. He must combine both goals in his thought and his emotion. Our teacher Moses, of blessed memory, presented the first personality in which the quest for God, heaven-searching study and meditation, were wedded to a ceaseless passion for the fellow-man, a program of dedicated teaching, counselling and helping.

Such fruitful combination of divergent tendencies is very rare. Joshua, the servant of Moses, disturbed by the frequent prophesying of common people, cried to him, *"Master, hold them back!"* Rashi, in his classic commentary, explains the plea thus: "Put community burdens upon them and they will cease!" But Moses protested the suggestion that he oppose any prophetic messengers.

It is well-nigh impossible for the normal human being to combine a successful discharge of intellectual tasks with the solution of practical problems. Where it is achieved, it is done at the cost of life itself. All admiration for the world-oblivious giant of law notwithstanding, the Torah insists on his obligation to aid the community. No man whose knowledge enables him to offer decisive counsel to any group may escape this duty, even if it involves major sacrifices, such as curtailment of his work for spreading of Torah-ideas and ideals.

It is through immersion in his neighbors' misery, rather than through preoccupation with ivory-tower problems, that a leader reaches genuine heights. Of the heroes of our national gallery, the Torah says that they were *"Holkhe Tamim"* (walking in perfection), which means that theirs was a harmony of relation toward both God and man.

Modern science is troubled by specialization as a major achievement of the intellectual. America is believed to have spread the concept of visible success as criterion of an individual's worth and thereby to have undermined the *temimut,* his inner balance and harmony.

Within the Jewish camp, too, the schism between life and letters has been generally deplored. No strengthening of Jewish religious life is possible, save through leaders dedicated to the absolute maintenance of spiritual values as a supreme asset. Such a man, serving God and the people fully, constantly, and harmoniously—at once a great scholar, a great fighter, and a great leader—was Joseph Wohlgemuth.

I.

EARLY YOUTH

He was born in 1867, in Memel, on the border between Prussia and Lithuania. His father and grandfather were Jewish leaders, distinguished by fine minds and deep faith. In his infancy, the family moved to Hamburg, where Rabbi Isaiah, the grandfather, functioned as *Klausrabbiner* (a scholar freed from the obligation of community work and enabled to spend all his time in the study of Torah). He enjoyed great popularity for his extraordinary knowledge, no less than because of his modesty. Elijah, his son, was a devoted adherent of the *Mussar* movement. His major goal was to deepen the inward sense of Jewishness, as well as to protect our ancient faith from modern detractors and misinterpreters. Because of inner scruples, all his modesty notwithstanding, he never became a popular leader. Throughout his life, he was a "Litvak", devoted to the search for truth and to the quest for moral improvement—yet, in his manner, somewhat of a stranger in a western milieu.

The grandparents and the family tradition exerted a powerful influence on young Joseph. From them was derived his abiding

bond with the Jewish people. His mother would tell him about
their sufferings under the Tsars and of the horrors of "Nicholas'
soldiers" (young boys snatched from their mothers' arms, and
exiled to terrible Siberia), to many of whom she would offer the last
meal before their tragic journey. To her he owed his profound
sympathy with their agonies and his passionate devotion to righteousness. From early adolescence he had to help his family. He
never overcame the accumulated burden of their problems, but
they founded his religious philosophy. His steady preoccupation
with the problems of God's relation to man, of the sufferings of
the righteous, of reward and punishment, was due not to mere love
of intellectual adventure, but to his having had to face almost every
day the tragedy of Jewish life in general and of individual Jews
in particular.

II.

ADOLESCENCE IN HAMBURG

Hamburg's Jewry impressed Joseph by its integrity and piety,
by the dignity of its communal life, and its broad cultural interests.
He combined with his special appreciation of the Lithuanian Jewish
tradition a clear recognition of Hamburg's moral values. He was
fortunate enough to be trained in the *Johanneum,* the city's famous
humanistic high school. The positive elements of German culture
emanated from this noble institute and helped the eager student to
search for truth also outside the camp of Israel and to hail ethical
assets everywhere.

But since early youth he knew that many-sided interests pre-
clude thoroughness. His desire to prepare a successful career did
not ignore the danger derived from too multi-faceted stimulations.
His spiritual integrity demanded a balancing of outside influences
with the solid possession of a set of principles and a point of view,
to assure an inner equilibrium. His devotion to the study of Jewish
lore was extraordinary, yet he often regretted his failure to dedicate
himself exclusively to this discipline. Always aware of non-Jewish
cultural values, he emphasized as his ideal type the *Rov* of
old, thoroughly nourished by the soil of rabbinic Judaism. He never
lost sight of human motivations with all their imperfections, the

frequent lack of truthfulness, the common failures of a society serving social ambition at a cost of loyalty to the faith.

Joseph Wohlgemuth attained immaculate literary achievement and reputation, uncompromising adherence to integrity, and profound consciousness of the spiritual miseries of his contemporaries. But he always emphasized the paramount duty of staying aware of, and devoted to, Torah as creed and life. The translation of the ideals and attitudes of the Torah into the fabric of modern life he considered the essence of all Jewishness.

III.

BERLIN

From Hamburg he moved to Berlin, where he stayed until 1932. For four decades he studied, taught, and exerted steady influence in that city. Because of Berlin's social leaders, who stood above all for secular enlightenment and because of the famous *salons* of its assimilated Jews, that community had acquired a bad reputation among the pious Jews of Eastern Europe. From the end of the 18th Century on, "Berliners" spelled to them freethinkers, assimilationists, would-be escapists from Judaism. The spiritual disintegration of the period was the harvest of the fashionable "enlightenment" of the French Revolution and the Napoleonic Wars. Within the Jewish community of Berlin and other cities of the age, there was a miserable record of flight from the camp. Wohlgemuth knew many Jews who had only feeble ties with the Jewish community, but there were many others who lived in accord with the Jewish tradition and in genuine unity with the Jewish people. There were countless small private synagogues in East Berlin whose members studied the Torah assiduously and practiced charity nobly. Hassidic movements had their private *stuebels* (small places of worship) which combined a sense of independence from German Jewry with a true appreciation of its pedagogical and social patterns. They agreed to disagree agreeably on matters which elsewhere provoked strife. German Jewry was of timeless value in the regeneration of the Jewish people everywhere. It may not be too bold to assert that without the work of the Berlin and Hamburg Jewish community, those in England, America, and Israel might never have reached their social, educational and charitable level. For the uninterrupted stream of Jewish refugees from the persecution in Russia passed almost exclusively through Berlin and Hamburg towards their goal across the ocean. In these cities, without the fanfare and the extravagancies of contemporary public collections, tremendous sums were provided to supply the tragic multitude with food, clothing, and passage money. Jews all over the world ought to think of the communities of Hamburg and Berlin with gratitude and respect.

German Jews may, perchance, be rightly accused of excessive economy in expressing sentiment. But it is not right to ignore their fast and purposive action in times of emergency, their effective help to brethren in distress. Berlin Jewry created precious patterns. Even the non-traditional Jews contributed generously. The absolute integrity of the leaders (*Justizraete, Sanitatsraete,* and *Universitatsdozenten*)* was wedded to warm personal interest. They never failed to appear at the railroad station to help their oppressed brethren in a personal way, looking upon *Tzedakah* as self-evident duty. Joseph Wohlgemuth greatly praised the conscientiousness with which every Jew kept his *Maasser-book* (detailed accounting of the tithe of his income). He himself led community efforts on behalf of the Lithuanian *yeshivot* during the First World War.

He had come to Berlin to obtain the diploma at the Hildesheimer Rabbinical Seminary. Ezriel Hildesheimer had commenced his work in Berlin with the establishment of an independent Torah-true community. Reform Jewry had gone to extremes in that city. They met with derision the requests of the Orthodox for proper attention to their religious need. That would be futile, they claimed, for "Torah-true Judaism is on its deathbed." The last quarter of the nineteenth century brought Berlin unprecedented prosperity in which the Jews shared. Torah-true Jews from small rural communities labored against the massive success of Reform. Rabbi Hildesheimer's small independent community could not make much headway, especially since many of the newcomers or older residents among the loyalists remained attached exclusively to their private institutions. They were unwilling to consider the advantages of affiliation with official Jewish communities, no matter what their attitude was to the sanctuaries of our faith. Many of

---

*These titles (Judicial Counsellor, Medical Counsellor, University Lecturer) were government-bestowed upon lawyers, physicians and other professionals as recognition of their professional attainment or social service.

them lacked a sense of community consciousness for which German Jews have been noted. The *Bet Hamidrash* catered to the religious and educational needs of the small group but remained unaware of larger associations and responsibilities. The need to stop reckless assimilation never dawned upon them. Too, gradually the Jewish community adopted a friendlier attitude and, indeed, subventioned them.

The rapid growth of Berlin scattered the Jews into many directions and Hildesheimer's one synagogue (*Adath Israel*) was too small to hold them all. Its own membership was heterogeneous. It lacked the assets of an old milieu, such as the revered communities of Frankfort, Mainz and Hamburg offered. That Rabbi Hildesheimer was able to forge it into a single-purposed instrument for Jewishness was a measure of his genius. His work essentially was educational. He trained the youth in his *Religionsschule* (School of Religious Instruction) so thoroughly in the traditions and the philosophy of life of Judaism that they represented a unique glory in the capital. Even Jews removed from Torah-true life sent their children to that school.

There they received tender care, perfect pedagogy and attained joyous identification with Jewish religious values and deep love of learning. The fascinating personalities emerging from that school created a wondrous unity with the parents and stopped the plague of assimilation.

For well-nigh thirty years Joseph Wohlgemuth served there as teacher of the Bible. Many hundreds of Jewish men have had the advantage of his instruction. To him they owed not only a thorough knowledge of the Hebrew language but the ability to study the holy text in the original and to attain from its own sources the Jewish philosophy of life. This educational achievement spelled not only a vital contribution to the spiritual endowment of the Torah-true Jew, but it also had devastating effects upon the "pastoral pretenses and superficial soul-guidance" of Reform teachers. Many Zionists from Germany now in leading positions in Israel aver their abiding obligation to the unique Berlin *Religionsschule Adath Israel* and to Joseph Wohlgemuth, one of its most potent teachers.

That school served as model for many others of its type. Its students had learned how unwise it is for a Jew to stay satisfied with a pre-digested knowledge akin to catechism. Not all of them became Torah-true Jews because often their parents had not reached that level, but they remained within the Jewish people and accepted their task to serve them loyally and fully.

Before admission to the seminary, Joseph Wohlgemuth had started teaching at the Adath school. He remained in that service, although his appointment as "dozent" (lecturer) at the seminary gave him his major task. He wanted to be not merely a "great professor", but a communal leader serving his group. To increase the spiritual prowess of the youth was his lifelong ambition. He could never understand how one could derogate that work in favor of important academic or literary projects. It was an ideal society that had assumed that burden in the Adath Israel. Wohlgemuth himself describes it in a brilliant essay in one of the volumes of his *Jeschurun*. The teachers of the school in main were derived from the students of the Rabbinical Seminary. Theirs was a living contact with the sources of the Torah, a strong sense of responsibility and above all, awareness, abiding and powerful, of the problems of the time. Hence there was no stagnation in their educational enterprise but constant revision of approach and method. To his colleagues, Joseph Wohlgemuth served as a model. They revered his wide and deep knowledge and his strong emotional appreciation of Jewish values. He demanded solid results from every hour of teaching, both in increased knowledge, as in its effect upon the Torah-true loyalty of his students. There is much truth in the saying, "Science is the art of elimination." He understood "the art of elimination", leading the pupil very fast to essentials. He was severe in his demands. Thus he would insist that students know whole chapters of the Hebrew Bible by heart in the original.

In 1899, when Wohlgemuth became betrothed, his top class presented him with the Song of Songs in Heinesque verses. Unfortuately, Hitler's hellhounds destroyed this unique piece of work. This extraordinary translation by a class of high school students was a page of glory for themselves and their teacher, as well as a symbol of the camaraderie that united them. The top class of girls was augmented by a "Selecta—Special Group" whence, within a short time, well-trained girl-teachers of religion emerged to whom the education of the next generation was entrusted, another living testimonial to Joseph Wohlgemuth.

His work for the city's young merchants blazed a trail. He invested considerable time and energy in lectures at their Montefiore Society, designed to warn them against the moral dangers of metropolitan life. He used Luzzatto's *Messilat Yesharim* (The Path of the Righteous) as his text, expatiating on self-discipline and inspiring them with the philosophy of the *Mussar* movement. Modern professors of Jewish law, as well as rabbis in our own days, might well follow that pattern of vital interest in the youth of our day, who are half-attached or not attached to our faith and who stay without effective direction.

It was because of his pedagogic power that young Wohlgemuth was appointed as lecturer in religious philosophy and homiletics at the Rabbiner Seminar. In those days the luminaries of that institution were Ezriel Hildesheimer, David Hoffman, and Jakob Barth. They gathered around themselves a group of gifted and dynamic students whom they hoped to develop into great authorities of the Torah.

To repel the constant attacks on the faith of our fathers, to offset widespread assimilation and systematic attempts to emancipate Jews from Judaism, it was vital to train rabbis with special aptitudes to maintain and strengthen the Orthodox position in the community. Many of them, all their fine tuition notwithstanding, became rabbinic communal leaders rather than *Gedole Torah* (great scholars), whose penetration with the spirit and the letter of the Torah would have resulted in. a more satisfactory generation of Torah-true laymen. In the compact homogeneous communities of Eastern Europe, our people were untouched by Western culture and by the problems of cultural pluralism which beset the Jews in the German communities. The latter had to fight an unceasing battle against the distintegration of the faith through the free-thinking social leaders of the time, who were on their knees in unintelligent worship of the intellect.

There was also a constant struggle against local intrigue to prevent Torah-true rabbis or teachers from gaining a hold in the community. It meant fighting day by day, place by place, against the deliberate stratagem of reformers to fill vacancies with ignorant, often unprincipled diplomés of their own seminaries. The Hildesheimer Academy hence was compelled to emphasize in its curriculum rhetorical and pedagogical prowess. The best methods had to be inculcated to preserve the laity for the traditions of our faith, to strengthen them inwardly and to immunize them against pernicious infection.

Ezriel Hildesheimer, who gradually had to rely more and more on David Hoffmann for the teaching program in the institution, was not only an extraordinary scholar, but like his colleagues, Barth and Hirsch Hildesheimer, shone as expert in scientific propaganda for the faith, and spent himself generously in the solution of social problems.

These men were unable to give their students more than instruction and inspiration. For decades it was Joseph Wohlgemuth who functioned as real guide, philosopher and friend of the student body. The qualities which distinguished his work in the *Religionsschule* came to full flowering on the higher level of the Rabbinical Seminary. Every student knew that he could approach him with personal, financial or ideological problems. He bewitched them by his warm freshness and youthful enthusiasm, as well as by the utter honesty of his personal religiousness. Wohlgemuth detested all intellectual pretense. The Friday evenings in his house were most effective sessions for the maturing personalities of his disciples. His gracious wife Rosa (née Lachman), through her spontaneous hospitality alike to poor and rich, to Westerners and Easterners, to college students and businessmen, had a considerable share in the blessing that these evenings spelled to these young men. Her wise and harmonious personality was of abiding benefit to her husband. She was his technical and literary assistant in the years when he edited *Jeschurun,* his monthly magazine "for Jewish life and teaching." When in 1927 she passed away, he suffered an irreplaceable loss, a diminution both of *joie de vivre* and creative power.

IV. Wohlgemuth as Philosopher of Religion

Three terms are basic to his thinking and writing: self, preservation, and spirit. This highly cultured European never denied the origin of his Lithuanian piety. He would reject any system based on overemphasized principle, on only intellectual foundation. The object to be treated should speak to us without the phraseology of a philosophical system. Its concretized work should inspire us. As we make it our own, it will evoke those vital reactions which will convey insight, an apprehension of its essence. True to the idea of the *Mussar,* he remained ever self-critical. He anticipated the danger of interpreting our intention into the text, of eliciting from it the solution of a problem that appeals to us, of submitting to the illusion that our spiritual situation is abiding. To subject the questing human self to the timeless pressures of the transmitted spirit, that was Wohlgemuth's work in the field of religious philosophy. He would reject any search which did not penetrate to the original source. The problem of religious philosophy he would always find first in the Holy Bible and in the world of the Talmud before approaching the philosophic literature of the Middle Ages.

Even when attacks of Christian theologians or modern free-thinkers were to be met by Jewish scholars, he would have the spirit of Judaism speak for itself. In that respect, too, he was a *tamim,* a thorough man of faith. His integrity was absolute. He had a holy horror for any attempt to explain away any difficulty, for any logical fallacy or other trick. It was a unique wedding of rationalism and childlike faith which inspired Wohlgemuth's work. But if the problem painstakingly pursued seemed to find no solution, he would go from the holy text straight to the atmosphere of living Torah, to the vital Jewish spirit represented by the Jewish people. From the Psalms of David he learned to rely on the strength of philosophical conviction and the deep faith possessed by the heroes of our past: on the rocklike strength of Torah-true Jews.

His students and readers learned from him that one must remain aware of the depth and breadth of the whole problem before offering a solution. He neither looked upon philosophy as valid by itself, nor did he regard it, like some Christian theologians, as the *"ancilla theologiae"* (handmaid of theology), but, rather, as a bearer of light which, from a definite angle, may illumine the teaching of Judaism as translated into life. Light stems from the realm of living spirit and returns to it. A philosophy of Judaism, as far as he was concerned, could never come from without. It must originate from the sources of our Torah-world and lead back to them. For "Science is but re-won naiveté." That philosophy of religion is necessary for sheer survival. It is true that the essence of Torah is unaffected by the problems of any particular epoch, the thought of any generation, of the superficiality of any fleeting fury of assimilation. Nevertheless, there are spiritual problems which no Torah-true Jew can ignore. Anyone who, as a matter of principle, would avoid confrontation with a hostile philosophy of life, thereby derogates the power of the Torah and causes his spiritual being to become stunted.

On the one hand, Wohlgemuth, deeply interested in all the problems of the time, was honest enough to condemn "hunting for problems." Occasionally he would warn against preoccupation with philosophy because of its danger to the simple faith. Refreshing was his often repeated warning that philosophy on its own merit will never win the race or produce the stone of the wise. But on the other hand, he was no less eloquent in his condemnation of dishonest pietism and in emphasizing the duty to meet courageously any challenge to the Torah.

He aimed at the preservation of our ethical and spiritual assets: "It is not to be gained by leaving the essence of Jewish thoughts in books. One must present it to contemporary man and especially for the Jew who wishes to be both a good son to his parents and a good father to his children. For one must dedicate oneself to the preservation of the stream of Jewish consciousness which started at Mount Sinai and will not end at the time of the Messiah."

V. WOHLGEMUTH AS TEACHER OF HOMILETICS

He trained his students in the art of using the raw materials of the past for a coinage of the present. Himself a master of style, he taught the art of preparing fruitful sermons. He stressed thought, clarity, and tight survey in the presentation of the material so emphatically that many a student, too much in love with unlimited eloquence, resented his teacher's proposed straightjacket. But Wohlgemuth wished to implant an abiding awareness in the minds of his students that a sermon represents an all-important opportunity for clarification of the Jewish *Weltanschauung* (world view). They should not merely stimulate but teach and serve to conquer superficiality. Therefore, the teacher was to be trained to be lucid in style and competent in presentation of content.

VI. Practical Rabbinics

There was one more discipline which Joseph Wohlgemuth taught in the seminary: *Horaah,* which means the ability to decide matters of Jewish law, covering the laws of *Kashrut,* with all their infinite details, and the many issues of marriage and divorce, as well as problems in civil law. Rector Hoffmann, because of his exceedingly burdensome program, found himself obliged to urge the assumption of this heavy task upon Wohlgemuth. The latter accepted it only after prolonged search had failed to produce an acceptable candidate. To render a *Halakhic* decision, one must be familiar with the whole Talmudic background of the question involved. Excellent answers in written examinations are not sufficient evidence of such ability to penetrate the core of the problem. Many of the students had studied at *yeshivot* before coming to, or graduating from, the Seminary; others continued their studies after obtaining their rabbinic diploma (*Semikhah*). It was fortunate that this studying at the *yeshivah* became increasingly the custom among the students.—Whatever Wohlgemuth offered was methodically perfect. But his painstaking preoccupation with both the realities and the legal finesse of the problem involved often exhausted his energies and restricted his work in the field of religious philosophy.

VII. Wohlgemuth as Journalist

In his younger years he published many articles about matters of Jewish *Weltanschauung* in *Der Israelit* and the *Juedische Presse.* His style, with all the weightiness of the content, was always vivid and intelligible to the man of average education. From time to time he would use a *bon mot* to enliven the subject. His articles dealing with important persons were both polite and ruthless. In 1917 he wrote a celebrated essay on *Achad Haam and Torah-true Judaism.* On a visit to that thinker at a Berlin convalescent home, he inquired about his reaction to that article. The latter replied, "Never has an Orthodox man treated me more nobly nor more devastatingly."

Up to 1914, Wohlgemuth had only the above two weeklies to fall back upon for his shorter publications. Then appeared the

Richtlinien (Guilding Principles) for a program of Reform Judaism, which, as exponent of Torah-true Judaism, he attacked in a memorable article. That battle of the books revealed the immediate need of a publication of Torah-true Judaism of a high scientific caliber, to take care both of its positive informative work, as well as of its defense against ideological attacks. Wohlgemuth undertook also the whole burden of providing the financial means for his monthly, the *Jeschurun*. Such reviews must be subsidized because subscribers never cover the major part of the budget. During the war and its agonizing aftermaths, it was an overwhelming job to keep the publication of that monthly going. *"Fuer Lehre und Leben im Judentum"* (for Jewish lore, law, and life)—its purpose was not only to create an organ on a thoroughly academic level, but also a watchtower from which the lights and shadows of modern Torah-true life could be viewed and illumined. Between 1914 and 1930, *Jeschurun* made incredible contributions towards strengthening Torah-true Judaism and Jewish national consciousness both in Germany and beyond its frontiers. Not all the writers thought and wrote on the level of the editor. Not every issue reflected his lofty spirit; but all those who, in the turbulence of those times yearned for an objective judgment, an unprejudiced expression of Torah-true Judaism, awaited every issue with bated breath. They knew that the editor and the other contributors were ever circumspect and sensitive. Wohlgemuth would always react to political or ideological problems touching upon the fields of religion, literature and esthetics, out of full knowledge of the Jewish tradition and in the light of its perennial position. Whenever public interest took hold of a historical personality, or the modern version of an ancient problem, weighty reference would be found in the pages of the *Jeschurun*. There are some book reviews of those *Jeschurun* years, potent and vivid enough even in our own days. Even those who profoundly disagreed with him praised his unfailing thoroughness and objectivity. To this day the *Jeschurun* has served as a reference library for questions of Jewish ideology, the science of the Talmud, or literary questions in the light of Torah-true Judaism. For some years the monthly carried a Hebrew appendix, enriched by fundamental contributions of his younger colleague, Abraham Eliyahu Kaplan, a giant of rabbinic lore, a deep thinker and resourceful scholar, poet and teacher of ethics, whose sudden death Wohlgemuth viewed as the greatest loss Judaism had sustained after the First World War.

VIII. WOHLGEMUTH AS AUTHOR

Among his books of abiding value is *The Jewish Religious Law in its own Light* (*Das Juedische Religionsgesetz in Juedischer Beleuchtrung*). His two essays on the *Halakhah and The Duties of the Heart* reveal the ultimate purpose of religious behavior.

Of similar significance are *Immortality in the Bible, Guilt and Punishment, God's Justice, Israel as a Chosen Nation, Peace, Consciousness of Guilt, The Consciousness of Guilt in Talmudic Literature, The Penitent and the Sinless Person, Of the Root of the Jewish Religion* (touching upon the problem whether Judaism has dogmas), and *The Concept of Piety in the Talmud*.

History will remember Joseph Wohlgemuth for his powerful work of enlightenment that drew an imperishable law of demarcation between the assimilationist Reform, represented by the *Richtlinien* ministers of religion and the Torah-true masses who would brook no contact with the parsons of radical reform. His pamphlets: *Review of the Richtlinien, Torah-true and Liberal Judaism,* inspired all Orthodox rabbis of Germany to sign their names in a definitive proclamation against Reform and established a well fortified rampart against its attacks. It ended forever the ambitions of some Reform souls to gain leadership in German Jewry. It is Wohlgemuth's merit that the overwhelming majority of German Jewry, even those who were not conforming Torah-true Jews, repudiated the *Richtlinien*.

His series on *Zionism, Nationalism, and Torah-true Judaism* retains for future reference the traditional view against irreligious nationalism. What he had to say about problems of Orthodox organization in the Holy Land and the *Galut,* about the nature of Jewish nationality and the meaning of Jewish history, all contemporary background notwithstanding, is of permanent significance. He felt close to the Agudat Israel and promoted its purposes (although he was not in agreement with its ideological rigidity and cherished the movement mainly for its practical goals).

His translations of the Pentateuch (a joint enterprise with Dr. Bleichrode) aided countless children and youths in an understanding of the main text of Judaism. Of similar significance was his translation of *Messilat Yesharim* which he dedicated to the memory of his mother. In many a synagogue this book was used also by women for edification, particularly during the High Holidays. It has helped them to understand the meaning of life and to achieve greater closeness to God.

His biographical essays on S. R. Hirsch, Moses Mendelssohn, Ezriel Hildesheimer, Jacob Barth, David Hoffmann, Abraham Elia Kaplan, and others, will remain significant; so will his description of a *Mussar Life in Our Own Time.*

Wohlgemuth paid his respects to the seminal thoughts of non-Jews. His review of representative thought of contemporary leaders of the spirit served in another way to spell out Jewish teaching and world view. His last work, *The Basic Thought of the Religious Philosophy of Max Scheler in the Light of Judaism,* offers not only the essence, but prepares the ground for comparison with the teachings of our faith without any diminution of its strength or depth. His article, *Consideration for the Animal in Judaism,* is based on an exhaustive study of the original sources and stresses the vital need for urbanized Jews to return to nature.

We must not slur over his series of pro-German articles published in the initial period of the First World War. Many people criticized them and in the light of the beastliness of the Third Reich they seem unintelligible. His accent, however, was not on "patriotism" but on his love for the Jewish people, whom he yearned to see redeemed from Czarist cruelty. For that achievement the German people seemed to him divinely ordained. The Nazi movement brought him a mortal disappointment. But 2,000 years ago, one of our greatest, Rabbi Akiba, took the calculated risk of aiding Bar Kochba in his effort to save Israel from the brutal power of Rome. Akiba, too, failed. But who would condemn great souls who erred in a noble cause?

In all the facets of his life, as communal leader, thinker, teacher and writer, Wohlgemuth awarded primacy to his responsibility in the service of God and Israel. He spent himself intensively, ceaselessly in his work. His nature was very sensitive. He had profound empathy and sympathy for those near and far, in a unique manner, for all humanity.

Wohlgemuth was also a *homo politicus,* deeply interested in current events and anxious to find in them, according to the classic Jewish way, not only signs of the Divine purpose, but also the foreshadowing of the Messiah. A political atrocity reported in the newspaper would make him jump from the table in righteous indignation. His major interests were righteousness in the life of the human family and the just cause of the Jewish people. He could not bear their horrible affliction in his own days. He could not accept what happened to the millions of his brothers in Eastern Europe. In 1932 he foresaw the bestiality of the German mobs and foretold the horrors that were to come.

For ten more years this self-sacrificing champion of the Jewish people had to live a life of terrible excitement alternating with stages of utter apathy. This intellectual giant had to vegetate almost without a mind. His family and friends did everything to lighten the burden. A benign Providence spared him the consciousness of Germany's moral abyss and of the implementation of a ruthless heathen plan for tthe destruction of the Jewish people.

The sanitarium protected him against the horrors of Nazism. The bloody hand of the Germans never touched this suffering Jacob. On the 22nd of Shevat 5692 he was called to the Academy on High. He found his last resting place near that of the man whom he revered as one of the great heroes of Judaism: Samson Raphael Hirsch.

EZRA MUNK

(1867-1940)

By Elie Munk and Hillel Seidman

(translated by Moses Jung, from the Hebrew)

EZRA MUNK

By Elie Munk and Hillel Seidman

When, in 1938, Hitler's Germany compelled Ezra Munk to leave his beloved Adass Yisroel Congregation in Berlin, where he had served for almost forty years, a significant epoch in the life of Jewry in that country came to an end. His death in 1940 in Israel evoked widespread mourning for a leader who had carried on his shoulders the full burden of the Torah-true communities of Germany. He was prominent as rabbi and outstanding as leader in the Union of Orthodox Congregations in Germany in the Agudat Israel, the National Central Office for Problems of Shehitah, and in many other organizations.

I.

Ezra Munk was born in Altona, Germany, on the 27th of Heshvan 5678 (November 25, 1867). His father was Rabbi Eliyahu and his mother Jenny, a sister of Rabbi Ezriel Hildesheimer, the founder of the famed rabbinical seminary and Adass Yisroel Congregation in Berlin. His family boasted a number of well-known scholars, such as Loeb Munk of Graetz, Tzevi Hirsch of Meseritz, and Meir Posen, author of *Bet Meir*.

He received his Jewish training from his father and the teachers of the renowned Altona community. Later, he attended the Hildesheimer Seminary in Berlin, from which he received his ordination (*Semikhah*). That famed institution was based on the principle of *"Torah im Derekh Eretz"*, the harmonious synthesis of the Jewish tradition with modern thought. It taught living Judaism, loyalty to the *mitzvot* in all phases of life. At Berlin University, Munk studied philosophy and Oriental languages. There he learned exact scientific method, painstaking investigation, and careful analysis of sources.

In 1893, at the age of twenty-six, he received a call to the rabbinate of the Adass Yisroel Congregation in Koenigsberg, a city which, at that time, was a citadel of Reform. It was his task to guard the independence of his congregation and to assure its adherence to the fundamentals of Judaism. The philosophy of

Immanuel Kant exerted great influence on educated Jews in that city. Rabbi Munk, whilst not surrendering to its views, utilized in his fight against Reform and its estrangement from tradition, the very methods of modern thought, in the role of "one who seized the spear from the Egyptian."

In Koenigsberg he passed the acid test of spiritual apprenticeship for his life's work. Here he came to understand the fundamental problems, religious and communal, of Orthodox Jewry in Germany. Here he found a laboratory for the development of his qualifications, acquiring extensive and intensive knowledge for successful labors as rabbi and teacher.

In Koenigsberg he married Selma Sandler, his faithful mate, invaluable both in the religious education of their children and in his manifold communal activities.

II.

The decisive turn in his career came in 1900 when, on the death of his uncle, Ezriel Hildesheimer, he was elected rabbi of the Adass Yisroel Congregation in Berlin. During his long service, his congregation developed a remarkable sense of responsibility for the strengthening and enlarging of the foundations of Torah-true Judaism.

In course of time, he became a recognized leader of German Orthodox Jewry, a position for which he qualified by dint of his personality and his great Torah-erudition. There was not a single Orthodox group in Germany in which he did not play a leading role. His rabbinical authority was unquestioned in a period of great men. There were many who turned to him for decisions in matters of ritual, as well as personal and communal relations. In his day there were in Germany a considerable number of Torah-true leaders and recognized Talmudic authorities, such as David Hoffmann, Rector of the Hildesheimer Seminary, Joseph Wohlgemuth and Avrohom Eliya Kaplan, professors at the same institution, Eduard Biberfeld, Spitzer of Hamburg, Herman Klein of Berlin, Solomon Breuer and Dayan Posen of Frankfurt-am-Main, Heinrich Ehrentreu of Munich, and Joseph Carlebach of Altona. Among the survivors of that period should be mentioned the world-renowned *Gaon,* the last rector of the Hildesheimer School, J. J. Weinberg (now at Montreux, Switzerland), Abraham Klein (formerly of Nuerenberg), now in Haifa, Jacob Rosenheim, Moses Auerbach, and Samuel Gruenberg in Tel Aviv.

The task inherited by Ezra Munk was hard, indeed. Ezriel Hildesheimer, and his great contemporary, Samson Raphael Hirsch, recognized during the spiritual crisis of German Torah-true Judaism that there was no assurance of its continuation unless it achieve an autonomous independent organization. It was for this reason that they made their congregations into a bulwark, stemming widespread religious defection.

Hildesheimer's successor had not only to preserve the inheritance intact, but to enlarge and develop it in accord with changing needs. The conditions confronting the young leader in Berlin required special skill, tact, and almost superhuman endurance. After a few decades, Adass Yisroel was an outstanding triumph of his leadership. Whilst remarkable in its *kashrut* institutions, its greatest accomplishment was the establishment of an autonomous school-system, which catered to seven hundred students. Its upkeep required outstanding financial contributions, which Adass Yisroel put at Dr. Munk's disposal. The schools illustrated not only the sacrificial fervor of his congregation, but developed into a national fortress of Torah-true Judaism.

Up to the year 1920 every Jew, by State law, was a member of his local congregation, irrespective of his views. Due to the assimilationist trend in the 19th Century, many congregations were ruled by liberals and reformers. In some cases, separate synagogues were run for Liberals and Orthodox, but under the same authority. Special acts of Parliament were required to allow Orthodox Jews to form their own congregation and leave the general community. Hildesheimer was a propagandist of "Independent Orthodoxy" (*Austritt*).

Hildesheimer was by nature a sociable type, and was inclined to cooperation in definite projects with persons of different persuasion without lessening in the slightest degree his independence or modifying even minor *minhagim* (customs). The bitter struggle, during the 19th Century, particularly in its second half, between Orthodoxy and Reform was well-nigh forgotten at the beginning of the Twentieth. It was precisely the *Austritt,* which had led to a weakening of the antagonisms. The parties kept their individual lives apart from each other. Hence frictions were rarer and whatever fighting remained lost its bitterness. On the other hand, there developed an approach to the Judaism of Eastern Europe, which until then had been removed from the pious folks in Germany. Western Jewry, with its customs and way of life, had created a barrier between themselves, the adherents of *"Torah im Derekh Eretz"*, and the Eastern coreligionists, who stood for *"Torah by Itself"*, unaffected by modern culture.

The First World War had brought about a rapprochement. Soldiers and officers from Orthodox circles in Germany came to Poland and Lithuania with the Kaiser's army and before their eyes there was suddenly revealed a new world—near to them in basic law and thought and strange in its externalities, its customs and ceremonies. Out of the darkness of the small towns and ghettoes there burst upon them the light of Torah and *Hassidism,* an effervescent Jewish life, powerful and complete, faithful in all its manifestations.

The union of effort between German and Polish and Lithuanian Jews through Agudat Israel brought about closer relations and mutual influence. Rabbis Pinchas Kohn, Emanuel Carlebach, and Dr. Leo Deutschlander founded a system of elementary Jewish religious schools in Lithuania and Poland.

One of the blessed results of this new attachment was the trend, especially among the Orthodox German rabbis, to send their sons for prolonged study to the *yeshivot* in those countries. It was not easy to move to Eastern centers of Torah learning, for there was a marked difference in living conditions between the poor hamlets of Lithuania and the conditions in Germany.

All these changes from within and without influenced Adass Yisroel more than any other community in Germany, because it was located in the capital, much closer to the East.

Together with these large responsibilities, Ezra Munk carried the great burden of many local duties: They included leadership of three large synagogues and various Orthodox institutions, supervision of kosher eating places, of *Shehitah,* and milk supply; personal charitable efforts and administration of charity funds.

The educational problem facing the religious community of Berlin was most difficult, comparable to the Jewish educational picture in America a quarter of a century ago.

Existing Jewish schools laid no emphasis on Jewishness. The public school, which attracted all, also Torah-true Jewish children, served the cause of assimilation and led to complete alienation from Judaism. The Orthodox school system of classes in religion

supplied only a minimal training in Jewish education, usually as
unwelcome additions to general education.

Long before, Ezriel Hildesheimer had made some efforts, unfortunately unsuccessful, to establish Orthodox day schools. Munk,
together with a group of Orthodox leaders, among them Eduard
Biberfeld and Meir Hildesheimer, mobilized all their resources
to establish one. After many disappointments, they realized their
aim.

At first there were only two classes of one hundred students
each and only three teachers. They faced the competition of the
public schools, which possessed ample and attractive classrooms,
supplied by the City Fathers with modern equipment and nourished by a generous government-supplied budget. Among the
difficulties of the Orthodox schools was also the wide distribution
of the Jewish population throughout various districts in the city
and in suburbs distant from one another. Transportation presented an almost insoluble problem. Because of the lack of buildings and building material in the war years (1914-1919) and
afterwards, it was well-nigh impossible to find a suitable place
for the school, or to obtain permission to erect an appropriate
structure.

In 1919 permission was obtained from the City Council to
open a private elementary school. "Eventually an impressive
(school) building was erected in the western part of Berlin. Within two years after the opening of the school, there were in existence
four educational institutions, viz., an elementary school for boys
with over 200 pupils; an elementary school for girls with 108
pupils; a secondary school for girls, and a technical secondary
school with 129 girls and 147 boys.

"In 1927, for the first time, there were held final examinations—
under the supervision of the city educational authorities—and in
their wake a charter was granted to the last two institutions. This
success prompted the congregation to add to the secondary school
three additional upper classes, the successful completion of which
would enable the boys and girls to enter college." (Mordecai
Elias in his "Study of the Orthodox School System in Germany".)

Rabbi Munk dedicated his time and energy to this network
of Jewish education. Under his guidance and the headmastership
of Dr. Nathan Schlesinger, education resulted in a deepening of
Torah-true consciousness, for they cultivated a spirit of loyalty
to faith and practice; the students acquired not only considerable

knowledge of Torah and Judaism, but also a religious outlook on life and self-evident attachment to the *mitzvot*. But Rabbi Munk was not satisfied with the organization and supervision of education, and his responsibility to obtain financial support. He taught Torah himself. To his lectures to the *Baale Batim* (heads of households) of his congregation, he added also sessions in the Talmud to the young people.

His method in the teaching of the Talmud was distinguished by marvelous exactness and lucidity. To clarify the various aspects of a controversy, he would use the blackboard, emphasizing in vivid manner opinions of Tannaim and Amoram (teachers of *Mishnah and Gemara*) until the issues were clearly understood.

At the completion of *sugyot* (themes) under discussion, he taught his students to write summaries of the problems and their solution; in this manner he encouraged independent thinking and also tested their knowledge.

One should emphasize his cordial relations with the youth of his congregation, which helped him greatly in the success of their education. Even small children looked at him with love and respect. The *Rov's* visit to their parents was a festive occasion. Young people, together with adults, would visit his home on Sabbaths and festivals and no one ever left the *Rov* without learning words of Torah. Thus a close personal bond was forged between the *Rov* and his pupils; he trained them not merely through his lectures, but through his attitudes and actions.

III.

His activities spread from Adass Yisroel to all the Orthodox congregations of Germany. To quote from Hermann Schwab, the historian of Orthodox Judaism in Germany:

"His activities in connection with the Society of Torah-true Rabbis (*Vereinigung traditionell-gesetzestreuer Rabbiner*) embraced the whole sphere of religious affairs: the promotion of Sabbath observance, of religious instruction, the provision of suitable textbooks, the training of teachers and community officials, especially *Shohetim,* the production of ritual appurtenances, arrangement of *halakhic* discussions at periodic conferences, the provision of kosher food, the supervision of kosher eating places

at home and abroad, in cooperation with the *Hamburg Verein*
(society for the promotion of kosher eating houses. This organization was founded in 1900 in Hamburg and for forty years
carried on its work first in Germany, gradually embracing all
Palestine, North America, and South Africa)."

Rabbi Munk was called upon to decide many *Shélot* (questions
of Jewish Law). His activities as *Ab Bet Din* (head of the rabbinic court) of the Adass Yisroel were woven into the tapestry of
Germany Jewry, as well as that of world-wide Orthodox Judaism,
in the framework of Agudat Israel. His thorough knowledge of
the *Shulhan Arukh* enabled him to weigh every responsum carefully and examine precedents throughout early and later rabbinical literature; if the subject matter required the opinion of a
scientist, legal or medical authority, he would invite them to cooperate. He was equally judicious in matters affecting individuals
and the community. His responsa, at times the result of consultation with other rabbinical authorities, were uniformly couched in
concise language. Because of the pressure of his routine labors,
unfortunately only a few of them were preserved. Those published
by Rabbi H. Klein testify to his thoroughness and close cooperation with his colleagues.

The Society of Jewish Academicians (*Bund Juedischer Akademiker*) was a powerful force in the Jewish life of Germany. He was
one of its founders, together with Dr. Isaac Breuer and Dr. Moses
Auerbach.

While Isaac Breuer was its philosopher and the creator of its
ideology, Rabbi Munk determined the schedule of its scientific
work, its lectures, discussions, investigations, and conferences, and
functioned as one of the editors of its publications. In Jewish
political matters, the society was neutral. Its sole aim was to unite
Jewish university students and graduates of all parties in the cause
of Torah.

Munk established a central office for the protection of *Shehitah*,
which gradually enlarged its scope to defend Judaism against all
detractors. He composed pamphlets and books, obtained testimoni-
als and opinions from recognized authorities.

He induced non-Jewish experts in physiology, veterinary science, and medicine in various European countries to submit statements on *Shehitah*. This material is still being used today whenever

Shehitah is under attack and has found remarkable support in the scientific opinions of American university professors in our day.[1]

For decades Ezra Munk held the honorary post of *Sachver-staendiger fuer Juedische Angelegenheiten* (expert for Jewish questions) at the Prussian Ministry for the Affairs of Cults. In this capacity he had to render opinions on all legal and political problems concerning Jews in Germany and was often called upon by the government to testify in the *Reichstag, Landtage,* and local parliaments. He enjoyed the highest confidence and respect of the government and the general public.

Whilst closely linked to his congregation, land, and times, Rabbi Munk stood out as an unusual personality, independent and original. He took into steady account local and contemporary exigencies. He knew the mind of German Jewry and used his broad secular knowledge to spread Torah and *Yirat Shamayim* (reverence for our Heavenly Father). Faithful to the philosophy of *Torah im Derekh Eretz,* he put the emphasis on Torah as both the fundamental way and goal. He was not satisfied with an isolated Torah-corner, but conquered for her a public place in the social life of his city. Adass Yisroel was absolutely independent, yet, when no matter of principle was involved, Rabbi Munk worked together, in well-defined areas, with non-Orthodox circles. Because of its perceptive consideration for the difference in cultural and civic patterns, and the consistent emphasis on the need of *basic harmony* in *Klal Yisrael,* Adass Yisroel became pivotal in efforts at cooperation between German and Eastern European Jews.

The same Ezra Munk who, even in 1938, when already in Jerusalem, warned its leaders in Berlin to guard its autonomy zealously, never surrendered the hope for the religious reclamation of the non-conforming majority, separation from whom he had battled for. His Torah-true conviction made him fight false ideas, but his democratic impulse refrained from personal attacks. Hence neither he nor his congregation were ever pushed into the corner. Ezra Munk succeeded in maintaining a central position in Jewish affairs, especially in protection of Jewry or the Jewish religion against anti-Semitic agitation, such as in the field of *Shehitah* or defense of Talmud.

---

[1]In 1946, his son, Michael L. Munk, together with Isaac Lewin and J. Berman, published in New York *Religious Freedom—the Right to Practice Shehitah,* which comprises all important data and has become the most important source book in this area.

He secured considerable support from persons and institutions who were not Orthodox. He labored in two areas: the struggle against the enemies of his faith and people, and in a systematic effort to interpret Judaism to its enemies and to those in the Jewish community who were estranged from Torah and *mitzvot*. Thus the eyes of important members of the general community, hitherto blinded by non-Jewish thought, by Reform outlook or the delusions of emancipation and assimilation, were opened to the beauty and power of our holy traditions.

Rabbi Munk knew both how to adapt himself to the choir and how to sing solo. He strove unceasingly to unite his people for the sake of Judaism, but when he saw some weaken or withdraw, he "girded his loins" and worked in isolation. His energy and persistence eventually drew people to him. The echo of his message survived him and to this day has both cheered and challenged the remnant of his flock. His was a personality, austere and tender, of extraordinary moral discipline, considerate of human frailty and unceasing in his challenge to the best in the men and women whom he led.

Like other leaders of integrity, Ezra Munk believed that educational enlightenment would suffice to banish moral darkness. He could not understand that there was ingrained in some people a festering curse, which was out to destroy; he could not imagine the dreadful happenings—between 1933 and 1945—in Germany and the rest of Europe.

He passed away in Jerusalem on the 1st of Heshvan 5701 (November 2, 1940) and was laid to rest on the Mount of Olives.

His wife passed away on the 10th of Nisan 5718 (March 31, 1958).

NEHEMIAH ANTON NOBEL

(1871-1922)

By Eugen E. Mayer

NEHEMIAH ANTON NOBEL

By Eugen E. Mayer

> *Open thou mine eyes, that*
> *I may behold wondrous things*
> *out of thy law.*
>
> Psalm CXIX, 18

In a note entitled *Sephiragedanken* (Thoughts on the period between the festivals of *Pessach* and *Shavuot*), Nobel, then in his early twenties, wrote: "To me, there is no division between 'rigid' *halakhah* and 'flowing' prophetism, between the sobriety of the law and the intoxication of poesy." This concord of law and life, of their reciprocal creativeness, was to become one of the *leitmotifs* of his many sermons, addresses, and writings, and indeed of his whole life. He once illustrated it by the famous story of Ben-Azzai, the Tanna, whose head was said to have been surrounded by flames while he was engrossed in the study of the Torah. Questioned about it by Rabbi Akiba, he said: "All I did was to join words of the Torah to those of the Prophets and words of the Prophets to those of the Writings, and they were as joyous as when they were given on Sinai."[1]

The same burning fire and rapturous absorption were overwhelmingly apparent when Nobel expounded the words of "The Book", stringing them together like pearls. It is this impression of him that first comes to mind when one attempts to portray this remarkable man.

YEARS OF STUDY AND FRUITION

Born in Nagy-Med, a small place in Hungary, on October 8, 1871, Nehemiah Tzevi Anton Nobel came to Germany in 1878,

---

NOTE: In the preparation of this article, which is partly based on a contribution on the same subject to *Misrachi Festschrift* (Berlin, 5687-1927), the author has had the privilege of consulting a substantial collection of manuscripts in German and Hebrew, left by Rabbi Nobel and now in the possession of his daughter, Mrs. Ruth Meyer-Nobel, in Haifa.

[1] *Midrash Shir Hashirim* I, 10: *"Thy cheeks are comely with circlets, thy neck with beads."* The Hebrew word *haruzim*, which the King James translation renders "chains of gold" and the Jewish Publication Society translation "beads," also denotes "lines of verse."

when his father, Joseph Nobel, was appointed rabbi of the "Klaus" synagogue in Halberstadt, a stronghold of traditional Judaism. There, under the guidance of his father and Rabbi Auerbach, he continued his intensive education in Bible, Talmud and rabbinical literature, studying at the same time at the *Domgymnasium,* where he acquired his excellent command of Latin and Greek. In an autobiographical note he says that, for four generations, his family had considered it their pride to devote their sons to the rabbinate.[1a] Following this tradition, he went, after matriculation, to Berlin to study at the Rabbiner-Seminar under such outstanding scholars as Ezriel Hildesheimer, David Hoffmann, Jacob Barth, and Abraham Berliner. He was already so advanced in his knowledge of the Talmud that Hildesheimer entrusted him with the *Gemara* lesson when he himself was prevented from giving it. Simultaneously, Nobel studied at the Berlin University under a galaxy of academic teachers. The courses of E. Zeller and E. Curtius on Greek philosophy and history, of W. Dilthey on literature, H. Steinthal on psychology, exerted a lasting influence on his formative years. During his three and a half years in Berlin, he frequently officiated as rabbi in private synagogues and gave many lectures to associations of students.

On the completion of his studies and after obtaining his ordination, he did his year's military service and was in 1896 appointed rabbi of the Hevrat Talmud Torah Congregation in Cologne. There he found time to finish his thesis on *Schopenhauer's Theorie des Schoenen,* in which he attempted to demonstrate the philosopher's dependence on the teachings of Kant; he received his degree as doctor of philosophy at the neighboring university of Bonn. In Cologne he met and married in 1898 Julie Weyl of Viersen (Rhine-

---

[1a] Both his parents, Rabbi Josef Nobel (1837-1917) and his mother Esther, née Bruck (1842-1917), could number among their immediate ancestors such distinguished rabbis as Josua Falk Hacohen, author of a commentary on the *Shulhan Arukh;* Zvi Hirsch Broda; Yechiel Naftali Bruck of Pressburg, a Kabbalist; Josef Kuttna and his son, Aron, both of Totis in Hungary. Among the publications of the father, a critical refutation of Rohling's *Talmudjude, Thabor,* a commentary on the *Haftarot,* and *Libanon,* a commentary on the Psalms, are noteworthy. The rabbinical tradition continued in the children: Israel, one of the three sons (born 1878) was rabbi of the Berlin community from 1925 to 1940 and is the author of several publications, including a translation of the Book of Job with commentary; another son, Gabriel, a dental surgeon, wrote an important work on dentistry in the Talmud; and Henriette, the only daughter, married Rabbi Emanuel Donath. (These data on the family were kindly supplied by Rabbi Israel Nobel, who lives now in retirement in Jerusalem.)

land), and their only child, his beloved Ruth, was born to them. His wife died in 1938 in Haifa.

After several years in Cologne, he accepted an invitation to become rabbi of the Adath Israel Congregation in Koenigsberg, but he seems not to have been happy in that *Austrittsgemeinde* (Separatists community) and resigned after a few months. At that period, a great change must have affected Nobel's whole outlook. Whether he felt a pressing need to concentrate on a more thorough study of the fountains of religion, morals and philosophy, or whether he altogether doubted his chosen vocation—we do not know, and maybe he did not know himself. At all events, he must have felt an irresistible urge to probe into "these supreme and most important questions confronting the human mind," as he says in his unsuccessful application of April 30, 1897 for the post of communal rabbi in Cologne—a most remarkable document. And so he went to Marburg, to study under Hermann Cohen, the great exponent of Kant, head of the so-called "Marburg School" of philosophy, and at the same time deeply attached to the values of Judaism. No other teacher had a more decisive influence on Nobel's mental growth; for here, in the strict discipline of methodical thought, he found his own way, a way different from that of his master, as far as the fundamentals of Judaism are concerned.

During all of his life, Nobel gratefully acknowledged his admiration for Hermann Cohen. On several occasions, this gratitude found eloquent expression, notably in 1902 and 1912, on Cohen's 60th and 70th birthdays, and in a memorial address of 1920. It is most interesting to observe Nobel's effort to delve ever deeper into his teacher's thought, to follow and interpret the evolution of his system and his evaluation of Judaism as "religion of reason."[2] While Nobel's own philosophical training is revealed in his analysis of Cohen's relation to Plato and Kant, he shows himself at his best in a critical comparison of his own and Cohen's views on rationalism and Judaism. "Judaism," he says,[3] "could never have become a universal religion, had it confined itself to a system of abstract thought." The prophets, he argues against Cohen, are not concerned with morals alone; they are not opposing the observance of the law, but its mechanical observance, "the miserable

---

[2]Cohen's great work, *Religion der Vernunft aus den Quellen des Judentums,* was posthumously published in 1919.

[3]In an article written for the *Juedische Presse,* 1902.

belief which has always been the catechism of *Werkheiligkeit*
(sanctimoniousness) and which holds that man can have religion
without morality." Moreover, he adds, here again opposing Cohen's
views, "the prophets are possessed of that healthy nationalism
which, as Cohen himself remarks, is compatible with world citizenship." A characteristic sidelight on Nobel's way of expression is
to be found in his second tribute to Cohen.[4] Recalling that in
Talmudic times a university was not called *alma mater,* but *kallah,*
i.e. bride, he finds in both names an indication of "creative love,"
a concept very dear to him.

In the address of 1920, the most comprehensive of Nobel's
expositions and appreciations of Cohen's theories, he finds the
historic achievement of Judaism in the fact that it has created
"a new relationship between God and Man." Cohen has surpassed his predecessors, and Kant in particular, with his doctrine
of the sovereignty and creativeness of the human intellect. And
here, says Nobel, is the starting point of Cohen's philosophy of
Judaism: not that the world exists, but that it is what it is (*"Dasein"*
and *"So-sein"*), that there is moral law, and that Israel's prophets
were the first to point out this aspect of the Creation, of the direction of the Divine towards the Human.

Nobel's admiration for Cohen is not dimmed by his own views
on the tenets of Judaism, and he insists that serious consideration
should be given to Cohen's profound theories of the relationship
between religion and morals, the importance of the God-idea in
the religious concept of the world, and the moral purposes of state
and society.

We know that Cohen was greatly impressed by Nobel's personality; he even remembered better than Nobel himself one of
his early sermons. Thus it was a fitting monument to their friendship that the following four lines, written by Nobel after Hermann
Cohen's death, were inscribed on his tombstone:

> *Platons strahlende Welt und Kants erdunkelnde Tiefen*
> *Strahlten Dir, Grosser, in Eins. Musisch erklangen sie Dir.*
> *An der prophetischen Glut entbrannte die lodernde Fackel.*
> *Sterbliches bargen wir hier; lodere heller, o Glut.*[5]

---

[4]Printed in *Mitteilungen der Grossloge fuer Deutschland,* 1912.
[5]In a very inadequate paraphrase:

Platon's radiant world and Kant's profoundness and darkness
Fused together in you, Muses intoning the tune.
Ardour of prophets did kindle the glow of the torch and its blazes.
Buried are mortal remains. Glow ever brighter, oh torch!

In the Zionist Movement

Nobel's metacritical attitude towards Hermann Cohen also found expression in their different approach to Zionism. Early adherence to the Zionist movement—he participated in the foundation of Mizrachi at the Pressburg Conference of 1904—was the natural outcome of Nobel's views on historical Judaism and the religious nationalism of the prophets, whereas Cohen's uncompromising opposition to political Zionism was an equally natural product of both his philosophy of Judaism and his German patriotism.

Those first two decades of the 20th century were the days when the Jews of Germany could believe that their century-long struggle for full emancipation had at long last come to an end. The short-lived Weimar Republic had all the appearances of a millenium. In that heyday of "assimilation"[6] the delusion was so complete that few Jews had forebodings of their standing on the brink of an abyss. Facing a political mirage, they honestly mistook for bliss what was in reality euphoria. Not without a melancholy smile does one remember a period when in the Jewish communities Orthodox and Liberal fought each other, and both united in fighting the Zionists.

"These fellows want to be happy," said Cohen of the Zionists,[7] understandably enough in a man of his intellectual integrity and his anti-utilitarian, anti-hedonistic views. Nobel, on the other hand, was deeply convinced that a new epoch in Jewish history was dawning and, quoting Goethe, he said: "And you may say that you have been present."[8]

While the early discussion of "Zionism and Religion" lost much of its interest when even the most Orthodox groups began to engage in practical work for and in Eretz Israel, the controversy on the political plane raged all the more fiercely and reached its culminating point with the publication, in 1915, of Cohen's *Deutsch-*

---

[6]A rather amusing sidelight on "assimilation" appears in the following episode. Speaking in 1894 at the Foundation Day of *Dibbuk Haverim*, the students' association of the Berlin Rabbiner Seminar, Nobel concluded his address with a call, "according to old German students' custom," for a "salamander" in honour of Ezriel Hildesheimer and their other teachers. (The "salamander" consisted in everybody standing up, circling their beer glasses on the table and draining them to the last dreg—surely a peculiar performance by an assembly of future rabbis.)

[7]See F. Rosenzweig, *Kleinere Schriften,* Berlin 1937, p. 347.

[8]In an address to the Zionist Association at Leipzig, in 1903.

tum und Judentum. Nobel wrote a reply to Cohen, but it seems in retrospect that this whole debate on "divided loyalties" was foreign to his way of thought. Party slogans, including "Orthodox" and "Liberal," could not appeal to a protagonist of "Klal Israel," or in Solomon Schechter's felicitous phrase, "catholic Judaism." But the larger issues involved continued to occupy his mind, and in the last year of his life he summed up his position in a letter to Max Warburg in Hamburg, dated April 10, 1921, in which he says:

". . . I cannot clearly state how the creative synthesis of religious positivism and happy recognition of purely philosophic values works in me. I only know that the genius of religious thought sways me and that I submit to it. Nor can I clearly express how it is that I am able to harmonize far removed and even antogonistic elements through the perception of the beautiful and the aesthetic with which I am blessed. But I know that this harmonization is vouchsafed me in certain supreme hours of revelation.

"The same applies to my national conviction. I have no doubt whatsoever that the history of Israel is not to be assessed on religious values alone. It is likewise the exponent of national development. The prophets looked upon the decline of the Jewish state as the decisive breach of its own existence. Despite all the great and comforting things which they and their keepers of the seal—the Talmudists and the rabbis—find to say about the Diaspora, it can only be regarded as sporadic. I am rooted in the sphere of national Jewish thought. It is not a conviction that I have absorbed: it is my very life. But, on the other hand, I cannot conceive of this life without Goethe, the poet of the Germans. There works in me this synthetic force, which binds together and unites both nationalisms. I realize that each one in itself is strong enough to be allied with the other.

"I warmly and heartily welcome your sweeping statements about the religious form of everything taking shape in Eretz Israel. I agree with you that Eretz Israel should never become another little Balkan state in Asia—nor even just an English colony. . . . Religious renaissance must be the ultimate aim of the new achievement. It is not through narrowmindedness and intolerance that we shall instill the spirt into Eretz Israel.

"The Zionist Organization has undertaken to declare the religious law as binding on its official shaping. At present that is all that can be required of it. With the Mizrachi movement, of which

16 years ago I was a co-founder, a strongly religious federation has taken up its stand within the general Zionist Organization. I support the Mizrachi and all its claims on all essential questions.

"Any attempt 'to create religion' through opposing organizations and by strife, quarrel and mutual recrimination can only indicate a complete misconception of the spirit of religion. Genuine exponents of the religious ideal are not so fearful as to be intolerant. Religion only flourishes on fertile soil. Orthodoxy itself is in need of resurrection. The Holy Land will produce a noble maternity and bring about a new re-birth. . . ."

THE LAST YEARS

The Marburg *caesura* marked a turning point in Nobel's life and the end of his years of apprenticeship. In 1901, he accepted a rabbinical position in Leipzig, in 1906 he was appointed communal rabbi in Hamburg, and in 1910 he succeeded Marcus Horovitz in Frankfort-on-Main, where he died, in his 51st year, on January 24, 1922. Of Hamburg he writes (in Hebrew) at the end of a Responsum on rabbinic law: "After years of wandering, I have here found a place of rest for the study of the Torah, as much as my heart could wish." The great impression he made, especially on the younger generation, is fully reflected in Oskar Wolfsberg's study.[9]

By now he had reached his full stature. In the two great communities of Hamburg and Frankfort he found not only the widest scope for self-expression, but also a measure of respect and admiration far beyond his own congregation, such as is granted to few religious leaders. He repaid this general affection when he declined the great honour of an offer to become Chief Rabbi of Vienna. A few weeks before his death, friends and disciples, as if in a premonition of the imminent loss, honoured him on his 50th birthday with a *Festschrift*.[10] He was deeply moved by this homage, all the more so because the contributors, who included Martin Buber and Franz Rosenzweig, represented a cross-section of the whole community. His unique position within the rabbinate had found expression in 1919, when the Union of German Rabbis elected him

---

[9]*Nehemias Anton Nobel*, Frankfort a.M. 1929.—Dr. Wolfsberg-Aviad became a leading figure in the Mizrachi movement; he died in August 1957 as envoy of Israel to Switzerland.

[10]*Gabe Herrn Rabbiner Dr. Nobel zum 50. Geburtstag dargebracht von* (follow the names of 13 contributors). Frankfurt a.M., 5682.

as their president, or—as Leo Baeck said—did not have to elect him, since he was there as their "given leader."[11]

His community paid him the supreme honour of burying with him a scroll of the Torah. A golden *kiddush* cup was donated in his memory to his synagogue at the Boerneplatz, and the *Lehrhaus* instituted an annual "Nobel Lecture." When after the seven days of mourning the *Gemara shiur* was resumed, R. Jacob Posen introduced the lesson with a reference to a Talmudic interpretation (in *Sanhedrin* 37a) of the right attitude towards those who are no longer observant and who asked after the death of Rabbi Zeira: "Until now this little man has prayed for us; who will now take care of us? That made them consider their ways and they returned to the fold" (See "Nachrufe," p. 33). No finer tribute could have been paid to the late rabbi.

INTERPRETER OF THE LAW

Nobel's personality drew its strength from three sources: the study of the Torah in the widest sense of the word, his understanding of the realities of life, and the spoken word. As in a precious ring, they were combined in him by the humanity that shone forth from his fine head, his deep, beautiful eyes, and even from his expressive hands.

The study of the law and its practical application were always his favourite occupation. It was one of the unfulfilled dreams of his later years that he could not retire for a year or two to one of the great Lithuanian *yeshivot,* to devote all his time to study, for study's sake. From his childhood onwards, he was exceptionally well trained, but he was well aware of the Herculean task to attain mastery of the immense domain of the Talmud and all the other sources of rabbinical law. Notes and excerpts from leading textbooks show the extent to which he had also studied general jurisprudence, Roman law in particular. It was these studies that taught him the value of the comparison of different legal systems. In addition, he was unusually well read in the classics, in European literature, and in philosophy.

With this rich background, his penetrating mind was able to see ever new aspects of the *Gemara.* He not only succeeded in making every *shiur* a source of increased knowledge, but—and this

[11]*Nachrufe auf Rabbiner N.A. Nobel* (ed. by the writer of this article), Frankfurt a.M. 1923, p. 28.

distinguishes the true master from the average teacher—he provoked questions and offered a wealth of suggestions for independent inquiry. His way of teaching was not, by any means, what is
usually called "systematic." He used to skip whole pages when he
thought it necessary to demonstrate the evolution and essence of
certain institutions of religious law and their legitimate claim to
observance. Always carefully prepared, every *shiur* thus became an
unforgettable experience.

His mastery of more time-honoured forms of exposition found
an outlet in his addresses on halakhic subjects, his opinions on
questions submitted to him, and his writings on legal issues. Among
the latter, special mention must be made of his studies on the
Talmudic law of lien, in the *Festschrift* for Hermann Cohen (Berlin,
1912), and on *shi'buda d'R.Nathan,* a doctrine of the assignment
of debts, in the *Festschrift* for David Hoffmann (Berlin, 1914).
Here, a learned discussion of controversies in rabbinical literature
on the nature of mortgage loans on real and movable property,
and the resulting rights and duties of creditor, debtor, and guar-
antor, and a comparison of Talmudic and Roman law led Nobel
to the conclusion that, with all its intricacies, the former represents
a higher level of legal practice because, unlike the Roman system,
it accords a certain measure of protection to the debtor. In this
humane approach, which tends to subordinate the strict provisions
of the law to moral principles, Nobel saw one of the great achievements of the masters of the Talmud. The truth of *summum jus,
summa injuria* was ever present in Nobel's mind.

Of greater actuality, however, was the treatise in which he
stated, in the classic style of the Responsa literature, the reasons
for his decision to institute an *Eruv* in Frankfort.[12] Although
the rabbinate of the *Israelitische Religionsgesellschaft,* the separate Orthodox community, opposed his decision, it was generally
accepted. Even today, this treatise impresses the reader by its
great learning and the force of the argument, but not less by the
author's sense of responsibility. He had, of course, made his
decision in constant consultation with his Bet-Din: the honorary
Dayan Jacob S. Posen (1857-1926), who, like his father, the
house rabbi of the pious Baron Wilhelm v. Rothschild, was one
of those merchants to whom, as the Talmud says (in Berakot 35b),
their Torah is a permanent, and their business a part-time, concern;

---

[12]*Porat Joseph, Kuntres Odot Tikkun Eruvin* (Frankfort a. M. 1914).

and the learned Haim Eliezer Lipinsky (1873-1931), who had come from Russia to Frankfort as a young man, became Dayan in 1904 and served three rabbis. Intermittently, though without any practical results, a small group continued to attack the *Eruv,* and R. Jacob Posen wrote, after Nobel's death, another treatise on the subject.[13] Published anonymously, it carries as a characteristic motto the words: "Why does one erect an *Eruv?* For the sake of peace."[14] Even as late as 1931, Nobel's successor, Rabbi Jacob Hoffmann, found it necessary to reaffirm, in a solemn statement from his pulpit, Nobel's decision and its *halakhic* foundation.

Equally learned and instructive were the great rabbi's lectures on difficult Talmudic passages which, according to custom, he used to give on the Sabbath before Passover and on *Sukkot,* and which always attracted a large audience, not only from his own congregation. The subjects he chose on such occassions covered a wide field, from problems of personal status to the law of *Prosbul* in a sabbatical year, or the chapter of "the stolen *Lulav*". His notebooks are full of sketches for the numerous lectures he gave through the years, sometimes only a few lines, indicating the various sources to which he proposed to refer, but sometimes a more elaborate synopsis; they also include a 15-page Hebrew manuscript on "a most difficult question" raised by Rabbi Akiba in connection with the kindling of the lights on *Shabbat Hanukkah.*

What made these lectures so attractive, despite their difficult subject matter, was his constant quest for the spirit behind the letter of the law, and his passion for bringing it home to his listeners. If the Torah is called "a tree of life," he saw more in this expression than a merely convenient metaphor for homiletic exercises. To him it meant exactly what it said: an appeal to observe the commandments, *"that you may live,"* or *"he shall live by them."* As in his *shiur,* he did not mind in the least, when the talmudical scholars who filled the first rows—Jacob Klatzkin, son of the *Gaon* of Lublin, used to be among them—fired questions at him, for such was his command of the subject that he was able to dispose of them effectively.[15]

---

[13]*Divre Shalom ve-Emet* (Frankfurt a.M. 1922).

[14]*Talmud Yerushalmi, Eruvin,* III.

[15]In this, as in so many other respects, Nobel was "different." On one occasion, when one of his opposite numbers relied in his *halakhic derashah* on a certain passage in Rambam, R. Jacob Posen, one of the greatest talmudical authorities of Frankfort, interjected: "It does not say so in *my* Rambam"; whereupon a notice appeared on the billboard of the synagogue: "It is forbidden to interrupt the Herr Rabbiner."

Nothing could be more welcome to him than such challenges. The saying in the Ethics of the Fathers, "Turn it (the Torah) and turn it over again, for everything is in it," meant in Nobel's interpretation the same as Faust's "Earn it anew, to really possess it."

Another aspect of Nobel's preoccupations is revealed in the many addresses he gave over the years on subjects of a different kind. As he used to point at the shelves in his study, distinguishing the "holy" from the "profane", "Here are my *sefarim* and there are my *books*," so he could deal with themes outside the normal province of a rabbi, as well as with more conventional ones. Goethe was his favorite, closely followed by Schopenhauer, but he also gave comprehensive lectures on the centenary of Herder's death and on the problem of ethics in our time. In his younger years he treated at considerable length, Hamlet and other plays of Shakespeare. Then there were papers on the 700th anniversary of the death of Maimonides and on Philo's relation to the Persian, Babylonian, and Greek civilizations. When still in his twenties, he dealt, in an address on Yohanan ben Zakkai and his times, with the question whether time creates man, or man his time, incidentally criticizing Mommsen's views on the Roman conquest of Judea. In yet another address, on the God-idea in the works of Ibn Gabirol and Spinoza, he maintains that Spinoza's "substance" is but "a metaphysical Nothing." One of his most important papers is a highly interesting essay of 1894 on "The Song of Songs", a wide-flung survey of the various interpretations given to this book in Jewish and non-Jewish sources, where he concludes that, on the basis of these interpretations, one could write a whole history of spiritual movements in Judaism. Mention may also be made of a lengthy review of the "Ethics of Judaism" by M. Lazarus, and of his sharp reply to a criticism of the historian Isaac Halevy's *Dorot Harishonim*. A good example of his far from stereotyped way of speech is provided by his presidential address at the Frankfort session of the Union of German Rabbis in 1921, where he interpreted the thrice repeated "Holy" as thesis, antithesis and synthesis in the Creation.

Unforgotten by those who were privileged to listen to him, were Nobel's lectures on "The Spirit of *Halakhah*," on the Sabbath, and his weekly lessons on the Psalms. The Sabbath, in particular, meant to him more than just a day of rest. Man and Sabbath together, he once said, have completed the Creation; and as the great revelation of divine freedom, the Sabbath became the proclamation of human freedom. He saw in its crowning the six days of toil and exaltation of human labor, an alliance between religion and social justice. He also liked to point out that the sanctification of the Sabbath was the only ceremonial law in the Decalogue. This conception was further developed in a much-quoted essay.[16]

In his personal life, he bore striking witness to the belief that the Sabbath day lends an "additional soul" to his observers. There was almost a halo about him when he intoned his own *niggun* of Yehuda Halevi's poem, *Al ahavatekha eshteh gevi'i.*[17] And he felt on firm traditional ground when sometimes he summoned the Sabbath to complete the number of three at table for grace after the meal.

In his lectures on the Psalms he frequently departed from an interpretation of their historical and religious content, to draw attention to the overwhelming beauty of their language. Here, his deep understanding of Hebrew enabled him to disclose many hidden treasures. It is not surprising that he was tempted to translate several psalms into German.[18]

All these various activities entered in the spectrum of Nobel's conception of the rabbi's calling. In his above-mentioned letter of 1897 to the Cologne community, he speaks of "the dignity and the burden" of the modern rabbi's function and continues: "I hold that a rabbi can fulfil his task successfully only if he stands above all parties within and outside of his community. He himself must have a firm and unflinching standpoint on all religious issues of his time. For myself, this standpoint is that offered by Judaism in its historical tradition. This alone seems to me to guarantee development and sound progress. But I consider it my duty to examine every religious trend within Judaism, to meet it with objective arguments only, to treat opponents with respect and, in my public activities, to lay greater stress on that which different trends have in common than on that which separates them."[18a]

However, to stand above the parties, does not mean, as he said on another occasion, that the Jewish priest surrounds himself with

---

[16]*Der Sabbath,* in the volume *Soziale Ethik im Judentum,* Frankfurt a.M. 1913. This essay is also included in the widely read Hebrew anthology *Sefer Ha-Shabbat,* ch. 4 (publ. in Tel Aviv).

[17]See F. Rosenzweig, *Jehuda Halevi,* 2nd ed., p. 212.

[18]Two of these translations, Ps. 23 and 42, were published, on the 10th anniversary of Nobel's death, in *Frankfurter Israelitisches Gemeindeblatt,* January 1932.

[18a]It is characteristic that, in his induction address at Frankfurt, he paid tribute not only to Marcus Horovitz, his predecessor, but also to Samson Raphael Hirsch.

clouds of incense, far removed from the burning issues of his time; or that, in order to satisfy all and sundry, he should renounce his own opinions. In that case he would stand, not above, but beneath the parties. And in 1902, in his great sermon at the 25th jubilee of Rabbi L. Munk in Marburg, he recalls that the hall of the Synhedrion was divided into a "holy" and a "work-a-day" half, and this division leads him to a searching inquiry into the place of religion in life and the responsibilities of the rabbi who, as the priest of old was subject to the judgment of the people's highest court, must always be conscious of his duty towards the community.

As a minister of religion, he considered it one of his principal duties to stress the ultimate purpose of all religion. A great thinker of Jewish descent has said of the philosophers that they are content to interpret the world, when their proper task was to change it; likewise, Nobel saw religion as a decisive force on the road to a new world order, that unending road towards the goal which the magnificent *Alenu*-prayer predicts, "when the world will be perfected under the Kingdom of the Almighty."

The Preacher

Describing his first impression of Nobel, Franz Rosenzweig says that the first sermon he ever heard—it was in 1920, on Passover—enthralled him once for all. "It was the first time in my experience," he continues, "that thoughts, real thoughts, were strewn about from a pulpit, and in lavish profusion . . . they were metaphysical *kashyes* and—not at all metaphysical, but religious *tirutzim*. To put it differently: human questions and divine answers."[19]

In these words, one of the secrets of Nobel's influence is revealed. He was not a professional philosopher, but, as Alexander Altmann says, he was perhaps "the only true philosopher amongst German-Jewish orthodoxy."[20] It was given him, as he himself said, to unite historical insight with a metaphysical urge. What T. S. Eliot calls "the intersection of the timeless with time" was one of the ever recurring counterpoints of his sermons; in the blessing after the reading of the Law, for instance, "the Lord who has planted everlasting life in our midst," he found that same link between the passing and the eternal.

---

[19]*Nachrufe,* p. 44.
[20]*Theology in Twentieth-Century German Jewry,* in *Year Book I* of the Leo Baeck Institute, London 1956, p. 211.

The medium which best served the expression of his thoughts was the spoken word. It burst from him like a torrent, flooding listeners—and himself. Watching him, one had the impression of a man struggling with a rising tide, with a demonic "It" that obsessed him, ordered him to speak, and spoke out of him. These were not sermons in the customary sense, and it is significant that in his numerous notes, as well as in the full text which he frequently wrote down afterwards, he avoids the word *Predigt* and uses *Rede* instead, instinctively aware of the telling difference between these two words. His notes also afford a glance into his workshop. Apart from certain official occasions, he did not prepare his sermons in the ordinary way, but chose his subject, jotted down a few relevant passages from Scripture, Talmud and Midrash, and this raw material started a chain reaction in his mind, setting in motion a creative process, over which he was no longer master. Once on his pulpit, "the word obeyed his call." Sometimes a familiar line was the source of inspiration, and sometimes a single word. Thus, the lines in Psalm 148, "Praise the Lord from the heavens—praise the Lord from the earth", became the vehicle for a whole series of profound observations on the two roads open to man: from above to below, or the road of faith, and from below to above, or the way of scientific inquiry. This leads him to conclude that, like the Mounts of Gerizim and Ebal, representing blessing and curse, there are the mounts of faith and knowledge, and between them the valley of life.

He could connect Sarah's hospitality with the hospitality offered by Judaism to the great ideas of other nations; the word *hevrah* became a clue for the element of holiness in human society; from the word "all" in *"speak unto* all *the congregation of Israel"* (Levit. XIX, 1) he drew inspiration for an exposition of the perennial theme of the mutual relation between individual and society—a subject he frequently dealt with. Likewise, in one of his many memorable interpretations of the Joseph story, the linguistic implications of the Hebrew name "Joseph" presented an opportunity for dwelling on the "too much" and the "too little" which, he thought, were characteristic of the genius whom his brothers fail to recognize.

It is easy to imagine what he made of the parable of the "two staves of beauty and the bands" (Zechariah 11, 7), or the words of the daily prayer, "Blessed be He who spoke and the world came into being." Or again, pointing out that the first rule of

the civil law of the Torah (Exodus XXI, 2) concerned the dis-
inherited who had to sell his freedom, he developed a whole
philosophy of freedom and social justice in Judaism.

One of the most magnificent sermons he ever gave, was his
vision of Kohelet, with whom he apparently had a personal affinity.
"You love of my younger years, you joy of my manhood," he
addressed him in the last year of his life. Little did he care when
Kohelet lived, whether he was a merchant or a king. It was he
who revealed to him the four great forces of the human heart:
hope, memory, love, and faith; and from him he learned that all
contrasts of life, national and religious, individual and social, are
resolved in the praise of Israel and his Lord.

Carried away, as he was, on the wings of the word, Nobel
was not by any means unworldly. He could find sharp words
against "higher criticism" of the Bible and became the spokesman
of the whole conservative community of Germany when he demonstrated the fallacies of the *Richtlinien,* proclaimed by the liberal
rabbis in 1912. The care for the needs of the younger generation,
for adult education, were always in the forefront of his interests.
And in the controversy of the early 'twenties about women's fran-
chise, his opinion that they should be granted both active and
passive right of election prevailed, and Frankfurt was the first
great community where a woman was elected to the Board.

While it is true that, like Pinehas, "he rose from the midst of
the congregation," he knew, already as a young student, that "the
recognition of the truth in the Torah is more important than its
beauty." And much later, in a *Shavuot* sermon, he said, "Mankind needs more than enthusiasts; it needs every single one of
you—the merchant, the scholar, the workman—to fulfil his daily
duty, and then every day will renew the Day of the Giving of the
Law." But he also maintained that reading and learning alone
was not enough, if "the great commentary of life" was missing.

These examples must suffice. There was something indefinable,
mystical, about the atmosphere in the crowded synagogue when
Nobel began to speak. Surely, not all his listeners could capture
the full meaning of all his thoughts, and yet they were spellbound,
as if witnessing a miracle. And in those hours, the congregation
itself became a sublime multitude, a *"Menge, die schoen wird
wenn das Wunder sie ergreift."*[21]

---

[21]Stefan George, in *Der Siebente Ring.*

Conclusion

When the Frankfort community approached Nobel with the offer to become their rabbi, he answered with a brief telegram: "Ja. Is., LXI, 1." In that passage Isaiah speaks of his mission, beginning with the words: *"The spirit of the Lord is upon me, because the Lord has anointed me to bring good tidings unto the humble."*

At a first glance, this reference may seem presumptuous. But far from it! Nobel was well aware that, like the prophet, whatever he had to say, he said as the Lord's messenger, acting, as it were, under orders. To be chosen, as people or as individual, always meant in Jewish tradition a privilege, not of rights and prerogatives, but of duty and submission. In this humble sense alone did Nobel conceive his mission, and throughout his all too brief life he was conscious of being a messenger.

He has delivered his message. We still hear his voice.

AARON LEWIN

(1879-1941)

By Isaac Lewin

AARON LEWIN

By Isaac Lewin

During the many years that I was privileged to serve my father, I occasionally dreamt of writing his biography. I collected every scrap of printed paper pertaining to his life. But that vast collection was lost in the holocaust of the Second World War. I have nothing to rely on but memory.

My father was a Talmudic scholar of brilliance and versatility,[1] a dynamic orator, and a champion of the Almighty's cause, whose life was devoted to his brethren and who shared the tragic fate of six million Jewish victims of German bestiality in the most horrible *Hurban* of our history.

YOUTH

On the fourteenth of Heshvan, 5640 (October 31, 1879), in the city of Przemysl, Galicia, a son was born to Rabbi Nathan Lewin, the son-in-law of the community's rabbi, Rabbi Isaac Shmelkes, who, in 1875, had published the first part of his great work, *Bet Yitzhak* on *Shulhan Arukh Orah Hayyim*.

The author, in his introduction, declared that he issued *Bet Yitzhak* to establish a memorial to his only son, Rabbi Aharon, who, in 1871, had passed away in the prime of life. Rabbi Aharon had left behind Talmudic novellae and, on the day of his death, asked his father to publish them. These novellae, called *Minhat Aharon,* bear the evidence of fine scholarship.

Rabbi Yitzhak established more than a literary monument for his son. The new infant of his son-in-law was named Aaron in memory of the deceased son. This grandchild was trained to continue a Torah dynasty of several centuries.[2]

---

[1] My father's books: (1) *Davar be-itto* (Krakow, 1899), (2) *Mate Aharon* (Krakow, 1905), (3) *Birkhat Aharon* (Drohobycz, 1913), (4) *Ha-Drash ve-ha-Iyyun* on Genesis (Bilgoray, 1927), Exodus (Bilgoray, 1931), Leviticus (ib. 1937) on Numbers, part one (Bilgoray, 1939), (5) a book of responsa, *Avne Hafetz* (Bilgoray, 1934), and a huge collection of articles and addresses in several languages.

[2] The ancestry of Rabbi Yitzhak Shmelkes extended to Rabbi Eleazar Rokeah of Amsterdam, author of the *Tevuot Shor,* and to that of R. David Halevy, author of *Ture Zahav,* on his father's side; to the "Maharam of Lublin", the "Maharam of Padua", and the "Hakham Tzevi", on his mother's side. Rabbi Shmelkes was famous for his power of analysis and the depth of his reasoning.

The grandfather dedicated himself to Aaron's education. The child's father, Rabbi Nathan, his main teacher, later became rabbi of Rohatyn and Rzeszow-Reisha, and after the author's death, published the sixth part of the *Bet Yitzhak* with his own comments.

The entire community of Przemysl crowded into the main synagogue when the young lad became Bar Mitzvah and ascended the pulpit. They were spellbound, both by the content of his dissertation and his manner of delivery. Young Aaron soon assumed an important place among the *Gaon's* students, who astounded Galicia by their astuteness.

When, in 1895, Rabbi Shmelkes, the chief rabbi of Lwow (Lemberg), published the third part of *Bet Yitzhak,* the grandson, aged fifteen, compiled the index and added his own novellae. In the subsequent parts of that work, one may find the young scholar's copious annotations.

Aaron soon became an important rabbinical figure in Lwow, the capital of Galicia, then an *"Ir ve-em be-Israel"* (a mother city in Israel). Men of all kinds—scholar, writers, hassidim, "maskilim" (followers of modern "enlightenment"), government and municipal dignitaries, streamed to Rabbi Shmelkes' home.

The grandfather discussed everything with his grandson, whose preaching power developed. At the age of nineteen, he delivered a Passover sermon, including *Halakhah* and *Agadah,* before a large congregation in the Kovea Ittim Le-Torah Synagogue. The enthused listeners insisted that he publish it. Thus the book, *Davar be-itto,* was issued.

Once, when he and his grandfather addressed a large audience, Rabbi Yitzhak asked Solomon Buber, the famous editor of the Midrashim, for his opinion of his grandson's speech. He replied, "I shall respond with Scripture (Samuel 1, 18.7) *'Saul has smitten his thousands and David his tens of thousands'."* Rabbi Yitzhak laughed and said, "Be at ease, for you have put me at ease." He remembered this *bon mot* and repeated it many times, for the rising star of his beloved grandson gave him more satisfaction than anything else.

The latter did not content himself with his trophies in the field of Torah. With the consent of his grandfather, he learned the two languages of the area, German and Polish, soon mastering both. He began to write articles in Polish.

In 1902 he married Doba (Dora), the daughter of Mr. Eliash Hirsch Friedmann, widely known for his generosity, of Wieliczka, near Krakow. After his marriage, he resided for a while in the home of his father-in-law. There his children were born: a daughter, Priva (Pauline), and three sons, the present writer and his twin brothers, Samuel and Marcus. In 1904 he was called to Sambor, in Eastern Galicia, to the pulpit previously held by leading rabbis. On the Sabbath of *Parshat Hukkat* (the 12th of Tammuz 5664), he delivered his first sermon.

The Rabbinate in Sambor

The selection of the young rabbi astounded Galicia. It was unprecedented to have a man, not yet twenty-five years old, as the spiritual leader of a community of 10,000. A famous *Tzaddik*, Rabbi Ori Yolles, whose Hassidic followers numbered in the thousands, resided in Sambor. The head of its rabbinic court was Rabbi Yitzhak Trau, an old and great Talmudic scholar. All wondered how so young a rabbi could prevail in a city of such outstanding men. But they learned soon that the young rabbi had captured the scholars by his brilliance and charm. He gained Rabbi Yolles' confidence and the affection of the people because of his communal work. He was aided by the experience acquired in his grandfather's home, but had already attained the qualities necessary for a successful rabbi. His first sermon in Sambor, published as *Mateh Aharon* (1905), expressed his views. It was based on a passage in the *Midrash Tanhuma (Vayishlah)*: *Elijah is destined to deliver three things to Israel: the container of manna, the dish of oil, and the dish of water; some say also the staff of Aaron.* He expounded: "The rabbi's duties are characterized by these items. The container of manna symbolizes his charitable activities: Manna for the poor. The dish of oil stands for his educational activity as the teacher of the people, anointed with the oil of Torah. The dish of water represents his purifying them by showing them the proper way of life. Aaron's staff is the symbol of peace, to which every rabbi must aspire in his community."

He carried out this program not only in Sambor, but wherever he could. He was invited to preach in many cities. He once spoke in Yaroslav, and was subsequently elected rabbi of that community. However, Sambor would not allow him to leave; its *parnassium* decided to summon the community of Yaroslav to a

Din Torah. The rabbi decided to remain in his first community. He rejected also a call to the important congregation in Czernowitz, Bukovina. The community of Sambor quickly learned to appreciate him. At the elections for the municipal council he received the greatest number of votes. He was the moving spirit in all communal activity.

But this work did not interfere with his scholarship. He spent eight years preparing a major commentary, *Birkhat Aharon,* (Drohobycz, 1913), on the tractate *Berakhot,* which blazed new trails in the explanation of the Talmud. The book contained 310 complete essays on various subjects related to that tractate. In depth and method of analysis, it is modeled after the *Bet Yitzhak,* but excels in the organization of its material and in the lucidity of its style.

His father, the *Gaon* Rabbi Nathan of Rzeszow (Reisha), in the preface, quoted the Talmudic statement (*Baba Metzi'a,* 85a) : "If one is a scholar, and his son one, and his grandson also one, the Torah shall never depart from his descendants." The Tossafot states this condition for the promise: *"It shall not depart from your mouth, the mouth of your seed, and the mouth of the seed of your seed."* "The *Bet Yitzhak,*" continues Rabbi Nathan, "who loved you like a son, will be made happy in his holy place in the heavens above, by the Torah novellae that issue forth from your mouth, my beloved son." One achievement in the community of Sambor was the establishment of an *eruv* around the town. The underlying *halakhic* principles may be found in *Avne Hafetz,* (Resp. 20).

WORLD WAR I

About a year before the First World War, Galician Jewry was thrilled by the fact that the rabbi of Sambor was appointed Crown Councillor (*Kaiserlicher Rat*), by the Emperor of Austria.

This was the first time that any Galician rabbi had gained such recognition. The entire country saw the award as the Emperor's recognition of the young rabbi's abilities.

In 1914, soon after the outbreak of the war, the Russian army captured Galicia and the Jews fled westward. Tens of thousands of refugees arrived in Vienna and in other Austrian and Bohemian cities. Their economic and spiritual condition was very critical. To organize their religious life, the Austrian government appointed the rabbi of Sambor, who arrived in Vienna in September 1914, and was respectfully received. With indefatigable energy he organized the refugee rabbis and presented the claims of the wandering Jews to the authorities, who urged him to assume the supervision of displaced persons' camps in the provinces (Nikolsburg, Bruck, Pohrlitz, and Gaya). He devoted himself to his task, appointed *shohetim,* and built synagogues. The Galician Jews in Austria saw that someone was concerned with their welfare and their spirits soared.

The rescue of hundreds of rabbis and rabbinical students about to be drafted into the Austrian army was one of Rabbi Lewin's great accomplishments during this period; the Austrian government exempted all ordained students from the draft and recognized the authority of ten Galician rabbis.

A few months later, the Russian army was defeated and Galicia returned to Austrian rule. At the first opportunity, Rabbi Lewin returned to Sambor, with the scope of his activity ever widening. Frequently called to meetings in Lwow and Krakow, he was appointed to a central committee for the care of war orphans. In Sambor he erected two large asylums for them.

The date of the Austrian and German debacle approached rapidly. In October 1918, a new Poland arose, but the city of Sambor was in the war zone between Poland and the Ukraine. The Jews organized autonomous committees in all of eastern Galicia which replaced the old *Kehillot.* Rabbi Aaron Lewin was among the first to participate.

Poland eventually proved victorious, and Sambor and all of Galicia were included in its boundaries. Aaron Lewin, a master of the Polish language, found a new field of activity.

The frame of his accomplishments reached Warsaw. In 1920, he received word that the leaders of that community (Leibish Davidson, Shaya Rosenboim, and Shackna Avrech) wanted to offer him the pulpit of Warsaw, Poland's capital. But, because the legal status of the Warsaw rabbinate had not been clarified, it was impossible to elect a chief rabbi.

Ten years later, the Warsaw *parnassim* were again frustrated in their attempt to elect him their chief rabbi. By then, Rabbi Lewin already was the representative of Warsaw in Parliament.

THE FIRST ELECTION TO THE SEJM (THE POLISH PARLIAMENT)

Poland voted for its first parliament in 1918, when Eastern Galicia was in the hands of the Ukrainians. The second elections were scheduled for November 5, 1922, and the Jews of Sambor requested their beloved rabbi to represent them. About twenty other cities, along with Sambor, constituted the district. Rabbi Lewin submitted his name on the slate of the United Jewish Bloc and was elected to the Sejm.

New horizons now opened for him. He was appointed a member of the Sejm's cultural committee.

When, clad in the garb of an Orthodox Jew, he rose on the floor of the Sejm to demand justice for his people, his exceptional spiritual powers revealed themselves immediately. He was soon hailed as one of the leading orators. His speech for the abolition of capital punishment received particular attention. At its conclusion he quoted the Mishnah (Makkoth 7): "A Sanhedrin which executes one person in seven years is called destructive. Rabbi Eliezer ben Azariah says, 'One in seventy years'; Rabbi Tarfon and Rabbi Akiva say, 'Were we in the Sanhedrin, nobody would ever have been killed'." The Polish legislators had never known of these Talmudic thoughts. They were accustomed to anti-Semites like Lutoslavski heaping abuse on rabbinic literature. Now they heard a Jewish spiritual leader, in superb Polish, revealing its ethical level. That address left a deep impression on their minds and even Lutoslavski conceded that he was taken aback by its content and style. The Polish Jew-haters sensed that here was a man over whom they could have no control. Whenever Rabbi Lewin rose to the rostrum, an atmosphere of respect prevaded the auditorium.

The Jewish representatives frequently chose him to speak on behalf of their parliamentary faction, especially when the budget of the ministry of religion and education was being discussed.

His work in the Sejm was only a small part of his burdens. Delegations and individuals streamed to him from all over Poland. His residence in Warsaw was soon recognized as the central point of Polish Jewry, for rabbis, *Tzaddikim,* and communal leaders came and went, presenting their problems and soliciting his help.

According to the law, a member of Parliament could not intercede on behalf of an individual whose case had already reached the courts. Rabbi Lewin often disregarded this rule and when a Jew was in straits, hurried to his aid. His patriarchal appearance made a profound impression on high officials, and his command of the Polish language hypnotized them into compliance with his requests.

From Tuesday to Thursday, when the Sejm was in session, he would spend in Warsaw. Leaving Sambor for Warsaw on Monday evenings, he would arrive there on Tuesday morning, fifteen hours later. Thursday evening he left for home.

During the long hours of the trip he would study and write novellae. Members of parliament were entitled to travel first class, in special cars marked "for members of the Sejm only". In this adequate accommodation his book, *Ha-drash ve-ha-Iyyun,* came into being.

In his introduction to the first volume, he wrote:

"This work is particularly dear to me because I labored on it as I travelled, on the wings of transportation, from my home to the capitol in Warsaw, where I represented my brethren in Parliament. I thank God that with all my engagements in public affairs, which snatch sleep from my eyes and slumber from my eyelids (for the needs of Israel are many in these days, as our enemies are so numerous, and the Jewish representatives must stand in constant watch to protect our people), His grace did not abandon me and I was privileged to cull pearls from the words of our Sages whose souls repose in Eden, and to enjoy their sayings."

He worked not only in the train, but would put down his thoughts in his room in Warsaw, in the Sejm and in the reception rooms of various ministries and governmental offices.

He would concentrate on some Torah thoughts before each speech in Parliament. In one responsum in *Avne Hafetz* (Nr. 35) he writes:

"Last week I addressed Parliament in Warsaw, and spoke from painful knowledge about our desperate situation. The economic crisis that has currently engulfed the country, has hit every level of our people and left many desolate. May the Almighty have mercy on us and bring our sorrows to an end. Before I ascended the rostrum, I concentrated for a short while on Torah to beseech mercy for myself and those who sent me. Among the thoughts that flashed through my mind, I remembered the comment of Rabbi Moshe ben Habib in his book, *Kappot Temarim,* that he who blows the *Shofar* on Rosh Hashanah is not the emissary of the community but the emissary of the Almighty. When I returned home for the holy Sabbath, I decided that since the thought had come to me at a time when it had some symbolic significance, I would pursue it a bit further. And I shall record several thoughts that occurred to me, as I hurried on my way to return to a session of Parliament. . . ."

Agudat Israel

When, in 1912, the Agudat Israel was founded in Kattowitz, Rabbi Lewin was among the first to endorse this independent Orthodox organization. He greatly aided it in Eastern Galicia during its early years after the rebirth of Poland.

When Rabbi Moshe Eliahu Halpern of Lodz, its representative in the first Polish Sejm, passed away in 1920, a memorial meeting was held in the largest synagogue in Lwow. The two leaders of Agudat Israel, Rabbi Aaron Lewin of Sambor and Rabbi Meir Shapira of Gliniany, came there to mourn the loss and to impress the religious element in the country with the need of dynamic work. The eulogy was publicized throughout the country, and Galicia's religious Jewry began to awaken from its slumber.

Rabbi Lewin was the only Galician rabbi elected to the Sejm on November 5, 1922. (Rabbi Meir Shapira of Sambor was simultaneously elected in Congressional Poland). He contacted the Agudat Israel deputies elected in Warsaw, Lodz, and elsewhere, and they formed the Parliamentary Club of *Agudat Shlome Emune Israel* (the name, at that time, of Agudat Israel in Poland).

At the first *Knessiah Gedolah* (World Congress) convened in Vienna in Elul, he reported on the defense of *Shehitah* against anti-Semitic attacks in various countries. At the conclusion of the *Knessiah,* he was elected President of the Central Council of the Agudat Israel World Organization, which acted as the movement's conscience and legislature.

In his opening address to the second *Knessiah Gedolah* (1929), he referred to the slaughter of the Hebron martyrs and turned to the nations of the world with the cry: "How is it possible? Where are you, the powers of Europe and America? Why do you remain silent, nations of the universe, when the small people which gave you the Book of Books, the Bible, is slaughtered before your eyes? Why don't you extend us a helping hand? Know that if you do not aid us, our nation will rise of itself and rebuild its ruins, *'And the blood will be a sign for you on the houses'* (Exodus XII, 13): The spilt blood of our martyrs will be a sign to us to rebuild the destroyed houses in the Land of Israel!"

He compared Agudat Israel and its Torah leadership to *"a rainbow which is in a cloud on a rainy day—so is the vision of light around it a vision of God's glory."* (Ezekiel I, 28). At a time when atheism was increasing throughout the world, Agudat Israel appeared on our nation's horizon. *"And it shall be that when I bring a cloud on the earth, a rainbow shall be visible in the cloud . . ."* (Genesis IX, 14).

In his opening address at the third *Knessiah Gedolah* in 1937, he described the bitter plight of the people, especially due to Nazi cruelty: "The Jewish nation and race have been scoffed at, mocked, and debased. We, the chosen people, who stood at Mount Sinai and heard the commandments from God's mouth, have been trampled beneath the feet of the wicked and the cruel."

He quoted Rabbi Issiah Hurwitz, the author of *Shne Luhot Habrit:* "Israel is destined to recite *shirah* (a song) in the future, not only on the redemption that they will see with their own eyes, but on the redemption that is destined to come. *Don't* despair! Be strong and faithful of heart, those who have faith in God! Know, my people, that our enemies who believe that they can destroy us, God forbid, are completely mistaken. More wicked, more cruel, and mightier tyrants have on more than one occasion been arrayed against us, and God has always rescued us from their hands. *They* succumbed and collapsed and *we* arose and were inspired. Thus shall we also safely emerge from the jaws of the beasts of prey of our times, strengthened and purified, and a period of glory and prosperity will commence for our people." At that time, the partition of Palestine was being broached. Aaron Lewin inspired the delegates with his call to strengthen Torah, with the cry that became famous: *"Hadliku et haner!"* (Light the candle!) Then he continued:

"The Land of Israel today is the focal point of our nation's problems. Our eyes are turned to our land and soil. 'Our hearts are in the East and we are in the West.' At this moment when Jacob is a prey to his enemies and Jewish property is in the hands of looters, the building of our land is of utmost importance, for it is a ray of light penetrating our exile, breaking through the clouds of darkness. The hope for our own land is the only one that hovers over the chasm of despair that has gripped our camp.

"For Torah Jewry, Israel is not simply an aspiration or the materialization of a dream or a national ideal. Its rebuilding is one of the great principles of our faith, of the holiest commandments. Experience has shown us that spiritual power is stronger, more dynamic, than nationalistic impulses or ideals!

"Hundreds of years ago, before the word "Zion" became a motto to inspire the masses, many thousands of God-fearing individuals, from far and near, made their way to our Holy Land, although it was a place of constant danger. They travelled across deadly deserts to reach the Land, which is *before God's eyes every day of the year*. They considered themselves fortunate when they could embrace its stones and pour forth their hearts like water at the Wailing Wall. Who can say whether this vanguard of the Lord's army did not cause the land to remain ours? Who knows that it is not because of the prayers and tears of these pioneers before the Wailing Wall that we are privileged to see the Land of Israel at the beginning of its rebirth?"

He quoted Rabbi Yehuda Halevi, *"How can one find pleasure in eating and drinking while dogs drag your lions?"* "We must state now, once and for all, that the Land of Israel can only be built on the Torah transmitted to us at Sinai. Without it, its builders labor, and its guardians watch, in vain. The Sabbath and the education of children in the land of our forefathers must be based on the foundations of Torah. Under no circumstances can we be satisfied with a mere nationalistic education, language, and day of rest. God's perfect Torah must have unlimited sovereignty in our land."

The Rabbinate in Rzeszow (Reisha)

After several years, he became a semi-legendary figure. Every address in the Sejm won great applause, every appearance at a Jewish conference caused a spiritual uplifting. He became the people's favorite champion.

The community of Grodno sent him a rabbinical contract in 1926. But, almost at the same time, he was compelled to accept another pulpit, in Rzeszow (Reisha).

His acceptance of the Reisha pulpit was unique. His father, who had been its rabbi since 1904, passed away on the fifth day of Elul 5688 (1926). During the *Shivah* a delegation from the community appeared to request that he accept its pulpit. His reply was that before making any decision he must first know whether the people really wanted him. To ascertain that fact, a petition was placed in the communal offices and all those who desired the rabbi of Sambor to be elected rabbi of Reisha were invited to come and sign their names. Many thousands trooped to the offices to do so.

A delegation of the Reisha's *parnassim* brought the petition to Sambor. The rabbi still hesitated, until Marcus Eckstein, one of the influential Hassidic leaders in Galicia and for fifty years a leader in Rzeszow's affairs, urged: "Jewish law recognizes the right of *hazakkah* (succession). Hence, when a rabbi passes away, his son normally presents his claim to the father's post. This right of succession surely cannot be one-sided. In the name of the community of Reisha, I claim the right of succession— *hazakkah*—to the rabbi. The rabbinate of Reisha is not of rank lower than Sambor's, and I believe that the rabbi must not refuse this offer, for it will imply a derogation of his sainted father's honor."

"You have conquered me," replied Rabbi Lewin. He accepted on condition that the formal election be by popular vote (and not only by that of the *parnassim,* as was customary in Galicia). It was unanimous.

Reisha was a city of many scholars, a metropolis of central Galicia. Rabbi Nathan Lewin had captivated the hearts of the people by his scholarship and character. When Rabbi Aaron came to serve in Reisha, the honors extended to him were great, indeed. He was elected to the City Council. His addresses were major events in communal life.

Various Polish and other European communities extended calls to him, among them Frankfort-on-the-Main. In that city there still lived a member of the congregation which, in 1851, had elected Rabbi Samson Raphael Hirsch, previously rabbi of Nikolsburg, spiritual head of Moravia and also a member of parliament. An old *parnass* of Frankfort called on Rabbi Lewin to waive his seat in the Polish legislature and accept the spiritual leadership of Frankfort, as Rabbi Hirsch had done. The letter made a strong impression on Rabbi Lewin, but the Polish Jewry insisted on Rabbi Lewin's presence. Very reluctantly he rejected Frankfort's offer, brought to him by one of his dearest friends, Jacob Rosenheim.

ELECTION TO THE SEJM IN WARSAW IN 1930

His greatest personal triumph was his election to the Sejm in Warsaw in 1930. At the parliamentary elections of 1928, religous Jewry did not succeed in winning a single mandate (despite the fact that they polled about 200,000 votes in various districts). Polish Jewry again was disunited for the elections three years later. The struggle was principally in Warsaw and Lodz. The candidates were Yitzhak Gruenbaum on the Zionist slate, and, opposing him, Rabbi Aaron Lewin of Reisha, nominated by the Agudat Israel.

His address in Warsaw, Lodz, and other cities (he headed the slate in many districts) attracted tens of thousands of Jews who saw him as the paragon of a political leader, constantly concerned with his people's needs. He was elected to the Parliament in Warsaw, the capital of Poland, and reached the peak of his political career, because election on an independent ticket in Warsaw was like enthronement in the highest political position of Polish Jewry.

In his first address in the new Sejm, on December 16, 1930, he made it clear that he stood above all politics when the good name of Polish Jewry was at stake. After describing their bitter economic plight and making a powerful demand for governmental aid to Jewish education institutions, he touched upon a very painful subject. Representative Gruenbaum, in the previous Sejm, had not hesitated to accuse religious Jewry of supporting the oppressive Russian, Austrian, and German governments when Poland was divided among these countries. According to Gruenbaum, religious Jews accepted every government without showing any loyalty to their native Poland. Rabbi Lewin, in answering this terrible and unfounded charge, showed that Poland's religious Jews had always aided their government. He mentioned Rabbi Meisel's active participation in the revolt against the Russians in 1863 and the aid extended to Marshall Pilsudski's armies by religious Jewry. Finally he declared:

"I don't want to create any misunderstanding. I did not cite these facts for you to emphasize the loyalty of religious Jewry as contrasted to other segments of Polish Jewry. I shall not imitate Mr. Gruenbaum and use this rostrum to condemn our political antagonists. On the contrary, I maintain that all Jews living in Poland, regardless of their political affiliation and without exception, are loyal Polish citizens and are devoted to their country. I was, however, obliged to establish for the future historian the fact that the derogatory remarks about religious Jewry in the previous Sejm were incorrect. What pains us most is that this was done by one of our own nation's sons, who, instead of defending our interest from this parliamentary rostrum, hurled false accusations at us." (Minutes of the meeting of the Sejm, December 16, 1930, pg. 103).

Aware that the anti-Semites in the Sejm would eagerly welcome the spectacle of the Jews feuding with each other, Aaron Lewin decided to protect the honor of the entire Jewish nation. He did not want someone later to charge that although the religious Jews were loyal citizens, other Jews were enemies of the state. His declaration could not be clearer. *All* Jews fulfill their obligations to the state, *all* are loyal. This approach made an unusual impression on the Sejm and the entire country.

During the years 1930-1935 he was burdened with an extremely heavy load. He had to do the work that thirty-four Jewish Sejm representatives had done in 1922-1927. In 1930, Rabbi Lewin was the only one elected on the Orthodox slate and was registered in the Sejm as the independent representative of Agudat Israel. His two Agudist colleagues (Leib Mincberg and Asher Mendelsohn), who also entered the Sejm and Senate that year, were members of the Governmental Bloc and had to accept its discipline. Several other Jewish representatives organized themselves into the Jewish Club. Rabbi Lewin stood alone.

Enjoying immense prestige among the Polish members of the Sejm, he was elected a member of the committee whose primary task was the revision of the country's constitution.

But his major concern was the welfare of the Jewish people. On occasion he employed very strong words in his debates with the representatives of the Polish parties. When on March 16, 1931, the Sejm discussed the supply of corpses to the universities, he declared: "There is no power in the world that can force us to transgress even the minutest part of our religious laws, which our nation has carefully preserved for many generations and for which it has sacrificed all of its possessions, sacrifices unparalleled in human history.

"I urge the faculties and students of the universities to put an end to religious polemics. Let their zealousness be that of scholars to broaden knowledge and science that will quench the strange fires of religious hatreds which wanton persons have kindled."

But the flames of hatred were too strong. Jewish students in Polish universities suffered greatly from their Polish colleagues and early in the academic year 1931-32 the latter organized pogroms.

In Warsaw and Cracow, older Jews, together with Jewish students, were beaten in the streets. Rabbi Lewin, addressing the Sejm on November 7, 1931, stated:

"The terrible incidents that took place in the Warsaw and Cracow universities bring disgrace upon their good name. Is this the Polish intelligentsia of the future, destined eventually to supply the nation with its leaders, which now so brutally attacks its Jewish colleagues? . . . Repetition of such incidents in the universities must be prohibited. If these 'strong arm' men feel that they have excess energies, let them utilize them for worthwhile purposes, for the benefit of science and the state, and not against unarmed Jews."

Whenever the budget of the Ministry of Religion and Culture was discussed, Rabbi Lewin presented the demands of religious Jewry. The Polish legislators heard, for the first time, about *yeshivot* in Radin, Mir, Baranowich and Lublin. He described the wonderful spirit prevailing in these institutions and the idealistic figures, such as the "Hafetz Hayyim", who directed them. He spoke of the Beth Jacob Seminary in Cracow, of the Jewish communities in Poland and their characteristics, he defended the Sabbath in connection with Sunday "blue laws", declaring that to restrain Jews forcibly from working on Sundays, was a tragic injustice.

In the course of the debate on the nation's budget, he described the economic plight of Polish Jewry: "The Jewish merchants are on the brink of complete disaster. I would be bringing coals to Newcastle, were I to list all the troubles oppressing Jewish merchants. They have almost crushed them! Well-nigh total absence of credit, the high cost of money, and lack of faith in economic relations, have removed the foundations from under their feet. The excessive taxes have robbed them of their economic existence. The primary need in the area of the state's relations with the merchants is a fundamental change in the tax system and the remittance of old tax debts. The finance minister has informed the Sejm that the accumulated debts of delinquent taxes reach the figure of 1-2 billion zlotys. These debts cannot be collected and must be quickly obliterated so that a sword be removed from over the head of the tottering businessman and that vital confidence be restored. Every attempt to increase, by new monopolies, state inference with the national economy should be abandoned, because it hurts both the state and the merchants. It is in the best interest of the state to abolish the existing monopolies, especially the whiskey monopoly, which is causing a deficit to the country." (Minutes of the Sejm's meeting on February 4, 1932, page 70).

In the course of an address on the tax imposed on regular commercial transactions, he quoted statistics that astounded the Sejm. He showed that in one line of business three categories of merchants existed within the state: "The wealthiest paid a few pennies tax on their merchandise; the second group paid much more; and the third, the poorest, paid ten times as much as the wealthiest ones." How could the poor merchant survive with this kind of competition from the rich dealers? His question impressed itself strongly on the government and the tax burden was somewhat eased. But Rabbi Lewin did not cease his efforts. He continued to portray the agony of thousands of Jews.

The result was that official circles began to consider the presence of the rabbi in the Sejm as undesirable. The new election laws of 1935 gave the government a decisive vote in presenting the slates of candidates. (Local election boards, rather than the voters, set up the slates.) The tens of thousands of Jewish voters in Warsaw and Lodz could no longer determine their parliamentary representatives. When Prime Minister Slavek finally decided against Rabbi Lewin, the wishes of the masses who specifically desired his election were ignored. Slavek's dictatorial ink toppled him from the Sejm's rostrum in 1935.

THE LAST YEARS

Polish Jewry saw Rabbi Lewin as its leader, whether he sat in the Sejm or not, and all public matters were brought to him. During the last years before the Second World War, the esteem of the Sejm in the state decreased, for the representatives who had passed through the "needle's eye" of the electoral boards (this was the popular description of the process) lacked stature to react properly to the injustices perpetrated upon the masses.

When various problems, such as prohibition of ritual slaughter, arose during the years 1936-1939, the rabbinic leaders and the delegates in the Sejm called upon him, and he travelled to Warsaw to advise on what was to be done. Some of the letters of the "Hafetz Hayyim" published in the collection *Mikhtve Hafetz Hayyim* (New York, 1935), indicate that he consulted Rabbi Lewin on all pertinent matters. Rabbi Hayyim Ozer Grodzenski of Vilna did not undertake any important step without him. The

"Gerer Rebbe," A. M. Alter, brought to him his difficult questions (Rabbi Lewin's *Avne Hafetz* contains two important responsa from his pen).

The three Hassidic *rebbes* of Ger, Alexander and Sochatchev, who had the allegiance of the majority of the *parnassim* of the Lodz Jewish community, decided that the rabbi of Rzeszow should be elected the Chief Rabbi of Lodz because his presence in that community would greatly elevate the religious life in the entire country. It was to have taken place towards the end of 1939. But, suddenly the Second World War broke out.

A committee was founded in Poland to protect the Jewish community from the dangers of expanding Hitlerism. Aaron Lewin was elected to its presidium. At the beginning of 1939, the Jewish communal leaders decided to send a delegation to London, to discuss with Lord Winterton and other British officials problems pertaining to the emigration of Polish Jewry. Again Rabbi Lewin was a member of this delegation.

He utilized the little free time that he had from his public duties and trips to Warsaw, for the study of Torah. The years of 1936-1939 were the most fruitful in his *halakhic* work. He prepared his second volume of responsa. It was lost in the Nazi holocaust. He had completed his work, *Ha-drash ve ha-Iyyun,* on the five books of the Torah and the five scrolls. Only the first part of the fourth volume was published. The second part, already in print in Bilgoray, and the manuscripts on Deuteronomy and the scrolls, too, were destroyed.

THE DESTRUCTION

On Roth Hashanah of 5700 (1939) the war broke out. On the fifth day of the war, it was apparent that Nazi Germany would defeat Poland.

Rabbi Lewin knew the fate in store for him if he would fall into the hands of the Germans. He was on their blacklist as a member of the presidium of the anti-Hitler committee. He could not remain in his community, most of which had already fled eastward. He also turned eastward with his wife and two youngest sons, and arrived in Lwow, where his daughter, married to Dr. Abraham Blatt, resided. But it was impossbile to tarry in Lwow, for the Nazis were approaching the city. He reached the town of Kuty, close to the Rumanian border. When the Hassidic rabbi of

Kossow (in Rumania) learned that Rabbi Lewin was on the other side of the Polish-Rumanian border, he sent a special messenger to escort him. The border was on a bridge over the Dniester River. Rabbi Lewin reached the bridge but could not cross it. Meanwhile Soviet Russia had captured the eastern part of Poland and the immediate danger of death passed. Russia did not demand the bodies, but rather the souls, of the refugees.

Rabbi Lewin returned to Lwow and remained there three months. At the end of December 1939, he left the city to travel to the Polish-Lithuanian border, over which thousands of Jews then passed into Lithuania. He tried to cross, but was seized by the border guards and arrested. Here a remarkable thing occurred. His jail was in Radin, in the house of the "Hafetz Hayyim." The Russian staff encamped in Radin, where it dealt with the fate of the refugees. There his friend, Rabbi Israel Meyer Hacohen, had resided. The "Hafetz Hayyim," several years before his death, had planned to travel to Rzeszow to visit Rabbi Lewin, but he could not manage it. Nor did Rabbi Lewin succeed in reaching Radin during the life of the "Hafetz Hayyim", but now, when the *yeshivah* hall had been converted into a Russian jail, the leader of Polish Orthodoxy suddenly found himself in this house!

He was released after a short imprisonment. The Russian judges did not know this old man, among the hundreds of people on trial for wanting to cross the Lithuanian border. All were acquitted. The word soon spread among the residents of Radin that Rabbi Aaron Lewin was being detained in the city. Baruch Mordecai Senderowitz, the Hafetz Hayyim's secretary, recognized him, and he resided with him for awhile. The Jewish communists in Radin also heard of his presence and decided to spy on his every movement. After three weeks, a man was sent from Vilna to take Rabbi Lewin to the Lithuanian city. The spies, who were observing his house closely, signalled the Russian police, who pursued the carriage in which Rabbi Lewin and his wife were travelling.

In Radin, in a letter to his sons, he wrote:

"To the anguish of my heart, overflowing with pain and sadness, the second attempt also was a failure. Our latest misfortunes are many times greater than our earlier ones, for when we were already on our way and had covered some ground, we were overtaken by a group of cavalrymen. We were brought to the city, where all our possessions were taken from us. . . . It is very bitter to return to Lwow after all the hardships suffered during the last few weeks. . . . But I see that this is the Almighty's will and I accept all that has happened to me. I fortify myself with the hope that God will send forth universal redemption and I shall gain personal salvation, so that my fortunes will rise, because of my sainted forefathers and because of the many people for whom I have toiled since my early youth. For when alone, I see myself weak and broken, and *'If Thy Torah were not my delight, I would be lost in my plight.'* Thank God that even while I am here I have busied myself with Holy Writ and have written some papers on *Halakah* and *Agadah* . . . I hope to Almighty God that we shall be together with you again and that I shall be privileged together with your mother (who in piety and great dignity of soul accepts lovingly all that came upon us and whom I have learned to know even more during these terrible days, a pillar of support during these tribulations) to rejoice in your happiness and to see your success and greatness. I shall flourish because of you, and I will not be lonely and abandoned in my old age as I am now. May the Almighty have mercy on me and give me the strength and fortitude to bear all."

Rabbi Lewin travelled towards Lwow and remained in the border town of Lida. All sorts of rumors were spread. Not Lida but the city of Swieciany would be annexed by Lithuania. He went to Swieciany, and from there to the village of Ayducishki, to await border changes. In the meantime, new efforts were made to transport him to Vilna. But all was in vain. The border remained unchanged and to cross it at night without the proper documents was extremely difficult. He returned to Lwow in the month of Nissan 5700 (April, 1940).

After Passover, a wave of expulsions from Eastern Galicia to Siberia commenced. Once Russian soldiers ordered him and his wife out of their residence because he was supposed to be transported to Siberia. He waited in the streets of Lwow to be taken to the transportation center. Apparently, the Russians forgot about them and they returned to their house.

Days, weeks, and months, passed. His sons had meanwhile made their way from Vilna to Japan, where they obtained a Chilean passport for him. When the pasport reached Lwow, Rabbi Lewin attempted in vain to obtain an exit permit. Germany launched its attack on Soviet Russia, her soldiers entered Lwow on July 1, 1941, the sixth day of Tammuz, 5701.

On that day, his brother, Dr. Ezeckiel Lewin, on his way to plead with Archbishop Szeptycki to order the Ukranians to spare the Jews, was seized by German policemen and taken to the Brygidki jail.

There he met Rabbi Aaron. The German police had discovered their old enemy. They had dragged him, torturing him horribly on the way, to the jail. There the brothers were murdered on the same day.

Rabbi Aaron's fate was for a long time unknown. His wife and daughter, then in Lwow, did not know what had happened. When American Jewry heard that Rabbin Lewin had been arrested by the Germans, a determined series of efforts were made on his behalf. President Roosevelt and ex-President Hoover both were deeply interested. The Chilean government was urged to demand that the Germans release him, for he had a Chilean passport. The Jewish community in Buenos Aires elected him as their rabbi. The Argentine ambassador in Berlin demanded his release, but the German government replied that "it is impossible to release Rabbi Aaron Lewin currently."

These efforts were all in vain for Aaron Lewin was no longer alive.

His wife, Dora, the golden-hearted companion of his life, and his daughter, a brilliant scholar in French phonetics, survived him. But in August, 1942, a search was made by the Gestapo in the house in Lwow (Theodor Place No. 4), where a group of Jews were hiding in a "bunker". The Rebbetzin of Reisha was among those discovered. She was taken to the extermination camp of Belzetz. As she was seized, a young Jewess, of her own free will, joined the transport. It was Pauline, who did not want to be separated from her mother. Both went together to Belzetz, where on the twelfth of Elul, 5702, they died, sanctifying the Name of God.

Pauline's only daughter, Hadassah, a sweet girl of eleven years, was still kept in hiding among friends in the Aryan part of Lwow. Ultimately, the Nazi hellhounds seized the litle girl, recognized her as Jewish, and shot her. The work of destruction was accomplished with true German thoroughness.

No generation is orphaned if Menahem
belonged to it (Mekh. Bo)

MENAHEM ZIEMBA OF PRAGA
(1882-1943)

By Israel Elfenbein

MENAHEM ZIEMBA OF PRAGA

By ISRAEL ELFENBEIN

In the epic of the Warsaw Ghetto (1937-1947), men of faith, rather than statesmen, poets or philosophers, have written their names large for posterity. Their acts of daily heroism and martyrdom were manifest everywhere in the hours of great terror. This was true in large measure of the last three members of the Warsaw Rabbinical Council, the *Va'ad Harabbanim,* who guided the destiny of the community. Their names are recorded in golden letters in the annals of the Jews in Poland.

They were: the youngest member, David Szapiro,[1] the middle-aged, Samson Stockhammer,[2] and the senior, Reb Menahem Ziemba of Praga.

I. GAON IN HALAKHAH—CHAMPION OF RESISTANCE

Of the latter, recognized by his contemporaries as the "lion of the group" *(ari she 'be 'haburah),* we present this study, on the basis of his *halakhic* writings,[3] as well as of the first-hand data

---

[1]The only surviving member of the Warsaw rabbinical council, who was the son-in-law of Reb Hayyim Ychoshua Gutschechter, dean of the Rabbinate of Warsaw—*Zekan harabbonim.*

[2]And not Simon Stockhammer (correct the statements of Dr. Hillel Seidman, Dr. Philip Friedman, Samuel Nigger, and others).

[3]Some of his works are:

Zera Abraham (Warsaw 5680; New York, 5709)—responsa, bearing the name of his grandfather, Reb Abraham Ziemba, who was a disciple of Reb Isaac Meir of Gur. These *She'eloth u-Teshuvot* were directed to his learned contemporary and correspondent, Abraham Luftbier, the son-in-law of *Gaon* Meir Simhah of Dwinsk.

Gur Aryeh Yehudah (Warsaw, 5688)—responsa, bearing the name of his middle son, Judah, who had died at the age of 18 years.

Totsa'ot Hayyim (Warsaw, 5681)—bearing the name of his father-in-law, Hayyim Yeshaiah Zederbaum—is a compendium on the "39 categories of labor" prohibited on the Sabbath.

O'Tiot Porhot—select sayings of Ziemba.

She'elot u-Teshuvot Remaz—bearing the initials of the author's name, Reb Menahem Ziemba.

Mahzeh l'Melekh—Novellae on Maimonides' code, *Yad ha-Hazakah,* which won the award from the Warsaw *Va'ad ha-Kehillot.*

Menahem Yerusholayim—Novellae on the Talmud Yerushalmi, bearing his first name.

Novellae on the Talmud Babli and the *Shulhan Arukh* in four parts, were destroyed in the Warsaw ghetto fire.

obtained from some of his intimate contemporaries.[4] They are survivors of the Warsaw Ghetto—now residing in Fuerth, Bavaria; Haifa and Natanya, Israel; New York City, Chicago and Amityville,[5] New York. We interviewed and corresponded with, virtually anyone who might have anything of value to tell. We corrected a number of items offered by some of the diarists[6] of the Warsaw Ghetto. We hope that this study may provide ample data,[7] hitherto unavailable, on the Warsaw Ghetto—as gleaned from the *unpublished diary* of Streicher of Hitlerite Germany.

It was on a Tuesday, the third day of the week, the eighth of December 1942, in the ghetto of Warsaw. A specially urgent session of the remaining leaders had been convened at the office of the communal archives. Those present (statesmen, rabbis, educators, poets, novelists, journalists and philosophers) sat in dead silence, gripped by an over-riding sense of fear and helplessness, a forerunner of the horror that was to follow.

Historians, like Dr. Isaac Schipper and Dr. Emanuel Ringblum, lost control of their historical perspective. Educators, such as Brandstaedter and J. L. Orleans, found themselves divested of direction. It remained for a gentle, slender man of less than medium height, whose deepest yearning was for solitude, prayer and meditation in the Torah, to present a message that would warm the heart and lift the spirit of the entire group.

It was the *Gaon* Ziemba, the spokesman of the Warsaw rabbinate, who arose to utter words of simple faith:

---

[4]These survivors are:

Rabbi David Szapiro, of Julianastrasse 2, Fuerth, Bavaria; K. Shab'thai, Hebrew journalist of *D'var* in Israel; Mosheh Lest'ni—his *"shtub-mensh"*—of Natanya, Israel; and the two sons of his older brother, Avigdor Aryeh Ziemba—Rabbis Abraham and Isaac Ziemba of New York and Chicago, respectively. To all of these contemporaries we are, indeed, very grateful.

[5]Daniel Casen of Amityville, New York, formerly war correspondent of the Chicago Tribune, the proud owner of the *unpublished* "Tagebuch" of Streicher in the author's handwriting (Hurwitz). This horrible, historic document supplies hitherto unknown material about the murderous decisions against Polish Jews in the last days of the Warsaw ghetto.

[6]Such as: Hillel Seidman, Shmuel Nigger, Philip Friedman, and others.

[7]It is rather deplorable to find that the diarists of the Warsaw Ghetto devote a single paragraph of meager description to Ziemba. Even the heads of the "Yivo" archives, recognized as specialists in the period of the Warsaw Ghetto—hardly have any new material or information available which would be of value to a researcher.

"We all have one need in common. We require spiritual healing and Divine guidance. I would urge you all to turn to Him on High for help through the medium of Torah, with its perennial message of serenity and *bittahon* (implicit faith). We must discipline ourselves to His mercy and goodness. What one heart cannot bear alone a *minyan* of faithful hearts, in unison with our loving Father, can bear. His Divine guidance and protection is surely at hand. Our sacred lore teaches us that in the long run the inward attitude is more important than outward conditions."

"Let us, *rebbe,* pray that at least our health and food provisions hold out," interjected one of the leftist leaders.

"Oh, no!" corrected Reb Menahem, gently, but firmly. "Let us pray that the faith of our fathers holds out. 'What would you do if you were afraid?' a member of the royalty asked of a famous moralist. He replied, 'I would do what Joan of Arc advised King Charles of France to do: 'I would act as if I were not afraid.' "

To this advice, the *Gaon* added his own paraphrase of the words of the Psalmist:[8] "The way of the righteous, when faced by terror, is to exclaim with inward conviction: *'The Lord knoweth best'* (*Yode'a ha-Shem*)—whatever the Merciful doeth, it is for a good purpose, for the benefit of us mortals. But the way of the wicked is to assert cynically: 'There is no hope for you. Of necessity, you and the others must perish (using the Hebrew *tovad,* in the second person).' It is the verdict of history, that the world is built on moral foundations. In the long run, it is ill with the evil doer and well with the just."

With these words of the *Gaon,* the *Stimmung* changed. The atmosphere now became surcharged with expectancy; the meeting ended with the chant of *"Ani ma'amin b'viat ha Mashiah"*—"I believe in the accelerated advent of the redeemer—Messiah ben David." Thus, each one was wending his way back to his bunker, and Ziemba to his at 7 Kupiecka Street.

The magic of his personality, his character and spirit accounted for the fact that, although by nature gentle and meek and physically frail from early childhood, Menahem Ziemba since 1940 had occupied the center of gravity in both the spiritual and political scenes of the Warsaw community. His influence was felt in all spheres of communal life, although, as a matter of principle, he would never have used the title of 'Rov.' Indeed, all responsa and letters he signed as "Menahem Ziemba of Praga" or "Menahem, a member

---

[8] Ps. I, 6.

of the Council" (*Haber l'Va'ad*). For years, he strictly adhered to his principle not to accept any offer to serve the community in an official rabbinical capacity. He would rather support his family from the earnings derived from the wholesale metal business on 34 Targowa Street, in Praga.

Almost against his will, his prestige gradually extended far beyond the inner circles of the Warsaw ghetto. One would have to turn to the history of the Jews in medieval Spain to find a parallel for such vast influence wielded by a humble, but firm, man of the spirit.

His contemporaries of varied shades of opinion speak of him as an efficient leader of his people in the hour of its gravest crisis.

In all likelihood, it was his mastery of the Polish tongue, together with his boundless love of his people and a profound grasp of the international scene and his noble soul that combined to make him the perfect spokesman of his people before the Catholic hierarchy in Warsaw (and at times even before the Hitlerite government in Poland). These higher echelons could have overruled his verdicts affecting the welfare of his brethren. In reality, however, they rarely ran athwart his directives.

II—HIS PRAGMATIC APPROACH

The *Gaon's* success in his efforts in behalf of his people was due to the fact that whilst strictly conforming to the *Din Torah* in his private life, he was liberal in his relations to those of divergent schools of thought. His approach was pragmatic, rather than dogmatic. Never would he condemn those in the Warsaw ghetto who did not emulate the pattern of his life. From the very start, Reb Menahem was reconciled to the various trends of Jewish life in the community, though he would never be reconciled to heresy.

In his abundant works of goodwill, he never failed to take into account a rapidly changing world. Never would he excoriate "His Majesty's opposition groups". Thus, though from his earliest days he had been closely identified with Agudat Israel, serving as member of the presidium of its supreme Torah authority[9] and attending all their world conclaves,[9a] he never permitted himself to be involved in inter-party strife. He would term all such

---

[9]The *Moetzet Gedole ha-Torah.*
[9a]At the most successful one of 1923 in Vienna, I was privileged to chat with Ziemba, in the company of the sainted moralist, Hafetz Hayyim, at the home of the Schreiber family.

bickerings a waste the Jewish community could not afford. In fact, all his life he aimed to promote fellowship and mutual understanding. And while he had issued a special call to dispel aggressive designs within the Warsaw ghetto and to work for closer cooperation and united strength, he also emphasized the danger of confusing unity with uniformity and would never permit the surrender of basic principles and ideals. The *Gaon* retained an authoritative, though not authoritarian, grip on all aspects of social and communal life by the sheer power of his personality and by his sagacity—the recognized spokesman of Torah and *K'lal Yisrael.* Even his consistent critics (in the ranks of radical Zionists and the extreme leftist circles) looked up to him as a fairminded and considerate opponent.

Thus, practically all parties had united in urging Ziemba to accept the office of membership in the Warsaw rabbinate. As early as 1932, we are reliably informed, such leaders as Dr. Gottlieb and Simhah Petrushka strongly favored his candidacy for the high office as head of the Warsaw Rabbinical Council (*Zwiazek Rabbina Ortodoksa*). This honor he had not sought and for a number of years consistently rejected, until the radical change in the economic status of Polish Jewry had affected his metal trade. Then the *Gaon,* against his better judgment, was forced to permit himself to be drafted for the high office. It marked a new chapter in his life as spokesman for his community. He discharged his new duties understandingly and successfully. Apparently, his warmth of heart, his compassion for the "underdog", and the love of his people, aided by an innate sense of humor, joined to give his presence rare dramatic force. Neither his aloneness of spirit and a ceaseless longing for concentrated study of Torah by day and by night, nor his craving for intimate communion with the Divine in the silence of prayer and meditation, would ever dull the impact of the *Gaon* upon the many whom he would continue to meet and encourage to carry on against all odds.

III—His New Approach to "Kiddush Hashem" Concept

The *Gaon's* attitude manifested itself in his work during normal times. It was exhibited at its best in the moments of the great terror, which brought in its wake the liquidation of the Warsaw ghetto. It spelled a new approach to the concept of *Kiddush ha-Shem,* self-immolation for the sanctification of the Divine Name.

To him the true meaning of this sublime ideal changed with the needs of the times and the temper of the age. It is neither to be evoked as a fixed formula or a stereotyped and static concept. It is born anew with every act of supreme fulfillment. Our appreciation of its glory grows with our experience. It is an act of wedding the ephemeral to the enduring. To paraphrase the thought of a medieval moralist and mystic: *"Kiddush ha-Shem* is the reaching out to the highest point of eternity in the flux of temporality." Out of the darkness of the hour comes a voice that discloses the ineffable in man. It helps us to bear the heaviest burdens and leaves in its wake neither regrets nor frustrations. That divine voice is not utterly silent in our age. There are many ways in which the Eternal communicates with us mortals and transplants us into the realm of the immortal. The soul of man is ever in need of consecration. When we are gasping with despair, when science and art have failed to save us from a sense of utter futility, then the faith of our fathers shows us the path of hope—the circuitous ways towards the accelerated steps of the Messiah. It makes us realize the tremendous implications of *Kiddush ha-Shem,* with its emphasis upon the divine dignity of human personality and the supremacy of the Jew, impervious to outward conditions. It gives us the assurance that the intimacy and compassion of our loving Father is near at hand and that we are destined to prevail over all evil.

With the *Gaon* this approach was not an abstract thought, but an integral part of his personal experience and a product of the times. It enabled him to react consistently and to influence others by his example.

IV—The Memorable Session of January 14, 1943

A session of the communal leaders was convened in the Warsaw archives at short notice on January 14, 1943. Its primary objective was to decide on the most propitious directive to be followed in the hour of gravest peril. "We all sense that catastrophe is near at hand," exclaimed A. G. Friedenson with great emotion. "The very atmosphere is saturated with some explosive, that may be hurled at us with terrible momentum, like a bombshell. But we are at a loss to know its exact nature. What should be the most effective *modus operandi* for us to pursue?"

Reb Menahem rose to the occasion: "Of necessity, we must resist the enemy on all fronts. . . . We shall no longer heed his instructions. Henceforth we must refuse to wend our way to the 'Umschlag-platz,' which is but a blind and a snare—a veritable stepping-stone on the road to mass annihilation. . . . Had we lived up to our presumed status of a *'people endowed with wisdom and understanding,'*[10] we would have discerned *ab initio* the enemy's plot to destroy us as a whole, root and branch, and would have put into operation all media of information in order to arouse the conscience of the world. As it is now, we have no choice but to resist. We are prohibited by Jewish law from betraying others, nor may we deliver ourselves into the hands of the arch-enemy. . . . Our much-vaunted prudence—not to be identified with genuine wisdom and true understanding—blurred our vision and turned out to be more devastating than folly and stupidity. To paraphrase the words of our Sages, 'Korah of old accentuated his innate aptitude for prudence to such an extent, that it blurred his vision and, in the end, it was his folly that brought about his ultimate doom.' "[11]

This reply to Friedenson's inquiry, spoken by Ziemba earnestly, softly, and almost with embarrassment, aroused a heated debate on the part of some of the leading participants. A semblance of order was restored, when Reb Menahem continued to speak with the authority of a *Halakhist* and uttered these noble words on the varied ways of approaching self-sanctification. A hush permeated the entire assembly hall, as he said: "Sanctification of the Divine Name manifests itself in varied ways. Indeed, its special form is a product of the times we live in. Under the sway of the first Crusade, at the end of the eleventh century, *Halakhah*—as an echo of political events of the times—had determined one way of reacting to the distress of the Franco-German Jews, whereas in the middle of the twentieth century, during the onrushing liquidation of the Jews in Poland, *Halakhah* prompts us to react in an entirely different manner. In the past, during religious persecutions, we were required by the law 'to give up our lives even for the least essential practice.'[12] In the present, however, when we are

---

[10]Deut.
[11]Tanh. Korah V.
[12]Tor. Shabb. XVI, 17.

faced by an arch foe, whose unparalleled ruthlessness and total annihilation purposes know no bounds, *Halakhah* demands that we fight and resist to the very end with unequaled determination and valor for the sake of the sanctification of the Divine Name."[13]

At once all debates ended. The *Gaon* of Praga had the final say. The *Pesak-Din* of the Warsaw *Bet-Din,* issued in 1943, buttressed by an earlier *Halakhah* verdict, in 1161, from the Fustat-Cairo *Bet-Din* of Maimonides, was unanimously accepted by Polish Jewry. *Kiddush ha-Shem* is more than a free-will offering of the select few alone. It is the paramount duty and a *Halakhah P'sukah* (clear decision) incumbent upon all of us.

V—FINAL SESSION WITH THE CATHOLIC HIERARCHY

Thus the historic struggle of resistance to the very end for a supreme religious cause (*Milhemet Mitzvah*)—[in contradistinction to a war for secular and political causes alone (*Milhemet Hareshut*)]—was enacted. It was pursued vigorously by the last three members of the Warsaw Rabbinical Council.

Suddenly, on the morning of April 19, 1943, Menahem Ziemba, together with his younger colleagues, Samson Stockhammer and David Szapiro, were summoned before the higher echelons of the Church authorities. When they reached the headquarters of the Catholic hierarchy, they were placed in an antechamber. There they were presented with the following ultimatum: "The dignitaries of the Roman Catholic Church have decided to save your lives, provided you three leave the Warsaw ghetto within twenty-four hours. At the lapse of this period, we, the representatives of His Holiness, shall no longer be responsible for the safety of your lives. Your fate will be that of your wretched people. You are given one hour to deliberate upon this final offer. The ultimate choice rests with you—to be or not to be."

In this ante-death chamber—so labelled by Samson Stockhammer—a dramatic silence had ensued, which gnawed at their burdened and heavy-laden hearts for quite a while. No one either moved or dared speak. Suddenly Rabbi David Szapiro arose to utter these memorable words: "We—the teachers and exhorters of our people—simply cannot abandon our wretched brethren on the 'last mile.' Truly, we cannot help them any longer materially.

---

[13]Cp. Maim., Teshubot ed. Leipzig 1859 II 14 b, c; J. Q. R. XIII 5-39.

But we are commissioned by Him on High to be near them and not to abandon them. This act of grace will serve as a 'balm of Gilead' to fortify their courage and warm their hearts and lift their spirits. We have no other choice but to reject the offer of the clergy with no regrets."

Thus spoke the youngest member of the council of three. All sobbed with relief, that they had withstood temptation and in a terrible dilemma had found the right solution.

Each of them was destined to meet his specific fate at a different time and place. Samson Stockhammer, originally an inmate of the Budzin concentration camp, twenty-six miles from Lublin, was killed by an American bombshell two days prior to V-E Day, in Schwartzfeld camps. David Szapiro alone wears "the ghastly crown of the last rabbi of the Warsaw ghetto." He is still among the living. To this very day he serves as the shepherd of his flock in the community of Fuerth, Bavaria, a living witness of the Warsaw ghetto.

Menahem Ziemba, we are reliably informed, was privileged to officiate on the first Passover Seder night, at his bunker on 7 Kupietska Street, in the company of only one of his daughters, Rosa Miriam, and of some nephews and nieces. In the midst of his persistent clarion-call for resistance—just before the door was opened for the symbolic entrance of the prophet Elijah—he uttered these last words of faith and admonition to the younger leaders of the resistance movement: "On this Seder night of watchfulness, we remember with reverence and love the blameless men and women and little ones, who perished at the hands of a tyrant, more wicked than the Pharoah of old who had enslaved our fathers in Egypt. *'Come,'* said he to his minions, *'let us cut them off from being a people, that the name of Israel may be remembered no more.'*[14] On this, the first day of national liberation, rise ye up as the remnant in the Warsaw ghetto against the adversary for the sanctification of the Divine Name. Do not permit yourselves to be divided from within. Let not brother turn against brother. In the end, united action will bring comprehensive redemption to Israel throughout the world."

And all present at the Seder lifted their voices in unison, chanting their song of faith in the advent of the *Messiah ben David* —the song of the martyrs in the ghetto and liquidation-camps.

[14]Ps. LXXXIII, 5.

VI—THE MARTYRDOM OF ZIEMBA AND HIS FAMILY

The festival of freedom in the company of relatives and friends was cruelly marred on Sabbath afternoon, the fifth day of Passover in 1943, when, at 4:10 P. M., Ziemba was killed by a Nazi while crossing Kupieca Street. On Sunday, the 20th day of Nisan 5703 [after having been immersed in compliance with the rigid *Taharah* practice of the Hassidim of Gur], the remnants of the Ziemba household brought Reb Menahem to temporary burial in the courtyard on 4 Kupieca Street near his home.

Nearly all his children and grandchildren met a martyr's death in the liquidation camps of Treblinky and Maidanek during the months of Elul-Tishre of 1942.

In the camp of Treblinky his wife Mindele, together with her two unmarried daughters, Leah and Debby Rachel, died in the gas chambers. There, too, Menahem had lost his married daughter, Hannah, together with her husband (Rabbi Samuel Leib ben David Baer,[15] who had served as member of the Warsaw *Bet Din*) and their two children, Yankele and Sarah.

In the camp of Maidanek perished his unmarried son, the prodigy, Aaron Naphtali Ziemba, and his oldest son, Simeon Eleazar, together with his wife, Pessie Yokhebed Rothblatt, and their five children, Handel Leah, Hanoah Heneh, Pinkhos, Leibel, and Rebecca. There, too, were killed his daughter, Rosa Miriam, and her husband, Rabbi Israel Weidenfeld. His son, Judah Ziemba, had died a natural death in 1926, at the age of 18. To his memory Reb Menahem dedicated a volume of his responsa, bearing the title *Gur Aryeh Yehudah* (Warsaw, 1927).

VII—ZIEMBA—GAON IN HALAKHAH

Reb Menahem, while ever active in communal endeavor, was by nature and predilection primarily a devotee of Torah, which he studied in solitude at night. To him the study of Torah in times of trial and tribulation had always been an act of faith and a source of moral strength. He was wont to repeat the words of Maimonides: "The life of the scholars and students without the study of Torah is tantamount to experiencing a lingering death."

---

[15]Correct accordingly Zera Abraham, Introduction p. 1.

His Method of Study

In his responsa and other *halakhic* works, he presents the subject exhaustively and avoids repetition and rhetorical language. In the study of both Talmudim, as well as of the Rambam, he did not altogether avoid the use of the pilpulistic method (in line with the long-established tradition of the Warsaw school of casuists). In the main, however, the *Gaon* developed in the course of time the analytical method of the Vilna and Volozin schools of learning. This he achieved through close contact with such giants of the intellect as Reb Hayyim Brisker and Reb Meir Simhah Hacohen of Dvinsk. This fact alone may account for his success in reducing most of the *halakhot* to their component parts.[16] Again, in his compendium on the thirty-nine categories of labor [prohibited by law on the Sabbath], he opened new horizons for the student of *Halakhah,* occasionally plumbing the very depths of the Talmudic text.[17]

Some of his contemporaries, such as the *Gaon* of Dvinsk and others, speak of Ziemba as a consummate master of *Halakhah,* who was endowed with the versatility and expertness of Reb Joseph Rosen of Dvinsk (the *Gaon* of Rogatchov), the profundity of the *Gaon* of Sochatchov, the ingenuity and pungency of Reb Meir of Gur (author of *Hiddusheh La-RIM*), the casuistic subtley of Reb Isaac Shmelkes of Lemberg, and the creativity of Reb Joseph Engel.

VIII—THE LIFE OF ZIEMBA—THE MAN

He was born in August, 1882, in Praga, the suburb of Warsaw. There his father, Elazar Lippa, and his mother, Hannah, eked out a meager livelihood from retail merchandising. From early childhood he was destined for greatness. He received a comprehensive training from Abraham Ziemba, his grandfather, himself a great disciple of Isaac Meir of Gur. Menahem married at an early age Mindele, the daughter of Hayyim Isaiah Zederbaum of Praga, who had amassed great wealth in the wholesale metal trade. The experience of the members of the Zederbaum household in the metal industry had enabled Mindele to conduct her own establishment in the iron trade on 34 Targowa Street in Praga for a period of well-nigh thirty years. Her commercial success enabled Reb Menahem to continue his advanced studies in both Talmudim and in the works of the Rambam.

---

[16]Cp. ib. p. 33-53.
[17]*Totzaot Hayyim,* 9, 16, 22.

Ziemba's Sense of Humor

Menahem, in a humorous vein, was wont to repeat: "My father-in-law, Reb Hayyim Zederbaum, must have invested at least 50,000 Polish zlotys on Menahem, to have him moulded into a perfect instrument. But, what a pity! The value he actually received in return for his investment is rather questionable."

The *Gaon* proved to be a natural wit on numerous occasions. He would admonish litigants who appeared before him at the *Bet Din*: "I would like you to realize that I am able to drink strong tea with its pure essence, not watered down in the brew." But he could be severe enough. When some carping critic referred to a member of the Warsaw rabbinate in derogatory terms, Menahem answered: "My friend, the Warsaw rabbinate as a whole is definitely above suspicion, irrespective of the questionable character of one of its individual constituents. The council as a body is reputed for Torah, wisdom, fear of Heaven, and unsullied character. They would never deviate from justice for lust for money."

His Ethical Personality

His conduct was one of austerity by precept and example. In no way, however, would it divest him of grace in dealing with his fellow men. It may not be amiss to quote some specimens of his sayings:

"Be careful not to snarl at life and people. The world today may be out of joint. Human misery may be appalling, but do not succumb to self-pity and hysteria."

"Keep thyself from everything that even appears ugly." He consistently refused to look at those daily Polish and German newspapers that plastered the likeness of Adolph Hitler on their front page, lest he himself become tainted with the evil machinations of this arch-protagonist of destruction and thereby have his vision blurred by just glancing at them.

IX. Summary

The serenity and lofty spirituality of Menahem Ziemba, and his supreme work during the last days of the Warsaw Ghetto are recorded in indelible letters in the annals of our people.

The synthesis of *Gaon* and champion, saint and martyr, in the harmonious personality of Reb Menahem Ziemba is as unique as it is precious beyond words.

ISAAC BREUER

(1882-1946)

By Salomon Ehrmann

(translated by Hebe R. Mayer-Bentwich, from the German)

ISAAC BREUER

By Salomon Ehrmann

If a future historian with sufficient perspective were to attempt to comprehend the events of Jewish history in the last 150 years—approximately from Mendelssohn to the establishment of the State of Israel—and to appraise their seemingly so varied and disconnected aspects, the following bold outlines of a picture might result: In the train of Jewish emancipation, the French Revolution opened up, at first in the West, and gradually throughout the Jewish ghettoes, the whole hitherto unrevealed wealth of European culture. In the struggle of ideas which ensued between this and the old Jewish national culture based on the recognition of God and of the Torah given on Sinai, the latter was seriously threatened. The ideal of humanism, the free individual, as well as the enticing vistas opened up by a spectacular development in natural science, the materialistic conception of life, the tearing down of the barriers between Jewish and non-Jewish citizenship—all these stood out in sharp contrast to a Judaism which was not only the spiritual banner-bearer of belief in God and the ideal conception of life, but which also made an absolute claim on the Jewish individual's practical life in all his undertakings from the cradle to the grave.

The first result of this schism was a mass secession from Judaism—by way of baptism or mixed marriage. One of these baptized Jews coined the apt expression of the certificate of baptism being "the ticket of admission to European culture".

Leaders of the so-called "Reform Movement" thought to counteract the process of disintegration threatening Judaism by a basic reduction of Jewish religious *mitzvot*. Vital traditions were abrogated, all references to the Messiah and to Zion were expurgated from the prayer-book: all means were tried to make of the Jew a citizen without an individuality of his own and without a land of his own; a mimicry with a hidden private appendage of a separate religiosity. The openly admitted aim was an assimilation as complete as possible to the non-Jewish environment. This attempt at an adjustment of the two cultures, lasting over a period of three to four generations, ultimately failed not only on account of its inherent falsity, but mainly because of the growing anti-

Semitic movement which hit the assimilated Jew all the harder for his having done all in his might—barring the renunciation of Judaism—to avoid any friction with his environment.

Thus there set in a new development in the interpretation of Hegel's law of thesis and antithesis which can best be described by the term of *counter-assimilation*. Assimilation no longer indicated, as hitherto, an approximation of Judaism to the non-Jewish culture, but a conscious approximation of the latter to the undiluted, uncompromising Jewish tradition which had merged from ideal into reality since the revelation on Sinai. Whereas hitherto the spiritual life of the non-Jew had been adopted as the criterion for Judaism, the Jewish conception of truth was taken by the counter-assimilationists as the criterion for the determining of what factors in the general cultural life could safely be incorporated into Judaism without concession of any kind. It is true that after decades of estrangement, large circles had lost all knowledge of the Jewish criterion. They saw in Judaism nothing more than a people's national union to which they proudly belonged and, by virtue of which pride, they refused to term themselves *"Weltbuerger"* (world citizens) or adherents of any other nation. Actually their being Jewish resolved itself into a unity of being but not into a unity of duty. But the inalienable one-ness of the Jewish *"Sein"* (Jewishness—the Jewish Being) united with such elements of European culture as did not conflict with Jewish duties, presents the characteristic trait of the counter-assimilation introduced and established by Rabbi Hirsch of blessed memory. Therewith was initiated a new epoch of revival of the Torah. The task was immense: The first object was to overcome the ignorance of Jewish ideals in which a whole generation had grown up. The full armor of modern education had to be mobilized to reinstate the Jewish religion with the incorporation of all that was true, noble and good in European culture. A strong conviction was needed to combat the widely prevailing adulteration and levelling of Jewish conceptions in communities and organizations and to substitute better ones in their place. In this conflict it was important to give clear and definite indication that the attack was on un-Jewish principles but in no way on individuals. It was further a matter of bringing to bear against the superficiality of a materialistic view of life the whole armory of a fundamental, philosophic schooling. Finally, it was essential that the peculiar character of the Jewish people as God's people and of the Jewish land as God's land, should be displayed in a light so clear and unequivocal as to baffle all tendencies of secularisation. An increasing number of distinguished personalities were continuously engaged, with more or less success, in the attempt to tackle the aspects of the problem. But it was vouchsafed to few to follow consciously in Rabbi Hirsch's footsteps in all the new paths that he had mapped out. One of the most outstanding figures among these pioneers breaking ground out of the ghetto, across the 20th century to the threshold of the Jewish State, was Isaac Breuer.

I.

It is not easy to introduce to a wide circle of readers this religious philosopher and Jewish leader. The perspective for a historical appreciation is not yet obtainable in matter of either time or material. As regards time, although more than a decade has passed since his death on the 13th of Menachem Av 5706 (1946), two of his most mature works were published only after his death and four manuscripts are still unprinted. As regards matter, it is yet too early to estimate to the full the extent of his influence. Isaac Breuer set the stamp of his philosophy on the oncoming generation in the *Golah* and in Israel, but only now is the fruit of the seed which he scattered gradually maturing. The attempt made here to draw a picture of the great Jew and of the spiritual treasures revealed in his works, is due to an extraordinary "accident"—in so far as such a term is applicable to a Jewish train of thought. Among the unpublished writings of Isaac Breuer is the manuscript of an autobiography, *Mein Weg,* of over 150 typed pages, on which this study is based, whence many quotations are given literally. The story of the development of his thought—given with strict discrimination between subjective and objective aspects, the account of what he aimed at and only partially attained, is a moving testimony to that profound self-scrutiny to which the author submitted himself again and again to establish whether or not he had moved a hair's breadth from the tradition sacred to him of Jewish philosophy and the Jewish view of life which had been transmitted to him from his ancestors.

YOUTH

Isaac Breuer, son of Rabbi Salomon Breuer, and grandson, on his mother's side, of Samson Raphael Hirsch, was born in Pápa

(Hungary) on the 10th Elul 5642 (1882). At eight years of age, he came to Frankfort-on-Main, where his father had been appointed rabbi of the *Religionsgesellschaft* (the famous Separatist community established by his grandfather). After graduation at the Jewish *Realschule* (secondary school) he entered a *yeshivah* at the age of fourteen. He had already received a thorough grounding in Talmudic knowledge from private teachers, so that on entering the *yeshivah* he was able to follow the *Shiurim* (the lectures) with full understanding. The Talmudic training which he imbibed in this *yeshivah* was of determining significance for the rest of his life. We quote a passage from the above-mentioned manuscript on the method of teaching which characterized it:

"Down to the present day my ambition is still to master a page of the Talmud—literally to conquer it with my modest abilities, by the same method as that which I followed so many years in deep admiration. For my father always studied with his pupils page for page (*"am Blatt"*). The *Gaon* never presented foregone conclusions; he never confined himself to those passages on which he—with his fertile genius—really had some new light to shed. The aim of his whole method of teaching was that the pupils should learn how to 'learn,' how to tackle the given page, how to extract the *shitot* (various principles or basic attitudes) by thorough examination of sentence for sentence, word for word in the text and in Rashi's commentary—how to approach the *Rishonim* (commentators before 1500 C. E.) and how, finally, to evaluate the *Aharonim* (the later ones). This was for me the perfect pattern of real Jewish scholarly approach, real Jewish criticism, and as such, it remains with me as model even after coming under the influence of non-Jewish scholarly method. Up to today I can 'learn' in no other way than the way he taught me.

"Father made no distinction between the *Halakhic* (preceptive) and *Agadic* (non-preceptive) sections of the Talmud. The habit of skipping over the latter, of relegating them to the private industry of his pupils or of treating them in a less scholarly manner, was foreign to him. In the *Halakhic* section he omitted no opportunity of touching on *Weltanschauung* in general, of referring to the principle involved, of teaching the fear of God, of strengthening belief in the truth of tradition and even, with a moving smile, of touching on problems of the day.

"Perhaps it was my life's good fortune that Judaism was presented to me from the outset in the objectivity of the Talmud, which can certainly not be looked upon as merely a work of religious edification and from which nothing is further removed than the cadging of disciples or the eliciting of a 'Placet' for assentient conviction. It presents Judaism much more as a spiritual phenomenon—as the revealed national privilege of the Jewish people—assuming God's existence, His creation, His revelation, His kingdom, to which Abraham's descendants became attached and which bound them forever to the Land—all these national-historical facts being unassailably drawn into the living experience of the nation itself. The Talmud presents this privilege, analyzes it and endeavors to prove it by its consequences and in its relations to practical life, so that the allegiance of the nation and its adherents may absorb the whole content of the Divine privilege and manifest it. The revelation of this national privilege of the Talmud from which it emanated, proved my mainstay and support on the road to God."

The train of thought revealed in this passage was analyzed and developed in one of the fundamental literary productions of Isaac Breuer, *Lehre, Gesetz und Nation* (Doctrine, Law, and Nation), a critical-historical investigation into the essence of Judaism. Throughout his life he remained true to his love of the Talmud. In Frankfort, and later in Jerusalem, he "stole the time" to give a daily *Shiur*—a Talmudic lecture—to a large circle of listeners. A few months before his death he stated that none of his literary and political activities seemed to him of such importance and none gave him such inner satisfaction as his daily *Shiur* on the Talmud and the results of his Talmudic studies.

II.

The second decisive factor in the spiritual development of Breuer was his absorption in the works of Rabbi Samson Raphael Hirsch. They became his criteria for the general conception, the main lines of which have been set out above, and also for his whole Jewish political activity which admitted of no concession to pact-making of any kind with un-Jewish communities or organizations. With clear vision he brought together the philosophies of his grandfather and his father to produce a stupendous whole. They had indicated two different paths—the path of the Torah to the world and the path of the world to the Torah: these two ways became one in the life of Breuer, the grandson and son. He looked upon the world with all its dazzling and confusing phenomena from the exclusive vantage point of the Torah: in his vision he saw the world in its incredible unity. And on the other hand, he drew the whole cosmos into the magic circle of the Torah.

III.

The reader of Breuer's works, which extend over nearly four decades and appear in an incxhaustible variety of literary forms, is arrested by the single-minded purposefulness of his life's work. From his autobiography it can clearly be seen that the basic ideas of his religious-philosophical works, *Lehre, Gesetz und Nation, Messiasspuren* (Traces of the Messiah), *Wegzeichen* (Signs of the Way), *Elijahu, Die Welt als Schoepfung und Natur* (The World as Creation and Nature), *Elisha,* and *Der Neue Kusari (The New Kuzari)*, has been fully revealed to the author in his young years as a university student. No better or more concise résumé of the works can therefore be formulated than the account of his intellectual development in his student days given by Breuer himself. This is a unique monument to the remoulding and independent adjustment of a profane field of knowledge to fit into the sphere of innately Jewish thought and purpose.

When Breuer left the *yeshivah,* having taken his matriculation (college entrance) as an external student, he continued his studies at the Universities of Strasbourg, Berlin and Giessen, concentrating on philosophy, particularly Kantian, general history and jurisprudence, the study of which he pursued with the greatest zeal. Acquiring of the subject matter was, for Breuer, only the first step. He proceeded to digest the newly gained knowledge in a ceaseless effort to bring it into line with the Jewish view of life and philosophy which he had absorbed from his home environment and from the *yeshivah.* To quote from his autobiography:

Philosophy

"My main interest was in Kantian philosophy. Lectures on this subject afforded me but little help. I got to know Kant by sheer hard work. First of all, I set out to read him myself and to apply to him as much mental effort as I was used to reserving for a difficult passage of the *Maharsha* (a classic commentary on the Talmud) ; and that is how I mastered 'my Kant.' It is my deep conviction that the God and King of Israel sends enlightened men among the nations from time to time, called and destined to play a part in Jewish 'Meta-history' and to exert a healthy influence on it. Not only Nebuchadnezzar and Titus were staves in God's hands—Cyrus also was one of God's anointed. Gutenberg did wonders for the preservation and dissemination of the oral law.

And when the hour of great controversies struck, when the Messianic time broke upon the world, in which Israel, under the start of social and national emancipation, had to protect herself against the pressures of the outside world—when everything depended upon her holding her own in the face of a thousand physical and spiritual oppressions—God caused to rise among the nations the exceptional man Kant, who, on the basis of the Socratic and Cartesian scepticism, brought about that "Copernican turn", whereby the whole of man's reasoning was set in steel limits within which alone perception is legitimized. Blessed be God who, in His wisdom, created Kant! Every real Jew who seriously and honestly studies the 'Critique of Pure Reason,' is bound to pronounce his 'Amen' on it. 'Go not about your own heart and your own eyes' or in Kantian language, 'pursue not the messages of your inner and outer experience—'for, pursuing them thou wilt be unfaithful to Me': the whole Kantian theory of perception is the most adequate commentary on this fundamental injunction of the Torah.

"In the pre-Messianic age, the Jewish individual approaching maturity is more than ever constrained by outer and inner experience. According to the evidence of the Torah itself, this experience as such is never in accordance with the Torah: if it were, the latter would be superfluous. The relation of the Torah to experience cannot be regulated by way of a constantly changing compromise nor by way of a continuous retreat into hidden recesses where the broom of 'reason' or 'science' has not yet penetrated. As radical and final as the above-quoted command of the Torah must be the answer to it. It cannot call forth the dishonesty of a confession of belief in a 'double truth.' It can only produce a sure insight into the value of an 'experience' conditioned only by the clear knowledge of the invariable limits by which it is circumscribed and outside of which it is bound to pursue on purely illegitimate 'Kundschaft' (spying adventure). The 'Critique of Experience' alone can fundamentally safeguard the Torah once and for all against an objectionable exceeding of its own competence. Neither 'heart'—the source of inner experience, nor 'eye'—the source of outer experience: remove from thyself outer and inner experience. What remains? Thy will remains—thy will redeemed from heart and eye—thine own free will! The Torah bids thee 'experience' with heart and eye: but 'rule' with thy will delivered from heart and eye! Rule in sanctity—for sanctity is God! The will—to whom actually is the will addressed? Above all—who determines the will? Certainly not the law: Here the wheel comes full circle. This is where Kant's 'Critique of Perception' leads directly back to the Talmud—to the national law of Judaism—to the nation of the law, the community of the law. . . .

"I studied Kant from the Jewish point of view. From the first moment I foresaw that I would find in his arsenal the weapons I sought to protect the sacred terrain of the Torah and the people of the Torah from the increasingly bold incursions of the spying emissaries (*Kundschafter*) in our time—to defend it effectively against the sallies of the eye and the heart without banning them or underestimating them; for that would mean a cleavage and destruction of the unity of the Jewish personality.

"For me Torah is 'The Torah of Life'. Kant became a weapon in my hand to protect Judaism effectively from the presumption of the *Kundschafter* of our times and from the paralysis of pre-mature —and, therefore, harmful—compromise, which is mostly naught but capitulation in disguise. It was a weapon for the time-conditioned mobilization of Judaism—but it was enlightenment for the recognition of Judaism. I did not carry the banner of Kant into Judaism. Just as I studied Kant from the point of view of the Jew, so all the more did I study Judaism.

"Nor did I make the whole standpoint of Judaism dependent on Kant. For full understanding of the spiritual basis of our present generation, Kantian reasoning is, nevertheless, indispensable. The fundament of his 'Critique' remains uncontested. If at some time or other, a completely new epoch should arise and break up this fundament, I am convinced that Divine dispensation would bring about another Kant to arise, the results of whose scholarship would again establish the truth of the Torah. In that case it is not the Torah, but rather my books, that would be outdated. What would that matter—seeing that they have achieved what they were intended to achieve? Kant stands on the threshold of Judaism—but he proceeds no further than that. Within himself he sensed the universal moral law, just as he sensed within himself the theoretic universal law. He was, indeed, the discoverer of the latter; for the Creator, who created man in 'His image', had endowed him with the ability to recognize that which exists and to dominate it. But Kant did not discover the universal moral law, for the moral universe is not what is but what should be. The conception alone of that universe and the striving for it has been instilled in mankind by the Creator in order that he may hear, obey, and perfect.

Kant confounded this yearning for the universal moral law with the law itself and thus came to his conception of the autonomy of human will and to complete negation of the moral heteronomy (of laws given not by oneself, but by someone else), even though it is God that stands for the Heteros. Ultimately it was the serpent that spoke out of his mouth: 'You will be as God, knowing good and evil.'

"The way of Judaism is completely different. It starts out with the heteronomy of God's Law and it leads to an autonomy to a 'sanctity' which embodies God's will completely in the will of self. My first attempt at setting this down in writing was in the study, *Lehre, Gesetz und Nation* (Doctrine, Law, and Nation), which dates from the time when I was a young apprentice-lawyer."*

Jurisprudence

When Breuer entered the university, he had not yet chosen a profession. It is only later that he decided to take up law, having previously promised his father to devote his legal knowledge to the service of the Jewish cause.

He kept this promise. Another literary product of his law-student's time is the work on *Friedhof und Feuerbestattung* (Cemetery and Cremation), which deals with the question of the burying of funeral urns in Jewish cemeteries. The book, written at the request of the Union of Orthodox Rabbis in Germany, appeared in 1912 and was well received by experts, particularly in a leading law journal. A second work, which appeared in 1919, *Die Preussische Austrittsgeseligehung und das Judentum* (The Prussian Law of Secession and Judaism), was published at first as a series of articles in the *Israelit,* as an answer to the *Richtlinien* published at that time by the Reform rabbis. Breuer's arguments culminate in the proof of the impossibility for any thinking Jew combining into one, two diametrically opposed views of life—that of the *Richtlinien* and that of the Torah—without degrading the concept of Judaism to an empty, barren shell of words without content.

At first the young student attended the law lectures, not for a choice of profession, but because of an inner urge to clarify the relation between Jewish law and the law of the nations. In his first law term he was particularly attracted by constitutional law. At-

---

*This is a systematic work, an important introduction for the Talmud-rooted Jewish student to the history, philosophy and law of the nations.

tending the lectures of the two well-known academic teachers, Laband and Ihering, he became fully aware that even the "law" itself is not the ultimate goal of modern consciousness. Law itself has another goal—namely, the state. Beyond the state there is no law. From this conception there results what is still the ruling doctrine in politics—that the state and its interests stand above the law. Modern law admits of no definition of itself isolated from the state. The concept of state is the foundation of law and constitutes its content. Breuer, in his autobiography, characterizes the contrast to the Jewish conception of law in the following passage, adding the remark that this point of view was of determining influence for all the time that followed:

"The Jewish nation received its law outside the country and before the foundation of the state. It achieved national unity through acceptance of the law. With this law it enters the Land, with this law it founds the state: but in the midst of the state it remains the nation of the law and it is not the state which is sovereign, but the law. When the state broke up, the law did not crumble; and even without the state, the nation remained the nation of the law, the Land remained the Land of the law. . . . With the Talmud in my mind and in my heart, I got to know the structure of the non-Jewish state better and better and thus came to a fuller understanding of the historical phenomenon of Judaism. . . ."

The philosopher of law, Stammler—also of the Kantian school of thought—exerted an important influence on Breuer; for he also recognized the problem presented by a concept of law serving only the state, having nothing to do with the ideal of justice; and he admitted the right of the individual to freedom as "the purpose of law"—or, as he expresses it—as "the law of laws." Naturally this was only a formal conception—the setting of a goal for this free will being left undetermined. Breuer writes about this: "That which applied to Kant's ethics, applies also to Stammler's philosophy of law. 'To act freely' is no law—it is only an aspiration. 'To rule freely—to form a community of seekers for freedom' is likewise an expression of aspiration for a society ruled by the law of freedom. Where is the law of free human intercourse? In his doctrine of the *Richtige Recht* (The Right or Proper Law), derived from the idea of social freedom, Stammler attempted to draw practical legal conclusions. I never considered him successful in this. The nations and mankind are still waiting for—a revelation; for the Torah is the law of free human action. The Torah is the law of a non-covetous society."

A legal-philosophical work of Breuer's, "The Concept of Law on the Basis of Stammler's Social Philosophy", appeared in the year 1912 as an appendix to the *Kant Student*. Breuer remained a member of the Kant Society until he left Germany, and it was in their publication that many of his contributions appeared—particularly book reviews, which were highly appreciated. His thesis presented at the end of his legal studies bore the title "The Legal Nature of a Patent-License".

Bund Juedischer Akademiker

One of the finest products of Germany's orthodox Jewry was the *"Bund der juedischen Akademiker"*, an organization rooted in the Torah. The moving spirit was Moses Auerbach, who had founded the first society of Jewish students (V. J. A.) in Berlin. Isaac Breuer, together with other like-minded young men, formed a V. J. A. in Strasbourg; similar groups were set on foot in Munich and Marburg; and in the summer of 1906 these societies formed themselves into a league—the "Bund Jeudischer Akademiker". Isaac Breuer was the first league president and worked out a scheme of instruction for freshmen (*Fuxen*) which was in use for years, and an extension of which can be found in his work, *Moriah,* published in 1945. Until his departure from Germany, Breuer was, with short breaks, *"Fux major"* i.e. instructor of freshmen for the V. J. A. in Frankfort. He describes in the following words the influence of the V. J. A. on him and the nature of the league.

"I loved the V. J. A. It formed my character in the years before my dear wife added the finishing touches.

"In a lengthy article in the *Israelit* in 1907, I gave a full description of the situation of the Jewish student at that time under the tile *Homeward Bound to the Land of the Philistines* —thus introducing the V. J. A. to the public. I may refer also to my book, *Ein Kampf um Gott* (A Battle About, or For, God), 1920.

"The intellectual trends of German Jewry were most pronounced at the universities because here they were not influenced by any practical considerations. There was the "K. C." (*Kartell-Convent*) and there were the Zionist societies. Both demanded a 'conscious Judaism'—the former on the basis of German nationalism, the latter on that of Herzl. The K. C. did not deny its Judaism—on the contrary, it stressed it. And true to the academic

tradition of outspokenness, it did not seek to hide it under the
veil of 'religion'. For the K. C. German Jews were a tribe developed under particular historical conditions in the midst of the
German tribes; though not Germanic, they had earned for themselves the full right not only to be tolerated but to be honorably
admitted to the league of German tribes, just like others of non-
Germanic origin, by virtue of their settlement for hundreds of
years on German soil, of their centuries-old entanglement with
German fate and their important contribution to German culture
and civilization.

"The Zionist societies also cultivated 'conscious Judaism'.
Here again 'conscious Judaism' had no direct relation to Torah
and Talmud. For them also, Jewish history was in no way the
meta-history of the chosen among peoples. They read this history
through Herzl's eyes and the result was, therefore, quite different
from that attained by the K. C. The stream of their 'conscious
Judaism' flowed not into Germany but into Palestine. And as
students are in no way called upon to take an active part in the
creation of a 'legally assured home for the Jewish nation,' it is
just in the universities that Zionism found its profoundest interpretation as an intellectual movement. It was this 'conscious
Judaism,' propagated at the universities by the Zionist societies,
that ultimately determined my anti-Zionism. Their victims among
the 'religious' students were legion. The university professors
on the one hand—and this 'conscious Judaism' so far removed
from Torah and Talmud, on the other—it was just too much . . .!

"The V. J. A. was originally founded as an Orthodox religious
society. As such it was not a real student-organization; for the
latter, far from being content to appeal only to a particular side
of the student, sought to take hold and mould the whole man. In
its early days, the V. J. A. included members who were also
affiliated with Zionist societies. To a certain extent, it took care of
the religious needs of these members, who attained their real ends
in the Zionist societies; accordingly, the V. J. A. only had a complementary religious function for them. It is easy to see how the
great problems dividing the traditional Jewry of Germany into
two camps were here reflected in the student body. At a decisive
meeting in Berlin, a motion for the abolition of double membership
was passed. Therewith the V. J. A. became a "totalitarian" student
league and its actual development dates from then.

"This is not the place to speak of the importance and the achievements of the V. J. A., which has its place in the history of German Judaism. But I may be permitted to acknowledge gratefully how much I, personally, owe to the League. It is here that I made friends—friends for life. Years of separation and complete stoppage of correspondence had no effect on these friendships. Were we to meet again tomorrow, we should pursue the conversation from the point where we had broken off yesterday. And as I write these words, I greet you all, friends far and near, the living and those of you who are no more. It was well with us and it is well with us and we remain faithful to each other. It is to the V. J. A. that I owe the joy of argument, the difficult art of listening, the still more difficult art of sympathy and the most difficult of all, that of mutual understanding. I greet you all—my "foxes" throughout the world (you were the little foxes who were to set fire with your torches to the fields of the Philistines). It was through you that what I felt attained form and substance—what I thought ripened to maturity and what I was dubious about achieved clarity and confirmation. My book, *Die Welt als Schopfung and Natur* (The World as Creation and Nature), is yours as much as mine. What I taught you I taught myself. You returned to me twofold what you received from me."

Without exaggeration we may say that what Isaac Breuer did for the V. J. A. was decisive for its future development. This was his first opportunity of translating his dream world into reality and of proving himself as an educator, and he exploited it to the full. In the twenties the V. J. A. had almost one thousand members.

Breuer left the university in 1909; in 1913 his legal apprenticeship culminated in the opening of a lawyer's office in Frankfort-on-the-Main.

Barely a year later, in August 1914—it was the 9th of Ab 5674 —a new epoch in world history was ushered in with the outbreak of the First World War. From April 1915 until the end of the war, Isaac Breuer was mobilized at first on guard duty and later, as legal advisor to the home command of the XVIIIth Army Corps. In the many lonely months and years of semi-occupation in his army service, Breuer found the time to think out and conceive the plan of the major works which, after the end of the war, he bestowed upon the Jewish world. In his autobiography he gives a short description of this conception, which may serve as an introduction to the reading of the works themselves:

"From the very first hour, the war illustrated and brought to life for me the Jewish theory of history as foretold by the prophets of Israel in such a forcible way that I could not free myself from the spell that it cast upon me and was compelled to bring all subsequent events into relation with it. This theory is essentially based on the distinction between meta-history and perceptible history—on the contrast between the Jewish people as a direct factor of meta-history and the nations as pillars of perceptible history—on the perpetual controversy between the idea of meta-history, based on the Divine plan of the Creation and the realities of perceptible history—a controversy the ultimate goal of which will be the meeting point of the two, at the end of time when creation and nature converge. In the vicissitudes of perceptible history, the war appeared to me as the explosive accentuation of the contrast to meta-history; the war of nations with its inevitable intense suffering for the Jewish people was revealed to me as the unmistakable symptom of the Messiah wrestling his way into existence. This completely conscious experience of prophetic history gave me the strength unreservedly to indicate the character of a living nation for Jewry in *Das Judenproblem* (The Jewish problem)—despite Zionism and perhaps because of Zionism— and to abjure the latter on national grounds. The war gave me an insight into the Messianic character of the epoch ushered in by the war of nations, and it induced me in my book, *Messias Spuren* (Traces of the Messiah), to call for the raising up of a nation and of all its members to the heights of prophetic prediction, for their mobilization for the decisive contests between meta-history and perceptible history—in short, for Messianic realization. At the end of the book, in apprehensive foreboding, I posed the question whether Agudat Israel would be able to find the way to this Messianic reality. In the light of this experience, Zionism appeared to me not only as an attempt made by false prophets and, as such, to be opposed with all our might—at a national reform of our people in the sense of a national assimilation to other nations and their perceptible history; I also saw in it an instrument in the hand of the God of meta-history for making the Jewish nation more active than it had been for 200 years in perceptible history, for its taking more active steps in the maturing of its predestined goal whilst the perceptible history of the other nations hastened more and more uncontrollably to its predestined end. In the Balfour Declaration and the Mandate—prepared and

achieved by Zionism—I saw the possibility of such an effect revealed by God to his people: I saw in them the unutterably difficult
but splendid task set by God for His people, in the time of the Messiah wrestling into existence—the task which, whilst far from
absolving from other tasks or from making them appear worthless
or superfluous, yet provides them with guidance and direction and
with unifying cohesion. Thus I conceived the idea of God's people
and God's Land everlastingly bound up with each other by the
Divine Law, separated for 2000 years by the Divine will, stepping
out of perceptible history, each facing the other directly under
God's marvelous direction. And both call out to us, both appeal to
us: awake, awake, be mindful of this—our God-given opportunity,
bring us together, so that the Divine glory and Divine presence may
unite us once more forever if ye have earned your redemption.

"I had already published my book, *Neuorientierung* (Re-
Orientation), during the war some time before *Messias Spuren*.
If the latter was intended to open the gates to a new future, I
attempted in *Neuorientierung* to clear away the rubble of the
past. Both works were the product of great inner upheaval; both
were the outcome of the terrible fear that Orthodoxy in the end—
like all the Philistines—might experience this war merely as an extremely unpleasant episode—that, like all the Philistines, it might
venture to begin again after the war where it had stopped before
the war and to tie up what the war had so disastrously torn apart.
For I felt—indeed, I knew—that this war was no episode—that it
was epoch-making and that the new epoch presented our people with
a completely new task unkown to them in the 2000 years of *Galut*
'the mobilization of the Jewish people and the Jewish Land for their
reunion under the sway of the Divine Law!'

"This quotation is taken from a little essay, *Die Idee des
Agudism* (The Idea of Agudism), which I published in 1919. It
is based entirely on *Messias Spuren* and is intended to develop
the program of 'Agudist Messianism.' The sentence quoted above
is a summary of all the points of this program. . . .

"When Wilson announced his 'Fourteen Points', when the
Balfour Declaration was given to our people, and the League of
Nations began to rise like a gentle moon over all the dark and
ghastly happenings, I experienced one of those great moments
in the progress of mankind when meta-history and perceptible
history meet, and Esau, overcome by love, bestows on Jacob the
kiss of brotherhood. I believed in Wilson. I believed in the

League of Nations. I believed in a just peace such as the tormented world had not yet known. It was only a great moment. Great enough to reveal the possibility of the National Home. But then the ways parted again. Esau went back to Seir. Esau dictated a peace, no better than any that had preceded. It was, indeed, no just peace. But it was incorporated in the legal acts of the League of Nations, thus maintaining law's guard over the lordship of force. Then I knew that the *Galut*-history of Esau and Jacob had only entered upon a completely new phase but that it was not yet ended. I realized that this war of the nations had only been the first of the Messianic wars and that our people would have to build up its Home in the midst of the fiercest of temporal storms, in the midst of a growing strike between metahistory and perceptible history.

"My aim was to arouse and to muster the people of the Torah for this fight. I recognized in Zionism the nationalism of perceptible history—the national *Yetzer Hara* (evil inclination or imagination), destined to arouse the national *Yetzer Hatov* (good inclination or imagination), which imbues the people of the Torah with a conscious sense of history, making them capable of action as a living nation for the first time for 2000 years and bringing them into active relation with the Land of the Torah. The *Yetzer Hara* is a productive force: one cannot and one should not evade it, but one must face up to it and conquer it and force it into the service of the good. It seemed to me that Orthodoxy up to that time, in its fleeing from the national *Yetzer Hara,* had got out of line with history—denying the national element altogether and estranging itself in timid anxiety from the national Land. I felt that Orthodoxy, in its fear of the national *Yetzer Hara* had withdrawn under the blanket of individualistic 'religion' in order to face the threatening impulses of the age of 'national emancipation' with the reinforced practice of Torah and *mitzvot.* But had it not struck out in the same path in the age of 'social emancipation' and had this not led in West and Central Europe to the most terrible of catastrophes?

"But was not the age of 'national emancipation' a thousand times more dangerous than that of 'social emancipation'? No! There was no such thing as flight from the national *Yetzer Hara,* if it was brought upon us by the Divine Providence—just as there was no flight from the individual *Yetzer Hara.* Flight from the national *Yetzer Hara* amounted to national suicide, to capitulation, just as flight from the individual *Yetzer Hara* means negative asceticism and barren monasticism. For this reason the kindling of genuine Jewish nationalism seemed to me to be the urgent call of the hour. My Jewish nationalism, deeply rooted in meta-history, enlightened my attitude to Zionism. It brought me to the realization that the fight of Rabbi Hirsch for the essence (*"Wesen"*) of the Jewish community *in nuce* had already signified the fight for the *Wesen* of the Jewish nation—long before Herzl. The 'neutral' Jewish nation was ultimately the outcome of the neutral Jewish community, whereas the community of the Torah was the primeval cell of the nation of the Torah."

Founding a Family

It was during the war in 1916 that Isaac Breuer chose the wife whom he eulogizes in his autobiography in the following words:

"I experienced the great blessing of establishing with my dear wife the Jewish national home in my own house. I can well call it a national home, for Zion and the Divine Law of Zion held sway over it. We fostered in our children loyalty and love for Zion and Jerusalem and, through these, loyalty and love for the Torah. If I failed to prevail in the Agudah with my 'preparedness program' I think I succeeded in doing so in my own home. That is something—it is a great deal. Perhaps it is—everything.

My home life did not clip my wings—on the contrary, it gave me additional strength. There was scarcely a single manuscript that my dear wife did not read and approve before it went to the press. Only occasionally she expressed her opinion of the style being 'too difficult.' And she opened our doors to guests of all kinds—especially to young people—and made them welcome with kindness and comfort. It was she who pleaded with me to have patience when success in the Agudah was not forthcoming; and she comforted me when disappointments came my way. In the end she returned with me gladly and joyfully to the sacred Homeland, where she fulfilled her exalted task better then ever."

AGUDAT ISRAEL

If some day in the future the unwritten history of Agudat Israel should be published, it would be the fitting place for a full presentation of Isaac Breuer's importance for that ideology and, in no small degree, for its political achievements. A short sketch is all that the scope of this biography allows.

As at the foundation gathering in Kattowitz in 1912, Breuer took an active part in all the great international conferences of the Agudah (with the exception of the Second Knessiah Gedolah). He was at first a member of the Provisional Committee of 1914 and later, after the First World War, member of the Chief Administration in *Vaad Hapoel,* the executive of which had its seat in Frankfort-on-Main. He undertook his first visit to the Holy Land on behalf of the Agudat Israel in 1926. At the First Knessiah Gedolah he was responsible for the Agudist Constitution, and later in Eretz Israel he was likewise a leading member of the World Executive, whose seat had meanwhile been transferred to the Holy Land. Nearly all the European national organizations— especially the Eastern ones—enjoyed the pleasure of his visit and of listening to his stirring Agudist speeches. But all this only reflects the external extent of his Agudist activity. Far more significant was the extent to which Breuer's philosophy, as set out in Agudist writings, influenced Agudat Israel in its present status: its whole approach to the new problems of the present day originated with him.

It took years—even decades—for Breuer to achieve recognition, even in the most select circle of his colleagues, for his program and for the range of his ideas for which he pleaded with holy zeal in the spoken and the written word. As opposed to the static program of "a solution of the task of the community, at any given moment, in the spirit of the Torah", he was of the opinion that the Agudah could only be worthy of its historic task if it consciously opposed a Torah-nationalism to the secular nationalism of the Zionists—in other words, if it professed to the above quoted "Program of Preparedness". At first people tried to discredit this program by labelling it "Palestino-centric", thus excluding the possibility of the whole world movement concentrating on Eretz Israel to the complete disregard of the task of the *Golah.* Breuer points out the fallacy of this reproach in the following words:

"I protest absolutely against the accusation of being 'Palestino-centric.' The only centre which I recognize is God and God's Torah. That is why the *yeshivot* in Tels, in Mir and in Frankfort are as important, in my opinion, as the school system in Palestine; the flourishing of the *Golah* is as near to my heart as the development

of Orthodoxy in the National Home. It is not a question of any re-
valuation, but purely of an historical insight into the nature of our
time and our task within it. Certainly a pre-condition is the
recognition that our people in the *Galut* are a living, though sorely
suffering nation, that the Torah is its valid and fundamental,
though sorely suffering law, that Eretz Israel is its everlasting,
eternally promised though sorely suffering Land, and that, finally,
this threefold sore suffering is the suffering of separation. History
without these premises has no appeal for us. Given these premises,
the outbreak of social emancipation and as a result of it the outbreak of Zionism; the outbreak of the World War, and the Balfour
Declaration impossible without it; the League of Nations, and the
Mandate unthinkable without it; the outbreak of "World Peace"
with all its unheard of dangers—all these things appeal to us in such
eloquent terms that only a deaf ear could ignore them. God calls
upon us! It behooves us to answer! The nation of God's Land calls
upon us! It behooves us to answer! The Divine Land of the Torah
calls upon us! It behooves us to answer! What, in all this, is
'Palestino-centric'? To be prepared is everything! My aim is to
make our people turn to the Land, and the Land turn to our people,
and both turn to the God of the people and of the Land! Were our
ancestors 'Palestino-centric' when they, the blessed ones, were
settled in 'their' Land? Are we to be so termed because, following
God's call, we prepare ourselves and the Land for a reunion? And
does not the preparedness of the nation include in itself the most
active support of the *yeshivot* in Tels, in Mir and in Frankfort?
Can we mobilize our people without *Yeshivah?* I am not 'Palestino-
centric' but 'Torah-centric.' But I place the Torah in the center—
of history."

Isaac Breuer found wide acknowledgment—particularly in the
East, but also to a great extent among West-European youth.
But he did not succeed in persuading the Agudah—as he had
hoped—to make his program the official one. The urge was
always upon him to test and re-test his national Agudism and to
explore deeper into it. He proceeded to write a number of books
which may be termed Agudist. Mention is made here of one of his
masterpieces, the *Neue Kusari,* but no attempt shall be made in
any short résumé of the contents to weaken the impression which
an intensive study of the work must make upon the reader.

There were a series of other points which challenged Breuer's
criticism even at the time when the Agudah steered its actions

according to the Kattowitz Program; he dwells on these, in part, in his two pamphlets, *Die Idee des Agudism* (The Idea of Agudism) and *Fünfundzwanzig Jahre Agudas Israel* (Twenty-five Years of Agudah). Despite all the disillusions which he experienced, he could not persuade himself to break with the Agudah. He gives the following reasons:

"This Agudah, in all its static insufficiency, was an exact organizational reflection of the nation of the Torah; not only the Agudah as such, but also the nation of the Torah itself, was estranged from history—recognizing only the tasks of the present and in the ultimate end uninspired by the completely novel confrontation of Nation and Land which the age of national emancipation has summoned up as a historical task. But this Agudah was for me not merely a society. The great men of Israel had stood at its cradle—had bestowed upon it their acknowledgment and their blessing. I would not care to separate myself from the Agudah and therewith from the people of the Torah. My place could only be in this static Agudah, in the ranks of the opposition, exhorting and warning, urging on and constraining and leaving the outcome to Providence. It was not easy to wait patiently. It was not easy to bear the growing cleavage between my Agudism and the actual Agudah. But it had to be. . . ."

ALIYAH TO ERETZ ISRAEL

Isaac Breuer was twice in Eretz Israel, in 1926 and in 1933, and with his characteristic clarity of perception, he was quick to notice light and shadow. On his return to Europe, he gave a full account to his friends of all he had experienced of the great economic boom, the blossoming of the soil, the fluctuating variety of the national society in process of development, the paucity in numbers of those who were determined and able to fight for the Torah and its recognition. His articles in *Nahlat Tzevi,* his lectures in Frankfort, Berlin and in the Polish, Lithuanian and Hungarian Torah centers, will go down in history. In the meantime, the criminal group of National Socialists had come to power and proclaimed open war against the Jewish nation. Isaac Breuer's farewell greeting to the German Orthodox youth was a lecture given in the Rabbi Hirsch Society, wherein he depicted Rabbi Hirsch not only as a great man of the past decade, but as a path-finder in history—a guide leading us to our Land, to Eretz Israel, where Torah and *"Derekh Eretz"* faced each other in quite a different way from anything possible in Frankfort, with a far more direct impact and a more far-reaching compass. The two had to be brought into relation with each other, and he termed this task *"Torah im Derekh Eretz Israel"*—"Tedaismus."

On the 8th Adar 5696 (1936), Isaac Breuer landed for the third time on the soil of Eretz Israel in Haifa—this time for good, with his family. He took up residence in Jerusalem and, after passing his law exams, opened up a lawyer's office. It is moving to read how his mind and his heart consciously expanded day by day under the influence of life in the Holy City. Limitations of space allow of only one quotation:

"At home in 'destroyed' Jerusalem! Woe to those who no longer see—no longer feel the destruction! It is easier to yearn for Jerusalem in Frankfort than—being in Jerusalem, to yearn for Jerusalem! Blessed be the Almighty who has given me the strength to yearn for Jerusalem in Jerusalem. Those who live in exile yearn for the home of their fathers, destroyed as it may have been for years. But if, returned to the house of his fathers, he yearns even there, and more than ever there for his father's house—this yearning is the greater and the purer, for it aspires to—the Father.

"How beautiful art thou—'destroyed Jerusalem!' Beautiful in the morning sunrise, in the evening sunset; and when, in daytime, the sun shines above, it is like a festive illumination. How beautiful are thy nights, oh, destroyed Jerusalem, bathed in the beams of the caressing moon, with the stars twinkling in ardent desire of thee! How beautiful is thy heavenly dome, oh destroyed Jerusalem, encompassing and preserving thee for the coming of God's glory. Beautiful are thy hills, diminutive domes of heaven surrounding thee as God surrounds His people. Beautiful are thy streets, oh destroyed Jerusalem, in which even today, in the image of tomorrow, people from all over the world and not only Jewish people have their trysting-place, filling them with bustling life. Beautiful are thy gardens, blooming again, as once before, two thousand years ago. Beautiful is the voice of thy birds, resounding once more in thy breezes. Everything stirs—everything rights itself: Will He not soon appear—the Father? Beautiful with an unearthly beauty are thy Sabbaths, oh destroyed Jerusalem, week by week. Great is their might over thy streets—even today in thy destruction. Faithful guardians see to it that this might should not decrease. And is it not as though, week by week, thou didst raise thyself, oh sacred City of Kings, on each one of thy Sabbaths

from the horror of destruction—'For thou hast dwelt long enough
in the valley of tears—and the Merciful One has mercy upon
thee.' Do I not, week by week, on thy Sabbaths feel myself
fanned by the breath of peace and of everlasting life? Do I not
often hear on thy Friday evenings the creation song of thy
stars, on Sabbath mornings the creation rejoicing of thy sun?
Is it not, indeed, week by week a prophetic foretaste of the delights
of the day that cometh, which shall be 'wholly Sabbath'?

"But the happenings of the war years brought with them heavy
suffering for Jerusalem. Twice did the army of the evil-doer stand
at thy gates, oh Jerusalem, and twice did the Almighty hold His
hand protectingly over thee, whilst millions of thy sons and
daughters sank down in the world outside. The world is 'destroyed' because and as long as thou art 'destroyed,' oh Jerusalem.
He who does not sense this connection and understand it in his
innermost being is a prey to the terrible upheavals of a meaningless
present. No smile can stir the lips—no drop of joy can relieve the
heart of him for whom death signifies the catastrophic final end:
between him and the smile, between him and the joy there stands
a million-fold death. But thou, oh destroyed Jerusalem, didst
teach me day by day the death in life and the life in death. Life
in thee is the life of destruction and death in thee is, indeed, more
than even destroyed life—but always and forever—life—*Har
Hazetim* (Mount of Olives—the timeless cemeteries) and thy
Har Hazetim is near, quite near thy *Har Habait* (Temple
Mount). For thy God is a God of life, of the whole of life—of
destroyed life and resurrected life. Where is thy sting, oh Death?
Even in *Har Hazetim* one is here at home—in life as in death—
at home."

Years of Maturity in Eretz Israel

Today, after the establishment of the State of Israel with the
attendant attitude of the Agudat Israel and its attempt to create
a united religious front at least in Parliament, and after the growth
of the opposition between the Neture Karta and Agudat Israel,
it has become abundantly clear that Isaac Breuer foresaw this
development with prophetic insight and confirmed in his writings
and in his ardent speeches the truth of the Sages' maxim: "*Hakham
minabi*" (A wise man is preferable to a prophet). His book, *Das
Juedische Nationalheim* (The Jewish National Home), his
articles in *Nahlat Tzevi* and in *Knesset Israel,* the account of

the representation of Agudat Israel before the Peel Commission, and finally his Agudist educational vade necum, *Moriah,* must be thoroughly studied and cannot possibly be adequately summarized here. He did not live to reap the recognition which was accorded to his pioneering direction of the world organization of Agudat Israel at the beginning of the establishment of the State. This came in the form of the publication of the "Guiding Principles" drafted by him for Agudist action in the Jewish State in Parliament and Government, as well as for an amalgamation into one front of the religious groups.

Isaac Breuer had fought with his life's blood for the idea of an organization of *Am Hatorah* (The people of the Torah). He ardently took up the cause of the Agudist worker, as an integral factor of the Agudist world organization. He assumed the presidency of the Poale Agudat Israel. His was not the mere dignity of office, but a total investment of his energy, ingenuity, ability to help *Poalim* blossom ideologically, no less than organizationally, and in all practical aspects of the young labor movement.

Countless problems arose which required the empathic support of the mother organization. At the third *Kenessiah*—held at Marienbad—Breuer stressed this request with all his persuasive power. He sought—in vain—to bring about the realization of the ideal of a union of all workers acknowledging the Torah, at a time when it was still possible to avoid the split which now prevails. He was tireless in his efforts to induce contemporary Torah scholars to summarize in systematic form the applicaton of the Divine law to the economic conditions and the technical foundations of a modern state, and thus to create an Agudist program for the constitutional and economic law systems of the country. In his lucid analysis of the new tasks in Eretz Israel, Breuer had reserved for himself the greatest and the most difficult of all—namely the application of the law of the Torah to come into effect not only within the communities, as in the *Golah,* but to have complete sway over the whole Jewish National Home. There was a time when it was thought that Breuer laid himself open to the charge of self-contradiction in his conception of the National Home, which clashed with his earlier views imbibed from Rabbis Hirsch and Breuer on the character of a Jewish organization. He himself was emphatic in denying this. Let the great man speak for himself in defense of the fact that in all his public offices and in all his writings he never swerved a hairsbreadth from the path conforming to the essential character of the independent organization of Torah devotees:

"In the *Golah,* the actual educational task of the communities consisted in supplying their adherents with the armor enabling them to withstand the challenge of a social life moulded essentially by the governing nation and not subject to the rule of the Torah.

"In the National Home, only organized societies embracing a social life of their own, in which the moulding sway of the Torah is tested and proved, can be called communities in the full, national sense of the word. In the National Home, it is not only meat that has to be 'ritually' prepared—but the whole of human co-existence.

"The contention is twofold—to suit the Torah to society and to suit society to the Torah. 'To suit the Torah to society' is a dangerous precept if not rightly interpreted. The Torah is eternal. But the facts which the Torah covers are not eternal. Modern economic life displays phenomena quite different from those in the time of Abaye and Rabo or that of Rabbi Joseph Caro. For centuries, a Jewish economic life in the fullness of its potentialities has not been brought in contact with the Torah. There is really no sense in demanding the rule of the Torah over economic life in the National Home, and this claim remains an empty phrase, as long as the official representatives of the Torah fail to make themselves well acquainted with the phenomena of this economic life and fail to bring them face to face with the eternal precepts of the Torah so that the eternal actuality of the latter may be proven.

"Society under the Torah: a difficult and adventurous road, at the end of which there beckons nothing less than the right of the redemption of the nation. This and nothing else is the issue in the era of national emancipation. True to Agudist principles, it is our task to set up the organization of an exclusively dominating Torah in the midst of the society of the National Home—to fit an organized people of the Torah into this society as an active factor. The day will never come, must never come, when the organization representing the dominating claim of the Torah renounces the sovereignty of the nation, thus demonstrating its recognition in the form of party, faction or any other form. It is bad enough that the Torah does not yet rule society. But organization of the Torah is possible today and is, therefore, our paramount duty. It should stand as the signpost of the unassailable sovereignty claim of the Torah. It should stand as the signpost of the indestructible nation of the Torah, which neither knows nor recognizes any Jewish nation besides itself and beyond its bounds.

"Its first and greatest responsibility should be education. In the midst of a society in which the Torah still has to fight for every inch of recognition and authority, it should work for a future society by fostering a generation of Jewish people completely rooted in the Torah, for whom being a man and being a Jew is one and the same thing, and who pay homage to no other nationalism than that of the Torah—a generation which makes no distinction between the commandments which bind man to God and those which bind man to his fellowman—a generation for whom social injustice is as cursed as 'ritual injustice'—a generation socially prominent for, and distinguished by, justice and equity, whose whole manner of life demonstrates the beauty of the ways known as the ways of the Torah—a generation of clear-sighted people who need not fight shy of controversy, withstanding the spirit of the age not by virtue of ignorance but by virtue of superior knowledge, opposing the profound seriousness of their conviction to superficiality and flippancy, their idealistic striving to covetousness and of sensuality— a generation of loving human beings unburdened by self-righteousness or presumption, in brotherly communion with all the sons of their people encompassed by the indivisible bonds of unity of the Torah—willing and able to be the leaders in the return to Israel's Father-King, of those who have gone astray. This education should set its aim *at* society, not *against* it, and the more deliberately it follows the Torah in the name of its exclusive sovereignty, in the name of subordinating nationality, the less it need fear society or proclaim the flight from society as its battle-cry. *Independence of the organization of the ruling Torah should not signify its isolation from society.* On the contrary: its fixed aim must remain the conquest of society. It must, therefore, make it its prime endeavor to fit social life into the Torah.

"Immutable for the organization of the Torah is the principle of its independence—immutable, also, the principle of non-responsibility for actions of commission or omission running counter to the Torah. This remains so, even if we vote against these actions and afterwards allow ourselves to be outvoted. An overwhelming majority cannot absolve us from our liability. The laws of the Torah cannot constitute an object for a vote. Voting in itself signifies rebellion.

"Organizational independence, and the rejection of any responsibility for actions committed or omitted contrary to the Torah—on these two points there can be no change or adjustment. But while strictly observing these two conditions, the Agudah today can and must contribute to a correspondingly reorganized Jewish Agency: it can and it must have a claim to the support of the Keren Kayemet and Keren Hayesod. Moreover, the Agudah must have a fitting share in the United Jewish Appeal. The collections of the United Jewish Appeal are definitely made in the name of Eretz Israel as a whole. Isn't the Agudah also part of Eretz Israel? Is it not bound up today with the National Home, for good or ill? The further exclusion of the Agudah can only be set down to shameful injustice and antagonism.

"One can and one should demand of Zionist leaders an understanding attitude towards the Agudah; they should not expect of it what it could never undertake, even under threat of dissolution—namely, the sacrifice of its organizational independence, or acceptance of responsibility for transgression of the Torah. They will have to admit, sooner or later, that as long as there exists an opposition between Agudism and Zionism, the Agudah cannot possibly be regarded as a faction within the Zionist organization. They will have to realize that the Agudah can only take its place in the Jewish Agency if ways are found of absolving it from responsibility for things which it cannot answer for. Such ways can be found if there is *sufficient good will on both sides.*"

When Isaac Breuer wrote these words, the Jewish State was not yet in existence. Hence the repeated use of the term "National Home". He has his own opinion as to whether the Torah-observing Jew should recognize this National Home as such, and if so, under what conditions; or whether he should look upon it as a danger to be guarded against. He writes: "Affirmation of the National Home and the task which it entails for the people of the Torah requires an unshaken optimistic conviction that gradually, after the intensest of inner conflicts, it may be possible to bring the whole content of national-social life under the sway and the shaping influence of the Torah. He who boasts no such optimistic faith is forced to the conviction that the National Home signifies the most terrible temptation that has ever assailed the people of the Torah, and the only task he will admit is rejection—fleeing from temptation, in order to preserve for himself and his children his faith in the Torah. He will see in the social life within the National Home not the true object of the sovereignty of the Torah, which alone is worth pursuing, but an ungodly affair which, just because it is staged exclusively by Jews, is further removed from the Torah by far than the social life of the *Golah,* whose relation to the Torah being absolutely un-Jewish, was quite naturally not antagonistic, but rather one of complete detachment."

As mentioned above, Breuer had already then drawn up guiding principles for the attitude to be taken by the Agudah in a Jewish State, whether in the government or in the opposition. Unfortunately, it was not given to the Agudah or to Breuer himself to represent the former in the State. But in his latter years he gathered round him a circle of people, thus creating a vanguard for the conflict within the social sphere. In the concluding sentences of the *Neue Kusari* he describes, in his attractive way, the aims of this conflict, the tasks of these young people.

Whoever had the good fortune of knowing him personally will remain under the impression that he incorporated the ideal type of the Jewish nation—described by our Sages (*Midrash Shemot,* par. 42) as a "stiff-necked" people: "You might think this stiff-neckedness is a fault, but no—it is Israel's pride. Either one is a Jew or one is not. It is with good reason that Ahiyah Hashiloni compared Israel to a reed: the reed stands in water, its stump renews itself; it has roots, and though all the storms in the world rage against it, they cannot move it from its place." Isaac Breuer was just such a Jewish character who knew how to withstand the storms of his times with all the unbending and unyielding of his Jewish conviction and his Jewish consciousness. That is why, in a time of instability and darkness, he was a guiding star for the deluded and the faltering: he made of them personalities able to face the bewildering pressure of the outer world with an inner conviction. But over and beyond his personal influence, Breuer continues to live in his writings. Here he opens the doors to all sons of Jewish mothers. He believes in the dawn—even while it is still night and he spoke and continues to speak with Isaiah's watchman of the night: *"if ye will enquire, enquire ye: return, come!"*

On Shabbat Nahamu—the 13th of Menahem Ab 5706 (1946) —the day of the *Brit Milah* of one of his grandchildren—he entered into his eternal rest, at the age of sixty-three. He found his last resting place on Har Hazetim. The inscription on his grave proclaims him:

"A great man in Israel who sanctified his life for the people of the Torah and the Land of the Torah."

BIBLIOGRAPHY

of the Principal Writings of Dr. Isaac Breuer

A. Published Works

Lehre, Gesetz und Nation—historical-critical enquiry into the essence of Judaism (1910)

Friedhof und Feuerbestattung (1912)

Die Preussische Austrittsgesetzgebung und das Judentum (1912)

Der Rechtsbegriff auf Grund der Stammlerschen Sozizialphilosophie (1912)

Messiasspuren (1918)

Ein Kampf um Gott (1920)

Die Idee des Agudismus (1921)

Judenproblem (1922)

Falk Nefts Heimkehr (1923)

Wegzeichen (1923)

Eliyahu (1924)

Die Tragik des Misrachi (1925)

Das juedische Nationalheim (1925)

Die Welt als Schoepfung und Natur (1926)

Elisha (1928)

Programm oder Testament (1929)

Der Neue Kusari (1934)

Erez-Yisrael Briefe (1936)

Fuenfundzwanzig Jahre Agudas Jisroel (1937)

Am Hatorah Hameurgan (Hebrew) (1944)

Moriyah (Hebrew) (1945)

Nahaliel (Hebrew) (1951)

B. In Manuscript

Ich und der Krieg (1915-1918)

Weltwende (1938)

Sha'ali S'rufah (in memory of German Jewry) (1942)

Mein Weg (Autobiography), 1946

JOSEPH CARLEBACH
(1883-1942)

By B. S. Jacobson

(Translated by Adolf Rimberg, from the German)

JOSEPH CARLEBACH

By B. S. Jacobson

I.

The scion of a rabbinical family, Joseph Carlebach was born in 1883 in Lubeck, Germany. His father, Rabbi Shlomoh, headed its congregation for almost half a century, revered for his scholarship, beloved for his dynamic compassion and democratic impulse, no less than for his gentleness.

Joseph Carlebach was and wanted to be a teacher. Throughout his life, his guiding star remained the concept of a rabbi in its traditional meaning—a teacher in Israel. While attending the Rabbinical Seminary in Berlin, he simultaneously studied natural science, philosophy and art, receiving his doctorate in mathematics. At the age of twenty-two, he went to Palestine for three years to join the staff of the Ezra Seminary, and then continued to teach science at a high school in Berlin. Not until 1914 was he ordained a rabbi. His teachers were the great luminaries David Hoffmann, A. Berliner, Hirsch Hildesheimer, Jacob Barth, and Joseph Wohlgemuth.

During the German occupation in World War I, the German Military High Command, recognizing his capabilities, entrusted Dr. Carlebach with the assignment to organize Jewish high schools in Kovno and Riga.

In 1919, as rabbi of the Lubeck congregation, he left Eastern Europe to succeed his sainted father. But a few years later he resigned that post in order to become principal of the Talmud Torah High School in Hamburg. Upon this famed institution he implanted deeply the mark of his personality. In 1925 he became Chief Rabbi of Altona, and ten years later, accepted the office of Chief Rabbi of Hamburg. The tragedy of his deportation from Hamburg by the Nazi murderers, in 1942, is at once deepened and enhanced by the glory of his heroism: he had scorned all avenues of escape offered to him and decided to stay with his congregation, come what may.

II.

Joseph Carlebach was an outstanding pioneer in the field of modern Jewish education, combining great knowledge with ineffable charm and wit. He fascinated his students, young and old, by his masterly art of shedding new light on Biblical exegesis, Talmudic teaching and Jewish philosophy—even when discussing a subject of secular literature, he knew how to demonstrate the eternal truth of Judaism and its immutable validity for every generation.

His joining, in 1905, the Ezra Teachers' Seminary in Jerusalem, as its first staff member trained in Western Europe, was of profound effect upon both the study program and the entire student body. The pupils reacted enthusiastically to his unique methods of instruction, as well as to his social activities. He pioneered in teaching mathematics and natural science in Hebrew, for which he created a new terminology. He introduced round-table discussions, excursions into the countryside, youth services on the *Shabbat,* and brought the spirit of his dynamic personality into the school. The love of his students knew no bounds. On the other hand, through his work in the Holy Land, Carlebach attained a breadth of view and a richness of experience unique among German rabbis and educators.

Still more impressive was his success in the assignment to establish secular Jewish high schools in Poland and Lithuania, in replacement of the local *heder.* The splendid achievements of the students astonished the authorities, who had resolved to have the old-fashioned *heder*-system disappear. The school in Kovno alone soon had some 800 students registered who, imbued with ardent Jewish nationalism, received instruction in all Jewish topics in Hebrew and made the holy language their vernacular. This Kovno high school was named after its founder, Dr. Carlebach, and remained open until the holocaust of the Second World War.

Carlebach's work in Lithuania and Poland brought him into close contact with all spheres of Eastern Jewry, with their amazing vitality and deep-rooted sense of unsophisticated Jewishness. Of open heart and mind, he rejoiced in this way of life, in which he saw the realization of Jewish ideals so dear to his soul. He came to see this spirit brought to its highest fruition in the great *yeshivot* which left their indelible mark upon his own concepts of Jewish education and were reflected in his extensive studies of the problem:

> "Is it the task of the school to educate people to be able independently to create cultural life for themselves and their fellow citizens, or has any milieu a right to utilize the school for educating its students to be merely the inheritors of contemporary cultural concepts? . . . But if there is a cultural constant, if there is a timeless, eternal goal in possible development where all differentiation and all individuality converge freely, as we Jews are sure there is, then our Jewish school may safely draw its norms and measures from these eternal values which are the true basis of development, today and in future, for educators and pupils alike. Children in school are the Messiahs, their teachers the prophets of the Messianic Kingdom to come! We must beware of a schematic answer to all the problems. The infinite depth and height of the Torah must be brought home to the student—a glimpse of its inexhaustible eternality, of its unlimited horizons.

> Let me say to all educators: I believe in religious individuality. The Torah was revealed to 600,000 Jews, but for each according to his capabilities, according to his style of life. I believe that, on Jewish grounds, there is no serious inconsistency between authority and freedom, between individual and general precepts, because our Torah, even though we are subjected to its law, is not man-made, but stems from the Creator of all diversification in individuality. Just let us learn again to avail ourselvs of the Torah's fullness and we shall see the spiritual richness of the individual student happily challenged and aided by the overwhelming wealth of our Torah.

> In working with our pupils, we must put this new synthesis to work, not as their superiors but as their leaders. We must detach the Jewish school from the narrow interests of the local community, must widen its horizon and restore the old Jewish ideals and values. We must create a distinct Jewish atmosphere, by reviving the Hebrew language and by picturesque presentation of Hebrew symbols. We must establish the religious workshop, on cooperative basis, for teacher and student, and, at long last, do away with the superstitious belief in old, outworn methods of education.

> I venture to say that these ideals of modern pedagogy have even been practiced already for quite some time. Where? In the *yeshivot* of Lithuania, which know of no compulsion, no extraneous auxiliary for education, of no thought of any teacher's clamor for authority and obedience. Nothing more or less do they intend to be than guides of a self-conscious youth who looks up, with spontaneous awe and admiration, to those masters of mind and spirit. They have one distinct educational

aim: the creative absorption of Torah. In the shadow of this aim, all intellectualism is subdued. They live united in religious wholeness, the brilliant students alongside with the less gifted, all striving towards the same goal: to learn for the sake of learning. Barely a breath of the outside world reaches into their inner sanctum. The rude realities of life are not permitted to stifle the atmosphere of pure idealism.

I do not know whether we shall ever attain again this orientation for our own schools here. But we must never weaken in our effort at rehabilitation, at mastering anew the problem of educating the Jewish child along the lines of development and progress."

No wonder that this glowing image of Yeshivah-life in the East followed Carlebach on his way back to Germany and made him implant it there. Shortly after his return to his home-town, he invited the illustrious *Rov*, Shmuel N. Rabinow of Kovno, to join him in founding a *yeshivah* in Lubeck. When elected Principal of the Talmud Torah High School in Hamburg, he succeeded in securing the Board's approval to establish another *yeshivah* in that city, calling again Rov Rabinow to head it.

III.

Master of the school, master of the pulpit, Joseph Carlebach relentlessly pursued his first and foremost urge: to teach Torah. His lectures on *T'nakh,* attended by many hundreds of people, kept the audience spellbound from beginning to end. He opened for them new vistas of the perception of the Divine Word, of the visions of the prophets, and the Jewish way of life. Beyond explaining difficult passages in Biblical writings in accord with the classic authorities, he made his listeners live through, in dramatic presentation, the torments of Hiob, the exalted poetry of *Shir Ha'shirim,* the philosophy of Kohelet, the historic period of the prophets as a revelation of their own inner ego and helped them realize the intimate connection of their own life with the long chain of generations down to the dim past. Said he in his inaugural sermon as Hamburg's Chief Rabbi:

". . . Thus should it be possible to serve best the many who, through wrong education and the short-sighted ideology of assimilation, have been estranged from the word of our Torah. To them we shall open the gates, build the golden bridge to bring them back. All my experience as rabbi and teacher has

convinced me of a deep-seated yearning, even among our alienated brethren, for a pure Jewishness—a longing much stronger
than we are led to believe. They sense the timelessness of our
Torah, they know we do not barter away any of the eternal
values of our religion. They know that the steadfastness of the
Jewish ideal shields their souls against the vicissitudes of life.
They crave to belong, for themselves and for their children.
So let us make this synagogue the center wherein to gather all
those who long to hear the undiluted word of God, above all
our youth which, in the word of the prophet, wilts away,
languishing for the truth which they do not find. They shall
find us ready wherever, whenever they are willing to come and
to listen."

His lectures attracted a wide variety of believers, Orthodox and
others, scholars and laymen, young and old, and inspired them
with new insights, understanding, and faith. When the fateful
year of 1933 broke over German Jewry, his inspired leadership
reached a climax in religious guidance, spiritual comfort and sheer
humane help, surpassing all his past achievements and culminating
in his open challenge to the powers of destruction by his demon-
strations, in word and deed, of the immortality of the Jewish
people and the Jewish Faith.

IV.

Carlebach's approach to the problems of progressive education,
to the changing tasks of the rabbinate, to the rejuvenation of
Biblical understanding and Jewish ideals, was but an expression of
his independent personality and of his belief in religious individuality. Indeed, his entire lifework bears the imprint of this characteristic. It also acted as a barrier against his sharing in political
leadership of Orthodox Judaism. To be sure, he joined and supported the Agudat Israel movement, but without sacrificing his
right to evaluate its strengths and its weaknesses. Attending its
second Kenessiah Gedolah (The "Torah Parliament") in Vienna,
he was deeply moved by this "mighty demonstration of faithfulness
to the Law of Israel and its rabbinical leadership" and he could
"sense the heartbeat of the pious great Jewish mass":

"Agudat Israel is a religious movement, neither more, nor less.
Every one of its meetings is divine service, rather than parliament, its language more sermon than discussion. Here Judaism
appears openly and clearly as a religious community and noth-

ing else. Its body politic is religion, its subject matter—worship, and the absolute authority of the Rabbinical Council the mark of distinction for the whole assembly.

But this is also the borderline of the Kenessiah where inherent danger begins. The Agudah swings too high above the earth and threatens to lose the ground under its feet. It affects our soul with excitement, but lends no will nor power for action. Abandoned to lofty ideals, it shrinks away from any concrete planning for their realization, from organizing the many into an advance-guard of practical workers, yes, collectors of taxes to bring up the wherewithal to give effect to an ultimate purpose. Here Agudat Israel fails seriously.

After all, what is to be the true nature of Agudat Israel? Shall it be considered a union created, above all, to preserve the purity of Jewish ideals, to demonstrate to the world the existence of a broad body of adherents to the historic structure of the Jewish people on the basis of Torah and *mitzvot?* Or is it a union for the purpose of giving effect to the actual and urgent needs of Orthodoxy? I believe only in the latter, for I do not worry about the eternality of Judaism and its purity as long as there is the Torah with its tradition as our unshakable foundation.

Thus, the concept of the Agudah as an ideological union appears to me a mistake, precipitated by the still more serious dominating error of the day, Zionism, with its concept of a Jewish nationalism fashioned after the materialistic trend of modern history. Neither can Zionism be reconciled with the institution of Judaism as a God-created Messianic ideal; it is wrong to consider the Jewish people merely a certain unit, without seeing in it the bearer of a creative higher principle devolving for all time in every individual Jew and in the whole of the people as well. But the attempt by Agudah to react upon these concepts of Zionism may well lead to the opposite mistake of underestimating the folk-realities of Judaism and eventually producing an ideology which overlooks fundamentals of collective existence in favor of common convictions, moral attitudes and a conformity in the conduct of life. In short, it will result in ignoring the national element—and this is, indeed, what already happens within the Agudah. At the very moment when language, country and common origin should govern our thinking, these concepts find no consideration and are pushed aside as irrelevant and incidental. But it is not an answer to Zionism's emphasis on country and common origin merely to make recognition of Torah and a devotion to *mitzvot* the only earmarks of the Agudah Movement. The Agudah's silence about the national element in Judaism and its deliberate evasion of open discussion about our positive orientation towards this national element is intolerable."

Carlebach's critical mind prevented him from following Agudah wholeheartedly, from throwing the full weight of his energies to its total organizational scheme. He chose to fight even alone, wherever the preservation of Jewish essentials seemed to him at stake. But his major targets were the advocates of Reform and the Jewish protagonists of modern Bible Criticism. Travelling from place to place and in numerous publications, he relentlessly attacked the ill-famed *Richtlinien* (Guiding Principles) set up by the leaders of Reform, exposing their incompatibility with the tenets of Judaism, their contravention of Jewish concepts and the fateful weakness of the entire program. Equally strong were his attacks on those "Renegades of the Spirit" whose concoctions in interpreting the Bible stirred his soul to the point of physical pain and made him condemn their work in strongest terms:

> "We reject every scholar of the Jewish faith who, in his work on the Bible, knowingly or by sheer ignorance, disregards any of the traditional commentaries beginning with the Talmud, via Rashi, Ibn Esra, Redak to the Ma'bim, S. R. Hirsch, D. Hoffmann and the authorities up to the very recent day. We reject every scholar of the Jewish faith who does not appraise Jewish values from the Jewish viewpoint, but takes his guidance from the non-Jewish, or even anti-Jewish, world."

V.

Carlebach's amazing capability of recreating before the eyes and ears of his listeners the spiritual assets of Jewish literature, and especially of the Bible, into living culture, his mastery in unveiling, through captivating oratorical presentation, the synthesis between the teachings of yore and contemporary values, is revealed in his books on *Shir Ha'Shirim, The Three Great Prophets: Isaiah, Jeremiah, and Ezekiel,* and *Kohelet—An Attempt at Interpretation.* They were edited after his lectures on these subjects and still reverberate the fervor of his voice breathing new life into Biblical words and shedding new light on them:

> "Unfathomable, as love itself, is *Shir Ha'shirim.* Its song illuminates love's holy mystery by the vibrating sound of words which stir our emotions even when we do not know what exactly they say—like the distant glow of the city's nightly lights guiding the stranger to the unknown place. Enough for us to know that the glory of love is the ultimate meaning of *Shir Ha'shirim,* that the divine flame of love burns in it and sings to us. As to the

question whether *Shir Ha'shirim* is allegory or a real song of love: It testifies to the high concepts of the Jewish people that the emotions of love, by metaphysical transfiguration, were made moral sign or symbol of Israel's boundless attachment and devotion to God. In the last analysis, it becomes rather irrelevant whether it pictures a real pair of lovers named Salomo and Sulamith or whether it is the expression of a metaphysical ideal. It means both and so we find the theme songs of *Shir Ha'shirim* sounding through later-day liturgical poetry and Jewish folk-song as well."

In his book, *The Three Great Prophets,* Carlebach penetrates deeply into the prophetic spirit, taking issue with the attempt to rationalize the phenomenon of prophetic vision on mere psychological grounds. He demonstrates brilliantly the eternal validity of the prophetic words in the light of mankind's history:

"Is there genuine prophecy or is there not? That is the very problem of religion. It is the acid test of our authentic meeting with God, whether or not He really revealed Himself. It has to do with the certainty of God's existence, about the reality of all religion. Like a towering rock in the ocean of time is the word of the great Jewish prophets in the literature of the world. Of all Biblical writings, the greatest importance was attached to them. What accounts for this distinction? Why does the world see in them the classics of religion? Evidently, because they are a clearer manifestation of higher inspiration, a more powerful expression of the divine spirit, a more immediate introduction to universal religiosity than any other spiritual work. Here, man feels himself addressed, actually and inescapably, by the Absolute.

But this very confrontation, by the prophetic word, of man with God, also made these books of the Prophets the largest problems to a science inclined to disbelief and to the assumption that all happenings in the world develop according to innate, logical laws like any system of natural science—an attitude unwilling to tolerate the veto of a timeless power. Are the prophets really the envoys of a higher will, they ask, authorized and competent to invoke such intervention? And by twofold answer do they propose to negate their title of validity. For one, they go so far as to question their legitimacy. For the other, they would not deny their mission but would re-interpret the prophetic message by transposing it into a surrealistic world, thinking of no real urgency, no actuality as to the present. They would turn the prophets into apocalyptists proclaiming something celestial but nothing of this earth, saying and prognosticating something about divine Providence but leaving mankind very much to itself.

Both arguments are equally sinister. The first makes the prophets outright liars, makes prophethood a self-deception. The other turns prophecy into an illusion, the prophets into dreamers. Both distort the prophetic word, are rooted in misconception of the nature of religion.

Revelation must be true and truthful. It cannot be reconciled with the concept of a God of Truth that these supreme teachers of self-inspection and rigorous veracity, these fiery attackers of falsehood and vanity, could have dared a frivolous venture with the legitimacy of their own mission. According to Jewish teaching, even the wisest of men, whose spirit might carry him to the loftiest heights, is rejected as messenger of eternal precepts when he becomes guilty of any moral wrong. Such "prophet" is incompatible with the honor of God and the dignity of religion.

True prophethood breaks through the barriers of the rational while, at the same time, the contents and the directive of veritable prophecy are rational. Revelation must be realizable, attainable by man, otherwise it would run counter to human dignity and reason. The great prophets are not soothsayers and prognosticators of fate, nor conjurers of celestial power for salvation or disaster. They are the great exponents of life, the scrutinizers of destiny, the guides into a bright future which, however, would not arrive automatically but rather, so the prophets admonish us, should be formed and shaped by ourselves, by our own effort. Nowhere do our prophets entertain the thought that human distress had gone too far for human power to save; that our earth is too deeply enmeshed in guilt and misery for a way out of the crisis; that the world must be destroyed and God Himself must intervene in order to lead up the new world. This despair in man, this complete passivity towards the rottenness of the momentary state of mankind, has been characteristic, not of the Hebrew Bible, but of the Apocalypse: 'Only as spectator is man admitted to experience God's day of world-renewal, be it as happy beneficiary of new salvation or as the one doomed to be crushed under its impact.'

But we cannot say it often enough or strongly enough that the trust in an all-powerful God is equalled by the trust in the infinite moral power of righteous man. . . . The majesty and holiness of God is correlated to the holy efficacy of the human being who absorbs the Law into his volition and identifies himself with the ultimate intents of Providence. It is not that salvation is for the chosen ones, but rather are they chosen for salvation. They are to bring it, to make it a reality. . . ."

Rabbi Carlebach's interpretation of *Kohelet* is unique among the traditional commentaries on this baffling work with its apparently pessimistic outlook on life, so contrary to Jewish concepts. He postulates that nothing of the kind may be read into that book. Its author merely intended to show the vanity, the utter emptiness of a life built only upon the material fortunes of this earth without any higher ideals, any absolute values, without the performance of *mitzvot* and orientation towards God. The picture of such life, with its key-words *"I"*, *"under the sun"*, and *"futile"*, repeated again and again, furnishes indeed a most forceful argument that the affirmation of life demands something else to make it worthwhile, to raise us above the animal level towards a constant, eternal goal:

> *"Kohelet* is the book of a subdued joy of life, of joy knowing about the tragedy of existence. It is the book of humility, of the human being without pretension to be a god, without craving absolute power. Its intent is to teach that nothing in the world should tempt us to see the only purpose of living in secure possession, honors and public recognition, power and success. Its immutable meaning lies beyond any of these. It can be found only in relation to God and His commandments."

Joseph Carlebach was also a prolific author of essays, most of which appeared in the *Israelit* of Frankfort and in the *Jeschurun* of Berlin. The wide range of subjects covered by these essays is indicated by their titles, such as "The Psalter of David in the Change of Time", "Style and Personality", "Morality as Polity", "Nature and Evaluation of the Minhag in Israel", "Services in the Synagogue of the Present", "Rabbinical Courts of Arbitration", and many others on educational problems and philosophy of religion. Several of Carlebach's writings were dedicated to Franz Rosenzweig, for whom he had a feeling of close attachment.

VI.

Carlebach's lifework grew to real magnitude. It was marked by a titanic effort to spread knowledge of Torah and to implant understanding of its values into his countless followers. But it is still another thing to evaluate his stature. Its greatness can never be adequately measured because his manifest achievements in meeting the emergency which befell his congregation and all European Jewry are but a fraction of his whole record: of the deeds of charity he passionately pursued, by day and by night, on lonely errands to help, to comfort, to counsel. In those dark hours he heard only the call of his inner voice to give more and more of himself, to verify his own profound understanding of the "trying problem of theodicy", the problem of suffering.

"Why all this torment? That is the question of the *Galut*. Why the suffering of the good, the noble, the pious, the righteous? This question is answered by Isaiah in his book of consolation and his answer is merely a slight variation of the question itself. We should not ask: 'Why does the servant of God suffer? but: 'What does he suffer for?' Why does he suffer? It hardly needs explanation: simply because mankind is not as yet messianic, because this world is not according to the will of God, not in the image of God. The only question then is: What does man suffer for? And there the Prophet assures us: You do not suffer in vain, not without aim and purpose! You suffer because through your suffering alone the world of the future can arise, because through this martyrdom the people of Israel is to help bring about the accomplishment of the ultimate messianic form of life in its normal, innate course of development. The suffering in the world would be unbearable were it senseless. But all suffering, all torment is still endurable to the noble soul if it serves towards the ultimate, highest purpose of earthly existence."

Joseph Carlebach stood this supreme test as a "servant of God" in the very sense of Isaiah's word. His blessed memory will stay with the eternal people an undying source of faith and strength.

MOSHE AVIGDOR AMIEL

(1883-1945)

By Solomon Kerstein

MOSHE AVIGDOR AMIEL*

By Solomon Kerstein

With the untimely death of Moshe Avigdor Amiel, beloved Chief Rabbi of Tel Aviv, a brilliant luminary of the rabbinic and scholarly world was extinguished.

He died on his birthday. There was deep mourning in all circles of traditional Judaism in the *Yishuv,* notably in the Mizrachi movement, of which he had been a pillar. He was at the height of his creative powers at his passing. He had brought breadth and perfection in many Jewish fields of his extraordinary creativity in his works on *Halakhah* and *Agadah,* and his addresses at Mizrachi conventions and Zionist Congresses. His studies, both in Hebrew and Yiddish, on the national religious ideology were preeminent.

Not long before his passing, the religious *Yishuv* had celebrated his sixtieth birthday and his fifty years of accomplishment for Torah and Zion. His work in behalf of Judaism, the national revival, and the upbuilding of the land, elicited full recognition from the entire *Yishuv.* In his honor, *Hatzofeh,* Mizrachi daily, brought out a special literary supplement.

I.

When twenty-seven years ago the community of Tel Aviv, first all-Jewish city, turned to Rabbi Amiel to succeed the late Rabbi Shlomo Hacohen Aronson, the populace rejoiced. But the Antwerp community, which he was serving with such distinction, was loath to let him go. (Soon after, however, Antwerp was compensated when the Mizrachi leader and rabbi of Lipneh, Samuel Halevi Brod, now a member of the Supreme Court in Jerusalem, came to assume the mantle of Chief Rabbi.)

---

*This article, expanded from a eulogy of my distinguished teacher of blessed memory, was written soon after his demise on the twelfth day of Nissan, 5705 (1945). He would now have been seventy-five years old. The article was included in the new American edition of Amiel's homiletic work, *Derashot el Ami* (Vol. 1, N. Y., 1952). The first edition (1923) appeared in Warsaw before his appointment as Chief Rabbi of Antwerp, my native city, where I was privileged to read the galley proofs of his subsequent volumes.

Amiel's achievements during his decade in Tel Aviv cannot be compassed in a brief review. One of his major successes was the academy he founded, known as The Yeshivah of the New Yishuv, now Yeshivat Ha-Rav Amiel. There was no dearth of distinguished *yeshivot* in Eretz Israel. But this project was revolutionary. Amiel had sensed the need of a Torah center in Israel which should be in keeping with the new *Yishuv*. His institution was to combine Torah and all other scholarly activities of the land in one curriculum, with all subjects taught in *Hebrew*. Its impress on the new *Yishuv,* particularly the youth groups, was immediately discernible. Later his project was proven a deed of foresight; for hundreds of religious-national youths, after graduation from *yeshivot ketanot* and high schools, streamed to it.

During the seven years when Rabbi Amiel stood at its helm, the *yeshivah* brought forth many rabbis and scholars who were to become a glory of the *Yishuv.* He founded his "network of Talmudic education"—Talmud Torahs and *yeshivot ketanot* to serve as preparatory schools for the central *yeshivah.* These schools are today found in Tel Aviv and its environs, in *moshavot* and *kevutzot.* For the adults and workers, Amiel established many centers for evening study. One of his final accomplishments was The Writers' Assembly, (*Kinnus Sofrim*), a group of rabbis who charted new courses in study of the Torah *"lishmah"* (for its own sake). The rabbi headed this group until his passing; its great task has been that of forming a unified system out of the Six Orders of the Mishnah.

Rabbi Amiel's ramified educational enterprises won the support of important groups in the *Yishuv* and outstanding individuals in the United States.

But Rabbi Amiel's signal talents were revealed in fields besides *Halakhah.* He was magniloquent as preacher, as well as educator and public servant. He excelled as stylist and publicist. His religio-philosophic essays have been adjudged an invaluable contribution to Hebrew thought. The late Chief Rabbi Kook remarked that on receiving a new book by Amiel, he would utter the blessing of *Sheheheyanu* over it, as one does on receiving or accomplishing something completely new. The rabbi's homiletic works are considered models in content, originality, unique style, and timeliness. Like his *halakhic* books, they have gone through four editions.

II.

Moshe Avigdor Amiel was born in 1883 (5643) in the town of Porozov, near Grodno. His father, Rabbi Jacob Joseph, a noted scholar, imparted much knowledge to his son until his Bar Mitzvah. The son cites several of his father's interpretations in his *halakhic* works.

At thirteen, he was sent to the celebrated *yeshivah* at Telz, where he studied for two years. He soon became known as a genius, being dubbed by his fellow students "the *illuy* (infant prodigy) of Porozov". Thence he journed to Vilna, the Jerusalem of Lithuania, to study under Rabbis Hayyim Soloveitchik and Hayyim Ozer Grodzenski.*

His first ministry was in the city of Schwintzan, which is near Vilna. Then only twenty-two, he had been called to replace the noted Rabbi Isaac Jacob Reines, founder of the Lida Yeshivah and of the Mizrachi movement. During his first years in Schwintzan, he was invited by Baron Guenzburg, in the name of the St. Petersburg community, to become a candidate for the Chief Rabbinate of this distinguished and aristocratic congregation. His youth, however—he was twenty-five—aroused opposition to his election.

In 1913 Amiel was named rabbi of Grayevo, a mature and much respected community. This city, on the German border, was first to suffer the barbarities of World War I. But it was then that the rabbi was able to demonstrate his talent for public service and his devotion to the war-stricken.

III.

The first important turn in his life came when Amiel departed from Poland in 1920 to head the Antwerp community, then one of the greatest in Western Europe. As Chief Rabbi, with broader horizons looming before him, he was enabled to utilize all his faculties. His fame soon extended to the entire Jewish world.

It was in that very year, 5680, that Amiel made his first appearance on the world Jewish stage, at the World Mizrachi Convention

---

*Among the Geonim who ordained him, at eighteen, were Rabbi Shlomo Hacohen of Vilna, Rabbi Zvi Hirsch Rabinowitz of Kovno, Rabbi Moshe Kokoshawski of Slobodka, Rabbi Meir Simcha Hacohen of Dwinsk, and the famed "Rogatchover", Rabbi Joseph Rosen of Dwinsk.

held in Amsterdam. As representative of Polish Mizrachi, his brilliant address on Mizrachi ideology and on Zionist problems profoundly impressed all in the assemblage. It was at this convention that the Antwerp delegation pressed him to remain in their city. Antwerp provided a broad field. The community, numbering forty thousand, had not been properly organized since the first years of the war. Through Amiel's leadership and the magic of his personality, peace and unity were established among all groups.

He founded *Tachkemoni,* the Hebrew high school, Talmud Torahs, a *yeshivah;* taught a daily class of the Talmud; strengthened the city's charitable institutions; and systematically organized the conduct of *kashrut.*

When many immigrants passed through the port city after the war on their journey to America, Amiel labored to assist them. He gained their gratitude and respect by insisting on *kashrut* in the immigrant hostels. A great victory was the consent of the heads of the precious stones exchanges to close their establishments on Sabbaths and holidays. He successfully established new congregations in Belgium's small cities.

The rabbi's home, with its large library, was a meeting place for scholars, rabbis, merchants, writers, and newspaper men—a spiritual center. Rabbi Amiel was beloved by the Zionist youth, notably those of Mizrachi and Torah Va-avodah. His reputation for hospitality and liberality grew apace. Privileged to serve him as his personal secretary, and with the freedom of his house, I was able to study the man and his deeds at intimate range.

An interesting fact, which came to light during Amiel's first days in Antwerp, indicates the nobility of his soul. When he received his salary, he would set a considerable part of it aside for charity, so that there was not sufficient remaining to supply necessities for Mrs. Amiel. The leaders of the community at once understood that they could not "trust" their rabbi with his salary. They would hand it to the *rebbetzin,* who assumed control of all household matters.

IV.

The spiritual legacy of Rabbi Amiel is being administered and enhanced by his descendants. He left a wife, a woman of distinguished ancestry and a scholar in her own right; six daughters;

and two sons—Eliezer, a lawyer, and Levi Isaac, graduate of the agricultural school, Mikveh Israel.

The rabbi gloried in his sons-in-law. One, Rabbi Levi Isaac Rabinowitz, became Chief Chaplain of the British Eighth Army, and later was elected Chief Rabbi of Johannesburg, South Africa. Rabbis Koppel of Paris and Saltzer of Marseilles distinguished themselves in the Zionist division of the Maquis, the French underground. The former was miraculously snatched from the clutches of the Gestapo. These two, again living in France, are helping restore the religious life of the Jewish youth there. The fourth son-in-law is Dr. Selbourne of Manchester, England. Another one, Nathan Lindenbaum, of blessed memory, a diamond trader and onetime president of Young Mizrachi in Antwerp, lived in New York. His widow married Max Stern, philanthropist, president of the New York Jewish Center, founder of Stern College, and leader in Torah-true Judaism in the U. S. One daughter is married to the noted Israeli public worker, Mr. A. Mann.

V.

Moshe Avigdor Amiel was known to the Jewish world as an outstanding preacher, who greatly influenced his generation. He was among the few Jewish leaders whose strength was equal in speaking and writing. As a *Rosh yeshivah,* he delivered his lucid lectures on the Talmudic themes. His books on law were outstanding in style, as well as in content. His spoken thoughts were always clear and well arranged. Many rabbis still employ his homilies as source material for their own sermons.

In his preface to *Derashot el Ami,* the author declares, "My sermons are not philosophical research, nor hairsplitting dissertations, nor examples of mysticism, but simply the Torah speaking in human language." He named his book *Derashot el Ami* (Sermons to my People) not only as a play on his own name, but as a hope that his works would achieve true popularity.

In addition to preaching, Rabbi Amiel taught *Halakhah* at his *yeshivah,* and the Mishneh Torah of Maimonides at the Great Synagogue of Tel Aviv. His articles appeared in *Sinai* and other periodicals; most impressive were his essays on "The Perplexed of This Era" in *Hamishor.*

Amiel's radiant image shines from his works, *Darke Moshe* and *Hamiddot Leheker Halakhah,* which cover the entire range of Talmudic and legal literature.

However, his writing does not sparkle with paradox. Completely original, logical, and lucid, he never tries to "lead an elephant through the eye of a needle."

FROM THE SELECTED WRITINGS OF RABBI MOSHE AVIGDOR AMIEL*

The Holiday of Spring and the Festival of the First Fruits

"*Pessah* and *Shavuot* each have an additional name—'the Holiday of Spring, and 'the Festival of the First Fruits'. These names convey their significance.

In the Spring Holiday, we bring forth flowers, while on the Festival of *Shavuot,* we present fruit. The former serves as the means, while the latter realizes the ends.

"Thus, *Pessah* represents the flowering of the Jewish nation, but *Shavuot* manifests its fruitfulness. For a free people without Torah, can be likened to flowers without fruit. Flowers, to be sure, are a delight to the eye, but, in themselves, they cannot satisfy. Fruit, on the other hand, while it may not please the sense of sight, is nevertheless vital to the sense of taste. And our fruit ripened only after the giving of the Torah.

"In short, the exodus from Egypt is the means; the giving of the Torah, the end."

The Holiness of the Jewish People

"There are those who understand Judaism through its aspect of holiness (*kedushah*) ; and there are those who appreciate it for its differentness (*havdalah*), in that it makes us distinct from all other nations on the face of the earth.

"And even as we conceive of Judaism, so do we consider the Jews; for Israel is unlike other peoples. Other nations *observe* their traditions, but their traditions do not *preserve* them, whereas in the case of the Jewish People, to a far greater extent than we *observe* the Torah, the Torah *preserves* us. 'It is a tree of life to those who cling to it'."

---

*I wish to express my indebtedness to Mr. Haskel Lookstein of Yeshiva University, for his English rendition of some of these excerpts.

Automatic Sanctification

" 'The vessels of the sanctuary sanctify their contents with or without the intent of the owner'. The Land of Israel is the sanctifying vessel of the Jewish People which resides therein; it sanctifies that people with or without its intent."

Two Great Mitzvot

"Consider carefully: There is one great *mitzvah* in the Torah, 'Thou shalt love thy neighbor as thyself', and not all are scrupulous in its observance. Whereas, in the case of the *mitzvah,* 'Thou shalt purge the evil from thy midst,' every Jew scrupulously goes about purging this evil—*from his fellow Jew.*

"In the *Haggadah shel Pessah* it is written about the wicked son: 'Because he removed himself from the general rule, he denied the principle'; and I say—because he denied the principle, he removed himself from the general rule."

Rabbi Amiel, observing the construction of *yeshivot* in Israel, thus paraphrased a remark of Saadia Gaon: "Our land is not the Land of Israel, except through its Torah."

On Partition of Palestine

". . . Indeed, those whose desire is merely 'to be like other nations,' will be satisfied with a small portion of the land, for there are other similarly unfortunate nations. But those to whom the Land of Israel is a land of life and holiness, will never accept the principle of partition. Only the dead can be dissected, never the living; and just as we never tolerated dissection and renovation of the Torah, so shall we never allow the dissection of Palestine. And if heaven has decreed that we accept this evil and painful situation, we shall accept it in part; the entire Land of Israel without a Jewish State, but not a Jewish State without the entire Land of Israel."

On the Subject of Sabbath

" 'Verily, you shall keep my Sabbaths, for it is a sign between me and you.' From the word 'sign' we learn that *Tephillin* are not donned on the Sabbath. For *Tephillin* are themselves a sign, as it is written: *'And you shall bind them for a sign upon your hand.'*

"We might inquire how the 'sign' of the Sabbath supersedes the 'sign' of *Tephillin*. Perhaps the opposite should be true, that the 'sign' of *Tephillin* ought to supersede the 'sign' of the Sabbath, and one who dons *Tephillin* on the Sabbath ought to be excused from the obligation of observing the Sabbath?

"Obviously, there are 'signs' and 'signs.' When we say that *Tephillin* are a sign, they are so called because they are placed on the head (the seat of thought) and opposite the heart. The Sabbath, however, is in itself the mind and heart of Judaism. It contains the essence of its thought and emotion, of the idea and the song of Judaism. The Sabbath is not only a 'source of blessing,' it is also a wellspring of Jewish thought and song. There is no natively Jewish thought, nor any authentically Jewish song whose content and spirit are not firmly embedded within the Sabbath. In it we perceive the vision of everything, and from it we derive our ideals and yearnings. If, God forbid, the Sabbath were ever to be abolished, the authentic Jewish mind and heart would disappear with it."

Next Year in Jerusalem

"If you will ask why we do not recite 'Next year in Jerusalem' seven times, as is our custom at the end of *Neilah* with 'The Lord is *the* God', I shall reply, that essentially, in this case, action speaks louder than words, and he who is short on words and long on deeds is all the more deserving of praise.

"Consequently, it has been prescribed that we pronounce 'Next year in Jerusalem' but once, for there is not time to waste on speech, since we are listening for the 'Great Shofar' which calls for the ingathering of the exiles. Immediately it is incumbent upon us to begin the work of building an everlasting and eternal structure. Immediately, upon hearing the blast of the *shofar,* we shall say with utmost haste, 'Next year in Jerusalem', and once we shall run homeward, the torch of our soul in hand, in order to begin fulfilling the *mitzvah* of '*succah*': to reestablish and bring to reality 'the Fallen Succah of David.'

"Then, most certainly, God willing, 'Next year in Jerusalem.' "

The Individual and the Public

"In every single individual, no matter how lowly, there exists a Divine image. If he commits any crime, he suffers pangs of conscience. But collective crimes do not even bring in their wake conscience-pangs. Only very few individuals are so unique as to have transgressed *'Thou shalt not kill'*. Clearly, however, is there a nation in existence which can say that as a nation it has not violated this prohibition? If every man possesses a 'Divine voice which walks within him', when this same man merges with the group, that group serves as an iron rampart cutting him off from the Divine voice within him.

"And when God revealed himself to the People of Israel on Mt. Sinai, he gave the Ten Commandments in the singular, directing them at every single person individually. 'I am the Lord *thy* God . . . Thou shalt have no other gods. . . .'"

Collective and Individual Righteousness

"If we should desire to summarize briefly all the distinctions between the general and the Jewish views of righteousness, we might best include them in one slogan, and put it thus: the general view is that righteousness rests on the principle of 'the part is only representative of the whole', whereas the Jewish view maintains just the reverse, that 'the whole is only equal to the sum of its parts'. The general view is that man—the part—is vital only insofar as his existence benefits society—the whole. The Jewish view sees the opposite, namely, that society was created exclusively in order to ameliorate and improve the lot of man— man, who is precious in and of himself.

"It follows from this premise, that the criteria which operate in their view of righteousness are to be found in the welfare of the collective community. An act which contributes to the welfare of the group is a righteous one, while one which adversely affects the collective welfare is viewed as sinful.

"As far as the group itself is concerned, in its relations vis-à-vis the individual, 'anything goes'. Whereas our view considers the criteria by which to determine the ethical nature of a particular act, as being the good and welfare of every single individual."

The image of Rabbi Amiel is still engraved on the souls of thousands of his students and admirers in Israel and other lands. May his memory remain an eternal blessing. *Zekher Tzaddik Livrakhah.*

BIBLIOGRAPHICAL NOTE

Sefer Hayovel, a jubilee volume edited by Rabbi J. L. Maimon on the occasion of Rabbi Amiel's sixtieth birthday (Mosad Harav Kook, Jerusalem, 1943), contains a bibliography of his writings, compiled by Isaac Werfel (Raphael). It contains 306 items, from 1929 to 1943, his most creative period. Articles in Hebrew and Yiddish, and in German and French translation, appeared in newspapers the world over.

Amiel's major works, on *Halakhah* and *Agadah,* have been published in many editions—in Poland, Belgium, and Israel. They are considerel classics.

This is the listing:

Darke Moshe, two volumes

Derashot el Ami, three volumes (English edition, Vol. I, "Unto My People", translated by Rabbi L. J. Rabinowitz, London, 1936)

Habayot Haruhniyot Shebetzionut

Hegyonot el Ami, three volumes

Hayesodot Ha-idiologiyim shel Hamizrachi

Hamiddot Leheker Hahalakhah, two volumes

Hatzedek Hasotziali Vehatzedek Hamishpati

Linevukhe Hatekufah

Am Segulah

Shabbat Malketa

ELIYAHU ELIEZER DESSLER

(1891-1953)

By Lion Carmell

ELIYAHU ELIEZER DESSLER

By Lion Carmell

Introduction

Every age produces the great men it most needs. The needs of our orphaned age are great, in the spheres of both theory and practice. In the realm of theory we need a twentieth-century Samson Raphael Hirsch[1], able to convey the eternal wisdom of the Torah to the contemporary mind. In the practical sphere, we need organizing genius, allied to vision, self-sacrifice and incandescent sincerity, to ensure the survival and expansion of Torah-institutions after the ravages of the Great Destruction.

One personality of our time combined both these faculties to an extraordinary degree. Because of his self-effacing mode of life and work, the wider world knew little or nothing of him, but his influence in both spheres was great and it is cumulative in effect. Only the future will reveal its true extent. That one was Rabbi Eliyahu Eliezer Dessler.

He was born in 1891 at Gomel, Russia, into a family famous for wealth and learning. His father, Rabbi Reuben Dov, had been a pupil of Rabbi Simhah Zissel Ziff[2] (one of the foremost disciples of Rabbi Israel Salanter),[3] from childhood, and had married a granddaughter of Rabbi Israel Salanter.

For a lengthy period—until the family fortune was lost in the Russian Revolution—the Dessler family were amongst the chief supporters of the famous *Mussar* academy, the Talmud Torah at Kellem, Lithuania, founded by Rabbi Simhah Zissel. Perhaps this upbringing amongst material abundance and in the spirit of self-criticism of the *Mussar* tradition, accounts for the fact that so much of Rabbi Dessler's teaching is directed against the temptations of materialism and selfishness, stressing man's task of creating good, for which all the material and spiritual gifts with which he is endowed are God-given tools.

---

[1]See pp. 263-299.
[2]See pp. 317-335.
[3]See "Jewish Leaders," pp. 197ff.

KELLEM

Unusual gifts of memory and logic appeared early in his life. Rabbi Hayyim Ozer Grodzenski of Vilna referred to him as *"a modner kind"* (an extraordinary child). Rabbi Dessler's father sent him to Kellem at the age of twelve. Though a boy amongst men, he achieved equal footing amongst those picked scholars. His application and concentration were a by-word: it became a game amongst local children to try to distract "Elinke the *Matmid"* (the industrious student).

His chief teacher was Rabbi Hirsch Braude, but he was greatly influenced also by Rabbi Simhah Zissel's son, Rabbi Nahum Wolf, as well as by his own father, under whom he studied in a refugee *yeshivah* (during the First World War when Kellem was under German occupation).

When the Communists came to power, the family were persecuted, but escaped to Latvia. Eliyahu Eliezer returned to study at Kellem. In 1919 he married Blume, a daughter of Rabbi N. W. Ziff, whose life embodied the great *Mussar* traditions of her illustrious family.

Rabbi Hayyim Ozer invited his nephew to become a *Dayan* at Vilna, but, in the family tradition of "trying not to make a living out of Torah", Dessler declined this opportunity and went to Riga, where, with his father, he attempted to restore the family business. The attempt failed, and it took him many years to repay, from his meager earnings, the debts of that failure.

Then began years of wandering, which led him also to America. (There are letters still extant from this period, in which his father warns him against the materialist influence of the local "golden calves".)

LONDON

In 1927 Rabbi Dessler settled in London with his wife and young son and daughter. He became rabbi in a well-known community, but this work did not satisfy him. His attitude may be summed up in a remark he made to its lay leaders: "Of all the hundreds of children attending our Talmud Torah, the only real achievement is with one we manage to send away to a full-time *yeshivah*. The rest will, unfortunately, probably not remember enough Hebrew even to say *'Kaddish'*." What he thought of the

Anglo-Jewish education of the period is shown by the fact that he kept his son out of school, himself teaching him and hiring a private teacher for the secular subjects demanded by the law of the land. As soon as possible, he sent him to the *yeshivot* of Vilkomir and Telz.

What did give him satisfaction was the private tuition he imparted to a small number of local boys. He selected his pupils carefully, with due regard to their talents and potentialities, and concentrated his great personal charm upon winning them for Torah. Having gained their interest and attachment by his profound Talmudical teaching, he introduced them gradually to the outlook on life taught by the *Mussar* school. Thus he managed to turn a number of businessmen's sons, who had never been to a full-time *yeshivah,* into Torah-personalities of considerable achievement and influence; they, in turn, are spreading his teaching now.

The strongest ingredient in his teaching was perhaps the object lesson of himself as a product of *Mussar*—his wonderful character, his kindness and consideration to all, his readiness to help with all his might anyone in any kind of difficulty.

One aspect of this help was to lend the full weight of his powerful mind to the solution of any problem brought to him. Since these pupils had received a modern education, it fell to Rabbi Dessler to resolve certain conflicts which had arisen in their minds relating to Torah and modern thought. This interest developed eventually into a new synthesis, based on the profound insights of the *Mussar* ideology and producing results which are a genuine and noble contribution to Jewish philosophy. Some of the fruits of this research are included in the posthumously published selection from his writings, *Mikhtav Me-Eliyahu* (London, 1955). Yet his attitude towards this kind of endeavor is characterized by his remark after proposing a particularly profound thesis: "Would that we never had this sort of problem! For those who, in their innermost heart, are really imbued with the spirit of the Torah, these are not problems at all. . . ."

Crisis

The Second World War, with its catastrophe for the Jewish people, imposed upon Rabbi Dessler a terrific spiritual burden, which eventually brought out his hidden reserves of power. His wife and daughter had gone to visit his son and other relatives in

Lithuania, and were stranded there at the outbreak of war. For a long time their fate was in doubt. Only those familiar with his sentitive nature could imagine his suffering, but he did not show how he felt. So, far from burdening his friends with his heartache, he did his utmost to comfort them in their own troubles. A clue to his feelings at this time may, however, be found in an *en passant* statement of his: "I need not worry about my family; since they are with such a righteous man as my brother-in-law, Rabbi Daniel,[4] it is well with them."

Eventually, his wife and children escaped from Europe—his wife and daughter to Australia, and his son[5] to America—and he was reunited with them only after the war.

On the other hand, his participation in the troubles of Israel knew no bounds. All his lectures of the period reveal the impact of the disaster. One problem in particular gave him no rest: "To what end has God left *us* alive?"

Decision

In 1941 Rabbi Dessler received the answer to this question, so far as he was concerned. There arrived a letter from Rabbi David Dryan, the *Shohet* of Gateshead, proposing the establishment of a *Kolel* (Institute of Higher Rabbinical Studies) for great Torah scholars, refugees from the great *yeshivot* of Poland and Lithuania who, at that time, were dispersed all over Great Britain, and requesting his cooperation.

The small Jewish community at Gateshead, in the north (virtually, so far as its main Gentile population is concerned, a working-class suburb of Newcastle), was even then a Jewish settlement unique for England: it was composed entirely of Torah-observing and Torah-loving Jews, who applied *"heimishe"* standards to their choice of leaders and of their way of life. Their *Shohet,* too, was a unique man, who ceaselessly stimulated the community to the creation of institutions far beyond its numerical or financial importance. Already before the war, he had been instrumental in creating the now famous *yeshivah.*

---

[4]Then head of the Kellem Talmud Torah and later a victim of the Nazis.
[5]Now Rabbi N. W. Dessler, Principal of the Hebrew Academy of Cleveland, Ohio.

When Rabbi Dessler received that letter, he knew that his hour of decision had come.

The project seemed impossible: communal life was disrupted by war conditions; all normal business was at a standstill, and the better-known philanthropists were hard to reach at all in the villages to which they had fled from the bombing. The existing *yeshivot* found it hard to obtain the barest necessities —who could think of starting a new institution?

Furthermore, even in normal times, gigantic efforts would have been needed to establish an institution of this particular kind. Few enough in England were they who understood the need for *yeshivot;* the conception of a *Kolel*—to keep grown and able-bodied men with their families at public expense, merely to allow them to continue studying—was beyond the mental horizon of even the best of them. Who would be able to propagate the idea, to carry the responsibility for such an enterprise and such a budget, involving raising funds entirely from individual donors? He, a shy and retiring man who had never taken the limelight? He, a man of fifty who had never been of robust health?

On the other hand, he saw the need only too clearly.

Many students, including one complete *yeshivah,* had come into England as refugees. There were many of them—young men who were studying Torah eagerly amidst danger and poverty, and married men who had already been forced to take up unsuitable rabbinical positions—who refused to relinquish the hopes they had had when in the great *yeshivot,* of reaching a high standard of Torah-learning. Amongst students still younger, who had not managed to go to the great *yeshivot* at all, there was a "hunger for the word of God." There was a dearth of the *yeshivah*-environment, of great Torah-personalities who would make it their task, as formerly, to care for the future—both spiritual and material—of the individual students.

He saw this, and more. Who would decide *halakhic* problems in twenty years' time? Where would our future *Geonim* (great authorities) come from? Whence our future spiritual leaders if every student, after only a few years in a *yeshivah,* would be compelled to seek a position or a trade?

These thoughts revolved in his mind when he received the letter from Rabbi Dryan with his far-sighted proposal.

But he felt, too, and most strongly, his own unworthiness for such an epoch-making task. Looking around, however, he found no one else prepared even to consider such an undertaking. He saw that he alone had been called to bear this burden, and this was to be his contribution to the rebuilding of Torah-life on the ashes of the European destruction.

He saw the hand of Providence, too, in the apparent misfortune of the separation from his family: he was free to travel at will through the length and breadth of Great Britain, and to devote himself to the great spiritual goal.

However, another problem presented itself. What of his existing groups of disciples, who had come to rely on him for their spiritual guidance and sustenance? Were they to be sacrificed for the overriding communal cause?

His beneficent spirit could not contemplate this. The only alternative that he could see was to continue this personal work, and integrate it somehow with his new commitments.

Activity

By an effort—which in his state of health bordered on the super-human—and by an extraordinary degree of co-ordination and self-discipline, he managed to do four "full-time" jobs: to be in effect, though not in name, principal and director of the *Kolel;* to raise most of its budget; to deliver weekly *Mussar* lectures at the *Kolel;* to deliver weekly lectures to old and new study circles in London, Letchworth, Chesham, and Manchester.

All this involved an enormous amount of traveling, which, in the difficult war-time conditions, was a great physical strain. For the next four years he was to spend almost every week in the following way: two to three days devoted to private lessons, for some of which he received payment, which he used for his own needs and for the support of his family. For he had decided from the start not to take any salary from the *Kolel*. Most of the lessons, however, were unpaid—he could neither allow his old study groups to lapse, nor refuse to accept new students. If the day was not sufficient, he gave regular lessons at night, often through the night. During the rest of the weekdays, and between lessons, he went out to raise money. The long-distance traveling he did usually overnight: on Friday mornings he was back at Gateshead, where he spent the *Shabbat* and, if necessary, also Sunday, when he would normally set out once more on his weekly itinerary.

In spite of this, he remained accessible to anyone who asked for his advice on private or public problems, and wrote a flood of letters: to his family, to students and friends who, though scattered by the war, were determined to remain in touch with him and his teaching.

What is perhaps most surprising is that the same period was most fertile, both in the discovery of profound and original ideas (together with explanations of *Agadot,* Midrashic and Zohar passages which revealed hidden depths of *Mussar* and psychology), and in arranging them for lectures and articles.

That one man would do all this appears incredible even to those who witnessed it, but at the time it seemed very natural to us, because it was so to him—an illustration of his unassuming way of life.

That way is reflected also in the organization of the *Kolel:* he was no more than a member of the committee of students which made the decisions. However, though his vote was equal to that of any other, his stature and his work for the *Kolel* naturally lent weight to his opinions.

The work required was tremendous: it was part of the constitution that no member was allowed outside earnings, or, indeed, any outside activity if it intruded on the ten or more hours per day fixed for study. In return, the *Kolel* had to find bursaries to keep its members in modest comfort. Starting with five selected men, it doubled its numbers in a year and went on growing. And it was a principle with him not to incur debts. His success surprised no one more than himself. He seems to have had this in mind when he said in one lecture:

> "In war-time, promising candidates are taken from the ranks of ordinary soldiers and, by a prodigious expenditure on skilled instruction and other requirements, are turned into officers in a fraction of the time normally required. So in times such as ours, when capable men are scarce, anyone who shows willingness to tackle a vital problem has Divine assistance heaped upon him. It turns the incapable into successful men, not because they deserve it but because the world needs them."

The *Kolel's* influence on the town—and ultimately far beyond its boundaries—was immense. The Gateshead Yeshivah grew in stature and increased its numbers several times over in a few years (it now has over 150 full-time students). Some of the new staff required came from the *Kolel.*

With Rabbi Dessler's planning and cooperation, further institutions arose in Gateshead, which by now have become famous in their own right. These include: The Jewish Teachers' Training College (the celebrated "Girls' Seminary"), the Boys' Boarding School, and the Sunderland Yeshivah. Recent years have seen also the rise of the Gateshead Centre of Jewish Learning, and the Gateshead Jewish Primary School, in addition to similar institutions established by his disciples and in his spirit, in London, Aix-les-Bains, Trilport, Tangiers and elsewhere.

His theory of how to found and maintain a Torah institution was original, if not unique. It could be summed up thus: one personality per institution, and one institution per personality. The personality who was selected as supremely fitting for the institution to be built up, was to own—and be owned by—the institution absolutely. It was to be *his* institution; and all his prestige and status, his very livelihood and that of his family, were to be bound up with its success. At the same time, the institution was to own him. He was to be its willing slave, serving it single-mindedly and always, with no other interest in life than to see it prosper. This put into practice one of the basic principles of *Mussar* psychology. The basic drives of the human personality were to be harnessed in the service of idealism.

He himself remained in the background. His advice and active co-operation in general or detailed planning was always available— but only on demand.

ISRAEL

After the war, factors accumulated requiring a change.

One of these was that his over-work had left its mark on his constitution. He had long tried to arrange the *Kolel* so that it would eventually run itself without his continuous presence and supervision. It now became clear that it would soon have to do so, one way or the other.

When, in 1948, Rabbi Josef Kahaneman of Ponevez Yeshivah, Bne Brak, Israel, offered him the position of *Mashgiah* (spiritual guide) at that great *yeshivah*, he accepted. He imposed, however, conditions allowing him to continue a measure of contact with England, both for the sake of his individual disciples, whom he had never neglected, and of the institutions he had helped to establish.

With his arrival, with his wife, at Bne Brak, there began another epoch in his life. After years of uninterrupted great physical stress, he found himself more free to pursue his researches. He did not, however, allow himself the slightest relaxation of effort. The whole of his great energies were re-chanelled into the sphere of creative thought. During the war, over a thousand lectures of his had been published on stencilled sheets. Now he continued his original researches with great concentration. Three times a week, at least, he addressed the Yeshivah. Much work, sometimes as many as twenty-five hours, went into the preparation of each of these lectures, profound studies of *Agadot, Mussar* and psychology, dealing with subjects of paramount importance to Jewish life and thought. This was a fruitful period. Many new principles appeared for the first time; others grew from mere points into fully developed themes. He still kept up correspondence with his English students and concerns. Almost every year he spent his vacations visting them, giving advice, planning new ventures.

When, in 1951, his wife died, he devoted himself even more to his life-study. His fame had spread in Israel and he was in great demand as a speaker before large audiences, as one of the influential minds, in his chosen field, of our generation.

His health continued to deteriorate, but he kept up his regular lectures until shortly before his death on the 25th Tevet 5714 (31st December 1953).

His works survive mainly in the form of brief notes published only as aides-memoire for his pupils, though many of the Bne Brak lectures are more fully preserved. It was only about a year before his death that he began to plan a selection to be published in book form. He did not live to carry out this plan, but a first series (in Hebrew) was published a year after his death, edited by the present writer, in collaboration with Rabbi S. A. Halpern. There are hundreds of manuscripts still to be sifted. The appended excerpts represent one of the first attempts to make Rabbi Dessler's teaching available in English. Through the teaching and writing of a number of his disciples, his work is continuing to contribute to contemporary Jewish thought and life.

RABBI DESSLER'S THOUGHT

I. Preface

His thought was first and foremost that of a *Baal Mussar* (an exponent of Jewish ethics). He judged his work only by the degree of his success in raising the intensity of spiritual life in his disciples. Problems of philosophy, Midrashic and Agadic themes, Biblical topics and figures, so prominent in his works, are never treated as ends in themselves, but only for the insights they may yield into the problems of personality, behavior and the integrated service of God.

In the fronts of contact between his thinking and the problems of contemporary thought, he had a unique contribution to make. As against the task of contemporary Jewish thinkers to re-state the truths of Torah in terms of modern thought, his achievement was to express and re-evaluate the axioms of modern thought in terms of Torah.

The work of the great *Mussar* thinkers who had preceded him had established the intellect as the tool of personality. Therefore, the extent to which it could reach true conclusions in the moral sphere was in direct ratio to the degree of a person's genuine attachment to truth. Such fealty, however, does not come naturally. A person is naturally more attached to the ideas and ways of thought which flatter his ego, lighten the burden of responsibility and make smoother the way to untrammeled material enjoyments. This natural bias, which may function unconsciously, can vitiate all judgments in the sphere of morals and Torah, no matter how powerful the intellect which propounds them. In fact, the stronger the intellect, the greater the danger, because, with it, the conceal- ment of the unconscious bias is more effective and the arguments to support the desired conclusion more plausible.

According to the teaching of *Mussar,* this bias can be eradi- cated only by long years of constant moral effort, aided by the disciplines of Torah-life and Torah-study.

Hence no weight at all attaches to the opinions, however sin- cere, of anyone who has not yet eradicated in himself the uncon- scious sources of this bias, which may have its origin in his particular social and economic environment, as well as in the human situation as such. The much-vaunted "unprejudiced intellectual approach" to the problems of Torah thus stand exposed as one of the myths of our day.

Rabbi Dessler subjected current non-Torah and anti-Torah views to searching criticism in the light of Torah-wisdom, and revealed the hidden premises and unconscious bias on which they are based. Thus he demonstrated their logical inadequacy.

So successful did this method prove, that one of his followers, if faced with a conflict between a widely-held contemporary view and a tenet of Torah, instead of putting himself on the defensive and groping for apologetics, will immediately endeavor to bring to light the bias, individual, social or otherwise, which has given rise to the divergent viewpoint. By way of illustration, we give below a few examples of his questioning of widely-held current opinions and beliefs, which consciously or unconsciously permeate the thinking even of those who consider themselves Orthodox and orthoprax:

Is the material world primary and the spiritual world secondary, or vice versa?

Is "nature" a reality or a myth?

Is human life the absolute value?

Is human happiness the highest good?

Is it true that every increase in knowledge can only bring greater good to humanity?

Is man naturally good, evolving towards good, perfectible by education, perfectible by eugenics?—or can he achieve good only through self-conquest by the exercise of individual moral effort?

Can human progress be measured in terms of increase in material standards of living?

Can higher living standards always be equated with increased happiness?

Has humanity outgrown the "primitive?"

At the present day, should "love" be the sole mainspring of service to the exclusion of "fear?"

Are honor and prestige worthwhile aims?

Is the aim of education independence of mind, or subjection to an absolute law?

It is not within the scope of this article to give Rabbi Dessler's solution to each of the above problems. Suffice it to say that he succeeded, in these and innumerable other cases, to demonstrate the unsupported nature of common assumption when measured against the eternal truths of Torah.

But he did not look upon this as his main task. He considered the intellect, with all its brilliance, as a very subordinate aspect of human activity. He saw its strength, but he saw, too, its fatal weakness—that it was in itself incapable of determining action. The springs of action lay elsewhere—in the dark realm of will, desire and feeling, both conscious and subconscious. He saw how a person's intellect could comprehend much wisdom, yet his action obey the dictates of his baser nature. How to gear knowledge to action? This tormenting question is the basic problem of Mussar, and to its solution Rabbi Dessler devoted his life's work.

In an age which valued intellect above all, he used intellectual brilliance as an instrument for the desired end. Having dazzled his hand-picked audience with the power of his thought and exposition, he insisted that the clarity achieved should not remain a mere intellectual attainment, but should immediately be translated into a heightened spiritual awareness and activity, into greater integrity in the service of God. His success varied; but one of the great attractions of his method, especially in the lectures of the earlier period, was the way in which he brought the most abstruse topics "down to earth," relating them to the spiritual level of his hearers, and enabling them to apply the principles so learnt to the resolution of their own inner conflicts.

The extracts that follow are by no means representative. They are in most cases only fragments taken out of a larger context. To give a rendering of even one of Rabbi Dessler's *Inyanim* (themes, lectures) in its entirety—premises, sources, illustrations and ramifications—would require space far in excess of this article. A typical lecture (delivered in Yiddish) would take between one hour and an hour and a half. In its written form (in Hebrew), stripped of the wealth of anecdote and illustration which enriched its delivery, it might consist of ten or twelve numbered paragraphs. Each of these could often have been expanded into a whole chapter of a normal book. Every point made pre-supposed a high degree of familiarity with the Bible and all the standard commentaries, Talmud, Midrashim, and the classical Jewish authors.

This inadequate rendering of a few of the less complex and abstruse of his themes may convey an idea of the varied scope of his thought.

II. FAITH

The Hebrew word for "faith," *Emunah,* means also "honesty," as in the expression *"nassaata ve-natata be-emunah."* (Hast thou dealt honestly in business?)

Faith, so far from being the result of uncritical belief, is in fact the consequence of subjecting one's inmost self to the criticism of utter honesty. When this searching self-criticism has burnt away the impurities, the dishonesties, and the self-deceptions, and has achieved "purity of heart," then faith will emerge automatically.

Faith means: being honest with oneself.

III. UNBELIEF

1. Why does a person deny the immortality of the soul? Perhaps it is because he has rejected that which is immortal in himself, and immortality is, therefore, no longer accessible to him.

2. Why does a person deny the reality of free-will? Perhaps it is because he has never exerted himself to exercise a free moral choice and thus has never experienced freedom.

3. Why does a person deny Divine Providence? Perhaps it is because, never having done anything to deserve Providence taking any particular interest in him, he has never experienced Providence in his own life. It is an old rule that "he who believes in natural causes is given into the hands of natural causes" (R. Bahya ibn Pakuda, (XI. Cent.) in his *Hovat Halevavot.*)*

IV. ILLUSION AND REALITY

What is illusion? That which contradicts experience. The human being can experience the world within a framework of the

---

*See "The Duties of the Heart" in the Jewish Library, vol. II, p. 167ff.

urges for self-gratification and power. He can also experience it within a framework of spirituality and self-surrender. Both types of experience exist in the inwardness of the human being. The first results in an existence full of gnawing hunger and pain; the second in an existence of joy and fulfillment. Since it is given to a person to experience the world in this second way no less than in the first, in what sense can this be called "illusion" any more than the other?

V. Sincerity

The learning of Torah and the fulfillment of precepts have value even when done from ulterior motives. There are three things, however, which if not done with utter sincerity are "not done at all": Repentance, prayer, and learning *Mussar*. Thus is the reason for the difficulty we experience in repenting. Other *mitzvot* can be commenced from ulterior motives in the hope that sincerity will ultimately be attained. Repentance must *commence* with sincerity.

VI. Interest

We often find people who are not interested in their work, although they may do it quite competently. What are they interested in? Perhaps a hobby: gardening, motoring, collecting stamps or old china. The hardest work, devoted to their hobby, is a pleasure; thoughts of the hobby fill their leisure moments; they read magazines about it during their lunch hour.

In Torah we also find people—perhaps ourselves?—who may carry out *mitzvot* with reasonable competence; who devote a necessary minimum of time to learning, but whose main interests lie elsewhere.

We must realize that as long as our interests are far from Torah, *we* are far from Torah. A person *is* where his interest is.

VII. Illusion and Reality

In a child's play-fantasy, his dream-world is real to him.

How much fantasy is there in the "real" objects of adult ambitions!

Take "prestige" and "honor," around which so much of our present-day activities revolve. Why are we so pleased when people around us recognize our virtues, and so hurt if they do not? Surely true "honor" resides in possessing the virtue itself: if we have this, then it makes no difference whether others know of it or not; if we have not, then what do we gain by the fact that others think we have? Nevertheless the illusion flatters us: if others behave as if we were admirable people, we can the more easily delude ourselves into thinking that we are. In fact, the less confidence we have in our own inner worth, the more we need the sop of other people's admiration.

We often see the illusion intensified. One enjoys adulation even when it is insincere. "Honor" is often given not because people really think one worthy of it, but because they want favors. Yet a person often is found to be satisfied with this double illusion: a show of "honor" in place of real admiration, and this itself in place of true inner worth.

A realistic view of human life would show the same fantasy— content of many of our other ambitions: happiness, security, material possessions, for example. Wealth and possessions do not bring happiness, but we nevertheless pursue them as a substitute for happiness. Again we accept the illusion as the reality.

Illusion is here used in no mystical sense. It refers to cases of demonstrable self-deception, a phenomenon which is verifiable in everyday life by anyone who cares to observe closely the behavior and motives of other human beings and of himself.

Those who are deeply involved in the entanglements of worldly life tend to describe the spiritual viewpoint as "escapism". Is this a projection of their efforts to escape from a realization of their own inner nature?

To go deeper still, on a realistic view all worldly activity is nothing in itself, but only the means to an end. The end is the attainment and realization of permanent spiritual values. Rabbi Shneour Zalman of Liady, in a famous epigram, said, "The philosophers say God created the world *ex niholo*—'something out of nothing.' I say that with the creation of the physical universe God made 'nothing out of something.' " Light and spirit and holiness did not need creating: they were already given in the existence of God. The truly creative act was the creation of the physical—that which can obscure the pure light of truth and spirituality. Yet this creation is not evil in itself; it was brought into being for a high end: the production of an environment adapted to the exercise of human free will.

The true realist is the one who sees through the bluff and humbug of so much of our wordly activities, and devotes himself and all his material possessions to the realization of true values—the inner values of the human personality.

VIII. National Honor

"And he himself passed over before them, and he (Jacob) bowed himself to the ground seven times until he came near his brother (Esau)." (Genesis, XXXIII, 3.) The Zohar reads, *"and He Himself* (the Divine Presence) *passed over before them,"* and it was to Him that Jacob bowed. The meaning is that Jacob accepted as a Divine decree his inferior *"Galut"* (exile) status, which necessitated his bowing to his brother. The bowing itself was of the body only, not of the mind. His mind remained directed towards the Almighty, to Whose will he subjected himself. His brother he saw merely as the tool of the Divine purpose.

This episode is the type of many similar confrontations in much later ages between the Jews and their *Galut* oppressors. How often did Jews find it necessary to fawn on their persecutors; yet this *Galut* necessity had no effect on their Jewish pride and self-esteem. They saw the necessity as a God-sent trial, but the enemies with whom they had to deal were of no account in their eyes; while dancing at their bidding, the Jews despised them in their hearts; the humiliations which they heaped on them had no more effect on their inner self-esteem than the actions of a wild animal. Today we feel this differently. Aping Gentile culture has become our ambition. In consequence, we tend to take others at their own evaluation, and to look on ourselves with their eyes. We feel, even in retrospect, a deep sense of shame at our ancestors' behavior. We feel they let down "the honor of Israel". How wrong we are! It is we who have compromised Jewish honor. Those earlier generations had a much higher sense of the honor of Israel than we can ever attain. Even while undergoing the greatest indignities, they remained supremely conscious of their high Jewish dignity: they saw themselves as so far above their enemies that they might have belonged to two different worlds. Nothing they could do to them could shake this inner consciousness of solid worth.

Only when our standards tend to approximate those of our neighbors do we tend to lose that sense of divine mission which is the true dignity of our people, and only then does the yoke of *Galut* become unbearable.

IX. Giving and Taking

1. Two Attitudes.

There are two attitudes to life and to one's fellow beings. They may be summed up as the "giving" attitude and the "taking" attitude.

The power of selfless giving is the most elevated of all human powers; in fact it is this power that the Torah refers to when it says that man was created *in the image of God* (Gen. I, 26).

"Taking" is the egoistic urge to draw to oneself whatever comes within one's orbit; to get as much as one can for oneself out of every situation and to give as little as possible in return. It has long been recognized that this attitude is the source of most of the trouble, unhappiness and evil in the world.

Every act, every motive of human behavior is governed by one of these two. There is no middle way.

2. The Spark.

There is no one in the world who has not at least a spark of the power of giving. Why is it that a person cannot enjoy himself properly alone? Whence comes that powerful and irrepressible urge for company, for society? Why is solitary confinement one of the most dreaded punishments? These are signs that the power of giving is inherent in every human being.

Every normal person wants children of his own. There are two aspects to this. One wants children as an extension of one's own personality. One wants them, too, because one feels the need of someone to love. This is the pressing need which makes childless people adopt children and which leads some to lavish their care on pets.

3. Love.

We always see love and "giving" develop together. Which is the cause and which the effect?

It is usually supposed that the love causes the "giving." But it might be said with greater justice that "giving" leads to love.

A person loves the work of his hands. A child he has brought up, an animal he has reared, a plant he has nurtured, even a house he has built—all these he loves because, as we say, "he has put something of himself into them." If I save somebody's life, I suddenly become interested in his future, even though he might have been a complete stranger to me before. All these are examples of love that comes from "giving."

A family was separated during the war; the father and son in one country, the mother in another. After the first joy of reunion they noticed something which hurt them considerably but which they were unable to remedy: the love and attachment between the father and son was much greater than that between the mother and son. The years of "giving" to each other had engendered a love in which the mother was unable to share.

If a person conquers his aversion to someone and does him a good turn, he will find his aversion has grown less.

To sum up: a "giver" never loses what he gives, but finds that he has created an extension of himself in his fellow being. This feeling of self-identification with the other we call "love."

4. LOVING ONE'S NEIGHBOUR.

We saw above that everyone possesses a spark of the power of "giving". Without it there would be no world; no marriage, no family, no society.

But undeveloped, this spark does not shed much light. A person usually chooses a very small circle for his "giving"; his family, a few friends, with these he can identify himself. Everyone else he considers strangers, "others", to be plundered and exploited as far as "decency" or convention will permit.

If one realized that one only has to "give" to love, one would come to see that there is no such thing as "the other"; he ceases to be "other" as soon as I have "given" to him. If one were to begin "giving" to *everyone* one comes into contact with, one would come to see that they are all "mine", all friends. In so far as I "give" to him, I must find part of myself in him. There is no human being in the world with whom I cannot identify myself by "giving".

For one who has reached this level of feeling and acting, the commandment to love one's neighbour as oneself (Lev. XIX, 18) presents no problems.[1]

If I have already "given" my neighbour something of myself, I can have no difficulty in loving him like myself, because I can recognize part of myself in him.

5. LOVE IN MARRIAGE.

Love between the sexes presents a special problem. Sexual desire and the longing for children are surely sufficient to satisfy the biological need. Whence come the tender love and affection which often accompany the phenomenon of "falling in love", and, more rarely, continue through married life?

The answer is, of course, that by fulfilling each other's needs and purpose they have become "givers" to each other, and this love is a result of the "giving." This love, of course, engenders further "giving", which in turn intensifies the love. "Giving" is therefore a dynamic, self-maintaining process.

Why, then, do we find that love so often fails during marriage?

Because the "giving" continued only as long as the couple found in each other the sole and best imaginable fulfillment of their biological needs. As soon as this vision faded, they reverted to their normal attitude to the "other"—the "taking" attitude. Under these conditions, love soon ceases.

My advice to young couples is, therefore: 'See that you each always make it your first concern to give the other pleasure and happiness; see that you each maintain that striving to "give" to the other which you both feel so strongly at the moment. You can be quite sure that the moment, God forbid, either of you departs from this attitude and begins making *demands* on the other, your happiness will be at an end.'

There are unfortunate people who have no desire to marry. This is because "taking" has so much power over them that it defeats even the biological urge to found a home.

Then there are those who—all too often in our generation—wish to keep the number of their children to a minimum. The "taking" urge has gripped them to such an extent that they cannot

---

[1]The correct translation, supported by the cantillation: *"Love thy neighbor. He is as thou"* endorses Rabbi Dessler's point. "He is as thou—becomest as thou—as thou lovest him."—Editor.

bear the thought of giving up anything, even though it would be their own children who would receive it.

We shall do well to consider these phenomena as maladies: as diminutions of the true human stature. A truly human relationship between man and wife is seen when both share the desire to "give". Then their love will be lasting, and their life will be filled with pleasure, happiness and contentment.

6. AMBITION.

Ambition is generally admired. We encourage our children to be ambitious. Someone once said: "Ambition is life."

But is it? Ambition is hunger; we feel a lack and the urge to make it good. Life involves hunger, but hunger is not life. Hunger is a mechanism implanted in the organism to bring to mind the needs of the body. The hunger of the animal is easily satisfied; not so the hungers of human ambition. The worldly aims we set ourselves are distant and difficult of achievement. A hard, bitter and protracted fight is needed to achieve even a part of them. In fact, a person can live to old age without even attaining half his ambitions, as our Sages say: 'No one leaves this world with half his desires fulfilled; if he has one hundred, he wants two; if he has two hundred he wants four' (*Kohelet Rabba* 1, 13).

The situation is aggravated by the natural concomitant of ambition—anxiety. Anxiety lest his ambitions are not fulfilled; anxiety lest he loses what he has got; anxiety about the ambitions of his children; anxiety about security even in the distant future.

Most often, the work and the worry involved in preparing all this do not even allow him to enjoy that part of his ambitions that he has achieved. Seeing this, his hunger increases still more, and becomes even less capable of fulfillment. Even the relatively more successful in the race usually end up ill, worn out, frustrated and physically and mentally strained. The unsuccessful—and they are the majority—suffer from all these and also from the bitter sense of failure.

This is the lot of the hungry ones.

But, you ask, do you want to deny the role of ambition in human life altogether? Are there no *good* ambitions?

There are. But here we come again to the difference between the "giver" and the "taker."

7. The Secret of "Giving."

Ambitions derived from the urge to "take" are self-frustrating. They are incapable of achievement because the apparent achievement is disappointing and gives rise to further hunger, which, in turn, cannot be appeased.

But the urge to "give" comes not from hunger but from fulfillment.

The way to fulfillment? By rejecting material ambitions and being satisfied with—no, by *rejoicing* in—one's lot. This is the blessing of the verse, *"And thou shalt eat and be satisfied"* (Deut. XI. 15)—"You shall eat a little, and it will be blessed in your inward parts." "Who is rich? He who rejoices in his portion" (Abot, IV, 1). It does not say he is "also rich", or "particularly rich"; it appears that he is the *only* one who is rich. Who is rich? He who has no more needs remaining unfulfilled. No matter how much a man may have objectively, he is not rich if he still hungers for more, for his needs are obviously not fulfilled.

A person in this state cannot be a "giver" in our special sense. His whole being cannot be centered on "giving", because he is still interested in "taking" for himself.

"Giving" arises only out of a state of complete contentment and fulfillment and the joy which this engenders. Like a river in flood, his joy spreads out in "giving" to all those with whom he comes into contact.

This is the completely happy man: who has replaced the hunger of material ambition by joy in the things of the spirit. Everything that he has is dedicated to his spiritual purpose; in every event of his life, great and small, he sees the beneficent hand of God. This is the only man who is capable of real "giving", and his service is the service of love. This is the man who has attained full human stature.

8. Ways and Means.

How can one achieve this state of completeness? If one finds oneself still dominated by the urge to "take", by what process can one free oneself from its joyless constriction and fill one's heart with the generous impulses of "giving"?

It is obvious that a person cannot achieve this immediately by a direct effort of will. The change must come gradually, and ways and means must be found to help the process along.

And here we must reveal the great secret of spiritual progress, expressed by our Sages as follows: "A man must always occupy himself with good things, even from the wrong motives, for impure motives can change to pure" (Nazir, 23b). In other words, we must make use of the powers we possess at the moment, whatever they are, to direct progress in the right direction. For example, a person who finds that the basic drives of his personality are still directed to "taking" for himself, should harness this drive in the service of the good. In matters between himself and God he can and must train himself to do what is right by involving *himself* in the outcome. Fear of punishment, fear of the pangs of conscience, hopes of reward, desire for prestige—all expressions of the urge to "take"—can be used to power a systematic program of right actions, which, if persisted in, can transform the personality; on one condition—that these external aids are looked on as crutches to be discarded as soon as they become unnecessary.

In our relations with our fellow men, in addition to all the aids mentioned above, we shall also find a very powerful ally in the imagination. We can force ourselves to imagine the other person's plight and so arouse in ourselves emotions of pity and commiseration. If these lead to right action, it does not matter at the moment that the motive may have been to some extent self-directed—to remove the unpleasant feelings aroused in *us* by the sight of the other person's misfortune. A person can become a real "giver" only by first, and for a long period, acting *as if* he were a "giver".

Again, a person who gives because he knows he ought to give is very far from being a "giver" in our sense. But the training can be extremely useful in our progress towards the goal.

9. GRATITUDE.

The "giver" and the "taker" can be distinguished also in their reaction to gifts or favors bestowed on them. The "giver" cannot bring himself to take something for nothing. The moment he receives anything from his neighbour his immediate reaction is to pay for it. If he cannot, his heart insists on paying back in thanks— genuine thanks, coming from the depths of his being.

The sign of the "taker" is that in his heart of hearts he takes everything for granted. His innermost conviction is that everything is there for him to take. When he receives anything, he therefore feels no inner urge to gratitude. He may, of course, give thanks, but it will be from the lips only and not from the heart. The apparent "giving" is itself "taking" in essence, because its purpose, recognized or unrecognized, is "taking"—either to obtain further favors in the future, or to conform with the conventions of respectable behavior.

10. LOVING GOD.

The service of God is founded on gratitude. This is one of the purest motives for service, as witness its introduction in the first of the Ten Commandments given to the whole of Israel in the great revelation on Mount Sinai: *"I am the Lord thy God who brought thee out of the Land of Egypt,"* and to awaken the emotions of gratitude still further: *"out of the house of bondage."*

Our Sages say: "Whosoever is ungrateful to his neighbor will eventually be ungrateful to God Himself." Rabbi Nahum Wolf Ziff of Kellem explained this saying as follows:

A person's behavior depends on his character. If he is of an irritable nature, he will react irritably to whatever interferes with his desires; and so with arrogance, kindness and indifference. One cannot borrow character-traits for special purposes and discard them at will. A person who is by nature ungrateful will be ungrateful not only in his relations with his fellow men but also in his relations with his Creator. The "taker" can, therefore, never serve God with all his heart.

The "giver", on the other hand, recognizing all the undeserved benefits he constantly receives from God's hand, will find in himself a constant urge to repay, and devote his whole life in gratitude to his Creator. He will eagerly search for ways to repay the unpayable, whether by praise or prayer, sacrifice or service. Finding that Torah and tradition clearly state the modes of behavior and service that God has graciously called acceptable to Him, he will eagerly pursue them, overjoyed that he, in all his littleness, has been given the opportunity to repay, or at least to be allowed to think he can repay, some infinitesimal part of the debt of gratitude he owes his Creator. Such pure "giving" as this always leads to love; and thus we have the crowning achievement of the power of "giving": that it leads to the greatest of all spiritual attainments— the pure love of God.

X. The Ego and the Worlds

1. Creation obscures the light of God's oneness.

2. What obscures this is in fact the ego in the creature.

3. Arrogance—inflation of ego—obscures this light excessively. It is, therefore, equivalent to idolatry (Zohar, I, 27b).

4. Humility—diminution of the ego—is equivalent to the life of the world to come.

5. There are angels which are created to sing once and vanish from existence. This means that the access of light is so great that their ego cannot maintain itself in separate existence.

6. The pleasure to be derived by the righteous from the radiance of the *Shekhinah* in the world to come is a delight in access of enlightenment. This enlightenment, however, will involve a diminution, not an inflation of ego, because the enlightenment will be assimilated by them not for themselves but for the glory of God. This assimilation of pleasure not for oneself but for the glory of God is the highest level attainable by a creature. This is the meaning of the saying: "In the world to come the righteous will sit *with their crowns on their heads,* enjoying the splendour, etc." (*Berakhot,* 17a). "Their crowns on their heads" signifies the enjoyment for the sake of God (*Lëshem shamayim*).

7. This level is unattainable in this world. The degree of obscurity necessary in this world to maintain the possibility of free choice precludes the diminution of ego beyond a certain point. The diminution of ego to the final point consistent with the separate existence of a creature is reserved for the world to come, which is, therefore, described as the world "no eye has ever seen but God's" (Isaiah, LXIV, 3).

8. There are, even in the world to come, an infinite number of degrees of approach to this final point. The degree to which one will be able to approach this existence will depend on the degree of diminution of ego attained under the conditions of this world, by the exercise of free will.

9. The main purpose of Torah and *mitzvot* in this world is to aid in the subjection of the will and ego of the creature to the will of the Creator.

10. *Mitzvot* done for ulterior motives or from habit or convention are valuable only as external aids. Only that *mitzvah*-act which involves the total subjection of will and ego to God can contribute to the ultimate goal of the personality in the life of the world to come.

THE CONTRIBUTORS

LEO JUNG. The editor is the rabbi of The New York Jewish Center, former President of the Rabbinical Council of The Union of Orthodox Jewish Congregations of America; Prof. of Ethics and Jewish Philosophy, Yeshiva University; Chairman of the J. D. C.'s Cultural and Religious Committee; translator (Soncino Edition) of two tractates of The Talmud, and author of *Fallen Angels, an Essay on Comparative Folklore, Mistranslations as Source of Lore, Living Judaism, Crumbs and Character, The Rhythm of Life, Harvest,* and other books, pamphlets and articles on Judaism and Jewish Law. He holds *Semikhah* at the hand of the *Gaon* David Hoffmann, and the degrees of M.A. (Cantab.), Ph.D. (London), D.D. (Yeshivah Univ.), and L.H.D. (N. Y. Univ.).

NIMA H. ADLERBLUM, Ph.D. Columbia University; Lecturer on contemporary philosophy. Member of the American Philosophical Association and of the Inter-American Congress of Philosophy. Elected by the Inter-American Congress of Philosophy of 1950 as editor of a contemplated edition of contemporary philosophical tendencies throughout the world. Active member of the American Committee (chairman, Professor Kilpatrick) for the translation and dissemination of John Dewey's and American philosophy through Latin America. Founder of the Hadassah National cultural work and for many years its cultural chairman and member of the National Board.

Research Work: 1934-1936 on problems and conflicts of minority nationalities in Central Europe and in Soviet Russia, on Nazism during the Hitler regime.

Immigration to Mexico: In 1938 she obtained concessions from former Mexican President Avila Camacho for the immigration of European refugees; in 1940 she took an active part in fighting anti-Semitism in Mexico.

Author: *A Study of Gersonides in his Proper Perspective*, Columbia University Press 1927, aiming at the vindication of Jewish philosophy, which had hitherto been regarded as a mere branch of scholasticism. Among her other contributions (in the

701

Journal of Philosophy and other magazines): *A Reinterpretation of Jewish Philosophy; A Perspective for the Study of Jewish Philosophy; The Emotional Content of Jewish Philosophy; Jewish Philosophical Romanticism; Medieval Jewish Philosophy; Jewish Ethics; Bachya Ibn Pakuda; Creative History; The Role of History; Main Currents and Thoughts of the 19th Century; Pragmatic Aspects of Jewish Philosophy,* etc.

Her book, *A Perspective of Jewish Life through its Festivals,* has been transcribed in Braille.

DR. ELIO TOAFF was born in Leghorn in 1915, the son of Professor S. A. Toaff, rabbi of that important community. Under his father's guidance, he attended the Rabbinical College in Leghorn, where, in 1939, he achieved the title of 'superior rabbi' (*Hakham ha-shalem*); in 1940 he received his Doctorate in Jurisprudence at the ancient University of Pisa. In 1941 he was appointed rabbi at Ancona, a post which he held during the whole period of the Second World War. In 1946 he became rabbi in Venice, where he was also appointed lecturer in Hebrew language and literature at the University Institute of Ca'Foscari. In 1951, after the death of Chief Rabbi Prato of Rome, he was appointed spiritual head of that ancient community, which post he still holds today.

DR. JOSEF UNNA graduated from the University of Frankfurt a.M. in 1920 (Doctorarum Politicarum) and received his *Semikhah* at the Hildesheimer Rabbinical Seminary in 1928. Since 1934 he has been living in Israel. He published *Statistics of Frankfurt Jews up till 1860* and a large number of scholarly papers in Israeli learned periodicals. Presently he is engaged in the edition of important rabbinical literature.

RABBI WALTER S. WURZBURGER B.A., Yeshiva University; M.A., Ph.D., Harvard University; *Semikhah,* Rabbi Isaac Elchanan Theological Seminary; Rabbi—Congregation Haye Adam, Boston, Mass., 1944-53; Rabbi—Shaare Shemayim Congregation, Toronto, since 1953. Ph.D. Thesis—*Pientano's Theory of A Priori Judgements.* Contributed articles and reviews to philosophical and rabbinical publications, as well as to the general and Anglo-Jewish press.

JACOB KATZ. Born Hungary, 1904. Educated in *yeshivot* in Hungary, Frankfort University, where he received his Ph.D. on the thesis, *The Assimilation of the German Jews.* Since 1936, teaching in Israeli secondary schools and Principal of Talpioth Seminary in Tel Aviv; since 1950, Hebrew University, Jerusalem, lecturing on Jewish social and educational history. Presently associate professor at Hebrew University. Publications: Articles related to above subjects; textbook of Jewish history; *Tradition and Crisis—Jewish Society at the End of the Middle Ages* (Hebrew, Mossad Bialik, Jerusalem, 1958—English translation in preparation).

DR. ARTHUR B. POSNER. Born in 1890, studied at the University and at the Hildesheimer Rabbinical Seminary of Berlin and obtained his *Semikhah* from the *Gaon* David Hoffmann and his Ph.D. at Tuebingen Univ.—Until 1933 rabbi of Kiel, he left for Israel; 1935-1953 he was Librarian of the Mizrachi Teachers' Seminary. He published a commentary on *The Book of Micah,* the Psalms; a book on *Prophetic and Liberal Judaism;* on Philo's *De Migratione;* articles on Rabbi E. L. Prinz and E. M. Lipschuetz. He collaborated in *Juesdisches Lexicon, Encyclopedia Ivrit,* and wrote many articles of geographical and historical import.

MOSES LEGIS ISAACS was educated in Cincinnati, holds a Ph.D. from the University of Cincinnati, has been Fellow in Bacteriology of the National Research Council, and Professor of Sanitary Science at Columbia University since 1916. He has been Professor of Chemistry at Yeshiva University since 1942 and Dean of Yeshiva College from 1942 to 1953.

NANCY ISAACS KLEIN is a graduate of Barnard College and a member of Phi Beta Kappa. She was associated in a secretarial capacity with the State University of New York.

MORDECAI BREUER. Born 1918 in Frankfurt a.M. Studied at *yeshivot* in Frankfurt and Jerusalem, as well as London University and Jerusalem Conservatoire. Member, Association of Jewish Composers in Israel. Co-founder of Ezra Youth Movement in Israel. Member of Poale Agudat Israel Central Committee. Published posthumous works of his father, Dr. Isaac Breuer. Editor of *Hama'ayan,* Orthodox Hebrew periodical. Former Director of Kfar Eliyahu, religious agricultural school in Israel.

DR. SAMUEL K. MIRSKY is Professor of Rabbinics and Director of the Israel Institute at the Bernard Revel Graduate School, Yeshiva University; founder and editor of *Talpioth,* a quarterly dedicated to Jewish history, philosophy and law, and of *Sura,* an annual devoted to study and research of Israeli problems.

Born in Russia in 1899, he received his Jewish education in Palestine, being ordained a rabbi in 1915 at the age of 16. Receiving a diploma from the Teachers College in Jerusalem in 1920, he graduated from the Palestine Government Law School in 1924 and was admitted to the bar in that country. He arrived in the United States in 1926 and received his B.A. from N. Y. U. in 1932, the M.A. and the Ph.D. from Columbia University in 1934 and 1952, respectively.

Dr. Mirsky is a past president of the Hebrew Academy of America.

He published *Hibbur ha-Testuvah la-Hameiri* (1950); *Commentary by Jonathan Lunel,* with introduction and notes, Jerusalem (1954); *Eretz ve Yamin* (1953); *Jewish Institutions of Higher Learning in Europe—Their Development and Destruction— Yeshiva of Volozin,* New York (1956); *Sheeltot De R. Acha*—a critical and annotated edition and translation of the Book of Genesis based on MSS—Jerusalem, 1957.

DR. ELIEZER EBNER. Born in Berlin, Germany, he studied at the *yeshivot* of Mir, Poland and Petach Tikvah, Israel. While in Israel he was also a member of a religious kibbutz and the leader of a Haganah unit. He came to the United States in 1941 and has held pulpits in Wilmington, Del. and Calgary, Alberta. At present he is the rabbi of the Brothers of Israel Synagogue of Long Branch, N. J. He has a Ph.D. degree from the Dropsie College of Philadelphia, Pa. in the Department of Education. He is the author of the recently published *Elementary Education in Ancient Israel* and has contributed articles and monographs to *Talpioth, Jewish Life,* rabbinical sermon manuals and other publications.

BENJAMIN DE VRIES. Born 1905 in Groningen, Holland; studied at the University of Amsterdam and at the Rabbinical Seminary there; obtained the degrees of Candidatum Linguarum

Semiticarum in 1928 and Litt. D. from the University of Leiden in 1938. He received his rabbinical diploma in 1930 and taught Biblical exegesis and Talmud at the Rabbinical Seminary of Amsterdam from 1930 to 1934. He was leader of the Mizrachi movement in Holland. Since 1934 he has lived in Israel, as school principal; from 1942 to 1951, as Inspector of Religious Schools; from 1951 to 1956, as teacher of the Talmud in high schools; since 1956, Lecturer in Talmud at the University of Tel Aviv and at the University Bar-Ilan. Dr. de Vries published books on folk-lore and history on the method of Judaic teaching. He serves as permanent critic of Judaistic studies in the Hebrew press.

JUDAH M. ISAACS was born in Cincinnati, Ohio, and comes from a family active in Orthodox circles for four generations in this country. He attended Harvard University, from which he was graduated magna cum laude with membership in the Phi Beta Kappa Society, and also attended Harvard Law School. At Harvard he specialized in medieval church history and prepared a treatise on Jewish communities in the Middle Ages. He has lectured from time to time on insurance at Columbia University and has contributed to the Atlantic Monthly.

DR. YESHAYAHU AVIAD-WOLFSBERG was born in Hamburg, Germany, in 1893, of an old rabbinic family. He traced his descent to Rabbi Isaiah Horowitz, the celebrated author of *Shne Luhot Habrit*. He was educated in the famous Talmud Torah and high school of his native city. At the University of Heidelberg, where he came under the influence of Hans Driesch, the neo-Vitalist, he studied biology and philosophy. He was deeply impressed by Rabbi Zalman B. Rabinkov. In Berlin, he studied medicine at the University, and Torah under David Hoffmann. He was a lifelong Mizrachi, the president of its movement in Germany. In 1934 he moved to Israel and for twenty years served as pediatrician, orator, author of countless articles in the general press, as well as in academic magazines. His many books are a luminous example of the synthesis in his own personality of Jewish teaching and the best of modern culture. He won golden opinions for his work as Israel's Minister in Scandinavia and as her Ambassador in Bern. His sudden loss was considered a national tragedy and felt all over the Jewish world.

DR. DAVID STRUMPF. Born 1892 in Mielec (Poland). Studied at the "Gymnasium" of Ausbach (Bavaria); at the Universities of Berlin, Munich, and Heidelberg; and at the Hildesheimer Rabbinical Seminary. He functioned as Rabbi and *Religionslehrer* in Cologne, Berlin, for a short time in Israel, and since 1934 in Zurich.

Publications: *The Jews in the Medieval French Mystery Plays*. Contributions in learned publications and periodicals on *The Spiritual Crises of our Time, Judaism and the Modern Point of View*.

DR. DARIO DISEGNI, Chief Rabbi of Turino, born in Florence in 1878, studied in the Rabbinic School directed by the Chief Rabbi S. H. Margulies, attended Genoa and Turin universities, and in Turin became Director of Arts. After obtaining the rabbinic degree at Florence, he filled rabbinic positions in Verona, Genoa and Turin. In 1930, the Italian Government entrusted him the reorganization of the Tripoli Jewish communities. Dr. Disegni published works on Jewish lore and translated into Italian the whole *Mahzor* according to the Italian *Minhag,* with notes. He wrote a brief biography of *Rov* Margulies as an introduction to the latter's book, *Sermons*. He also wrote some exegetical essays about the prophets and the psalms.

JUDA ARI WOHLGEMUTH, born at Berlin in 1903, graduated from the famous *Friedrichsgymnasium* in his native city and the Yeshivah of Telshi in Lithuania. At the Universities of Berlin, Leipzig, Marburg and Koenigsberg and the Hildesheimer Rabbinical Seminary he studied history, philosophy and education and obtained the title of Academic Teacher of Religion and *Studienrat*. He taught at the Jewish schools of Altona and Riga. From 1941-47 he lived in Siberia as war prisoner of the Soviets. Between 1953-57 he taught Judaism to the enthused Torah-true youth of Zurich. Wohlgemuth contributed many articles to German, Hebrew and Yiddish newspapers and learned periodicals and published *Reform—A Historical Perspective, Of the Thought and Faith of our Time, Yesodot Hinnukh ha-Dat Lador* and *Fragt immer—Gut oder Boese?,* his magnum opus. He died suddenly in 1957.

SALOMON EHRMANN (Ph.D., D.D.S.) studied at the Yeshivah of Frankfort, where he received his *Semikhah* at the hand of the sainted Rabbi Solomon Breuer. He obtained his secular education at the Universities of Munich, Berlin, Giessen, Kiel and Frankfort. He was honorary lecturer at the Yeshivah of Frankfort, member of the Supreme Council of Agudath Israel and Director of its Palestine Office. One of the founders of the inter-denominational Kepler Society, a member of the Kant-Gesellschaft, he served (1938-42) as rabbi in Paris and since has resided in Switzerland. There he developed a fruitful activity as rabbi in charge of refugees, as writer, lecturer and director of the world organization of Agudah. He edited *Unser Weg* (1908-10) of *The Bund Juedischer Akademiker,* the monthly *Nachalath Zvi* (1930-37) and contributed many essays and articles to the *Israelit, Die Juedische Presse, Der Tag* (Warsaw), *Unser Wort* (Vilna), *Kol Israel* and *Hamodia* (Jerusalem).

ISIDORE EPSTEIN, B.A., Ph.D., D.Lit. (University of London). Principal of Jews' College, London; formerly Rabbi, Middlesbrough Hebrew Congregation, England.

Publications:

The Responsa of R. Solomon b. Adret of Barcelona as a Source of the History of Spain; The Responsa of R. Simon b. Zemah Duran; Judaism of Tradition; Judaism (Great Religions of the East Series); *Jewish Way of Life; Man and His Creator; The Faith of Judaism; Judaism,* in the Encyclopedia Britannica 1955 Edition. Editor, Babylonian Talmud in English (35 vols.) Editor, Maimonides Centenary Memorial Volume. Advisory Editor, Chambers Encyclopedia, Jewish Sections. Joint Editor, Essays presented to Dr. J. H. Hertz, and contributor to various publications and journals.

JOSEPH BLOCH. The Nestor of the French Rabbinate and one of its leading rabbis. Has occupied various pulpits in Alsace-Lorraine, the country of his birth, and is at present rabbi in Haguenau. A pioneer in the field of Jewish education in France, he has published a number of books and pamphlets.

SIMON LANGER. Born in Alsace-Lorraine, he has been the rabbi of the well known Orthodox congregation in Rue Montevideo, Paris, from 1924 until the outbreak of the war in 1939. Having served as a chaplain in the French Army until the collapse, he came to the United States in 1941. In 1949 he succeeded the sainted Moses Hyamson as the rabbi of Orach Chaim.

RABBI DR. ELIE MUNK. Born in Paris in 1900, he received his rabbinical training at the Hildesheimer Rabbinical Seminary in Berlin and completed his secular studies at the University of Berlin.

In 1927, he was chosen rabbi in Ansbach (Bavaria) and the surrounding district, where he wrote his *World of Prayer* and *Ner Olam* (The Light of Eternity), dealing with Jewish mysticism.

In 1937, Rabbi Munk accepted his present position as rabbi of Congregation Adath Yereim in Paris. During the war years, when he was forced to flee to Switzerland, he wrote *La Justice Sociale en Israel*.

At the end of the war, Rabbi Munk returned to Paris, reorganized his community, and threw himself into the task of extending help and succor to the *She'erit Hapletah*. Recently appeared his *Vers L'harmonice,* dealing with Kabbalistic ideas and of their relation to Jewish and universal history, and *The World of Prayer* (a translation of his magnum opus).

HILLEL SEIDMAN, author of twelve books in Hebrew, Yiddish and Polish on Judaistic topics, has served as journalist of The Day-Morning Journal, New York, *Haboker, Heruth,* Tel Aviv; as editor of The Jewish Week, New York. Former Director of the Archive of the Jewish Community of Warsaw. Director, Ministry for Social Welfare, Israel (1950-1952). Former writer of the *Moment,* daily paper, *Dos Yiddishe Tagblat,* Warsaw. Radio commentator on WEVD, New York. Contributor to *Hadoar, Talpioth,* New York, *Encyclopedia Shel Galiot,* Jerusalem, and others. Author, *Diary of the Warsaw Ghetto* (in Hebrew and Yiddish), *Yeshivot in Poland* (in Hebrew), and other books.

EUGEN ELIAHU MAYER (Dr. Jur.). Born in Zweibruecken (Palatinate) as son of District Rabbi Dr. Israel Mayer and Johanna (née Mannheimer). Studied law and economics at Munich, Berlin and Heidelberg. From 1910 to 1914 at head office of Jewish Colonization Association (ICA) in Paris, on several missions to Russia. 1914 to 1918 on active service. From 1919 to

1933 Syndicus (head of administration and legal adviser) of *Israelitische Gemeinde,* Frankfurt-a.M. Since 1933 in Jerusalem. Until his recent retirement, on the editorial board of *The Jerusalem Post.*

DR. ISAAC LEWIN lived before the war in Lodz, Poland, where he represented the Jewish community in the City Council. In 1938 he was elected Rabbi of Sambor.

He is the author of *The Vienna Divorce; The Participation of the Jews in the Elections to the Diet in Ancient Poland; The Jewish Excommunication in Lithuania in the 17th and 18th Centuries; The Right of the Dissolution of Parliament; Contributions to the History of Jews in Poland; History of the Bar in Ancient Poland.* He contributed to many magazines and newspapers in Yiddish, Polish, Hebrew and German. His book of essays, *Past and Present* (Lodz 1939), studies in historical and literary problems, was published two months before the outbreak of the war.

Since 1941 in America, he published *The Protection of Jewish Religious Rights by Royal Edicts in Ancient Poland* (1943), *In the Struggle against Discrimination* (1958), and co-edited the *Black Book of Polish Jewry* (1943). In 1944 he became lecturer of history in the Bernard Revel Graduate School. Since 1943 he has been a member of the Polish Institute of Arts and Sciences in America.

ISRAEL ELFENBEIN. Born in Buczacz (Poland), he studied at the Pressburg Yeshivah and received *Semikhah* from three European *Gedolim* in 1906. In 1906 he came to U. S. A., attended Yeshivat Isaac Elchanan and obtained his M.A. at Columbia U., D.H.L. from the Jewish Theological Seminary in 1915. He served as rabbi in Chicago, New York City, and Sea Gate. Since 1939 he has been Executive Director Mizrachi Education and Expansion Program. Dr. Elfenbein contributed to REJ; JQR; *Tarbitz,* Zion, *Kiryat Sefer,* Sinai, *Hadoar, Bitzron,* J.E. and *Encyclopedia Talmudit,* and edited, 1929-1940: *Die Shtimme von Volk,* Brooklyn. His books include: *Sefer Minhagim of Meir of Rothenburg; Teshuvot Rashi* (in three parts); *Inside Palestine under Turkey; Maimonides, the Man; Sefer Minhagim Yeshanin m'Dura of Isaac of Dueren; Problems of Jewish Reconstruction in America; Hosafot v'Tikkunim l'Teshubot Rashi;* and *Teshuvot Rabbenu Hanannel.*

Rabbi B. S. Jacobson. Born 1901 in Hamburg, Germany. Studied Torah at the Yeshivah of Galanta and the Hildesheimer Rabbinical Seminary in Berlin; his academic work (philosophy and Semitic languages) he pursued at the Universities of Berlin and Hamburg. From 1924 to 1938 (when he left for Israel) he was Academic Teacher of Religion at the Talmud Torah High School of Hamburg. In Israel he teaches Bible at the Girls' Teachers' High School, and lectures at the *Hug Noar Dati* and the *Ihud Shivat Zion* in Tel Aviv. His books in German include translations and editions of Rambam's *Hilkhot Teshubah* and *Hilkhot Deot; Grundzuege der Aramaeischen Sprache des Talmud,* and *Festkunde.* His Hebrew books: *Madrikh Le'Iyob ve-Kohelet* 1949, *She-elot le-iyyun bi-Nebiim Rishonim* 1954, '55, *Binah be-Mikra* (translated into English as "Meditations on the Torah", 1956), 1953-1958, and *Hazon ha-Mikra,* 1957.

Solomon Kerstein. Born Antwerp, Belgium, September 7, 1901; attended Israelitische Realschule Yesodei Hatorah, Antwerp; Etz Chaim Yeshivah, London; Rabbi Jacob Joseph Yeshiva, New York. Vice-president, Bloch Publishing Company, New York City, since 1947, editor. Bloch's Book Bulletin; editor, *Unzer Shtimme,* since 1941; American correspondent, *Hatzofeh,* Tel Aviv daily, since 1937. A founder, secretary, Jewish Book Council of America; vice-president, Mizrachi National Education Commission. Author, *Jewish Libraries and Book Collections in American Jewish Institutions and Universities, 1945-46.* Contributor to Anglo-Jewish and Yiddish press in U. S., Canada.

Lion (Aryeh) Carmell, born in London, commenced studying under Rabbi E. L. Dessler in 1933 and maintained unbroken contact with him until the latter's death in 1953. He took in 1945 an external Science degree (in Estate Management) of London University. Mr. Carmell has been especially active in the sphere of adult education. He is Chairman of the Association for Promoting Torah Education in Great Britain, and of the Jewish Scholarship Centre, and Hon. Director of Studies of the Moreah Teachers' College, London. In addition to publishing a number of popular articles and essays, Mr. Carmell was co-editor of *Mikhtav Me-Eliyahu* (London 1955), the first published selection of the ethical and philosophical writings of Rabbi Dessler, and is at present engaged in editing hitherto unpublished manuscripts of the Agadic commentaries of Maharal of Prague.

Univ. of Tulsa Library
Tulsa, Oklahoma

THE JEWISH LIBRARY

Edited by Leo Jung

CONTENTS

Volume I (1928; second revised edition, 1943)

---

*Omitted in second edition.
**Only in the first edition.

5. The "Women's Branch" of the "Union of Orthodox Jewish Congregations of America", by Betty F. Goldstein, New York.

6. The "National Council of Jewish Women", by Hannah G. Solomon and Nannie A. Reis, Chicago.

7. The Jewish Woman in the Responsa, by Prof. I. Epstein, D.Lit., London (England).

8. The Grande Dame in Jewish History, by Rabbi Felix Aber, Ph.D., Bremen (Germany). Translated by Hugo Mantel, B.A.

9. Literature for Jewish Women in Medieval and Later Times, by Rabbi Arthur Posner, Ph.D., Anvers (Belgium). Translated by Rabbi A. Burstein, M.A.

10. Outstanding Jewish Women in Western Europe, by Dr. Cecil Roth, Ph.D., London (England).

11. Jewish Women in Social Service in Germany, by Dr. Else Rabin, Ph.D., Breslau (Germany). Translated by Rebecca Latz and I. S. Adlerblum.

12. The Jewish Lullaby, by Rabbi Israel Goldfarb, Brooklyn (N. Y.).

13. Art and the Jewish Woman, by Hebe Rahel Bentwich Mayer, Frankfurt am Main (Germany).

14. Taharah—A Way to Married Happiness, by Rivka Levi Jung, B.A., Iowa City (Ia.).

15. Neurosis and the Modern Jewess, by Dr. W. M. Feldman, M.D., London (England).

16. The Jewish Woman in Eastern Europe, by Studienrat Ari Wohlgemuth, Riga (Latvia). Translated by I. S. Adlerblum.

17. The Jewish Woman of Palestine, by Lotta Levensohn, Jerusalem.

18. The World Organization of Jewish Women, by Rebekah Kohut, New York.

19. The Élan Vital of the Jewish Woman, by Dr. Nima H. Adlerblum, Ph.D., New York.

VOLUME V (1946; second revised edition, 1949)

"ISRAEL OF TOMORROW"

RELIGION

1. Jewish Foundations of the New World Order, by Rabbi Leo Jung, Ph.D., New York.

2. Religion and the World of Tomorrow, by Siegmund Forst, New York (Translated by Eugenie A. Propp).

3. Judaism and the World of Tomorrow, by the late Isaac Breuer, LL.D. (Translated by I. S. Adlerblum).

RELIEF AND RECONSTRUCTION

4. J. D. C. In World Jewry—Past, Present, and Future, by Leon Shapiro and Boris Sapir, New York.**

LAW

5. Labor in Rabbinical Responsa, by Dr. Ch. W. Reines, New York.

6. Judaism and International Law, by Rabbi Philip Biberfeld, Ph.D., New York.

7. The Jewish Attitude Towards Peace and War, by Rabbi David S. Shapiro, Indianapolis.

8. Jewry-Law—Past, Present, and Future, by Professor Guido Kisch, New York.

8A. Anti-Semitism in the World of Tomorrow, by Professor M. L. Isaacs, New York.*

8B. The Attitude of the Hafetz Hayyim Toward Labor, by Rabbi Oscar Z. Fasman, Chicago.*

THE ARTS

9. The Halakhah and Aesthetics (Judaism of Tomorrow and the World of Art and Beauty), by Rabbi H. Raphael Gold, M.D., New York.

---

*Omitted in second edition.
**Only in the first edition.

10. Some Directives for Jewish Music of Tomorrow, by Rabbi Milton Feist, New York.**

11. Jewish Literature in the World of Tomorrow, by Professor Meyer Waxman, Chicago.

12. Gersonides in Jewish Thinking of Tomorrow, by Dr. Nima H. Adlerblum, New York.

SCIENCE

13. Natural Science and Problems of Judaism, by Professor Bruno Kisch, M.D., New York.

14. The Economic Prospects of American Jewry, by Professor Nathan Reich, New York.**

PALESTINE

15. The State of Israel and the United Nations, by Tamar de Sola Pool, New York.**

15A. Palestine in the Post-War World, by Tamar de Sola Pool, New York.*

16. The High Court of Justice in the Past and in the Future, by the late Rabbi Isaac Unna, Ph.D.

POLAND

17. Polish Jewry—Yesterday, Today and Tomorrow, by Dr. Wolf Blattberg, New York.

18. Religious Judaism in Independent Poland, by Dr. Isaac Lewin, New York. (Translated by Rabbi Abraham Burstein)

AMERICA

19. The Jewish Communal Organization of Tomorrow, by the late Rabbi Bernard Drachman, Ph.D.

20. America and Israel of Tomorrow, by Elisha M. Friedman, New York.

21. Yeshivah Education in America, by Professor Jacob I. Hartstein, New York.

---

*Omitted in second edition.
**Only in the first edition.

8. Isaac Leeser and the *Occident,* by Professor Moses Isaacs, Ph.D., Yeshiva University, and Nancy I. Klein, A.B., Yonkers, N. Y.

9. Samson Raphael Hirsch, by Mordecai Breuer, Kfar Eliyahu, Israel.

10. Isaac Elhanan Spector, by Rabbi Samuel K. Mirsky, D.D., Yeshiva University.

11. Simha Zissel Broida (Ziff), by Rabbi Eliezer Ebner, Ph.D., Long Branch, N. J.

12. Joseph Tzevi Halevi Duenner, by Doctorandus Benjamin de Vries, Tel Aviv, Israel (translated by Dr. Herman Axelrod, from the Hebrew; adapted by Vivienne H. Siegel).

13. Abraham Jacob Gershon Lesser, by Judah Isaacs, B.A., New York.

14. David Hoffmann, by the late Yeshayahu Aviad-Wolfsberg, M.D., Jerusalem, Israel.

15. Hirsch Hildesheimer, by Rabbi David Strumpf, Ph.D., Zurich, Switzerland.

16. Samuel Hirsch Margulies, by Chief Rabbi Dario Disegni, Turin, Italy (translated by Mitzi Feuerstein, from the Italian).

17. Joseph Leib Bloch, by the late Juda Ari Wohlgemuth, Zurich, Switzerland.

18. Tobias Lewenstein, by Moses Lewenstein, Kew Gardens, N. Y., and Rabbi Salomon Ehrmann, D.D.S., Zurich, Switzerland (translated by Moses Jung, LL.B., Ph.D., from the German).

19. Avraham Yitzhak Hacohen Kook, by Rabbi I. Epstein, D. Litt., London, England.

20. Ernest Weill, by Rabbis Joseph Bloch, Haguenau, and Simon Langer, New York.

21. Joseph Wohlgemuth, by the late Juda Ari Wohlgemuth, Zurich, Switzerland.

22. Ezra Munk, by Rabbi Elie Munk, Ph.D., Paris, France, and Hillel Seidman, Ph.D., New York (translated by Moses Jung, LL.B., Ph.D., from the Hebrew).

23. Nehemiah Anton Nobel, by Eugen Eliahu Mayer, Dr. Jur., Jerusalem, Israel.

24. Aaron Lewin, by Professor Isaac Lewin, Ph.D., Yeshiva University (translated by Rabbi Louis Bernstein, from the Hebrew).

25. Menahem Ziemba of Praga, by Rabbi Israel Elfenbein, D.H.L., New York.

26. Isaac Breuer, by Rabbi Salomon Ehrmann, D.D.S., Zurich, Switzerland (translated by Hebe R. Mayer-Bentwich, Jerusalem, Israel, from the German).

27. Joseph Carlebach, by Rabbi B. S. Jacobson, Tel Aviv, Israel (translated by Adolf Rimberg, from the German).

28. Moshe Avigdor Amiel, by Solomon Kerstein, New York.

29. Eliyahu Eliezer Dessler, by Lion Carmell, B.Sc., London, England.

INDEX